The Planning of Change

The Planning of Change

Third Edition

Edited by

Warren G. Bennis
University of Cincinnati

Kenneth D. Benne
Boston University

Robert Chin
Boston University

Kenneth E. Corey
University of Cincinnati

HOLT, RINEHART AND WINSTON
New York   Chicago   San Francisco   Atlanta
Dallas   Montreal   Toronto   London   Sydney

For permission to use copyrighted material, the author is indebted to the following:

p. 306 "Gestalt Prayer" by Frederick S. Perls. © Real People Press 1969. All rights reserved.

pp. 306–7 "The Madman" by Kahlil Gibran. From *The Wanderer: His Parables and His Sayings*, by Kahlil Gibran. Copyright 1932 by Alfred A. Knopf, Inc. and renewed 1960 by Mary G. Gibran. Reprinted by permission of Alfred A. Knopf, Inc., and William Heinemann Ltd., Publishers.

pp. 307–8 From "How Hard It is to Keep from Being King When It's in You and in the Situation" from *The Poetry of Robert Frost* edited by Edward Connery Lathem. Copyright © 1962 by Robert Frost. Copyright © 1969 by Holt, Rinehart and Winston. Reprinted by permission of Holt, Rinehart and Winston, Publishers, and Jonathan Cape Limited.

p. 308 From "On Silence" by Freya Stark, *Holiday Magazine*, December 1965, reprinted with permission of *Holiday Magazine*, © 1965 The Curtis Publishing Company, and John Murray (Publishers) Ltd.

Library of Congress Cataloging in Publication Data

Main entry under title:

The planning of change.

First-2d editions edited by W. G. Bennis, K. D. Benne, and R. Chin.
Includes bibliographies and index.
1. Social change—Addresses, essays, lectures. I. Bennis, Warren G. II. Bennis, Warren G. The planning of change.
HM101.P558 1976   301.24'08   75–41359

ISBN 0–03–089518–9

Preface

The first edition of *The Planning of Change* was published in 1961, the second in 1969. This third edition shows both continuities with the previous editions and departures from them.

All have sought to contribute to the unfinished task of merging and reconciling the arts of social practice and action and the sciences of human behavior. This task, as we see it, presents both an intellectual and a practical, moral challenge to those who would improve the quality of life in American society. Living in an age whose single constant is change, all men and women are in urgent need of whatever resources can be made available as they seek to understand and manage themselves and their environments, to understand and solve the unprecedented personal and social problems that confront them.

The intellectual challenge comes from the necessity to develop an adequate theory of the processes through which knowledge of human behavior and of human systems is applied and utilized. More particularly, a theory of applying and adapting theories of social, interpersonal, and personal dynamics to the special case of deliberate changing is required. All editions have sought to bring together some of the best current conceptualizations of various aspects of utilization and change processes.

The practical, moral challenge lies in inventing and developing social technologies, consistent with our best social and behavioral knowledge and adequate to the practical and moral requirements of contemporary change situations. All editions have sought to present discussions and evaluations of a rapidly growing body of change technologies, viewed not as isolated methods for achieving and guiding change, but rather in their intellectual, practical, and moral bearings and implications.

Another part of the practical challenge is the development of persons who can function effectively and responsibly as agents of planned change. This edition, as well as its predecessors, has been designed to provide material aid in the education of such agents. Change agents are now being educated in various departments of social and behavioral science as well as in various professional schools. We have tried to keep the needs of this scattered academic audience in mind. As in the case of its predecessors, this edition should prove useful in departments of psychology, sociology, and anthropology and in schools of public and business administration, social work, education, theology, nursing and other health professions, and public health as well.

How does this third edition differ from the second? About four-fifths of the readings in this edition are new. This change reflects the current rapid expansion and development of theory-building, research, and practical experimentation in applied social and behavioral science in this country and abroad. We have tried to reflect the contours of this developing field of study in this edition.

Changes of emphasis in applied behavioral science have also occurred in response to the turbulent social environment of the 1960s and the various liberation movements which that decade released. These changes have been reflected throughout the present edition. The addition of Professor Kenneth Corey to our editorial group has enabled us to give an emphasis to processes of planning, particularly planning for community action and development, which the earlier editions did not provide.

It is hard to know where to begin and where to end in acknowledging the contributions of the many people who have helped us, directly and indirectly, in preparing this book. Our most direct debt is to those contributors whose work we have reprinted. Specific acknowledgement of our obligation to each of them and to their publishers is made at the beginning of each selection.

The index shows many names in addition to those of our contributors. In a number of cases, these writers have published work that we wished to include. Space limitations made inclusion impossible. We are nevertheless grateful for their very real help in maturing our own thinking.

Dr. Gina Abeles gave valuable editorial and bibliographical assistance throughout the preparation of this third edition.

W. G. B.

K. D. B.

R. C.

K. E. C.

Boston University

University of Cincinnati

December 1975

CONTENTS

Preface   v

Introduction   1

PART ONE: Planned Change in Perspective   9

Chapter 1:   Planned Change in Historical Perspective   11

1.1   Planned Change in America   *Kenneth D. Benne,
      Warren G. Bennis, and Robert Chin*   13
1.2   General Strategies for Effecting Changes in Human
      Systems   *Robert Chin and Kenneth D. Benne*   22

Chapter 2:   Contemporary Differentiations in Theories and
             Practices of Planned Change   46

2.1   Strategies of Consultation   *Robert R. Blake and
      Jane Srygley Mouton*   48
2.2   The Current State of Planned Changing in Persons,
      Groups, Communities and Societies   *Kenneth D. Benne*   68

PART TWO: Diagnostics of Planned Change   85

Chapter 3:   Systems   87

3.1   The Utility of System Models and Developmental
      Models for Practitioners   *Robert Chin*   90
3.2   The Utility of Models of the Environments of
      Systems for Practitioners   *Robert Chin*   103
3.3   The Differentiation-and-Integration Model
      Paul R. Lawrence and Jay W. Lorsch   112
3.4   Some Notes on the Dynamics of Resistance to Change:
      The Defender Role   *Donald Klein*   117

Chapter 4:   Utilization of Knowledge   125

4.1   Science and Practice   *Kenneth D. Benne, Robert Chin,
      and Warren G. Bennis*   128
4.2   Evaluating Theories of Action   *Chris Argyris and
      Donald A. Schön*   137
4.3   The Process of Utilization of Social Research To
      Improve Social Practice   *Ronald Lippitt*   147
4.4   An Exploratory Study of Knowledge Utilization
      Ronald G. Havelock and Kenneth D. Benne   151
4.5   Educational Field Experience as the Negotiation of
      Different Cognitive Worlds   *Kenneth D. Benne*   164
4.6   Pedagogy of the Oppressed   *Paulo Freire*   171

Chapter 5:   Emerging Perspectives on Planned
             Organizational Change   175

5.1   The Evolution of Organizational Environments
      S. Terreberry   178
5.2   Contemporary Perspectives on Planned Social Change: A
      Comparison   *James E. Crowfoot and Mark A. Chesler*   188
5.3   Social Experimentation and the Changing World of Work
      Neal Q. Herrick, Susan Bartholomew, and John Brandt   205
5.4   Who Sank the Yellow Submarine?   *Warren G. Bennis*   219

Chapter 6:   Support in the Empowering and Legitimation of
             Change Efforts   228

6.1   Consciousness-Raising: A Five Stage Model for Social and
      Organizational Change   *Samuel A. Culbert*   231
6.2   Who Speaks for the Poor?   *Neil Gilbert and
      Joseph W. Eaton*   245
6.3   Drama and Advocacy Planning   *Lisa R. Peattie*   251

PART THREE: Interventions for Planned Change   261

Chapter 7:   Planning Structures and Processes   263

7.1   Structures in the Planning of Community Change:
      A Personal Construct   *Kenneth E. Corey*   265
7.2   Open Systems Planning   *G. K. Jayaram*   275
7.3   A Group Process Model for Problem Identification and
      Program Planning   *André L. Delbecq and
      Andrew H. Van de Ven*   283
7.4   Retracking America: A Theory of Transactive Planning
      John Friedmann   297
7.5   Life Planning   *Herbert A. Shepard*   305

Chapter 8:   Education and Re-Education   314

8.1   The Processes of Re-Education: An Assessment of
      Kurt Lewin's Views   *Kenneth D. Benne*   315

8.2 Process Consultation   *Edgar Schein*   327
8.3 Explorations in Consulting-Client Relationships
     Chris Argyris   331
8.4 Toward the Style of the Community Change Educator
     Richard Franklin   352

Chapter 9:   Power and the New Politics   359

9.1 Alternative to the Status Quo: Education at Sanctum
     Michael Rossman   363
9.2 Half Slave, Half Free   *Philip Slater*   370
9.3 Beyond the Carrot and the Stick: Liberation and Power
     without Control   *John E. McCluskey*   382
9.4 Male Power and the Women's Movement
     Barbara Bovee Polk   404
9.5 Foundations for a Radical Concept of Planning
     Stephen Grabow and Allan Heskin   413

PART FOUR: Values and Goals   **425**

Chapter 10:   Finding Direction in Planned Change   427

10.1 Learning To Image the Future   *Elise Boulding*   431
10.2 The Future as the Basis for Establishing a Shared Culture
      Margaret Mead   444
10.3 Toward a Protean Style of Self-Process
      Robert Jay Lifton   458

Chapter 11:   Some Value Dilemmas of the Change Agent   467

11.1 Ethical Issues in Social Intervention
      Donald P. Warwick and Herbert C. Kelman   470
11.2 The Moral Orientation of Laboratory Methods of
      Education and Changing   *Kenneth D. Benne*   496

Index   507

Introduction

In an important sense this world of ours is a new world, in which the unity of knowledge, the nature of human communities, the order of society, the order of ideas, the very notions of society and culture have changed and will not return to what they have been in the past. What is new is new not because it has never been there before, but because it has changed in quality. One thing that is new is the prevalence of newness, the changing scale and scope of change itself, so that the world alters as we walk in it, so that the years of man's life measure not some small growth or rearrangement or moderation of what he learned in childhood, but a great upheaval. What is new is that in one generation our knowledge of the natural world engulfs, upsets, and complements all knowledge of the natural world before. The techniques, among and by which we live, multiply and ramify, so that the whole world is bound together by communication, blocked here and there by the immense synapses of political tyranny. The global quality of the world is new: our knowledge of and sympathy with remote and diverse peoples, our involvement with them in practical terms, and our commitment to them in terms of brotherhood. What is new in the world is the massive character of the dissolution and corruption of authority, in belief, in ritual, and in temporal order. Yet this is the world that we have to live in. The very difficulties which it presents derive from growth in understanding, in skill, in power. To assail the changes that have unmoored us from the past is futile, and in a deep sense, I think, it is wicked. We need to recognize the change and learn what resources we have.

Robert Oppenheimer[1]

[1] Robert Oppenheimer, "Prospects in the Arts and Sciences," *Perspectives USA*, II (Spring 1955), 10–11.

THE PROBLEM

Richard Weaver once remarked that the ultimate term in contemporary rhetoric, the "god term," is "progress" or "change":[2] the world, as Oppenheimer remarks, alters as we walk in it. It would appear, then, that we are beyond debating the inevitability of change; most students of our society agree that the one major invariant is the tendency toward movement, growth, development, process: change. The contemporary debate has swung from change versus no change to the methods employed in controlling and directing forces in change. Dewey has remarked that ". . . history in being a process of change generates change not only in details but also in the *method of directing social change.*"[3] The predicament we confront, then, concerns method; methods that maximize freedom and limit as little as possible the potentialities of growth; methods that will realize man's dignity as well as bring into fruition desirable social goals.

Concerning the methods of change, we can observe two idea systems in the contemporary scene that are directly counterposed: the law of nonintervention and the law of radical intervention. The former stems from the natural-law and "invisible-hand" ideology of the laissez-faire doctrine—part economic analysis and part ideology. Tampering and social tinkering with man's natural and social universe interferes with the homeostatic forces, which, if left unfettered, will bring about the perfectly optimized good life. Keynesian and welfare economics, as well as the monopolistic structure of contemporary society, have all exposed the weaknesses in the natural-equilibrium position. (Keynes once remarked that classical economic doctrines may well work in the long run; but, he poignantly added, in the long run we'll all be dead.)

Marxian analysis, with its emphasis on conflict, inevitable class struggle, and radical intervention—occasionally at the price of human freedom—represents the other extreme. Although Marxian theory was developed as an indispensable antidote to the elegant rationalizations of the laissez-faire doctrine, it now also suffers from an obsolescence wrought by the accelerating changes of the world, including the Marxian world, which its basic theory could not predict or encompass.

Planned change, as we view it, emerges as the only feasible alternative to the methods; that is, a method which self-consciously and experimentally employs social knowledge to help solve the problems of men and societies. One may approve or deplore the concept of planned change—or look on it with scientific detachment. But no one will deny its importance. And this book

[2] Richard Weaver, "Ultimate Terms in Contemporary Rhetoric," *Perspectives USA,* II (Spring 1955), 123.

[3] John Dewey, *Liberalism and Social Action* (New York: G. P. Putnam's Sons, 1935), p. 83 (our italics).

was designed to bring about greater understanding of its developing methods, the social processes bearing on its use, its potentialities, its consequences, both ethical and pragmatic, as well as its limitations.

NATURE OF THIS BOOK

There is an old parable that has made the rounds about the grasshopper who decided to consult the hoary consultant of the animal kingdom, the owl, about a personal problem. The problem concerned the fact that the grasshopper suffered each winter from severe pains due to the savage temperature. After a number of these painful winters, in which all of the grasshopper's known remedies were of no avail, he presented his case to the venerable and wise owl. The owl, after patiently listening to the grasshopper's misery, so the story goes, prescribed a simple solution. "Simply turn yourself into a cricket, and hibernate during the winter." The grasshopper jumped joyously away, profusely thanking the owl for his wise advice. Later, however, after discovering that this important knowledge could not be transformed into action, the grasshopper returned to the owl and asked him how he could perform this metamorphosis. The owl replied rather curtly, "Look, I gave you the principle. It's up to you to work out the details!"

All parables, supposedly, contain a moral, and the moral here provides one of the main cornerstones of this volume: How can the man of knowledge utilize his hard-won knowledge to help clients and lay personnel? And conversely, how can the lay public provide information and insight that will aid the man of knowledge, the expert, in his role as helper as well as theory builder?

These are not simple questions, and unfortunately ways of answering them are not easily arrived at or even certainly known. And the conditions of the world today—with the often noted communication gap between actionists, practitioners and scientists, clients and professional helpers—and the ever increasing specialization and technocracy of the sciences, tend to exacerbate the problem. In another part of the essay quoted above, Oppenheimer states eloquently what can be taken as a central leitmotiv of this book of readings and text:

The specialization of science is an inevitable accompaniment of progress; yet it is full of dangers, and it is cruelly wasteful, since so much that is beautiful and enlightening is cut off from most of the world. Thus it is proper to the role of the scientist that he not merely find new truth and communicate it to his fellows, but that he teach, that he try to bring the most honest and intelligible account of new knowledge to all who will try to learn. This is one reason—it is the decisive organic reason—why scientists belong in universities. It is one reason why the patronage of science by and through universities is its most proper form; for it is here, in teaching, in the association of scholars, and in the friendships of teachers and taught, of men who by profession must themselves be both teachers and taught, that the narrowness of scientific life can best be moderated, and that the analogies, insights, and harmonies of scientific discovery can find their way into the wider life of man.[4]

Putting the problem a little differently, we can say that the major foundation of this book is the *planful application of valid and appropriate knowledge in human* affairs for the purpose of creating intelligent action and change. Thus, this is a book that focuses on *planned change*; conscious, deliberate, and collaborative effort to improve the operations of a human system, whether it be a self-system, social system, or cultural system, through the utilization of valid knowledge.[5]

Let us review briefly some of the organizing features of this volume. First, what is meant by valid and appropriate knowledge? The parable, of course, burlesques just this point. Yet we find that a substantial body of social science literature suffers an owlish deficiency. Whitehead, commenting pungently on this matter said: "In this modern world the celibacy of the medieval learned class has been replaced by a celibacy of the intellect which is divorced from the concrete contemplation of complete facts."[6]

The relationship between theory and practice must constantly be kept within the same field of vision in order for both to cope with the exigencies of reality. We have developed a substantial body of theory and certainly a rich body of practice, but somehow our failure has been to provide the necessary transformations and bridgings between the two. Kurt Lewin, one of the intellectual forebears of this volume, was preoccupied with this issue of the relationship between the abstract and concrete. He once compared this task to the building of a bridge across the gorge separating theory from full reality. "The research worker can achieve this only if, as a result of a constant intense tension, he can keep both theory and reality fully within his field of vision."[7] We seem, quite often, to become lost at the crossroads of a false dichotomy;

[4] Oppenheimer, p. 9.

[5] Ronald Lippitt et al., *Dynamics of Planned Change* (New York: Harcourt, Brace & World, Inc., 1958). This book would undoubtedly serve as an excellent companion text to this volume. Any book of readings, by definition, suffers from a lack of systematic integration of its content; Lippitt's book may provide a welcome format for readers of this text. On the other hand, *Dynamics* represents a more constricted view of change than the present volume.

A recent publication, K. Benne, L. Bradford, J. Gibb, and R. Lippitt (Eds.), *The Laboratory Method of Changing and Learning: Theory and Application* (Palo Alto, Calif.: Science and Behavior Books, 1975), significantly overlaps the content of this volume, particularly in the emphasis on the place of re-education in personal and social change. Readers of this volume who wish to explore some of the methodologies and technologies dealt with in this volume in summary fashion, may wish to consult this source.

[6] Alfred North Whitehead, *Science and the Modern World* (New York: Mentor Books).

[7] Remark attributed to Lewin by his wife, Getrud Weiss Lewin, in her introduction to *Resolving Social Conflicts* (New York: Harper & Row, Publishers, 1948).

the purity and virginity of theory on the one hand and the anti-intellectualism of some knowledge-for-what adherents on the other. This division oversimplifies the issue. The issue is far more complicated; it concerns the transformations and developmental conceptualizing that have to be undertaken before theory can become practical.[8]

Once these intellectual linkages between theory and practice are effectively established, we have to be concerned further with the social processes that bear on the infusion of knowledge into action and policy decisions. These two foci—practical theory and the social dynamics of utilizing knowledge in effecting change—make up two of the dominant themes in this volume.

One other meaning that has implications for the organization of this book can be drawn from our parable. The grasshopper, supplicant, comes to the expert owl for help. The owl listens to the problem, prescribes a remedy, and terminates the relationship. The owl did not discuss implementation or consequences of his therapy, nor did he seem to understand the *dependence* of the client, nor did he recognize the *transference* in the relationship. The owl simply proffered a rational *"solution."* The meaning, then, that now emerges from our parable has to do with the nature of the relationship between the man of knowledge, the expert, and his client. Our conviction, which is reflected in a number of articles in this volume, is that the extent to which knowledge can be effectively utilized by practitioners and clients— especially knowledge provided for social change—depends to a great extent on the nature of the relationship between the client and change agent.[9] In other words, we do not view science in and of itself as the panacea. This naïve technocratic viewpoint does not take into account the importance of the existential relationship between the man of knowledge (change agent) and the client system. Dewey once said that "Mankind now has in its pos-

---

[8] Harold Guetzkow writes about the conversion barriers in using the social sciences. "Little attention has been given," he says, "to the way the very structure of knowledge affects its conversion for application. In the social sciences the role of scientist, engineer, technician, practitioner, and policy-maker has not been well differentiated. It may be useful to sketch how the knowledge that the scientist develops may be converted by others for use and then to examine the impact of certain characteristics of basic knowledge upon the application process." This conversion process is one of the main concerns of this volume. See "Conversion Barriers in Using the Social Sciences," *Administrative Science Quarterly*, IV (1959), 68–81.

[9] These terms have been developed in conjunction with the National Training Laboratories and used by Lippitt et al. in *Dynamics of Planned Change* (New York: Harcourt, Brace & World, Inc., 1958). Client refers to the person or group being helped, thus client system whether it be person, group, organization, community, culture, family, club, or whatever. Change agent refers to the helper, the person or group who is attempting to effect change. These are fairly clumsy terms but we cannot think of ready substitutes, and they are coming into wider usage.

We might point out now that Lippitt et al. restrict the role of the change agent by defining him as exogenous to the client system, a person from the outside who attempts to effect change. We believe this is too narrow a view, and we have encompassed in our definition the idea that the change agent may be either in or outside the client system.

session a new method, that of cooperative and experimental science which expresses the method of intelligence."[10] In this book on the theory and practice of planned change we aim to stress the cooperative and collaborative aspects of the various relationships implicated in change—change agent to client, among clients, and among change agents—as well as the scientific findings related to change. (Too often social scientists neglect as legitimate inquiry the collaborative process and the interpersonal and methodological norms and rules distinctively required in the practices of an action science.)

We are now in a better position to express succinctly the nature of this book. Perhaps our greatest emphasis is on the processes of planned changing, on how change is created, implemented, evaluated, maintained, and resisted. The processes of change take us, given its enormous scope, into many fields. The exploration fans out into the various dimensions of change processes (from brainwashing to introducing change in a classroom or a factory), into the social and psychological consequences of change, into the antecedent conditions for effectively planning change, into strategic leverage points for effecting change. Included, also, are some of the major instruments which have been developed for creating and maintaining change: training, consulting, and applied research.

Focusing on the processes and instruments of change, however, does not provide an adequate picture of the complications of change and changing. We have to illuminate the targets or systems to which the change is directed. In this book we make a strong effort to keep in mind four types (or levels) of systems: self, role, interpersonal or group, and larger systems such as formal organizations, communities, and in some cases, cultural systems. "The educational task," Dewey once said, "cannot be accomplished merely by working on men's minds without action that effects actual changes in institutions."[11] We cannot overemphasize the importance of keeping the fact in mind that human behavior is like a centipede, standing on many legs. Nothing that we do has a single determinant. We emphasize this now because we believe there is a danger in focusing too narrowly on personality factors; elements in addition to the *personal* equipment of the client and the change agent must be considered.

In addition to the change processes and the various client systems, we will present material, touched on earlier, relevant to the nature of the collaborative processes in planned-change programs. Moreover, some attention will be given to the strategy and methodology of planned change, its complexities, vicissitudes, and outcomes.

George Santayana once observed that in our changing world we no longer salute our ancestors but bid them good-bye. The temptations to ungrateful impiety are great for all men but perhaps particularly great for practitioners and theorists of planned change with their typical present and future

[10] Dewey, op. cit., p. 83.
[11] Dewey, op. cit., p. 4.

orientation to human affairs. We have tried to resist this temptation to impiety in ourselves by giving attention to the historical roots of contemporary ideas about deliberate changing of men and societies. We have sought to salute our ancestors in this field of intellectual and moral endeavor, both ancestors who have fed our own chosen orientation and those who have nourished variant contemporary orientations. Statements about change become shrill and hollow, when they do not include attention to the conditions of stability and continuity in human life.

No discussion of planned change would be complete without some attention to the perplexing philosophical issues, axiological and ethical, which this subject generates. In these times of "hidden persuaders," brainwashing, "payola," conformity, and manipulation, lay and intellectual publics alike are exceedingly wary, lest social and psychological knowledge bring into actuality the specter of predictable—and thereby helpless—man. We share this concern, as a number of articles in this volume attest; but we also join Spinoza in saying that our job as men of knowledge is not to weep or laugh, but to understand.

One of our problems here is that our ethical-value positions are intimately related to our pragmatic positions. For example when we postulate that collaboration is a *sine qua non* of effective planned change, we are insisting on an ethical imperative as well as on a scientific objective. Value orientations color almost every statement in the book. The best we can hope to do is make our own values as explicit as we can. Throughout the course of the book we have attempted to do this.

A brief word about the outline of this volume is now in order. What is the outline of this third edition of the book, and how does it compare and contrast with the second edition? The present edition contains four parts. In Part One, we try to provide perspective on "planned change," as we define it, by discussing its underlying ideas and variant methodologies in two sorts of contexts. The first context is historical. How has thinking about "planned change" and its uses been influenced by the tortuous career of social science and social practice and action in American society? Our second edition was published in 1969 during the cresting of the civil rights and other liberation movements in America and in the midst of American involvement in the Vietnam War. We made no attempt to discuss the effects of the turbulent 1960s on the practice and prospects of planned change. In this edition, we try to assess these effects and to reflect our assessment in the readings selected for Parts Two to Four of the book. The second context we have chosen for placing planned change in perspective is a mapping of the internal differentiations in its methodologies and technologies which have emerged in its evolution, as a social movement and as a practice profession, in the fifteen years since our first edition was published in 1961. The second edition provided no such systematic typology of variant technologies of planned changing addressed to persons, groups, organizations, communities, and societies as targets of changing.

In the third edition, we have devoted Parts Two and Three to the "diag-nostic" and "intervention" aspects of planned change, respectively. The mean-ing and use of four families of concepts in diagnosing change situations are explored in Part Two—"social system," "knowledge utilization," "conflict, power and authority," and "support systems." Three intervention modes—"planning structures and processes," "re-education" and "the new politics"—are dealt with in Part Four. The readings in Parts Two and Three of the present volume differ from the corresponding parts of the second edition in three ways. (1) We have dealt directly with the structures and processes of "open systems" and "transactive" planning where these were touched only tangentially in the preceding edition. (2) We have sought a better balance between processes of changing in community and in organizational settings where the second edition focused primarily upon organizational change. (3) We have, in this edition, honored one legacy from the 1960s in dealing with the difficult problems of mobilizing the efforts and energies of "the poor" and "the oppressed" in pursuing changes which serve their interests as they articu-late these for themselves and which augment their continuing exercise of power in community life.

Part Four of this volume, like Part Four of the second edition, explores the dilemmas confronted by agents of planned change with respect to the directions and goals to which change programs should be oriented and with respect to the ethical and moral principles which should guide their decisions and actions. The readings in this volume deal more adequately than we were able to do in the second edition: (1) with difficulties of imaging the future both of persons and institutions and (2) with the ethical problems encount-ered at the level of public policy-making.

This, in a very general way, indicates the content and emphasis of the present volume. We hope that readers will recognize the editors' difficulties in constructing a book of readings that draw upon so wide a range of sources—from the major disciplines of the behavioral sciences, from the history and philosophy of these sciences, from social and personal ethics, and from theories of application and practice. However, that is, as we see it, the requi-site scope of our topic, and hence this book of readings.

Planned
Change in Perspective

PART ONE

Planned Change
in Historical Perspective

CHAPTER
ONE

One way in which people gain perspective on current events which are moving around them, indeed events which are moving in and through them since their choices and actions contribute to shaping the events, is to think of those events historically. How did the events come to be? What human needs, aspirations, and conflicts lent motivation to the events? What changes in life conditions gave them impetus and focus? And what ideas and ideals provided direction and justification for them? In this chapter, we attempt to place that evolving complex of events, which we have called "planned change," in historical perspective.

Another way to get perspective on a field of study and practice is to map the different varieties of thought and practice which have developed internally to the field. "Planned change" has undergone a rapid internal differentiation since the first edition of this book was published in 1961. In Chapter Two we try to make sense of current bewildering differentiations within the advocacy and practice of "planned change."

Our treatment of the history of planned change in this chapter must, of necessity, be impressionistic. No thorough historical study of it has yet been made. One strand in its history is the changing relationships between persons of knowledge and persons of action, between persons who are expert because of their special studies and persons who are in political and managerial control of institutions or who aspire to such control. For, as we have noted, planned change involves a new relationship between social scientists, students of human affairs on the one hand, and practitioners and action planners and leaders, on the other. Planned change requires collaboration between social scientists and action planners. This is in contrast to the segregation and conflict which have marked the relations between "theory" and "practice" traditionally and which persist in contemporary social organization, despite the widespread breaching of the walls of segregation in recent years.

Of course, the use of experts as advisers and consultants to rulers is much older than the relatively recent emergence of the social sciences or the helping professions as research and teaching disciplines in modern universities. In the past the experts may have been sages, priests, shamans, astrologers, or philosophers rather than scientists in the modern sense. George A. Kelly has outlined the changing history of these uneasy relationships in an illuminating essay, "The Expert as Historical Actor."[1]

Kelly makes clear the basis of many of the dilemmas of experts who are drawn into the service of action programs and projects. They must mediate between a system shaped to the production and refinement of knowledge and a system concerned centrally with the exercise and channeling of power in the service of practicable ends. Where the persons of knowledge may espouse a Utopian "sociological vision," they must deal with non-Utopian action leaders who are committed to the achievement of the possible and practicable within an existing system of power relationships.

As protagonists of planned change, we do not see a Utopian end to the contrasting and conflicting mentalities and characters selected and nurtured by systems of knowledge and by systems of power which Kelly's essay illuminates or an end to the tensions in relationship which result when persons from both systems attempt to collaborate in planning for the resolution and melioration of human issues and ills. But we do believe that such unwonted collaborations are increasingly required by an irreversible shift in our society from tradition-directed policies and practices to knowledge-based policies and practices and from unconscious historical selection of viable patterns and forms of living to deliberate human choice, invention, and evaluation of such patterns and forms. Part of the task of planned change is the linkage and re-education of hitherto segregated and conflicting groups toward the practice of creative collaboration. Another strand in the history of planned change would, therefore, be a documentation of this irreversible shift from a non-planned to a planned way of life in postindustrial societies.

In the first selection in this chapter, "Planned Change in America," the editors sketch shifting and conflicting attitudes and practices among social scientists, social practitioners, policy makers, and oppressed minorities in America with respect to several distinguishable aspects of planned change since the late nineteenth century. These aspects include consciousness of the need for planning changes in human life; the relations of social scientists to social practice and planning; the professionalization of change agents; and

---

[1] *Daedalus,* Volume 92, No. 3.

the place of popular participation in the direction and evaluation of programs of changing.

In "General Strategies for Effecting Changes in Human Systems," Chin and Benne attempt two tasks. They propose a three-way classification of the strategies of changing in current use. The authors of this volume are committed to one of these families of strategies, the "normative re-educative," as most appropriate to the conditions of contemporary life and to the advancement of scientific and democratic values in human society. But this commitment does not mean that the authors reject any place for the other two families of strategies—the "rational-empirical" and the "power-coercive," as Chin and Benne name them—in the armamentarium of change agents and change strategists in our time. It is probably safe to predict that all three kinds of strategies will continue to be used in action programs. However, we believe that continuing research, development, and training in the applied behavioral sciences will extend the use of normative re-educative strategies in local, national, and world society.

Chin and Benne also attempt to place the three classes of general strategies within recent historical streams of thought about man and society, which have fed these strategies and their sustaining and supporting rationales. This tracing of the intellectual roots of contemporary ways of thinking about planned change is designed to establish continuities with our past as well as to place alternative contemporary approaches to changing into clearer relief. Although this final piece was prepared primarily for an audience of leaders in public education, it should have meaning for change strategists in other institutional settings as well.

1.1   PLANNED CHANGE IN AMERICA

Kenneth D. Benne, Warren G. Bennis,
Robert Chin

The idea of social scientists participating in and actively influencing the planning and implementation of social change has been a center of controversy in America

This piece has been written for this edition. It incorporates material from the first edition of *The Planning of Change: Readings in the Applied Behavioral Sciences*, edited by Warren G. Bennis, Kenneth D. Benne, and Robert Chin. Copyright © 1961 by Holt, Rinehart and Winston, Inc.

since the emergence of the idea in the late nineteenth century. The idea of social planning and governmental employment of experts is, of course, much older. But the differentiation of the more behaviorally oriented social sciences—psychology, sociology, and anthropology—as distinct research disciplines, along with tentative acceptance of and support for them within the university structure in the late nineteenth and early twentieth centuries, gave new impetus to the Baconian dream of a New Atlantis governed by scientific thinkers and doers. Controversy over the idea has divided in varying degree action leaders, policy makers, social scientists, professional practitioners, and the "general public" from 1900 to the present.

The focus of the controversy has shifted during this time, along with the terms in which the issue is discussed. In fact, we see two major shifts in this continuing debate. One shift occurred between 1900 and the 1950s. The shift accompanied the co-optation of liberal progressivism by the New Deal and its domestication of a "brain trust" of professors into the service of government change programs. A new characteristic quality of the controversy is most apparent in the affluent 1950s.

The second shift in the controversy occurred during the 1960s. This period was marked by the emergence and cresting of the civil rights and other liberation movements, by the pressure of various "grass roots" protest movements against the established techno-structure,[1] by the emergence and spread of a survivors' mentality among various segments of American society, and by the Vietnam War and its aftermath. We are too close to these events of the 1960s to see clearly or fully either their motivations or their consequences. But it is clear that they did refocus attitudes toward planned change and affected its rationale, its opportunities and responsibilities, and its practices. Events, new thoughts, and occurrences in

[1] "Techno-structure" is Galbraith's term for the coalition between interests and their spokesmen within both the private and the public (governmental) structures of our political economy. The "military-industrial complex" is one often-mentioned aspect of this coalition. It is this coalition which makes decisions concerning the policies which control our economic and related social and political life. See J. K. Galbraith, *The New Industrial State* (Boston: Houghton Mifflin, 1967: 2d Revised Edition, 1971).

countries abroad have contributed direct and indirect waves of influence on American thinking about the need for and processes of planned change.

Let us return now to the history of planned change in America. In 1900, controversy over planned change was typically stated in sweeping ideological terms. Should or should not men seek, through deliberate and collaborative forethought in the present, to mold the shape of their collective future? Or should confidence rather be placed in a principle of automatic adjustment, operating within the processes of history to reequilibrate, without human forethought yet in the interest of progress and human welfare, the inescapable human upsets and dislocations of a changing society?

This issue raised a corollary issue concerning the proper relations of the emerging social sciences of the time, and of social scientists, to the guidance and management of practical affairs. In general, the "planners" saw an important place for social science in informing policies and in rendering social practice more intelligent and reality-oriented. Proponents of "automatic adjustment" tended to relegate social scientists to an observer role and to deny them participation or leadership in influencing the direction or the form of practical affairs. This conception of "nonintervening" social science fitted the mainline traditions of the natural sciences and of the older social studies—history, economics, and political theory. This view of the proper relationships between social science and social action was further reinforced by aspirations of the younger and more behavior-oriented sciences—psychology and sociology—to achieve and maintain their autonomy and "purity" within the academic world in which they were parvenus. The issue concerning "science" and "practice" has been raised anew as "applied social science" has been encouraged and supported by many policy-makers and social practitioners, and actively promoted by some social scientists.

Lester F. Ward was one of the earliest social scientists in America to proclaim that modern men must extend scientific approaches into the planning of changes in the patterns of their behaviors and relationships. He was well aware that men were already utilizing their accumulating collective and scientific intelligence deliberately to induce changes in their nonhuman environment. And he saw a major role for the emerging sciences of man in extending a similar planning approach into the management of human affairs.

Man's destiny is in his own hands. Any law that he can comprehend he can control. He cannot increase or diminish the powers of nature, but he can direct them. . . . His power over nature is unlimited. He can make it his servant and appropriate to his own use all the mighty forces of the universe. . . . Human institutions are not exempt from this all-pervading spirit of improvement. They, too, are artificial, conceived in the ingenious brain and wrought with mental skill born of inventive genius. The passion for their improvement is of a piece with the impulse to improve the plow or the steam engine. . . . Intelligence, heretofore a growth, is destined to become a manufacture. . . . The origination and distribution of knowledge can no longer be left to chance or to nature. They are to be systematized and erected into true arts.[2]

Ward's proclamation seemed foolish boasting, if not downright sacrilege, to many among his contemporaries. William Graham Sumner was one of the leaders in sociology who emphasized both the folly and sacrilege of prophecies like Ward's.

If we can acquire a science of society based on observation of phenomena and study of forces, we may hope to gain some ground slowly toward the elimination of old errors and the re-establishment of a sound and natural social order. Whatever we gain that way will be by growth, never in the world by any reconstruction of society on the plan of some enthusiastic social architect. The latter is only repeating the old error over again, and postponing all our chances of real improvement. Society needs first of all to be free from these meddlers—that is, to be let alone. Here we are, then, once more back at the old doctrine *laissez faire*. Let us translate it into blunt English, and it will read—Mind your own business. It is nothing but the doctrine of liberty. Let every man be happy in his own way.[3]

It may be fortunate or unfortunate that American controversies a half century later over the direction and management of social change seldom took the form of sweeping societal prescriptions and counterprescriptions or ideological debates—a form which Ward and Sumner, along with their contemporaries, gave to them. In any event, the form of the controversies shifted. In large measure subsequent events have foreclosed the factual basis for Sumner's argument. *Laissez faire* has been widely abandoned in practice as a principle of social management, whatever ghostly existence it yet enjoys in conservative political platforms and pronunciamentos. Human interventions designed to shape and modify the institutionalized behaviors of men are now familiar features of our social landscape. "Helping professions" have proliferated since Ward's and Sumner's day. Professions of industrial and public management have taken shape. The reason for being of all of these is deliberately

[2] Quoted in Henry Commager, *The American Mind* (New Haven, Conn.: Yale University Press, 1950), pp. 208, 210, 213–214.

[3] Quoted in Commager, op cit., pp. 201–202.

to induce and coach changes in the future behaviors and relationships of their various "client" populations. This is most apparent in "new" professions such as psychiatry, social work, nursing, counseling, management, and consultation in its manifold forms. But older professions too, such as medicine, law, teaching, and the clergy, have been pressed increasingly to become agencies of social change rather than of social conservation. Resistances to assuming the new role have, of course, developed along with the situational pressures to enact it.

Behavioral scientists, neo-Sumnerians among others, in the first part of the twentieth century, were drawn, with varying degrees of eagerness and resistance, into activities of "changing," such as consultation and applied research. "Helping professionals," "managers," and "policy-makers" in various fields of practice increasingly sought and employed the services of behavioral scientists to anticipate more accurately the consequences of prospective social changes and to inform more validly the processes of planning designed to control these consequences.

We were widely seeking to plan social changes in the fifties. And both the products and the methods of social research were being more and more widely utilized in the processes of such planning. Sumner's ideological advice had been widely rejected in practice.

But it is equally true that Ward's millennial hope seemed far—indeed very far—from realization. Attempts to apply social knowledge in planning and controlling changes tended to be fragmented by the division of contemporary agents of change into specialized and largely noncommunicating professions and disciplines. These attempts were thwarted too by noncommunication and noncollaboration among policy-makers and action planners in the various institutional settings where planning has become familiar

practice—industry, government, welfare, health, and education. Advocates and students of planned change became more cautious in their claims, less millennial in their hopes than Ward tended to be. The modal question shifted from "Should we seek to plan change?" to "How to plan particular changes in particular settings and situations?" Where the wider societal view had not been entirely lost the question was raised of "How to interrelate and link the various forms which the planning of change has taken in conventionally isolated but actually interdependent settings of social action and practice?"

Men in the fifties had thus widely come to believe that they had no actual choice as to whether somebody will seek to plan continuing changes in the patterns of their lives. Men must try to plan their changing futures, and this necessity is seen to be determined by cultural conditions, not primarily by the ideology men happen to hold. "Democratic," "communistic," and "fascist" peoples must alike try to plan social changes. This helped to account for the shift of many questions about planned change from an "ideological" to a "technical" form. This did not mean, as some who would reduce all questions of planning to technical form might believe, that questions about the values which should guide planners can or should disappear from discussions about planning or from the processes of planning. It meant rather that these questions too had taken new forms.

Both Ward and Sumner worked within a framework of common assumptions about the actuality and desirability, if not the inevitability, of Progress. Their ideological differences centered on varying ways of achieving the Progress which both generally assumed to be, in some way, America's destiny, and by patriotic extension, human destiny as well. (The pessimism of Sumner grown old came more from despair over the course of events about him than from relinquishment of this ideal.) Differing means of achieving Progress, of course, if carefully analyzed, meant different meanings of Progress as well. But the values of "rationality," "freedom," "universal education," and the "extension through science of human control over the natural environment" were, in general, values acceptable to "planners" and "antiplanners" as well. Both sought to settle value issues by an appeal to living traditions of "liberalism" and "democracy," traditions not usually clearly distinguished one from the other.

It was a living tradition of "liberal democracy" that could no longer be assumed or taken for granted in discussions of issues of planned change in the period after World War II. Intellectually and practically, consensus in the core values of "liberalism" and "democracy" had been eroded in America. And these values had never been a part of the living tradition of many national cultures outside America in both technologically developed and undeveloped nations. The possibility, desirability, and meaning of Progress, and most emphatically its inevitability, as defined and revered within the liberal tradition, had been challenged fundamentally.

Neoconservative critiques of "liberalism" had been familiar features of the American intellectual scene for a generation before the 1950s. "Liberal" theology had been attacked by religious neo-orthodoxies of various types. "Liberal" politics had been denounced as unrealistic and "soft" by political conservatives who sought to meet their security needs through maintaining a militarily strong capitalist state within a hostile world. "Progressive" education had been inveighed against by various conservative critics as negligent of "fundamentals" in knowledge and in morality.

As already noted, the focus of attention of most people interested in planning in the 1950s was on the technical ques-tions of how to plan in particular isolated social settings, rather than on the more fundamental questions of who should be involved in processes of planning and of what overarching values and purposes processes of planning should serve. The prevailing model of planning was an *engineering* model of applied science rather than a clinical model, in terms of Alvin Gouldner's distinction.[4] In the *engineering* model, plans are made by experts to meet the needs of the people affected by the plan as the experts interpret these needs, as well as relevant objective technical and economic conditions and requirements. After the plan is made, the consent of those affected to the plan is engineered by effective means of monologic persuasion. In the *clinical* model, the experts work collaboratively and dialogically with those affected by the policy to be made in order to inform them and to empower them toward participation in making, evaluating, and remaking operating plans. (It is, of course, apparent that the authors of this book are committed to the clinical rather than the engineering model.)

The New Deal, World War II, and the scientific management movement had familiarized our society in the uses of the expertise of economists and other students of people and of society according to the engineering model of planning. Only a minority of critics, for example, in the human relations movement in industry, in mental health, and in community work, advocated an alternative model of participatory planning and of the deployment and use of social science resources. We believe that this preference for "technological" solutions to human problems in the 1950s was by no means accidental.

For the liberal faith in progress in America had become intertwined, in both

[4] Alvin W. Gouldner, "Explorations in Applied Social Science," *Social Problems,* Vol. 3, No. 3, January 1956, pp. 173–181.

learned and popular minds, with a faith in technology as the guarantor of progress. Many people believed that the only realistic and dependable index of progress was the development and utilization of an ever more refined and powerful technology. A changing technology, so Veblen and others argued, was the principal motor of social change. Each technological advance involved us in new social and human problems. But the devotees of technology, and these included most Americans, believed that a new technology would be invented to solve these problems with a minimum of effort, travail, or responsibility on the part of most people. The technological experts would eventually save us.

It was the evidence of cataclysmic historic events, rather than the criticisms already noted, that cast convincing doubt upon the inherent beneficence of the technological god. After the day in August 1945 when a U.S. Bomber dropped a nuclear bomb—a stupendous technological achievement—upon Hiroshima, many sensed that mankind had moved, in Karl Jaspers' term, into a new Axial period of human history. Man's ingenious and inventive cultivation of technology had given him the power to pollute his planet irreparably and to destroy all terrestrial life.

Actually, the germ of the mentality of the lucky and guilty survivors of holocaust was planted during World War II by Nazi genocide and the real possibilities of irreparable nuclear pollution. This mentality did not flower until the 1960s. Most of us persisted through the 1950s in role-playing a dying faith in technological solutions to human problems and watched the increasing gross national product and the proliferation of ingenious gadgets to add to human comfort as evidences of a societal health and growth in which we no longer deeply believed.

This is no place to write the history of the turbulent 1960s in America. But several of its developments have thrown the discussions and practices of planned change into new relief. It is these developments which we will note and attempt to interpret in their influence on the practice of planned change.

The 1960s were marked by a wave of liberation movements which stemmed from persons and groups of persons who felt alienated from the mainstream of American life, alienated from themselves and their "real" nature and potentialities, oppressed by the forms and conventions of established society. Protests against oppressive conditions of life and against those who defended and maintained these conditions began with racial groups, particularly Blacks in America, and spread to students and younger people, to poor people, to women, to homosexuals, to American Indians, and to environmental conservationists.[5]

Almost invariably the language and rhetoric of protest was a language and rhetoric of "power"; the goal of protest, in addition to local and occasional goals,

[5] It is interesting to note that the U.S. Supreme Court in its decision in *Brown* vs. *Kansas* in 1954 gave unprecedentedly strong weight to the evidence and recommendations of social scientists concerning the educational effects of racial segregation. Thus, this landmark decision, which gave impetus to the civil rights movement, created conflicting public images of "social science" and its relation to the making of public policy. Within the minds of those who opposed the decision, suspicion of "social scientists" as "radicals" was created or reinforced. Within the leadership of the Black community and of other militant supporters of the civil rights movement, this significant contribution by social scientists may have created unrealistic expectations of their continuing support which were partly destroyed and replaced by disillusionment in the light of the neutrality shown by many social scientists when, during the height of the civil rights movement, polarization and conflict deepened and violence flared.

was a redistribution of maldistributed power. Protests were "mass" movements but most often the professed aim was to encourage oppressed persons to lift themselves out of the reactive mass, to encourage individuals to become proactive, to accept and affirm themselves as persons, to reject the attributions of inferiority, powerlessness, and helplessness which those in charge of established society place upon them. The "new" consciousness-raising aimed toward politicizing traditional relationships by exposing and emphasizing their "power" dimension. But the consciousness-raising and self-affirming actions advocated and practiced were "therapeutic" in intention as they sought self-acceptance and self-assertion for those whom the "establishment" had put down and kept down. And the protest movements also often embodied qualities of religious commitment, putting faith above conventional and "worldly" knowledge and wisdom. Institutionalized compartmentalizations of "politics," "therapy," and "religion" were broken down. Were new mergers of purpose and method and alternative institutions implicit in the razing of old boundaries and walls?

Some of the protest movements, especially those defined along generational lines, young *versus* old, cut across national boundaries and emerged in capitalist, communist, and socialist countries, in developed and developing countries.[6] Were there intimations of a nascent world culture in the youth movements, a nascent consciousness and culture, pressing against the confines of repressive and outmoded social organization and controls?[7]

[6] See, for example, Margaret Mead, *Culture and Commitment* (New York: Natural History Press, 1970).

[7] Charles A. Reich's, *The Greening of America* (New York: Random House, 1970), emphatically overstated this view.

How have these liberation movements and new experiences in grass-roots participation in community planning affected the status of planned change? What problems and opportunities have they precipitated for students and practitioners of planned change?

They exposed and in a measure cleared away some of the conventional debris that has clouded the realities of existing relationships in our society—the distorting effects of power differentials, the dysfunctional inhibitions of expression of affect, positive and negative, in many human relationships; the gap between professed values and values in use; and the dehumanizing effects of depersonalized relations in many of our bureaucratized institutions, political, industrial, and educational. These effects are clearly in line with the values of planned change of the sort we are advocating and are supportive of its continuing thrust.

They have unmasked the assimilationist myth of the American melting pot and revealed the pluralism inherent in American life, the variety of groups and group interests that are seeking their place in the sun, and they have thus placed the clarification and negotiation of differing values and value orientations as an inescapable priority upon the agenda of agents of change and their clients. Technical problems remain but they can no longer crowd out the clarification and negotiation of value stances. The stance of value neutrality on the part of applied social scientists and social practitioners has been effectively debunked.

In their emphases on redistribution of power, they have revealed inadequacies in their own conceptions of power and in the conceptions of power held by many of their adversaries as well. The assumption that power exists in a fixed amount and that one must take power away from those who wield it in order to gain power for one's self and one's group vitiated many of their well-intentioned programs of change. Power can be generated by peer support, by a more adequate self-concept, by shared values and goals, by access to more valid knowledge and information. Win-win strategies of changing can be built upon this latter conception of power. Win-lose strategies of changing which lead to destructive polarization are bolstered by the assumption that power exists in a limited and fixed amount. Agents of planned change have an important re-educative task in the conceptual clarification of power and in finding strategies for its generation and use.

This is illustrative of the fact that protestors often were clearer about their values and goals than they were creative in inventing methods and strategies of changing that were coherent with their values and goals and which led to effects consistent with their intentions. This clearly presents a re-educative task for the agent of change. But, we believe, liberation movements, in general, created a readiness for such re-education that was not there before.

We have stated that one of the values of planned change, as we see it, is the use of valid knowledge and information as a basis for plans and programs of change. And, we believe, much relevant valid knowledge lies in the tested concepts and methods of social scientists. It is at this point that some of our gravest misgivings about the effects of protest movements in America center. For many, protest movements have led to estrangement between the resources of the social sciences and the action strategists and planners of protest movements. They may, in some instances, have strengthened the anti-intellectualism which is always endemic in American life and which has always accompanied the growth of populist movements. This effect, if it in fact is an effect, is, of course not entirely the "fault" of those in liberation movements. For liberationists are partly right in seeing the resources of the applied social sciences as more oriented and avail-

able to the needs of guardians of the status quo than to those who are challenging that guardianship and in interpreting the claim of value neutrality which many in the social sciences still make for themselves as a mask for passive endorsement of the powers that be. But the liberationists are wrong in depriving themselves of resources that could make their projects of changing more coherent and more effective. This widened gap, insofar as it exists, between social scientists and those from the oppressed who take leadership in humanizing our institutions and relationships defines an important task for practitioners of planned change in America.

In characterizing the effects of American experience in the 1960s on the prospects of and challenges to planned change, we cannot fail to mention and assess the effects of that period's most cataclysmic event—American involvement in the Vietnam War. And, because we are still suffering deeply its painful effects, an adequate assessment is currently impossible. We could have no clearer demonstration of the failure of power-coercive strategies of change in the relations between nations and the need to invent and test more collaborative strategies at that level. Our attempt to coerce both North and South Vietnam and the Viet Cong into conformity to what our leaders defined as our national interest failed. In the case of North Vietnam and the Viet Cong, we showed the impotence of technological might against the human power generated by belief in a cause. Our show of force only solidified resistance to the imposition of our alien purpose. In the case of South Vietnam, we showed our inability, though our material investment was stupendous, to engineer popular acceptance of a regime in which people did not believe and to induce high popular morale under the leadership of that regime.

It remains to be seen whether we as a people and a government will be able to face and acknowledge our failures, to learn from them, and to take the lead in instituting more collaborative, more creative, less fundamentally destructive ways of resolving conflicts among nations. Actualizing this desirable outcome should have a high priority on the agenda of agents of planned change in America.

The effects of our involvement in the Vietnam War upon the internal society of our nation were no less drastic than on our international relations. Our potential learning through our mistakes about processes of changing are equally great. The power that stems from the hoarding of relevant information by any elite was vividly illustrated. In the name of national security, access to relevant information was stringently limited to a few in the central government. This limited access left most people and their representatives in Congress relatively helpless in effectively criticizing, redirecting, and altering public policy with respect to the war. And it made possible the dissemination of highly selected and false information in an attempt to engineer acquiescence in the Executive's war policy. That this manipulation of information failed to engineer acquiescence or to still criticism and protest, that it eventually destroyed the credibility of two Presidents, may be a tribute to our system of civil liberties and to the commitment in our people to openness and authenticity in the relationship between leaders and followers. That the policy worked for so long, that it paralyzed public discussion and debate for so long, that it led to governmental invasion of the privacy of so many honest dissenters are facts that are sobering in their implications. More adequate management of the flow of information on which public policy is based and more effective protection of the rights of privacy and of dissent should be high priorities on the agenda of agents of planned change. And this applies to local as well as to national and international change programs.

We have spoken of the survivors'

mentality which emerged in America after the Nazi holocaust and the nuclear bombing of Hiroshima and which spread widely during the 1960s. This is a mentality that accepts the premise that the survival of *mankind, not just you or me,* has become problematic in our time and place. It is conjoined with the premise that the extinction of mankind, if it comes, will be through the agency of human beings themselves. Where acceptance of these premises does not lead to a paralyzing and guilty despair, it may engender a new sense of moral responsibility in persons. And this sense of responsibility may lead to a reassessment of even our most hallowed traditional moralities and policies against the criterion of their implications and consequences in terms of human survival.

Richard Means has expressed the contemporary ethical meaning of problematic human survival in this way:

If the survival of life is a basic good and can be accepted by people throughout the world, then this good is universal. On the practical level, the terror of atomic holocaust maximizes into reality the greatest good for the greatest number, that is, survival and life, as the basic ethical rule. It is the interconnection of terror, the intricate web of world destruction, that now ties us together and lends objectivity to the consequences of our values. Thus the values of industrial civilization, of the warring powers of the East and West, are universalized in their implication and consequences and must be judged in relation to a universal good—the fact of human survival.[8]

Agents of planned change must resist in themselves the despair and accept the deepened ethical responsibility both of which are implicit in acknowledgment of

[8] Richard L. Means, *The Ethical Imperative: The Crisis in American Values* (Garden City, N.Y.: Doubleday, 1969), p. 56.

the problematic character of human survival today. And they must invite their clients to open their values, personal, local, political, religious, to a test against this new universal criterion of good—human survival.

1.2 GENERAL STRATEGIES FOR EFFECTING CHANGES IN HUMAN SYSTEMS

Robert Chin, Kenneth D. Benne

Discussing general strategies and procedures for effecting change requires that we set limits to the discussion. For, under a liberal interpretation of the title, we would need to deal with much of the literature of contemporary social and behavioral science, basic and applied.

Therefore, we shall limit our discussion to those changes which are planned changes—in which attempts to bring about change are conscious, deliberate, and intended, at least on the part of one or more agents related to the change attempt. We shall also attempt to categorize strategies and procedures which have a few important elements in common but which, in fact, differ widely in other respects. And we shall neglect many of these differences. In addition, we shall look beyond the description of procedures in common sense

This essay was prepared especially for the 2d Edition of *The Planning of Change.* It was adapted from a paper by Robert Chin prepared for "Designing Education for the Future—An Eight State Project" (Denver, Colo., 1967). Kenneth D. Benne joined in revising and expanding sections of the original paper for inclusion in the 2d Edition. In the process of revision, what was in several respects a new paper emerged. The original focus on changing in education was maintained. Historical roots of ideas and strategies were explored. The first person style of the original paper was also maintained. Citations have been modified to include articles contained in the present volume, along with other references.

terms and seek some genotypic characteristics of change strategies. We shall seek the roots of the main strategies discussed, including their variants, in ideas and idea systems prominent in contemporary and recent social and psychological thought.

One element in all approaches to planned change is the conscious utilization and application of knowledge as an instrument or tool for modifying patterns and institutions of practice. The knowledge or related technology to be applied may be knowledge of the nonhuman environment in which practice goes on or of some knowledge-based "thing technology" for controlling one or another feature of the practice environment. In educational practice, for example, technologies of communication and calculation, based upon new knowledge of electronics—audiovisual devices, television, computers, teaching machines—loom large among the knowledges and technologies that promise greater efficiency and economy in handling various practices in formal education. As attempts are made to introduce these new thing technologies into school situations the change problem shifts to the human problems of dealing with the resistances, anxieties, threats to morale, conflicts, disrupted interpersonal communications, and so on, which prospective changes in patterns of practice evoke in the people affected by the change. So the change agent, even though focally and initially concerned with modifications in the thing technology of education, finds himself in need of more adequate knowledge of human behavior, individual and social, and in need of developed "people technologies," based on behavioral knowledge, for dealing effectively with the human aspects of deliberate change.

The knowledge which suggests improvements in educational practice may, on the other hand, be behavioral knowledge in the first instance—knowledge about participative learning, about attitude change, about family disruption in inner-city communities, about the cognitive and skill requirements of new careers, and so forth. Such knowledge may suggest changes in school grouping, in the relations between teachers and students, in the relations of teachers and principals to parents, and in counseling practices. Here change agents, initially focused on application of behavioral knowledge and the improvement of people technologies in school settings, must face the problems of using people technologies in planning, installing, and evaluating such changes in educational practice. The new people technologies must be experienced, understood, and accepted by teachers and administrators before they can be used effectively with students.

This line of reasoning suggests that, whether the focus of planned change is in the introduction of more effective thing technologies or people technologies into institutionalized practice, processes of introducing such changes must be based on behavioral knowledge of change and must utilize people technologies based on such knowledge.

A. TYPES OF STRATEGIES FOR CHANGING

Our further analysis is based on three types or groups of strategies. The first of these, and probably the most frequently employed by men of knowledge in America and Western Europe, are those we call empirical-rational strategies. One fundamental assumption underlying these strategies is that men are rational. Another assumption is that men will follow their rational self-interest once this is revealed to them. A change is proposed by some person or group which knows of a situation that is desirable, effective, and in line with the self-interest of the person, group, organization, or community which will be affected by the change. Because the person (or group) is assumed to be rational and moved by self-interest, it is assumed that he (or they) will adopt the proposed change if it can be rationally justified and if it can be shown by the proposer(s) that he (or they) will gain by the change.

A second group of strategies we call normative-re-educative. These strategies build upon assumptions about human motivation different from those underly-lying the first. The rationality and intelligence of men are not denied. Patterns of action and practice are supported by sociocultural norms and by commitments on the part of individuals to these norms. Sociocultural norms are supported by the attitude and value systems of individuals —normative outlooks which undergird their commitments. Change in a pattern of practice or action, according to this view, will occur only as the persons involved are brought to change their normative orientations to old patterns and develop commitments to new ones. And changes in normative orientations involve changes in attitudes, values, skills, and significant relationships, not just changes in knowledge, information, or intellectual rationales for action and practice.

The third group of strategies is based on the application of power in some form, political or otherwise. The influence process involved is basically that of compliance of those with less power to the plans, directions, and leadership of those with greater power. Often the power to be applied is legitimate power or authority. Thus the strategy may involve getting the authority of law or administrative policy behind the change to be effected. Some power strategies may appeal less to the use of authoritative power to effect change than to the massing of coercive power, legitimate or not, in support of the change sought.[1]

1. Empirical-Rational Strategies

A variety of specific strategies are included in what we are calling the empirical-rational approach to effecting change. As we have already pointed out, the rationale underlying most of these is an assumption that men are guided by reason and that they will utilize some rational calculus of self-interest in determining needed changes in behavior.

It is difficult to point to any one person whose ideas express or articulate the orientation underlying commitment to empirical-rational strategies of changing. In Western Europe and America, this orientation might be better identified with

[1] Throughout our discussion of strategies and procedures, we will not differentiate these according to the size of the target of change. We assume that there are similarities in processes of changing, whether the change affects an individual, a small group, an organization, a community, or a culture. In addition, we are not attending to differences among the aspects of a system, let us say an educational system, which is being changed—curriculum, audio-visual methods, team teaching, pupil grouping, and so on. Furthermore, because many changes in communities or organizations start with an individual or some small membership group, our general focus will be upon those strategies which lead to and involve individual changes.

We will sidestep the issue of defining change in this paper. As further conceptual work progresses in the study of planned change, we shall eventually have to examine how different definitions of change relate to strategies and procedures for effecting change. But we are not dealing with these issues here.

the general social orientation of the Enlightenment and of classical liberalism than with the ideas of any one man. On this view, the chief foes to human rationality and to change or progress based on rationality were ignorance and superstition. Scientific investigation and research represented the chief ways of extending knowledge and reducing the limitations of ignorance. A corollary of this optimistic view of man and his future was an advocacy of education as a way of disseminating scientific knowledge and of freeing men and women from the shackles of superstition. Although elitist notions played a part in the thinking of many classic liberals, the increasing trend during the nineteenth century was toward the universalization of educational opportunity. The common and universal school, open to all men and women, was the principal instrument by which knowledge would replace ignorance and superstition in the minds of people and become a principal agent in the spread of reason, knowledge, and knowledge-based action and practice (progress) in human society. In American experience, Jefferson may be taken as a principal, early advocate of research and of education as agencies of human progress. And Horace Mann may be taken as the prophet of progress through the institutionalization of universal educational opportunity through the common school.[2]

[2] We have indicated the main roots of ideas and idea systems underlying the principal strategies of changing and their subvariants on a chart which appears as Figure 1 at the end of this essay. It may be useful in seeing both the distinctions and the relationships between various strategies of changing in time perspective. We have emphasized developments of the past twenty-five years more than earlier developments. This makes for historical foreshortening. We hope this is a pardonable distortion, considering our present limited purpose.

a. BASIC RESEARCH AND
   DISSEMINATION OF KNOWLEDGE
   THROUGH GENERAL EDUCATION

The strategy of encouraging basic knowledge building and of depending on general education to diffuse the results of research into the minds and thinking of men and women is still by far the most appealing strategy of change to most academic men of knowledge and to large segments of the American population as well. Basic researchers are quite likely to appeal for time for further research when confronted by some unmet need. And many people find this appeal convincing. Both of these facts are well illustrated by difficulties with diseases for which no adequate control measures or cures are available—poliomyelitis, for example. Medical researchers asked for more time and funds for research and people responded with funds for research, both through voluntary channels and through legislative appropriations. And the control measures were forthcoming. The educational problem then shifted to inducing people to comply with immunization procedures based on research findings.

This appeal to a combination of research and education of the public has worked in many areas of new knowledge-based thing technologies where almost universal readiness for accepting the new technology was already present in the population. Where such readiness is not available, as in the case of fluoridation technologies in the management of dental caries, general strategy of basic research plus educational (informational) campaigns to spread knowledge of the findings do not work well. The cases of its inadequacy as a single strategy of change have multiplied, especially where "engineering" problems, which involve a divided and conflicting public or deep resistances due to the threat by the new technology to traditional attitudes and values, have thwarted its effectiveness.

But these cases, while they demand attention to other strategies of changing, do not disprove the importance of basic research and of general educational opportunity as elements in a progressive and self-renewing society.

We have noted that the strategy under discussion has worked best in grounding and diffusing generally acceptable thing technologies in society. Some have argued that the main reason the strategy has not worked in the area of people technologies is a relative lack of basic research on people and their behavior, relationships, and institutions and a corresponding lack of emphasis upon social and psychological knowledges in school and college curricula. It would follow in this view that increased basic research on human affairs and relationships and increased efforts to diffuse the results of such research through public education are the ways of making the general strategy work better. Auguste Comte with his emphasis on positivistic sociology in the reorganization of society and Lester F. Ward in America may be taken as late nineteenth-century representatives of this view. And the spirit of Comte and Ward is by no means dead in American academia or in influential segments of the American public.

b. PERSONNEL SELECTION
   AND REPLACEMENT

Difficulties in getting knowledge effectively into practice may be seen as lying primarily in the lack of fitness of persons occupying positions with job responsibilities for improving practice. The argument goes that we need the right person in the right position, if knowledge is to be optimally applied and if rationally based changes are to become the expectation in organizational and societal affairs. This fits with the liberal reformers' frequently voiced and enacted plea to drive the unfit from office and to replace them with those more fit as a condition of social progress.

That reformers' programs have so often failed has sobered but by no means destroyed the zeal of those who regard personnel selection, assessment, and replacement as a major key to program improvement in education or in other enterprises as well. This strategy was given a scientific boost by the development of scientific testing of potentialities and aptitudes. We will use Binet as a prototype of psychological testing and Moreno as a prototype in sociometric testing, while recognizing the extensive differentiation and elaboration which have occurred in psychometrics and sociometrics since their original work. We recognize too the elaborated modes of practice in personnel work which have been built around psychometric and sociometric tools and techniques. We do not discount their limited value as actual and potential tools for change, while making two observations on the way they have often been used. First, they have been used more often in the interest of system maintenance rather than of system change, since the job descriptions personnel workers seek to fill are defined in terms of system requirements as established. Second, by focusing on the role occupant as the principal barrier to improvement, personnel selection and replacement strategies have tended not to reveal the social and cultural system difficulties which may be in need of change if improvement is to take place.

c. SYSTEMS ANALYSTS AS
   STAFF AND CONSULTANTS

Personnel workers in government, industry, and education have typically worked in staff relations to line manageagement, reflecting the bureaucratic, line-staff form of organization which has flourished in the large-scale organization of effort and enterprise in the twentieth century. And other expert workers—systems analysts—more attuned to system difficulties than to the adequacies or inadequacies of persons as role occupants within the system, have found their way into the staff resources of line management in contemporary organizations.

There is no reason why the expert resources of personnel workers and systems analysts might not be used in nonbureaucratic organizations or in processes of moving bureaucratic organizations toward nonbureaucratic forms. But the fact remains that their use has been shaped, for the most part, in the image of the scientific management of bureaucratically organized enterprises. So we have placed the systems analysts in our chart under Frederick Taylor, the father of scientific management in America.

The line management of an enterprise seeks to organize human and technical effort toward the most efficient service of organizational goals. And these goals are defined in terms of the production of some mandated product, whether a tangible product or a less tangible good or service. In pursuing this quest for efficiency, line management employs experts in the analysis of sociotechnical systems and in the laying out of more efficient systems. The experts employed may work as external consultants or as an internal staff unit. Behavioral scientists have recently found their way, along with mathematicians and engineers, into systems analysis work.

It is interesting to note that the role of these experts is becoming embroiled in discussions of whether or not behavioral science research should be used to sensitize administrators to new organizational possibilities, to new goals, or primarily to implement efficient operation within perspectives and goals as currently defined. Jean Hills has raised the question of whether behavioral science when applied to organizational problems tends to perpetuate established ideology and system relations because of blinders imposed by their being "problem centered" and by their limited definition of what is "a problem."[3]

We see an emerging strategy, in the use of behavioral scientists as systems analysts and engineers, toward viewing the problem of organizational change and changing as a wide-angled problem, one in which all the input and output features and components of a large-scale system are considered. It is foreseeable that with the use of high-speed and high-capacity computers, and with the growth of substantial theories and hypotheses about how parts of an educational system operate, we shall find more and more applications for systems analysis and operations research in programs of educational change. In fact, it is precisely the quasi-mathematical character of these modes of research that will make possible the rational analysis of qualitatively different aspects of educational work and will bring them into the range of rational planning—masses of students, massive problems of poverty and educational and cultural deprivation, and so on. We see no necessary incompatibility between an ideology which emphasizes the individuality of the student and the use of systems analysis and computers in strategizing the problems of the total system. The actual incompatibilities may lie in the limited uses to which existing organizers and administrators of educational efforts put these technical resources.

d. APPLIED RESEARCH AND
   LINKAGE SYSTEMS FOR
   DIFFUSION OF RESEARCH RESULTS

The American development of applied research and of a planned system for linking applied researchers with professional practitioners and both of these with

centers for basic research and with organized consumers of applied research has been strongly influenced by two distinctive American inventions—the land-grant university and the agricultural extension system. We, therefore, have put the name of Justin Morrill, author of the land-grant college act and of the act which established the cooperative agricultural extension system, on our chart. The land-grant colleges or universities were dedicated to doing applied research in the service of agriculture and the mechanic arts. These colleges and universities developed research programs in basic sciences as well and experimental stations for the development and refinement of knowledge-based technologies for use in engineering and agriculture. As the extension services developed, county agents—practitioners —were attached to the state land-grant college or university that received financial support from both state and federal governments. The county agent and his staff developed local organizations of adult farm men and women and of farm youth to provide both a channel toward informing consumers concerning new and better agricultural practices and toward getting awareness of unmet consumer needs and unsolved problems back to centers of knowledge and research. Garth Jones has made one of the more comprehensive studies of the strategies of changing involved in large-scale demonstration.[4]

All applied research has not occurred within a planned system for knowledge discovery, development, and utilization like the one briefly described above. The system has worked better in developing and diffusing thing technologies than in developing and diffusing peo-

[3] Jean Hills, "Social Science, Ideology and the Purposes of Educational Administration," *Education Administration Quarterly* I (Autumn 1965), 23–40.

[4] Garth Jones, "Planned Organizational Change, a Set of Working Documents," Center for Research in Public Organization, School of Public Administration (Los Angeles: University of Southern California, 1964).

ple technologies, though the development of rural sociology and of agricultural economics shows that extension workers were by no means unaware of the behavioral dimensions of change problems. But the large-scale demonstration, through the land-grant university cooperative extension service, of the stupendous changes which can result from a planned approach to knowledge discovery, development, diffusion, and utilization is a part of the consciousness of all Americans concerned with planned change.[5]

1) Applied research and development is an honored part of the tradition of engineering approaches to problem identification and solution. The pioneering work of E. L. Thorndike in applied research in education should be noted on our chart. The processes and slow tempo of diffusion and utilization of research findings and inventions in public education are well illustrated in studies by Paul Mort and his students.[6] More recently, applied research, in its product development aspect, has been utilized in a massive way to contribute curriculum materials and designs for science instruction (as well as in other subjects). When we assess this situation to find reasons why such researches have not been more effective in producing changes in instruction, the answers seem to lie both in the plans of the studies which produced the materials and designs and in the potential users of the findings. Adequate linkage between consumers and researchers

was frequently not established. Planned and evaluated demonstrations and experimentations connected with the use of materials were frequently slighted. And training of consumer teachers to use the new materials adaptively and creatively was frequently missing.

Such observations have led to a fresh spurt of interest in evaluation research addressed to educational programs. The fear persists that this too may lead to disappointment if it is not focused for two-way communication between researchers and teachers and if it does not involve collaboratively the ultimate consumers of the results of such research—the students. Evaluation researches conducted in the spirit of justifying a program developed by expert applied researchers will not help to guide teachers and students in their quest for improved practices of teaching and learning, if the concerns of the latter have not been taken centrally into account in the evaluation process.[7]

2) Recently, attempts have been made to link applied research activities in education with basic researchers on the one hand and with persons in action and practice settings on the other through some system of interlocking roles similar to those suggested in the description of the land grant–extension systems in agriculture or in other fields where applied and development researches have flourished.

The linking of research-development efforts with diffusion-innovation efforts has been gaining headway in the field of education with the emergence of federally supported Research and Development Centers based in universities, Regional Laboratories connected with state departments of education, colleges and universities in a geographic area, and

[5] For a review, see Ronald G. Havelock and Kenneth D. Benne, "An Exploratory Study of Knowledge Utilization," selection 4.4 in the present volume.

[6] Paul R. Mort and Donald R. Ross, *Principles of School Administration* (New York: McGraw-Hill, Inc., 1957). Paul R. Mort and Francis G. Cornell, *American Schools in Transition: How our Schools Adapt their Practices to Changing Needs* (New York: Bureau of Publications, Teachers College, Columbia University Press, 1941).

[7] Robert Chin, "Research Approaches to the Problem of Civic Training," in F. Patterson (ed.), *The Adolescent Citizen* (New York: The Free Press, 1960).

with various consortia and institutes confronting problems of educational change and changing. The strategy of change here usually includes a well-researched innovation which seems feasible to install in practice settings. Attention is directed to the question of whether or not the innovation will bring about a desired result, and with what it can accomplish, if given a trial in one or more practice settings. The questions of *how* to get a fair trial and *how* to install an innovation in an already going and crowded school system are ordinarily not built centrally into the strategy. The rationalistic assumption usually precludes research attention to these questions. For, if the invention can be rationally shown to have achieved desirable results in some situations, it is assumed that people in other situations will adopt it once they know these results and the rationale behind them. The neglect of the above questions has led to a wastage of much applied research effort in the past.

Attention has been given recently to the roles, communication mechanisms, and processes necessary for innovation and diffusion of improved educational practices.[8] Clark and Guba have formulated very specific processes related to

and necessary for change in educational practice following upon research. For them, the necessary processes are: *development*, including invention and design; *diffusion*, including dissemination and demonstration; *adoption*, including trial, installation, and institutionalization. Clark's earnest conviction is summed up in this statement: "In a sense, the educational research community will be the educational community, and the route to educational progress will self-evidently be research and development."[9]

The approach of Havelock and Benne is concerned with the intersystem relationships between basic researchers, applied researchers, practitioners, and consumers in an evolved and evolving organization for knowledge utilization. They are concerned especially with the communication difficulties and role conflicts that occur at points of intersystem exchange. These conflicts are important because they illuminate the normative issues at stake between basic researchers and applied researchers, between applied researchers and practitioners (teachers and administrators), between practitioners and consumers (students). The lines of strategy suggested by their analysis for solving role conflicts and communication difficulties call for transactional and collaborative exchanges across the lines of varied organized interests and orientations within the process of utilization. This brings their analysis into the range of normative-re-educative strategies to be discussed later.

The concepts from the behavioral sciences upon which these strategies of diffusion rest come mainly from two traditions. The first is from studies of the diffusion of traits of culture from one cul-

[8] Matthew B. Miles, *Some Propositions in Research Utilization in Education* (March 1965), in press. Kenneth Wiles, unpublished paper for seminar on Strategies for Curriculum Change (Columbus, Ohio, Ohio State University). Charles Jung and Ronald Lippitt, "Utilization of Scientific Knowledge for Change in Education," in *Concepts for Social Change* (Washington, D.C.: National Educational Association, National Training Laboratories, 1967). Ronald G. Havelock and Kenneth D. Benne, "An Exploratory Study of Knowledge Utilization," David Clark and Egon Guba, "An Examination of Potential Change Roles in Education," seminar on Innovation in Planning School Curricula (Columbus, Ohio: Ohio State University, 1965).

[9] David Clark, "Educational Research and Development: The Next Decade," in *Implications for Education of Prospective Changes in Society,* a publication of Designing Education for the Future—An Eight State Project" (Denver, Colo., 1967).

tural system to another, initiated by the American anthropologist Franz Boas. This type of study has been carried on by Rogers in his work on innovation and diffusion of innovations in contemporary culture and is reflected in a number of recent writers such as Katz and Carlson.[10] The second scientific tradition is in studies of influence in mass communication associated with Carl Hovland and his students.[11] Both traditions have assumed a *relatively passive recipient of input* in diffusion situations. And actions within the process of diffusion are interpreted from the standpoint of an observer of the process. Bauer has pointed out that scientific studies have exaggerated the effectiveness of mass persuasion since they have compared the total number in the audience to the communications with the much smaller proportion of the audience persuaded by the communication.[12] A clearer view of processes of diffusion must include the actions of the receiver

as well as those of the transmitter in the transactional events which are the units of diffusion process. And strategies for making diffusion processes more effective must be transactional and collaborative by design.

e. UTOPIAN THINKING AS A STRATEGY OF CHANGING

It may seem strange to include the projection of utopias as a rational-empirical strategy of changing. Yet inventing and designing the shape of the future by extrapolating what we know of in the present is to envision a direction for planning and action in the present. If the image of a potential future is convincing and rationally persuasive to men in the present, the image may become part of the dynamics and motivation of present action. The liberal tradition is not devoid of its utopias. When we think of utopias quickened by an effort to extrapolate from the sciences of man to a future vision of society, the utopia of B. F. Skinner comes to mind.[13] The title of the Eight State Project, "Designing Education for the Future" for which this paper was prepared, reveals a utopian intent and aspiration and illustrates an attempt to employ utopian thinking for practical purposes.[14]

Yet it may be somewhat disheartening to others as it is to us to note the absence of rousing and beckoning normative statements of what both can and ought to be in man's future in most current liberal-democratic utopias, whether these be based on psychological, sociological, political, or philosophical findings and assumptions. The absence of utopias in current society, in this sense, and in the sense

[10] Elihu Katz, "The Social Itinerary of Technical Change: Two Studies on the Diffusion of Innovation," in W. Bennis, K. Benne, and R. Chin, *The Planning of Change* (2d Edition, New York: Holt, Rinehart and Winston, 1969), Chap. 5, p. 230. Richard Carlson, "Some Needed Research on the Diffusion of Innovations," paper at the Washington Conference on Educational Change (Columbus, Ohio: Ohio State University). Everett Rogers, "What are Innovators Like?" in *Change Processes in the Public Schools,* Center for the Advanced Study of Educational Administration (Eugene, Oregon: University of Oregon, 1965). Everett Rogers, *Diffusion of Innovations* (New York: The Free Press, 1962).

[11] Carl Hovland, Irving Janis, and Harold Kelley, *Communication and Persuasion* (New Haven: Yale University Press, 1953).

[12] Raymond Bauer, "The Obstinate Audience: The Influence Process from the Point of View of Social Communication," in *The Planning of Change,* 2d Edition, Chap. 9, p. 507.

[13] B. F. Skinner, *Walden Two* (New York: Crowell-Collier and Macmillan, Inc., 1948).

[14] "Designing Education for the Future— An Eight State Project" (Denver, Colo., 1967).

that Mannheim studied them in his now classical study,[15] tends to make the forecasting of future directions a problem of technical prediction, rather than equally a process of projecting value orientations and preferences into the shaping of a better future.

f. PERCEPTUAL AND CONCEPTUAL REORGANIZATION THROUGH THE CLARIFICATION OF LANGUAGE

In classical liberalism, one perceived foe of rational change and progress was superstition. And superstitions are carried from man to man and from generation to generation through the agency of unclear and mythical language. British utilitarianism was one important strand of classical liberalism, and one of utilitarianism's important figures, Jeremy Bentham, sought to purify language of its dangerous mystique through his study of fictions.

More recently, Alfred Korzybski and S. I. Hayakawa, in the general semantics movement, have sought a way of clarifying and rectifying the names of things and processes.[16] While their main applied concern was with personal therapy, both, and especially Hayakawa, were also concerned to bring about changes in social systems as well. People disciplined in general semantics, it was hoped, would see more correctly, communicate more adequately, and reason more effectively and thus lay a realistic common basis for action and changing. The strategies of changing associated with general semantics overlap with our next family of strategies, the

normative-re-educative, because of their emphasis upon the importance of interpersonal relationships and social contexts within the communication process.

2. Normative-Re-educative Strategies of Changing

We have already suggested that this family of strategies rests on assumptions and hypotheses about man and his motivation which contrast significantly at points with the assumptions and hypotheses of those committed to what we have called rational-empirical strategies. Men are seen as inherently active, in quest of impulse and need satisfaction. The relation between man and his environment is essentially transactional, as Dewey[17] made clear in his famous article on "The Reflex-Arc Concept." Man, the organism, does not passively await given stimuli from his environment in order to respond. He takes stimuli as furthering or thwarting the goals of his ongoing action. Intelligence arises in the process of shaping organism-environmental relations toward more adequate fitting and joining of organismic demands and environmental resources.

Intelligence is social, rather than narrowly individual. Men are guided in their actions by socially funded and communicated meanings, norms, and institutions, in brief by a normative culture. At the personal level, men are guided by internalized meanings, habits, and values. Changes in patterns of action or practice are, therefore, changes, not alone in the rational informational equipment of men, but at the personal level, in habits and values as well and, at the sociocultural level, changes are alterations in normative structures and in institutionalized roles and relationships,

---

[15] Karl Mannheim, *Ideology and Utopia* (New York: Harcourt, Brace & World, Inc., 1946).

[16] Alfred Korzybski, *Science and Sanity* (3d ed.; International Non-Aristotelian Library Publishing Company, 1948). S. I. Hayakawa, *Language in Thought and Action* (New York: Harcourt, Brace & World, Inc., 1941).

[17] John Dewey, *Philosophy, Psychology and Social Practice,* Joseph Ratner (ed.) (Capricorn Books, 1967).

as well as in cognitive and perceptual orientations.

For Dewey, the prototype of intelligence in action is the scientific method. And he saw a broadened and humanized scientific method as man's best hope for progress if men could learn to utilize such a method in facing all of the problematic situations of their lives. *Intelligence,* so conceived, rather than *Reason* as defined in classical liberalism, was the key to Dewey's hope for the invention, development, and testing of adequate strategies of changing in human affairs.

Lewin's contribution to normative-re-educative strategies of changing stemmed from his vision of required interrelations between research, training, and action (and, for him, this meant collaborative relationships, often now lacking, between researchers, educators, and activists) in the solution of human problems, in the identification of needs for change, and in the working out of improved knowledge, technology, and patterns of action in meeting these needs. Man must participate in his own re-education if he is to be re-educated at all. And re-education is a normative change as well as a cognitive and perceptual change. These convictions led Lewin[18] to emphasize action research as a strategy of changing, and participation in groups as a medium of re-education.

Freud's main contributions to normative-re-educative strategies of changing are two. First, he sought to demonstrate the unconscious and preconscious bases of man's actions. Only as a man finds ways of becoming aware of these nonconscious wellsprings of his attitudes and actions will he be able to bring them into conscious self-control. And Freud devoted much of his magnificent genius to developing ways of helping men to become conscious of the main springs of their actions and so capable of freedom. Second, in developing therapeutic methods, he discovered and developed ways of utilizing the relationship between change agent (therapist) and client (patient) as a major tool in re-educating the client toward expanded self-awareness, self-understanding, and self-control. Emphasis upon the collaborative relationship in therapeutic change was a major contribution by Freud and his students and colleagues to normative-re-educative strategies of changing in human affairs.[19]

Normative-re-educative approaches to effecting change bring direct interventions by change agents, interventions based on a consciously worked out theory of change and of changing, into the life of a client system, be that system a person, a small group, an organization, or a community. The theory of changing is still crude but it is probably as explicitly stated as possible, granted our present state of knowledge about planned change.[20]

Some of the common elements among variants within this family of change strategies are the following. First, all emphasize the client system and his (or its) involvement in working out programs of change and improvement for himself (or itself). The way the client sees himself and his problem must be brought into dialogic relationship with the way in which he and his problem are seen by the

[18] Kurt Lewin, *Resolving Social Conflicts* (New York: Harper & Row, Publishers, 1948). Kurt Lewin, *Field Theory in Social Science* (New York: Harper & Row Publishers, 1951).

[19] For Freud, an interesting summary is contained in Otto Fenichel, *Problems of Psychoanalytic Technique* (Albany: NT Psychoanalytic Quarterly Inc., 1941).

[20] W. Bennis, K. Benne, and R. Chin, *The Planning of Change* (1st ed.: New York: Holt, Rinehart and Winston, 1961). R. Lippitt, J. Watson and B. Westley, *The Dynamics of Planned Change* (New York: Harcourt, Brace & World, Inc., 1958). W. Bennis, *Changing Organizations* (New York: McGraw-Hill, Inc., 1966).

change agent, whether the latter is functioning as researcher, consultant, trainer, therapist, or friend in relation to the client. Second, the problem confronting the client is not assumed *a priori* to be one which can be met by more adequate technical information, though this possibility is not ruled out. The problem may lie rather in the attitudes, values, norms, and the external and internal relationships of the client system and may require alteration or re-education of these as a condition of its solution. Third, the change agent must learn to intervene mutually and collaboratively along with the client into efforts to define and solve the client's problem(s). The here and now experience of the two provide an important basis for diagnosing the problem and for locating needs for re-education in the interest of solving it. Fourth, nonconscious elements which impede problem solution must be brought into consciousness and publicly examined and reconstructed. Fifth, the methods and concepts of the behavioral sciences are resources which change agent and client learn to use selectively, relevantly, and appropriately in learning to deal with the confronting problem and with problems of a similar kind in the future.

These approaches center in the notion that people technology is just as necessary as thing technology in working out desirable changes in human affairs. Put in this bold fashion, it is obvious that for the normative-re-educative change agent, clarification and reconstruction of values is of pivotal importance in changing. By getting the values of various parts of the client system along with his own, openly into the arena of change and by working through value conflicts responsibly, the change agent seeks to avoid manipulation and indoctrination of the client, in the morally reprehensible meanings of these terms.

We may use the organization of the National Training Laboratories in 1947 as a milestone in the development of norma-tive-re-educative approaches to changing in America. The first summer laboratory program grew out of earlier collaborations among Kurt Lewin, Ronald Lippitt, Leland Bradford, and Kenneth Benne. The idea behind the laboratory was that participants, staff, and students would learn about themselves and their back-home problems by collaboratively building a laboratory in which participants would become both experimenters and subjects in the study of their own developing interpersonal and group behavior within the laboratory setting. It seems evident that the five conditions of a normative-re-educative approach to changing were met in the conception of the training laboratory. Kurt Lewin died before the 1947 session of the training laboratory opened. Ronald Lippitt was a student of Lewin's and carried many of Lewin's orientations with him into the laboratory staff. Leland Bradford and Kenneth Benne were both students of John Dewey's philosophy of education. Bradford had invented several technologies for participative learning and self-study in his work in WPA adult education programs and as training officer in several agencies of the federal government. Benne came out of a background in educational philosophy and had collaborated with colleagues prior to 1943 in developing a methodology for policy and decision making and for the reconstruction of normative orientations, a methodology which sought to fuse democratic and scientific values and to translate these into principles for resolving conflicting and problematic situations at personal and community levels of human organization.[21] Benne and his colleagues had been much

[21] Raup, Benne, Smith, and Axteile, *The Discipline of Practical Judgment in a Democratic Society,* Yearbook No. 28 of the National Society of College Teachers of Education (Chicago: University of Chicago Press, 1943).

influenced by the work of Mary Follett,[22] her studies of integrative solutions to conflicts in settings of public and business administration, and by the work of Karl Mannheim[23] on the ideology and methodology of planning changes in human affairs, as well as by the work of John Dewey and his colleagues.

The work of the National Training Laboratories has encompassed development and testing of various approaches to changing in institutional settings, in America and abroad, since its beginning. One parallel development in England which grew out of Freud's thinking should be noted. This work developed in efforts at Tavistock Clinic to apply therapeutic approaches to problems of change in industrial organizations and in communities. This work is reported in statements by Elliot Jaques[24] and in this volume by Eric Trist. Another parallel development is represented by the efforts of Roethlisberger and Dickson to use personal counseling in industry as a strategy of organizational change.[25] Roethlisberger and Dickson had been strongly influenced by the pioneer work of Elton Mayo in industrial sociology[26] as well as by the counseling theories and methodologies of Carl Rogers.

Various refinements of methodologies for changing have been developed and

tested since the establishment of the National Training Laboratories in 1947, both under its auspices and under other auspices as well. For us, the modal developments are worthy of further discussion here. One set of approaches is oriented focally to the improvement of the problem-solving processes utilized by a client system. The other set focuses on helping members of client systems to become aware of their attitude and value orientations and relationship difficulties through a probing of feelings, manifest and latent, involved in the functioning and operation of the client system.[27] Both approaches use the development of "temporary systems" as a medium of re-education of persons and of role occupants in various ongoing social systems.[28]

a. IMPROVING THE
PROBLEM-SOLVING
CAPABILITIES OF A SYSTEM

This family of approaches to changing rests on several assumptions about change in human systems. Changes in a system, when they are reality oriented, take the form of problem solving. A system to achieve optimum reality orientation in its adaptations to its changing internal and external environments must develop and institutionalize its own problem-solving structures and processes. These structures and processes must be tuned both to human problems of relationship and morale and to technical problems of meeting the system's task requirements, set by its goals of production, distribution, and

[22] Mary Follett, *Creative Experience and Dynamic Administration* (New York: David McKay Company, Inc., 1924).

[23] Karl Mannheim, *Man and Society in an Age of Reconstruction* (New York: Harcourt, Brace & World, Inc., 1940).

[24] Elliot Jaques, *The Changing Culture of a Factory* (New York: Holt, Rinehart and Winston, 1952).

[25] William J. Dickson and F. J. Roethlisberger, *Personal Counseling in an Organization. A Sequel to the Hawthorne Researches* (Boston: Harvard Business School, 1966).

[26] Elton Mayo, *The Social Problems of an Industrial Civilization* (Cambridge, Mass.: Harvard University Press, 1945).

[27] Leland Bradford, Jack R. Gibb, and Kenneth D. Benne, *T-Group Theory and Laboratory Method* (New York: John Wiley & Sons, Inc., 1964).

[28] Matthew B. Miles, "On Temporary Systems," in M. B. Miles (ed.), *Innovation in Education* (New York: Bureau of Publications, Teachers College, Columbia University Press, 1964), pp. 437–492.

so on.[29] System problems are typically not social *or* technical but actually sociotechnical.[30] The problem-solving structures and processes of a human system must be developed to deal with a range of sociotechnical difficulties, converting them into problems and organizing the relevant processes of data collection, planning, invention, and tryout of solutions, evaluation and feedback of results, replanning, and so forth, which are required for the solution of the problems.

The human parts of the system must learn to function collaboratively in these processes of problem identification and solution and the system must develop institutionalized support and mechanisms for maintaining and improving these processes. Actually, the model of changing in these approaches is a cooperative, action-research model. This model was suggested by Lewin and developed most elaborately for use in educational settings by Stephen M. Corey.[31]

The range of interventions by outside change agents in implementing this approach to changing is rather wide. It has been most fully elaborated in relation to organizational development programs. Within such programs, intervention methods have been most comprehensively tested in industrial settings. Some of these more or less tested intervention methods are listed below. A design for any organizational development program, of course, normally uses a number of these in succession or combination.

1. Collection of data about organizational functioning and feedback of data into processes of data interpretation and of planning ways of correcting revealed dysfunctions by system managers and data collectors in collaboration.[32]

2. Training of managers and working organizational units in methods of problem solving through self-examination of present ways of dealing with difficulties and through development and tryout of better ways with consultation by outside and/or inside change agents. Usually, the working unit leaves its working place for parts of its training. These laboratory sessions are ordinarily interspersed with on-the-job consultations.

3. Developing acceptance of feedback (research and development) roles and functions within the organization, training persons to fill these roles, and relating such roles strategically to the ongoing management of the organization.

4. Training internal change agents to function within the organization in carrying on needed applied research, consultation, and training.[33]

Whatever specific strategies of intervention may be employed in developing the system's capabilities for problem solving, change efforts are designed to help the system in developing ways of scanning its

[29] Robert R. Blake and Jane S. Mouton, *The Managerial Grid* (Houston: The Gulf Publishing Company, 1961).

[30] Jay W. Lorsch and Paul Lawrence, "The Diagnosis of Organizational Problems," in *The Planning of Change,* 2d Edition, Chap. 8, p. 468.

[31] Stephen M. Corey, *Action Research to Improve School Practices* (New York: Bureau of Publications, Teachers College, Columbia University Press, 1953).

[32] See contributions by Miles *et al.,* "Data Feedback and Organizational Change in a School System," in *The Planning of Change,* 2d Edition, Chap. 8, p. 457, and Jay W. Lorsch, and Paul Lawrence, "The Diagnosis of Organizational Problems," in *The Planning of Change,* 2d Edition, Chap. 8, p. 468.

[33] C. Argyris, "Explorations in Consulting-Client Relationships," in the present volume, Chap. 8. See also Richard Beckhard, "The Confrontation Meeting," in *The Planning of Change,* 2d Edition, Chap. 8, p. 478.

operations to detect problems, of diagnosing these problems to determine relevant changeable factors in them, and of moving toward collaboratively determined solutions to the problems.

b. RELEASING AND FOSTERING
   GROWTH IN THE PERSONS WHO
   MAKE UP THE SYSTEM
   TO BE CHANGED

Those committed to this family of approaches to changing tend to see the person as the basic unit of social organization. Persons, it is believed, are capable of creative, life-affirming, self- and other-regarding and respecting responses, choices, and actions, if conditions which thwart these kinds of responses are removed and other supporting conditions developed. Rogers has formulated these latter conditions in his analysis of the therapist-client relationship—trustworthiness, empathy, caring, and others.[34] Maslow has worked out a similar idea in his analysis of the hierarchy of needs in persons.[35] If lower needs are met, higher need-meeting actions will take place. McGregor[36] has formulated the ways in which existing organizations operate to fixate persons in lower levels of motivation and has sought to envision an organization designed to release and support the growth of persons in fulfilling their higher motivations as they function within the organization.

Various intervention methods have been designed to help people discover themselves as persons and commit them-selves to continuing personal growth in the various relationships of their lives.

1. One early effort to install personal counseling widely and strategically in an organization has been reported by Roethisberger and Dickson.[37]

2. Training groups designed to facilitate personal confrontation and growth of members in an open, trusting, and accepting atmosphere have been conducted for individuals from various back-home situations and for persons from the same back-home setting. The processes of these groups have sometimes been described as "therapy for normals."[38]

3. Groups and laboratories designed to stimulate and support personal growth have been designed to utilize the resources of nonverbal exchange and communication among members along with verbal dialogue in inducing personal confrontation, discovery, and commitment to continuing growth.

4. Many psychotherapists, building on the work of Freud and Adler, have come to use groups, as well as two-person situations, as media of personal re-education and growth. Such efforts are prominent in mental health approaches to changing and have been conducted in educational, religious, community, industrial, and hospital settings. While these efforts focus primarily upon helping individuals to change themselves toward greater self-clarity and fuller self-

[34] Carl Rogers, "The Characteristics of a Helping Relationship," in *The Planning of Change,* 2d Edition, Chap. 4, p. 153.

[35] Abraham Maslow, *Motivation and Personality* (New York: Harper & Row, Publishers, 1954).

[36] Douglas M. McGregor, "The Human Side of Enterprise," in W. Bennis, K. Benne, and R. Chin, *The Planning of Change* (1st ed.; New York: Holt, Rinehart and Winston, 1961), pp. 422–431.

[37] Dickson and Roethisberger, cited above.

[38] James V. Clark, "A Healthy Organization," in *The Planning of Change,* 2d Edition, Chap. 6, p. 282. Irving Weschler, Fred Massarick, and Robert Tannenbaum, "The Self in Process: A Sensitivity Training Emphasis," in I. R. Weschler and E. Schein (eds.), *Issues in Training,* Selected Reading Series No. 5 (Washington, D.C., National Training Laboratories).

actualization, they are frequently designed and conducted in the hope that personal changes will lead to changes in organizations, institutions, and communities as well.

We have presented the two variants of normative-re-educative approaches to changing in a way to emphasize their differences. Actually, there are many similarities between them as well, which justify placing both under the same general heading. We have already mentioned one of these similarities. Both frequently use temporary systems—a residential laboratory or workshop, a temporary group with special resources built in, an ongoing system which incorporates a change agent (trainer, consultant, counselor, or therapist) temporarily—as an aid to growth in the system and/or in its members.

More fundamentally, both approaches emphasize experience-based learning as an ingredient of all enduring changes in human systems. Yet both accept the principle that people must learn to learn from their experiences if self-directed change is to be maintained and continued. Frequently, people have learned to defend against the potential lessons of experience when these threaten existing equilibria, whether in the person or in the social system. How can these defenses be lowered to let the data of experience get into processes of perceiving the situation, of constructing new and better ways to define it, of inventing new and more appropriate ways of responding to the situation as redefined, of becoming more fully aware of the consequences of actions, of re-articulating value orientations which sanction more responsible ways of managing the consequences of actions, and so forth? Learning to learn from ongoing experience is a major objective in both approaches to changing. Neither denies the relevance or importance of the noncognitive determinants of behavior—feelings, attitudes, norms, and relationships—along with cognitive-perceptual determinants, in effecting behavioral change. The problem-solving approaches emphasize the cognitive determinants more than personal growth approaches do. But exponents of the former do not accept the rationalistic biases of the rational-empirical family of change strategies, already discussed. Since exponents of both problem-solving and personal growth approaches are committed to re-education of persons as integral to effective change in human systems, both emphasize norms of openness of communication, trust between persons, lowering of status barriers between parts of the system, and mutuality between parts as necessary conditions of the re-educative process.

Great emphasis has been placed recently upon the releasing of creativity in persons, groups, and organizations as requisite to coping adaptively with accelerated changes in the conditions of modern living. We have already stressed the emphasis which personal growth approaches put upon the release of creative responses in persons being re-educated. Problem-solving approaches also value creativity, though they focus more upon the group and organizational conditions which increase the probability of creative responses by persons functioning within those conditions than upon persons directly. The approaches do differ in their strategies for releasing creative responses within human systems. But both believe that creative adaptations to changing conditions may arise *within* human systems and do not have to be imported from *outside* them as in innovation-diffusion approaches already discussed and the power-compliance models still to be dealt with.

One developing variant of normative-re-educative approaches to changing, not already noted, focuses upon effective conflict management. It is, of course, common knowledge that differences within a society which demand interaccommodation often manifest themselves as conflicts. In the process of managing such conflicts, changes in the norms, policies, and relationships of the society occur. Can conflict management be brought into the ambit of planned change as defined in this volume? Stemming from the work of the Sherifs in creating intergroup conflict and seeking to resolve it in a field--laboratory situation,[39] training in intergroup conflict and conflict resolution found its way into training laboratories through the efforts of Blake and others. Since that time, laboratories for conflict management have been developed under NTL and other auspices and methodologies for conflict resolution and management, in keeping with the values of planned change, have been devised. Blake's and Walton's work represent some of the findings from these pioneering efforts.[40]

Thus, without denying their differences in assumption and strategy, we believe that the differing approaches discussed in this section can be seen together within the framework of normative-re-educative approaches to changing. Two efforts to conceptualize planned change in a way to reveal the similarities in assumptions about changing and in value orientations toward change underlying these variant approaches are those by Lippitt, Watson, and Westley and by Bennis, Benne, and Chin.[41]

[39] Muzafer and Carolyn Sherif, *Groups in Harmony and Tension* (New York: Harper & Row, Publishers, 1953).

[40] Robert Blake *et al.*, "The Union Management Inter-Group Laboratory," in *The Planning of Change,* 2d Edition, Chap. 4, p. 176. Richard Walton, "Two Strategies of Social Change and Their Dilemmas," in *The Planning of Change,* 2d Edition, Chap. 4, p. 167.

[41] R. Lippitt, J. Watson, and B. Westley, *Dynamics of Planned Change* (New York: Harcourt, Brace & World, Inc., 1958). W. Bennis, K. Benne, R. Chin, *The Planning of Change* (1st ed.; New York: Holt, Rinehart and Winston, 1961).

Another aspect of changing in human organizations is represented by efforts to conceive human organization in forms that go beyond the bureaucratic form which captured the imagination and fixed the contours of thinking and practice of organizational theorists and practitioners from the latter part of the nineteenth through the early part of the twentieth century. The bureaucratic form of organization was conceptualized by Max Weber and carried into American thinking by such students of administration as Urwick.[42] On this view, effective organization of human effort followed the lines of effective division of labor and effective establishment of lines of reporting, control, and supervision from the mass base of the organization up through various levels of control to the top of the pyramidal organization from which legitimate authority and responsibility stemmed.

The work of industrial sociologists like Mayo threw doubt upon the adequacy of such a model of formal organization to deal with the realities of organizational life by revealing the informal organization which grows up within the formal structure to satisfy personal and interpersonal needs not encompassed by or integrated into the goals of the formal organization. Chester Barnard may be seen as a transitional figure who, in discussing the functions of the organizational executive, gave equal emphasis to his responsibilities for task effectiveness and organizational efficiency (optimally meeting the human needs of persons in the organization).[43] Much of the development of subsequent organizational theory and practice has centered on problems of integrating the actualities, criteria, and con-

[42] Lyndall Urwick, *The Pattern of Management* (Minneapolis: University of Minesota Press, 1956).

[43] Chester I. Barnard, *The Functions of the Executive* (Cambridge: Harvard University Press, 1938).

cepts of organizational effectiveness and of organizational efficiency.

A growing group of thinkers and researchers have sought to move beyond the bureaucratic model toward some new model of organization which might set directions and limits for change efforts in organizational life. Out of many thinkers, we choose four who have theorized out of an orientation consistent with what we have called a normative-re-educative approach to changing.

Rensis Likert has presented an intergroup model of organization. Each working unit strives to develop and function as a group. The group's efforts are linked to other units of the organization by the overlapping membership of supervisors or managers in vertically or horizontally adjacent groups. This view of organization throws problems of delegation, supervision, and internal communication into a new light and emphasizes the importance of linking persons as targets of change and re-education in processes of organizational development.[44]

We have already stressed McGregor's efforts to conceive a form of organization more in keeping with new and more valid views of human nature and motivation (Theory Y) than the limited and false views of human nature and motivation (Theory X) upon which traditional bureaucratic organization has rested. In his work he sought to move thinking and practice relevant to organization and organizational change beyond limits of traditional forms. "The essential task of management is to arrange organizational conditions and methods of operation so that people can achieve their own goals best by directing their own efforts toward organizational objectives."[45]

Bennis has consciously sought to move beyond bureaucracy in tracing the contours of the organization of the future.[46] And Shephard has described an orgnizational form consistent with support for continual changing and self-renewal, rather than with a primary mission of maintenance and control.[47]

3. Power-Coercive Approaches to Effecting Change

It is not the use of power, in the sense of influence by one person upon another or by one group upon another, which distinguishes this family of strategies from those already discussed. Power is an ingredient of all human action. The differences lie rather in the ingredients of power upon which the strategies of changing depend and the ways in which power is generated and applied in processes of effecting change. Thus, what we have called rational-empirical approaches depend on knowledge as a major ingredient of power. In this view, men of knowledge are legitimate sources of power and the desirable flow of influence or power is from men who know to men who don't know through processes of education and of dissemination of valid information.

Normative-re-educative strategies of changing do not deny the importance of knowledge as a source of power, especially in the form of knowledge-based technology. Exponents of this approach to changing are committed to redressing the imbalance between the limited use of behavioral knowledge and people technologies and the widespread use of physical-biological knowledge and related thing technologies in effecting changes in human affairs. In

---

[44] Rensis Likert, *New Patterns of Management* (New York: McGraw-Hill, Inc., 1961).

[45] McGregor, pp. 422–431.

[46] W. G. Bennis, "Changing Organizations," in *The Planning of Change*, 2d Edition, Chap. 10, p. 568.

[47] H. A. Shephard, "Innovation-Resisting and Innovation-Producing Organizations," in *The Planning of Change*, 2d Edition, Chap. 9, p. 519.

addition, exponents of normative-re-educative approaches recognize the importance of noncognitive determinants of behavior as resistances or supports to changing— values, attitudes, and feelings at the personal level and norms and relationships at the social level. Influence must extend to these noncognitive determinants of behavior if voluntary commitments and reliance upon social intelligence are to be maintained and extended in our changing society. Influence of noncognitive determinants of behavior must be exercised in mutual processes of persuasion within collaborative relationships. These strategies are oriented against coercive and non-reciprocal influence, both on moral and on pragmatic grounds.

What ingredients of power do power-coercive strategies emphasize? In general, emphasis is upon political and economic sanctions in the exercise of power. But other coercive strategies emphasize the utilization of moral power, playing upon sentiments of guilt and shame. Political power carries with it legitimacy and the sanctions which accrue to those who break the law. Thus getting a law passed against racial imbalance in the schools brings legitimate coercive power behind efforts to desegregate the schools, threatening those who resist with sanctions under the law and reducing the resistance of others who are morally oriented against breaking the law. Economic power exerts coercive influence over the decisions of those to whom it is applied. Thus federal appropriations granting funds to local schools for increased emphasis upon science instruction tends to exercise coercive influence over the decisions of local school officials concerning the emphasis of the school curriculum. In general, power-coercive strategies of changing seek to mass political and economic power behind the change goals which the strategists of change have decided are desirable. Those who oppose these goals, if they adopt the same strategy, seek to mass political and economic power in opposition. The strategy thus tends to divide the society when there is anything like a division of opinion and of power in that society.

When a person or group is entrenched in power in a social system, in command of political legitimacy and of political and economic sanctions, that person or group can use power-coercive strategies in effecting changes, which they consider desirable, without much awareness on the part of those out of power in the system that such strategies are being employed. A power-coercive way of making decisions is accepted as in the nature of things. The use of such strategies by those in legitimate control of various social systems in our society is much more widespread than most of us might at first be willing or able to admit. This is true in educational systems as well as in other social systems.

When any part of a social system becomes aware that its interests are not being served by those in control of the system, the coercive power of those in control can be challenged. If the minority is committed to power-coercive strategies, or is aware of no alternatives to such strategies, how can they make headway against existing power relations within the system? They may organize discontent against the present controls of the system and achieve power outside the legitimate channels of authority in the system. Thus teachers' unions may develop power against coercive controls by the central administrative group and the school board in a school system. They may threaten concerted resistance to or disregard of administrative rulings and board policies or they may threaten work stoppage or a strike. Those in control may get legislation against teachers' strikes. If the political power of organized teachers grows, they may get legislation requiring collective bargaining between organized teachers and the school board on some range of educational issues. The power struggle then shifts to the negotiation table and compromise between competing interests may become the expected goal of the intergroup exchange. Whether the augmented power of new, relevant knowledge or the generation of common power through joint collaboration and deliberation are lost in the process will depend on the degree of commitment by all parties to the conflict to a continuation and maintenance of power-coercive strategies for effecting change.

What general varieties of power-coercive strategies to be exercised either by those in control as they seek to maintain their power or to be used by those now outside a position of control and seeking to enlarge their power can be identified?

a. STRATEGIES OF NONVIOLENCE

Mahatma Gandhi may be seen as the most prominent recent theorist and practitioner of nonviolent strategies for effecting change, although the strategies did not originate with him in the history of mankind, either in idea or in practice. Gandhi spoke of Thoreau's *Essay on Civil Disobedience* as one important influence in his own approach to nonviolent coercive action. Martin Luther King was perhaps America's most distinguished exponent of nonviolent coercion in effecting social change. A minority (or majority) confronted with what they see as an unfair, unjust, or cruel system of coercive social control may dramatize their rejection of the system by publicly and nonviolently witnessing and demonstrating against it. Part of the ingredients of the power of the civilly disobedient is in the guilt which their demonstration of injustice, unfairness, or cruelty of the existing system of control arouses in those exercising control or in others previously committed to the present system of control. The opposition to the disobedient group may be demoralized and may waver in their exercise of control, if they profess the moral values to which the dissidents are appealing.

Weakening or dividing the opposition through moral coercion may be combined with economic sanctions—like Gandhi's refusal to buy salt and other British manufactured commodities in India or like the desegregationists' economic boycott of the products of racially discriminating factories and businesses.

The use of nonviolent strategies for opening up conflicts in values and demonstrating against injustices or inequities in existing patterns of social control has become familiar to educational leaders in the demonstrations and sit-ins of college students in various universities and in the demonstrations of desegregationists against *de facto* segregation of schools. And the widened use of such strategies may be confidently predicted. Whether such strategies will be used to extend collaborative ways of developing policies and normative-re-educative strategies of changing or whether they will be used to augment power struggles as the only practical way of settling conflicts, will depend in some large part upon the strategy commitments of those now in positions of power in educational systems.

b. USE OF POLITICAL INSTITUTIONS TO ACHIEVE CHANGE

Political power has traditionally played an important part in achieving changes in our institutional life. And political power will continue to play an important part in shaping and reshaping our institutions of education as well as other institutions. Changes enforced by political coercion need not be oppressive if the quality of our democratic processes can be maintained and improved.

Changes in policies with respect to education have come from various departments of government. By far the most of these have come through legislation on the state level. Under legislation, school administrators have various degrees of discretionary powers, and policy and program changes are frequently put into effect by administrative rulings. Judicial decisions have played an important part in shaping educational policies, none more dramatically than the Supreme Court decision declaring laws and policies supporting school segregation illegal. And the federal courts have played a central part in seeking to implement and enforce this decision.

Some of the difficulty with the use of political institutions to effect changes arises from an overestimation by change agents of the capability of political action to effect changes in practice. When the law is passed, the administrative ruling announced, or the judicial decision handed down legitimizing some new policy or program or illegitimizing some traditional practice, change agents who have worked hard for the law, ruling, or decision frequently assume that the desired change has been made.

Actually, all that has been done is to bring the force of legitimacy behind some envisioned change. The processes of re-education of persons who are to conduct themselves in new ways still have to be carried out. And the new conduct often requires new knowledge, new skills, new attitudes, and new value orientations. And, on the social level, new conduct may require changes in the norms, the roles, and the relationship structures of the institutions involved. This is not to discount the importance of political actions in legitimizing changed policies and practices in educational institutions and in other institutions as well. It is rather to emphasize that normative-re-educative strategies must be combined with political coercion, both before and after the political action, if the public is to be adequately informed and desirable and commonly acceptable changes in practice are to be achieved.

c. CHANGING THROUGH THE RECOMPOSITION AND MANIPULATION OF POWER ELITES

The idea or practice of a ruling class or of a power elite in social control was by no means original with Karl Marx. What was original with him was his way of relating these concepts to a process and strategy of fundamental social change. The composition of the ruling class was, of course, for Marx those who owned and controlled the means and processes of production of goods and services in a society. Since, for Marx, the ideology of the ruling class set limits to the thinking of most intellectuals and of those in charge of educational processes and of communicating, rationales for the existing state of affairs, including its concentration of political and economic power, are provided and disseminated by intellectuals and educators and communicators within the system.

Since Marx was morally committed to a classless society in which political coercion would disappear because there would be no vested private interests to rationalize and defend, he looked for a counterforce in society to challenge and eventually to overcome the power of the ruling class. And this he found in the economically dispossessed and alienated workers of hand and brain. As this new class gained consciousness of its historic mission and its power increased, the class struggle could be effectively joined. The outcome of this struggle was victory for those best able to organize and maximize the productive power of the instruments of production—for Marx this victory belonged to the now dispossessed workers.

Many of Marx's values would have put him behind what we have called normative-re-educative strategies of changing. And he recognized that such strategies would have to be used after the accession of the workers to state power in order to usher in the classless society. He doubted if the ruling class could be re-educated, since re-education would mean loss of their privileges and coercive power in society. He recognized that the power elite could, within limits, accommodate new interests as these gained articulation and power. But these accommodations must fall short of a radical transfer of power to a class more capable of wielding it. Meanwhile, he remained committed to a power-coercive strategy of changing until the revolutionary transfer of power had been effected.

Marxian concepts have affected the thinking of contemporary men about social change both inside and outside nations in which Marxism has become the official orientation. His concepts have tended to bolster assumptions of the necessity of power-coercive strategies in achieving fundamental redistributions of socioeconomic power or in recomposing or manipulating power elites in a society. Democratic, re-educative methods of changing have a place only after such changes in power allocation have been achieved by power-coercive methods. Non-Marxians as well as Marxians are often committed to this Marxian dictum.

In contemporary America, C. Wright Mills has identified a power elite, essentially composed of industrial, military, and governmental leaders, who direct and limit processes of social change and accommodation in our society. And President Eisenhower warned of the dangerous concentration of power in substantially the same groups in his farewell message to the American people. Educators committed to democratic values should not be blinded to the limitations to advancement of those values, which are set by the less than democratic ideology of our power elites. And normative-re-educative strategists of changing must include power elites among their targets of changing as they seek to diffuse their ways of progress within contemporary society. And they must take seriously Marx's questions about the re-educability of members of the power elites, as they deal with problems and projects of social change.

The operation of a power elite in social units smaller than a nation was revealed in Floyd Hunter's study of decision making in an American city. Hunter's small group of deciders, with their satellite groups of intellectuals, front men, and implementers, is in a real sense a power elite. The most common reaction of educational leaders to Hunter's "discovery" has been to seek ways in which to persuade and manipulate the deciders toward support of educational ends which educational leaders consider desirable—whether bond issues, building programs, or anything else. This is non-Marxian in its acceptance of power relations in a city or community as fixed. It would be Marxian if it sought to build counter power to offset and reduce the power of the presently deciding group where this power interfered with the achievement of desirable educational goals. This latter strategy, though not usually Marxian inspired in the propaganda sense of that term, has been more characteristic of organized teacher effort in pressing for collective bargaining or of some student demonstrations and sit-ins. In the poverty program, the federal government in its insistence on participation of the poor in making policies for the program has at least played with a strategy of building countervailing power to offset the existing concentration of power in people not identified with the interests of the poor in reducing their poverty.

Those committed to the advancement of normative-re-educative strategies of changing must take account of present actual concentrations of power wherever they work. This does *not* mean that they must develop a commitment to power-coercive strategies to change the distribution of power except when these may be necessary to effect the spread of their own democratically and scientifically oriented methods of changing within society.

A. RATIONAL—EMPIRICAL   ## B. NORMATIVE—

VIEWS OF THE ENLIGHTENMENT AND CLASSICAL LIBERALISM   VIEWS OF THERAPISTS,

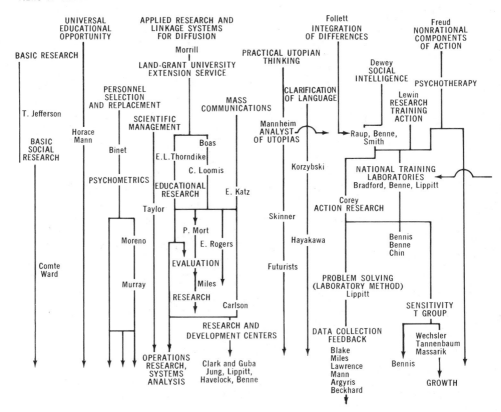

FIGURE 1   Strategies of Deliberate Changing

RE-EDUCATIVE

C. POWER—COERCIVE

TRAINERS, AND SITUATION CHANGERS

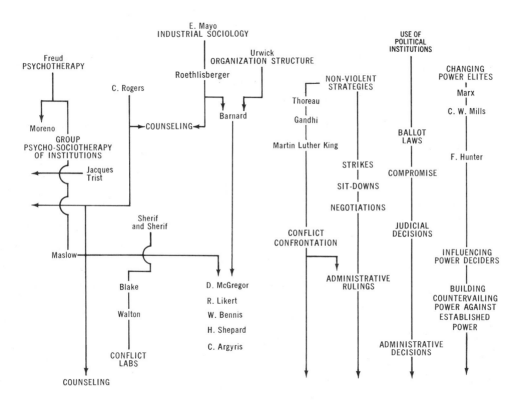

Contemporary Differentiations in Theories and Practices of Planned Change

CHAPTER TWO

As awareness and acceptance of the need for continuing changes in interpersonal and intergroup relations, institutions, social structures, and ways of life have widened and deepened in the consciousness of contemporary men and women, the volume and variety of efforts to introduce planfulness and deliberateness into processes of social and personal change have expanded correspondingly. The bewildering multiplicity of "therapies," "consciousness-raising methodologies," "development technologies," and "planning-action models" which today confront the student and practitioner of planned change evokes a search for meaningful patterns within this multiplicity.

The functions of a cognitive map of the current profusion of innovations and experimentations in the diagnosis and development of human systems are, at one and the same time, intellectual and practical. Intellectually, it is clarifying to get a meaningful view of the entire scope of the field of planned change. This means a way of identifying the differentiations among prevailing practices and rationales—a categorization that both accounts for the descriptively discernible differences in practice and makes it possible to compare and contrast these differences in their interrelations. Practically, it is useful for a change agent to see the range of approaches available for possible use as that agent confronts situations calling for his or her responsible intervention and shapes an intervention appropriate to himself or herself and to the requirements of the context of decision and action.

In the preceding chapter, Chin and Benne presented a mapping of the field of planned change in terms of "families" of intervention strategies. The bases of differentiation among these generalized strategies were varying images of man and of ways in which changes in human behavior and relationships are best effected, images with historically traceable roots in Western culture and history.

In this chapter, we are seeking to map contemporary differences in the practices and rationales of planned change without reference to their historical origins. Probably the most apparent basis for differentiating practices of planned change is the unit of human organization which is seen and taken as the target of change. The unit may be an individual person. It may be a group or an interpersonal relationship. Or perhaps the target of change is an intergroup complex or interface. An entire organization may be the focus of a change effort. Other change agents may take a society or some societal pattern or practice as their chosen target of changing. The relevant point here is that methods of diagnosis and intervention do vary as the unit-target of change varies.

Blake and Mouton have identified five types or kinds of interventions which applied social scientists are currently making into organizations in the interest of organizational change. These they name acceptant interventions, catalytic interventions, confrontation, prescriptive interventions, and the application and utilization of principles, models, and theories concerning the determination of human change. When Blake and Mouton combine their five types of intervention with the five target-units of change previously identified, a diagnosis/development matrix with twenty-five cells is generated. They provide examples of change efforts, along with bibliographical references, to illustrate the meaning of each cell in their matrix.

While Blake and Mouton recognize variations in the practice of changing as different human units are focused upon, their entire map is designed to clarify the current field or *organizational* diagnosis and development. Thus their concern with personal change, whether through acceptant, catalysis, confrontation, or prescription, is limited to changes of persons within an organization, undertaken in the interest of organizational development. And, similarly, their treatments of group, intergroup, and societal change are subsumed under their central concern with the changing of organizations.

There is a general point concerning the changing of human systems which the work of Blake and Mouton makes clear. The various levels and units of human organization as targets of change cannot be dealt with adequately in arbitrary isolation one from the other. For persons, groups, intergroup complexes, organizations, and societies are in actuality overlapping open systems. But a change agent can and does focus attention and effort on one level of human organization or another.

While Blake and Mouton's matrix illuminates admirably differentiations in the current practices and practice-rationales in organizational development, it leaves other areas of change practice and rationales unmapped. In essay 2.2 in this chapter, Benne attempts to map other areas of current practice in deliberate changing, where the focal purpose is not organizational development. His essay has been written to supplement the work of Blake and Mouton and thus deals only tangentially with processes and programs of organizational change.

2.1 STRATEGIES OF CONSULTATION

Robert R. Blake, Jane Srygley Mouton

In the process of our studies we have come to recognize that five different kinds of interventions characterize what applied behavioral scientists do as they work with people in organizations. They intervene, in any of these five ways, in five different settings or units of change. So a matrix of twenty-five cells is necessary to describe the significant change efforts that are going on. We would like to explain what these cells are, provide a brief bibliography to pinpoint work going on in each, and provide a few examples that describe the respective intervention/development assumptions that each contains.

You will notice that Figure 1 is called the D/D (Diagnosis/Development) Matrix. This is because diagnosis and development are two aspects that are more or less interdepedent in planned change efforts, although occasionally they need to be separated for purposes of analysis.

The *rows* of the matrix represent types of interventions. One is acceptant. The next is catalytic. A third is confrontation. The fourth is prescriptive. The fifth and last includes use of principles, theories and models as the determinants of change. Selection of any particular intervention, of course, is a judgmental decision taken on the basis of prior diagnosis.

The *columns* of the matrix refer to

settings within which change occurs. The first column identifies the individual *per se* as a unit of change. The second, or team, column refers mainly to small groups, projects, departments, and managerial "family" groups, but it also includes interpersonal relations on a one-to-one basis. The third column is for intergroup relationships. Examples of intergroup diagnosis/development units are interdivisional, headquarters-field, union-management, and other relationships between any organized groupings within or semi-external to the organization. The fourth column refers to the organization considered as a whole or as a system. The fifth we have labeled "society" because of the broader implications of training and development for planned change of society at large.

ACCEPTANT INTERVENTION

Now let's go along the top. What an "acceptant" intervention does is to enter into contact with the feelings, tensions, and subjective attitudes that often block a person and make it difficult for him to function as effectively as he otherwise might. The developmental objective is to enable him to express, work through and resolve these feelings so that he can then return to a more objective and work-related orientation. This is not the whole area of counseling as it relates to therapy. It is that aspect of counseling which takes place within the framework of organizations and which is intended to help a

FIGURE 1 The D/D Matrix[1]					
	Unit of Change				
Types of Intervention	*Individual*	*Team (group, project, department)*	*Intergroup (interdivisional, headquarters-field, union-management, etc.)*	*Organization*	*Society*
Acceptant	A	B	C	D	E
Catalytic	F	G	H	I	J
Confrontation	K	L	M	N	O
Prescriptive	P	Q	R	S	T
Principles, Models, Theories	U	V	W	X	Y

[1] This way of organizing intervention strategies led us to introduce a third dimension called *focal issues*. There are four: power/authority, morale/cohesion, norms/standards, and goals/objectives. See R. R. Blake, and Jane Srygley Mouton, *Consultation* (Reading, Mass.: Addison-Wesley, 1976).

person perform better. Certainly it is a very important application of counseling.

Here is an example of counseling with individuals from Cell A in the matrix. During the 1930's, at the Hawthorne plant of the Western Electric Company, it was discovered that many employees were blocked, taut, seething with tensions of one kind or another. Generally these tensions were either work-focused or home-focused, or an intricate combination of both. For some years Hawthorne management provided a counseling service that enabled people to be aided through counseling to discharge the emotion laden tensions. We say "to discharge" tensions, as distinct from resolving them more or less permanently. The procedure was, in effect, "Any time you feel overcome by tension, get a slip from your supervisor and go see a counselor." This is comparable—if we adopt an oil-industry analogy—to "flaring off" subterranean natural gas rather than piping it to wherever it can be productively used.

In the peak year of the program, 1948, Hawthorne's department of coun-seling was manned by fifty-five people. That's a large complement of counselors. This very interesting experiment has been documented by its originators, who were able to return to the scene of their effort and to study the consequences thirty years after the program began.

An example I would like to para-phrase for you is from their book (Dickson & Roethlisberger, 1966, 225–226). The situation takes place in the counselor's office. Charlie enters. He is a semi-skilled worker who has been with the company for some time but has recently been trans-ferred to a new inspection job from another one he had formerly mastered and enjoyed. He is unhappy with his new job.

Counselor: Hi 'ya Charlie, how are you?
Charlie: Glad to see you. We all set to go?
Counselor: Sure, any time you're ready.
Charlie: Well, I'm ready any time to get out of this g.d. place. *You know, you get shoved around from one place to another.*
Counselor: You mean you don't have one steady job?

Charlie: Steady, hell. When I came from the first floor I was supposed to do this particular bank job. I stayed on that for two or three weeks, not even long enough to learn it, then I got transferred up here. . . . Of course you know what I got. It got me nothing, just this job here which was a cut.*

Counselor: Then all that work didn't pay off?

Charlie: Pay off? There's no payoff at all.

As you can see in this brief example, Charlie is ventilating his feelings and frustrations and the counselor is "reflecting"; trying to aid Charlie to clarify them by feeding him back a summary of those tensions so that Charlie might get an understanding of what they are, rather than just feeling the hurt and distress of them. You will notice that the counselor is not attempting to help Charlie solve his "transfer with pay cut" problem. That's one point of application that involves counseling with an individual to promote catharsis.

In recent years—and "way out" from Hawthorne—the continuum of learning through experience has been extended and enriched through experimentation with action oriented, non-verbal approaches. An advantage here is that the modalities through which an individual is able to experience himself in situations are increased. Results and experiences can be more directly *felt,* in the sense that words are unnecessary to convey whatever emotions are involved. The way in which any particular approach is used, of course, determines its location in the matrix. One of the most common uses of "encountering" is in the effort to promote personal growth through individual cathartic experiences (Watson, 1972, 155–172).

Now let's look to Cell B. This in-

* (in his hourly rate of pay)

volves acceptant interventions at the team or group level. Here the idea is that before a team can do an effective job of dealing with its work problems, it may have to deal with emotional tensions and feelings that exist within and between its members.

Gibb has for a considerable time been aiding teams to discharge tension in a cathartic way. This example is from his account of his methods (Gibb, 1972). He describes how, in the process of team building, he may begin with what he calls a "preparation meeting." He brings together the people who are going to be leaders of different teams in order to prepare them for their experience. Why does he start this way? "The primary constraint," he says, ". . . is, of course, fear. Participants are given . . . perhaps the first half-day to share and fully explore as many of their fears as they are able to verbalize." What help is this? "Fears dissipate as they are brought into awareness, shared with others, lived with, listed on the board, made public, and made acceptable. The public expression of the fear may take many forms." (Gibb, 1972, 38) So the effort begins with group exploration which aims to remove these constraints so that constructive sessions can take place.

Cell C identifies approaches to planned change utilizing catharsis at the intergroup level. For example, I am sure that many readers have experienced the tensions and emotions that underlie many union-management relationships. Bickering at the bargaining table is a constant feature and, many times, the topics discussed are not the relevant ones that need to be resolved. Sometimes the relevant ones can't even be expressed! Rather, the issues that people concentrate on seemingly are brought to the table in order to provoke a fight. Often such intergroup dynamics emerge from emotions and frustrations which never get uncovered but stay beneath the surface. Catharsis at the intergroup level has as its purpose to uncover feelings that are barriers to problem-solving interaction; to provide the opportunity for them to be made public; and, in this way, to escape from their hidden effects.

Here is an example from a union-management situation we happen to be familiar with. Contract bargaining was underway. It was hopeless. It was going nowhere. We heard management voicing its frustrations and bitching about the union, and we suggested that perhaps the needed activity was to get *away* from the union-management bargaining table and to sit down together in a special conference for the sole purpose of exploring the feelings these groups held toward one another. This was done. The tensions discharged in those three days were destructive, deep-rooted, intense. The grudges and fantasies from the past that were blocking present effectiveness finally got unloaded, and this freeing-up permitted bargainers to get back to their deliberations.

Here is just one example of the many fantasies unveiled during these days. At one time, actual events which were the source of the fantasy had occurred, but now the "truth" of these events was a matter of history. At the present time the varied feelings about these events were in the realm of fantasy.

"In 1933," (this cathartic session took place in *1963*) the union told the management, "you s.o.b's had us down and out because of the depression. And what did you do? You cut everybody's pay in half and, having done so, then you turned us out into the yard to dig up all the pipe and repack it. How do you expect us to bargain with a bunch of cutthroats that would do that to human beings who are down?"

The managers, hearing this, did a retake and said, "Oh, but golly, that was not *us;* that was five dynasties of management ago!" But this disclaimer didn't

mollify the union. Eventually, 1963 management walked the 1963 union back through the time tunnel in an attempt to reconstitute the thinking that 1933 management had undertaken. This was "We shouldn't let people go home with no job. We should keep them 'whole.' We can't employ them full time because we don't have that much production scheduled—market demand is way down. Rather than laying off people *en masse,* the humane thing to do is to keep everyone on the payroll, but to make the cost burden bearable by reducing wages. Also, we have to keep them occupied somehow. With operational activities currently at such low levels, the only thing we can do that has long-term utility to it is to dig up the yard pipe and repack it."

So the 1933 management's intentions were probably well-meant, but the union's legend regarding those intentions portrayed them as very malicious. Yet eventually the 1963 union, after reconsidering that management's dilemma, agreed that it had taken the most humane alternative open to it. So the old legend dissolved away. Only by getting this kind of emotional muck out in the open and discharged was it possible for these union and management representatives to get back to a businesslike basis of working toward a contract. That's an example of acceptant at the intergroup level.

There are many examples of acceptant interventions at the organization level, Cell D.

In another company the entire management engaged in an "acceptant" experience prior to bargaining. The reason was that even though management, at an intellectual level, desired to interact on a problem-solving basis with the plant's independent-union representatives, there were many deeply-rooted antagonistic attitudes which continually surfaced and stifled the effort. Why? The ostensibly humane attitudes of people who have received formal education sometimes only serve as a mask for deeper feelings of resentment and antipathy. Often there is a lot of hate among managerial people toward the work force. Such feelings are particularly prevalent among engineers, supervisors and foremen who have, in their own careers, only recently risen above the level of the "blue-collar stiff."

The consultant determined that to work solely with the bargaining committee would be insufficient as they could only move in a problem-solving direction if they had the support of the rest of management. Thus a series of conferences were held. Participants were the top 100 members of management, who represented all levels of supervision except first and second line foremen. The stated purpose of these meetings was to develop shared convictions in regard to answering the key question, "How can we create better relations between union and management?"

Participants were put into three "cross-section" groups during each conference. Quinn, the plant manager, sat in one group. Van, the operations superintendent, sat in another group and Wes, the personnel chief, in a third. The groups struggled with the problem of how to improve union-management relations. It was fascinating to watch because a fairly substantial cross-section of the managerial group considered the key question a hopeless one to answer. "There is no way to bring about any improvement vis-à-vis the thugs, thieves and crooks who presently are running the union. How can you cooperate and collaborate with such a rat pack?"

Then as the question got debated, their deep-lying attitudes and feelings were expressed in detail and were looked at from many points of view. A new concept began to appear. Consciousness dawned that one can never look forward to an improvement in union-management relations unless this governing attitude—

namely that the union is composed of thugs, thieves and crooks—is erased or at least given an experimental adjournment in the minds of management. After the discharge of emotions was completed, it was concluded in group after group, "Regardless of what the union officers are personality-wise and what their history has been, the only conceivable way of bringing about a resolution of conflict is through treating the union officers as officers and according them the dignity and respect due to people who are duly elected. It is not our place to judge the people who have been chosen by their membership as lawful representatives. This is not our role. Our role is to meet with these people and to search for whatever conditions of cooperation and collaboration are possible."

As a result of this cathartic experience, it was possible thereafter for management's bargaining team to take a more collaborative stance (Blake & Mouton, 1973).

At the level of society shown in Cell E, there also are mechanisms that provide for catharsis. Religious institutions are one example. More so in American history than now, but still persisting, is the role of the clergyman as one of the persons to whom people turn when in deep emotional trouble, with the expectation of his providing the disturbed person an opportunity to talk through his feelings. In addition, the doctor, teacher, and school or private counselor are often turned to for help during periods of emotional turmoil, as indeed may be true for parents as well. Beyond these, whenever there is a trauma in society it frequently happens that *ad hoc* mechanisms are created which help people work through their distressed emotional feelings. Well remembered American examples include the two Kennedy funeral processions that were carried by television to many parts of the world. These occasions aided people to mourn. Mourning, in this sense, means working through and discharging tensions of a painful emotional character which currently are preventing people from going on living in their customary ways. As is true in the individual case, societal catharsis mechanisms may not have any direct and systematic connection to potential problem-solving steps, although they sometimes stimulate remedial action of one kind or another.

CATALYTIC INTERVENTIONS

Let's move to the next row down: catalytic interventions. "Catalytic" intervention means entering a situation and adding something that has the effect of transforming the situation in some degree from what it was at an earlier time. That's quite different from catharsis. When a training manager or consultant is acting to induce catharsis, he is reflecting or restating the problem—or perhaps simply listening in a fashion that gives empathic support. But when a person makes a catalytic intervention, he might provide a suggestion that causes the problem to be seen in a different and more relevant perspective. Or he might suggest a procedure that will lead to a different line of action being adopted.

Here is a catalytic intervention at the individual level, Cell F in the D/D Matrix. In one particular company they have a career-planning project. A young man who had been employed for some time came in to talk about his career hopes. The interviewer said, "What are your aspirations? Where would you like to end up in the company?"

The young man replied, "Well, I think I would like to be president or chairman."

Now then, the interviewer might have said something in a cathartic or reflective way. But he didn't. He said, "Well, that's an interesting aspiration. I would like to think it through with you. How many years of education do you have?"

"Six."

"How many promotions have you had in the last two years?"

"One small wage increase."

"Have you taken any courses on your own initiative?"

"No."

And as the discussion continued, the young man began to see the unrealism in his aspiration to be president. Currently there was *no* realistic possibility either in terms of some evidence of upward progression, or of autonomously achieved preparation, or in terms of anything else he was doing. The consultant thereby brought him to the choice point of whether he was prepared to make the additional sacrifices necessary for him to generate upward movement, or whether he was simply content to go on projecting an unrealistic career fantasy (Gould, 1970, 227–228). That's a catalytic intervention at the *individual* level.

Another example, which uses a laboratory setting for life/career planning, is premised on catalytic intervention at the individual level (Fordyce & Weil, 1971, 131–132).

Catalytic intervening at the *team* level, Cell G, is one of the most popular applied behavioral science developments of the past twenty-five years, and has become a central intervention in industrial life. There are a whole host of names that come to mind at this point. There are people who engage in team-building sessions where the purpose of their interventions is not to direct the team or merely to reflect back members' feelings, but to facilitate the interaction process so that the team comes to have a better understanding of the problems and pitfalls it's gotten into, and so on.

The following is an example of Schein, a consultant, facilitating group action by focusing attention on how the agenda for meetings was determined.

In the Apex company I sat in for several months on the weekly executive-committee meeting, which included the president and his key subordinates. I quickly became aware that the group was very loose in its manner of operation: people spoke when they felt like it, issues were explored fully, conflict was fairly openly confronted, and members felt free to contribute.

What did this mean to Schein?

This kind of climate seemed constructive, but it created a major difficulty for the group. No matter how few items were put on the agenda, the group was never able to finish its work. The list of backlog items grew longer and the frustration of group members intensified in proportion to this backlog.

How did members themselves diagnose the situation?

The group responded by trying to work harder. They scheduled more meetings and attempted to get more done at each meeting, but with little success. Remarks about the ineffectiveness of groups, too many meetings, and so on, became more and more frequent.

But what did it look like to Schein?

My diagnosis was that the group was overloaded. Their agenda was too large, they tried to process too many items at any given meeting, and the agenda was a mixture of operational and policy issues without recognition by the group that such items required different allocations of time.

So what did Schein propose?

I suggested to the group that they seemed overloaded and should discuss how to develop their agenda for their meetings. The suggestion was adopted after a half-hour or so of sharing feelings.

Was Schein passive and reflecting or active in a facilitative way?

It was then decided, with my help, to sort the agenda items into several categories, and to devote some meetings entirely to operational issues while others would be exclusively policy meetings. The operations meetings would be run more tightly

in order to process these items efficiently. The policy questions would be dealt with in depth. (Schein, 1969, 106)

Another example of facilitative or catalytic interaction occurs between boss and subordinate as they engage in "management by objectives." Quite frequently, however, in the introduction of MbO in an organization, people other than just the boss and subordinate are used to develop and facilitate the program. Here is a description of what such facilitators do. It is taken from Humble's work with management by objectives (Humble, 1967, 60). He calls these internal people "company advisers."

Company Advisers must be selected and trained to a highly professional standard in the various techniques. . . . An Adviser is a source of professional advice on the whole programme. He develops suitable techniques and methods with managers; counsels each, individual manager in the Key Results Analysis preparation; is present at first Reviews; helps to analyse training plans. He is an "educator" and "catalyst," *not* a man who states what the standards should be, nor what the priorities are and how the problems should be solved. That is management's task.

In this description we see a clear distinction between what we later on call prescriptive interventions—where the intervention is for the purpose of telling people what to do—and the facilitative or catalytic type of intervention where the goal is to aid a process of change or development to occur.

Data-gathering procedures frequently are used in a catalytic way. This is where data are intended to add something to the situation in order to change it (Likert, 1961). When these data are returned to their users, the expert's own personal participation is best described as catalytic.

Usually he doesn't tell people what the data mean, but he does ask them questions that aid them to probe meanings more directly.

Next to Cell H, intergroup. Catalysis here denotes adding something *between* two groups, in order to enable existing difficulties to rise to the surface or be placed squarely on the examining table so that they can be dealt with.

An intergroup intervention example is described by Beckhard. What he describes is a situation where people from a higher level meet with people from a lower level. The goal is to aid the lower-level people to communicate with the higher-level managers, or discuss specific problems with them, or to bring forth their feelings, attitudes, opinions and ideas regarding what actually is happening in some existing situation. Usually they have been unable, on any prior occasion, to communicate their ideas directly through organizational channels.

The person who organizes and leads the meeting is acting in a catalytic way. He is inserting a procedure into the situation that is facilitating in the sense that it helps the situation to develop toward resolution. In the following description, the meeting leader gives an assignment to each of the groups—say, to a top level group and a middle management group. He does not give directions as to what specifically should be discussed, but he indicates a way to get started on a facilitative discussion.

Think of yourself as an individual with needs and goals. Also think as a person concerned about the total organization. What are the obstacles, "demotivators," poor procedures or policies, unclear goals, or poor attitudes that exist today? What different conditions, if any, would make the organization more effective and make life in the organization better? (Beckhard, 1967, 154)

Then each unit goes off and discusses this separately. Beckhard's instructions are sufficiently general to permit people to put into their discussion whatever it is that is specifically troubling them in their particular jobs and situations. Then the meeting leader, from there on, continues in his procedurally facilitative role by helping the two units collect their data, analyze their feelings and facts, evaluate and compare them, and generally make progress. A similar example of catalytic intervention with multiple membership groups is provided by Bennis (Bennis, 1970, 158–160). Sometimes this approach is called a confrontation meeting, but this is a misnomer, because it entails no confrontation of the sort correctly described by Argyris (Argyris, 1971) which will be discussed later. Rather, the proceedings have a "group suggestion box" quality.

At the organization level (Cell I), intervention by an "ombudsman," who is empowered to bypass ordinary channels when he problem-solves on behalf of people who are burdened with difficulties because of some mistake or lack of response on the part of his particular company or government department, is catalytic in character, particularly in its facilitative aspects (*Commerce Today*, 1972, 29; Foegen, 1972, 289–294).

At the level of society there are many endeavors that are essentially catalytic, as specified in Cell J. We wish it were possible to say they were being systematically implemented within comprehensive and coherent frameworks of development. But there are some that, considered individually, have become quite systematic by now. Taking a census every five or ten years, one which describes the state of the nation "as of" a given point in time and permits comparisons to be made across several decades, is one way of aiding citizens to review their situation, of aiding national leadership to formulate policy, and of aiding industries to see the contemporary shape of markets, population trends, and many other things. The census is a powerful force in society. So are opinion polls. These are becoming ever more significant in the eyes of the public. Unfortunately their uses are somewhat limited to political affairs, but there are many other points of application that are possible for polling mechanisms, ones that can have a catalytic effect in terms of how society sees itself conducting its affairs.

CONFRONTATION

Let us now look along the next row, which deals with *confrontation* strategies. These represent quite different intervention styles from catalysis and very different from cathartic interventions. Confrontation has much more challenge in it. It's a much more active intrusion into the life experience of other people than could possibly be implied by a catalytic approach, and certainly much more than would be implied by a cathartic one.

There's another distinction here. As you move from catharsis and catalytic approaches into the next three, what you find is that, under the first two, there is no challenge of the *status quo* by the intervener. In other words, he accepts the definition of the problem, and the associated values and attitudes usually as these are given by the client, and then helps the client to adjust better to the *status quo*. Under a confrontation mode you frequently find a shifting across some kind of "gap"—the existence of this gap having been identified in the locus of the challenge that the intervener implies.

In different ways, each of the next three approaches is much more likely to cause people to challenge the *status quo* and to reject the existing situation as being less preferable than a stronger situation that could be designed to replace it. That's a very important shift in thinking—from simply aiding people to conform or adjust, to assisting people to redesign the situations in which they live and work.

First, we'll describe a confrontation type of intervention at the individual level (Cell K). This occurred in a multinational company where the New York president visited the subsidiary president and said to him, in effect—though it was a whole day in the doing—"Look, Henry, I want you to know that we're very unhappy with how your company is operating. As we look at it, in comparison with other companies in our worldwide group, your profit performance is far below the best, and we just don't see you taking the vigorous action necessary to solve your problems."

Henry *said*—that is, he didn't reply to the specifics of that statement: he couldn't hear them—"If you'll look at our 1949 figures and then look at our latest performance records relative to 1949 when I took over, you'll see that over the years we have made a dramatic shift for the better."

And so they went at it, this way and that, all day, and neither heard the other. From the New York Headquarters president's point of view, this was a company they would willingly sell, because they couldn't exert influence upon it. From the subsidiary president's point of view, a valiant effort over many years that had produced betterment was being disregarded. Now the confrontation was this.

The next day, one of us said to Henry, "My hearing is that two quite different *perspectives* are being employed to evaluate this company's performance. The perspective of the New York president is a here-and-now perspective. He doesn't care what you did for him yesterday, he is asking. 'What are you doing for me today?' By comparison, your perspective is historical. You're saying, 'How much better we're doing now than yesterday and last year and five years ago.' So unless you two can get onto a common perspective and reason from there, I see very little possibility of any collaborative effort occurring." Well, they did eventually get onto that common perspective basis. Once both of them understood what the central issue was, and that they weren't just totally unresponsive to each other, then some very significant changes took place in the subsidiary company, ones which are continuing to have enlivening effects. That's a confrontation that has caused development to get underway. And the *status quo* has been radically changed from what it previously had been.

Gestalt approaches, several of which are engineered to dramatize an encounter between the participant and an absent person, between two or more imaginary people, or even to dramatize ambivalent feelings within the person's own personality, are confrontational in character, even though cathartic elements are present. Conflicts, contradictions, incongruencies, and so on, are focused by the situation as the intervener structures it—or directly through the intervener's own words—in such a way as to permit more insightful resolutions through the elimination of contradictions, rationalizations, etc. (Herman, 1972).

Now let's examine confrontation at the team level (Cell L). An example of this comes during a team-building session conducted by Argyris. During this team-building session, and for the last several hours, members had been insisting that the company has a soft, manipulative, ineffective philosophy. Yet they had not really pinned down examples but were just talking in terms of generalities. So he said, "It is difficult to deal with such an answer, namely that the whole company is at fault. Could you give a specific example?" Nobody could. He continued very directly, saying, "OK fellows, are you going to be soft on these issues? You speak of integrity and courage. Where is it? I cannot be of help, nor you for that matter, if all you do is accuse the company of being ineffective. You said you were ready to talk—OK, I'm taking you at your word." (Argyris, 1971, 84) He is confronting them with the discrepancies between what they can be specific about and the abstractions.

Confrontation at the intergroup level (Cell M) usually involves each in coming to terms with the other. This interaction is not in terms of discharge of emotional tensions—as in the example of union and management given earlier—but in terms of gaining a shared and realistic sense of what their relationship is.

Here is an example. This one involves the headquarters' Division of Manufacturing in a large company and its major plant, which is located thirty miles away. The Division is headed by a vice president. A general manager runs the plant. These two had gotten more and more out of phase with each other over the years until they had nearly reached total impasse. It was very difficult for anyone to see how their misunderstandings had originated and grown into crisis proportions.

Eventually it was arranged for the vice president of manufacturing, and eight or ten people who reported to him, and the plant's general manager and the twelve people who reported to him to get together to study their relationship. The task was for each group to describe what the relationship between headquarters and the plant would be like if it were really a good one. Thereafter, they were to describe what the relationship actually was, here and now. The vice president of manufacturing's group worked in one room and put on newsprint a description of what, from their viewpoint, an ideal relationship would be like. The plant manager's group did the same thing, but in another room. Then they came back together and put their newsprints on the wall so that it could be seen by all what both sides thought a sound relationship would be like. The descriptions were similar and this similarity gave a lot of encouragement. Differences were discussed and resolved.

The next step, working separately, was for each group to describe the relationship as it actually existed here and now. They did this, and brought back their newsprints. Now it seemed like the relationship being described, as viewed from the headquarters point of view, was "totally" different from the relationship being pictured from the plant point of view. These dramatic divergences stimulated confrontation between the two groups on the issue of what, in fact, did characterize their mutual relationship. For several days, with close management of this situation and the interaction maintained by the interventionist to avoid an uncontrolled explosion, they thrashed through many aspects until a more accurate picture of the present relationship emerged. Now it became possible for both groups to see the many deep problems that in fact existed. They then designed some strategies for improvement steps that could lead toward resolution.

There is a comprehensive description of confrontation at the organization (Cell N) level (Jaques, 1951). The project was one of the innovative applied behavioral science interventions of the early post-war period and took place within the Glacier Metal Company in England. Jaques describes how he and others on his research team continually confronted the organization with the character of its internal relationships and objective performance.

At the societal level are found a good many institutionalized as well as informal mechanisms through which problems are confronted. What these are is a function of the kind of society you are looking at. The two-party system provides way of confronting issues by challenging what's going on. When one party publicizes its point of view, the other side is confronted with the necessity of either accepting the point of view as expressed, or identifying flaws in it. This is not to imply that in *any* political system this is done particularly well. We are only suggesting that two-party mechanisms, as these link into and work through a nation's executive branch, legislatures and public media, constitute one important way of confronting the problems of society and getting them into definition so that actions can be taken in behalf of solving them. Furthermore, the spread of the union-management confrontation mechanism into government, school, university and professional settings has resulted in this mechanism of intervention taking on social dimensions. Beyond that the entire legal system provides mechanisms by which confrontation with redress of injustice is provided for.

PRESCRIPTIVE

Now let's consider the *prescriptive* row. These are the most forceful types of intervention, ones which I rather doubt are widely practiced by training and development people. But they are widely applied by outside consultants in conjunction with managers in industry, commerce, and government. Higdon describes the prescriptive approach as used in various consulting firms such as McKinsey and Company; Arthur D. Little; Booz, Allen and Hamilton, and many others (Higdon, 1969). The basic procedure is that management asks an expert in, and he and his associates study the situation and provide a recommended solution. The "mainstream" consultant is not working with emotions in a cathartic sense. He is not working catalytically. He is not confronting. He is telling. His recommendations would be directions, if he had the authority of rank. But he is certainly prescribing, and these prescriptions sometimes are very complete and fundamental. Often they involve changing an organization's structure, or getting out of one product line and into another, or applying a more efficient theory of business. Many times they involve firing or laying off people, and so they can have impactful consequences on the development of an organization. Sometimes the prescription is rejected out of hand. Sometimes, when taken, it results in a healthful bracing up of part or all of the organization. There have been numerous instances, however, of consultant prescriptions becoming very frustrating to the organization in terms of the difficulties and side effects left in their wake. These include lowered morale, people leaving because they no longer can give their commitment, and so on.

Here's a description of prescriptive strategy at the individual level (Cell P). It is where a consultant is trying to hold up a mirror in front of a manager to help him see what he is like, and then to prescribe, in concrete and operational terms, what he'd better do. The client is a plant manager who has trouble with his chief accountant, who is a rather "cold and formal" individual. To obtain better results than he was presently getting from this man, the plant manager—a genial fatherly person who likes to develop warm personal relations with his subordinates—was advised to take a forceful, direct, impersonal approach with him. This, the consultant predicted, would resonate much better with the accountant's psyche than the manager's more typical approach had been doing. On the matter of delayed reports the manager was to say the following, "I want your report on my desk at nine o'clock Friday morning, complete in every detail, and no ifs, ands, or buts about it." Having delivered that ultimatum, he was to turn around and leave. The plant manager did just that, although, being the kind of person he was, it was hard for him to do. The new approach brought striking results. The report came in on schedule and it was one of the finest the plant manager had ever received (Flory, 1965, 158–159). The client had been told specifically how he should act and he followed it through in strict accordance with the consultant's plan. In this case it produced effective results. Inciden-

tally, the developing area of "behavior modification" (Krumboltz, 1965) is a training strategy that has prescriptive qualities.

An example of a prescriptive intervention at the group level (Cell Q) is offered by Cohen and Smith. They think this kind of intervention is most suitable toward the end of a group experience. At that time the total group is divided into subgroups of four or five members who are given the following instructions.

> . . . In each subgroup one person will leave the room for ten minutes. During that time the remaining members will first diagnose this person's typical style of interacting with others, and secondly try to pinpoint definite, specific, helpful suggestions as to how he might be helped to engage in atypical but productive behavior both for himself and the group. I must stress the terms 'definite' and 'specific.' Don't make abstract generalizations like 'you're too much of an introvert, so try being an extrovert for a while.' Instead, give him definite and specific prescriptions to carry out that are generally atypical but productive. Thus, one person might be told to express anger toward the group more directly and verbally instead of remaining quiet. The process continues until everyone has been given a 'behavioral prescription.' We will all meet back here in 'X' minutes to see what sort of changes have occurred. (Cohen & Smith, 1972, 103)

Robert's Rules of Order are prescriptive rules for conduct at the group or team level [Robert (1876), 1970]. They tell the leader how to operate meeting procedures. This rather mechanical set of criteria, if followed, prescribes the process parameters of the meeting, provides for expressions of differences, and offers a voting mechanism for resolution.

The third party arbiter is used at the intergroup level to provide for the resolution of differences, and to speed thinking toward further progress (Cell R). Typically, it operates in the following way. Two groups—say, management and a union—reach an impasse. Both agree to submit the disagreement to binding arbitration. The arbitrator, characteristically a disinterested outsider, hears evidence or otherwise studies the case and renders his decision. This usually takes the form of a prescription which both sides in the dispute are obligated to take (Linke, 1968, 158–560, Lazarus *et al*, 1965).

Prescriptive approaches at the organization level are shown in Cell S. One is vividly described in a case study from *Fortune*. Top management of Philco had engaged an outside firm to study the organization and to propose needed changes. Here's how a crucial meeting was described.

James M. Skinner, Jr., president of Philco Corp., (arrived) . . . for a momentous meeting that had been six months in the making. Waiting for Skinner in suite 1808 were nine somewhat apprehensive men from Arthur D. Little, Inc., the technical consulting firm of Cambridge, Massachusetts.

. . . Donham spoke first, outlining in general terms what A.D.L. hoped to accomplish with its reorganization plan. What he was proposing, in brief, was a massive reorganization of Philco's marketing setup, which would: make the job of marketing all of Philco's consumer products the responsibility of one division; fix profit responsibilities at precise points in the company; get day-to-day pressures off the backs of men who should be doing long-range planning; and provide much closer support for Philco's independent distributors and dealers. (Thompson, 1959, 113–114)

Levinson, operating out of a psychoanalytic tradition, has described his model of organization diagnosis in step-by-step terms. The approach he depicts is prescriptive in character, as demonstrated in the following excerpt which gives a few of the diagnostician's recommendations regarding the improvement of personnel practices at "Claypool Furniture and Appliances."

The recommendations to be made, following the logic expressed in the last discussion, are as follows:

Personnel Practices The company should establish descriptions and standards and objectives for all positions. It should develop orientation and training programs to properly prepare people for for their jobs and provide appraisal devices by which personnel and their superiors can assess progress and training needs. Positions and training in supervision and management are to be included in this process. A procedure for identifying prospective managerial talent should be evolved. The representative council should be abolished, and it should be replaced by employee task forces appointed to solve specific intraorganizational problems. Such groups, to include stock personnel, would end the isolation of the stock people and contribute to organizational identification and group cohesion.

A continuous and open evaluation of the wage and salary structure below the managerial levels should be undertaken, with the intention of creating and maintaining an equitable and competitive salary structure. . . . (Levinson, 1972, 491)

The Hoover Commission was an effort to use prescriptive techniques of diagnosis and development at the societal level. Ex-president Herbert Hoover and other members of the commission comprised a prestigious group. The presumption was that the voice of their authority behind recommendations would be sufficient, along with a responsive incumbent President, to bring about the recommended reformations in terms of restructuring the design and operations of the executive branch of the government.

The usual procedure, applied on all

levels of government in the United States, is to set up a formal inquiry into existing conditions, in the hope of bringing forth concrete recommendations with a fair chance of adoption. Inquiries of this type on the federal level include the President's Committee on Administrative Management with Louis Brownlow as chairman (reporting in 1937) and the (first) Commission on Organization of the Executive Branch headed by former president Herbert Hoover (reporting in 1949). (Willson, 1968, 632)

PRINCIPLES, THEORIES, AND MODELS

The first row of the matrix identifies diagnostic and developmental efforts which focus upon aiding people to acquire insights derived from principles, theories, or models. The assumption is that deficiencies of behavior or performance can be resolved best when people responsible for results use relevant principles, theories, or models in terms of which they themselves can test alternatives, decide upon and take action, and predict consequences. It is an approach which emphasizes intervention by concepts and ideas rather than by people.

With regard to Cell U, the particular significance to an individual of theory, principles, and models is that they are capable of providing a map of valid performance against which actual behavior and actual performance can be contrasted. When gaps exist between theory specifications for sound conduct and actual behavior, then change can be introduced which reduces the gap by increasing the congruence between the two. In this sense—and also, importantly, in the sense of removing self-deception—systematic concepts involving theories, principles, or models constitute a "theory mirror" which has the unique power of enabling people to see themselves, their present situations or future potential more clearly than if reliance is on subjective notions that something feels "right," "natural," or "okay,"

or simply that others "approve" it. Here are some examples:

Transactional Analysis is a conceptual formulation which provides a mirror into which people can look as a way of seeing themselves. Training designs have been created which enable participants to identify "Parent," "Child," and "Adult" oriented behavior both directly and with the benefit of colleague feedback and to study and practice ways of shifting toward more adult-like behavior (Blansfield, 1972, 149–154).

Also at the individual level, there is the Kepner-Tregoe system which provides managers with a model through which to design an analysis of any given problem and evaluate the quality of decisions they make. The objective is to reduce impulse, spontaneity and reliance on past practice and to shift to a rationality basis for problem analysis and decision making (Kepner & Tregoe, 1965).

There are a variety of theories, principles or models regarding individual behavior, some of which are accompanied by intervention strategies calculated to make the models functionally useful in concrete situations. Some of the more widely known include Theories X and Y (McGregor, 1960), Grid® formulations (Blake & Mouton, 1964, 1968, 1970; Mouton & Blake, 1971), and Systems 1 through 4 (Likert, 1967). However, the approach described by Likert does not involve man-to-man feedback on actual performance. Thus provisions are unavailable for penetrating and correcting self-deception.

Examples of theory orientation at the individual level include four Grids: Managerial, Sales, Customer, and Marriage; each of which describes several alternative models—9,9, 9,1, 1,9, 5,5, and 1,1—as well as mixed, dominant and backup theories. Once a person has learned the various theories, they can be used to diagnose his own behavior. In addition, he can select any theory as a model to change toward, but the most likely endorsed one is 9,9. He can then study and practice ways of increasing the congruence between his actual behavior and the model (Blake & Mouton, 1968, 34–66).

Some approaches to team building (Cell V) use principles, theories and models as the basis for diagnosing and feedback and for implementing development activities. Central issues, which, for the top team of a large chemical plant, demonstrated the gap between a diagnosis of their present ways of functioning and a model of what they considered ideal, are shown in Figure 2. This actual/ideal comparative diagnosis was used for designing strategies of change to be implemented within the next four months (Blake & Mouton, 1968, 120–157).

Theory, principle and models also have proved useful in strengthening intergroup relations (Cell W). Phase 3 of Grid Organization Development, for example, begins with two groups convening for the purpose of describing what would be an ideal model for their particular relation-ship. This ideal model is itself based on theories of intergroup conflict and cooperation (Blake & Mouton, 1964; Blake, Shepard & Mouton, 1964). It culminates with an *in situ* design which spells out the properties of a sound and effective relationship in a particular, concrete setting. The modeling stage is followed by implementation strategies for converting "what is" to "what should be." An example of the properties of an ideal management-union relationship as described by one company is shown in Figures 3 and 4.

The development of an Ideal Strategic Corporate Model in Phase 4 of Grid Organization Development is an example of the use of models at the organization level (Cell X). Phase 4 enables a top group, particularly, to isolate itself from the *status quo* long enough to design what would be an "ideal" company, given its realistic access to financial resources. Issues considered include, "What should be the key financial objectives that the company should strive after?" "What should be the nature of the company's

---

FIGURE 2   Actual vs. Ideal Top Team Culture in a Chemical Plant

Actual	*Ideal*
Persons only do what is expected of them. Each man runs his own shop. The boss calls the shots.	Synergism is exploited, issues are talked through, and solutions and decisions based on facts are fully thrashed through to understanding and agreement.
Plans come down from the boss without opportunity to review, evaluate, or recommend changes by those who implement them.	Plans based on analysis of facts permit real issues to be treated soundly; plans are produced jointly by those who should be involved; individual responsibilities are clear.
Traditional ways of doing things are rarely questioned; they represent the tried and true operating standards.	Elements of culture are continually evaluated in the light of requirements for peak performance and, if necessary, they are modified or replaced through thoughtful discussions and agreement among team members.
Results are what count, no matter how achieved.	Team members are fully committed to excellence, results are achieved because members are motivated to exceed.

FIGURE 3 What a Sound Union-Management Relationship Would Be as Described by Management

The Management Would:

Maintain open communications with the union in the following areas:
  Economics of industry and company
  Goals and objectives of company
  Long range company plans
  How company profits handled and distributed
  Problems facing company
  Growth opportunities—company and individual
  Security and development of employees
  Employee induction and orientation—where person fits in total scheme of things
Participate in prebargaining discussions to:
  Identify and clarify current economic climate
  Identify and understand company's competitive position
  Assess and evaluate indexes for productivity
  Identify and agree upon appropriate and objective cost of living standards
  Identify and understand employee attitudes and concerns
  Assess strengths and weaknesses of present contract
  Identify possible obstacles and barriers that could arise during negotiations
Adopt bargaining strategy to:
  Develop frame of reference for agenda
  Explore problem areas jointly
  Explore opportunity areas
Have more joint problem solving—e.g., on:
  Evaluating impact on employees from operational changes
  Work simplification
  Benefits and pension programs
  Techniques of training
  Job safety
Handle complaints and grievances as follows:
  First line supervisors would discharge responsibility for resolving complaints and grievances and act with dispatch
  Participate in continuing joint efforts leading to clear interpretation and uniform application of contract clauses at working level
  Maintain open door policy—union executives have free access to management executives and vice versa
  Establish and maintain open, upper level labor-management dialogue—ongoing critique
  Endeavor to understand problem confronting union officers within their frame of reference in their relationship with membership.

The Union Would:

Develop comprehensive understanding of specific nature of the business and concern for it
Understand and consider nature of competition as it relates to company performance and needs for change
Develop understanding of relationships of productivity to wages and benefits
Because of peculiar nature of industry, understand long range impact on both company and employees from work stoppages
Recognize implications of taking fixed positions in approaching problems—win-lose trap
Recognize harm in intragroup (within union) conflict resulting in company and employee backlash
Subdue personal interests in favor of overall company and union objectives
Accept responsibility to communicate facts to employees without prejudice.

Source: Blake, R. R. & Mouton, J. S. *Corporate excellence through grid organization development: A systems approach.* Houston: Gulf Publishing, 1968, 181–182. Not to be reproduced without permission.

FIGURE 4   What a Sound Union-Management Relationship Would Be as Described by the Union

---

The Management Would:

Exercise authority on complaints, grievances, questions, decisions needed, etc., without needless delay, particularly first level managers

Adopt uniform education program for all supervisors, vertical and horizontal, on understanding, interpreting, and applying the contract

Interpret the contract in an honest and aboveboard way

Consult employees on changes in working schedules, shifts, transfers, location, etc.

Apply a system of seniority and rotation without favoritism, e.g., assigned overtime, easy jobs, time off, vacations, best working schedules, etc.

Rate employees' performance on a uniform, systematic, and fair basis and with employees told where they stand

Coordinate and communicate effectively between department supervisors to prevent needless work by employees and cut down costs and wasted effort.

The Union Would:

Represent all employees fairly

Communicate problems, complaints, contract infractions to management

Have access to top management without runaround at lower levels

Be concerned with costs and amount of production

Insure employee has correct rating for skills he has and that he is paid for job he does, not the classification he has.

(Union had insufficient time remaining to complete this activity.)

Source: Blake, R. R. & Mouton, J. S. *Corporate excellence through grid organization development: A systems approach.* Houston: Gulf Publishing, 1968, 183. Not to be reproduced without permission.

---

business, and the nature of its markets?" "What should its structure be?" "What policies should it operate under?" Finally, "What are development requirements for getting from where it is to where it would go if it were to approach the ideal model?" An example of the change in thinking about financial objectives at the corporate level during Phase 4 is shown in Figure 5.

The use of principles, models and theories also can be seen at the level of society (Cell Y). The Magna Charta is a well-known historical example. The U.S. Constitution describes the kind of behavior, freedom and control which American society was expected to be modeled after. Over nearly two centuries, several constitutional amendments have updated the model in the light of contemporary perspectives. Legislative and executive actions are always being tested against the Constitution.

Lilienthal's work in Iran can be viewed as intervention at the societal level to bring about change through assisting the eventual users to design models of "what should be" as the basis of specific implementation plans. Lilienthal is a notable industrial statesman who led first the Tennessee Valley Authority and then the U.S. Atomic Energy Commission in their beginning years. He has described his later consulting work (Lilienthal, 1969) when, with his own and his colleagues' vast knowledge of hydro-electric engineering, community rehabilitation, and agri-business, they helped the Iranian government

FIGURE 5   Genuine Concern with the Organization's Earning Capacity Results from Designing an Ideal Strategic Model

From	To
Maintain or increase market share while living within a budget.	Optimal 30, minimum 20 percent pretax return on assets employed with an unlimited time horizon.
Dollar profit should improve and not fall behind last year. Return on investment computed and discussed on an after-the-fact calculation which exerted little or no influence on operational decision making.	Each business should have a specified profit improvement factor to be calculated on a business-by-business basis. The objective should be an earnings per share level which would within five years justify a price-earnings ratio of 20 to one or better.
	Share of market objectives should be established within the framework of return on assets and cash generation objectives.

Source: Blake, R. R. & Mouton, J. S. *Corporate excellence through grid organization development A systems approach.* Houston: Gulf Publishing 1968, 233. Not to be reproduced without permission.

design a model for water and electric-power resources for the future of its then undeveloped Khuzestan province. That model is being systematically implemented through the building of dams, power irrigation systems, and so on, as well as infrastructure developments such as agricultural advisory programs, health and educational facilities, etc. This is an example of how a consultant can work, not in a prescriptive mode, but as a skillful teacher in aiding people to learn to design and implement complex models. Lilienthal thus has enabled a vast development to occur, one that otherwise would have been piecemeal, suboptimizing, and possibly impractical.

Skinner's recent writings about society are derived from theory and principles and also rest on a model concept (Skinner, 1971).

SUMMARY AND CONCLUSIONS

The D/D Matrix provides a way of encompassing a wide range of activities now underway for strengthening human performance through diagnosis and development. Illustrations of each approach have been provided without trying to be inclusive.

Using this matrix, anyone who wishes to do so can identify the assumptions underlying his own work, and evaluate their probable consequences for increasing the effectiveness of individuals, groups, groups in relationships with one another, organizations, and society. The acceptant approach of emotional barrier-reduction and the catalytic approach of helping people to make progress in dealing with given situations are most likely to aid individuals and groups to do a better job within the existing *status quo.*

Confrontation and prescription are useful in a "fixed" or "frozen" situation. They provide alternatives to those currently present in the *status quo.* Both rely heavily on outside expertise.

The history of society and its capacity to identify and grapple with complex and interrelated problems of the physical environment, new technologies, and community development is significantly linked with the production and use of principles, theories and models for understanding, predicting—and, therefore, managing—natural and human environments. Approaches to diagnosis and development which rely on the use of principles, theories, and models for understanding emotional, intellectual and operational events provide the most powerful and impactful approach to the implementation of planned change.

It is highly unlikely that any single approach will be based solely on one intervention mode. Rather, the likelihood is that several intervention modes will be included, with one of them being central or dominant. For example, the Dickson-Roethlisberger counseling program appears to have been a very "pure" individual-cathartic approach, with minor reliance on counseling as catalytic intervention. Process consultation, as depicted by Schein, relies heavily upon catalytic intervention, with some use of acceptant interventions and very infrequent use of the confrontation mode, Schein makes practically no use of the prescriptive mode, and makes theory interventions only after the fact.

The intervening in T Groups is mainly catalytic, with secondary reliance on the cathartic mode. "Encounter" relies very heavily on catharsis. Grid OD concentrates on theory, principles and models; but it also provides at key points for confrontation, catalytic intervention, and cathartic release. Other approaches can be analyzed in a similar manner.

No one can say, in an abstract sense and without regard to a particular situation, that there is "one best way." While principles, theories, and models constitute the strongest approach, they may lack feasibility until emotional blockages have been reduced through cathartic intervention. Or, perhaps, opening up the possibilities of systematic OD may take little more than a timely catalytic intervention which enables managers to see possibilities not previously envisaged. Statements of a similar character can be made with regard to confrontation and prescription.

In the final analysis, however, acceptant, catalysis, confrontation or prescription constitute means to an end, rather than ends in themselves. The ultimate goal is that people become capable of effective living through utilizing principles, theories and models as the basis of human enrichment.

References

Matrix

Cell

L   Argyris, C. *Organization and innovation.* Homewood, Ill.: R. D. Irwin, 1965.

L   Argyris, C. *Intervention theory and Method.* Reading, Mass.: Addison-Wesley, 1970.

L   Argyris, C. *Management and organization development.* New York: McGraw-Hill, 1971.

H   Beckhard, R. The confrontation meeting. *Harvard Business Review,* March-April, 1967, 149–155.

H   Bennis, W. G. Organization development: What it is and what it isn't. In D. R. Hampton (Comp.) *Behavioral concepts in management* (second edition). Encino, Calif.: Dickinson, 1972. Pp. 154–163.

U   Blake, R. R. & Mouton, J. S. *The managerial grid: Key orientations for achieving production through people.* Houston: Gulf Publishing, 1964.

W   Blake, R. R., Shepard, H. A. &

Mouton, J. S. *Managing intergroup conflict in industry*. Houston: Gulf Publishing, 1964.

C   Blake, R. R., Sloma, R. L. & Mouton, J. S. The union-management intergroup laboratory: Strategy for resolving intergroup conflict. *Journal of Applied Behavioral Science*, 1965, *1*, 1, 25–57.

U, V,   Blake, R. R. & Mouton, J. S. *Cor-*
W, X   *porate excellence through grid organization development: A systems approach*. Houston: Gulf Publishing, 1968.

U   Blake, R. R. & Mouton, J. S. *The grid for sales excellence: Benchmarks for effective salesmanship*. New York: McGraw-Hill, 1970.

X   Blake, R. R. & Mouton, J. S. *How to assess the strengths and weaknesses of a business enterprise*. Austin, Tex.: Scientific Methods, Inc., 1972, 6 vols.

D, I   Blake, R. R. & Mouton, J. S. *Journal of an OD man*. Forthcoming, 1973.

U, V   Blansfield, M. G. Transactional analysis as a training intervention. In W. G. Dyer (Ed.), *Modern theory and method in group training*. New York: Van Nostrand Reinhold, 1972. Pp. 149–154.

Q   Cohen, A. M. & Smith, R. D. The critical-incident approach to leadership in training groups. In W. G. Dyer (Ed.), *Modern theory and method in group training*. New York: Van Nostrand Reinhold, 1972. Pp. 84–196.

I   *Commerce Today*, 2, April 3, 1972, 29.

A   Dickson, W. J & Roethlisberger, F. R. *Counseling in an organization: A sequel to the Hawthorne researches*. Boston: Division of Research, Graduate School of Business Administration, Harvard University, 1966.

P   Flory, C. D. (Ed.) *Managers for tomorrow*. New York: The New American Library of World Literature, 1965.

I   Foegen, J. H. Ombudsman as complement to the grievance procedure. *Labor Law Journal*, May 1972, *23*, 289–294.

F   Fordyce, J. J. & Weil, R. *Managing with people: A manager's handbook of organization development methods*. Reading, Mass.: Addison-Wesley, 1971.

B   Gibb, J. R. TORI theory: Consultantless team building. *Journal of Contemporary Business*, 1972, *1*, 3, 33–41.

F   Gould, M. I. Counseling for self-development. *Personnel Journal*, 1970, *49*, 3, 226–234.

K   Herman, S. M. A. Gestalt orientation to organization development. In W. Burke (Ed.) *Contemporary organization development: Approaches and interventions*. Washington, D. C.: NTL Institute for Applied Behavioral Science, 1972.

S   Higdon, H. *The business healers*. New York: Random House, 1969.

G   Humble, J. W. *Improving business results*. Maidenhead, Berks.: McGraw-Hill, 1967.

N   Jaques, E. *The changing culture of a factory*. London: Tavistock, 1951.

U   Kepner, C. H. & Tregoe, B. B. *The rational manager*. New York: McGraw-Hill, 1965.

P   Krumboltz, J. D. (Ed.) *Revolution in counseling: Implications of behavioral science*. Boston: Houghton Mifflin, 1965.

R   Lazarus, S. *et al. Resolving business disputes: The potential of commercial arbitration.* New York: American Management Association, 1965.

S   Levinson, H., with Molinari, J. & Spohn, A. G. *Organizational diagnosis.* Cambridge, Mass.: Harvard University Press, 1972.

G   Likert, R. *New patterns of management.* New York: McGraw-Hill, 1961.

U   Likert, R. *The human organization, its management and value.* New York: McGraw-Hill, 1967.

Y   Lilienthal, D. E. *The journals of David E. Lilienthal.* Vol. IV. *The road to change, 1955–1959.* New York: Harper & Row, 1969.

R   Linke, W. R. The complexities of labor relations law. In R. F. Moore (Ed.), *Law for executives.* New York: American Management Association, 1968.

U   McGregor, D. *The human side of enterprise.* New York: McGraw-Hill, 1960.

U   Mouton, J. S. & Blake, R. R. *The marriage grid.* New York: McGraw-Hill, 1971.

Q   Robert, H. M. *Robert's rules of order* (newly revised). Glenview, Ill.: Scott, Foresman, 1970. First published, 1876.

G   Schein, E. H. *Process consultation: Its role in organization development.* Reading, Mass.: Addison-Wesley, 1969.

Y   Skinner, B. F. *Beyond freedom and dignity.* New York: Knopf, 1971.

S   Thompson, E. T. The upheaval at Philco. *Fortune,* February 1959, 113-116+

A   Watson, G. Nonverbal activities— why? when? how? In W. G. Dyer (Ed.), *Modern theory and method in group training.* New York: Van Nostrand Reinhold, 1972, Pp. 155–172.

T   Willson, F. M. G. Government departments. *Encyclopaedia Britannica.* Vol. 10. Chicago: Encyclopaedia Britannica, Inc., 1968.

2.2   THE CURRENT STATE OF PLANNED CHANGING IN PERSONS, GROUPS, COMMUNITIES AND SOCIETIES

Kenneth D. Benne

Without discounting in any way the admirable clarity with which Blake and

This essay was written especially for this volume as a supplement to Selection 2.1 by Blake and Mouton. The "matrix" was designed to map and clarify various current practices and rationales in organizational development. This essay seeks to characterize and clarify the present state of planned change efforts in which the focus of the effort is upon some human system other than the organization, more particularly the bureaucratic organization.

Mouton have mapped current practices in the complex field of organizational diagnosis and development, I recognize at the outset that my task of mapping the terrain of planned changing outside the organizational setting is a more difficult one. I recognize further that my mapping will not achieve the elegance or completeness which Blake and Mounton have achieved.

The kinds of practices I am trying to categorize cover a wider spectrum of change targets, stretching from the human individual, through the small group and interpersonal relations, through inter-group relations, to which I have annexed the "community" as a local intersystem of group and organizational systems to the macrosystems of societies and cultures. The ideological element is probably stronger between identifiable streams of practice focused on individual changing than among various practitioners of or-ganizational development. Certainly, the ideological element is much more visible in practices designed to stimulate and guide processes of community and societal changing. And there is probably more collegiality, more sharing of experimental results, more reading of each other's papers and journals, among practitioners of organizational development than among practitioners in any other part of the spectrum of planned changing.

Yet, though we can rightly be more dubious about the clarity of the results, the effort may be worth a try.

I. THE HUMAN INDIVIDUAL AS THE TARGET OF CHANGING

A generation ago, most informed people would have identified two main forms of social practice, whose aim was deliberately to effect changes in human individuals. One form of practice was psychotherapy, the other education. At that time the two forms of practice seemed relatively easy to distinguish. In general, psychotherapy dealt with the treatment of pathologies and deviations from the norm. It was, therefore, reasonable to assume that the practice of psychotherapy should be car-ried on or at any rate supervised by special-ists from the medical profession—psychia-trists. A division of labor was beginning to occur with nurses, social workers, occu-pational and physical therapists, and clini-cal psychologists getting into the therapeu-tic act. But the "therapeutic" or medical model was for the most part intact.

Education, on the other hand, was identified with the transmission of selected cognitive and skill elements, drawn from the cultural conserve, to "normal" human individuals, more particularly to those who were chronologically immature. This trans-mission process was designed to equip the individual with the knowledge and skills thought to be required in coping with his or her adult responsibilities as person, as citizen, and as a member of one vocational group or another. The site of education was the school and the class-room, though supervised experiences in field settings were included as part of voca-tional and professional education.

It is the breakdown of these relatively neat categories and institutions of educa-tion and psychotherapy that has led to the differentiation and proliferation of method-ologies and technologies designed to facili-tate individual changing which now con-front the student and practitioner of plan-ned changing. A brief examination of the critiques that have led to the breakdown of the walls between education and therapy may help us to understand the spate of "new" methodologies for individ-ual changing which have followed and suggest a more apt basis for their classi-fication.

There has been a revolt within the medical profession itself against the patho-logical or medical model of changing.[1] One set of objections to the pathological model is that it draws attention away from the life conditions and environmental stresses which have induced the individual difficulty or trauma. Resources, includ-ing the resources of health professionals,

[1] Thomas Szasz, "The myth of mental illness," *American Psychologist*, 1960, *15*, 113, and R. D. Laing and A. Esterson, *Sanity, Madness and the Family* (New York: Basic Books, 1964), represent two quite different forms that revolt, from within the medical profession, against the domination of the pathological model in therapy has taken.

should be focused on changing the life conditions and environmental stresses which induce individual difficulties in functioning. This critique often is phrased as a plea for a *preventive* rather than a therapeutic approach to health problems, for *positive* conceptions of health, particularly of mental health, rather than a negative conception of health as the absence of pathology. This approach, it should be noted, would draw a significant part of the energies of health professionals away from treatment and into processes of prevention. And the core of preventive interventions is a process of *education* and *re-education*. It is consistent with this approach to take treatment, rehabilitation, and re-education processes away from segregated hospital institutions and back into the families, neighborhoods, and work settings of the clients. This requires, of course, a redeployment and reorganization of professional persons and resources.

Another objection to the pathological model in therapy has been that it brings the stereotype of a disease entity between the professional helper and his or her client, be it a stereotype of "schizophrenic," "manic-depressive," or "character disorder." The helper is tempted to treat a disease entity, rather than to deal with a unique, holistic client as a person in all the complexities of his or her strengths, limitations, difficulties, and aspirations. This objection is often combined with a purpose of rehumanizing "treatment" relationships. Here, as elsewhere, stereotypy may obstruct the mutually growthful meeting of persons.

Related to these revolts within "therapy" are claims, supported by some evidence, that responsibility for therapy should be diffused from the psychiatrist and shared with all who have contact with the patient or client—nurses, social workers, psychologists, paraprofessionals, and, indeed, his or her peers—other patients and clients. This would redefine the role of the psychiatrist as counselor,

educator, and re-educator to a diversified staff group. This idea is behind movements toward group psychotherapy and reaches its culmination in the idea of a therapeutic community.[2]

Comparable revolts have been taking place, or at least are being advocated, on the educational side of the divide. A central object of criticism has been the transmissive model of education. This model, it is argued, diverts the attention of the educator from his or her client in his or her wholeness and uniqueness and introduces a standardization and rigidity into the curriculum which reduce the responsiveness of the school to the service of variegated learning needs and to the utilization of unanticipated learning opportunities. A model, alternative to a transmissive model, is often termed a model of personal growth or of personal and cultural renewal.

Here, as in therapy, the concept of the learning client as a whole person challenges the almost exclusive preoccupation of the traditional school with cognitive development and encourages the assumption of responsibility by the school for the affective and conative development of students as well. In other words, the subject matter of the school should include feelings, values, and interpersonal relations as well as facts, concepts, and intellectual skills. This kind of alternative school is sometimes named humanistic education. It is interesting to note a convergence at this point between the programs of such alternative schooling and preventive-oriented programs in mental health.

Again, as in the case of psychotherapy and the psychiatrist, the traditional centrality and essentiality of the teacher-pupil relationship have been questioned

[2] See Maxwell Jones, *The Therapeutic Community* (New York: Basic Books, 1953), for a description of a pioneer attempt to create and utilize a therapeutic community.

and diffusion and sharing of responsibility for help in learning called for. Not only the teacher but teacher aides and other paraprofessionals, other students—age peers, younger and older students—and community persons, and most of all the student himself or herself—come to share responsibility for the purposing, planning, and evaluation of learning projects. Here, as in the case of the psychiatrist in therapy, the teacher must change to include functions as consultant, team builder, and trainer to other human parts of learning teams within the scope of his or her responsibilities.

A criticism of the segregation of schools from the ongoing life around the schools is also implicit in the revolt against the transmissive model of schooling. On this view, field experiences for students of any and all ages become an expected part of the learning program. Extensions of educational opportunities to individuals at any age or juncture of living are also an implication of this alternative model of education. Finally, this view of education counters the preoccupation, which has characterized many recent "innovators" in schooling, with the elaboration and refinement of thing technologies—audiovisual and multimedia equipment, teaching machines and other "teacher-proof" electronic devices. The view does not oppose the use of such technological aids to learning. It does reassert the view of the educative process as centrally an interpersonal—a social—process.

It should now be clear that the traditional categories of "therapy" and "education" as ways of differentiating processes of individual changing have been breached and broken—deeply, in thought and aspiration, and significantly, though with great resistance, in patterns of practice. Significant "new" methodologies for aiding, stimulating, and supporting individual changing have emerged that are difficult or impossible to classify in traditional

terms. Such methodologies are being utilized at present both in health centers and clinics and in "alternative schools." They are probably still practiced most frequently and fully in the "temporary systems" of "growth centers," human relations training laboratories and workshops, and programs of informal continuing education.

How can we classify these methodologies? They vary significantly in their conceptions of the human individual or of the aspect of the human individual that is seen as most strategic in processes of individual changing in our own period of human history. *I felt it convenient to note the aspect of the individual which each methodology seeks to support clients in rediscovering and reevaluating.* I realize I will do an injustice to the complexities of each methodology thus classified. In partial expiation for this injustice, I have noted a reference which includes a more adequate description of the methodology and its rationale.

I have selected representative instances to illustrate my subcategories rather than attempting a complete coverage. My selection has not been grounded in a value judgment that the ones chosen are "better" than those omitted. My basis of selection has been rather to identify the methodologies which are now "better known" both to me and to the general public.

a. THE REDISCOVERY
   AND REEVALUATION
   OF THE SELF

Müller-Freienfels, in his history of early twentieth-century psychology, noted that much "modern" psychology is a study of man without a psyche or self. This is a pardonable exaggeration which emphasizes the behavioristic cast of the main line of "academic psychology" in the first half of this century. There have been strong reactions against the "neglect" of the self by various clinical and humanistic psychologists in recent years. And some of the newer methodologies of individual changing seek to involve individuals in clarifying their self-concepts and self-images and in more fully understanding and affirming themselves as selves.

1) Rogerian counseling and its extension from a two-person setting into the encounter group clearly belongs in this classification. The effort is to create the conditions which allow free persons to learn about themselves, to perceive and affirm the clarified and undistorted image of self that emerges within the interchanges between the learner and the therapist and/or the members of the encounter group. The focus is on the client and his or her needs to learn and grow, not upon the propagation of the values and preferences of the therapist or facilitator.[3]

2) In Gestalt Therapy attention is focused, usually in the presence of other clients, if not in a developed group, upon the client's discovery and acceptance of his or her boundaries as a self as over against the boundaries of other selves. Great emphasis is placed upon each client discovering and owning, in the sense of assuming responsibility for, his or her own feelings and actions and disowning responsibility for the feelings and actions of others. Various ingenious exercises, including spontaneous drama and fantasy, are utilized in the achievement of the change objective.[4]

3) Transactional analysis is an outgrowth and simplification of Freudian analysis. Its practitioners regard the individual as a "family" of introjected selves, including an internalized father, mother, infantile child, growing-learning adult, and so on. When the internalized father, for example, is ascendant in an individual, the other in an interpersonal relationship becomes a child to that individual. Interpersonal relations are confused and strained by this kind of distortion of the other to fit the unconscious role-playing needs of the individual. The goal of changing is to lift the interpersonal games he or she plays into consciousness through interaction with others and interpretation of the interactions. Presumably, such consciousness reduces the compulsion of the individual to play interpersonal games and enables the individual to build and enact more authentic and reality-oriented relationships with others.[5]

4) The T-group, or Training group, was developed on the basis of ideas of self as a social emergent which characterize such social psychologies as those of Kurt Lewin, John Dewey, and George Herbert Mead. Selves emerge within social processes as biologic individuals incorporate significant memberships symbolically into their ways of functioning as differentiated members of a society. The first T-groups focused on helping persons to rediscover and reevaluate themselves as members of groups and of other interpersonal relationships as they helped to build an assemblage of strangers into a functioning group and reflected on their experiences in doing so. The original T-groups also were designed to help members learn experientially about small group development and processes, as we will note later. As clinical psychologists and psychiatrists came to work with T-groups, the emphasis on learning about group processes and membership was relaxed and a variant of T-groups, often called sensitivity groups, sought to focus the learning of

[3] See Carl R. Rogers, *Client-Centered Therapy* (Boston: Houghton Mifflin, 1951), and Carl R. Rogers, *Carl Rogers on Encounter Groups* (New York: Harper & Row, 1970).

[4] See Fritz Perls, *Gestalt Therapy Verbatim* (Lafayette, Calif.: Real People Press, 1969).

[5] Eric Berne, *Games People Play* (New York: Grove Press, 1964).

members upon expanding awareness of their idiosyncratic selves.[6]

5) A variant learning group has been developed by Max Birnbaum under the name of "clarification group." The process of the clarification group is designed and directed to stimulate and support members in rediscovering and reevaluating their "social selves." This involves a reassessment by members of the influences of racial, ethnic, religious, age, and sex groups to which they belong or have belonged upon their ways of seeing, valuing, and thinking about their social worlds with emphasis upon the influence of these memberships upon their relations with members of other social and cultural groups. This method of self-study was designed originally to augment the self-objectivity of persons who work and live in multiracial, multiethnic, and multireligious community settings. It belongs also, therefore, in the later section of this essay which deals with training and consultation in intergroup and community relations.[7]

6) The last methodology to be noted in this subsection actually unites an emphasis upon the rediscovery and reevaluation of the self with an emphasis upon the rediscovery and reevaluation of the body. This is the "personal growth laboratory" originated and developed by John and Joyce Weir. The laboratory is designed to support participants in achieving self-differentiation and in developing guidelines for their continuing *psychic, somatic,* and *spiritual* development. Methods include bodily movement, fantasies, and

spontaneous dramatization and ritualization of significant life events. It seems clear that the Weirs work with a biosocial concept of the individual and of individual growth.[8]

b. REDISCOVERY AND REEVALUATION OF THE BODY[9]

In another connection, I wrote recently:

My social self, as I along with others construct and imagine it, may or may not include my body. But, in a healthy person, the body is lifted up into membership within the inner society of selves and speaks openly and unashamedly, though in its own language in the dialogues through which decisions are made and personal integrity is sought and achieved. This is to accomplish that naturalistic

---

[6] See L. P. Bradford, J. Gibb, and K. D. Benne (Eds.), *T-Group Theory and Laboratory Method* (New York: Wiley, 1964).

[7] See Max Birnbaum, "The Clarification Group," chapter 15 in Benne, Bradford, Gibb, and Lippitt (Eds.), *The Laboratory Method of Changing and Learning* (Palo Alto, Calif.: Science and Behavior Books, 1975).

[8] John Weir, "The Personal Growth Laboratory," chapter 13, in Benne, Bradford, Gibb, and Lippitt (Eds.), op. cit.

[9] I have found difficulty in fitting the methodology of individual changing through behavior modification into my classification. It is an application of behaviorist learning theory to processes of unlearning dysfunctional behaviors and of learning more functional behaviors in a wide range of practical settings. It is built primarily upon the theory of learning as operant conditioning originated by B. F. Skinner. It clearly rejects a "pathological" model for explaining dysfunctional behavior and eschews "consciousness" and "inner processes and structures" like self as significant factors in processes of learning and relearning. It seeks to extinguish dysfunctional responses and to instate functional responses to environmental stimuli by programming the rewards which are presented along with the stimuli. See B. F. Skinner, *Beyond Freedom and Dignity* (New York: Knopf, 1971), for an explication of the rationale of behavior modification as a methodology of individual changing.

resurrection of the body for which Norman Brown pleads in his *Life Against Death!*[10]

It is the "naturalistic resurrection of the body" to which another set of methodologies concerned with changing human individuals is devoted. Many persons, it is believed, lose touch with their bodies, lose awareness of their bodies in the mazes of their shame and guilt-ridden, value-laden social-symbolic worlds which they must negotiate in living. In the interest of personal wholeness and integrity, the body must be rediscovered and affirmed.

1) I have already mentioned the emphasis in the Weirs' Personal Growth Laboratory on expanding and deepening awareness of bodily processes, both autonomic processes and cerebrally controlled processes, through methods which involve both relaxation and concentration upon feeling and listening to the body.

2) A methodology known as bioenergetics, strongly influenced by the organismic psychology of Wilhelm Reich, has been developed to help persons expand awareness of their own bodies. It also coaches persons in becoming aware of the bodily correlates of their psychic functions and dysfunctions and, through such awareness, toward altering dysfunctional aspects of their behavior.[11]

3) A most powerful tool for facilitating awareness of bodily processes is biofeedback. Information about their own bodily functioning is fed back to individuals by converting the electromagnetic waves which accompany organ functioning into forms which they can receive through their own senses. Although *biofeedback* is in an experimental stage as a method for the treatment of bodily dis-

orders, one observed result is of particular behavioral significance. Individuals can come, through biofeedback, to control consciously processes which are ordinarily experienced as involuntary, as under control of the autonomic nervous system—blood pressure, heart beat, and so forth.

This ability to control involuntary bodily processes achieves the same ends which Yogins, Zen Buddhists, and others had sought to achieve and had in some measure achieved through the "non-technological" means of meditation, relaxation, and "mental" concentration. The frontiers of "biofeedback" research and practice have recently been intertwined with methodologies for rediscovering and reevaluating the transpersonal or spiritual dimension of human functioning.[12]

c. REDISCOVERY AND REEVALUATION
    OF THE TRANSPERSONAL

Along with the penchant for naturalistic, biosocial explanations of individual development and dynamics, which has flourished in secularized academic and "enlightened" circles in modern Western and Westernized civilizations, belief in a transpersonal, spiritual reality in which human individuals do and/or should participate has coexisted in Western civilization and more emphatically in parts of Eastern cultures as well. And "methodologies" for individual changing—prayer, meditation, mystical experience, religious conversion—have developed concurrently with this belief.

With loss of confidence in established

---

[10] Kenneth D. Benne, "Something There Is That Doesn't Love a Wall," *Journal of Applied Behavioral Science,* Vol. I., No. 4, 1965, p. 334.

[11] See Alexander Lowen, *The Betrayal of the Body* (New York: Macmillan, 1967).

[12] See, for example, G. S. Schwartz, "Biofeedback, Self-Regulation and the Patterning of Physiological Processes," *American Scientist,* June 1975, Vol. 63, No. 3, 314–324; and J. Kamiya, L. V. DiCara, T. X. Barber, N. E. Miller, D. Shapiro, and J. Stoyva, (Eds.), *Biofeedback and Self-Control: An Aldine Reader on the Regulation of Bodily Processes and Consciousness* (Chicago: Aldine-Atherton, 1971).

ways of education and therapy in America and other parts of "the West," already noted and described, it is not surprising that methodologies for guiding persons into rediscovery and reevaluation of the transpersonal and spiritual dimensions of their lives have emerged, along with others which have emphasized rediscovery and reevaluation of self and body. Jungian therapy and analysis and some forms of pastoral counseling were precursors of these developments in Europe and America.

In general, two main kinds of methodological developments concerned with planfully guiding individuals into rediscovery and reevaluation of the transpersonal are now apparent in America. The first is an outgrowth from indigenous "Western" ways of thinking about the spiritual dimension of life. The second is a more or less conscious acculturation and adaptation of "Eastern" modes of spiritual discovery, ascesis, and development.[13]

1) The best-known example of the first kind of development is probably psychosynthesis, a methodology of therapy and education originated by Robert Assagioli. Assagioli is a medical doctor and psychiatrist who became convinced that the human unconscious was inhabited not only by repressed instincts and emotions but by a superconscious as well. Assagioli does not deny the "reality" of the "lower" unconscious but has sought ways of helping clients to gain access to, to become conscious of the "higher" unconscious as well in growing toward fuller self-realization and self-actualization. The methods of psychosynthesis include meditation, inner dialogues, guided imaginative fantasies, and interpersonal encounter. These methods are unified around the notion of a higher self at the core of each individual that can direct the harmonious development of all aspects of personality. Beyond personal synthesis lies access to creativity, transpersonal experience, and spiritual development.[14]

2) The second kind of methodology is more difficult to illustrate with one example. Yogin techniques and techniques from Zen Buddhism have found their way fragmentarily into various approaches to stimulating and supporting personal growth. In its more fully developed forms, it often embodies a radical disjunction between the individual "ego" which involves individuals in falsely ascribing "reality" to sensate and material objects and events that are inherently "illusory" and "Self" which is achieved through union with a transpersonal principle that is inherently "real." The approach of the ARICA Institute and its founder, Oscar Ichazo, may be taken as representative of this latter point of view.[15]

II. THE SMALL GROUP AS MEDIUM AND TARGET OF CHANGING

It is not accidental that the small, face-to-face group has come to occupy a strategic place as a *medium* of planned changing in recent years. This is true for several reasons. The small group is a link between the individual and the larger social system

[13] Some attention is now being given to developing a distinctively indigenous American way of gaining access to the transpersonal dimension of human life. This is illustrated by interest in the ethnographic reports by Carlos Castenada on the spiritual powers of the Amerindian wise man, Don Juan. See, for example, Carlos Castenada, *Journey to Ixtlan: The Lessons of Don Juan* (New York: Simon and Schuster, 1972).

[14] See Roberto Assagioli, *Psychosynthesis: A Manual of Principles and Techniques* (New York: Viking, 1971).

[15] Sam Keen, " 'We Have No Desire To Strengthen the Ego or Make It Happy': A Conversation about Ego Destruction with Oscar Ichazo," *Psychology Today*, July 1973.

of which he or she is a part. This is readily apparent in a formal organization, e.g., an army. The individual soldier belongs to a small group, a squad or a tank or bomber crew. This is, social-psychologically, his or her link to the larger army. And similarly with the student in a classroom which links him or her with the school-building system and in turn with the larger school system. The same is usually true, though not so obviously, of an individual's linkage with less formally organized systems like communities and racial and ethnic groupings. Thus the small group is potentially a medium for influencing both the persons who are its members and the larger system of which their group is a part.

Larger social systems ordinarily depend on small groups in formulating and maturing their policies and programs, whether the small group is a committee, cabinet, or board. Thus, change in the composition and functioning of such a strategic small group may produce change also in the wider social system which is dependent upon that group for guidance and direction.

Human individuals develop value orientations originally through internalizing the norms of small groups on which they depend, notably families. Changes in value orientations of individuals may be accomplished by their seeking and finding significant membership in a small group with norms that are different in some respects from the normative orientation these individuals bring to the group.

Finally, whatever else it is, a small group is an organized social system. Individual members can learn about the general characteristics of social systems directly and experientially by becoming aware of the social system characteristics of a small group to which they belong.

a) For all of these reasons, the small group, as its structure and dynamics have recently become an object of psychological study and research, has come to be a strategic contemporary medium in programs both of personal and of social changing. It can, therefore, be argued that a core part of the training of change agents, whatever their specialized target of changing—person, organization, community, or macrosystem—is training in the diagnosis and management of small group processes. Such training takes two principal forms in contemporary America.

1) The first, the T-group, has been discussed in the preceding section as a methodology of individual changing. It was noted in that discussion that the T-group was originally used as a medium for learning experientially about the formation, processes, and development of small groups. And it is still used for this purpose in the training of change agents. In such training programs T-group experiences are ordinarily supplemented by conceptual seminars and skill-practice sessions, in which skills of group diagnosis and intervention are practiced, followed by feedback of observed effects, and analysis and evaluation.[16]

2) The second form of group training follows what is frequently called the "Tavistock Model." This model for developing awareness and understanding of group structures, cultures, and processes has its intellectual roots in the psychoanalytical work of Melanie Klein and W. W. Bion. It is ordinarily conducted in a conference setting with from 50 to 70 participants. Participants experience group and organizational processes and structures in small study groups of 9 to 13 members, in the total conference group, and in an intergroup exercise. Their experiences are interpreted by the use of Bion's categories of emotional group states and other psychoanalytic and sociological con-

---

[16] For a discussion of skill practice and development see Eva Schindler-Rainman and Ronald O. Lippitt, "Awareness Learning and Skill Development," chapter 9, in Benne, Bradford, Gibb, and Lippitt, op. cit.

cepts. The goal is an understanding of group behavior and of the influence of structure on behavior rather than the development of change-oriented strategies as in the T-group.[17]

b) Both forms of training just discussed create temporary groups under "laboratory" conditions in order for group members to learn experientially about small group formation and functioning. But ongoing groups with an indefinite life tenure may also be taken as targets of changing. Blake and Mouton, in their D/D matrix, discuss such change efforts as they occur in organizational development under the name of "team-building." "Team-building" may be applied to various work units, staffs, and boards in formal organizations. And similar team-building efforts are used in planning councils, committees, commissions, and task forces at the community and macrosystem level as well.

1) A distinctive approach to group changing is represented by Virginia Satir's work with families. Family members are induced to objectify and analyze patterns of interaction in the functioning of the family as a small group. They are supported in trying out and evaluating alternative patterns where established patterns are seen to lead to unsatisfactory effects.[18]

III. PLANNED CHANGING AT THE INTERGROUP RELATIONS AND COMMUNITY LEVEL

Many Americans carry an ideal image of local community in their heads which may becloud a clear view of the realities of the

[17] See W. W. Bion, *Experiences in Groups* (London: Tavistock Publications, 1961), and Boris Astrachan, "The Tavistock Model of Laboratory Training," chapter 14, in Benne, Bradford, Gibb, and Lippitt, op. cit.

[18] Virginia Satir, *Conjoint Family Therapy* (Palo Alto, Calif.: Science and Behavior Books, 1967).

contemporary community—urban, suburban, or rural. The ideal image is of a relatively undifferentiated neighborhood, with people, who know each other and who talk the same language, getting together periodically in a New England town meeting or its equivalent to thrash out differences about the public business, to levy taxes on themselves, and to select leaders from among themselves to carry out their mandates and to account for their stewardship to the people at their next public meeting.

Now, all of us "know" that local communities are no longer like that, even small-town and rural communities. We know also that the idealized image of the ways people can get together to direct and handle their public business is not practicable under contemporary conditions. Yet the values implicit in the ideal image, values that account for its hold on the mentalities of many Americans, may still be valid, though the ways in which they can be translated into practice must be much more complicated and vastly different from the pattern of a town meeting and of selectmen directly responsive and responsible to that meeting.

These values are easy to state, however difficult they are to actualize in public practice. People affected by public policies and plans should participate in making them and in evaluating their consequences as they are acted upon. People should be informed about public issues and prepared to make intelligent choices and decisions with respect to them. Conflicts in interest among people should be confronted publicly and worked through to a viable and acceptable "trade off," if not consensus. Public officials should be responsible and accountable to the people who have endowed them with their authority. The initiation of changes should come from "volunteers" as well as from professionals and technicians, however much "volunteers" may need the services of professionals and technicians in converting their ideas for change into actuality. These, if I am not mistaken, are the values that lie behind most programs and projects in community development in America today.

We can get a mental hold on the complexity of contemporary communities, especially urbanized communities, by noting that they are differentiated both areally and functionally. A community, by definition, has spatial boundaries, though these may be difficult to define for purposes of planning and development. For example, the public safety of a community may be in the hands of a number of separate police forces—city, metropolitan, state, and federal. The boundaries of educational, public health, and judicial districts rarely coincide. Within its spatial boundaries, subareas may be specialized for particular kinds of land use under zoning laws and regulations—industrial, business, residential, and so on. Residential subareas are often differentiated by race, by ethnicity, and by social class.

Students of local communities recognize various lines of functional differentiation as well. These include religious, educational, recreational, welfare, health (physical and mental), political, economic, mass media, public safety, and cultural subcommunities. Each of these subcommunities is more or less separately organized. And indeed some subcommunities are divided by many separate internal organizations, for example, the religious subcommunity.

Efforts to actualize the values inherent in community development programs and projects must take these social-psychological realities of areal and functional differentiation into account.

a) It helps to map the kinds of planned changing going on in contemporary communities to recognize that much community development is organizational development. It is easy to recognize that the functional subcommunities do their many kinds of work through organizations. Some organizations are governmentally controlled and supported, others are privately supported and funded, others draw funding from both nongovernmental and governmental sources. And other organizations follow areal lines—neighborhood improvement associations, area planning councils, and so on.

And just as business and industrial organizations, confronted with the challenges of changing personnel, changing markets, and turbulent and unpredictable environments, have been seeking and, in some measure, finding ways of planning for change in their internal and external relations, so have nonbusiness and nonindustrial community organizations. All of Blake and Mouton's 25 varieties of organizational diagnosis and development are probably being tried here and there by welfare departments, churches, temples, schools, hospitals, Campfire Girls, Junior Leagues, area planning councils, labor unions, television stations, political parties, War Resisters' Leagues, police forces, etc., etc., as well as by business and industrial organizations. Methodologies, of course, need to be adapted to differing organizational sizes, purposes, traditions, and degrees of sophistication. Blake and Mouton's analysis serves admirably in mapping this organizational aspect of community development.

b) But how does community development differ from organizational development, more particularly when a community change project or program requires interagency, interareal and interprofessional collaboration, as most significant change projects and programs do? Eva Schindler-Rainman has specified seven differences between community development and organizational development:[19]

[19] Eva Schindler-Rainman, "Community Development," chapter 19 in Benne, Bradford, Gibb, and Lippitt, op. cit., pp. 447–448.

1. In the community, the process is always *intergroup*, that is, between groups and organizations who must collaborate on given projects, while in the organization the process is within one organization. . . .

2. The second difference has to do with *loyalty*. Within the geographic community there are many loyalties to be dealt with, loyalties to several different organizations; often loyalty to the geographic community itself; loyalty to subcommunities; and loyalty to a variety of causes. In the organizational context there may be loyalty to the organization, and perhaps to one's department or superior, but it is a different kind of thing than the many different "loyalty hats" people wear within a community.

3. A third factor is the *commitment* factor. In an organization, part of the commitment, if an employee has it, is due to the fact that he is paid in money for his services. Commitment to community causes is often of a different variety. There may be strong religious, ethical, or philosophical commitments to particular causes or particular projects.

4. Another difference is that in the community one almost always works with both *professionals and volunteers,* while that is not true in most organizations.

5. Also, the *multiple agenda of* communities need to be considered. While there might be the question of child care centers and improved education within the community, there are many other agenda. There will be many other kinds of things equally important to various people, all the way from urban-suburban planning to passing the bonds for the water district, to electing new board of education members, to rapid transit plans. Within the organization, though there may be multiple agenda, their extent is not nearly so vast or complicated as those of the total geographic community.

6. Another difference is that often in community development projects the *efforts* of people, both professional and volunteer, *are voluntary;* that is, people can be asked, requested, but not required, to come to meetings, and participate in a planning or action process. But in an organization it is possible for management to require participation of employees. The participation may or may not be willing, but it can be required. This is much harder to do in a community setting.

7. Another possible difference is that in community development there is a maximum effort to include *different sectors* of community population, and this is probably a more various group to draw from than would be found in any organization, even if all the different sectors of an organization were included in the development and . . . planning processes.

I will comment on current methodologies of changing in relation to two of the differences which Schindler-Rainman has identified and in relation to another aspect of current community development practice which she has not discussed.

1) "In the community, the [developmental] process is always intergroup." And among the intergroup relations that must be dealt with and handled are relations between racial groups, ethnic groups, and religious groups. These relationships are often marked by strong feelings of fear and hostility and by historically imbedded stereotypes. As we noted in "Planned Change in America" in Chapter I, boundaries between ethnic and racial groups became more sharply articulated in the 1960s in America. Identification with such groups became more closely intertwined with the personal identities of many of their members.

Rational collaboration in community planning and action between such groups and their members is virtually impossible unless methodologies can be found to develop understanding of these nonrational factors within the members and leaders of such groups. We discussed Max Birnbaum's clarification group earlier as a way of helping individuals to rediscover and affirm their own distinctive "social selves" and in the same process to understand and appreciate the distinctive and different social selves of members of other groups. This methodology has shown promise in training both professionals and volunteer, indigenous leaders who live and work in racially, ethnically, and religiously mixed community settings. For this purpose, clarification group training is conducted in a residential, "community development laboratory" with a mixed intergroup population. Clarification group experience is supplemented by conceptual inputs and by community diagnostic and planning activities.

Clarification group experiences have also been used successfully, in modified form, in actual community settings torn by interracial and interethnic conflicts, in laying the groundwork for intergroup participation in resolving the conflicts.[20]

2) "Another difference is that in the community one almost always works with both professionals and volunteers." The "ideal image" of community life with which we began this section, stressed the *voluntary* character of the initiation, control, and evaluation of community changes by the people of the community. While this image is idealized, it reflects an historical reality in American life. Local problems were probably solved more by volunteer local citizen initiative and effort in small-town and rural America than in any other nation. There was less dependence on centralized initiatives and directives to induce and direct changes in local community life than in other nations.

While this tradition of volunteer effort never died completely in America, it was more and more restricted as various

[20] See Thomas J. Cottle, "Strategy for Change," *Saturday Review,* September 20, 1969, for a description and evaluation of one such use of the methodology.

public services came increasingly to be delivered to people through the agency of complex and bureaucratized organizations and as the management and control of these organizations were increasingly turned over to paid and specially trained professionals. This was the trend in education, in churches, in the delivery of health services, in the distribution of public welfare, and in public safety. Volunteers tended to work more and more under the control of technically trained professionals, even in many of the volunteer boards and councils which were nominally in control of community agencies and organizations.

Some public-spirited citizens who were committed to the value of voluntary initiative and effort in American community life documented, deplored, and criticized this trend. But it was the populist protest movements of the 1960s which decelerated and perhaps (it is too early to say) reversed the trend. The unresponsiveness of established agencies and organizations to client and consumer needs, the "elitist" attitudes of professionals toward clients, the lack of popular participation in the direction of agencies on which people's lives depended were charges leveled against schools, churches, health and welfare agencies, and police forces among others. Some changes in structural arrangements to facilitate popular participation in community agencies and organizations have been made in response to protests and demands—decentralized "community" schools, "community" controlled health clinics, lay councils in churches, citizens' review boards for police forces, etc., etc.

But if such structural arrangements are to be maintained, extended, and made to work, programs of training and re-education for both volunteers and professionals in new, collaborative ways of working and relating must be planned, carried through, evaluated, and replanned. Such efforts are currently under way in many communities and under many auspices, though few would say that they are now adequate to their difficult task.[21]

3) I have suggested the multiplicity of community organizations which currently complicate processes of community-wide planning and action but which do serve as channels for getting a hearing for their members' interests and viewpoints into the councils of the community. But with all this multiplicity of organizations, there are numbers of people in most communities whose interests and views are not articulated or organized and who exert virtually no proactive influence in processes of community policy-making and planning, even though their lives are affected by the policies and plans which others make. Such people are the poor, members of racial and ethnic minorities, homosexuals and other deviates, and sometimes women, the old and the young.

They have often internalized majority attitudes toward themselves as incapable of participating actively and openly in public decision-making. They feel powerless to influence other people or their environments in any significant way. We noted earlier the effort of liberation movements to alter the attitudes of such persons by supporting them in defining and publicly asserting their own needs and worth and in altering their self-defeating images of themselves.

Discussions of some of the methodologies that have developed recently for facilitating this change objective have been included in later sections of this book. See Peattie, "Drama and Advocacy Planning" (selection 6.3), Gilbert and Eaton, "Who Speaks for the Poor?" (selection 6.2), and Paulo Freire, "The Pedagogy of the Oppressed" (selection 4.6).

IV. PLANNED CHANGING IN MACROSYSTEMS

The uses of methodologies of planned changing, as we have defined it, in macrosystems—for example, in changing national policies or cultural patterns or in resolving issues between nations—are very much less frequent and, therefore, less differentiated than in change programs and projects targeted to persons, small groups, organizations, and local communities.

This may be in part due to the preference of practitioners of planned changing for a clinical model of applied social science over an engineering model, to use Gouldner's distinction.[22] It is easier to work "clinically" with even a large organization or community than with a nation or an international complex.

But I doubt if the limited penetration of planned changing into macrosystems is mainly due to the preference or orientation of change agent practitioners. Organizational development programs have been conducted in a number of departments and agencies of national government in the U.S.A. and in other nations as well. And methodologies of planned changing are widely used in in-house training and consultation programs of staff development in many units of state and federal governments. Most of these uses have been undertaken in efforts to improve internal communications, work satisfaction, and productivity. They have not led to differentiations of methodologies beyond those noted in Blake and Mouton's matrix and in my survey. And they have not pene-

---

[21] See Eva Schindler-Rainman and Ronald Lippitt, *The Volunteer Community: Creative Use of Human Resources* (Washington, D.C.: Center for a Voluntary Society, 1971), for a discussion of current methodologies for empowering volunteer efforts of various sorts and for re-educating professionals to support and collaborate with volunteer initiative and assumption of responsibility.

[22] Alvin W. Gouldner, "Explorations in Applied Social Science," *Social Problems*, Vol. 3, No. 3, January 1956, pp. 173–181.

trated into processes of crucial policy and decision-making.

I suspect that the limited access of our sort of agents of planned change to crucial national and international meetings is rather due to deeply entrenched traditional attitudes and practices of governmental and intergovernmental policymakers. Their strategies of changing tend to be power-coercive, rather than normative-re-educative, to use Chin and Benne's distinction. Law and administrative and judicial decree are traditionally power-coercive instruments. Those who influence the making of laws and decrees work from carefully prepared positions. The process of exchange between "positions" tends to follow an adversary model of attack and defense. And the outcome, if the power behind various "positions" is fairly equal, is at best a compromise, not a creative synthesis which involves the meeting and merging of minds and interests into some new common view which is commonly acceptable and which could not have been formulated by any member or representative in advance of meeting and deliberation. It is the *mutually re-educative* processes out of which creative syntheses emerge upon which normative-re-educative strategists of changing basically depend. The use of such strategies requires of participants openness, trust, and a willingness to make themselves vulnerable to the influence of those who oppose them. The entrenched methodologies of governmental and intergovernmental policy-making are premised upon a distrust of those very qualities of exchange. Until the tragic wastefulness of human resources implicit in and consequent upon present processes of policy-making comes home to those in government, there will be little openness to seeking and developing alternative processes.

1) Meanwhile, it has been found that persons can experience and gain insight into the dynamics and development of macrosystems under laboratory conditions.

This can be accomplished by setting conditions in a conference which lead to human phenomena analogous to, if not isomorphic with, those that develop historically in nations. Those who experience the phenomena can reflect upon their experiences and extract learnings from them that are applicable to their choices and functioning as citizens within the politico-economic scene. "History" can be put upon a humanly encompassable and observable stage.

Max Pages has described and analyzed the experiences that developed in a human relations laboratory in France when the usual initial structures of subgroupings were not provided and participants and staff accepted the task of building a miniature society from the ground up and of extracting learnings from their experiences.[23] Comparable experiences have been conducted in Denmark, in England, and in the United States. Perhaps a strategic step would be to recruit persons high in positions of governmental and intergovernmental policy-making for participation in such laboratories.[24]

[23] Max Pages, "The Flexible Structures Laboratory," chapter 17 in Benne, Bradford, Gibb, and Lippitt, op. cit.

[24] Such experiences are analogous to simulation techniques which have been developed for research and training purposes in organizational and community settings not accessible for field experimentation. Simulation can also be used as a way of anticipatory try-out, practice, and revision of plans where a try-out in the "real" situation is seen as too costly or dangerous. See William A. Gamson, *SIMSOC: Simulated Society* (New York: Free Press, 1969), for a discussion of simulation methodologies.

Simulation is, of course, akin to psychodramatic and sociodramatic methodologies which were pioneered in psychotherapy and action training by J. L. Moreno. In these methodologies, human situations and difficulties are not only talked about but are dramatically acted out to provide rich "inner" and "outer"

2) Some attempts to use methods of planned changing in actual situations of transnational conflict have been reported. One of these was a study of groups of representatives of Ethiopia and Eritrea, who met with applied behavioral scientists in trying to settle a long-standing dispute about national boundaries and to try different and, hopefully, more effective ways of settling such disputes. Methods of collaborative management of conflict, developed in organizational development studies, were employed.[25]

Another reported experiment was to test the applicability of and results of T-group methods in an extended meeting in Israel of a group composed of Israeli and Arab members.[26]

Although the results of such experiments are in no way definitive, and though they have led to no differentiations in methods of practice, they are promising enough to warrant further efforts to extend methodologies of planned changing into the international field.

---

behavioral data, which, when analyzed, often lead to vivid, convincing, and applicable insights and learnings for the participants. See J. L. Moreno, *Psychodrama* (Beacon, New York: Beacon House, Inc., 1946). For a concise survey of current developments in psychodrama, sociodrama, and role-playing, see Hilarion Petzold, "Psychodrama and Role-Playing," chapter 16 in Benne, Bradford, Gibb, and Lippitt, op. cit.

[25] Richard E. Walton, "A Problem-Solving Workshop on Border Conflicts in Eastern Africa," *The Journal of Applied Behavioral Science*, Vol. 7, pp. 453–489.

[26] Martin Lakin, in collaboration with Jacob Lomrantz and Morton S. Lieberman, *Arab and Jew in Israel* (Washington, D.C.: NTL Institute, 1969).

Diagnostics
of Planned Change

PART

TWO

SYSTEMS

CHAPTER

"Systems analysis" is a tool of the mind for observing, diagnosing, and intervening in the complex web of interdependencies which must be taken into account in processes of planned change. The articles in this chapter represent the technical use of the concept of system; they avoid the error of reification, that is, making "the system" into an active causal or resisting agent in the social dynamics of change.

Systems vary in size, complexity, and concreteness. The unit size may be an individual, a small group, an organization, a community, a nation-state, or indeed the world. As we become more acquainted with a given system and as more and more diagnostic frameworks of analysis are forged by the theorist, researcher, and practitioner, the limitless complexity of more and more elements and aspects to take into account in a system analysis has to be cut back to the practitioner's ability to handle no more than a few at a time.

The concrete organizational systems encountered in industry, in education, in health and social services, and in justice are treated as similar in systems dynamics; yet there are major differences between them and unique characteristics of each. In comparing or locating a system we suggest six dimensions representing differences that determine the system analysis:

(1) The "goals" of organizational systems can be assessed for the degree of their clarity-ambiguity, simplicity-diversity, and localization-diffuseness of responsibility. For example, school systems, compared to industrial systems, have ambiguous, diverse, and diffuse goals, with attendant consequences for evaluation of the effectiveness of the school system. The specificity of methods

and means for achieving the goals are also relatively ambiguous, diverse, and diffuse. Social service systems too vary along similar dimensions.

(2) The degree of interdependence of parts of the system varies greatly. Industrial organizations, and the human body as a system, have a relatively high degree of interdependence of the parts, and an identifiable relationship to the environment. On the other extreme of loose interdependency, there is the despairing wail by an exasperated college president: "The college is a collection of rugged individualists held together by a common struggle over parking spaces." The processes of resource allocation, budgeting, and the exercise of influence, power, and authority may be diffuse and not differentiated in location of responsibility.

(3) The degree of internal structural differentiation may vary from simple role differentiation to highly complex and hierarchical functional segregation of jobs and specialities. The processes of a face-to-face small group as the ideologically preferred way of functioning have been applied to organizations as part of the struggle in creating and maintaining organizational systems embodying human values. The use of the small group analysis has led to blind spots about hierarchies and segmentation.

These dimensions have led to the label of the sociotechnical systems, or the sociotechnical approach to systems. In this approach the issues of goals, the means most appropriate for achieving these goals, and the human and social relationships suffusing these technical activities have become the mode of analyzing industrial organizations, with attempts to apply these to educational, mental health and social service systems as well. Although once used to indicate the necessity of human beings obeying the rational dictates of the technical systems, there are now efforts to give primacy to how the human and social systems can affect the creation of the technical systems not only of its means but also of its goals.

Decentralization into subsystems, creation of parallel and highly autonomous systems within the larger system, such as alternative schools or satellite operations in industry, and the creation of new interstitial systems such as coordinating councils, or new consortia, collaboratives or cooperatives for accomplishing tasks are new forms of systems.

(4) The degree of vulnerability to outside pressures varies significantly. Vulnerability is highly characteristic of public and secondary educational systems, and social service systems. These systems incorporate the ideologically valued form of client and community control. There is required a response to short-run demands or pressures which may be incompatible with the long-range goals of the system.

(5) Time perspective. Systems vary in the degree to which they are fixed in their dynamics around periodicity of activities and processes. Educational systems have been rigidified with the time calendar and its attendant processes. In addition, each system's development and growth over time phases and periods vary according to distinctive system properties and to historically differentiated institutional systems.

(6) Stability and resistance to change. Practitioners approach a system in terms of its readiness or resistance to change. The degree of interdependence, differentiation, and boundary vulnerability are bases for the analysis of stability and resistance to change.

Systems analysis may also be applied to the analysis of selected segments of a concrete system, such as the communications, power, or value subsystems.

In selection 3.1, "The Utility of System Models and Developmental Models for Practitioners," Chin shows how to draw back from observed behaviors to examine the mind-sets, the models, by which conceptualizations are organized. Chin identifies the properties of the model of an open or closed system in contrast to a developmental model. In addition to presenting these well-known and often-used models, the essay outlines the implications of each for a practitioner's approach to changing human systems. The intersystem model may be applied to the relationship of the change agent and client system as well as to analysis of systems in relation to other systems.

Practitioners have increased need for understanding and coping with the environment of the system as interdependence has increased and rigid boundaries have loosened. Essay 3.2, "The Utility of Models of the Environment of Systems for Practitioners," shows the ways in which the environment of a system may be viewed and what particular structures of the environment are of use to the practitioner. Managing the environment of systems is an increasingly difficult task. Chin shows how the turbulent environment and the future perspective toward the environment may be differentiated into an articulated turbulent environment. The essay points to the importance of doing so lest agents of planned change plan only for reactions to turbulent, unpredictable, and swooping forces. Terreberry's article "The Evolution of Organizational Environments" (5.1) also details the concept of turbulent environment in Chapter 5.

Lawrence and Lorsch's article, "The Differentiation and Integration Model" (3.3), shows the necessity for organizations to increase their internal differentiation and to focus on the resultant necessary processes of integration. The position is parallel to that occurring in the psychological processes of identity, increased differentiation of self, and integration with others.

Klein's article, "Some Notes on the Dynamics of Resistance to Change: The Defender Role," offers a perspective on resistance to change. He suggests that what the practitioner sees as resistance to change may well be the testing of the thrust of the change by members of the system. After all, not all proposed changes are equally valuable, and some persons must perform roles in the system as the gatekeepers of standards of acceptability. Klein reminds us that the change agent may often define change in such ways that those who do not agree are seen as blind resisters of change. It is as if the change agent is saying, "We have values; the clients have psychological mechanisms." It seems more appropriate to view the occasion as an opportunity of working with the internal roles of the system, including those who defend the status quo, to foster mutually desirable change.

The ways in which practitioners see how constituent elements of a human system are put together shape the approaches to dealing with forces and expected resistances to change. It is proposed here that practitioners may find an economical set of ideas and concepts which organizes a number of perplexing and disorderly cacophonies, alters the mind-set of the change agent (which itself could well be the most major intervention possible) and points up bases for evaluating the effects of contemplated interventions. With such conceptual schemas seemingly useful for all occasions and all settings and which mold the reality of the perceiver and function in judging the actions to be undertaken, we do need some caution. Systems concepts comprehend stability of what exists and thus guide the approaches to change and changing. Do such functional aproaches to system dynamics tend to be conservative and justificatory of the status quo? We don't think so when systems analysis is used to uncover the tensions of goals and realities and do not preclude or hide the normative evaluations which must be made by the members of the systems and by the change agent as well.

3.1   THE UTILITY OF SYSTEM MODELS AND DEVELOPMENTAL MODELS FOR PRACTITIONERS

Robert Chin

All practitioners have ways of thinking about and figuring out situations of change. These ways are embodied in the concepts with which they apprehend the dynamics of the client-system they are working with, their relationship to it, and their processes of helping with its change. For example, the change-agent encounters resistance, defense mechanisms, readiness to change, adaptation, adjustment, maladjustment, integration, distintegration, growth, development, and maturation as well as deterioration. He uses concepts such as these to sort out the processes and mechanisms at work. And necessarily so. No practitioner can carry on thought processes without such concepts; indeed, no observations or diagnoses are ever made on "raw facts," because facts are really observations made within a set of concepts. But lurking behind concepts such as the ones stated above are assumptions about how the parts of the client-system fit together and how they change. For instance, "Let things alone, and natural laws (of economics, politics, personality, etc.) will work things out in the long run." "It is only human nature to resist change." "Every organization is always trying to improve its ways of working." Or, in more technical forms, we have assumptions such as "The adjustment of the personality to its inner forces as well as adaptation to its environment is the sign of a healthy personality." "The coordination and integration of the departments of an organization is the task of the executive." "Conflict is an index of malintegration, or of change."

Reprinted from the first edition of *The Planning of Change: Readings in the Applied Behavioral Sciences,* edited by Warren G. Bennis, Kenneth D. Benne, and Robert Chin. Copyright © 1961 by Holt, Rinehart and Winston, Inc.

"Inhibiting forces against growth must be removed."

It is clear that each of the above concepts conceals a different assumption about how events achieve stability and change, and how anyone can or cannot help change along. Can we make these assumptions explicit? Yes, we can and we must. The behavioral scientist does exactly this by constructing a simplified *model* of human events and of his tool concepts. By simplifying he can analyze his thoughts and concepts, and see in turn where the congruities and discrepancies occur between these and actual events. He becomes at once the observer, analyzer and modifier of the system[1] of concepts he is using.

The purpose of this paper is to present concepts relevant to, and the benefits to be granted from, using a "system" model and a "developmental" model in thinking about human events. These models provide "mind-holds" to the practitioner in his diagnosis. They are, therefore, of practical significance to him. This suggests one essential meaning of the oft-quoted and rarely explained phrase that "nothing is so practical as a good theory." We will try to show how the "systems" and "developmental" approaches provide key tools for a diagnosis of persons, groups, organizations, and communities for purposes of change. In doing so, we shall state succinctly the central notions of each model, probably sacrificing some technical elegance and exactness in the process. We shall not overburden the reader with citations of the voluminous set of articles from which this paper is drawn.

We postulate that the same models can be used in diagnosing different sizes of the units of human interactions—the person, the group, the organization, and the community.

One further prefatory word. We need to keep in mind the difference between an "analytic" model and a model of concrete events or cases. For our purposes, *an analytic model* is a constructed simplification of some part of reality that retains only those features regarded as essential for relating similar processes whenever and wherever they occur. *A concrete model* is based on an analytic model, but uses more of the content of actual cases, though it is still a simplification designed to reveal the essential features of some range of cases. As Hagen[2] puts it: "An explicitly defined analytic model helps the theorist to recognize what factors are being taken into account and *what relationships among them are assumed* and hence to know the basis of his conclusions. The advantages are ones of both exclusion and inclusion. A model lessens the danger of overlooking the indirect effects of a change of a relationship" (our italics). We mention this distinction since we find a dual usage that has plagued behavioral scientists, for they themselves keep getting their feet entangled. We get mixed up in analyzing "the small group as a system" (analytic) and a school committee as a small group (concrete) or a national social system (analytic) and the American social system (concrete) or an organizational system (analytic) and the organization of a glue factory (concrete). In this paper, we will move back and forth between the analytic usage of "model" and the "model" of the concrete case, hopefully with awareness of when we are involved in a semantic shift.

THE "SYSTEM" MODEL

Psychologists, sociologists, anthropologists, ecomonists, and political scientists have been "discovering" and using the system

[1] "System" is used here as any organized and coherent body of knowledge. Later we shall use the term in a more specific meaning.

[2] E. Hagen, chapter titled "Theory of Social Change," unpublished manuscript.

model. In so doing, they find intimations of an exhilarating "unity" of science, because the system models used by biological and physical scientists seem to be exactly similar. Thus, the system model is regarded by some system theorists as universally applicable to physical and social events, and to human relationships in small or large units.

The terms or concepts that are a part of the system model are "boundary" "stress or tension," "equilibrium," and "feedback." All these terms are related to "open system," "closed system," and "intersystem" models. We shall first define these concepts, illustrate their meaning, and then point out how they can be used by the change-agent as aids in observing, analyzing or diagnosing—and perhaps intervening in—concrete situations.

The Major Terms

System Laymen sometimes say, "you can't beat the system" (economic or political), or "he is a product of the system" (juvenile delinquent or Soviet citizen). But readers of social science writings will find the term used in a rather more specific way. It is used as an abbreviated term for a longer phrase that the reader is asked to supply. The "economic system" might read as: "we treat price indices, employment figures, etc., as if they were closely interdependent with each other and we temporarily leave out unusual or external events, such as the discovery of a new gold mine." Or in talking about juvenile delinquency in "system" terms, the sociologists choose to treat the lower-class values, lack of job opportunities, ragged parental images, as interrelated with each other, in back-and-forth cause-and-effect fashion, as determinants of delinquent behavior. Or the industrial sociologist may regard the factory as a "social system," as people working together in relative isolation from the outside, in order to examine

what goes on in interactions and interdependencies of the people, their positions, and other variables. In our descriptions and analyses of a particular concrete system, we can recognize the shadowy figure of some such analytic model of "system."

The analytic model of system demands that we treat the phenomena and the concepts for organizing the phenomena as if there existed organization, interaction, interdependency, and integration of parts and elements. System analysis assumes structure and stability within some arbitrarily sliced and frozen time period.

It is helpful to visualize a system[3] by drawing a large circle. We place elements, parts, variables, inside the circle as the components, and draw lines among the components. The lines may be thought of as rubber bands or springs, which stretch or contract as the forces increase or decrease. Outside the circle is the environment, where we place all other factors which impinge upon the system.

Boundary In order to specify what is inside or outside the system, we need to define its "boundary" line. The boundary of a system may exist physically: a tightly corked vacuum bottle, the skin of a person, the number of people in a group, etc. But, in addition, we may delimit the system in a less tangible way, by placing our boundary according to what variables are being focused upon. We can construct a system consisting of the multiple roles of a person, or a system composed of varied roles among members in a small work group, or a system interrelating roles in a family. The components or variables used are roles, acts, expectations, com-

[3] A useful visual aid for "system" can be constructed by using paper clips (elements) and rubber bands (tensions) mounted on a peg board. Shifting of the position of a clip demonstrates the interdependency of all the clips, positions, and their shifting relationships.

munications, influence and power relationships, and so forth, and not necessarily persons.

The operational definition of *boundary* is: the line forming a closed circle around selected variables, where there is less interchange of energy (or communication, etc.) *across* the line of the circle than *within* the delimiting circle. The multiple systems of a community may have boundaries that do or do not coincide. For example, treating the power relationships may require a boundary line different from that for the system of interpersonal likes or dislikes in a community. In small groups we tend to draw the same boundary line for the multiple systems of power, communications, leadership, and so on, a major advantage for purposes of study.

In diagnosing we tentatively assign a boundary, examine what is happening inside the boundary, if necessary. We examine explicitly whether or not the "relevant" factors are accounted for within the system, an immensely practical way of deciding upon relevance. Also, we are free to limit ruthlessly, and neglect some factors temporarily, thus reducing the number of considerations necessary to be kept in mind at one time. The variables left outside the system, in the "environment" of the system, can be introduced one or more at a time to see the effects, if any, on the interrelationship of the variables within the system.

Tension, stress, strain, and conflict

Because the components within a system are different from each other, are not perfectly integrated, or are changing and reacting to change, or because outside disturbances occur, we need ways of dealing with these differences. The differences lead to varying degrees of tension within the system. *Examples*: males are not like females, foremen see things differently from workers and from executives, children in a family grow, a committee has to

work with a new chairman, a change in the market condition requires a new sales response from a factory. To restate the above examples in conceptual terms: we find built-in differences, gaps of ignorance, misperceptions, or differential perceptions, internal changes in a component, reactive adjustments and defenses, and the requirements of system survival generating tensions. Tensions that are internal and arise out of the structural arrangements of the system may be called *stresses and strains* of the system. When tensions gang up and become more or less sharply opposed along the lines of two or more components, we have *conflict*.

A word of warning. The presence of tensions, stresses or strains, and conflict within the system often are reacted to by people in the system as if they were shameful and must be done away with. Tension reduction, relief of stress and strain, and conflict resolution become the working goals of practitioners but sometimes at the price of overlooking the possibility of increasing tensions and conflict in order to facilitate creativity, innovation, and social change. System analysts have been accused of being conservative and even reactionary in assuming that a social system always tends to reduce tension, resist innovation, abhor deviancy and change. It is obvious, however, that tension and conflict are "in" any system, and that no living system exists without tension. Whether these facts of life in a system are to be abhorred or welcomed is determined by attitudes or value judgments not derivable from system theory as such.

The identification of and analysis of how tensions operate in a system are by all odds *the* major utility of system analysis for practitioners of change. The dynamics of a living system are exposed for observation through utilizing the concepts of tension, stress and strain, and conflict. These tensions lead to activities of two kinds: those which do not affect the structure of the system (dynamics), and those which directly alter the structure itself (system change).

Equilibrium and "steady state" A system is assumed to have a tendency to achieve a balance among the various forces operating within and upon it. Two terms have been used to denote two different ideas about balance. When the balance is thought of as a fixed point or level, it is called "equilibrium." "Steady state," on the other hand, is the term recently used to describe the balanced relationship of parts that is not dependent upon any fixed equilibrium point or level.

Our body temperature is the classic illustration of a fixed level (98.6° F.), while the functional relationship between work units in a factory, regardless of the level of production, represents a steady state. For the sake of simplicity, we shall henceforth stretch the term "equilibrium" to cover both types of balance, to include also the idea of "steady state."

There are many kinds of equilibria. A *stationary equilibrium* exists when there is a fixed point or level of balance to which the system returns after a disturbance. We rarely find such instances in human relationships. A *dynamic equilibrium* exists when the equilibrium shifts to a new position of balance after disturbance. Among examples of the latter, we can observe a *neutral* type of situation. *Example:* a ball on a flat plane. A small push moves it to a new position, and it again comes to rest. *Example:* a farming community. A new plow is introduced and is easily incorporated into its agricultural methods. A new level of agricultural production is placidly achieved. A *stable type of situation* exists where the forces that produced the initial equilibrium are so powerful that any new force must be extremely strong before any movement to a new position can be achieved. *Example:* a ball in the bottom of a goblet. *Example:* an organization encrusted with tradition

or with clearly articulated and entrenched roles is not easily upset by minor events. An *unstable type of situation* is tense and precarious. A small disturbance produces large and rapid movements to a new position. *Example:* a ball balanced on the rims of two goblets placed side by side. *Example:* an organization with a precarious and tense balance between two modes of leadership style. A small disturbance can cause a large swing to one direction and a new position of equilibrium. *Example:* a community's balance of power between ethnic groups may be such that a "minor" disturbance can produce an upheaval and movement to a different balance of power.

A system in equilibrium reacts to outside impingements: (*1*) By resisting the influence of the disturbance, refusing to acknowledge its existence, or by building a protective wall against the intrusion, and by other defensive maneuvers. *Example:* a small group refuses to talk about a troublesome problem of unequal power distribution raised by a member. (*2*) By resisting the disturbance through bringing into operation the homeostatic forces that restore or re-create a balance. The small group talks about the troublesome problem of a member and convinces him that it is not "really" a problem. (*3*) By accommodating the disturbances through achieving a new equilibrium. Talking about the problem may result in a shift in power relationships among members of the group.

The concepts of equilibrium (and steady state) lead to some questions to guide a practitioner's diagnosis.

a.   What are the conditions conducive to the achievement of an equilibrium in this case? Are there internal or external factors producing these forces? What is their quality and tempo?

b.   Does the case of the client-system represent one of the typical situations of equilibrium? How does judgment on this point affect intervention strategy? If the practitioner feels the situation is tense and precarious, he should be more cautious in intervention than in a situation of stable type.

c. Can the practitioner identify the parts of the system that represent greatest readiness to change, and the greatest resistance to and defense against change? Can he understand the functions of any variable in relation to all other variables? Can he derive some sense of the direction in which the client system is moving, and separate those forces attempting to restore an old equilibrium and those pushing toward a new equilibrium state?

Feedback Concrete systems are never closed off completely. They have inputs and outputs across the boundary; they are affected by and in turn affect the environment. While affecting the environment, a process we call output, systems gather information about how they are doing. Such information is then fed back into the system as input to guide and steer its operations. This process is called feedback. The "discovery" of feedback has led to radical inventions in the physical world in designing self-guiding and self-correcting instruments. It has also become a major concept in the behavioral sciences, and a central tool in the practitioner's social technology. *Example:* in reaching for a cigarette we pick up tactile and visual cues that are used to guide our arm and finger movements. *Example:* our interpersonal communications are guided and corrected by our picking up of effect cues from the communicatees. *Example:* improving the feedback process of a client system will allow for self-steering or corrective action to be taken by him or it. In fact, the single most important improvement the change-agent can help a client system to achieve is to increase its diagnostic sensitivity to the effects of its own actions upon others. Programs in sensitivity training attempt to increase or unblock the feedback process of persons; a

methodological skill with wider applicability and longer-lasting significance than solving the immediate problem at hand. In diagnosing a client system, the practitioner asks: What are its feedback procedures? How adequate are they? What blocks their effective use? Is it lack of skill in gathering data, or in coding and utilizing the information?

Open and Closed Systems

All living systems are open systems—systems in contact with their environment, with input and output across system boundaries. What then is the use of talking about a closed system? What *is* a closed system? It means that the system is temporarily assumed to have a leak-tight boundary—there is relatively little, if any, commerce across the boundary. We know that no such system can be found in reality, but it is sometimes essential to analyze a system as if it were closed so as to examine the operations of the system as affected "only by the conditions previously established by the environment and not changing at the time of analysis, plus the relationships among the internal elements of the system." The analyst then opens the system to a new impact from the environment, again closes the system, and observes and thinks out what would happen. It is, therefore, fruitless to debate the point; both open and closed system models are useful in diagnosis. Diagnosing the client as a system of variables, we have a way then of managing the complexity of "everything depends upon everything else" in an orderly way. Use of system analysis has these possibilities: (a) diagnosticians can avoid the error of simple cause-and-effect thinking; (b) they can justify what is included in observation and interpretation and what is temporarily excluded; (c) they can predict what will happen if no new or outside force is applied; (d) they are guided in categorizing what is relatively enduring and stable, or changing in the situation; (e) they can distinguish between what is basic and what is merely symptomatic; (f) they can predict what will happen if they leave the events undisturbed and if they intervene, and (g) they are guided in selecting points of intervention.

Intersystem Model

We propose an extension of system analysis that looks to us to be useful for the problems confronting the change-agent. We urge the adoption of an intersystem model.

An intersystem model involves two open systems connected to each other.[4] The term we need to add here is *connectives*. Connectives represent the lines of relationships of the two systems. Connectives tie together parts (mechanics) or imbed in a web of tissue the separate organs (biology); connectives in an industrial establishment are the defined lines of communication, or the leadership hierarchy and authority for the branch plants; or they represent the social contract entered into by a therapist and patient; or mutual role expectations of consultant and client; or the affective ties between family members. These are conjunctive connectives. But we also have conflicts between labor and management, teenage gang wars, race conflicts, and negative emotional responses to strangers. These are disjunctive connectives.

Why elaborate the system model into an intersystem model? Cannot we get the same effect by talking about "sub-systems" of a larger system? In part we can. Labor-management conflicts, or interpersonal relations, or change-agent and client relationships can each be treated as a new

[4] A visualization of an intersystem model would be two systems side by side, with separately identified links. Two rubber band–paper clip representatives can be connected with rubber bands of a different color, representing the connectives.

system with sub-systems. But we may lose the critical fact of the autonomy of the components, or the direct interactional or transactional consequences for the separate components when we treat the sub-systems as merely parts of a larger system. The intersystem model exaggerates the virtues of autonomy and the limited nature of interdependence of the interactions between the two connected systems.

What are some of the positive advantages of using intersystem analysis? First, the external change-agent, or the change-agent built into an organization as a helper with planned change does not completely become a part of the client-system. He must remain separate to some extent; he must create and maintain some distance between himself and the client, thus standing apart "in another system" from which he re-relates. This new system might be a referent group of fellow professionals, or a body of rational knowledge. But create one he does and must. Intersystem analysis of the change-agent's role leads to fruitful analysis of the connectives—their nature in the beginning, how they shift, and how they are cut off. Intersystem analysis also poses squarely an unexplored issue, namely the internal system of the change-agent, whether a single person, consultant group, or a nation. Helpers of change are prone at times not to see that their own systems as change-agents have boundaries, tensions, stresses, and strains, equilibria, and feedback mechanisms which may be just as much parts of the problem as are similar aspects of the client-systems. Thus, relational issues are more available for diagnosis when we use an intersystem model.

More importantly, the intersystem model is applicable to problems of leadership, power, communication, and conflict in organizations, intergroup relations, and international relations. *Example:* Leadership in a work group with its liaison, negotiation, and representation functions is dependent upon connectives to another group and not solely upon the internal relationships within the work group. Negotiators, representatives, and leaders are parts of separate systems each with its own interdependence, tensions, stresses, and feedback, whether we are thinking of foreign ministers, Negro-white leaders, or student-faculty councils.

In brief, the intersystem model leads us to examine the interdependent dynamics of interaction both within and between the units. We object to the premature and unnecessary assumption that the units always form a single system. We can be misled into an utopian analysis of conflict, change-agent relations to client, and family relations if we neglect system differences. But an intersystem model provides a tool for diagnosis that retains the virtues of system analysis, adds the advantage of clarity, and furthers our diagnosis of the influence of various connectives, conjunctive and disjunctive, on the two systems. For change-agents, the essence of collaborative planning is contained in an intersystem model.

DEVELOPMENTAL MODELS

Practitioners have in general implicitly favored developmental models in thinking about human affairs, while social scientists have not paid as much attention to these as they have to system models. The "life sciences" of biology and psychology have not crystallized nor refined their common analytic model of the development of the organism, despite the heroic breakthroughs of Darwin. Thus, we are forced to present only broad and rough categories of alternative positions in this paper.

Since there is no standard vocabulary for a developmental model, we shall present five categories of terms that we deem essential to such models: direction, states, forces, form of progression, and potentiality.

The Major Terms

Developmental models By developmental models, we mean those bodies of thought that center around growth and directional change. Developmental models assume change; they assume that there are noticeable differences between the states of a system at different times; that the succession of these states implies the system is heading somewhere; and that there are orderly processes which explain how the system gets from its present state to wherever it is going. In order to delimit the nature of change in developmental models we should perhaps add the idea of an increase in value accompanying the achievement of a new state. With this addition, developmental models focus on processes of growth and maturation. This addition might seem to rule out processes of decay, deterioration, and death from consideration. Logically, the developmental model should apply to either.

There are two kinds of "death" of concern to the practitioner. First, "death" or loss of some part or subvalue, as a constant concomitant of growth and development. Theories of life processes have used concepts such as katabolic (destructive) processes in biology, death instincts in Freud's psychology, or role loss upon promotion. On balance, the "loss" is made up by the "gains," and thus there is an increase in value. Second, "death" as planned change for a group or organization— the dissolution of a committee or community organization that has "outlived its purpose and function," and the termination of a helping relationship with deliberateness and collaboration of participants is properly included as part of a developmental model.

Direction Developmental models postulate that the system under scrutiny—a person, a small group, interpersonal interactions, an organization, a community or a society—is going "somewhere"; that the changes have some direction. The direction may be defined by (a) some *goal* or end state (developed, mature); (b) the *process* of becoming (developing, maturing) or (c) the degree of achievement *toward* some goal or end state (increased development, increase in maturity).

Change-agents find it necessary to believe that there is direction in change. *Example:* self-actualization or fulfillment is a need of the client-system. When strong directional tendencies are present, we modify our diagnosis and intervention accordingly. A rough analogy may be helpful here. A change-agent using a developmental model may be thought of as a husbandman tending a plant, watching and helping it to grow in its own natural direction of producing flowers. He feeds, waters, and weeds. Though at times he may be ruthless in pinching off excess buds, or even in using "grafts," in general he encourages the plant to reach its "goal" of producing beautiful flowers.

Identifiable state   As the system develops over time, the different states may be identified and differentiated from one another. Terms such as "stages," "levels," "phases," or "periods" are applied to these states. *Example:* psychosexual definition of oral, and anal stages, levels of evolution of species, or phases of group development.

No uniformity exists in the definition and operational identification of such successive states. But since change-agents do have to label the past, present, and future, they need some terms to describe successive states and to identify the turning points, transition areas, or critical events that characterize change. Here, system analysis is helpful in defining how parts are put together, along with the tensions and directions, of the equilibrating processes. We have two polar types of the shifts of states: (a) small, nondiscernible steps or increments leading to a quali-

tative jump. (*Example:* black hair gradually turning gray, or a student evolving into a scholar); (b) a cataclysmic or critical event leading to a sudden change. (*Example:* a sickness resulting in gray hair overnight, or an inspirational lecture by a professor.) While the latter type seems more frequently to be externally induced, internal factors of the system can have the same consequence. In other words, the internal disequilibration of a balance may lead to a step-jump of the system to a new level. Personality stages, group stages, and societal phases are evolved and precipitated from internal and from external relations.

Form of progression   Change-agents see in their models of development some form of progression or movement. Four such forms are typically assumed. First, it is often stated that once a stage is worked through, the client-system shows continued progression and normally never turns back. (Any recurrence of a previous state is viewed as an abnormality. Freudian stages are a good example: recurrence of a stage is viewed as regression, an abnormal event to be explained.) Teachers expect a steady growth of knowledge in students, either in a straight line (linear) or in an increasingly accelerating (curvilinear) form.

Second, it is assumed that change, growth, and development occur in a *spiral* form. *Example:* A small group might return to some previous "problem," such as its authority relations to the leader, but now might discuss the question at a "higher" level where irrational components are less dominant.

Third, another assumption more typically made is that the stages are really phases which occur and recur. There is an oscillation between various states, where no chronological priority is assigned to each state; there are cycles. *Example:* Phases of problem-solving or decision-making recur in different time periods as essential to progression. Cultures and societies go through phases of development in recurrent forms.

Fourth, still another assumption is that the form of progression is characterized by a branching out into *differentiated* forms and processes, each part increasing in its specialization, and at the same time acquiring its own autonomy and significance. *Example:* biological forms are differentiated into separate species. Organizations become more and more differentiated into special task and control structures.

Forces First, forces or causal factors producing development and growth are more frequently seen by practitioners as "natural," as part of human nature, suggesting the role of genetics and other inborn characteristics. At best, environmental factors act as "triggers" or releases," where the presence of some stimulus sets off the system's inherent growth forces. For example, it is sometimes thought that the teacher's job is to trigger off the natural curiosity of the child, and that growth of knowledge will ensue. Or the leadership of an organization should act to release the self-actualizing and creative forces present in its members.

Second, a smaller number of practitioners and social scientist think that the response to new situations and environmental forces is a coping response which gives rise to growth and development. Third, at this point, it may be useful to remind ourselves of the earlier discussion of the internal tensions of the system, still another cause of change. When stresses and strains of a system become too great, a disruption occurs and a set of forces is released to create new structures and achieve a new equilibrium.

Potentiality Developmental models vary in their assumptions about potentialities of the system for development, growth, and change. That is, they vary in assumptions about the capabilities, overt or latent, that are built into the original or present

state so that the necessary conditions for development may be typically present. Does the "seed"—and its genetic characteristics—represent potentialities? And are the supporting conditions of its environment available? Is the intelligence or emotional capability or skill-potential sufficient for development and change in a social and human process?

Change-agents typically assume a high degree of potentiality in the impetus toward development, and in the surrounding conditions that effectuate the potential.

Utility to Practitioners

The developmental model has tremendous advantages for the practitioner. It provides a set of expectations about the future of the client-system. By clarifying his thoughts and refining his observations about direction, states in the developmental process, forms of progression, and forces causing these events to occur over a period of time, the practitioner develops a time perspective which goes far beyond that of the more here-and-now analysis of a system-model, which is bounded by time. By using a developmental model, he has a directional focus for his analysis and action and a temporal frame of reference. In addition, he is confronted with a number of questions to ask of himself and of his observations of the case: Do I assume an inherent end of the development? Do I impose a desired (by me) direction? How did I establish a collaboratively planned direction? What states in the development process may be expected? What form of progression do I foresee? What causes the development? His diagnoses and his interventions can become strategic rather than merely tactical.

THE CHANGE-AGENT AND MODELS

The primary concern of this paper has been to illustrate some of the major kinds of analytic models and conceptual schemas that have been devised by social scientists for the analysis of change and of changing human processes. But we need to keep in mind that the concern with diagnosis on the part of the social scientist is to achieve understanding, and to educe empirically researchable hypotheses amenable to his methods of study. The social scientist generally prefers not to change the system, but to study how it works and to predict what would happen if some new factor were introduced. So we find his attention focused on a "theory of change," of how the system achieves change. In contrast, the practitioner is concerned with diagnosis: how to achieve understanding in order to engage in change. The practitioner, therefore, has some additional interests; he wants to know how to change the system, he needs a "theory of changing" the system.

A theory of changing requires the selection, or the construction, by theoretically minded practitioners, of thought-models appropriate to their intended purpose. This has to be done according to explicit criteria. A change-agent may demand of any model answers to certain questions. The responses he receives may not be complete nor satisfactory since only piecemeal answers exist. At this period in the development of a theory of changing, we ask four questions as our guidelines for examining a conceptual model intended for the use of change-agents.

The first question is simply this: does the model account for the stability and continuity in the events studied at the same time that it accounts for changes in them? How do processes of change develop, given the interlocking factors in the situation that make for stability? Second, where does the model locate the "source" of change? What place among these sources do the deliberate and conscious efforts of the client-system and change-agent occupy? Third, what does the model assume about how goals and directions are determined? What or who

sets the direction for movement of the processes of change? Fourth, does the model provide the change-agent with levers or handles for affecting the direction, tempo, and quality of these processes of change?

A fifth question running through the other four is this: How does the model "place" the change-agent in the scheme of things? What is the shifting character of his relationship to the client-system, initially and at the termination of relationship, that affects his perceptions and actions? The question of relationship of change-agent to others needs to be part and parcel of the model since the existential relationships of the change-agent engaged in processes of planned change become "part of the problem" to be investigated.

The application of these five questions to the models of systems and models of development crystallizes some of the formation of ingredients for a change-agent model for changing. We can now summarize each model as follows:

A "system" model emphasizes primarily the details of how stability is achieved, and only derivatively how change evolves out of the incompatibilities and conflicts in the system. A system model assumes that organization, interdependency, and integration exist among its parts and that change is a derived consequence of how well the parts of the system fit together, or how well the system fits in with other surrounding and interacting systems. The source of change lies primarily in the structural stress and strain externally induced or internally created. The process of change is a process of tension reduction. The goals and direction are emergent from the structures or from imposed sources. Goals are often analyzed as set by "vested interests" of one part of the system. The confronting symptoms of some trouble are a reflection of difficulties of adaptability (reaction of environment) or of the ability for adjustment (internal equilibration). The levers or handles available for manipulation are in the "inputs" to the system, especially the feedback mechanisms, and in the forces tending to restore a balance in the system. The change-agent is treated as separate from the client-system, the "target system."

The developmental model assumes constant change and development, and growth and decay of a system over time. Any existing stability is a snapshot of a living process—a stage that will give way to another stage. The supposition seems to be that it is "natural" that change should occur because change is rooted in the very nature of living organisms. The laws of the developmental process are not necessarily fixed, but some effects of the environment are presumably necessary to the developmental process. The direction of change is toward some goal, the fulfillment of its destiny, granting that no major blockage gets in the way. "Trouble" occurs when there is a gap between the system and its goal. Intervention is viewed as the removal of blockage by the change-agent, who then gets out of the way of the growth forces. Developmental models are not very sharply analyzed by the pure theorist nor formally stated, usually, as an analytic model. In fact, very frequently the model is used for studying the unique case rather than for deriving "laws of growth"; it is for descriptive purposes.

The third model—a model for "changing" is a more recent creation. It incorporates some elements of analyses from system models, along with some ideas from the developmental model, in a framework where direct attention is paid to the induced forces producing change. It studies stability in order to unfreeze and move some parts of the system. The direction to be taken is not fixed or "determined," but remains in large measure a matter of "choice" for the client-system. The change-agent is a specialist in the technical processes of facilitating change, a helper to the client-system. The models

for changing are as yet incompletely conceptualized. The intersystem model may provide a way of examining how the change-agent's relationships, as part of the model, affect the processes of change.

We can summarize and contrast the three models with a chart (page 102). We have varying degrees of confidence in our categories but, as the quip says, we construct these in order to achieve the laudable state of "paradigm lost." It is the readers' responsibility to help achieve this goal!

THE LIMITATIONS

It is obvious that we are proposing the use of systematically constructed and examined models of thought for the change-agent. The advantages are manifold and—we hope—apparent in our preceding discussion. Yet we must now point out some limitations and disutility of models.

Models are abstractions from the concreteness of events. Because of the high degree of selectivity of observations and focus, the "fit" between the model and the actual thought and diagnostic processes of the change-agent is not close. Furthermore, the thought and diagnostic processes of the change-agent are not fixed and rigid. And even worse, the "fit" between the diagnostic processes of the change-agent and the changing processes of the "actual" case, is not close. Abstract as the nature of a model is, as applied to the change-agent, students of the change-agent role may find the concepts of use. But change-agents' practices in diagnosing are not immediately affected by models' analyses.

Furthermore, there are modes of diagnosing by intervening, which do not fall neatly into models. The change-agent frequently tries out an activity in order to see what happens and to see what is involved in the change. If successful, he does not need to diagnose any further, but proceeds to engage in further actions, with

Assumptions and Approaches of Three Analytic Models

	Models of Change		
Assumptions and Approaches to:	*System Model*	*Developmental Model*	*Model for Changing: Intersystem*
1. *Content*			
Stability	Structural integration	Phases, stages	Unfreezing parts
Change	Derived from structure	Constant and unique	Induced, controlled
2. *Causation*			
Source of change	Structural stress	Nature of organisms	Self and change-agent
Causal force	Tension reduction (creation?)		Rational choice
3. *Goals*			
Direction	Emergent	Ontological	Deliberate selection
Set by	"Vested interests"		Collaborative process
4. *Intervention*			
Confronting symptoms	Stresses, strains, and tensions	Discrepancy between actuality and potentiality	Perceived need
Goal of intervening	Adjustment, adaptation	Removal of blockages	Improvement
5. *Change-Agent*			
Place	Outside the "target" system	Outside	Part of situation
Role	External diagnoser and actor	External diagnoser and actor	Participant in here and now

the client. If unsuccessful, however, he may need to examine what is going on in more detail.

The patch work required for a theory and model of changing requires the suspension of acceptance of such available models. For this paper has argued for some elements from both the system models and the developmental models to be included in the model for practitioners, with the use of a format of the intersystem model so as to include the change-agent and his relationships as part of the problem. But can the change-agent wait for such a synthesis and emerging construction? Our personal feeling is that the planning of change cannot wait, but must proceed with the available diagnostic tools. Here is an intellectual challenge to the scientist–scholar of planned change that could affect the professions of practice.

3.2   THE UTILITY OF MODELS OF THE ENVIRONMENTS OF SYSTEMS FOR PRACTITIONERS

Robert Chin

Organized models for the analysis of the environment of a system are increasingly necessary for the rapidly changing and interdependent world of the practitioner of planned change. Policy-makers, front-line practitioners, strategists, futurists, systems theorists, and planners regularly do make use of conceptions of environment because the operations of a system are intermeshed with the features of its environment. (*Illustrations:* "The person's high ego strength will cope with whatever social pressures he encounters." "The school board exists in a hostile environment." "Our organization must not only react, but must anticipate the social revolutions in its environment." "Our markets are shifting." "Change the environment, not the person." "Future shock." "We must train teachers to teach kids to live in a world 80 years off.") The social environment is forcefully impactful, and must be reacted to in deliberate ways. Are there different models of the environment, models with common dynamics? What are some of the useful models that can guide the observations, diagnoses, and possible interventions about the environment and its impacts on the systems called individual, group, organization, or community?

The first part of this article reviews the system-environment relationships; the second examines conceptual models of what I shall call textures of and clusterings in the environment; the third identifies selected contents of environments; and the last part suggests some ways for practitioners to use the proposed conceptions. The notions of systems and of development are presented elsewhere.[1]

[1] See R. Chin, "The Utility of System Models and Developmental Models for Practitioners," 3.1 above.

I. SYSTEM-ENVIRONMENT RELATIONS

Contemporary systems feel anguish over the loss of control of the "outside" forces. Worse yet, these outside forces are confusing and changing and arise from very distant and at times unknown origins. Impacts strike unexpectedly, frequently, and are unaccompanied by clear alternatives of problem-solving or adaptive responses by the system. In short, the environment causes turbulent and acute effects on the individual, group, organization, and community. The supercharged reality of these dynamics is a constant theme of social commentators. The responses of a planned change practitioner, whether internal or external manager or facilitator-consultant to a system and its environment, require an organized set of models of types, structures and dynamics, and conceptions for managing the environment and its relation to a system in order to develop rational approaches. An effective strategy and thought model for planned change is dependent upon several factors: the selection of the target unit as a system (person, group, organization, community); the location of the boundary defining what is a part of the system and what is in the environment; the ability to analyze the environment in orderly fashion; the intervention theory, practices, and needed professional competencies for changing the system or the environment; the models used for the system—its interrelations and its development, direction, and form—and the assumed directions of flow of causal forces of the system and of its environment.

The operational definition of a boundary of a system—the demarcation fencing in that which contains greater commerce within than across the demarcation—conceptually separates a system from the environment—a definition in terms of the system's internal interdependency. Tackling the issue of the demarcation from the stance of the environment can restate what to include or exclude from a system conceptually. The boundary between the environment and the system, between internal and external factors, is always somewhat arbitrary, as is the choice of the size of unit forming the system. Convenience and utility are the main bases for these deliberate decisions in forming either a discipline of knowledge or a discipline of practice.

What have been some models of conceptualizing the environment-system relations?

The front-line practitioner's typical procedure for deciding what factors to place in the environment is usually determined by answers to two questions: Does the factor make a difference in achieving the system's objective? Can I do anything about this factor? If the factor is seen to make a major difference in achieving some objectives of the system and nothing can be done about it directly or immediately, then the factor is placed in the environment. The environment is thus conceptually used as a reserve category of factors to be taken into account later or as conditional to the actions to be undertaken but not directly attended to for intervention.

As interdependency of the parts of a system and its environment became both a recognition of reality and a crystallized value of practitioners, closed and open system models have been drawn upon for their convenience of thought for observations, diagnostics, and interventions. In focusing on systems theory for the analysis of the individual, group, organization, and community, the practices have tended to focus on the internal characteristics of parts, and the relationships of parts to other parts of the system. In contrast, "open systems" theory

(Bertalanffy, Emery, and Trist)[2] pointed up the responses of the system to its environment, such as the system's open commerce across a boundary while still maintaining the integrity and avoiding the dissolution of the system, the proactive relation of the system to its environment, the equally effective multiple pathways available to a system to achieve its goals (namely equifinality), and the adaptive responsiveness of a system to the changes in the environment. (*Illustration:* counseling or consulting, training, organizational development, fact-gathering research and the internal climate supporting the problem-solving, planning, decision-making capabilities and flexibilities.) The theory and practice are focused to enhance the adaptive survival and growth of the system.

In intersystem theory, interdependency is broadened to describe and analyze the structured relations of a system to an organized part of the environment, namely another system. (*Illustration:* "The social environment of the child is the family." "The committee must deal with another committee to get the job done." "Alternative schools, as an organization, must maintain relationships with the administrators of the regular school system and to the various constituencies of students, parents, teachers, and to the changing social scene.") Each of these depicts the interdependency of a system (an individual, group, organization) and another system—an intersystem model. There is a need for extending the analysis of the interdependency of a system and its environment to encompass more of the essential features of the environment than intersystem theory permits.

Planning and embodying the future in the present require some differentiated models of the environment of the system. The fearsome blob of the future, often experienced as undifferentiatingly over-

[2] See Terreberry (5.1) in this volume.

whelming and catastrophic, can be focused, or at least brought under conceptual control, if more specific models of the future environment are used in the analysis. The emergent field of futurism—its approaches, values, and technologies for envisioning the future and reconstructing its possible shape, is presently based upon using known and specific variables of the environment. (*Illustrations:* The social indicators of the population and the state of societal trends in youth rebellion, housing, or psychological ideals in humanistic psychology or in self-actualization.) But there is a trap in the practices of futurology, because the specific factors to be encountered in the future may indeed be substantively different from those seen as important in the present environmental phenotypes. Concrete planning for middle- and long-range futures is thus handicapped without models for examining the genotypic or underlying features of the environment.

There is a set of existing models to describe the features and dynamics of the system-environment relations. A common analogue is similar to the forces and their operations in the physical universe. Factors arising from the sun, planets, stars, meteors, and other events impact on the earth; the earth is a "spaceship" with an enclosed system acting as an environment for man. In this metaphor there is a postulated order and a regularity. Unexpected events are merely knowledge gaps, the limitations of the time-span to take into account. The causal forces scientifically are understood as system dynamics. In addition, man has used astrology and geomancy as ways of fitting conceptions of man's nature and behavior as affected by the forces of the physical universe.

The environment of an animal or species of animal is conceived of as consisting of a balance of forces plus an occasional major upheaval or a cataclysmic event such as a flood or a forest fire. This ecological model is that of a shifting balance of food in the environment and numbers within each and among the varieties of species forming an equilibrium. More recently, this equilibrium has been recognized as upset by man in his ruthless alterations and wanton activities, such as the consumption of resources in the environment without undertaking the restorative or recycling process to replace resources or the tipping of the balances between forces thus permanently upsetting the equilibrium. This model of the environment for a biological system is the basic balance of a steady state, with predictable transformations of resources and processes, and with the disastrous intrusion of exogenous directional forces. The environment is treated as a macrosystem or ecosystem occasionally disrupted by catastrophic forces. Basically the intrinsic nature of a particular system is fixed (by genes, or "human nature"), with the environmental forces selecting survivals.

The metaphors for man-made or social environments center around conflict and control. Research psychologists have struggled with the polarity of heredity versus environment in the formation of behavior patterns. Situationalists in social psychology and sociology have demonstrated the utility of concentrating upon the setting and its field of forces as governing behavior and action. Perception of the environmental field of forces (Lewin's psychological environment, subjective environment) and phenomenological analysis of the individual or group have dominated these research approaches. Practitioners in the applied social sciences have developed wide-angle conceptions to take account of "what's really out there" and its actual, potential, and perceivable impact.

A common metaphor is that the environment is composed of supernatural forces. Daemonic forces, some positive and some evil, abound. Halfway between the deities and man, the daemons act willfully and are a bit more fathomable and placable than gods, but still in essence not under man's control. In the contemporary scene in America, the revival of the exploration of inner states of man and the techniques of shamans, witch doctors, faith healers, and seers are intended to bring these daemonic forces into the service of man's desires to shape the environment.

Metaphors of social environments tend to be anthropomorphic (complex forces are personified as person or group actions), full of perceived causal attributions of the motivations of other individuals or groups (they are conspiratorial, they intend willfully some outcome), restrictive or repressive (individuality is suppressed by society) and focused upon the possibilities of bringing the environment under control. The environment is to be conquered (man over nature) or altered by deliberate effort (reconstruction, normative re-education, social change, socialist construction). In other cultural assumptions, man fits into nature (Taoism).

These conceptions tend to focus on the system with notions of the environment of the system treated as relatively undifferentiated. When the environment is studied, it is seen as a system, thus jumping to a different-sized unit directly. Can we derive concepts of the environment as environment? I propose to examine models of the textures of and clusterings in the environment and then some selected aspects of the environment as environment of a system.

II. MODELS OF TEXTURES OF AND CLUSTERINGS IN THE ENVIRONMENT

The *texture* of the environment of a system may be seen as having varying amounts of organization, pattern, and/or clustering. A simple conception of the texture of the environment is that of a plain and featureless ground in which the system exists as figure. No clusterings or salient features exist in the environment.

Impacts on the system from the environment are random in time, place, and effects. Illustrative instances might be an infant without a differentiated environment, or an isolated prisoner-of-war camp with all-powerful and randomly behaving guards. Such a conception of the environment is also implicit when the focus of conceptualization is on the system and its input—an input that is itself isolated, contextless, and without necessary meaning or regularity. Such a system does not have any predictability about the environment. Experimental researches using single stimulus variables often taken on the characteristics of isolated inputs from the environment. The individual, group, organization, or community, however, rarely is in this simple an environment, except under pathological conditions. Furthermore, such systems will tend to create some image of what their environments are and will attribute some regularity and causal efficacy to the forces impacting from the environment.

Thus, a second model of the environment is that it is composed of a single bold and salient cluster of knowable probabilities of effects. The cluster in the environment may or may not be sufficiently organized internally to be treated as a system with its own internal dynamics. The impacts of this environment on a system arise directly from the cluster. Intersystem theory is applicable in treating the environmental parts and dynamics of the interacting system. (*Illustrations:* husband as a system with wife as the other system in the environment engaged in mutually reinforcing or interactive neurotic dynamics; a team as a system in interaction with another group in its environment in intergroup competition where intragroup activities of one system of individuals affect the intragroup dynamics of the other system's individuals.)

The third model of the texture of environment is when the environment is composed of several interlinked clusters and systems. Effects of the environment's clusters and systems result from the characteristics of each of the clusters and/or from the interactive nature of the clusters and systems with each other. (*Illustration:* husband as a system with wife and children as environment, with the interactional dynamics of children and mother resulting in impacts separate from the individual impacts of the wife or child; a team with another team and a supervisory group in an organization.)

A word of caution: These three models of the environment are differentiated by the degree of clustering represented and by conceptions of the dynamics of the clusters, with varying predictability of the environmental systems. They are not solely defined by the number of elements contained in the environment. The focus is on the kinds of interactions of the parts of the environment with each other.

The fourth model of the texture of the environment which reflects the complexity of the environment is often called a turbulent environment (Emery and Trist).[3] A turbulent environment has multiple clusters and multiple systems, each with its own dynamics interacting with the other dynamic processes arising from the field of the environment itself, as well as from the interactive forces of the multiple systems. In this model the environment is a "field" of forces. It is rapidly changing in both its structures and its dynamics. Each part of the system of the environment is a source of change, with its interactive processes producing new forces for the system. This conception avoids an oversimplified linear determinism of impacts on the observing system. The stability of the impacts is seen through some second-order concepts (the rate of change, the speedup or slowdown of growth, the narrowing and widening of boundaries of the field of forces). The unforeseeable consequences of these interactions from

time to time create a new field of forces. Under these conditions the environment as a total system will "step-jump" into new levels of functioning, forming new levels of steady state or balance. The noticeable tendency is for these step-jumps to occur more frequently in a given present than they did in the past. Revolutions in and of the structure and organization of the environment become commonplace. In the long run, it is possible to expect these step-jumps to have some limits. A set of principles for analyzing the dynamics of these processes of a turbulent environment is not at hand; rather attention is paid to how the system can learn to adapt to a turbulent environment. (*Illustrations:* new levels of consciousness for future shock, the process emphasis for managing of change, the flexible structures of organizations for proactive management of new problems.)

Such fluid processes, in this conception of the environment, alter the channels of commerce across the boundaries: new ones will develop, and old ones will diminish in importance. These interactions, which are the essence of the complex and turbulent environment, do not appear to have the characteristics of steady-state or even stable relationships. The step-jumps in the equilibrium and the structures of the systems forming the environment interrelate with more and more distant systems, interpenetrating with more and more layers of the environment. The result is a conception stretching the limits of its useful properties. Is a new conception of these structures and dynamics of the environment called for?

A fifth model, the articulated turbulent environment, identifies the nodules, envelopes, and layers in the environment which organize, channel, and process the turbulent forces and information about them for the system. These special clusters and/or systems in the environment select, organize, focus, filter, dampen, amplify, translate or transform the forces in the

---

[3] See Terreberry (5.1) in this volume.

turbulent environment. These articulations exist in the environment and are different from those parts of the system which perform essentially the same functions for the system internally. (*Illustrations:* credibly wise or trusted informants, such as parents, teachers, and advisors; news and information media, technical consultants; social indicators; research assessments, "intelligence activities"; early warning systems.) These sources for transmission to the system may in turn become a dynamic part of the field of forces, such as the mass media have progressed beyond being a passive conduit or messenger, or research reports hopefully can become. As such, they themselves become an interactive and dynamic cluster in the environment.

Articulating the turbulent environment has also been accomplished by the active and participative creation by systems of special temporary systems in the environment as an integral phase of planned change. These special temporary systems are constructed as a contrived arrangement in the environment of the system which is "not for real." The system reaches beyond its own boundaries in creating with others in a cultural island a try-out of a different way of managing in relating to its turbulently changing environment. This articulated temporary system in the environment (and not "in the system") is temporary; an alternative to regular ways of performing; a pattern of partial commitment and emotional investment; experimental; and, oriented to data and data collection on how the new ways relate to the turbulent environmental forces, fits, and produces effects and longer-range consequences. (*Illustrations:* for the individual, the cultural island of a training group such as the T-group; for the small group and organization, the simulation and/or pilot programs, or alternative organizational patterns.) Some dilemmas and conflicts do arise in the active creation of these temporary systems.

First, the main system is viewed to be "inauthentic" in creating the temporary system in the environment which is not part of the system. The system does not seem to invest energy and make "real" commitments. Another dilemma is the condition of irreality and play acting deemed useful for experimenting artificially and creating potentially valued alternatives, as compared to dealing with the practical realities of the system and its environment. The transfer of the implications to the system of the trying out of new ways in the temporary system in the turbulent environment has been another dilemma. In reference to these dilemmas, some practitioners of planned change have abandoned the practice of constructing temporary systems and have developed practices aimed at direct change in the system, losing the virtue of concretizing and trying out the new visions of managing the turbulent environment. The practices for a model of the articulated turbulent environment allow for more experimentation, a major virtue and response to the dynamics of a turbulent environment.

These models of textures of the environment are descriptive of general features of environments. The next section identifies selected contents of environments

III. CONTENTS OF THE ENVIRONMENT

Five content aspects of the environment are selected for their relevance to planned change: (1) the means in the environment for transforming the environment; (2) the patterns that structure power and authority environment relations to the system; (3) the resources that I shall call nutriments because they serve functions of the system; (4) the available information in the environment for the system; and (5) the structures representing potential feedback loops to the system.

The means existing in the environment for transforming the features of the environment are a powerful source of social change. Technologies, physical and social, are increasingly present to alter the environment of systems. These crucial technologies are an exploding and accelerating source of change in the environment itself, and breed additional environment-alteration means.

Social technologies, such as re-educative techniques, knowledge-building techniques, the transformation of the nature of man's impulses, have not been as consequential as the means for transforming the physical environment. Yet the recognition of the necessity for making better use of the social technologies is constantly thrust forward as even more crucial than the physical means.

Practitioners have been concentrating upon these innovations in social technologies and assessing their impacts with the use of models of a plain or cluster environment.

Structures of authority and power are in the environment. The balances or ratios of dominance/subordination in influence of clusters or forces in the environment are defined for the system. The ratios of influence as perceived by the system become psychological issues of whether locus of control over the system is within the system or in the environment of the system. Materialistic determinists, along with fatalists, share a conviction that places power and influence over the individual, group, organization, or community system in key factors in the environmental structures. In addition to directly exercising authority and power, these structures also provide information for the system about its potentials and limits with respect to influence, control, and countercontrol.

Power, influence, authority, and control in turbulent environments are shifting and unstable coalitions in the environment, creating an intolerable condition for the system. A frequent reaction of the system is to attempt to apply a simpler conception of texture, to see a "power structure" even when such conceptions are not realistic. Applying an articulated turbulent model can lead to discovering the specific clusters and nodules which can or do mediate the environment's total influence relationships and which also create conditions to examine untested information about influence or lack of influence.

The next aspect of the environment we will examine is the resources in the environment. These resources are viewed by us as nutriments with objects, functions, and dynamics involved in them (e.g., money, food, jobs, services, and psychological need fulfillment). These resources become nutriments supplying the system insofar as the system's survival and development are dependent upon the regular input of the resources as nutriments. Nutriments are promotive of repair and of growth.

The dynamics of the environmental structures for the delivery of nutriments for any given individual, group, organization, or community are often assumed to be based on a win-lose competition for limited or depleting supplies. This view is usually called a "zero-sum" assumption; that is, gains for one system require an equal loss for another system; the sum of the gains-losses equals zero; the size of the pie to be divided is fixed. (*Illustrations:* money, food supply, number of jobs, love from parents, intergroup striving for power and influence, an industrial firm's share of the market for its products.) Another possible assumption is that resources are expanding or expandable by transforming the conditions and resources, so that gain for one system can be accompanied by gain rather than loss for another system.

The social and psychological nutriments range (probably hierarchically) from the physiological to the psychologically based need for actualization of self. The analysis of the availability of these nutriments in the environment has to indicate how the texture shapes the nutriment structures of the environment. The individual, group, organization, or community cannot draw upon the environment unless the supplies are present, or in increasing supply, or are potentially expandable. (*Illustration:* a highly stressed unemployed parent can't easily be warm and supportive to a child.)

The environment is teeming with signals, symbols, and events as potential information to a system. This potential information in the environment may not ever be translated or organized as information for a system. (Some theorists of systems have restricted the term "information" to that which actually makes a difference in the actions of the system. Here we are treating information as that content in the environment which has the potential of altering the deliberate processes, strategies, and plans of the system.) Information is by symbols and codes to be scanned and decoded by the system. Clarifying the processes of communications in the environment and between system and environment are key approaches for practitioners in dealing with how as well as what is communicated.

The information may exist in a plain environment, and be thus conceptually managed as an input to the system, a convenience for researchers and theorists, but hardly a sufficient model for the practitioner. Clustered information, both by content, source, and by an organized structure of some coherency, may exist.

The conflict of the reliability and validity of information clusters (credibility), areas of distortions, the double-bind, the paradoxical action cues and demands, and risks of the consequences of undertaking action, become criterial for the work of temporary systems in an articulated turbulent environment.

Lastly, the identification of the available feedback sources and their dynamics in the environment are necessary to the activities of the practitioner. Feedback has been conceptualized as a characteristic of the system of the individual, group, organization, or community. The identification of the potential feedback arrangements of the textured *environment* of a system provides a setting for the analysis, diagnosis, and improvement of the internal feedback processes.

In summary, the models for analysis of the environment of systems directly deal with conceptions of how the environment is organized and what is in the environment.

IV. UTILITY OF CONCEPTIONS TO PRACTITIONERS

Conceptions of the texture and aspects of the environment are of use to the practitioner for diagnosing and intervening for planned change. The type of use depends upon the approach to change and the role of the agent of the change, whether as a technical or process consultant, facilitator, trainer, or action researcher in the laboratory mode of planned change, or as a policy-maker, advocate, or engineering consultant.

Three fundamental approaches to changing the relationships of a system to its environment are possible: (1) change the properties of the environment of the system; (2) change the interrelationship of the system to the environment; and (3) change either the internal characteristics of the system such as its awareness, perceptions, and images of the environment, or its internal responsiveness to the changing environment.

1. Changing the properties of the environment of the system involves acting directly to change the features of the environment. These changes of the environment are not necessarily made by the target system, the ultimate beneficiary of the changes of the features of the environment.

2. Changing the intersystem relationships between the system and its environment involves moving the boundary in or out, or establishing direct links between

features of the environment and parts of the system, in order to regulate and manage the channels of relationship between the system and the environment, or lessening the disjunctive connections between the system and the environment.

3. Changing the internal characteristics of the system as related to the environment typically works to improve the system's scanning and sensing mechanisms, such as the individual's ability to see and hear; to create more roles in groups and organizations for scouting and researching the environment (survey research, market research); or to clarify the mechanisms and roles for transforming acquired information into action implications (Research and Development centers), thus clearing up the noisy channels of the inputs of the system. Improving the feedback mechanisms internal to the system to gather data about the effects, or consequences, of a system's actions on the environment is one of the most strategic and valued procedures for a normative re-educative approach. Additionally, efforts to alter the attributed dynamics and causes have been central to the changing of the internal characteristics of a system. (*Illustration:* feedback scanning by an individual; use of a process observer by a committee or by an organization.)

In order to illustrate the utility of the presented notions of the texture of the environment for these approaches, we will make use of a grid which interrelates somewhat mechanically the conceptions of texture with aspects of the environment. The grid itself opens the possibility of strategizing and selecting the conceptual model for planned change. For example, my suggestion is that the practitioner might begin with the assumptions of a turbulent environment for diagnosis of the case and its context. For more dissection, he could move to analyze the texture of the environment as multiclustered and then move to a cluster analysis. And for planned change, the practitioner could make use of the conceptual model of an articulated turbulent environment. The first set of activities shapes the diagnosis; the latter suggests the ways of managing the turbulent environment. Each practitioner probably evolves his/her own strategy and process of fitting together a set of conceptual models for the purposes of planned change of the environment of a system. And, practitioners may locate how he/she typically does approach an analysis of the environment.

There are uses of the conceptions in each cell. For example, the cell M-A, multicluster patterns of authority and power in the environment, suggests the analysis of how the multiclusters manage their definitions of self and other with each other, and eventually with the system. The pat-

Textures of E	(M) Means in E for Environment Transforming	(A) Patterns of Authority and Power in E	Contents in E (N) Nutriments and Resources in E	(I) Potential Information in E	(F) Feedback System in E
(P) Plain E	P-M	P-A	P-N	P-I	P-F
(C) Cluster E	C-M	C-A	C-N	C-I	C-F
(M) Multicluster E	M-M	M-A	M-N	M-I	M-F
(T) Turbulent E	T-M	T-A	T-N	T-I	T-F
(AT) Articulated Turbulent E	AT-M	AT-A	AT-N	AT-I	AT-F

tern of several teams in an organization in relation to top management is the clustered pattern of authority (environment) for a manager (system) in one section. Intervening can be directly into the environment by consultation techniques with top management, or can be on the reporting relationships or management techniques of supervision, or can be consultation or training the manager and how he perceives and relates to authority and power. The techniques for facilitating change in the multicluster environment may well be different.

The cells are probably not of equal importance. Practitioners may train themselves to use each of these conceptions for the mindholds about the environment. Each conception can be intertwined with applied and basic social science, on the one hand, and the accepted role, agency policy, and the procedures of planned change.

In conclusion, a focus on the environment brings to saliency as figure that which has been treated as background to the figure of a system. Practitioners of planned change are increasingly attending to the texture and aspects of the environment as a wider definition of the discipline of planned change.

Methodologically, this essay has presented models of the environment. Models represent organized conceptual schemas, the abstract tools with which concrete theories are built. My emphasis on models is because practitioners can use this form of social science for the many disciplines of social practices as first-line practitioners as well as second-order practitioners who are generalizing, theorizing, and researching.

3.3 THE DIFFERENTIATION-AND-INTEGRATION MODEL

Paul R. Lawrence, Jay W. Lorsch

The notions of differentiation and integration and associated concepts dealing with the management of intergroup conflict have been presented as a comprehensive conceptual model elsewhere.[1] We want

Originally appeared within Chapter 2, "Concepts for Developing Organizations," in *Developing Organizations, Diagnosis and Action*, by Paul R. Lawrence and Jay W. Lorsch (Reading, Mass.: Addison-Wesley, 1969).

References in the deleted portions of this essay have been removed and the remaining references renumbered.

[1] P. R. Lawrence and J. W. Lorsch, *Organization and Environment: Managing Differentiation and Integration*. Boston: Div. of Research, Harv. Bus. School, 1967.

only briefly to summarize them here. In doing so, we need to emphasize two points.

1. The model is based on empirical study of ten organizations in three different environments. Further, these findings have been corroborated by our consulting activities in several additional settings.

2. The model is fully consistent with the view of organizations as systems. That is, instead of providing a universal prescription of the one best way to organize, it provides a framework, based on the demands of the organization's environment, by which we can understand what organizational characteristics are required if an organiza-

tion is to perform effectively in its particular environment.[2]

DIFFERENTIATION

To understand the environmental demands on an organization, we start first by looking at how much differentiation should exist among the various groups. As already suggested, this depends upon what internal characteristics each group must develop to carry out planned transactions with its assigned part of the environment. More specifically, it depends primarily upon the extent to which the certainty of information within the various parts of the environment is similar or different. If these parts of the environment (e.g., the market, scientific knowledge, technoeconomic or manufacturing factors) are fairly homogeneous in their degree of certainty, the units will need to be fairly similar in formal organizational practices and members' orientations. If these parts of the environment have quite different degrees of certainty, the units will need to

[2] As we shall explain in more detail below, the relationship between organizational performance and internal organizational characteristics can lead to effective performance, but feedback of results also affects the way organizational states and processes develop. For example, in a high-performing organization, knowledge of success may create an atmosphere where differences in viewpoint are more acceptable and where conflict involves less tension. However, in this discussion, we will deal with the relationship as unidirectional—certain organizational characteristics leading to effective performance. We feel justified in doing this because from the viewpoint of managers or consultants concerned with corrective action, changing these internal organizational characteristics provides the best opportunity for ultimately improving performance. The reader should realize that awareness of the need to make changes is a result of feedback in the other direction (about past organizational performance).

be more differentiated. Our evidence indicates that these needed differences are not minor variations in outlook but, at times, involve fundamental ways of thinking and behaving.

INTEGRATION

This model focuses attention not only upon the degree of differentiation necessary but also upon the integration required among organizational units. We need to be concerned with two aspects of the integration issue: which units are required to work together and how tight the requirement is for interdependence among them. But there is a strong inverse relationship between differentiation and integration. As we have suggested, when units (because of their particular tasks) are highly differentiated, it is more difficult to achieve integration among them than when the individuals in the units have similar ways of thinking and behaving. As a result, when groups in an organization need to be highly differentiated, but also require tight integration, it is necessary for the organization to develop more complicated integrating mechanisms. The *basic* organizational mechanism for achieving integration is, of course, the management hierarchy. In organizations with low differentiation, we have found that this is often sufficient to achieve the required intergroup collaboration. However, organizations faced with the requirement for both a high degree of differentiation and tight integration must develop *supplemental* integrating devices, such as individual coordinators, cross-unit teams, and even whole departments of individuals whose basic contribution is achieving integration among other groups. By using this model, then, we are able to understand not only the pattern of differentiation and integration required to deal effectively with a particular environment, but also the formal structural devices needed to achieve this pattern.

Conflict Management Variables

This model also points to another set of variables which are important—the behavior patterns used to manage intergroup conflict. As individuals with different points of view attempt to attain unity of effort, conflicts inevitably arise. How well the organization will succeed in achieving integration, therefore, depends to a great extent upon how the individuals resolve their conflicts. Our work indicates that the pattern of behavior which leads to effective conflict resolution varies in certain respects depending upon environmental demands, and in other respects is the same *regardless* of variations in environmental demands.

Those conflict management factors which vary with environmental demands include the pattern of influence of power within and among groups. The influence within groups means the organizational level *at which influence or power resides* to make decisions leading to the resolution of conflict. If conflict is to be managed effectively, this influence must be concentrated at the point in the various group hierarchies where the *knowledge* to reach such decisions also exists. Obviously, this will vary depending upon the certainty of information in various parts of a particular environment. The required pattern of influence among groups also varies with environmental demands. The groups which have more critical knowledge about environmental conditions are the ones which need to have high influence in resolving intergroup conflict if the organization is to be effective in resolving such conflict.

The factors which lead to effective conflict-resolution under all environmental conditions are the mode of conflict resolution and the basis from which influence is derived. In organizations existing in quite different environments, we have found that effective conflict management occurs when the individuals deal openly with conflict and work the problem until they reach a resolution which is best in terms of total organizational goals. In essence, effective organizations confront internal conflicts, rather than smoothing them over or exercising raw power or influence to force one party to accept a solution.[3]

In organizations dealing effectively with conflict, we have also found that the individuals primarily involved in achieving integration, whether they be common superiors or persons in coordinating roles, need to have influence based largely upon their perceived *knowledge and competence*. They are followed not just because they have formal positional influence, but because they are seen as knowledgeable about the issues which have to be resolved.

To summarize, the differentiation and integration model provides a set of concepts which enable us to understand what characteristics an organization must have to be effective in a particular set of environmental circumstances. It directs our attention to environmental demands on the organization in terms of the degree of differentiation, the pattern and degree of integration, integrative mechanisms, and conflict-resolving behaviors. In sum, it provides a way of understanding much of what needs to happen at both the organization-and-environment and group-to-group interfaces.

SUMMARY OF THE CONCEPTUAL FRAMEWORK

We shall now summarize several points about organizations and their development that have been covered earlier in varying levels of detail. At the simplest level, we

[3] This finding is consistent with the theory and findings of others. See especially *Managing Intergroup Conflict in Industry* (Blake, Shepard, and Mouton. Houston: Gulf Publishing Co., 1964).

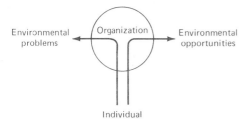

Environmental problems ← Organization → Environmental opportunities

Individual

FIGURE 1

have seen that organizations start with individuals who take collective action and form an organization so that they will improve their ability to cope with their environment. In this way, the organization becomes a device of mediating between the individual and his wider environment. It provides a setting that structures and channels his transactions with the environment. It helps him engage with problems. Figure 1 symbolizes this process.

Figure 2 takes our analysis one step further. Here we see individual contributors each tied to a specific task (a dot). The individual contributors are grouped (by the triangles) into organizational units. The environment is now depicted not as

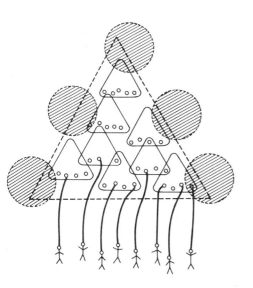

FIGURE 2

an undifferentiated mass, but as having different sectors (circles). Certain contributors are linked to these sectors to indicate their specialized task of conducting transactions with that environmental element. Each unit has developed different characteristics depending upon its part of the environment. But each unit is shown as having an integrated relationship to other units.[4] While, for simplicity, we show the integration being achieved through a shared member, we have already indicated that other mechanisms also exist to achieve integration. Finally, achieving differentiation and integration depends upon the organization members' capacity to manage conflict. In sum, this diagram depicts the basic features of our definition of organizations:

1. the transactions between individual contributors and the organization;
2. the pattern of differentiation of such systems as they manage the transactional strategy for dealing with the environment; and
3. the means for achieving integration.

In Fig. 3 we take the final step in summarizing our conceptual framework by showing the key variables we have explored in a dynamic relationship to each other. This suggests the two key features of systems analysis that are stressed above —the *interdependence* of system parts, and the organization's *morphogenic* property. The variables we have placed in this model need little further explanation except to say that the rectangle denotes the organization's boundary.[5]

[4] This follows the "linking pin" idea developed by Likert in *The Human Organization* (New York: McGraw-Hill, 1967).

[5] The boundary of an organization is particularly resistant to definition because of the fact that organizations can readily modify their own structure. For example, we would ordinarily expect to place a supplying sub-

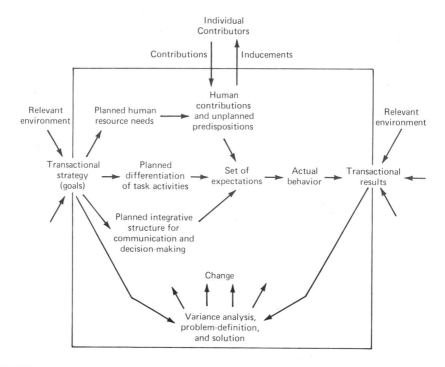

FIGURE 3

We see the now familiar transactional strategy as straddling the boundary with the environment. The concept of goals has been introduced simply to indicate that a strategy includes an expected target. We see that this strategy is tightly related to three internal elements: planned human-resource needs, planned differentiated task-activities, and a planned integrating structure for the necessary intergroup communication and decision-making. Planned human-resource needs are one determinant of the actual human contributions realized

from working out the contribution-inducements contracts with individual contributors.

As these contributions actually occur, we must recognize that they consist of not only planned-for skills and talents but also unplanned characteristics of the whole person who appears at work with all of his built-in predispositions. The total mix of planned and unplanned human needs, differentiated activities, and integrating structures and procedures combine to create a complex set of expectations among organizational contributors. Individual members come to expect of themselves and others certain specified activities, interactions, and even certain sentiments and attitudes. These include expectations about certain informal groupings of people that were not planned in the differentiated task activities.

It is this complex set of expectations that directly condition and guide the actual

---

contractor outside the formal legal boundary of a business organization, but his relation to the organization may become so close, so exclusive, and so interdependent that, for other purposes, it would make sense to treat the subcontractor as *inside* the boundary. The placement of organizational boundaries will continue to be a difficult issue simply because of this characteristic of organizations.

overt behavior of people—the actual activities performed, the interactions that occur, and the attitudes and sentiments that are held and expressed. Of course, it is this resultant behavior that, *in toto,* generates the results or outcomes in the transactions actually conducted with the environment on behalf of the organization. Was the delivery actually made according to the planned time? Were all the parts put in their proper place? Were new supplier contracts discussed, agreed and signed? Were collections made as planned so that cash deposits match cash disbursements as planned? And so on, for the thousands of behavioral events that generate (or do not generate) the surplus of resources for the organization that are essential if it is to survive and grow. Reviewing how results compare with goals, members will consider, as described above, changes in goals, procedures, and structure. As the arrows indicate, these considerations are fed into the decision-making process and may result in certain changes in the next cycle of operations. . . .

In concluding this summary, we need to emphasize again the feedback process that is indicated on the bottom of Fig. 3. This feedback loop is the way we characterize the organizational-development process. As organization members get information about the results of their activities measured against the organization's plans and goals, they may make changes and adjustments at any or all of the interfaces we have discussed. If they make the "right" choices, they will enable the organization to develop.

3.4   SOME NOTES ON THE DYNAMICS OF RESISTANCE TO CHANGE: THE DEFENDER ROLE

Donald Klein

The literature on change recognizes the tendencies of individuals, groups, organizations, and entire societies to act so as to ward off change. Though it is generally acknowledged that human beings have a predilection both to seek change and to reject it, much of the literature has isolated the latter tendency for special emphasis. In fact studies of change appear to be taken from the perspective or bias of those who are the change agents seeking to bring about change rather than of the clients they are seeking to influence. It

Reproduced by special permission from *Concepts For Social Change,* "Some Notes on the Dynamics of Resistance to Change: The Defender Role," Donald Klein, Cooperative Project for Educational Development Series, Vol. 1, National Training Laboratories, Washington, D.C., 1966.

seems likely, therefore, that our notions of change dynamics are only partially descriptive. It is interesting that Freud used the term "resistance" to identify a phenomenon which from his point of view, had the effect of blocking the attainment of his therapeutic objectives. One wonders whether patients would use just this term to refer to the same sets of interactions between themselves and their therapists.

Freud, of course, emphasized that resistances were a necessary and even desirable aspect of the therapy. He pointed out that without resistance patients might be overwhelmed by the interventions of the therapist, with the result that inadequate defenses against catastrophe would be overthrown before more adaptive ways of coping with inner and outer stimuli had been erected.

DESIRABILITY OF OPPOSITION

It is the objective of this paper to suggest that, as in patient-therapist dyads, opposition to change is also desirable in more complex social systems. It is further suggested that what is often considered to be irrational resistance to change is, in most instances, more likely to be either an attempt to maintain the integrity of the target system to real threat, or opposition to the agents of change themselves.

Opposition to Real Threat

Change of the kind we are considering consists not of an event, but of a process or series of events occurring over a period of time, usually involving a more or less orderly and somewhat predictable sequence of interactions. Though it involves the reactions of individuals, it also entails reorganization of group, organizational, or even community behavior patterns and requires some alteration of social values, be they explicit or only implicitly held.

Few social changes of any magnitude can be accomplished without impairing the life situations of some individuals or groups. Elderly homeowners gain little and sometimes must spend more than they can afford for new public school buildings or for the adoption of kindergartens by their communities. Some administrators may lose their chances for advancement when school districts are consolidated to achieve more efficient use of materials and resources. Other examples of real threat could be cited from public health, urban renewal and other fields. There is no doubt that some resistance to change will occur when individuals' livelihoods are affected adversely or their social standings threatened.

However, there are more fundamental threats posed by major innovations. Sometimes the threat is to the welfare of whole social systems. Often the threat is not clearly recognized by anybody at the time the change occurs; it emerges only as the future that the change itself helped shape is finally attained.

For example, the community which taxes property heavily in order to support kindergartens or costly educational facilities may very well be committing itself to further homogenization of its population as it attracts young families wealthy enough to afford the best in education and drives out working class groups, elderly people, and those whose cultural values do not place so high a priority on education. The community which loses a small, poorly financed local school in order to gain a better equipped and perhaps more competently staffed district facility may also be committed to a future of declining vigor as its most able young people are as a result more readily and systematically siphoned off into geographically distant professional, industrial and other work settings.

It is probably inevitable that any major change will be a mixed blessing to those undergoing it in those instances when the status quo or situation of gradual change has been acceptable to many or most people. The dynamic interplay of forces in social systems is such that any stable equilibrium must represent at least a partial accommodation to the varying needs and demands of those involved. Under such circumstances the major change must be desired by those affected if it is to be accepted.

Maintenance of Integrity

Integrity is being used here to encompass the sense of self-esteem, competence, and autonomy enjoyed by those individuals, groups, or communities who feel that their power and resources are adequate to meet the usual challenges of living. Unfortunately such integrity sometimes is based on a view of reality that is no longer tenable. When changes occur under such circumstances they force us to confront the fact that our old preconceptions do not fit present reality, at least not completely. Dissonance exists between the truths from the past and current observations. In some cases relinquishing the eternal verities would resolve the dissonance but would also entail a reduction of integrity. However irrational, the resistance to change which occurs in such cases may have as its fundamental objective the defense of self-esteem, competence and autonomy.

In our complex, changing world the assaults on individual, group and community integrity are frequent and often severe. The field of public education is especially vulnerable to such assaults. So much so, in fact, that one sometimes wonders whether there are any truly respected educational spokesmen left who can maintain the self-esteem, sense of competence, and necessary autonomy of the schools against all the various changes which are being proposed and funded before they have been adequately tested.

Resistance to Agents of Change

The problem is further complicated by the growing capacity, indeed necessity, of our society to engage in massive programs of planned change and by the development of ever-growing cadres of expert planners capable of collecting and processing vast bodies of information, of organizing such information into designs for the future apparently grounded on the best available expertise, and of marshalling arguments capable of persuading great numbers of political, business, and other civic leaders that action should be taken. The difficulties which arise stem from the very magnitude of the changes being projected, from the rapidity with which such changes can occur, and from the troubling realization that these changes often are irreversible as well as far reaching, thus ensuring the prolongation of error as well as of accuracy.

Most important of all, however, as a generator of defense would appear to be the frequent alienation of the planners of change from the world of those for whom they are planning. The alienation is one of values as much as it is one of simple information. It exists in many fields but is perhaps most apparent in the field of urban renewal, where planners have yet to devise mechanisms whereby they can adequately involve their clients in the planning processes. Many examples can be cited. Health professionals feel that matters of the public health should be left in the hands of the experts most qualified to assess the facts and to take the necessary action. They often decry the involvement of the public in decisions about such matters as fluoridation through referenda or other means. Educators, too, are often loath to encourage the development of vigorous parent groups capable of moving into the arena of curriculum planning, building design, or other areas of decision making.

Few expert planners in any field are prepared to believe that their clients can be equipped to collaborate with them as equals. What can the lay person add to the knowledge and rationality of the technical expert? And is it not true that the process of involving the client would only serve to slow down if not derail the entire undertaking? The result is that each planning project proceeds without taking the time to involve those who will be affected by the planning until such a point when it is necessary to gain the client's consent. And if decisions can be made and implementation secured without involving his public, the planner's job is greatly simplified.

It is little wonder, therefore, that planners typically do not engage in collaborative planning with clients on specific projects. It is costly, time consuming, irritating, frustrating, and even risky.

However, the failure of planners to work collaboratively with those for whom they plan contributes to the well known American mistrust of the highly trained, academically grounded expert. Under the most benign circumstances, the client may be skeptical of the planner's recommendations. Given any real threat to livelihood or position, or given any feared reduction in integrity, clients' skepticism may be replaced by mistrust of planners' motives and open hostility towards them.

The motives of innovators are especially apt to be suspect when the planning process has been kept secret up until the time of unveiling the plans and action recommendations. By this time the innovators usually have worked up a considerable investment in their plans, and are often far more committed to defending than to attempting to understand objections to them. They are not prepared to go through once again with newcomers the long process of planning which finally led them to their conclusions. And they are hardly in the most favorable position to entertain consideration of new social data or of alternative actions which might be recommended on the basis of such information. The result often is that opposition to the recommended change hardens and even grows as the ultimate clients sense that their reactions will not materially influence the outcome in any way short of defeating the plan in open conflict.

DEFENSE AS PART OF THE PROCESS OF INNOVATION

Studies in such fields as agriculture and medicine have helped clarify the sequence of processes involved in successful innovation of new practices. Even in such technical fields where results can be more or less objectively judged in terms of profit, recovery rates, and the like, successful innovation occurs only after initial resistances have been worked through.

Innovation in any area begins when one or more people perceive that a problem exists, that change is desirable and that it is possible. These people then must decide how best to go about enlisting others to get the information needed to assess the problem further and to develop the strategy leading to implementation of a plan of action. However, we know that those people who are prepared to initiate change within their own groups, organizations or communities are often in a very unfavorable position from which to do so. In stable groups especially it is the marginal or atypical person who is apt to be receptive to new ideas and practices or who is in a position where he can economically or socially afford to run the risk of failure.

Thus it has been found necessary to carry out sustained efforts at innovation in which experimentation with new ideas can be followed by efforts at adapting or modifying them to fit more smoothly into existing patterns until finally what was once an innovation is itself incorporated within an altered status quo.

The Importance of Defense in Social Change

Up to this point, this paper has touched on some of the factors contributing to the inevitability of resistance to change and has presented but not developed the major thesis, which is that a necessary prerequisite of successful change involves the mobilization of forces against it. It has suggested that just as individuals have their defenses to ward off threat, maintain integrity, and protect themselves against the unwarranted intrusions of other's demands, so do social systems seek ways in which to defend themselves against ill-considered and overly precipitous innovations.

The existence of political opposition virtually ensures such defense within local, state and national government to the extent that the party out of power is sufficiently vigorous. The British system of the loyal opposition perhaps even more aptly epitomizes the application of the concept of necessary defense in the area of political life.

In more implicit ways, non-governmental aspects of community life have their defenders. These latter individuals and groups constitute the spokesmen for the inner core of tradition and values. They uphold established procedures and are quick to doubt the value of new ideas. Their importance stems from several considerations:

First, they are the ones most apt to perceive and point out the real threats, if such exist, to the well-being of the system which may be the unanticipated consequences of projected changes;

Second, they are especially apt to react against any change that might reduce the integrity of the system;

Third, they are sensitive to any indication that those seeking to produce change fail to understand or identify with the core values of the system they seek to influence.

The Defender Role

The defender role is played out in a variety of ways depending on such factors as the nature of the setting itself, the kind of change contemplated, the characteristics of the group or individual seeking to institute change, and the change strategy employed. In a process of orderly and gradual change, the defender role may be taken by a well established, respected member of the system whose at least tacit sanction must be gained for a new undertaking to succeed. In a situation of open conflict where mistrust runs high the defender role may be assumed by those able to become more openly and perhaps irrationally vitriolic in their opposition. These latter are often viewed by the proponents of change as impossibly intractable and are dismissed as "rabble rousers" or "crack pots." This was frequently the attitude on the part of pro-fluoridationists toward the anti's.

Though crack pots may emerge as defenders under certain circumstances, it is suggested here that, so long as they are given support by a substantial segment of the population even though it may be a minority, they are expressing a reaction by all or part of the target system against real threat of some kind. In one community, I observed a well educated group of residents vote overwhelmingly against fluoridation at town meeting even though (as I viewed it) the small body of antifluoridationists expressed themselves in a highly emotional, irrational way. In later conversations it appeared that many who voted against actually favored fluoridation. They were influenced not by the logic of the defenders but by other dynamics in the situation which presumably the defenders also were reflecting. Some of those who voted "no" were unprepared to force fluorides on a minority; others pointed out that those presenting the case for fluorides had neglected to involve the voters in a consideration of the true nature and extent of the problem of tooth decay; and a third group wondered why the health officer and others fighting for the change were so insistent on pushing their plan through immediately rather than asking the town through the more usual committee procedure to consider the problem at a more leisurely pace. The pro-fluoridationists, on the other hand, were discouraged by the vote, felt rejected by fellow townspeople, and had grave doubts about bringing the issue up again in view of the fact that "they don't want to protect their children's teeth."

In the instance of fluoridation the defenders usually have been drawn from the ranks of those who do not hold public office and who do not consider themselves to be members of the Establishment. This is not always the case, however. In civil rights controversies the change agents typically are the disenfranchised; the defenders occupy public office or appear to be close to the sources of existing power. But no matter whether the innovation comes from top down or bottom up, in each situation the defenders are representing value positions which have been important not only to themselves but to larger groups of constituents, and presumably to the maintenance of the culture itself.

In the Boston controversy over de facto school segregation the School Committee Chairman was elected by an overwhelming vote of those who, however bigoted many of them may be, believe they are defending their property values, the integrity of neighborhood schools, and their rights to stand up against those who are trying to push them around. If any of us were faced in our neighborhoods with the prospect of a state toll road sweeping away our homes, we, too, might convince ourselves that we could properly rise up in defense of the same values. The point is not whether the schools should remain segregated; they should not. Rather as change agents we must be concerned with the values held by the opposition and must recognize that, to a great extent, their values are ours as well. Moreover, it would help if we could grant that, in upholding these values, the defenders—however wrong we believe they are in the stands they take and the votes they cast—are raising questions which are important in our society and which we must answer with them. It is far too easy to dismiss neighborhood schools as a reactionary myth or to hold that they are unimportant in face of the larger objective of reducing intergroup barriers. The issues become far more complex, however, when we grant that neighborhood schools were established because in the judgment of many educators and citizens they had merits apart from the current controversy over segregation. Once having granted this, the problem becomes one of seeking solutions which can minimize the losses in respect to such merits and maximize the gains in respect to integration. I would predict that, if it were

possible for the change agents to consider seriously the concerns of the defenders in the case of school integration, many of the latter would no longer feel so embattled and would no longer require the kind of leadership which in Boston has just been renominated overwhelmingly for the School Committee.

But what about the motives of those who lead the opposition to good causes? Are they not apt to seize on virtuous issues simply as ways to manipulate opinion and to rally more support? No doubt this is true. Nonetheless, I think the point still holds that the virtues are there to be manipulated. They can be used as a smoke screen by demagogues only so long as those who follow them are convinced that the agents of change are themselves unscrupulous, unprincipled, and unfeeling. Therefore, we add to the anxieties and opposition of those who are being rallied by the demagogues if we dismiss the latter and fail to come to grips with the concerns of those who uphold them.

Of course, demagogues, and rabble rousers do more than articulate the values of their followers. They also dare to give voice to the frustrations and sense of helpless rage which these followers feel but usually cannot express. Those who are the targets of change usually do not feel it is safe to give vent to their true feelings. The man who is a demagogue in the eyes of his opponent is usually a courageous spokesman to the follower whom he is serving as a defender.

How the Change Agent Views the Defender

Thus an important implication for the change agent is that the defender, whoever he may be and however unscrupulously or irrationally he may appear to present himself and his concerns, usually has something of great value to communicate about the nature of the system which the change agent is seeking to influence. Thus if the change agent can view the situation with a sympathetic understanding of what the defenders are seeking to protect, it may prove desirable either to modify the change itself or the strategy being used to achieve it. In certain situations the participation of defenders in the change process may even lead to the development of more adequate plans and to the avoidance of some hitherto unforeseen consequences of the projected change.

It is important, therefore, for those seeking change to consider the costs of ignoring, overriding, or dismissing as irrational those who emerge as their opponents. To ignore that which is being defended may mean that the planned change itself is flawed; it may also mean that the process of change becomes transformed into a conflict situation in which forces struggle in opposition and in which energies become increasingly devoted to winning rather than to solving the original problem.

Outcome of the Defender Role

What happens to the defender role during a period of change is no doubt a function of many factors, such as the nature of the issue, previous relationships between opposing sides, and the various constraints of time, urgency of the problem, and the like. We are all familiar with situations in which defenders and protagonists of change have become locked in fierce conflict until finally the defenders have either won out or been shattered and forced to succumb. Frequent examples can be found in the early history of urban renewal when entire urban neighborhoods, such as the West End of Boston, were destroyed and their defenders swept away as a consequence. It is also possible for conflict to continue indefinitely with neither side able to gain the advantage, to the extent that both sides contribute to the ultimate loss of whatever values each was seeking to uphold. Labor-management disputes

which shatter entire communities are instances where the interplay between innovative and defensive forces ceases to be constructive.

Often in communities the defenders of values no longer widely held become boxed in and remain in positions of repeated but usually futile opposition to a series of new influences. The consensus of the community has shifted in such a way as to exclude those who may once have been influential. In their encapsulation these individuals and groups are no longer defenders in the sense the term is being used here; for they no longer participate meaningfully in the changes going on around them.

Finally, as has already been suggested, the defenders may in a sense be co-opted, by the change agents in such a way as to contribute to an orderly change process.

School Administrator—
Defender or Change Agent

Within school systems the balance between innovation and defense must always be delicate, often precarious. The history of education in this country is full of examples of major innovations accomplished by an outstanding superintendent which, no matter what their success, were immediately eliminated by his successor. Sometimes disgruntled citizens who have been unsuccessful in opposing innovations are better able to mobilize their opposition when no longer faced with powerful professional leadership. Sometimes teachers and staff members who have conformed to but not accepted the changes feel more secure to express their opposition to the new superintendent.

It has been pointed out by Neal Gross and others that the superintendent of a public school system faces the almost impossible task of mediating between the conflicting demands of staff, community, and other groups. He is almost continuously confronted with the opposing influences of innovators and defenders, not to mention the many bystanders within the system who simply wish to be left alone when differences arise. Under the circumstances it may well be that one of the most important skills a superintendent can develop is his ability to create the conditions wherein the interplay between change agents and defenders can occur with a minimum of rancor and a maximum of mutual respect. As we have seen in New York City and elsewhere, however, controversies do arise—such as civil rights—wherein the superintendent seems unable to play a facilitating role.

In situations that are less dramatic and conflict laden, the superintendent and other school administrators are usually in a position where they can and indeed must be both change agents and defenders. In the face of rapid social change they face the challenge of learning how to foster innovation, while at the same time finding the most constructive ways in which to act in defense of the integrity of their systems. It is also important that they learn how to differentiate between change which may pose real threat and change which is resisted simply because it is new and feels alien. Perhaps most important of all, they have the opportunity of educa-

ting the change agents with whom they work, either those inside their systems or those who come from the outside to the point where the change agents perceive, understand, and value the basic functions and purposes of the schools.

The Force Field of the Defender

In human relations training we have frequently used Lewin's force field model as a way to introduce learners to the objective analysis of the forces driving towards and restraining against a desired change. Here, too, we have tended to view the change field through the eyes of the protagonists. I think it would be illuminating in any study of educational innovation to attempt to secure analysis of the force field from defenders as well as change agents at several stages of the innovative process. Comparative analysis of the views of protagonists and defenders might help illuminate the biases of the former and clarify more adequately the underlying origins within the target system of the opposition. It also should provide us with a better understanding of the dynamics of the defender role and how it can be more adequately taken into account in programs of social innovation.

UTilizATioN
of KNowlEdqE

CHAPTER

The use of valid knowledge is the crux of planned change. What is valid knowledge, its processes of generation and creation, forms, tests, and transformation for utilization? Some of the common types of valid knowledge are those of the social and behavioral scientists (including the researcher); the applied first-order and second-order social and behavioral practitioners; the learners in a variety of settings; and the potential knowers who are now suppressed or oppressed. The purpose of this chapter is to raise some selected issues of utilization of knowledge in planned change.

In some sense, our treatment of knowledge, including theory and fact, is focused around three questions. First, what exists in the conditions or case under study; second, how is it changing; and third, how can planned change be brought about intentionally. Chin and Downey ("Changing Change," *Handbook on Research in Teaching*, 2d Edition, chapter 17) warn about the elusive nature of the primitive and superficial definitions of change. The attainment of general valid knowledge about planned change and its utilization requires in instances clear families of different concepts for system and structural change, innovation-focused installation, and process-based definitions of change and changing.

For the social and behavioral scientist, *valid* knowledge is contained in the theories and empirical findings which emerge from obeying the rules of the scientific method. The underlying commitment is to the experiment and its basic language of proof. Issues of reliability and validity are the key tests of knowledge. These rules are applied both to the internal conditions of a study and to the external arrangements to assert the generalizability of the findings of the particular study of the particular sample. The method of work is to focus on the reduction of the probability of plausible alternative explanations so as to enhance the "true" explanations. These ideas, explanations, and theories, then, form the basis of knowledge seen as the "selectively retained tentatives," an evocative phrase proclaiming the evolutionary process of science and science-making. A more empirical thrust is embodied in the use of information, data embodied in files and records, and macro or aggregate information. Social policy processes are increasingly dependent upon these data treated as social indicators of the state of the society or its sectors. Utilization of knowledge for the first-line practitioner can be based upon these types of valid knowledge when suitably transformed into the specific case or instance in which the action and planned action is to be undertaken.

The first-order practitioner on the firing line of action builds up a body of "valid" knowledge of selectively retained tentatives embodied in practices and is guided by feedback as practices form. The second-order practitioner is explicitly evaluating these formulations, practices, and programmatic efforts and their summative outcomes to build a case for a discipline intending to tie in with the knowledge of what exists and how it changes. Evaluation research models have the challenge of expanding their boundaries to encompass issues of utilization for first- and second-order practitioners as well.

The learners in transmissive and experiential settings (academic and field) accept and build valid knowledge. Field experiences, apprenticeships, internships create a learning setting in which subjective knowledge becomes intersubjective with appropriate sets of rules for testing these tentatives.

And, in the world of liberation of the suppressed and oppressed, whether of minorities, peasants, workers, or groups such as women, socialized members of groups, organizations and communities, proponents claim valid knowledge is generated and tested. Indeed for Mao Tse-tung, theory and practice in tandem and combined is the sole basis of valid knowledge. For him, without Marxist *praxis*, there is no valid knowledge.

The issues in "Science and Practice" (4.1) deal with some of the processes involved in moving from general knowledge to specific knowledge, the interrelations of science and art in practice, the form of knowledge in generalizations and the issues of translation into cases confronting the practitioner, concepts versus feelings, the selection of conceptual tools, the usable aspects of theory and a few of the pitfalls we encounter in bridging between science and practice.

Underlying processes of the utilization of knowledge is what Argyris and Schön (4.2) point to as a discrepancy between espoused theories and theories-of-action-in-action. Espoused theories based on ideology and social science must give way to the formulation of the implicit and, at times, explicit theories-in-action, the theory of intervention. For theories-in-action tend to create a behavioral world that constrains or frees the individual. Argyris and Schön pick out criteria for the examination of theories-in-action: internal consistency, congruence between espoused theory and theory-in-use, effectiveness, testability, and valuation of the world created by the theory-in-use. They offer a pragmatic solution to the dilemmas and paradoxes occurring in the theory-in-action held by practitioners, and suggest ways in which these have been or could be sustained in a dialectic process. By their focus on theories-in-use, they offer a way to build an adequate behavioral examination of what theories-in-use create in the behavioral world.

How research utilization has brought into the "science-consumer system" new knowledge and evaluated practice is described by Lippitt in "The Process of Utilization of Social Research to Improve Social Practice" (4.3). Valid knowledge is seen as based upon research and evaluated or validated practice. The article points to the necessity for the training of the consumer in knowledge utilization. Havelock and Benne carry forward the analysis of the utilization process at the macro level, seeing the relations between science and practice as what was called in a previous chapter, an intersystem issue. In this article, "An Exploratory Study of Knowledge Utilization" (4.4), they lay the foundation for the direct study of the roles, linkages, and patterns in science and its utilization, generating specific issues for study of what has been an historical problem.

Benne, in his article on the utilization of knowledge in field experiences (4.5), moves beyond the usual scientific definitions of valid knowledge and evaluated practice to show how a certain type of valid knowledge is created in field experiences of the learner. Valid knowledge for the learner is present when the experiences encountered are elevated to more general meaning by the person engaged in field experience. Most important, Benne points to the epistemological principles which justify these processes of creating valid knowledge.

The excerpt from "Pedagogy of the Oppressed" (4.6) by Paulo Freire is couched in revolutionary language and is hampered stylistically because the original writing was in Portuguese. In this article, valid knowledge emerges and is utilized in the dialogical relations between the revolutionary leadership and beneficiaries of true liberation in humanistic revolutions. The utilization of knowledge is embedded in reflection and action directed to the structures to be transformed.

4.1   SCIENCE AND PRACTICE

Kenneth D. Benne, Robert Chin, Warren G. Bennis

The change-agent cannot afford to enjoy the intellectual luxury of the historian or archeologist who focuses upon understanding and delineating changes that are manifest only in the relics of completed events. Nor can he be satisfied with the stance of the detached observer who interprets changes, while they are going on, from some calculated vantage point of noninvolvement. Those who undertake the functions of a change-agent must not only diagnose the ongoing events in which they are involved but must also find ways to intervene in these events to maximize the valid human values implicit in the events. Ideally, the change-agent should combine in some measure the wisdom and sense of perspective of the historian and the penetrating acumen of the scientific observer, while putting into practice the skills and arts of appropriate and resolute action.

Can such paragons be produced among social scientists and social practitioners? The question cannot be fully answered before the event. But we consider it no less realistic to seek to fulfill hopes than to succumb to fears when both are realistically justified by an examination of the human situation. The answer to the question depends in part upon the type of "realism" men embrace in confronting their condition. We are voting here for the brand of "realism" that accepts the uncertainties and ambivalences of the contemporary situation, while trying to maximize

Revised version of "Science and Practice" by Benne, Bennis, and Chin, from the Second Edition of *The Planning of Change,* edited by Warren G. Bennis, Kenneth D. Benne, and Robert Chin (New York: Holt, Rinehart and Winston, 1969).

the hopes inherent in it. The notion of "change-agent" seems to us consistent with this brand of realism. It points to a prospect and program, in only the early stages of achievement, not to a finished fact. In this sense it is "realistic." It calls for a reorientation and reorganization in the patterns of thought, practice, and association widely prevalent among social scientists and social practitioners.

Such a call for reorientation and reorganization is disturbing both to social scientists and to social practitioners. The disturbance arises in part from the "realistic" difficulties always involved in effecting changes of any magnitude in existing patterns of thought and relationship. But the sense of disturbance may also reflect valuatively and attitudinally tinged issues concerning the place of "science" in human affairs and certain "conceptions" of behavioral science that we consider to be misconceptions. What are some of these issues and misconceptions?

SCIENCE VERSUS ART IN PRACTICE

A practitioner who shapes and forms—or better, re-shapes and re-forms—materials of a certain sort must be something of an artist. He must have a "feel" for the materials with which he works. His knowledge of these materials must go beyond "knowledge about" them to "knowledge by acquaintance with" them. The latter knowledge does not come to him by detached observation and theorizing primarily or alone but by direct "handling" of his materials, by learning to appreciate their reluctances and readinesses, learning to guide his "handling" by the qualitative reactions of his materials to the "handling." Learning the arts of practice comes through a process of apprenticeship, preferably under the guidance of an experienced practitioner who has mastered the art, not through academic tutelage in theories and hypotheses "about" the materials handled by his craft.

This "art" dimension in practice is clearly evident in the functioning and the education of skilled artisans of various sorts. It is equally evident in the functioning and education of "helping professionals," whom we seek to characterize collectively as "change-agents." In seeking for conceptual tools to guide the functioning of change-agents, are we denying the "art" dimension in their work or selling it short? Are we, more pointedly, seeking to substitute scientific knowledge about people and their conduct in stability (structures) and change (processes), in sickness and in health, for knowledge by acquaintance with people as particular persons or kinds of persons, as particular groups, particular organizations, etc.?

This is not what we are aiming to do, of course. What we are rather doing is to deny a logical gulf between the knowledge of the artist and the knowledge of the scientist, which, by assumption, frequently separates the functioning and education of social scientists and of social practitioners. This gulf, we believe, is widened by the conventions of traditionally institutionalized practice—conventions that masquerade as inherent logical contradictions in the thinking of many social practitioners and of many social scientists as well. The gulf has been institutionally bridged in some areas of practice more than in others. It is least bridged in the arts of practice where people are the "materials" practiced upon and best bridged in areas of practice where physical things and processes are the "materials" to be altered, re-shaped, and re-formed through practice.

What can we learn by analogy, from historical experience in the latter areas of practice? Unfortunately, confidence in such analogies is undermined by a historical circumstance that probably reflects the unbridged gulf in thinking about "science" and "practice" previously mentioned. We have thriving scholarly disciplines in the history and philosophy of the "sciences" and in the history and philosophy of the "arts." Scholarly studies in the philosophy and history of "engineering" have been relatively neglected. Yet the growth of "engineering" disciplines has been the cultural response to the bridging of the gulf between the "physical sciences" on the one hand and the "practical arts" of altering, re-shaping, and re-forming physical things and processes on the other.

Despite the lack of adequate studies in this history and philosophy of engineering disciplines, two analogies between the place of "science" and "art" in "physical engineering" and the place of these in "human engineering" may be suggestive.

1. Engineering uses scientific knowledge of physical things and processes to exploit "new" possibilities and potentialities in the practices of handling and developing these things and processes. It continually passes beyond conventional views of "natural potentialities" in things and processes that are actually rationalizations of present techniques of practice. It is doubtful if artisans working with coal tar, for example, would or could ever have developed the flood of colors, old and new, locked up in coal tar, a substance so qualitatively different from the dyes that may be made to issue from it. Physiochemical knowledge derived from basic research about dyes and pigmentation and about the chemical composition of coal tar opened up for engineering diagnosis hitherto closed "natural" potentialities" and led to the construction of "human artifacts" for actualizing these potentialities. In doing so, engineers transformed "nature" as conventionally seen by an addition to the arts of human culture. And "common sense" has generally absorbed this transformation

of "nature," at least in cultures with a highly developed chemical technology. Newly invented concepts in basic research led to engineering concepts of practical utility.

Are the possibilities so different within the processes of human engineering? Are we limited in our current view of the possibilities and potentialities of human nature by our present arts of handling, managing, and developing human beings? Can basic scientific concepts and knowledge of processes of human conduct be introduced into practitioners' diagnoses of human potentialities and can the creation of social artifacts to elicit and stabilize hitherto unrealized possibilities in "human nature" be thus stimulated and facilitated? Can new arts of guiding human growth and development become bridges of "engineering" between our present arts of education, organization, and policy-making and the beginnings of basic scientific knowledge about human beings in their personal and collective behavior?

We see no logical reasons why analogous "engineering" developments in social practice are impossible. And we see the best hope of directing and managing processes of technological change toward humane ends in thus extending our conceptions of the possibilities of human nature and in building cultural and institutional artifacts to elicit and stabilize these new possibilities. One barrier to realizing this hope lies in the fear that "human nature," as we know it now, will be destroyed in deliberately devising new technologies for its renovation. Is this fear groundless?

2. This question brings us to a second analogue. Our fears about the dehumanizing effects of engineering practice stem from our experiences with past decisions about the uses of engineering competence that have involved neglect of or insensitivity to important moral and esthetic values. Competences in physical engineering have frequently been employed

(or misemployed) by industrial and governmental bureaucracies to serve limited values, for example, maximization of economic advantages in the case of the former and maximization of "defense" advantages in the case of the latter. The effect has frequently been "selective inattention" by those with engineering competence to other human values at stake in the changes they have exercised their ingenuity to produce. Men fear that a similar "selective inattention" will work in the use of competences in social engineering as these develop. In fact, men can point to such "selective inattention" in "engineering" approaches to influence that have been widely publicized, for example, in manipulation of mass media by "hidden persuaders" or by votaries of "motivational research," and by the practitioners of "brainwashing."

The grounds for fear are evident enough. Where are the grounds for hope? We believe that they lie in the very fact that "values" have been served in the massing and utilization of engineering resources in the past. We need to unmask the pose of amorality that has, wittingly or unwittingly, been assumed by engineers, physical and social. A similar pose has been assumed widely by scientists and artists as well. Competitive economic advantage is a value and its disciplined pursuit a morality, albeit a limiting one. Similarly, competitive "defense" advantage in the cold war represents a value and its disciplined pursuit a morality, although again it is limited and constricting and probably eventually self-defeating, if exclusively employed in decisions about the development and utilization of engineering talent. No practitioner operates without the guidance of moral and/or esthetic norms however unexamined, inarticulate, and uncriticized these may be. Our hope lies in this fact and in the possibility of stimulating examination, articulation, and criticism of the values that engineering competence does and should serve on the part of engineers themselves and those who employ their talents.

There is a morality inherent in the human enterprise of engineering itself (just as we argued previously that there is a morality inherent in the human enterprise of science). Scholars like Veblen and Ayres have made this fact abundantly clear, however we may choose to criticize their particular articulations of its content.[1] As this inherent morality becomes clear to engineers and as they assume responsibility for extending and maintaining it in their work, it is doubtful to us that they will, be able to collaborate wholeheartedly in inhumane utilizations of their talents. Since their role is increasingly necessary to the maintenance of both economic and political structures in "developed" countries, their moral voice will be heard. This is now true for engineers concerned with the development of things. It will become increasingly true of engineers concerned with the development of human beings as well. Meanwhile, for many, the articulation of their moral voice remains an unfinished task.

GENERALIZATIONS AND CASES

As we have seen . . . , practitioners are certainly concerned with particular "cases," with their diagnosis and with planning treatments to effect improvements in them. Scientists, on the other hand, are concerned with particular "cases" primarily to verify or disprove generalizations about the relationships between variables that are somehow exemplified in the "cases." Claims for the utility of scientific findings for practitioners must take account

[1] Thorstein Veblen, *The Instinct of Workmanship* (New York: Crowell-Collier and Macmillan, Inc., 1914), and C. E. Ayres, *The Theory of Human Progress* (Chapel Hill: The University of North Carolina Press, 1944).

of this important distinction between the two orientations. This valid distinction may be used to lend plausibility to the sharp conceptual cleavage between "knowledge about" and "knowledge by acquaintance with"—a cleavage already noted.

How do generalizations function in the thinking of practitioners about "cases" with which they are concerned? It is easy for practitioners who are focused on the "unique" character of case-situations to forget the "deductive" aspects of their diagnostic processes. Yet these "deductive" aspects are always present, however, inarticulately. Previous experiences with other cases would have no meaning for this case if there were not some generalizations carried over from previous experiences and brought to bear upon the present one. An organizational consultant may have learned that some pattern of symptoms observed or revealed in the present instance connotes difficulties in communication upward in the hierarchy of the organization. Another pattern of symptoms may indicate unacknowledged competition between department heads. The practitioner thus develops "diagnostic orientations" in the course of his practice. And he deduces from these orientations meanings for observable symptoms and syndromes in the case he is diagnosing. Frequently these diagnostic orientations have not been well articulated by the practitioners themselves. The process of deduction of meanings from them may operate implicitly and the end-product of diagnosis may emerge into his consciousness as an "insight" that illuminates the complexities of the confronting case with a meaning and a direction for intervention in treatment of the case. Insight and intuition are then opposed sharply to logical operations from preformed theories or hypotheses. The value of stressing the uniqueness of the case is to reduce the prevalence of mechanical or nonorganic diagnoses accomplished only by derivations from previous knowledge. The disvalue may lie in producing the same effect through failure to examine and articulate the diagnostic orientations that are actually at work, wittingly or not, in the processes of diagnosis.

It is at the point of formulating, criticizing, or revising diagnostic orientations toward the cases with which he works that the practitioner finds the most direct use for scientific generalizations. For these generalizations are designed to point to meaningful connections between variables *possibly* at work within any situation being analyzed. A perfect science of human behavior, if one were available to practitioners, would still point to structures of *possibility* within the cases with which he deals. It would not obviate the necessity for reconnaissance of particular situations to find which variables are at work there, for judgment of which variables are crucial in explaining the difficulty in the case, for measurement of the magnitudes of these variables as they combine to contribute to the difficulty. The arts of diagnosis are thus still necessary to the practitioner, but they can be validly informed by scientific generalizations that have been integrated into the diagnostic orientations he brings to the cases with which he deals.

CONCEPTS VERSUS FEELINGS IN PRACTICE

The gulf between the artist and the scientist divides them, often deeply, in their approaches to the emotions and feelings of men. First of all, there is an ideologically created distinction between concepts about knowledge, information, and other cognitive processes and those about emotions, feelings, and interpersonal relations. Philosophers and scientists long ago organized separately the terms and concepts for talking about and interpreting the cognitive and the affective aspects of man's

behavior. Due to the process of abstracting, necessary for the creation of terms and concepts, a gulf between the two omnipresent aspects of man's behavior is made and widened. And we are then constrained to talk about separate and polarized entities: ideas versus emotions, rational versus nonrational, perceptions and cognitions as affected by emotions, rational task structures versus the structure of interpersonal relations in groups, and so on. What has been conceptually put asunder in the past by the use of separate terms has to be put back together again. The scientist takes his time in relating these polarized terms in his conceptual framework; the practitioner artist does it "on the fly" while working with a case. In so doing, the practitioner is led to another problem of his relationship to the scientist's concepts.

The gulf is widened when practitioners insist that the states of feelings or nonverbal emotional communications or the personal vocabularies of the emotions are destroyed or made trivial by the arid "scientific" concepts that are intended to capture, reflect, and analyze an emotional experience. The client's feelings, it is argued, can be understood primarily by the change-agent's apprehending the wholeness of the feelings, or some symbolic facsimile of them, and not through concepts intended to provide knowledge about the experiences of the client. It is as if the change-agent cannot know by conceptual and intellectual analysis, but can only comprehend by making use of his own feelings and reactions as a resonating instrument.

The impact of depth psychology upon man's view of man has both intensified and alleviated the struggle over the best way of apprehending man's feelings and emotions. Freud, on the one hand, stretched our horizons by redefining the range and explorable depths of the emotions, and thereby increased man's sense of awe and mystery about emotional manifestations and their role in man's behavior. In more recent times, Rogerian theory and therapy, existential psychology, and the widespread use of differentiated and complicated artistic mediums of emotional expression have strengthened assumptions about the fragile untranslatability of feelings and emotions into conceptual language. Further reinforcement for safeguarding the sanctity of the feelings and emotions comes from various defensive moves against the invasion of human affairs by "scientism" and from the poignant search of contemporary men for the wholeness and immediacy of experience that individual alienation and social fragmentation often deny him. Many seem to say "if you can talk about your feelings directly and conceptually, then they are not real, or have disappeared."

Yet, at the same time, Freud was using terms, concepts and constructions, metaphors and analogical language to provide a vehicle by which these very feelings and emotions could be organized and examined both by those who have them and by the analyst trained to recognize them to make them accessible to scrutiny and analysis by the person with troubling or immobilizing feelings. By putting into concepts the very stuff of the irrational and nonrational feelings and emotions, he advanced immeasurably the use of concepts to describe and analyze the emotions and also to bring them under self-control.

This dilemma of the change-agent cannot be brushed away lightly. He must acknowledge the polarization of "feeling" and "rationality" that operates in many situations, he must recognize the limitations of present attempts to bridge the gulf between "knowledge" and "emotion," and he must supplement his diagnostic orientations with acknowledgment of the reality of his own personal feelings and those of others. In brief, the change-agent can and must learn to use his own feelings and emotional apparatus, along with his conceptual paraphernalia, to achieve the best understanding he can of his client's feelings and emotions. Balancing these modes of understanding is part of the artistic skill required of the change-agent. Sharpening his conceptual tools is a necessary step in the controlled use of his own feelings and emotional reactions.

SELECTION OF CONCEPTUAL TOOLS

Contributing to the difficulty of the change-agent in making use of the knowledge of man contributed by social scientists is the sheer volume of clamorous and conflicting claims to primacy issuing from those in various scientific specializations. Shall he diagnose "role" difficulties? Or are personality mechanisms of the individuals concerned at the root of human difficulties? Or should the change-agent concentrate upon the power structure of the organization? How does the practitioner guide his selection from among the competing wares offered by various social sciences?

Two interrelated ideas are useful in sorting out and evaluating the conceptual tools that are of use to the change-agent. First, he needs to look at the functions and limitations of a "concept," "conceptual framework," or "model"; second, he must examine the size of human units and the level of analysis which are of central relevance to a particular change-agent.

Change-agents, accustomed to dealing with "facts," often find hard sledding in dealing with "theory." But, we reiterate, facts are always, in truth, observations made within some conceptual framework. Concepts are invented in order to fix a particular slant on reality and to guide the production of new facts. The preoccupation of behavioral scientists with new concepts unintelligible to present common sense is based on this supposition. The resistance by practitioners to "jargon" may be understandable but if pushed to the extreme would deny the cornerstone of the scientist's contributions to knowledge.

Change-agents themselves make use

of concepts and conceptual schemas, even while they are most vociferously attacking unfamiliar concepts in the name of naïve realism or common sense. Common sense itself is a loose collection of conceptual schemas, and is the end-product of cultural accretions, of folk wisdom, habitual modes of thought and hidden assumptions about human nature, and the social arrangements of man. An explicit formulation of concepts into a conceptual schema to be used by the change-agent allows him to reveal, examine, and refine his "common-sense" diagnostic orientations. Conceding the fact that there are very many possible conceptual schemas, what underlying unity operates among all of them? Unity can be sought, and at the same time, valid groupings of particular conceptual schemas can be found by examining the thought model lying behind assorted conceptual schemas. The thought models of "system" and of "development" can, we believe, fulfill the function of sorting out and evaluating various concepts for use by change-agents.

But which is the correct model, the most useful conceptual schema, the most relevant and powerful concept for a particular change-agent? Again, as we have insisted in preceding sections, the artistic skills of the change-agent must be in making such selective judgments. No cook book can tell him exactly what idea to use. He must select and combine from the available tools at hand and must create new tools when the existing stock is shown to be inadequate. He must in the last analysis create his own role and role relationships. But valid knowledge *will* be useful both in the process of creation and in evaluating its products.

Another assumption made by contemporary behavorial scientists is that when change-agents are dealing with an individual, a small group, an organization, or a community or nation, there are some similarities and some differences among these clients, regardless of size. All client-

systems are assumed to be like all others in some ways, like some others in certain other ways, and like no others in still other ways. For example, an individual, a small group, an organization, or a community or nation all are analyzable in terms of the interdependent nature of a social system.

The discussion of *levels* of analysis may best be approached by an anecdotal illustration. A group of spectators sat watching a football game. They saw two groups of eleven men facing each other, heard a whistle blow, then suddenly action erupted, followed by another blast of the whistle, whereupon everyone stopped. One of the spectators said, "That was a good draw play, we gained eight yards." When questioned about this jargon, he said, "Well, the quarterback handed the ball to the fullback, who counted off several seconds, waiting for the opposition to be drawn in, and then crashed into the middle of the line and advanced eight yards before being tackled and stopped. That's what is called a 'draw play.'" Someone asked a second spectator, "What did you see?" "Well," he replied, "I saw the acting out in different degrees of the needs for aggression and achievement in the players and the effects of how each views himself in relation to the other twenty-one men." A third spectator said, "I saw eleven men on either side engage in a pattern of coordinated behavior with very well worked out expectations of action for each position in regard to other positions, until these patterns were disrupted by the other side." A fourth spectator said, "I also saw your role relationship and integrations. But additionally, I saw a leadership structure, which included a man in one position calling signals during the play and a captain exercising some limited authority. I saw a social system of eleven men opposing another social system, each of which was composed of many subsystems and structures like leadership, conflict, plus a coach attached to each system." A fifth spectator said, "I saw two kinds of tradition: the ritualistic and emotional meaning of a game of this sort and the heightened excitement and tension of this particular game due to the traditional rivalry between these two teams. Both traditions reflect the competitive and peer values of our young adult culture."

Here we have a football fan's description and analysis of his "jargon." He has learned the concepts and conceptual schemas of football, and finds that it is a useful shorthand for describing a set of events. Also, we find an analysis of motives and self by the second spectator (perhaps an individual psychologist); a role analysis of expectations in a small task group by the third spectator (perhaps a small-group man); a portrayal of social structures and social systems by the fourth (no doubt a sociologist); and a statement of how the traditions and values of the culture affect behavior by the fifth (a cultural anthropologist). The statements and analyses are pitched at different levels of analysis, each using a different set of concepts and terms. The point is that no one level of analysis is the "real" one. Each is applicable for pointing up a different aspect of the behavior being observed and analyzed. It is conceivable that a football coach or a football player might find interpretations from any of these levels of analysis useful, depending upon the difficulty his team is encountering and the goals of improvement that have been agreed upon by coach and team.

Change-agents may not, in relation to the confronting case, be able to select their conceptual tools of diagnosis at one level alone. They may be forced to become multidisciplinary. Furthermore, the change-agent must select his tools of analysis on the basis of his preferred intervention strategy, his diagnosis of what he has power to do, the degree of accessibility of various variables to his influence, and the nature of his influence on and in relation to various parts of the client-system.

ASPECTS OF THEORY

Theory itself has differentiated aspects. In addition to a conceptual schema, there are constructs, conceptual hypotheses, middle-range theories, grand theories, models and meta-theories, in an ascending order of abstraction, all lumped together as "theory." These are all necessary for the proper role of theory in helping to order observations, to explain or to guide predictions. Constructs (hypothetical constructs or intervening variables) are deliberately created ideas or inferences with or without any directly observable reality, but which serve the heuristic function of allowing analysis and explanation to occur. As these are put together into some if-then statements, we generate hypotheses which can be translated into probes for empirical studies. Behavioral science is stocked with these hypotheses backed up with empirical probes and are organized as "middle-range theories," devoted to a limited range of phenomena. Verified findings of these organized "if-then" statements derived from the middle-range theories of power, reference groups, roles, interpersonal relations, communications, attitude change, etc., have been urged as the counterpart to the engineering and medical sciences model to create applied middle-range theories of consulting, training, feedback, and laboratory education. Counter arguments have been posed that such findings of middle-range theories, basic and applied, are bound by the historical time period in which these theories and their findings are generated. Grand theories have the seductive lure of all-encompassing architectonic assertions to explain behavior and changes in behavior. Freudian, Humanistic, Behavioristic theories, and variations of these grand theories, have been treated as if they are grand theories by practitioners without critical examination of their constructs, hypotheses, and internal middle-range theories. The ideas and framework of these middle and grand theories are organized by "models," such as the systems, intersystem, or developmental models. And, finally, there are analyses of the assumptions and values which form a body of meta-theory. These aspects of theory and their coordinate observations and "facts" need to be separated when we utilize knowledge. Some practitioners and behavioral scientists have insisted on making use of middle-range verified theories and their facts as a positivistic stance for applied behavioral science, while others have urged the utilization of knowledge based on conceptual schemas and models as the most useful aspect for creating a science of practice.

PITFALLS FOR THE UNWARY

In any hasty rapprochement between behavioral science and the arts of practice, we find some pitfalls.

1. One of these we may call the "etiological" pitfall. A major concern of many behavioral scientists is to find out how a given state of affairs came about; they are interested in "causes." In his eagerness to use scientific knowledge, the practitioner of planned change frequently has been booby-trapped into using a theory of origins of the problem as a basis for his intervening in helping to solve the here-and-now problem. We consider this search for "basic causes" by practitioners as a pitfall because identification of the "causes" of a state of disorganization in a social system does not mean that the change-agent can or should work at undoing or remedying these original "causes." The strategic intervention to help restore an organization to effective functioning may well require an entirely different action from that of trying to affect the "basic causes" of the problem, which are frequently located earlier in its history. In short, etiology, the "science of causes," may uncover both states and, in Allport's term, the functional autonomy of

the present. One way of avoiding this pitfall of extreme dependency upon "etiology" is for the change-agent to start with scientific formulations of a strategy of action and intervention and then test the relevance of the diagnosis of origins or causes against the proposed plan. The consequence of this procedure is that we limit the amount and kind of diagnosis performed to those diagnoses that reveal future consequences of presently alterable factors. A preventive program of action, compared to a corrective one, does frequently require more etiological knowledge.

2. Another issue revolves around predictability and control. The behavioral scientist seeks to unravel the complex causal connections in personal and social change processes, often under artificially controlled conditions, and to report his results as proven or disproven hypotheses. His example has sometimes lured the practitioner into thinking that a predictable specificity of consequences will follow if he but learns to act in the correct manner. But, as Merton and others have pointed out, unforeseen consequences are always built into any social action. A change-agent always encounters varying degrees of low predictability and lack of control. Therefore the despair of the change-agent over the limits of his ability to act "scientifically" must be converted to an acceptance of incomplete predictability as a condition of his work. We propose that a midpoint between unrealistic demands for predictability and control and defeatist acceptance of the all-too-true realities of unanticipatable consequences is the position for the change-agent to occupy. He must become a "probability expert." He should be a gambling man, who eschews "sure bets" and "long shots" simultaneously. But, like a professional gambler, he should seek the bets that give him a probability edge over pure chance. This is the best he can do in the immediately confronting problem, hoping in the long run he will

come out ahead. The position suggested is actually in line with much current thinking in the natural and behavorial sciences; namely, to substitute probability calculations for oversimple cause and effect thinking.

3. Another issue of paramount concern is the approach of the scientist and of the practitioner to the working contexts of "comprehension" and "verification." Using a simplified procedure, we suggest examining these two contexts as if they were separate dimensions. "Comprehension" and "understanding" are concerned with the exploration, formulation, and grasp of some phenomenon. "Verification" attempts to prove or disprove the "truth" of some hypothesis. It involves the cautious skepticism that demands more explicitly stated bases of demonstrating whether or not some diagnosis is "actually" so. The methods of the scientist typically emphasize the latter context through more and more rigorous procedures of demonstrating whether or not

something is so. On the other hand, "comeprehension" uses more personal, less elaborately codified procedures. The immersion in their materials on the part of historians, anthropologists, and practitioners such as psychiatrists, social workers, and consultants is reminiscent of the German sociological term for understanding, *Verstehen*. The "proof" of their conclusions by verification is not so easily obtained, at least within the predominant value system of the scientist. The point of this discussion is to suggest that we examine the issues surrounding our methods of diagnosing to assess the relative emphases to be placed on "understanding" and on "verification." Hopefully, we can maximize both; practically we may need to sacrifice some "comprehension" in achieving a high degree of "verification," and vice versa (and more typically), accept some lower degree of "verification" in order to achieve maximum "comprehension."

4.2   EVALUATING THEORIES OF ACTION

Chris Argyris, Donald A. Schön

To consider the interaction of theories-in-use and their behavioral worlds, we must look at their tendencies rather than at their cross-sectional properties at any instant in time. Whether theories-in-use tend to create a behavioral world that constrains or frees the individual depends on answers to the following questions: Are the theories-in-use and espoused theories internally consistent? Are they congruent? Are they testable? Are they effective? Do

we value the worlds they create? The relationships among these criteria are expressed in Figure 1.

INTERNAL CONSISTENCY

In a very simple sense, *internal consistency* means the absence of self-contradiction. But in the domain of theory of action, its meaning becomes more complex.

The most important kind of consistency lies not between propositions in the theory ("This man is generous," "This man is stingy") but among the governing variables of the theory that are related to

From Chris Argyris and Donald A. Schön, *Theory in Practice: Increasing Professional Effectiveness* (1974). Reprinted by permission of Jossey-Bass Inc., Publishers.

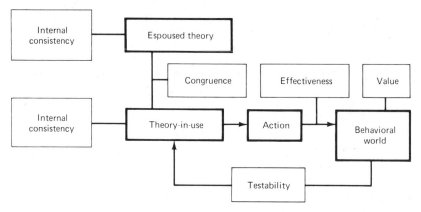

FIGURE 1

assumptions about self, others, and the behavioral setting. For example, a theory of action might require two propositions— "Keep people calm" and "Encourage participative government"; if participative government can come about only through heated action, the theory is internally inconsistent, although not logically inconsistent. It is not self-contradictory, as saying a horse is and is not white would be. However, efforts to achieve the governing variables would interfere with one another.[1]

Each of these variables has a range that is acceptable; within that range, there are levels of preference. As long as calmness does not rise to the point of inertness, we may prefer to have things as calm as possible. As long as participation does not rise to the point of anarchy, we may prefer to have as much of it as possible.

If two or more such variables are internally incompatible in a particular context, one cannot achieve as high a level of

preference for both of them taken together as one can for each of them taken separately.[2] If we call such a relationship *incompatibility,* we can reserve the term *internal inconsistency* for the special case in which one variable will fall out of its acceptable range if the other is brought into the acceptable range.

Whether governing variables are incompatible or internally inconsistent depends on a number of factors.

1. Other governing variables—for example, variables related to self-protection, courtesy, or protection of others —may limit the means for achieving some variables.
2. The array of actions envisaged in the theory-in-use may be too narrow. Outside of that array, there may be some

---

[1] We might have chosen to speak of two inconsistent values. But remembering our earlier discussion of the field of constancy, there is a much larger set of variables for which under a given theory-in-use one strives toward keeping values within a desired range. It is among larger subsets of these that relations of consistency or inconsistency hold.

[2] Not all governing variables need behave this way. For some, perhaps, there may be no question of degrees of achievement. One either achieves them or does not; they are binary. Perhaps justice or truth-telling can be taken to be such variables. When two such variables in a given behavioral context interfere with one another, they exhibit internal inconsistency. Given the behavioral context, the injunctions to achieve these two values are in relation to one another very much like a logical contradiction.

means for achieving one variable without dropping the other variable out of its acceptable range.

3. The acceptable range of each variable may be broadened or narrowed so as to make the two variables more or less incompatible.

4. The assumptions in the theory-in-use may be altered so as to make the governing variables more or less incompatible. For example, the assumption "People cannot address the problem of self-government without becoming excited" may be absent from theory-in-use but may be valid in the situation; in this case, the agent would find that he cannot reach acceptable levels of both variables, but he would not understand why.

5. The protagonist may act on his world so as to make it take on characteristics that are either conducive or resistant to the internal consistency of his theory. His behavior may somehow affect people's sense of responsibility in a way that enables participation in self-government without disruption. Or, his behavior may have the opposite effect. Since this behavior is itself a reflection of other aspects of the theory-in-use, theories-in-use may tend to make themselves internally consistent or inconsistent. In the worst case, increasing one's efforts to achieve governing variables decreases one's chance of achieving them; in the best case, increasing one's efforts increases the chance of achieving them.

If two or more governing variables in a theory-in-use are internally inconsistent, then, for given settings or ranges, arrays of strategies, assumptions about the situation, constraining variables, and influences of action on the behavioral world there is no way of falling into the acceptable range for one value without falling out of the acceptable range for the other.

It is important to notice the relationship between internal consistency and constancy. Theory-in-use may be regarded as a program for action designed to keep the values of certain variables constant within acceptable ranges. It is analogous to a computer program for an industrial process that is designed to keep conditions such as temperature and pressure within acceptable limits. The program's internal consistency and the acceptable limits of the variables determine one another. The internal consistency of the theory-in-use conditions the ability of the theory-in-use to achieve the desired constancies; the nature of the desired constancies partly determines the internal consistency of the theory-in-use.

CONGRUENCE

Congruence means that one's espoused theory matches his theory-in-use—that is, that one's behavior fits his espoused theory of action. A second (and much-used) meaning of *congruence* is allowing inner feelings to be expressed in actions: when one feels happy, he acts happy.

These two meanings are complementary and show an integration of one's internal (what one who is aware of my feelings and beliefs would perceive) and external (what an outsider who is aware only of my behavior would perceive) state. Lack of congruence between espoused theory and theory-in-use may precipitate search for a modification of either theory since we tend to value both espoused theory (image of self) and congruence (integration of doing and believing).

The caricature of a politician shows him advocating what looks like an espoused theory for the benefit of others, feeling no uneasiness over that theory's incongruence with his theory-in-use. Such an individual probably does not believe in the theory he is advocating although he does have an espoused theory he believes; incongruence between the latter theory and his theory-in-use may very well cause uneasiness and trigger a change in theory.

The degree of congruence varies over time. One's ability to be himself (to be what he believes and feels) may depend on the kind of behavioral world he creates. A behavorial world of low self-deception, high availability of feelings, and low threat is conducive to congruence; a behavioral world of low self-esteem and high threat is conducive to self-deception and incongruence. If one helps create situations in which others can be congruent, his own congruence is supported.

There is no particular virtue in congruence, alone. An espoused theory that is congruent with an otherwise inadequate theory-in-use is less valuable than an adequate espoused theory that is incongruent with the inadequate theory-in-use, because then the incongruence can be discovered and provide a stimulus for change. However, given the importance of congruence to a positive sense of self, it is desirable to hold an espoused theory and theory-in-use that tend to become congruent over the long run.

EFFECTIVENESS

A theory-in-use is effective when action according to the theory tends to achieve its governing variables. Accordingly, effectiveness depends on: the governing variables held within the theory; the appropriateness of the strategies advanced by the theory; and the accuracy and adequacy of the assumptions of the theory. A strong criterion of effectiveness would require that governing variables stay in the acceptable range once they have been achieved. Some theories-in-use tend to make themselves less effective over time. For example, if an agent tends to become more effective in ways that reduce the effectiveness of others, he may increase the dependence of others on him and make it more and more difficult for himself to be effective. Long-run effectiveness requires achieving governing variables in a way that makes their future achievement increasingly likely. This may require behavior that increases the effectiveness of others.

Long-run effectiveness requires single and double-loop learning. We cannot be effective over the long run unless we can learn new ways of managing existing governing variables when conditions change. In addition, we cannot be effective unless we can learn new governing variables as they become important.

Note that long-run effectiveness does not necessarily mean that action becomes easier. One may respond to increased effectiveness by addressing himself to new governing variables for which he begins by being less effective; progress in effectiveness may be reflected in the sequence of governing variables one tries to achieve.

TESTABILITY

Theories of action are theories of control, like the theories involved in engineering, in clinical medicine, or in agricultural technology. They are testable if one can specify the situation, the desired result, and the action through which the result is to be achieved. Testing consists of evaluating whether the action yields its predicted results. If it does, the theory has been confirmed; if it does not, it has been disconfirmed. This tests the effectiveness of the theory.

Special problems regarding testability stem from two related characteristics of theories of action: theories of action are normative (they set norms of behavior) and they are theories of the artificial (they are about a behavioral world that they help to create). There are three basic problems.

1. How can one test theories that prescribe action? How can norms or values be tested?
2. Given that theories-in-use tend to make themselves true in that world, how can they be tested?
3. In a situation of action (particularly in a stressful situation), we are required to display the stance of action —that is, confidence, commitment, decisiveness. But in order to test a theory, one must be tentative, experimental, skeptical. How can we, in the same situations, manifest the stance of action and the experimental stance?

Simple prescriptions ("Don't go near the water!") are not testable because they do not predict results, but if . . . then . . . prescriptions ("If you want to avoid catching a cold, stay away from the water in winter!") are testable. Testing may not be straightforward because assumptions, often hidden, accompany such if . . . then . . . prescriptions. It is assumed here, for example, that you will not expose yourself to other risks of catching cold. Only if we make such assumptions explicit and control for them can we interpret the failure or success of the experiment.[3]

A more challenging problem has to do with the testing of norms of values themselves. Can we test governing variables such as "stay healthy"? In one sense, the answer to this question must be no, because governing variables are not if . . . then . . . propositions and make no predictions. But if one looks at the entire range of variables—the entire field of constancy involved in a theory-in-use—it is meaningful to ask whether, over time, these values will become more or less internally consistent, more or less congruent

with the governing variables of espoused theory, and more or less effectively realized. For example, a set of governing variables that includes "stay healthy," "disregard advice," and "seek out dangerous excitement" may turn out to become increasingly incompatible. In this sense, one may test the internal consistency, congruence, and achievability of governing variables. But one may do so only in the context of a theory-in-use in interaction with its behavorial world over time.

The second basic problem of testing theories of action is their self-fulfilling nature. Here are two examples. A teacher believes his students are stupid. He communicates his expectations so that the children behave stupidly. He may then "test" his theory that the children will give stupid answers to his questions by asking them questions and eliciting stupid answers. The longer he interacts with the children, the more his theory will be confirmed. A second example involves a manager who believes his subordinates are passive, dependent, and require authoritarian guidance. He punishes independence by expecting and rewarding dependence with the result that his subordinates do behave passively and dependently toward him. He may test his theory by posing challenges for them and eliciting dependent responses. In both cases, the assumptions turn out to be true; both theories-in-use are self-fulfilling prophecies because the protagonist cannot discover his assumptions to be mistaken or his theory as a whole to be ineffective. The so-called testing brings the behavioral world more nearly into line with the theory, confirming for all concerned the stupidity of the students and the dependence of the subordinates. We call such a theory *self-sealing*.

An outsider may find that the teacher's and the manager's theories-in-use are incompatible with the outsider's perception of the situation. But the outsider operates on a theory-in-use of his own

---

[3] In nonlaboratory situations, the concept of experiment is not rigorously applicable; it is not usually possible, for example, to institute strict controls. But a similar sense of experiment is applicable. . . .

that is different from that of the protagonist. The protagonist himself cannot discover that his theory-in-use is mistaken
unless he can envisage an alternative
theory and act on it.

The protagonist may find that over
the long run his theory becomes less consistent, less congruent, and less effective.
This will depend on the stability of conditions under which he operates, the other
values that make up his field of constancy, and other factors. As time goes on,
the protagonist is less able to get information from others (students or subordinates) that might disconfirm his theory-
in-use. Others become less willing to
confront, to display conflict, to reveal feelings. In this sense, the protagonist's self-
sealing theory becomes progressively less
testable over time.[4]

Consider those affected by the protagonist's theory-in-use. The students, for
example, may deceive their teacher about
their real feelings and beliefs and still remain open to others who reveal that the
teacher's assumptions are inaccurate; after
all, the students live in many behavioral
worlds, not only in the world of the
school. But perhaps the students have no
behavorial world free of these assumptions. If so, others could not discover real
feelings and beliefs different from those

[4] . . . [It can be argued that] the testability of theories-in-use is essential to their
effectiveness over the long run because effectiveness over the long run depends on double-
loop learning. There is no learning without
testability.

If there is no requirement for double-
loop learning, the argument falls. But we will
argue further that circumstances of progressive change—the loss of the stable state—
make testability and double-loop learning an
essential feature of theories-in-use. Otherwise,
the protagonist cannot discover ahead of time
the changes in conditions that will influence
his effectiveness; and, when such changes
have occurred, he will not be able to discover in a differentiated way the aspects of
his theory that have failed him.

that confirm the teacher's theory. Deception of others would have been converted
to self-deception. In the behavioral worlds
created by such theories-in-use, there
would be no way to discover that the
teacher's theory is self-sealing. For this,
outside events would have to cause the
theory-in-use to fail, or someone with a
different theory-in-use would have to expose the students to a different behavorial
world long enough to recover their awareness of feelings and beliefs different from
these expected by the teacher.

The interaction of theory-in-use and
behavorial world has a political as well
as an experimental dimension. The continued exercise and confirmation of a
theory-in-use can be seen as a political
process that proceeds from suppressing certain kinds of behavior and information to
creating conditions in which others repress both elements. The theory has then
made itself true and, by its own lights,
effective. Orwell in *1984* and Laing in
The Politics of Experience both describe
such political processes. There need be no
conscious construction of theory and
reality on the part of a powerful protagonist; one might say that the theory constructs its own reality.

The third basic problem of testing
theories of action concerns the stance we
should take toward our theories-in-use.
One must regard any theory as tentative,
subject to error, and likely to be disconfirmed; one must be suspicious of it. However, one's theory-in-use is his only basis
for action. To be effective, a person must
be able to act according to his theory-in-
use clearly and decisively, especially under
stress. One must treat his theory-in-use as
both a psychological certainty and an intellectual hypothesis.

The apparent paradox is heightened
in unstable situations of action where one
is overwhelmed by information and unable
to develop a grounded theory of what is
going on. Here, norms for behavior substitute for knowledge. One need not know

precisely what is going on because, independent of such knowledge, norms provide a basis for action.

An interventionist is a man struggling to make his model of man come true. In an unstable and uncertain world that nevertheless demands action, he puts a normative template on reality. All the more paradoxical, then, the demand that theories-in-use be treated as hypotheses.

Hainer (1968) described this existential stance as one of "affirmation without dogmatism." He considers the here and now to be both prior to and more fundamental than one's theory about it, treating theories as perspectives on reality that are also bases for action. Operationally, we are ready to discover that our theory is mistaken and to change it; yet we are reluctant to make such a change since change implies unsteadiness or flightiness that would themselves be a basis for failure. The commitment to focus on the here and now lets us encounter the unpredictable and lets us deal with the next piece of reality when we encounter it, modifying our theory-in-use as events require.

Our ability to take such a stance and to be conscious of taking it (as a part of an ethic for situations of uncertainty) is a model of such behavior for others, reducing their need for here-and-now certainty and allowing them to be freer to test their own theories without giving them up as a basis for action. Their doing so, in turn, further encourages us to do so.

VALUES FOR THE WORLD
CREATED BY THEORY

Because theories-in-use are mutually interdependent with their behavioral worlds, it is revelant to ask not only "Is your theory effective?" but also "How do you value the behavioral world created by the theory?"

One cannot and should not clearly separate the questions of knowledge applicable to the construction of the theory and the questions of value applicable to the construction of reality. For, as we have seen, these processes determine one another.

Should a protagonist's theory meet all of the criteria we have described, one can still ask, "How do I value the world he has created?" Even if the theory-in-use is effective for its own values, successfully repressive of all others to the point that testability has no meaning, one may still ask this question.

The manager in our earlier example may become more and more convinced that all of his subordinates are passive and that all initiative in the organization must come from him. But he may also come increasingly to dislike the behavorial world of his organization in which expanding demands on him are accompanied by expanding resentment and distrust.

In short, the criteria so far elaborated provide a basis for judging theories of action, but they do not substitute for the evaluation of the world created by the theory.

It is clear how an outsider, with an independent theory-in-use, could engage in such an evaluation. If the protagonist, himself, is to do so, however, he must begin to make a connection between his own theory-in-use and those features of his behavioral world he most dislikes; otherwise his negative evaluation will have no bearing on this theory. And other governing variables than those contained in his theory-in-use must be alive, or becoming alive, for him; his ability to ask such a question implies that he is able to envisage, even to some small extent, a behavorial world different from the one he has created.

BRIEF REVIEW

We have so far described a conceptual framework for considering theories of action, their structure and role, their status as tacit knowledge, their interaction with the behavorial worlds in which they function, and the criteria that apply to them.

Theories of action are theories that can be expressed as follows: In situation S, if you intend consequence C, do A, given assumptions $a_1 \ldots a_n$. Theories of action exist as espoused theories and as theories-in-use, which govern actual behavior. Theories-in-use tend to be tacit structures whose relation to action is like the relation of grammar-in-use to speech; they contain assumptions about self, others, and environment—these assumptions constitute a microcosm of science in everyday life.

Theories-in-use are vehicles for achieving and maintaining governing variables within acceptable ranges; the governing variables constitute the field of constancy in which deliberate behavior takes place. Building theories-in-use involves learning about managing variables and learning about changing variables. Theories-in-use are theories of the artificial; they help to create as well as describe the behavorial worlds to which they apply. Hence, theory-construction and reality-construction go together. The constancy of theories-in-use is considered as valuable as the constancy of the behavorial worlds created by those theories.

The concept of theory-building or theory-learning, particularly the kind of learning that requires change in governing variables, involves a paradox. The impetus toward constancy of theories-in-use and behavorial worlds impedes change in governing variables.

THEORY-BUILDING PROCESS AND DILEMMAS

How, then, do theory-building and learning occur? Some theory-building is a linear increase of building-blocks of experience;

new microtheories that extend the application of old governing variables probably develop in this way. However, the kind of theory-building that involves both change in the governing variables and double-loop learning tends to be convulsive, taking the form of infrequent, discontinuous eruptions that are initiated by dilemmas. This pattern of change probably derives from the nature of dilemmas and from the characteristic patterns of response to them,[5] which will be described next.

Dilemmas consist of conflicts of requirements that are considered central and therefore intolerable. The dilemmas that are important to the development of theories-in-use may be organized around several criteria that apply to the relationship between theories-in-use and the behavorial world.

Dilemmas of incongruity arise out of the progressively developing incongruity between espoused theory (on which self-esteem depends) and theory-in-use. For example, a politician who sees himself as believing in participatory democracy is disturbed by the manipulative, rough-shod tactics he uses in his career. Another agent's espoused values of warmth and sensitivity turn out to be incompatible

[5] The concept of dilemmas and their role in precipitating change in values is not a new one. For example, Rokeach (1968) offers the following view: "The greatest pay-off should come about by bringing into an inconsistent relation the most central elements of the system. . . . Attention is thus drawn especially to . . . an inconsistent relation between two or more terminal values . . . since these terminal values are the most centrally located structures; having many connections with other parts of the system, we would expect inconsistencies which implicate such values to be emotionally upsetting . . . to dissipate slowly, to be long-remembered, to . . . *lead to systematic changes in the rest of the value system*, to lead to systematic changes in connected attitudes, and finally, to culminate in behavior change" (pp. 21–22).

with the pain he finds himself inflicting on others.

In order for such conflicts to become dilemmas, the elements of espoused theory must be central to the protagonist's self-image, and events must emphasize the conflict between espoused theory and theory-in-use in ways that overcome normal attempts to avoid noticing the conflict. A potential dilemma may exist long before it surfaces.

Dilemmas of inconsistency arise when the governing variables of theory-in-use become increasingly incompatible. For example, one person finds it increasingly impossible, in the behavioral world he has helped to create, both to win and to contain the hostility of others when he wins. But the person values both the winning and the repression of hostility. Another person finds it increasingly impossible, in the world of the family he has helped to create, to do his duty regarding his children by punishing them and to maintain their respect. This person needs both to do his duty and to retain the respect of his children for doing his duty regarding them (derived from Laing, 1970).

Dilemmas of effectiveness arise when governing variables, in a theory-in-use/behavorial-world interaction, become less and less achievable over time, finally reaching the point at which they fall outside the acceptable range. For example, a person seeks to keep others calm and controlled by suppressing conflict; the hostility engendered by the suppression reaches an unavoidable boiling point so that no one is calm and controlled. Another person values a strategy of combat because it is familiar, because he knows how to use it, and because its use carries high status with it. But conditions change (others become aware of the strategy) so that the strategy becomes less and less effective.

Dilemmas of value arise when the protagonist comes increasingly—and, finally, intolerably—to dislike the behavorial world his theory-in-use has helped to create. For example, the protagonist values trust within his own group and also values the progress of the group. To achieve this progress, the protagonist is devious and manipulative toward outsiders. Group members, who act as though they expect people to be generally consistent in their behavior, progressively mistrust the protagonist, and the atmosphere within the group becomes progressively more manipulative and devious.

Dilemmas of testability arise when the protagonist, who values his ability to confirm or disconfirm his assumptions, finds that he is eventually completely cut off from the possibility of doing so by the behavioral world he has helped to create. For example, a manager finds that his subordinates and peers, conditioned by the mistrust they have come to feel for him and by the punishment they feel they have received when they "leveled" with him, no longer give him any valid information at all.

These kinds of dilemmas are not mutually exclusive; for example, a dilemma of effectiveness may also be a dilemma of testability, depending on the perspective taken. However, all dilemmas share certain characteristics: there is conflict between some element of the prevailing theory-in-use and some criterion applicable to the theory. The protagonist experiences this conflict as a central one—that is, the values he places on the elements of theory-in-use and the criterion are central rather than peripheral; in the cycle of interactions between theory-in-use and behavorial world, the conflict gets progressively worse.

The dilemmas may be created suddenly, as conditions shift in the behavorial world, or they may emerge gradually through the cycles of interaction. In either case, change in the governing variables of theory-in-use tends to be convulsive because of a characteristic pattern of response to dilemmas.

The responses to emerging dilemmas are not characteristically efforts to effect substantive change in governing variables. We value the constancy of our theories-in-use and our behavorial worlds. Hence, theories-in-use tend to be self-maintaining. We tend to adopt strategies to avoid perceiving that data do not fit, that behavorial reality is progressively diverging from one's theory of it, that one's theory is not testing out.

The repertoire of devices by which we try to protect our theories-in-use from dilemmas displays great imagination. Some of the more striking devices follow.

We try to compartmentalize—to keep our espoused theory in one place and our theory-in-use in another, never allowing them to meet. One goes on speaking in the language of one theory, acting in the language of another, and maintaining the illusion of congruence through systematic self-deception.

We become selectively inattentive to the data that point to dilemmas; we simply do not notice signs of hostility in others, for example.

The protagonist adopts a political method of suppressing the offensive data; for example, he succeeds in frightening others enough so that they will not reveal their mistrust of him.

The protagonist acts, sometimes violently, to remove the offending elements or himself from the situation. He either gets the trouble-maker fired or—his behavorial world having become unbearable—he moves to California. Or he may resolve to break off relations with his son.

The protagonist acts in subtle ways to make a self-sealing, self-fulfilling prophecy of his threatened theory-in-use—like the manager or teacher in our earlier ex-amples—by using his authority to elicit the desired behavior from others and to cause the rest to be suppressed.

The protagonist introduces change, but only into his espoused theory—leaving his theory-in-use unchanged.

The protagonist introduces marginal change into his theory-in-use, leaving the core untouched.

These devices and others like them, individually or in combination, tend to maintain theory-in-use in the face of the emerging dilemma. Therefore, even if the signs of the dilemma have appeared gradually, the eventual change in governing variables tends to be convulsive. By the time the conflict becomes intolerable, the protagonist tends to have exhausted his stock of defenses; he is well into an explosive situation.

All of these dilemmas are, in a fundamental sense, dilemmas of effectiveness. If the protagonist finds intolerable the inconsistency of his governing variables or his inability to confirm or disconfirm his assumptions, it is because inconsistency and lack of testability also mean inability to achieve minimum realization of governing variables. If incongruity is intolerable, it is because the protagonist finds that he cannot realize the central governing variables of the espoused theory on which his self-esteem depends. If there were no need for effectiveness, there would be no dilemmas.

Hence, the basic dilemma is one of effectiveness and constancy. The protagonist strives to be effective and to keep constant his theory-in-use and the behavorial world he has created. When, finally, he cannot do both in spite of his full repertoire of defenses, he may change the governing variables of his theory-in-use. This dialectic shapes the theory-building process. . . .

References

Hainer, R. "Rationalism, Pragmatism, Existentialism." In M. W. Shelly and E. Glatt (Eds.), *The Research Society*. New York: Gordon and Breach, 1968.

Laing, R. D. *Knots.* New York: Pantheon, 1970.

Rokeach, M. "A Theory of Organization and Change within Value-Attitude Systems." *Journal of Social Sciences,* 1968, *24* (1), 21–22.

4.3   THE PROCESS OF UTILIZATION OF SOCIAL RESEARCH TO IMPROVE SOCIAL PRACTICE

Ronald Lippitt

My observations in this paper are based on some brief, but varied experiences with problems of science utilization encountered at our Center for Research on the Utilization of Scientific Knowledge at the University of Michigan. Our staff teams of sociologists, psychologists, and others are involved with such social problems as delinquency, illegitimate pregnancy of teen-agers, the educational motivation of culturally deprived children, the lack of creative teaching practices, leisure-time programs for central-city girls, the pathology of communication between parents and teen-agers, and the mental health and productivity problems of work groups in government and industry. In each project a special effort is made to focus on the process by which scientific knowledge and personnel can help develop and validate significant improvements in educational and social practice.

PATTERNS AND RESEARCH UTILIZATION PROCESSES

I want especially in this paper to distinguish between three patterns of research utilization which bring into the "science

From Ronald Lippitt, "The Process of Utilization of Social Research To Improve Social Practice," *American Journal of Orthopsychiatry,* XXV, No. 4 (1965), 663–669. Copyright © 1965, the American Orthopsychiatric Association, Inc. Reproduced by permission.

consumer system" new knowledge and validated practice from outside, and three other patterns which develop scientific knowledge within the system and then utilize it as a basis for improvement of practice.

1. In the first pattern, the scientist consultant in collaboration with a practitioner or practice group identifies and defines a problem of practice. This definition is used in retrieving research knowledge helpful in deriving both action implications and the design for an improvement of practice or the invention of new practice.

For example, a recent one-day consultation conference focused on the problem of how the several million citizens of a metropolitan area could be involved in the development of plans for the metropolitan region. A team of professional and political leaders from the metropolitan area spent the first half of the day interviewing invited resource people. Some of the outside resources were familiar with research and theory in this field and three of the outsiders were leaders of similar projects in other metropolitan areas. With a pre-developed schedule of research retrieval probes the host team conducted a guided conversation with the visiting resource people. All this retrieved information was tape-recorded. During the second phase of the day's activities the local leadership took active initiative in attempting to formulate implications of this inquiry for the development of a program for their own metropolitan situation, and they began to project the elements of a design for action that drew from the implications both of previous research and previous practice innovations. The next steps of developmental work were also clarified and agreed on.

A second example started from the definition by elementary school personnel of their problem of "the in-betweeners." These were defined as primarily older elementary school acting-out boys who were too disruptive to be acceptable in the classroom or other educational facilities of the school, but too young and not seriously delinquent enough to be appropriately in the hands of the police and the court. A "knowledge retrieval" session of school people and scientists from child development, educational psychology, social psychology, and sociology identified a variety of relevant research findings and then focused on producing a series of statements about the possible implication of the findings for "things that should happen to the clients" in order for a significant process of resocialization and education to be achieved. These statements of implications from research findings were used as a springboard for a brainstorming session with the practitioners about program design that might deal with the problem. An action design for reeducation emerged which was quite different from anything which either the researchers or the practitioners had visualized originally. This design was later tested for feasibility in two schools, evaluated as successful, and subsequently diffused to other schools.

2. The second pattern for importing knowledge from outside the system entails conducting an extra-system feasibility test of a design procedure to meet some social practice issue. This test is conducted by the applied science team under controlled conditions, and, if the test proves successful, the newly developed model for improved social practice is demonstrated and recommended for adoption by the target system.

An example here concerns the development by our staff of the so-called cross-age socialization design. From our previous research we hypothesized that one of the major potentials in most educational and socialization situations was going unused, namely, the potential influence of older peers on younger peers. We decided to test experimentally the feasibility of training ten-, eleven-, and twelve-year-olds to function as educational aids and socialization agents with five-, six-, and seven-year-olds. The experimental settings were a camp and an elementary school where teams of scientists and social engineers controlled the experimental programs. Results indicated it was feasible to train the older peers to assume creative teaching functions. There was very significant response on the part of the young, and the older children showed great personal growth in their own attitudes and achievement because of their experience of responsibility in collaboration with adults and their learning from the training seminars. It was possible thereafter to present this evidence to a school system concerned about the problems of achievement and motivation in young pupils. The school system adopted our model on a tryout basis and later made several creative adaptations in the process of carrying out and evaluating the design.

3. The third pattern of importation is a very exciting one to me. This is the process of identifying creative innovations invented by practitioners someplace else and developing procedures for getting appropriate documentation about these social inventions so that their relevance to local needs can be considered and the essential features of the practice adopted or adapted. One of the great tragedies in American education and social practice is that a large proportion of the creative inventions which are in line with good re-

search and theory never become visible and are never appropriately transmitted from one setting and one practitioner to another. What dissemination does take place is of such low quality that successful high-quality adoption is usually impossible.

An example of a model for coping with this problem is illustrated in a current Center project with a state teachers association. All teachers in a selected school system now have an opportunity to fill out a "Teaching Practice Nomination Sheet" identifying their invention of a teaching practice to cope with a particular type of educational problem (for example, stimulating more motivation to learn) or the invention of a colleague. These nomination sheets go to a screening committee which reviews the conceptual and research relevance, the practical significance, and the potential adoptability of each practice. This experiment seeks to discover the kinds of practices that can be communicated by this written form, the kinds that require additional steps of observation, and the types that require more intensive training and consultation. Above all, we have developed a procedure for identifying, describing, and importing new models into the system which have been developed by practitioners in other communities, agencies, or organizations.

Let us turn now to three patterns of utilization of scientific resources which differ from the foregoing in emphasizing the *local* development of the resource knowledge to be utilized.

1. The first pattern has the organization or agency contract with the scientist team to collect diagnostic data relevant to some problem, analyze the data, and feed the data back for the sponsor's use. A brief example will illustrate this pattern:

The Center's action research team recently conducted an intensive city-wide study of a sample of delinquents and matched nondelinquents to assess factors related to the development and maintenance of delinquent behavior. They also conducted an interview study of key educational and socialization policy leaders concerning their conceptions of delinquency and its prevention. These data were analyzed by the scientist team and were reported back to the community leaders in a series of community seminars to which the key community leaders were invited. Staff members were available during these seminars to provide interpretation of the findings and to react to the generalizations and implications formulated by the community leaders.

2. The second pattern has the outside applied researchers supervise a self-study process within the sponsoring organization or community or agency, training local staff members to collect information and to participate in the processing of data, interpretation of findings, and the spelling out of implications for the development of change.

Our classroom teaching study is an illustration of this pattern of science utilization. Thirty teachers from seven school systems volunteered to work with us on a diagnostic self-study of their classroom education climate and the possible implications for changes in their teaching practice. During the spring the action-research team provided the teachers with questionnaires to inquire into their own attitudes and orientations, and with rating and questionnaire tools to use in eliciting information from their classroom group concerning orientation toward learning, toward the teacher, toward each other, and many other aspects of classroom dynamics. During the summer the teachers met regularly with the staff to help tabulate and analyze the data, to develop the concepts needed to work on interpretation, and to think through the implications of the findings for possible changes in their own teaching role in the fall. Consultation was provided in this thinking-through process, and in clarifying the plans for the use of new teaching procedures.

3. The third and final pattern of internal mobilization is quite different from the other two. It focuses on the idea that the practitioner needs training in learning how to be a consumer of scientific resources before he can be a utilizer of scientific knowledge.

a. One of our activities in this connection is focused on training teachers in the techniques of social science problem-solving and providing them with a tool kit of diagnostic tools and conceptual orientations to assist them in collecting appropriate information and using it to solve their problems of classroom management.

b. In another project we have developed a laboratory course in behavioral science for elementary-school children. The students have an opportunity to discover who the behavorial scientists are and how their resources can be used, as well as to learn to carry their own inquiry projects on various problems of human relations. (It seems clear that part of the current negative orientation toward scientific resources, in mental health, education, and social welfare, is because of a serious lack of any such education about the nature and the utility of social research and the social scientists.)

THE ROLES AND TRAINING OF THE SOCIAL RESEARCH UTILIZATION AGENT

From our studies we have come to conceive the research utilization function of our staff as requiring them to be *linking* agents at various points in the flow of research utilization. We have to develop new skills of retrieving and organizing research-based knowledge so that it links up to the needs of the social practitioner or client population. Helping the practitioner to clarify his resource needs is, of course, another aspect of this linking responsibility. And there is a necessary linkage function in helping the practitioner work through the implications of new knowledge.

As I have noted in several examples, still another function of the research utilization agent is to serve as inquiry consultant or trainer, assisting the client population in carrying through its own diagnostic research and working through the meaning of the findings for changes of practice. We must also find effective and appropriate ways of linking creative innovations to their colleagues to facilitate the spread and successful adaptation of new practice.

Our own experience with graduate seminars and practicums has revealed that there are significant numbers of students, both in the behavorial science departments and in the professional schools, who are eager to explore these new roles. These students seek new skills quite different from the research production skills typically taught in behavorial science departments and from the skills of operating practice taught in the professional schools. Certainly the training of research utilization agents requires a grounding *both* in behavorial science discipline and in professional values and technology. This obviously puts a new strain on the fairly segregated curriculum designs and training sequences which still exist in most of our graduate programs. The challenge is great—*and* surmountable.

4.4   AN EXPLORATORY STUDY OF KNOWLEDGE UTILIZATION[1]

Ronald G. Havelock, Kenneth D. Benne

A. THE NEED TO STUDY UTILIZATION

In contemporary America, "science" is fast becoming an "establishment" in the political and industrial life of our society.[2] We use this term non-invidiously to indicate a social institution which is accorded continuing support and secure status apart from shifting and changing political and industrial leadership. This newly won estate raises serious questions about the organization of scientific effort and about the social responsibilities of the scientific enterprise. The scientists demand autonomy in developing their basic research and their abstract theoretical structures. The scientific rhetoric used in claiming support from society is based on the claim that accumulation of scientific knowledge is good in itself or on the promise that social investment in basic science will repay society by augmented practical usefulness at some future time, but only in ways that cannot be defined in advance.

We are not concerned at this point to question the validity of the scientists' claim to support and status. The fact is that the scientific rhetoric has been generally "successful" with political and industrial leadership. Scientists have received a degree of political and administrative autonomy, along with financial support, which is without precedent among men of knowledge in American public life. Yet it seems clear to us that the establishment of science within our political and economic life has stemmed from a widespread faith among our political and industrial elites that the cultivation of science will lead to more powerful, more realistic, more effective public policies and modes of practice. The hope of those who maintain scientists in their position of heightened support and esteem is a new version of the old hope of Francis Bacon, Benjamin Franklin, and Thomas Jefferson that science will provide men with great new powers to meet human needs. Jefferson and Franklin believed that science would fulfill this hope primarily through dissipation of ignorance and superstition as scientific knowledge is learned by people generally. A contemporary view is that this hope can be fulfilled by the effective utilization of scientific knowledge and scientific methodology for the improvement of policy and practice in many particular social settings where specialized expertise strongly influences decisions taken—in medicine, industry, agriculture, education, and even politics. This historic shift in the human hope in-

Reproduced by special permission from *Concepts for Social Change*, Cooperative Project for Educational Development Series, Goodwin Watson, ed., pp. 47–70, Copyright 1966 National Training Laboratories.

[1] Credit for many of the ideas and insights contained herein should be given the members of a consultative seminar on knowledge utilization problems which was held at the University of Michigan between December, 1962 and May, 1963. Senior researchers at the Institute for Social Research on different occasions interviewed representatives from agriculture, economics, medicine, public health, and other fields. The resulting transcripts provided the raw material from which the authors developed the conceptual model which follows. The seminar and the subsequent analysis were supported by a grant from the Ford Foundation. Unless otherwise specified, quotations in this text are direct extracts from the transcripts of these seminar sessions. A much more extensive and detailed report on the seminar is to be published subsequently.

[2] See Don K. Price, *The Scientific Estate*, for a full development of this theme.

vested in scientific research deserves further explanation.

While utilization is a hope for some and even a firm expectation for others, it remains, for most of us, a poorly defined and poorly articulated concept. On the one hand, we are aware of an enormous and ever-increasing body of specialized scientific knowledge and, on the other hand, we have a vague vision of this knowledge being used by people to make better washing machines, safer automobiles, better schools, more healthful and productive organizations or happier community relations. Yet there is no clear picture of how we get from one end of the utilization chain to the other. We know, or at least we feel, that science has been and will be useful, but we do not know much about the transition from science to improved action and practice.

Many have previously concerned themselves with this problem, and here and there within our society we find highly developed and sophisticated systems of knowledge utilization. Systems such as those operating in the American Telephone and Telegraph Company and in the Agricultural Extension Service show evidence of many years of self-conscious effort to build and improve linkages between basic science and use. Such organizations are pathfinders and exemplars and are worthy of careful study. But they are not likely to answer all of the important questions about effective utilization. Many questions will remain. Can the same processes be introduced into other areas of action and practice where quality and quantity of information differ, where goals are specified, and where vastly differing organization patterns prevail? Can utilization in these exemplary systems be improved? Are the criteria and the long-range goals explicit and implicit in these systems adequate for general use?

Questions like these cannot be answered easily. And they cannot be answered in a vacuum. We need to make comparisons; comparisons not only with other fields and other instances, but also with ideal conceptual models of utilization processes as well. In short, a body of knowledge and theory about the processes of utilization is necessary before fully meaningful and accurate commentary can be made with respect to particular systems.

This paper will offer one general model of factors involved in knowledge utilization. This model is derived in part from an informal study of existing utilization systems. So in a rough sense it could be termed inductive or empirical. The intent, however, was to provide as *complete* a picture as possible of the *whole* problem, so that in much of our labors we were compelled to go far beyond the limited data available to us. As a result it should be viewed primarily as a theoretical offering. It is hoped that it will be of some use to researchers and practitioners in mapping out this complex and poorly understood domain.

There seem to be two ways to conceptualize utilization. One way is as a *system* and the other is as a *process*. A system model of utilization uses concepts such as "organization," "group," "person," "agent," "position," "role," "channel," and "link." A process model includes such concepts as "relationship," "linkage," "transfer," "exchange," "translation," "diffusion," and "communication." Some of the materials from the sessions seemed to fit most naturally into a system model, while other materials fell nicely into a process model. This fact helped us to realize that knowledge utilization cannot be properly understood without using *both* models. It was obvious, on the one hand, that utilization comes about through the conveyance of information along a complex series of pathways which connect groups and individuals fulfilling many different roles. These roles are associated roughly with such areas of activity as "basic research," "applied research and development," "practice" and "consumption" or "clienthood." Yet, in each interchange, each connection between one person or group and another, a *process* of communication (and influence) was going on, a process which could be understood and studied without regard to the specific groups or persons involved in the interchange. In other words, the interchange between a basic scientist and an applied scientist, or between a practitioner and a consumer or client, are both acts of communication and influence and they have many common properties which can be grouped together when utilization is viewed as a process.

B. UTILIZATION AS A SYSTEM: THE STRUCTURE OF UTILIZATION

A utilization system may be thought of as analogous to the human body. First of all, there is a chain or a network of relationships which has the function of carrying information and producing need-fulfilling behaviors. This information-carrying system, the counterpart of the human nervous system, we have designated "the flow structure" of utilization. The basic research "establishment" functions in this flow structure like the new brain (cerebrum), abstracting, generalizing, and ruminating, while at the other end the consumer functions like the old brain (thalamus, hypothalamus), needing, demanding, willing.

But the flow structure, like the nervous system, does not exist and cannot exist by itself. The nervous system is supported, supplied, built and rebuilt, protected, and to some extent controlled by other organs and subsystems within the total body system. In the same way the flow structure is supported and controlled by many groups and individuals in the greater society who are not primarily or necessarily information carriers. Such groups and individuals, and the subsystems

of which they are a part, we have designated collectively as the "administrative" structure of utilization. Although there are probably more, we have isolated five aspects of this administrative backup to utilization. These are (1) education, (2) financial support, (3) legal or administrative control, (4) protection, and (5) growth or change maintenance. In the next few pages we will present what seem to be the important features, first of the flow structure and then of the administrative structures of utilization.

1. Flow structure Two concepts are essential for the understanding of the flow structure of utilization. These are "barrier" and "unit of information." "Barriers" are the defining and identifying limits of any group or any individual and they are the *differences* between the frame of reference of the sender and the frame of reference of the receiver. "Units of information" refers to the substance of knowledge which is being transmitted, whether it be in the form of an idea, an observation, working model, finished manufactured product, advertising copy, or professional service. "Units of information" also refers to requests, questions, demands, payments, agreements, and OK and distress signals of every variety, these latter being units typically employed in "feedback" or "control."

A complete utilization chain is a need-fulfillment cycle in which a "consumer" expresses a need to a "resource person," who in turn finds the resources for satisfying the need and transmits these back to the "consumer" in a form in which the consumer can use them to satisfy the need.

Figure 1 might represent the relationship between a mother (practitioner) and her crying infant (consumer or client). The infant has a problem (let's say hunger) which can *not* be solved within its own system. Therefore, it must somehow or other convey awareness of this

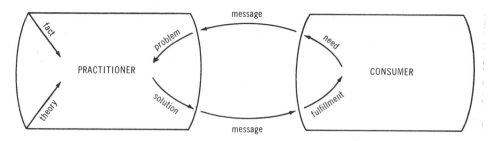

FIGURE 1   A Simple Utilization System

need to the mother, which it does by translating the need into a cry. This substitution of a noise for a felt need may be thought of as necessitated by the *barrier* between the infant's own body and the outside world. Once transmitted, however, the message must be heard and correctly interpreted by the mother, i.e., it must enter her system, thereby crossing a second barrier. The solution, once arrived at, must once again somehow leave her system and re-enter the system of the infant.

To complete any cycle, units of information must flow in both directions. Information which flows in the direction of the "consumer" may be termed "utilization flow." Information which flows in a direction away from the consumer may be termed "feedback."

When the practitioner is unable to fulfill the need by himself, he may have to rely on other more specialized resource persons for assistance. The cycle is thereby extended over three persons and it may be further extended to include any number of persons and/or groups. Typically, a chain member is identified by a specific role designation, which refers to his position relative to the consumer. Most immediately related to the consumer is the "practitioner," followed by "applied researcher" or "developer," and ending with the "basic researcher."

The significance of barriers to the understanding of utilization may be better understood as we progress to more complex utilization systems.

Barriers do not exist only between individuals. They also exist between groups of individuals, and it is perhaps a tautology or definitional statement that communication among members of a group is more easily attained than communication with others outside the group. If we return to the mother who hears the persistent cry, her first resource may likely be her husband. Even though the pediatrician is much more likely to help her solve her problem than is her husband, the latter is far more easily accessible. She can tell him when the first twinge of doubt about what she should do arises, without fear of rebuke for presenting him with trivia and without incurring a fee. Both of these factors represent barriers between the family and the outside group represented by the pediatrician. The fear of triviality may well be a barrier between herself and her husband, but it will be considerably less with members of her own family group, since the more formal barriers of fees, geographical distance, and restricted access are relatively absent within the family. The situation is presented diagrammatically in Figure 2.

A special advantage of the system approach to utilization lies in the great ease with which systems can be represented pictorially. The authors were able to build pictorial representations of the flow structure within each of the seven systems covered in the seminar sessions. These diagrams are especially helpful in highlighting organizational and psychological bar-

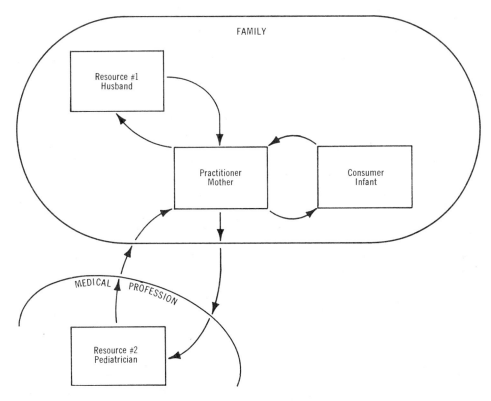

FIGURE 2   Group Membership Barriers. The above diagram illustrates the practitioner's resource access problem. The most qualified and appropriate resource may be relatively inaccessible because of group membership barriers.

riers and bonds at a gross level, and they are a most significant feature of the content analysis. It is to be hoped that with experience we will be able to refine our techniques of representation to include more features of a system and to show them with greater accuracy and clarity. Figure 3 is offered as an example of how a fully developed flow structure within a utilization system might look. As this diagram shows, the American Telephone and Telegraph Company contains within it a formal utilization scheme made up of several well-defined roles and subsystems.

The left hand side of this diagram, representing the academic community, is not actually tied into this utilization chain in any formal sense, but is shown here to suggest what the *orientation* of "basic" scientists employed by Bell Labs might be. Since these scientists are trained in universities, they thereby have status within various scientific disciplines, and membership in the learned societies.

In the total A.T.&T. scheme, division of labor has been carried out to a very high degree. As expected, at one end we have the basic research function, and at the other we have the practitioner function (the telephone companies) and the consumers of telephone service. But in between we have several separate phases of application. The "applied" and "development" research wings which exist within Bell Labs are concerned with general applications and the development of new devices, working models, etc. The phase which is concerned with development for actual production and distribution of the products which derive from research is carried on in a separate subsidiary of A.T.&T., Western Electric.

Utilization chains are beset by two principal kinds of difficulties, the impermeability of barriers and the overloading of resource persons. The extent of each tends to vary inversely with the extent of the other: the simplest chains which involve only a few resource persons and hence few barriers are continuously in danger of overloading, particularly where complex messages requiring many units of information are involved. Complex chains which contain many resource persons in separately defined roles tend to reduce the pressure on any one member, thereby reducing the danger of overloading. However, the addition of each new member means that the information must flow through additional barriers.

The problem of the proliferation of barriers is somewhat alleviated when the system makes effective use of the principle of *inclusion*. When division of labor occurs it is important to include the newly created roles within the pre-existing inclusive organization. It is especially important to maintain primary group ties which are so helpful in facilitating the free flow of information. The system depicted in the diagram just presented (Figure 3) utilizes this principle of inclusion to the maximum. Not only are all the major roles included in one company organization, but each suborganization includes a wide range of roles. Development and design engineers in Bell Labs have professional and functional ties with engineers employed by Western Electric, but organizationally they are tied to the basic researchers in Bell Labs. Likewise, by granting considerable autonomy and prestige to their basic researchers, Bell Labs attracts individuals who are respected members of the scientific establishment and who remain so. To facilitate permeability and at the same time to reduce overloading, some utilization chains contain one or more "linkage agents" whose roles are defined exclusively in terms of facilitating and controlling flow. For example, Bell Labs have introduced a special type of linkage agent whom they call the "systems engineer." The systems engineer must first and foremost have an overall "field view," a knowledge of the needs and resources of the entire organization and its relationships to the consumer. In addition, he must be conversant with the ongoing research efforts of Bell's basic scientists so that he can draw from these efforts information which can be utilized by the development branch of the organization. Actually, the systems engineer serves in several linkage capacities. He not only links basic research to development research, but he also links Bell Labs with other subdivisions of A.T.&T., and, most importantly, he provides a feedback link from each subdivision to every other subdivision.

Up to this point we have focused our discussion on those aspects of the flow structure which are formally laid down or institutionalized in a system of utilization. However, it has been universally observed by social scientists that there are certain informal channels which may carry a major traffic of communication within a system. These informal channels may serve to complement or buttress the formal structure, they may tend to undermine it, or they may render it utterly functionless by taking on all significant communicative tasks. An especially troublesome example of informal flow is what we have called the "by-pass." This occurs when certain consumers or practitioners, through their special knowledge of resources, are able to go directly to researchers for new knowledge useful to themselves, by-passing formally constituted linkage or application agents. For example, in agricultural exten-

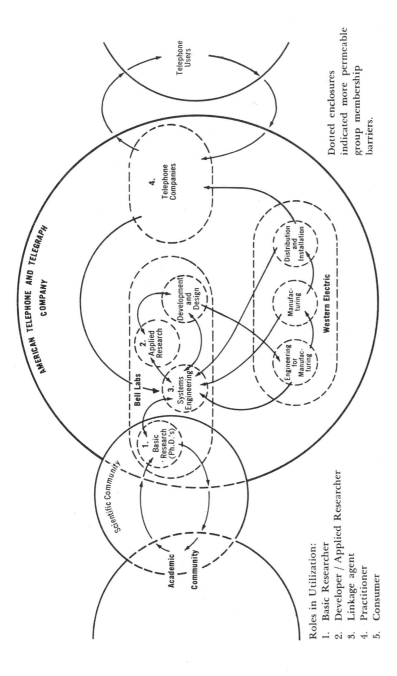

Roles in Utilization:
1. Basic Researcher
2. Developer / Applied Researcher
3. Linkage agent
4. Practitioner
5. Consumer

FIGURE 3 A Utilization System.[3] The above diagram outlines the knowledge utilization chain in a large corporation. Note especially the *linkage* role represented in this system by "systems engineering." Systems engineers are especially adept at deriving implications from basic research while leaving the basic researchers to pursue purely scientific interests without fear of company constraint.

[3] Constructed from information supplied by a participant in the utilization seminar and supplemented by material from J. A. Morton, "From Research to Technology," *International Science and Technology*, May, 1964.

sion it appears that the wealthiest and most knowledgeable farmers often by-pass the county extension agents and get new information directly from experiment stations and other scientific sources further up the chain.

Another reason for studying these informal channels is that they tend to be used to provide feedback where the formal system makes little provision for it. There is often a tendency to think of utilization as only a one-way process in which information flows from basic to applied levels and finally to the consumer, but the full utilization cycle requires information to flow also in the other direction. Thus, when the formal system ignores feedback, we may expect to find it occurring informally.

2. Administrative structures As mentioned previously, the administrative backup to utilization may be divided into five areas: (a) education, (b) financial support, (c) control, (d) protection, and (e) change. Let us look briefly at each of these in turn.

a. The educational structure provides for the replenishment of the professionals, the maintenance of standards, and, above all, the preparation of consumers for the use of knowledge. However, the educational system as a whole seems to lay greater emphasis on training for *basic* and for *practice* roles at the expense of the equally important roles of *development* and *consumption*. There has also been a tendency to concentrate on recruitment and training of *new members* at the expense of the equally important educational functions of continuing education and consumer information.

b. How financial support is administered may determine the fate of a utilization effort. The *amount* of money available for various projects may be a major factor in their success, but there are other aspects of support which may be of equal importance. *Reliable* and *stable* support makes possible long-range, well-planned projects. In addition, many sources of financial support have strings attached such as "for pure science only" or "for application only, not research" which tend to break up some of the vital linkages. However, the experience of certain creative funding agencies suggests that it is possible, through the careful and thoughtful allocation of financial support, to promote effective utilization of knowledge.

c. Utilization systems also need control structures. Successful utilization requires that goals be specified and that people coordinate their activities toward the fulfillment of these goals. Certain persons are therefore endowed with the powers to see to it that this is the case. An important question to be asked is, "Who should be so endowed?" Persons directly involved in some aspect of the *flow* structure of utilization ("on-line") were seen as being more conversant with the details of knowledge and practice in a given area; but such persons might be unable to take an objective view, a view which would reckon with every aspect of the process without any concern for self-interest or the special prejudices of one's own professional group. Other topics considered under control structure are the desirable degree of centralization, the aspects of behavior to be controlled, and the means of control.

d. A fourth administrative function which overlaps somewhat with both the educational and the control structures is the protection structure of utilization. What gate-keeping functions are necessary to keep one group from encroaching on another? What kind of licensing is necessary to protect the consumer from improper or premature utilization? What kind of patenting or copyrighting procedures are necessary to protect the creative researcher from exploitation? When we answer all these questions, we will have built up a coherent picture of what the protection structure of utilization systems is and might be.

e. Somewhat tentatively, we have proposed that there is a fifth administrative function which is served by what might be called a "change" or "growth" structure. Preparing for new developments, expected or unexpected, is an administrative function which is only recently beginning to receive major recognition. Within any utilization system provisions should be made to ensure adaptability to new knowledge and new circumstances, and to keep abreast of the changing needs of the consumer. It seems probable that utilization systems have to be open systems, flexible enough to gear themselves to changes in knowledge and in the technology of knowledge utilization and communication. The mechanisms which are employed in some fields and organizations to ensure this kind of flexibility—including training and development programs—can properly be called the "change structure" of these fields and organizations.

With the discussion of these five administrative structures, we round out our presentation of utilization as a system. To recapitulate, the system analysis of utilization was broken down into two parts which were called the flow structure and the administrative structure. Basic elements considered under flow structure were "barriers" and "units of information." Using these elements it is possible to construct diagrams which more or less faithfully depict the formal flow of information from basic science to the consumer. Such diagrams are helpful in diagnosing various problems in a system such as inadequate linkage, too many or too few barriers, overloading, and inadequacy of feedback or two-way flow. There are many activities necessary for the maintenance of a utilization system which do not fall properly within the flow structure itself, because they do not primarily involve information-carrying. These have been designated the administrative structures of utilization, and five have been identified: education, support, control, protection, and change.

C. UTILIZATION AS A PROCESS

The systems approach gives us a good overview of utilization. It shows us the number and variety of roles and subsystems involved in a utilization chain, and it gives some idea of how utilization fits into the structure of the society as a whole. But the system approach becomes more cumbersome when we want to get a more detailed picture of what is going on at each of the exchange points or "linkages" in the flow structure. A utilization chain involves countless communicative acts, exchanges of information, contacts between persons and between groups. To study each of these linkages as a discrete phenomenon occurring at one and only one point in the system would be excessively redundant and more confusing than enlightening. All these separate linkages have many features in common, and they may all be considered as separate instances of one overall *process.*

What kind of process is this process of utilization? We think of it as a unique process which shares many aspects of processes of communication and economic exchange without being precisely either of these. It is like *communication* in that a message of some sort is transmitted from a source to a receiver, but the message may not contain information in the usual sense. What is transmitted may be a service or a product or it may be a payment or a word of thanks. Moreover, the relationship of the sender to the receiver is likely to be of a special sort. If the sender is nearer the "basic" end of the utilization chain, he may be more likely to deal with information abstractly and theoretically, and he may share to some degree the common prejudices and value orientations of the scientific "establishment." If the receiver is nearer the "applied" end of the chain, he may only be tuned to receive information which is practical, concrete, and of clear relevance to consumer need. He may also share the common prejudices and values of any one of the many practitioner "establishments." The problem of utilization is not simply to get a given piece of information across from a sender to a receiver, but to change it, transform it, so that it can be recognized and accepted as something of value in a system which views information differently.

Utilization is like *economic exchange,* on the other hand, in that the cash value or need fulfilling value of the message is always of primary relevance. One of the shortcomings of the traditional communication model is the inadequate emphasis it places on the motivational context of any exchange process. People don't just send messages automatically. They do so because they want to or because they feel they have to, and the same applies to the receiving of messages. When we think of utilization as a process, this becomes especially clear. Utilization means gaining information and ordering it so that it can be put to *use* to fill needs. Of course, the exchange may not be economic in the narrow sense, as we can see from the example of the mother and her infant, but the sender must be paid off in some way, whether this payoff be in the form of cessation of any annoying cry, an expression of gratitude, a sum of money, or merely some sign that the message has been received accurately, with respect, and with good intent.

It seemed, then, that in analyzing the utilization process, we had to give major emphasis to this motivational aspect. Other features of the process could be broken down in two major categories. The first of these we have called "interpersonal and group membership issues"; these deal essentially with the permeability problem, the problem of how individuals with different normative orientations can trust one another enough to share their knowledge. The second we have called "technical issues"; these deal with the content of the message itself, the manner in which it is prepared and transmitted, and the medium through which it is transmitted. There are, then, three features to the process of utilization: first, the motivational; second, the interpersonal; and third, the technical. Let us briefly consider some of the categories under each.

1. Motivational aspects   When we discuss motivation, we should distinguish between motives which are based directly on consumer or client need and those which are not. Naturally, motivation comes from the consumer first and foremost. His needs are the *raison d'être* of utilization. Yet it would be too much to expect that every role on the utilization chain is filled by someone who has the consumer's need always in mind. In fact, people fill these roles for a variety of reasons, all related to their own needs.

With respect to consumer needs, there are two questions of special interest: first, how needs come into being; and second, how needs get communicated. With regard to the first, we feel it would not be profitable to present a catalogue of all human needs which can be satisfied by knowledge utilization. But we do feel that some appreciation should be extended to the range, flexibility, complexity and variability of such needs. In view of these facts, it would seem undesirable to assess prematurely the "use-value" of a given piece of knowledge as "good" or "bad." The assumption that *all* knowledge has various potential *use values* is supported by what we know about human motivation.

With regard to the communication of human needs, the seminar sessions brought to light some fascinating and paradoxical findings. One might have thought that the effective communication of a need bears a direct relation to its urgency, but there seems to be no obvious formula for determining *psychological urgency*. Mortal needs, for example, are not always viewed by the public as most pressing:

Sometimes there is more concern with disfigurements than there is with fatal things. In the public health area, for example, work on polio, which has a relatively low fatality rate, received tremendous support. This is a crippling disease, and people are afraid of being crippled.[4]

Another example:

How did we learn about fluoridation? We learned about this because there was a disfiguring coloring of the teeth which resulted from excess fluoride in water, and the time between the first adequate clinical description of this disease and the discovery of its cause—not cure, but prevention—was exactly sixteen years. This is an extraordinarily rapid development in the history of medicine.

Perhaps this all boils down to the fact that some needs are more visible than others, literally and figuratively. However, what is visible may not be most important for either the short-run or long-run welfare of the individual. This is a real problem in utilization. Some of the consumer's most desperate needs, like the need to overcome loneliness or the need to express feelings, have such a low visibility that chains of utilization do not readily work their way towards them.

Sometimes, urgency itself becomes a problem. Seminar participants discussed at least three circumstances in which the pressing nature of the need prevented effective utilization. First, there is the "too hot

to handle" situation, where anxiety inhibits appropriate action. Another is the impulse to say "don't stand there, *do something*" when the most rational course is hands-off. And lastly, the tendency to use applied researchers to "put out fires," i.e. to find ad hoc solutions without regard to long-range needs or wide-range uses.

Among the second group of motives, those not based on consumer needs, the most salient are a) ego involvement, b) the need to know, and c) the need to tell. We have a general impression that there is a cacophony of motives involved in the utilization process, some good, some bad, some helping utilization, some hurting. Many of the motives that lead to good utilization have no direct relevance to it. They are means to *other* ends, and utilization fruits are an incidental byproduct. This could be said of the need to know and the need to tell, and there are others: financial gain, status seeking, possibly even the need to control others. In each case, we might ask ourselves, "Does our end (good utilization) justify this means?"

Beyond these considerations is another. How are all these motives fitted together in the economy of the individual consumer or client to produce a good utilizer? The best way to answer this question and to conclude our motivation section is to quote an excerpt from one of the interviews.

I agree with what you've said, with the suggestion that you sort of look both to security and unrest. And it's the combination of security and unrest that makes for change, creative change. It's not revolution, but it results in some kind of improved condition.

A combination of security and unrest and uneasiness.

Confidence—security means a sense of confidence?

That's right, you have to be confident that you can be insecure.

The best college course I ever had was

---

[4] The quotations used in this paper were taken from the interviews with the informants representing the various fields previously mentioned.

called 'Planning for the Unplanned Program,' and the main topic of the course was creating divine discontent, which is discontent with security.

2. Interpersonal and group membership issues The process of communication is a matter of language, transmission, and having something to say, but this is only part of it. Communication is also contact and nonverbal exchange between persons and between groups. To be heard, a message must be received without suspicion. The sender must be trusted and believed. The receiver must be interested and receptive. There must be a rapport, a feeling of commonness of purpose or of spirit, or, at the very least, an implicit contract that what is said will be listened to.

In order to get a message through to another party, it is necessary to penetrate one or more interpersonal or intergroup barriers. There are innumerable individual and group differences which divide us from one another. Some of these differences are potential seeds of conflict, and can create noise and blockage in the communications between people.

We begin our outline of interpersonal and group membership issues by presenting a theoretical analysis of the concept of "permeability," reasoning that all barriers have common features regardless of their specific content. For example, all barriers may be characterized as having a greater or lesser degree of rigidity, durability, interconnectedness, and visibility; and the overall permeability of barriers is some function of these various properties. Among factors which seem to *cause* boundaries to be more or less permeable, we found references to age and education levels, geographical separation, cohesiveness (psychological distance), and perceived external threat (self-preservation).

Discussion in the seminar sessions focused more concretely on the various kinds of boundary conditions that create problems for utilization. Among these, *status differences* and *value differences* were by far the most frequently mentioned.

The comments dealing with status problems were divided into three categories: first, factors making for low status; second, factors making for high status; and third, observations on how status can be used as a vehicle of utilization. Factors making for low status included being young, being old, having too little education, imitating the practices of others, being associated with an applied discipline, and being associated with a young discipline. Factors making for high status included having a doctor's degree, belonging to an older profession, bypassing the practitioner, living in an "ivory tower," and being a specialist. Status barriers can be overcome or turned to the advantage of utilization in certain ways. There are certain persons in a group who have been identified by social scientists as opinion leaders, individuals whose ideas and practices are followed by other group members primarily because they hold high status. When dissemination efforts are aimed primarily at these opinion leaders, they have a greater chance of acceptance by the group as a whole. Interestingly enough, however, extremely low status persons may also be useful lead-ins to a target group because such persons present very little threat to high status professionals. . . .

Whether they are caused by values, by status discrepancies, or by other aspects of group identity, the differences between groups create special problems for persons who attempt to serve as linkage agents. Some of the key functions in utilization are served by persons who are in intermediate positions between one professional ingroup and another. Unfortunately, persons who occupy such positions are beset by many woes peculiar to this "in between" status. In short, they are "marginal" men. They exist on the periphery of one discipline because of their connections with another.

Yet these are the men who pass on information, who get it applied, who create the linkage. Therefore, it is of the utmost importance for us to understand their problems, and ultimately we must come up with solutions to their problems of marginality which will not only allow these people to carry on in security and esteem, but which will also attract ever-increasing numbers to take on similar roles in our society.

There are a number of ways in which linkage roles can be secured so that marginality does not undermine the persons who occupy them. It is of the utmost importance that linkage persons have a secure institutional base. Most efficient and desirable from the point of view of rapid and effective utilization would be the securing of a firm base for linkage persons in both basic and practice fields. This can only be achieved if genuine dual membership is possible and if the linking person is able to deal constructively with problems of dual membership. Another solution to the marginality problem might be the establishment, perhaps in a university, of a separate base such as an institute for research application. However, such a separate institutional base could not be an island unto itself. It would need to be organizationally tied to and overlap with basic research and practice fields. A third possibility discussed in the seminar would be the achievement of linkage through the periodic rotation of certain members from basic to applied research settings or from practice to research settings.

Viewing interpersonal and group membership issues as a whole, we can see certain broad themes appearing. Effective linkage requires that the giver and receiver both have a sense of *security* or *trust in themselves*. Beyond that, and building on that, they must have a sense of *trust in each other*. These conditions can be brought about when there is full recognition of the importance of *self-esteem, self-identity maintenance, group-identity maintenance, and group esteem*.

3. Technical issues The task of communication is not completed when interpersonal problems are solved. Even when there is an atmosphere of acceptance and mutual understanding, the message must be composed, transcribed, translated, transmitted, received, and checked back for errors. Although these operations may become entangled in *interpersonal* or *intersystem* "noise," they should also be considered separately from interpersonal issues as additional ways in which problems in the utilization chain may arise. We are now concerned, then, with the mechanics of the flow of information, or the *technical* issues of utilization.

The technical aspect of the utilization process has two phases. The first phase is the *preparation* of the message, including the gathering of information, coding in suitable discourse, screening, and possibly labelling or titling. The second phase is the *transmission* of the message, the process of actually getting the message to the receiver.

Preparation of a message involves four steps. The first of these is assembly, bringing together the relevant facts which are to become the "content" of the message. The effectiveness of this step will depend in part on the extent to which the sender's field is a rationalized and systematized body of knowledge. Thorough cataloguing and indexing in a field makes the task of assembly much easier.

The second step in the preparation of the message is recoding the information so that it is understandable and acceptable to the receiver. This may involve organizing it in the receiver's categories, using the receiver's special language, summarizing and simplifying, and possibly incorporating a latent or explicit value message which would make the information more acceptable to the receiver's value orientation.

The third step is screening. The message should be reviewed and re-evaluated with respect to a number of criteria including safety, reliability, validity, error, relevancy and redundancy.

Finally, when the utilization message has been assembled, recoded, and screened, it should be carefully packaged and labelled. The all-important first impression of a message is given by its title, or its label, or the container in which it comes. The receiver should have a reasonably accurate expectation of the contents of the message and more especially the value the message may have for him.

Transmission of the message involves another set of considerations somewhat different from those involved in preparation. The most serious problems encountered in transmission have been discussed previously under the headings of lag, overload, feedback, and static. These difficulties vary, to a great extent, with the properties of the medium which is chosen as the vehicle of transmission. Writing is the primary carrier of information in a complex technological culture and it has the advantages of accuracy and volume transmission with a minimum of static. On the other hand, it is often slow, tends to be overloaded, and is ineffective for feedback. The mass media of television, radio, and lectures to large audiences have advantages over writing in that they provide speed in presentation and distribution, but, like writing, they provide poor feedback channels and are highly prone to static. Face-to-face transmission within small groups of people provides the best feedback opportunity, but may be inefficient for mass dissemination. An ideal vehicle for transmission of new knowledge of a complex nature would appear to be comprehensive in-residence learning sessions. Most important and most effective of all is to provide the receiver the opportunity to *experience* the new information, either through observing a demonstration or by trying it out himself.

Under "technical issues" we should also consider certain broad strategic questions when information is transmitted. Among these are: What is the most effective way to approach a known barrier? What is the most effective way to present evidence or "proof" of the validity of findings? How can we best insure that new knowledge, once absorbed and tested, will be retained and kept in use? And finally, how can we instill in the receiver the desire to pass on his newly acquired knowledge to others who are similarly in need? . . .

4.5 EDUCATIONAL FIELD EXPERIENCE AS THE NEGOTIATION OF DIFFERENT COGNITIVE WORLDS

Kenneth D. Benne

In the decade just past, the boundaries

This article is part of a longer report which grew out of a research into educational field experiences, conducted at Boston University under a National Institute of Education grant (DHEW-NIE-3-1756, Robert Chin, principal investigator) on Learning to Utilize Knowledge and Experience.

between schools, colleges and universities and nonscholastic institutions in their environments have become more permeable. One evidence of this change is the growing educational use of student field experiences as a supplement, adjunct or sometimes as a coequal partner to academic instruction. Field experiences have, of course, been an established part of many programs of vocational and professional education for a generation and more in medicine, nursing, social work, engineering, preaching, teaching, and various vocational trades. But, in the past decade, field experiences have found their way into programs of general education and liberal arts as well. Attempts to incorporate nonacademic experiences for students into academically sponsored courses and programs of instruction have been perhaps most frequent in departments centered in behaviorial studies of human beings and human systems—psychology, sociology, political science, and anthropology. At any rate, it is these uses of field experiences with which this paper is concerned.

Students engaging in a combination of academic instruction with field experiences may be seen as *living out* a process of knowledge utilization. They are maintaining simultaneous memberships in a scholastic institution, professedly devoted to the production and/or dissemination of "basic" knowledge, and a practice institution or action setting in which knowledge and know-how are used in performing a social function or in meliorating a human condition. The student is placed in the position of a linking or bridging agent in two distinct social systems within the knowledge utilization chain.[1] The quality of learnings achieved by the student will depend upon how adequately he or she understands and manages this dual membership, upon how well he or she integrates the discrepant and sometimes conflicting demands of the two social settings upon his or her thought, conduct, and expenditure of energies.

Field experiences for students in preprofessional and vocational education have frequently been marked by conflicts be-

tween academic and field supervisors. For academic supervisors, students are in the field to augment, widen, and deepen their learning of professional knowledge and skills. For field supervisors, learnings by students are subordinated to maintenance of quality service to clients (patients for student nurses, occupational therapists, and physical therapists in hospitals, pupils for student teachers in schools, congregants for student preachers in churches, etc.). The student is at a point of conflict between priority objectives in the two institutions in which he or she is involved in his or her field experience. For example, the academic supervisor wants greater responsibility in working with pupils for the student teacher than the field supervisor can willingly permit, in light of the hazards to pupil learning and to the public relations of the school which might result from the "mistakes" of a student teacher, even though the "mistakes" might furnish excellent opportunities for professional learning. Or, if the field supervisor guides the student teacher into "safe," routine tasks in the school, the academic supervisor may feel that the student teacher is being exploited by being required to work for the school with little or no possibility of learning from such work.

Such conflicts do occur in preprofessional field experiences where academic and field supervisors belong to the same profession and where both institutions have a stake in "good" education for prospective professional members. The possibility of conflict, and the actuality too, are greater where students are undertaking field experience in order "better" to learn psychology, sociology, anthropology, or political science. For here the common professional bond between academic and field supervisors, and the student too, is missing. And the discrepancy between the norms of the two social systems, e.g., a university department of sociology and an urban police department, concerning ap-

---

[1] See 4.4 above, Havelock and Benne, "An Exploratory Study of Knowledge Utilization."

propriate thoughtways and behaviorways for their "members" is much wider.[2]

It is common, within academic circles, to attribute conflicts which students encounter in field experiences to differences between the norms and attitudes which operate in practice and field settings and the norms and attitudes characteristic of the academic setting, with resultant conflicting expectations as to how the student should invest his or her time and energy in work and learning. The fact that conflicts do occur for students in preprofessional and vocational field experiences, as noted above, indicates that such an explanation of the conflicts is partially true. For here, academic and field supervisors, and students too, hold a generally common view of the knowledges and skills which aspirants to professional status should acquire. The conflicts can be explained in some large part by *noncognitive* factors operating within and between the academic and nonacademic social systems involved.

But, in field experiences utilized for

purposes of general education of students in the behavorial sciences, we have noted another important dimension in the conflicts. This conflict focuses in the cognitive area itself. The student confronts different notions concerning the nature of knowledge and the ways in which knowledge claims are to be tested and validated. The conflicts which students encounter are grounded in *epistemological as well as normative and attitudinal* differences in the social systems which students are expected to bridge and link.

It is often difficult for persons in academic settings to accept the notion that people in practice and action settings possess and use "knowledge" in informing their choices and decisions and in guiding and evaluating their actions unless that "knowledge" is akin in form and organization to the "knowledge" which they build and test and communicate in their academic enterprises. And it is difficult for actionists and practitioners in field settings, especially when they have been schooled in academic ways of "knowing" and academic definitions of "ideal knowledge" to defend and affirm their practical "knowledge" as an alternative, in some respects at least, to the "knowledge" professed by academics.

A short detour into the history of epistemology, the science of knowing, may help to illuminate this difficulty. Traditionally, epistemology has been studied and taught as a part of philosophy. The goal of epistemological studies has been seen as normative or prescriptive, in the sense that the goal of true knowing is to see or to comprehend a universal reality which somehow underlies or transcends everyday experience. "Knowledge" has been distinguished from the "opinions," "beliefs," and "notions" by which those engaged in practice and action make sense, individual or common sense, of their often chaotic worlds and by which they guide and justify their decisions and actions.

The normative models for "real

---

[2] I realize that educational field experiences may be undertaken by students and their academic advisors with various learning objectives in mind. In fact, the staff of the research project, out of which this report came, was able to identify ten different models of field experience in current use. The different models emphasize various "product" and "process" learning objectives for students engaged in field experiences: Product models—Socialization model, Pre-professional model, Service model, Change agent model; Process models—Actualization model, Dialogic model, Inquiry model, Embedded model, Multiple membership model, Responsibility model. I am concerned here with two aspects common to all these models. First, field experience involves students in a process of "knowledge utilization." Second, field experiences place students in a linking relationship to social systems with discrepant norms concerning knowledge—its nature, its uses, and its validation.

knowledge" have been drawn from the processes and products of the efforts of persons who specialize in "knowing." These are scholars and basic researchers who are abstracted socially from the pushes and pulls of practical affairs and who are supported by one set of sponsors or another in pursuing their central purpose of adding to and refining the cultural stockpile of disinterested "knowledge." Western epistemologists, working for the most part, in modern times, in universities, have not drawn their models of valid "knowing" from the methods and products of thinking of men and women of action who guide, direct, and conceptualize the practical "makings" and "doings" of culture and society.[3]

[3] This is not to say that Western civilization has been devoid of "sages" or "technologists" among their men of knowledge, to use Znaniecki's distinction (F. Znaniecki, *The Social Role of the Man of Knowledge* [New York: Columbia University Press, 1940]). Plato might be taken as an archetype of the first and Leonardo da Vinci of the second. In brief, "technologists" cultivate knowledge of how to fit and organize means and energies effectively and efficiently into processes of achieving ends without focal or responsible concern for the validity or "rightness" of the ends served. "Sages" are concerned with the "rightness" or "wrongness" of ends to be served through collective action and only secondarily with the "truth" or "error" of the evidences and arguments which they use to justify the "rightness" of the ends they recommend or the "right" ways to achieve those ends. The role of "scholar" or "basic researcher" has been defined in the West as different from the roles either of "sage" or "technologist." The "scholar" or "basic researcher" seeks, tests, and refines disinterested "knowledge" of the ends and means of human cultures without developing or recommending more powerful and refined means to be employed or without attempting to justify "right" ends and means and to condemn "wrong" ones. It is the "scholar" or "basic researcher" who has furnished grist to the mill of the West-

The failure of Western epistemologists convincingly to demonstrate or exemplify their ideal of *absolutely* valid knowledge has evoked various criticisms of their ideal over the centuries. One notable recent example of such criticism is the work of John Dewey and other American pragmatists.[4] They sought to refocus epistemological studies in several ways which are relevant to our present discussion. They shifted their definition of "knowledge" from the products to the processes and methods of knowing, in their attack on "knowledge" as an unconditioned vision or comprehension of "reality." The subject matter of epistemological studies becomes the processes by which human knowers confront the confused and problematic in experience and seek to restore clarity and direction to experience. Inquiry, problem-solving, hypothesizing, verification became the focal concern of epistemologists. While the study of knowing processes in basic research and scholarly disciplines was not neglected by the pragmatists, Dewey and others included within the scope of epistemology "knowing" as it operates in practical judgments—planning, deciding, valuing. Dewey sought to formulate a generalized method of coming to know, which, while differentiating processes of knowing in various research disciplines and in "basic" and "applied" researches, sought to identify formal elements of a generalized

ern epistemologists in their search for canons and criteria of valid knowledge. It has been noted and argued that *traditional Chinese* epistemology drew its canons and criteria of valid knowledge from the functioning of the "sage" rather than the Western model of "basic" scholar or researcher. See, e.g., I. A. Richards, *Mencius on the Mind* (New York: Harcourt, Brace, 1932).

[4] Out of a wide range of possible examples, John Dewey, *How We Think* (Boston: Heath, 1933), may be taken as typifying this shift in emphasis.

method of inquiry common to all these ways of knowing.

Dewey's approach to learning and knowing has not been accepted universally either in academia or in nonacademic settings, but it has been influential in both. It has helped to release and empower *empirical* studies of knowing processes by both psychologists and sociologists. The idea of knowledge as an unconditioned vision of a universal "reality" has been widely abandoned by scholars and basic researchers themselves, not alone due to Dewey's and others' criticisms of the idea but also to comparative studies of ways of knowing in various human cultures with various views of "reality." Psychologists have emphasized both organic and environmental *conditions* which affect the development of cognitive organization and functioning in and by persons.[5] And sociologists have explored the relations between social organization, social movements, and social change and various forms and functions of knowledge.[6]

We may summarize the historical

[5] See, for example, Jean Piaget, *Psychology and Epistemology: Toward a Theory of Knowledge* (New York: Viking, 1971).

[6] See, for example, Karl Mannheim, *Ideology and Utopia* (New York: Harcourt, Brace, 1936), and F. Znaniecki, op. cit.

shift I have been describing in the focus of epistemological studies in the table below.

This brings us back to our exploration of the epistemological differences in field and in academic settings from which we departed in our brief historical detour. Two things should now be clear. First, the prevailing contemporary viewpoint in epistemological studies lends credibility to the search for differences in established ways of knowing in academic settings and in established processes of knowing in practice and action settings. Second, the history of epistemology suggests why, where the traditional assumption that academic ways of knowing are inherently closer to "reality" than other ways has not been surrendered or lost, learning situations involving encounters between academic men and women and men and women of action and practice are frequently defined hierarchically, with proponents of the "academic" definition of "knowledge" in the superior position.

Without specifying some of the typical differences in epistemological orientation between members of academic organizations and members of action and practice organizations, which I will attempt to do later, a few general principles concerning the conditions of optimum learning by students in field experiences may now be stated. The student should

From Emphasis On:	To Emphasis On:
Products of cognitive behavior	Processes of cognitive behavior
Retrospective reference to accumulated knowledge	Prospective reference to needed knowledge
Some *one* favored *ultimate* context of knowledge production and verification—the role of scientist, scholar, technologist, seer or sage.	Acceptance of *plural proximate* contexts in which knowledge claims are initiated, formulated, and variously tested.
Devotion to a criterion of certainty and verbal defensibility	Various criteria—usefulness, fruitfulness, illumination (insight), consensus of some validating community.
Sharp separation between processes of knowledge building and verification and processes of knowledge application and utilization.	Blurring of distinctions between knowledge building and knowledge application—between the "pure" and the "applied."

be oriented to think of his acquisition of "knowledge" through field experience as a two-way not a one-way flow. He or she should not expect merely to find concrete examples in the field to illustrate and clarify the "knowledge" he or she has acquired through instruction in academia —be it in psychology, sociology, anthropology, or political science. Nor will the student be able to report, summarize, and evaluate his or her cognitive learnings from field experiences fully or adequately in terms and concepts congenial to the academic disciplines. Rather the student should be oriented to explore two cognitive worlds and to clarify the differences and overlaps between these two worlds. The student is oriented to *utilize* the "knowledge" he or she finds and acquires in the field to confront relevant academic "knowledge" and to understand the strengths and limitations of both. This is in addition to the more familiar *utilization* of academic "knowledge" to illuminate processes of practice and action in the field.

Of course, students will not be fully empowered to engage in such fruitful inquiries, unless their supervisors, academic and nonacademic, share this conception of knowledge utilization as a two-way flow and support students in taking advantage of their opportunity for epistemological inquiry. In fact, a good way to facilitate such sharing and support is through seminars in which students, academic supervisors, and field supervisors participate. Such seminars may not only facilitate learning by students but build mutual understandings and appreciations by academic and nonacademic people of their different yet overlapping cognitive worlds as well. In such seminars, *noncognitive* blocks to communication will need to be faced and worked through—stereotypes one of another, status differentials between the two kinds of people and knowledges involved, and fears of exposure of inadequacy and incompetence. But the assur-

ance that there is "knowledge" to be gained by all parties to the exchange gives point and substance to the explorations.

Now let me suggest some of the typical differences which have been discovered to date in the form and organization of knowledge between academic persons and persons in practice and action settings. I hesitate to do this because a typology may be used by students and by academic and nonacademic supervisors to "stereotype" persons in the two worlds and to foreclose the *fresh* inquiries which need to be made by students and supervisors in each field and academic setting that is being used educationally. It is the inquiry which reveals the *actual* cognitive worlds that are involved and the actual learnings that may be derived from creative negotiation of these worlds. I trust that a partial typology (pp. 170–171) may guide and open up processes of inquiry and learning rather than foreclose or eliminate them.

I have, of course, emphasized differences between "scientists" and "practitioners" in my typology. My construct is of two "ideal types." Actual persons in academia or in field settings may and do incorporate complex mixtures and integrations of both types in their actual behavior and communication. In fact, the educational goal of field experiences, as I have analyzed these, is for students to attain consciousness and appreciation of the two forms of knowing and to integrate these into their cognitive repertoires. Students should be able to act appropriately, in one mode of knowing or the other, as their role and situation require it. And, as already suggested, academic and nonacademic supervisors should acquire the same understandings and flexibility of response.

Collaboration between academic persons and practitioners and action leaders is possible and often desirable. But effective collaboration requires recognition and affirmation of epistemological differences on both sides of the social di-

The Cognitive Worlds of Behavioral Scientists	The Cognitive Worlds of Social Practitioners and Action Leaders
1. People and human systems which they study are not of interest as particular cases but as instances to confirm or disconfirm generalizations about people and human systems. Knowledge is organized around verbally (and/or mathematically) articulated generalizations.	1. People and human systems are clients or constituents. The social practitioner and action leader are concerned with particular cases, situations and practical difficulties in order to help, improve or change these. Knowledge is organized around kinds of cases, situations, and difficulties and takes the form of effective ways of diagnosing and handling them.
2. The occasion for inquiry is some gap or discrepancy in a theory or conceptual scheme. "Success" in inqury is measured by attainment of more warrantable statements of variable relationships which fill the gap and/or obviate the discrepancy.	2. The occasion for inquiry is some difficulty in practice, some discrepancy between intended results and the observed-consequences of actions or excessive psychic and/or financial costs of established ways of working. "Success" in inquiry is measured by attainment of ways of making and/or doing which are more effective in fitting means to ends and/or in reducing costs of operation.
3. Scientists try in the course of their researches to reduce or to eliminate the influence of extraneous values (values other than "truth" value) from the processes of collecting data and determining and stating the meaning of the data within the research context. Their knowledge is relatively independent of the uses to which it may be put.	3. Practitioners and action leaders try to find and interpret data which enable them to serve the values which they are committed to serve—"productivity," "health," "learning (growth)" and, in more political contexts, the "power," "freedom," and "welfare" of their "clients" or "constituents." Their knowledge is consciously related to use for some purpose or set of purposes.
4. Scientists set up their researches to reduce the number of variables at work in the situations they study, by controlling the effect of other variables. Experimental results take the form of statements about the relationships of abstracted and quantified variables.	4. Practitioners and action leaders (like historians and anthropologists) work in field settings where multiple and interacting variables are at work. Their understanding of situations tends to be holistic and qualitative, though they may of course use quantitative methods in arriving at their "estimate of the situation." Unlike historians and anthropologists, they do not *attend* to all the variables involved in the *full* understanding of a situation but rather to variables which are thought to be influential and accessible to their manipulation in handling the situation in the service of their chosen values.
5. Time, in the form of pressing decisions, does not influence their judgments and choices so directly as it does those of practitioners. They can reserve judgment, waiting for the accumulating weight of evidence. A longer time perspective operates	5. Time presses the practitioner to decide and act—judgments cannot wait. He or she must judge in order to meet deadlines, whether the evidential basis for judgment is "complete" or not. They must depend on their own hunches and insights in at-

The Cognitive Worlds of Behavioral Scientists (Continued)	The Cognitive Worlds of Social Practitioners and Action Leaders (Continued)
in their judgments of what needs to be done now and later. Their statements of what they know are more qualified, less impregnated with their own hunches and insights as to what incomplete evidence means for purposes of action.	tributing meaning to incomplete or contradictory evidence. Their knowledge is impregnated with their own hunches and values. It is more personal, more dependent on their own ability to read a situation than the more impersonal knowledge which the scientist professes and communicates.

vide, not denial of differences on the ground that we are both persons of good will or polarization of differences into an impassable gulf between "theoretical" persons and "practical" persons.

My typology, in its emphasis on differences, is thus not formulated in the interest of thwarting but rather of furthering collaboration. It does suggest some of the kinds of differences which students in field experiences might explore in actual situations. It is such actual differences which students can use in negotiating discrepant cognitive worlds and in learning experientially and academically about the utilization of behavorial knowledge.

4.6   PEDAGOGY OF THE OPPRESSED

Paulo Freire

I shall start by reaffirming that men, as beings of the *praxis*, differ from animals, which are beings of pure activity. Animals do not consider the world; they are immersed in it. In contrast, men emerge from the world, objectify it, and in so doing can understand it and transform it with their labor.

Animals, which do not labor, live in a setting which they cannot transcend. Hence, each animal species lives in the context appropriate to it, and these contexts, while open to men, cannot communicate among themselves.

From *Pedagogy of the Oppressed* by Paulo Freire. © 1970 by Paulo Freire. Used by permission of The Seabury Press, Inc. British Commonwealth editions published by Sheed & Ward Ltd., London (cased edition) and Penguin Books Ltd. (paperback edition).

But men's activity consists of action and reflection: it is praxis; it is transformation of the world. And as praxis, it requires theory to illuminate it. Men's activity is theory and practice; it is reflection and action. . . .

Lenin's famous statement: "Without a revolutionary theory there can be no revolutionary movement[1] means that a revolution is achieved with neither verbalism nor activism, but rather with praxis, that is, with *reflection* and *action* directed at the structures to be transformed. The revolutionary effort to transform these structures radically cannot designate its leaders as its *thinkers* and the oppressed as mere *doers*.

[1]Vladimir Lenin, "What Is To Be Done," in *Essential Works of Lenin*, Henry M. Christman, ed. (New York, 1966), p. 69.

If true commitment to the people, involving the transformation of the reality by which they are oppressed, requires a theory of transforming action, this theory cannot fail to assign the people a fundamental role in the transformation process. The leaders cannot treat the oppressed as mere activists to be denied the opportunity of reflection and allowed merely the illusion of acting, whereas in fact they would continue to be manipulated—and in this case by the presumed foes of manipulation.

The leaders do bear the responsibility for co-ordination—and, at times, direction—but leaders who deny praxis to the oppressed thereby invalidate their own praxis. By imposing their word on others, they falsify that word and establish a contradiction between their methods and their objectives. If they are truly committed to liberation, their action and reflection cannot proceed without the action and reflection of others.

Revolutionary praxis must stand opposed to the praxis of the dominant elites, for they are by nature antithetical. Revolutionary praxis cannot tolerate an absurd dichotomy in which the praxis of the people is merely that of following the leaders decisions—a dichotomy reflecting the prescriptive methods of the dominant elites. Revolutionary praxis is a unity, and the leaders cannot treat the oppressed as their possession.

Manipulation, sloganizing, "depositing," regimentation, and prescription cannot be components of revolutionary praxis, precisely because they are components of the praxis of domination. In order to dominate, the dominator has no choice but to deny true praxis to the people, deny them the right to say their own word and think their own thoughts. He cannot act dialogically; for him to do so would mean either that he had relinquished his power to dominate and joined the cause of the oppressed, or that he had lost that power through miscalculation.

Obversely, revolutionary leaders who do not act dialogically in their relations with the people either have retained characteristics of the dominator and are not truly revolutionary; or they are totally misguided in their conception of their role, and, prisoners of their own sectarianism, are equally non-revolutionary. They may even reach power. But the validity of any revolution resulting from anti-dialogical action is thoroughly doubtful.

It is absolutely essential that the oppressed participate in the revolutionary process with an increasingly critical awareness of their role as Subjects of the transformation. If they are drawn into the process as ambiguous beings, partly themselves and partly the oppressors housed within them—and if they come to power still embodying that ambiguity imposed on them by the situation of oppression—it is my contention that they will merely *imagine* they have reached power.[2] Their existential duality may even facilitate the rise of a sectarian climate leading to the installation of bureaucracies which undermine the revolution. If the oppressed do not become aware of this ambiguity during the course of the revolutionary process, they may participate in that process with a spirit more revanchist than revolutionary.[3] They may aspire to revolution as a means of domination, rather than as a road to liberation.

[2] This danger further requires the revolutionary leaders to resist imitating the procedures of the oppressors, who "enter" the oppressed and are "housed" by the latter. The revolutionaries, in their praxis with the oppressed, cannot try to "reside" in the latter. On the contrary, when they try (with the oppressed) to "throw out" the oppressors, they do this in order to live *with* the oppressed—not to live within them.

[3] Although the oppressed, who have always been subject to a regime of exploitation, may understandably impart a revanchist dimension to the revolutionary struggle, the revolution must not exhaust its forces in this dimension.

If revolutionary leaders who incarnate a genuine humanism have difficulties and problems, the difficulties and problems will be far greater for a group of leaders who try (even with the best of intentions) to carry out the revolution *for* the people. To attempt this is equivalent to carrying out a revolution *without* the people, because the people are drawn into the process by the same methods and procedures used to oppress them.

Dialogue with the people is radically necessary to every authentic revolution. This is what makes it a revolution, as distinguished from a military *coup.* One does not expect dialogue from a *coup*— only deceit (in order to achieve "legitimacy") or force (in order to repress). Sooner or later, a true revolution must initiate a courageous dialogue with the people. Its very legitimacy lies in that dialogue.[4] It cannot fear the people, their expression, their effective participation in power. It must be accountable to them, must speak frankly to them of its achievements, its mistakes, its miscalculations, and its difficulties.

The earlier dialogue begins, the more truly revolutionary will the movement be. This dialogue which is radically necessary to revolution corresponds to another radical need: that of men as beings who cannot be truly human apart from communication, for they are essentially communicative creatures. To impede communication is to reduce men to the status of "things"—and this is a job for oppressors, not for revolutionaries.

Let me emphasize that my defense of the praxis implies no dichotomy by which this praxis could be divided into a prior

stage of reflection and a subsequent stage of action. Action and reflection occur simultaneously. A critical analysis of reality may, however, reveal that a particular form of action is impossible or inappropriate *at the present time.* Those who through reflection perceive the infeasibility or inappropriateness of one or another form of action (which should accordingly be postponed or substituted) cannot thereby be accused of inaction. Critical reflection is also action.

I previously stated that in education the attempt of the teacher-student to understand a cognizable object is not exhausted in that object, because his act extends to other students-teachers in such a way that the cognizable object mediates their capacity for understanding. The same is true of revolutionary action. That is, the oppressed and the leaders are equally the Subjects of revolutionary action, and reality serves as the medium for the transforming action of both groups. In this theory of action one cannot *speak of an actor,* nor simply of *actors,* but rather of *actors in intercommunication. . . .*

Scientific revolutionary humanism cannot, in the name of revolution, treat the oppressed as objects to be analyzed and (based on that analysis) presented with prescriptions for behavior. To do this would be to fall into one of the myths of the oppressor ideology: the *absolutizing of ignorance.* This myth implies the existence of someone who decrees the ignorance of someone else. The one who is doing the decreeing defines himself and the class to which he belongs as those who know or were born to know; he thereby defines others as alien entities. The words of his own class come to be the "true" words, which he imposes or attempts to impose on the others: the oppressed, whose words have been stolen from them. Those who steal the words of others develop a deep doubt in the abilities of the others and consider them incompetent. Each time they say their word without

4 "While we might obtain some benefit from doubt," said Fidel Castro to the Cuban people as he confirmed the death of Guevara, "*lies, fear* of the truth, complicity with false illusions and complicity with lies have never been weapons of the revolution." Quoted in *Gramma.* October 17, 1967. Emphasis added.

hearing the word of those whom they have forbidden to speak, they grow more accustomed to power and acquire a taste for guiding, ordering, and commanding. They can no longer live without having someone to give orders to. Under these circumstances, dialogue is impossible.

Scientific and humanist revolutionary leaders, on the other hand, cannot believe in the myth of the ignorance of the people. They do not have the right to doubt for a single moment that it is only a myth. They cannot believe that they, and only they, know anything—for this means to doubt the people. Although they may legitimately recognize themselves as having, due to their revolutionary consciousness, a level of revolutionary knowledge different from the level of empirical knowledge held by the people, they cannot impose themselves and their knowledge on the people. They cannot sloganize the people, but must enter into dialogue with them, so that the people's empirical knowledge of reality, nourished by the leaders' critical knowledge, gradually becomes transformed into knowledge of the *causes* of reality.

Emerging Perspectives on Planned Organizational Change

CHAPTER FIVE

Over the past five years or so, planned organizational change has undergone some profound, and altogether salutary changes. At least there are signs here and there; certainly at the mythic "leading edge" where the seminal minds can be found, planned organizational change has taken on a new maturity. If not found yet at Erik Erikson's eighth stage of development, it is certainly beyond the adolescent's acne and pubescent antics.

There is an emerging, new perspective regarding planned organizational change, one which casts some doubt on a number of assumptions more or less characteristic of somewhat older versions. For example, most previous writing:

1) Took organizations as a single class: instrumental, large-scale, science-based, international bureaucracies, operating under conditions of rapid growth. Service industries and public bureaucracies, as well as nonsalaried employees, were generally excluded, like the "underclass" they really were.

2) Paid practically no attention to the social ecology of interinstitutional relationships or to the boundary transactions of the organization. It was as if organizations were positioned in an environmental void, not unlike what Emery and Trist would call a "placid, random environment."

3) The *management* of conflict was emphasized, whereas the *strategy* of conflict was ignored.

4) Underplayed power of all types, while the role of the leader as facilitator—"linking pin"—using an "agricultural model" of nurturance and climate building was stressed.

5) Implied a theory of change based on gentle nudges of growth coupled with a "truth-love" strategy; that is, with sufficient trust and collaboration with valid data, organizations would "get it together," progress monotonically (and even monotonously) toward some vaguely defined vivid utopia where openness, risk-taking, self-actualization, and democratic values would triumph.

It is neither necessary nor possible to recapture what happened to us, individually and to organizations, since the last edition of this volume. It would take a Homer or Herodotus—or, better, a first-rate folk-rock composer —to sort out the tumult and tragedy of the past several years. The bitter agony of Viet Nam, the convulsive stirrings now, not only of black Americans, but gays, handicapped, aged, ethnics, veterans, women, and—yes, men. Our world has become more complicated, more interdependent, actually bypassing McCluhan's "Global Village," creating a "Global City" so that we can all see, for sure—but find it hard to comprehend—just what's going on. So we view the Black Panthers in America and the White Panthers in Jerusalem, the sprawling multinational behemoths, the not-so-subtle interaction between the Yom Kippur War, the OPEC oil squeeze, a realignment of the 77 nonaligned, so-called "Third World" nations with the promise of more transnational "producer blocs." All we know for sure is that our oil bills are higher, that our dollar brings in less, much less than two years ago, and that the problems we live with seem beyond our comprehension, beyond our national boundaries, and, worse, beyond our national control.

Nowadays, John Cage said not long ago, everything seems to happen at once and our souls are conveniently electronic or omniattentive. And it seems very difficult to solve our organizational problems because they infect, reflect the malaises of the greater society, and before you know it, our institutional lives. Very much like the way Machiavelli analyzed bad, unwise political judgments or any bad, fatal decision. He likened this to diseases. Those diseases, like TB for example, that are extremely easy to cure during the onset and first stages but almost impossible to diagnose then, are in their later stages all too easy to diagnose, but almost impossible to cure.

This is the consequence of living in an age that appears through a flickering TV screen that goes in and out of focus as it is expressed through the new, less familiar media, the strikes, injunctions, overnight shortages, disruptions, bombings, kidnappings, and other demonstrations which befuddle and often numb our responses or lead us into a messy metaphysical pathos.

In his *Report to Greco,* Nikos Kazantzakis tells us of an ancient Chinese imprecation: "I curse you; may you live in an important age." So be it. Our organizations are damned, encumbered, buffeted, and burdened by some new forces and some badly understood old forces making Planned Organization Change more challenging and perplexing than we thought it to be. Or want it to be.

What we discern about the nature of society says something about the deficiencies of some contemporary approaches to planned organizational change. In general, these have tended to be primarily oriented to the internal dynamics of organization, aimed at contributing to the established (and increasingly questioned) ethics and goals of economic and organizational growth (rather than quality), and relatively unconcerned with affected constituencies (within) and pivotal constituencies external to the organization.

Yet, what we detect is that there are increasing pressures in the political-cultural-economic environment of our institutions which call for new forms of planned change, new, still undiscovered strategies that will generate more responsiveness to external forces and interest groups. And to complicate matters even more, the internal governance, tasks, and divisions of labor will have to be confronted in ways that we are only beginning to understand. New strategies of power and politics have changed the rules of the game. The signs of this challenge are now inherent in the revolution of values discussed by such authors as Philip Slater (see Chapter Nine for further elaboration), Charles Reich, Saul Alinsky, Martin Luther King, and others.

The message in this for those of us involved in the field of planned organizational change is that our paradigms of planned change (or organizational development) desperately need to be broadened to account for the needs, aspirations, anger, and concern of outside interest groups and internal pressure groups and caucuses and to incorporate models of change which are more innovative and far-reaching in their definitions of who governs the organization. We seem to be living through a period when two dilemmas that confront almost every human institution have to be answered: First, how do we establish new forms of power when "nobody seems to be in charge"? And, secondly, how do we get everybody in the act and still get some action? We have also to better understand the only basic questions, according to Tolstoy, that interest human beings: How to live? What to live for?

Without such an effort, which we believe is based upon a realistic image of the forces of change now present in the environment, the contemporary organization will no doubt be forced to change anyway—but in ways it will find odious and even more intolerable—like Machiavelli's last phase of disease, painfully easy to diagnose, impossible to cure.

The articles included in this chapter do take into account many of the societal forces, and if we think about them as a conceptual collage, they tend to represent a new stage of organizational development. Implied in the Herrick et al. article (5.3) is a big question: whether the concerns for human warmth and love can be met without satisfying the old-fashioned concerns of meaningful work, recognition, mastery, and prestige.

Terreberry's article (5.1) takes as its focus of convenience the turbulent, dynamic, and most importantly, the causal texture of the environment and how that creates new problems and a growing uncertainty about our deepest human concerns, our work, quality of life, neighborhoods, child rearing, life styles, and law and order.

"Who Sank the Yellow Submarine?" (5.4) by Bennis suggests what happens to an organization (in this case, a university) when external forces—

unforeseen and powerful—impinge on a major, somewhat haphazard change program.

The authors represented in this chapter seem less chary of getting into questions of power, politics, and dissensus. They seem to understand—more than our so-called liberal politicians—what George Wallace understands and exploits: that there is an interesting (and potentially dangerous) shift away from an emphasis on race and ethnicity to economic *class*.

Taken as a whole, the articles examine (and sometimes career away from) threats to the legitimacy of authority, the growing tension between populist and elitist solutions, baffling forces which undermine the conditions under which democracy flourishes—fear.

These papers, in all fairness, are not fully evolved. On occasion their grasp exceeds their reach. And yet we like them, erratic and unfinished as they are. Perhaps we like them more because they are unfinished. One exception is the Crowfoot-Chesler article; they attempt—and partly realize—a systematic analysis of an emerging perspective.

For surely, they accurately reflect Jefferson's notion of the "American way," America, always, as "an unfinished revolution." And one that is unlikely ever to cease unless those forces that manage to intervene and mysteriously disarm our collective intelligence fail to be better understood.

5.1   THE EVOLUTION OF ORGANIZATIONAL ENVIRONMENTS

S. Terreberry

Darwin published *The Origin of Species by Means of Natural Selection* in 1859. Modern genetics has vastly altered our understanding of the variance upon which natural selection operates. But there has been no conceptual breakthrough in understanding *environmental* evolution which, alone, shapes the direction of change. Even today most theorists of change still focus on *internal* interdependencies of systems—biological, psychological or social—although the external environments of these systems are changing more rapidly than ever before.

INTRODUCTION

Von Bertalanffy (1956) was the first to reveal fully the importance of a system being open or closed to the environment in distinguishing living from inanimate systems. Although von Bertalanffy's formulation makes it possible to deal with a system's exchange processes in a new perspective, it does not deal at all with those processes in the environment *itself* that are among the determining conditions of exchange.*

Originally published in *Administrative Science Quarterly*, March 1968, Vol. 12, No. 4, pp. 590–613. Copyright © 1968 by Administrative Science Quarterly.

References and footnotes in edited portions of this paper have been deleted.

* [Editors' Note: Chin's paper, selection 3.2 in Chapter Three of this volume, proposes conceptual models for the textures of the environments of systems and discusses the utility of such models for practitioners of planned change.]

Emery and Trist (1965) have argued the need for one additional concept, 'the causal texture of the environment'. Writing in the context of formal organizations, they offer the following general proposition:

That a comprehensive understanding of organizational behavior requires some knowledge of each member of the following set, where L indicates some potentially lawful connection, and the suffix 1 refers to the organization and the suffix 2 to the environment:

$$L_{11} \quad L_{12}$$
$$L_{21} \quad L_{22}$$

L_{11} here refers to processes within the organization—the area of internal interdependencies; L_{12} *and* L_{21} to exchanges between the organization and its environment—the area of transactional interdependencies, from either direction; and L_{22} to processes through which parts of the environment become related to each other—i.e. its causal texture—the area of interdependencies that belong within the environment itself (p. 22).

We have reproduced the above paragraph in its entirety because, in the balance of this paper, we will use Emery and Trist's symbols (i.e., L_{11}, L_{21}, L_{12} *and* L_{22}) to denote intra-system, input, output, and extra-system interdependencies, respectively. Our purpose in doing so is to avoid the misleading connotations of conventional terminology.

PURPOSE

The theses here are: (a) that contemporary changes in organizational environments are such as to increase the ratio of externally induced change to internally induced change; and (b) that *other* formal organizations are, increasingly, the important components in the environment of any focal organization. Furthermore, the evolution of environments is accompanied —among viable systems—by an increase in the system's ability to learn and to perform according to changing contingencies in its environment. An integrative framework is outlined for the concurrent analysis of an organization, its transactions with environmental units, and interdependencies among those units. Lastly, two hypotheses are presented, one about organizational *change* and the other about organizational *adaptability;* and some problems in any empirical test of these hypotheses are discussed.[1]

CONCEPTS OF ORGANIZATIONAL ENVIRONMENTS

In Emery and Trist's terms, L_{22} relations, i.e. interdependencies within the environment itself, comprise the 'causal texture' of the field. This causal texture of the environment is treated as a quasi-independent domain, since the environment cannot be conceptualized except with respect to some focal organization. The components of the environment are identified in terms of that system's actual and *potential* transactual interdependencies, both input (L_{21}) and output (L_{12}).

Emery and Trist postulate four 'ideal types' of environment, which can be ordered according to the degree of *system connectedness* that exists among the components of the environment (L_{22}). The first of these is a 'placid, randomized' environment: goods and bads are relatively unchanging in themselves and are randomly distributed, e.g. the environments

[1] I am particularly grateful to Kenneth Boulding for inspiration and to Eugene Litwak, Rosemary Sarri and Robert Vinter for helpful criticisms. A Special Research Fellowship from the National Institutes of Health has supported my doctoral studies and, therefore, has made possible the development of this paper.

of an amoeba, a human foetus, a nomadic tribe. The second is a 'placid, clustered' environment: goods and bads are relatively unchanging in themselves but clustered, e.g. the environments of plants that are subjected to the cycle of seasons, of human infants, of extractive industries. The third ideal type is 'disturbed-reactive' environment and constitutes a significant qualitative change over simpler types of environments: an environment characterized by similar systems in the field. The extinction of dinosaurs can be traced to the emergence of more complex environments on the biological level. Human beings, beyond infancy, live in disturbed-reactive environments in relation to one another. The theory of oligopoly in economics is a theory of this type of environment.[2]

These three types of environment have been identified and described in the literature of biology, economics and mathematics.[3] 'The fourth type, however, is new, at least to us, and is the one that for some time we have been endeavouring to identify' (Emery and Trist, 1965, p. 24). This fourth ideal type of environment is called a 'turbulent field'. Dynamic processes 'arise from the *field itself*' and not merely from the interactions of components; the actions of component organizations and linked sets of them 'are both persistent and strong enough to induce

autochthonous processes in the environment' (p. 26).

An alternate description of a turbulent field is that the accelerating rate and complexity of interactive effects exceeds the component systems' capacities for prediction and, hence, control of the compounding consequences of their actions.

Turbulence is characterized by complexity as well as rapidity of change in causal interconnections in the environment. Emery and Trist illustrate the transition from a disturbed-reactive to a turbulent-field environment for a company that had maintained a steady 65 per cent of the market for its main product—a canned vegetable—over many years. At the end of the Second World War, the firm made an enormous investment in a new automated factory that was set up exclusively for the traditional product and technology. At the same time post-war controls on steel strip and tin were removed, so that cheaper cans were available; surplus crops were more cheaply obtained by importers; diversity increased in available products, including substitutes for the staple; the quick-freeze technology was developed; home buyers became more affluent; supermarkets emerged and placed bulk orders with small firms for retail under supermarket names. These changes in technology, international trade, and affluence of buyers gradually interacted (L_{22}) and ultimately had a pronounced effect on the company: its market dwindled rapidly. 'The changed texture of the environment was not recognized by an able but traditional management until it was too late' (Emery and Trist, 1965, p. 24)....

The first question to consider is whether there is evidence that the environments of formal organizations are evolving toward turbulent-field conditions.

[2] The concepts of ideal types of environment, and one of the examples in this paragraph, are from Emery and Trist (1965, pp. 24–6).

[3] The following illustrations are taken from Emery and Trist (1965). For random-placid environment see Simon (1957, p. 137); Ashby (1960, sec. 15/4; the mathematical concept of random field; and the economic concept of classical market).

For random-clustered environment see Tolman and Brunswick (1935); Ashby (1960, sec. 15/8; and the economic concept of imperfect competition).

For disturbed-reactive environment see Ashby (1960, sec. 7; the concept of 'imbrication' from Chein (1943); and the concept of oligopoly).

EVIDENCE FOR TURBULENCE

Ohlin (1958, p. 63) argues that the sheer rapidity of social change today requires greater organizational adaptability. Hood (1962, p. 73) points to the increasing complexity, as well as the accelerating rate of change, in organizational environments. In business circles there is growing conviction that the future is unpredictable. Drucker (1964, pp. 6–8) and Gardner (1963, p. 107) both assert that the kind and extent of present-day change precludes prediction of the future. Increasingly, the rational strategies of planned-innovation and long-range planning are being undermined by unpredictable changes. McNulty (1962) found no association between organization adaptation and the introduction of purposeful change in a study of their companies in fast-growing markets. He suggests that built-in flexibility may be more efficient than the explicit reorganization implicit in the quasi-rational model. (*Dun's Review* 1963, p. 42, questions the effectiveness of long-range planning in the light of frequent failures, and suggests that error may be attributable to forecasting the future by extrapolation of a non-comparable past.) The conclusion is that the rapidity and complexity of change may increasingly preclude effective long-range planning. These examples clearly suggest the emergence of a change in the environment that is suggestive of turbulence. . . .

The following are examples from two volumes of the *Administrative Science Quarterly* alone. Rubington (1965) argues that structural changes in organizations that seek to change the behavior of prisoners, drug addicts, juvenile delinquents, parolees, alcoholics [are] . . . the result of a social movement whose own organizational history has yet to be written'. Rosengren (1964) reports a similar phenomenon in the mental health field whose origin he finds hard to explain: "In any event, a more symbiotic relationship has come to characterize the relations be-tween the [mental] hospitals and other agencies, professions, and establishments in the community.' He ascribes changes in organizational national goals and technology to this inter-organizational evolution. In the field of education, Clark (1965) outlines the increasing influence of private foundations, national associations, and divisions of the federal government. He, too, is not clear as to how these changes have come about, but he traces numerous changes in the behavior of educational organizations to inter-organizational influences. Maniha and Perrow (1965) analyse the origins and development of a city youth commission. The agency had little reason to be formed, no goals to guide it, and was staffed by people who sought a minimal, no-action role in the community. By virtue of its existence and broad province, however, it was seized upon as a valuable weapon by other organizations for the pursuit of their own goals. 'But in this very process it became an organization with a mission of its own, in spite of itself.'

Since uncertainty is the dominant characteristic of turbulent fields, it is not surprising that emphasis in recent literature is away from algorithmic and toward heuristic problem-solving models (Taylor, 1965); that optimizing models are giving way to satisficing models (March and Simon, 1958); and that rational decision making is replaced by 'disjointed incrementalism' (Braybrooke and Lindblom, 1963). These trends reflect *not* the ignorance of the authors of earlier models, but a change in the causal texture of organizational environments and, therefore, of appropriate strategies for coping with the environment. Cyert and March (1953) state that 'so long as the environment of the firm is unstable—and predictably unstable—the heart of the theory [of the firm] must be the process of short-run adaptive reactions' (p. 100).

In summary, both the theoretical and case study literature on organizations suggests that these systems are increasingly finding themselves in environments where the complexity and rapidity of change in external interconnectedness (L_{22}) gives rise to increasingly unpredictable change in their transactional interdependencies (L_{21} and L_{12}). This seems to be good evidence for the emergence of turbulence in the environments of many formal organizations. . . .

In the short run, the openness of a living system to its environment enables it to take in ingredients from the environment for conversion into energy or information that allows it to maintain a steady state and, hence, to violate the dismal second law of thermodynamics, i.e. of entropy. In the long run, 'the characteristic of living systems which most clearly distinguishes them from the nonliving is their property of progressing by the process which is called evolution from less to more complex states of organization' (Pringle, 1956, p. 90). It then follows that to the extent that the environment of some living system X is comprised *of other living systems,* the environment of X is *itself* evolving from less to more complex states of organization. A major corollary is that the evolution of environments is characterized by an increase in the ratio of externally induced change over internally induced change in a system's transactional interdependencies (L_{21} and L_{12}). . . .

In the case of formal organizations, disturbed-reactive or oligopolistic environments require some form of accommodation between like but competitive organizations whose fates are negatively correlated to some degree. A change in the transactional position of one system in an oligopolistic set, whether for better or worse, automatically affects the transactional position of all other members of the set, and in the opposite direction, i.e. for worse or better, as the case may be.[4] On the other hand, turbulent environments require relationships between dissimilar organizations whose fates are independent or, perhaps, positively correlated.[5] A testable hypothesis that derives from the formal argument is that the evolution of environments is accompanied, in viable systems, by an increase in ability to learn and to perform according to changing contingencies in the environment.

The evolution of organizational environments is characterized by a change in the important constituents of the environment. The earliest formal organizations to appear in the United States, e.g. in agriculture, retail trade, construction, mining (See Stinchcombe, 1965, p. 156) operated largely under placid-clustered conditions. Important inputs, such as natural resources and labor, as well as consumers, comprised an environment in which strategies of optimal location and distinctive competence were critical organizational responses (Emery and Trist, 1965, p. 29). Two important attributes of placid-clustered environments are: (a) the environment is itself *not* formally organized; and (b) transactions are largely initiated and controlled by the organization, i.e. L_{12}. . . .

When the environment becomes turbulent, however, its constituents are a multitude of other formal organizations. Increasingly, an organization's markets consist of other organizations; suppliers of material, labor and capital are increasingly organized, and regulatory groups are more numerous and powerful. The critical response of organizations under these conditions will be discussed later. It

[4] Assuming a non-expanding economy, in the ideal instance.

[5] Emery and Trist argue that fates, here, are positively correlated. This author agrees if any expanding economy is assumed.

should be noted that *real* environments are often mixtures of these ideal types.

The evolution from placid-clustered environments to turbulent environments . . . can be summarized as a process in which formal organizations evolve: (a) *from* the status of systems within environments not formally organized; (b) *through* intermediate phases, e.g. Weberian bureaucracy; and (c) *to* the status of subsystems of a larger social system. . . .

INTER-ORGANIZATIONAL ANALYSIS

It was noted that survival in disturbed-reactive environments depends upon the ability of the organization to anticipate and counteract the behavior of similar systems. The analysis of inter-organizational behavior, therefore, becomes meaningful only in these and more complex environments. The interdependence of organizations, or any kind of living systems, at less complex environmental levels is more appropriately studied by means of ecological, competitive market, or other similar models.

The only systematic conceptual approach to inter-organizational analysis has been the theory of oligopoly in economics. This theory clearly addresses only disturbed-reactive environments. Many economists admit that the theory, which assumes maximization of profit and perfect knowledge, is increasingly at odds with empirical evidence that organizational behavior is characterized by satisficing and bounded rationality. Boulding (1965) comments that 'it is surprisingly hard to make a really intelligent conflict move in the economic area simply because of the complexity of the system and the enormous importance of side effects and dynamic effects' (p. 189). A fairly comprehensive search of the literature has revealed only four conceptual frameworks for the analysis of inter-organizational relations outside

the field of economics. These are briefly reviewed, particular attention being given to assumptions about organization environments, and to the utility of these assumptions in the analysis of inter-organizational relations in turbulent fields.

William Evan (1966) has introduced the concept of 'organization-set', after Merton's 'role-set' (pp. 177–80). Relations between a focal organization and members of its organization-set are mediated by the role-sets of boundary personnel. 'Relations' are conceived as the flow of information, products or services, and personnel (pp. 175–6). Presumably, monetary and legal, and other transactions can be accommodated in the conceptual system. In general, Evan offers a conceptual tool for identifying transactions at a given time. He makes no explicit assumptions about the nature of environmental dynamics, nor does he imply that they are changing. The relative neglect of inter-organizational relations, which he finds surprising, is ascribed instead to the traditional intra-organizational focus, which derives from Weber, Taylor and Barnard. His concepts, however, go considerably beyond those of conventional organization and economic theory, e.g. comparative versus reference organizations and overlap in goals and values. If a temporal dimension were added to Evan's conceptual scheme, then it would be a very useful tool for describing the 'structural' aspects of transactional interdependencies (L_{21} and L_{12} relations) in turbulent fields.

Another approach is taken by Levine and White (1961, p. 586) who focus specifically on relations among community health and welfare agencies. This local set of organizations 'may be seen as a system with individual organizations or system parts varying in the kinds and frequencies of their relationships with one another'. The authors admit that interdependence exists among these local parts only to the extent that relevant resources are not available from *outside* the local region, which lies beyond their conceptual domain. Nor do we find here any suggestion of turbulence in these local environments. If such local sets of agencies are increasingly interdependent with other components of the local community and with organizations outside the locality, as the evidence suggests, then the utility of Levine and White's approach is both limited and shrinking.

Litwak and Hylton (1962) provide a third perspective. They too are concerned with health and welfare organizations, but their major emphasis is on coordination. The degree of interdependence among organizations is a major variable; low interdependence leads to *no* coordination and high interdependence leads to merger, therefore they deal only with conditions of moderate interdependence. The type of coordinating mechanism that emerges under conditions of moderate interdependence is hypothesized to result from the interaction of three trichotomized variables: the *number* of interdependent organizations; the degree of their *awareness* of their interdependence; and the extent of *standardization* in their transactions. The attractive feature of the Litwak and Hylton scheme is the possibility it offers of making different predictions for a great variety of environments. Their model also seems to have predictive power beyond the class of organizations to which they specifically address themselves. If environments are becoming turbulent, however, then increasingly fewer of the model's cells (a 3 × 3 × 3 space) are relevant. In the one-cell turbulent corner of their model, where a large number of organizations have low awareness of their complex and unstandardized interdependence, 'there is little chance of coordination' (p. 417), according to Litwak and Hylton (1962). If the level of awareness of interdependence increases, the model predicts that some process of arbitration will emerge. Thus the model anticipates the inter-organiza-

tional implications of turbulent fields, but tells us little about the emerging processes that will enable organizations to adapt to turbulence.

The fourth conceptual framework available in the literature is by Thompson and McEwen (1958). They emphasize the interdependence of organizations with the larger society and discuss the consequences that this has for goal setting. 'Because the setting of goals is essentially a problem of defining desired relationships between an organization and its environment, change in either requires review and perhaps alteration of goals' (p. 23). They do not argue that such changes are more frequent today, but they do assert that reappraisal of goals is 'a more constant problem in an unstable environment than in a stable one', and also 'more difficult as the "product" of the enterprise becomes less tangible' (p. 24).

Thompson and McEwen outline four organizational strategies for dealing with the evironment. One is competition; the other three are subtypes of a cooperative strategy: bargaining, co-optation, and coalition. These cooperative strategies all require direct interaction among organizations and this, they argue, increases the environment's potential control over the focal organization (p. 27). In bargaining, to the extent that the second party's support is necessary, that party is in a position to exercise a veto over the final choice of alternative goals, and thus takes part in the decision. The co-optation strategy makes still further inroads into the goal-setting process. From the standpoint of society, however, co-optation, by providing overlapping memberships, is an important social device for increasing the likelihood that organizations related to each other in complicated ways will in fact find compatible goals. Co-optation thus aids in the integration of heterogeneous parts of a complex social system. Coalition refers to a combination of two or more organizations for a common purpose and is viewed by these authors as the ultimate form of environmental conditioning of organization goals (Thompson and McEwen, 1958, pp. 25–8).

The conceptual approaches of Levine and White and of Litwak and Hylton therefore appear to be designed for non-turbulent conditions. Indeed, it may well be that coordination *per se*, in the static sense usually implied by that term, is dysfunctional for adaptation to turbulent fields. . . .

INTEGRATIVE FRAMEWORK

Model

It is assumed that the foregoing arguments are valid: (a) that organizational environments are increasingly turbulent; (b) that organizations are increasingly less autonomous; and (c) that other formal organizations are increasingly important components of organizational environments. Some conceptual perspective is now needed, which will make it possible to view any formal organization, its transactional interdependencies, and the environment itself within a common conceptual framework. The intent of this section is to outline the beginnings of such framework.

A formal organization is a system primarily oriented to the attainment of a specific goal, which constitutes an output of the system and which is an input for some other system (Parsons, 1962, p. 33). Needless to say, the output of any living system is dependent upon input into it. Figure 1 schematically illustrates the skeletal structure of a living system. The input and output regions are partially permeable with respect to the environment which is the region outside the system boundary. Arrows coming into a system represent input and arrows going out of a system represent output. In Figure 2, rectangles represent formal organizations and circles represent individuals and *non-*

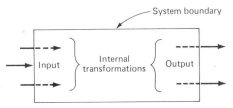

FIGURE 1   Structure of living systems such as a formal organization

formal social organizations. Figure 2 represents the *statics* of a system X and its turbulent environment. Three-dimensional illustration would be necessary to show the *dynamics* of a turbulent environment schematically. Assume that a third, temporal dimension is imposed on Figure 2 and that this reveals an increasing number of elements and an increasing rate and complexity of change in their interdependencies over time. To do full justice to the concept of turbulence, we should add other sets of elements even in Figure 2 below, although these are not yet linked to X's set. A notion that is integral to Emery and Trist's conception of turbulence is that changes outside of X's set, and hence difficult for X to predict and impossible for X to control, will have impact on X's transactional interdependencies in the future. The addition of just one link at some future time may not affect the super-system but may constitute a system break for X.

This schematization shows only one-way directionality and is meant to depict energic inputs, e.g. personnel and material, and output, e.g. product. The organization provides something in exchange for the inputs it receives, of course, and this is usually informational in nature—money, most commonly. Similarly the organization receives money for its product from those systems for whom its product is an input. Nor does our framework distinguish different kinds of inputs, although the analysis of inter-organizational exchange requires this kind of taxonomic device. It seems important to distinguish energic in-

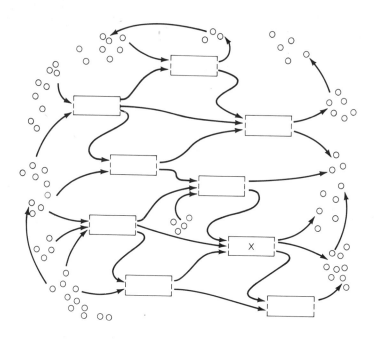

FIGURE 2   Illustration of system *X* in turbulent environment

puts and outputs from informational ones. Energic inputs include machinery, personnel, clientele in the case of service organizations, electric power, and so on. Informational inputs are not well conceptualized although there is no doubt of their increasing importance in environments which are more complex and changeable. Special divisions of organizations and whole firms devoted to information collecting, processing and distributing are also rapidly proliferating, e.g. research organizations, accounting firms, the Central Intelligence Agency. . . .

Our simplistic approach to an integrative framework for the study of organizations (L_{11}), their transactional interdependencies $(L_{21}$ and $L_{12})$ and the connectedness within their environments (L_{22}), gives the following conceptual ingredients: (a) units that are mainly formal organizations, and (b) relationships between them that are the directed flow (Cartwright, 1959) of (c) energy and information. The enormous and increasing

importance of informational transaction has not been matched by conceptual developments in organization theory. The importance of information is frequently cited in a general way, however, especially in the context of organizational change or innovation. Dill (1962) has made a cogent argument on the need for more attention to this dimension.

The importance of communication for organizational change has been stressed by Ohlin (1958, p. 63), March and Simon (1958, pp. 173–83), Benne (1962, p. 232), Lippitt (1958, p. 52), and others. Diversity of informational input has been used to explain the creativity of individuals as well as of social systems (see, e.g. Allport, 1955, p. 76, Ogburn and Nimkoff, 1964, pp. 662–70). The importance of boundary positions as primary sources of innovative inputs from the environment has been stressed by March and Simon (1958, pp. 165–8, 189) and by Kahn *et al.* (1964, pp. 101–26). James Miller (1955, p. 530) hypothesizes that up to a maximum, which no living system has yet reached, the more energy a system devotes to information processing (as opposed to productive and maintenance activity), the more likely the system is to survive. . . .

SUMMARY

The lag between evolution in the real world and evolution in theorists' ability to comprehend it is vast, but hopefully shrinking. It was only a little over one hundred years ago that Darwin identified natural selection, as the mechanism of evolutionary process. Despite Darwin's enduring insight, theorists of change, including biologists, have continued to focus largely on internal aspects of systems.

It is our thesis that the selective advantage of one intra- or inter-organizational configuration over another cannot be assessed apart from an understanding of the dynamics of the environment itself. It is the environment which exerts selective pressure. 'Survival of the fittest' is a function of the fitness of the environment. The dinosaurs *were* impressive creatures, in their day.

References

Allport, F. H. (1955), *Theories of Perception and the Concept of Structure*, Wiley.

Ashby, W. R. (1960), *Design for a Brain*, Chapman & Hall, 2nd edn.

Benne, K. D. (1962), 'Deliberate changing as the facilitation of growth', in W. G. Bennis *et al.* (eds.), *The Planning of Change*, Holt, Rinehart & Winston.

Boulding, K. E. (1965), 'The economies of human conflict', in E. B. McNeil (ed.), *The Nature of Human Conflict*, Prentice-Hall.

Braybrooke, D., and Lindblom, C. E. (1963), *A Strategy of Decision*, Free Press.

Cartwright, D. (1959), 'The potential contribution of graph theory to organization theory', in M. Haire (ed.), *Modern Organization Theory*, Wiley, pp. 254–71.

Chein, I. (1953), 'Personality and typology', *Journal of Social Psychology*, vol. 18, pp. 89–101.

Clark, B. R. (1965), 'Inter-organizational patterns in education', *Administrative Science Quarterly*, vol. 10, pp. 224–37.

Cyert, R. M., and March, J. G. (1953), *A Behavorial Theory of the Firm*, Prentice-Hall.

Dill, W. R. (1962), 'The impact of environment on organizational development', in S. Mailick and E. H. von Ness (eds.), *Concepts and Issues in Administrative Behavior*, Prentice-Hall, pp. 94–109.

Drucker, P. F. (1964), 'The big power of little ideas', *Harvard Business Review*, vol. 42, May.

Emery, F. E., and Trist E. L. (1965), 'The causal texture of organizational environments', *Human Relations*, vol. 18, pp. 21–31.

Evan, W. M. (1966), 'The organization-set: toward a theory of inter-organizational relations', in J. D. Thompson (ed.), *Approaches to Organizational Design*, University of Pittsburgh Press.

Gardner, J. W. (1963), *Self-Renewal*, Harper & Row.

Hood, R. C. (1962), 'Business organization as a class-product of its purposes and of its environment', in M. Haire (ed.), *Organizational Theory in Industrial Practice*, Wiley.

Kahn, R. L., *et al.* (1964), *Organizational Stress*, Wiley.

Levine, S., and White, P. E. (1961), 'Exchange as a conceptual framework for the study of inter-organizational relationships', *Administrative Science Quarterly*, vol. 5, pp. 583–601.

Lippitt, R. (1958), *The Dynamics of Planned Change*, Harcourt, Brace & World.

Litwak, E., and Hylton, L. (1962), 'Inter-organizational analysis: a hypothesis on coordinating agencies', *Administrative Science Quarterly,* vol. 6, pp. 395–420.

Maniha, J., and Perrow, C. (1965), 'The reluctant organization and the aggressive environment', *Administrative Science Quarterly,* vol. 10, pp. 238–57.

March, J. G., and Simon, H. A. (1958), *Organizations,* Wiley.

McNulty, J. E. (1962), 'Organizational change in growing enterprises', *Administrative Science Quarterly,* vol. 7, pp. 1–21.

Miller, J. G. (1955), 'Toward a general theory for the behavorial sciences, *American Psychologist,* vol. 10, no. 9, pp. 513–31.

Ogburn, W. F., and Nimkoff, M. F. 1964), *Sociology,* Houghton Mifflin, 2nd edn.

Ohlin, L. E. (1958), 'Conformity in American society', *Social Work,* vol. 3, p. 63.

Parsons, T. (1962), 'Suggestions for a sociological approach to the theory of organizations', in A. Etzioni (ed.), *Complex Organizations,* Holt, Rinehart & Winston.

Pringle, J. W. S. (1956), 'On the parallel being learning and evolution' *General Systems,* vol. 1, p. 90.

Rosengren, W. R. (1964), 'Communication, organization and conduct in the "therapeutic milieu' ", *Administrative Science Quarterly,* vol. 9., pp. 70–90.

Rubington, E. (1965), 'Organizational strain and key roles', *Administrative Science Quarterly,* vol. 9, pp. 350–69.

Simon, H. A. (1957), *Models of Man,* Wiley.

Stinchcombe, A. L. (1965), 'Social structure and organizational in J. G. March (ed.), *Handbook of Organizations,* Rand McNally.

Taylor, D. W. (1965), 'Decision making and problem solving', in J. G. March (ed.), *Handbook of Organizations,* Rand McNally, pp. 48–82.

Thompson, J. D., and McEwen, W. J. (1958), 'Organizational goals and environment', *American Sociological Review,* vol. 23, pp. 23–31.

Tolman, E. C., and Brunswick, E. (1935), 'The organism and the causal texture of the environment', *Psychological Review,* vol. 42, pp. 43–72.

Von Bertalanffy, L. (1956), 'General system theory', *General Systems,* vol. 1, pp. 1–10.

5.2 CONTEMPORARY PERSPECTIVES ON PLANNED SOCIAL CHANGE: A COMPARISON

James E. Crowfoot, Mark A. Chesler

All planned change efforts imply a commitment to certain ends, adherence to a certain view of reality, and acceptance of

Reproduced by special permission from *The Journal of Applied Behavioral Science,* "Contemporary Perspectives on Planned Change: A Comparison," James E. Crowfoot and Mark A. Chesler, Volume 10, Number 3, 1974, pp. 278–303, National Training Laboratories.

References and footnotes from edited portions of this paper have been deleted.

certain modes of realizing those ends. Those assumptions constitute the conscious or unconscious bases for selecting specific courses of action and thus they precede all tactical decisions. To the extent that change agents cannot identify those basic assumptions and their implications, they cannot explore the full range of effective strategies of change.

In this paper, we attempt to identify some presuppositions that undergird all change strategies and underlie all distinctions between person, organization, or system-oriented levels of analysis or intervention. The innumerable discussions of strategy and tactics within the field of planned change are inadequate because they are seldom explicitly rooted in or derived from a basic philosophical and experiential orientation to the world. Many syntheses of planned change practice therefore seem to rely primarily on classifications of strategies and tactics alone. For example, Hornstein *et al.* (1971) organize their work on the basis of a categorization of activities: e.g., individual, technostructural, data-based, organizational development, violence and coercion, and nonviolence and coercion, and nonviolence and direct action. Olmusk (1972) likewise generates a set of descriptive titles of modes of activity: fellowship, political, economic, academic, engineering, military, confrontation, and applied behavorial science. On the basis of a consensus/dissensus dimension on issues, Warren (1971) distinguishes among consensus, campaign, and contest strategies of planned change. Jones's (1965) work uses three categories of strategies—normative, utilitarian, and "others," which, though instructive, also fail to focus on the theoretical and normative assumptions that guide the selection and development of strategy. Coleman (1973) does, however, attempt to synthesize approaches to planned social change which are directed toward increasing control over resources or the conditions of existence, and he distinguishes between theories that assume change occurs as a result of altered social conditions and theories that locate the origin of social change in personal change. Nevertheless, though his effort begins to uncover the underlying assumptions of change strategies, it does not go far enough.[1]

Two of the best efforts to discover those root value assumptions and diagnostic orientations are Chin and Benne (1969)

and Rothman (1970). The former identify three meta-strategies of or perspectives on planned social change: empirico-rational, normative-reeducative, and power-coercive. Rothman also uses three categories in his review of community organizing practices: locality development, social action, and social planning. Although their work reflects rich insights and considerable sophistication in change projects as well as in the theoretical literature, they do not deal with some of the perspectives and currents in planned social change now at work in this society. Both writings appear to distort or to reflect important distortions in the field. The Chin and Benne emphasis on knowledge, and more particularly upon science, commits them to a professionalism that clouds the emergent power of scientific professionals in positions of technocratic influence. Both the normative-reeducative and empirico-rational approaches generally reflect strong elements of professional commitment in the language and analysis of consultants and clients. Cautions against social conflict and division are raised only in the context of the power-coercive approach, indicating the authors' priorities and preferences regarding social harmony and consensus. The Rothman typology, more circumscribed in historical origins, is more specific than Chin and Benne with regard to tactical and strategic implications. Rothman displays considerable acuity regarding the real nuances of power, with both his locality development and social action

---

[1] Several prominent writers collapse the differences in approaches to planned social change by defining the field in ways that considerably narrow legitimate alternatives. For instance, Bennis, Benne, and Chin state that "planned change is the only feasible alternative" to both radical interventionism and non-interventionism. "Radical interventionism" is then identified as Marxian analysis (Bennis, Benne, & Chin, 1969, p. 2). But Marx, and especially Lenin and his followers, did deliberately "plan change," and they planned it on the basis of both moral values and their own system of intellectual and empirical thought, as do Bennis, Benne, and Chin.

categories apparently of the power-coercive genre. The social planning approach, on the other hand, seems to combine broad aspects of the Chin and Benne empirico-rational and normative-reeducative approaches.

CONTEMPORARY APPROACHES TO PLANNED SOCIAL CHANGE

From our point of view, the contemporary field of planned social change may be divided into three perspectives, using criteria somewhat different from others reviewed.[2] One major segment of the field, represented by Rothman (1970) and Bennis, Benne, and Chin (1969) and their colleagues, is the "professional-technical" (PT) school of thought, which stresses the intellectual expertise of selected classes of people and their ability as well as their right to make decisions and plans for others in order to be "helpful."[3] Another major segment, avowedly "political" (P), stresses the organization of mass power, legitimate office, and the mobilization of elites.[4] The third major perspective is

[2] We wish to acknowledge the efforts of undergraduate and graduate students in our classes in social change at the University of Michigan for their help in developing and testing this typology.

[3] Some of the key works in this perspective on planned social change include: Argryis (1962), Bennis, Benne, and Chin (1969), Likert (1961), Lippitt (1958), Schein (1969), Watson (1966), Zetterberg (1962). These works, and this perspective, often dominate the scholarly literature in planned social change, probably because these professional scholars write in the journals available to other scholars.

[4] Seminal works in this perspective on planned social change include: Alinsky (1969), Carmichael and Hamilton (1967), Gamson (1968), Kahn (1970), Lenin (1943), Machiavelli (1957). Biographies and historical treatments of political leaders are also especially good sources of assumptive reflections and strategic insight to this approach.

"countercultural" (CC); redemptive in character, it stresses the unfolding nature of man and emphasizes communal organization as the building and rebuilding blocks of a new, unalienating society.[5]

Four questions permit us to identify and differentiate these approaches to planned social change, and thereby broaden our understanding of apparent tactical conflicts and basic strategic variations and choices:

1. What are their general images of society?
2. What are their general images of the individual?
3. What are their diagnoses of contemporary society?
4. What are their priorities with regard to change?

Professional-Technical Perspective

According to this perspective, society consists of many subsystems, which have complex interrelationships as well as differentiated internal structures and processes. Communities and organizations are functionally specialized structures geared to the division of labor necessary to achieve agreed-upon goals that fulfill a broader societal function (Durkheim, 1949). These collections of persons and social institutions are made interdependent by social and economic relations and moral obligations and their construction of a consensual ideology.[6]

[5] Key works in this perspective on planned social change include: Buber (1949), Fairfield (1972), Fromm (1955), Nearing and Nearing (1970), Schutz (1971), Slater (1970), and the Bible (New Testament especially). The redemptive character of this perspective has lent it a religious orientation in sacred states, and a strong humanist and anarchist cultural thrust in more secular states or times.

[6] This view of organizations has its scientific genesis largely in Weber's (1930) emphasis upon technical rationality. Bureaucratic

The professional-technical perspective thus considers society, and most organizations, to be basically sound, although they need to cope better with ongoing change, which is inevitable and related to the imperative of progress—to a rapidly developing technology, to an ever larger scale of production, and to the increasingly complex and dynamic problems of administration (Lawrence & Lorsch, 1967). Nevertheless, the bureaucratic press for organizational survival, usually translated into efforts to maintain an organization or community in its current form, may lead to dysfunctional adjustments to changing internal and external environments (Argyris, 1962; Katz & Kahn, 1966; March & Simon, 1958). Needs for rationally organized change should be met with systematic planning, guiding and direction by expert administrators, which often require professional consultant assistance.

Given this view of society and the individual, as well as its diagnosis of social problems, the PT perspective calls for constant planned incremental changes, a preference entirely congruent with its concern for stability and its belief in progress.

In working with social systems, this perspective usually emphasizes change within small working groups and organizations rather than change in individuals per se or change in society as a whole. Individuals are viewed as occupants of a role to which they are normatively committed and through which they perform rewarding social functions. They are de-

authority, vested in key system decision-makers and managers, operates according to rules and regulations agreed to or followed by all. The operations of subunits are oriented to the survival of the total organization, and operations of organizations are tuned to societal integration. This diagnostic perspective is tied clearly to "functional" social theories and to the concern for intersystem equilibrium in the organization of society (Parsons, 1951).

pendent upon the receipt and manipulation of information, particularly of the kind which leads to coordination with others, for adequate role performance. The individual's resistance to change is usually explained in terms of his or her fear of risk, lack of adequate information, or absence of opportunities and rewards for creative problem-solving behavior. The individual is often viewed as unable to make rational decisions on his own, partly as a function of organizational role pressures and partly as a function of inadequate intellectual preparation and access to information.[7]

Thus, a popular change strategy for groups, organizations, or communities is the creating of more rational problem-solving systems through which groups of individuals establish new norms, role definitions, and operating procedures. Collective problem-solving efforts are undertaken to help develop new responses to changing situations and to provide individuals with more satisfactory socio-emotional settings in which to perform (Sofer, 1964; Davis, 1967). Emphasis is usually placed upon more informal and open communication patterns, which generate new forms of

[7] Bennis and others argue against change efforts that minimize the reality of organizational forces and contexts acting upon persons. Change in individuals would not necessarily alter embracing organizational or role parameters. Individuals are changed through alterations in roles, groups, and organizations. Such change efforts attempt to reduce anxiety and support persons against their "irrational" fears (Jacques, 1951). The involvement of supervisors and peers, as well as the individuals themselves, is used to create this supportive atmosphere and to overcome resistance (Watson, 1966). In addition, new information or revised aspects of old information systems are key inputs in individual change efforts (Rogers & Shoemaker, 1971; Havelock, 1973). When it is necessary to focus on individuals, the most revelant aspects include their social views, skills, and role behaviors.

information transmission and social relationships; and functional face-to-face groups, whose members reflect different levels of status or authoritiy and engage in mutual problem solving, are preferred. Experts help the group become aware of its interpersonal processes and thus more rational about the social and technical issues to be solved. The development of good personal relations is considered to develop confidence and trust among organizational or community members and to overcome their resistance to change.

Although changing the society rather than the organization might seem a logical extension of this view, the PT perspective generally considers that objective beyond current scientific expertise and therefore an inappropriate focus of action. Nevertheless, social planning efforts or social policy formulations that emphasize diagnosis and prescription, but stop short of institutional and citizen mobilization, do represent efforts to apply this perspective at a macro-societal level. Here, diagnostic expertise and intellectual competence are considered applicable, without necessarily incurring the intellectual and operational risks and complexities involved in large-scale social action.

Political Perspective

The political perspective views society as composed of many different groups, each defined by the uniquely shared interests of its members. Groups may be defined on the basis of social function or role, race and ethnicity, socioeconomic status, political roles, sex, age ideology, and so forth. They may be loosely organized or coherently integrated into social categories and institutions. These groups and institutions, with different and often competing interests or goals, are the social units of primary concern.[8]

[8] The very goals of social organizations are to generate collective effort to gain re-

To the extent that resources are perceived as scarce, groups will compete for their control. Thus, competition and conflict over access to and control of such commodities as material goods, dominant symbol systems and ruling ideologies, information, technical skill, respect, and status are inevitable (Coser, 1967; Dahl, 1967). One key to the mediation or resolution of such conflict is the status or relative power of the groups involved. Social systems are seen to contain not only multiple interest groups but also particular distributions of power among those groups. In some cases, cross-group understandings or norms concerning certain groups' rights to or claims on resources may exist. Although those understandings may have temporary authority, they are ultimately rooted in the power positions of the constitutent groups and must be negotiated for the larger system to be integrated and stable.

Planned change originates in a group's discontent with the resources it is receiving or the way in which they are obtained (Gamson, 1968). Since resource allocation is a constant problem, so is relative discontent, and so is a press for change. To achieve change in the distribution of resources—whether in quality or quantity—always involves opposition by or resistance from groups that are satisfied with the pattern, typically elites or those groups currently in control.

The individual is viewed as necessarily interdependent with others. Essentially powerless to meet his needs alone, he must establish explicit interdependence with other individuals and groups in order to mobilize the power required to gain resources needed for survival and satis-

sources required for human fulfillment and to provide an arena for negotiations among different groups seeking similar resources (Dahrendorf, 1949). From the "political" perspective, this is the essence of the social contract.

faction and to advance common interests. Groups of individuals are, however, not always aware of their objective interests, which can be clouded by myths propagated by others—especially by elites. When a group acts on the basis of subjective interest alone its objective interests may not be realized and its members may be left with unmet needs.[9]

P proponents contend that the contemporary state apparatus opts for stability rather than equality in regulating the relations among groups and between groups and resources. The result is a high concentration of power in the hands of a few people or a few interest groups, which some advocates of the P perspective view as inevitable. Current patterns of resource allocation and regulation are usually seen as unfair and unjust by those who come from or are allied with a society's oppressed groups, but as fair or beneficial, though difficult to maintain, by those concerned primarily with the welfare of its elites. The oppressed are groups denied substantial participation or power in societal decision making, which typically reduces their share of the resources essential for their well-being.[10] Elite groups in society exercise their power to maintain control of the decision-making process, which in turn serves their self-interests. The decision-making system of any group at any moment may include laws, norms, and social intelligence systems (often referred to in this perspective as social science), all of which favor groups with high power over those with less power.

The political perspective's priorities for change diverge according to a concern for advancing the interests of either oppressed or elite groups. When the concern is for the former, gaining power to alter decision making and advance their welfare in political, economic, and social systems is advocated. A key prerequisite to the implementation of this strategy is that members of oppressed groups recognize their common character—their low power position or oppression—and see themselves as possessing objectively related interests.[11]

When priorities center on direct or indirect service to elites, they usually in-

---

[9] Balbus (1971) discusses the concept of objective interests as something the individual (or group) "is affected by." Accordingly, the individual does not have to be aware of that interest for it to be potent and relevant. By contrast, Balbus sees a subjective interest as something a person or group "is interested in," regardless of its real potency or lack thereof. Accordingly, persons or groups can have subjective interests that are incongruent with their objective interests (i.e., false consciousness) and objective interests of which they are unaware (i.e., lack of consciousness).

[10] *Typically*, because oppressed groups such as the poor, blacks, or students are occasionally provided with substantial resources for their survival and material welfare (Cloward & Piven, 1971). Sometimes this serves to stabilize and harmonize an inequitable system. Receiving resources without the power to control the process is the mark of a paternalist system, albeit perhaps a benevolent one (Jordan, 1968; Rhea, 1968). The cultural control that reflects this political outlook is described for colonized third-world minorities in Blauner (1972) and Fanon (1966).

[11] Often called consciousness raising and discussed in Balbus (1971), Bradley *et al.* (1971), Freire (n.d.), Peslikis (1970), Shapiro (1972), *Women* (1972). For Balbus, true and effectively raised consciousness would mean the coming together of both objective and subjective modes of interests within the individual or group. The most progressive situation would be one in which members of oppressor and oppressed groups are involved in separate forms of consciousness raising. Thus, third-world minorities and whites (Terry, 1970), women and men (Krichbaum, 1974), young and old, and poor and rich may become aware of the existence of, and their roles in, racism, sexism, age chauvinism, and class discrimination.

volve increasing elite satisfaction with resources or with their power and control of the process of allocation. Tactics may include increasing communication among elite members, facilitating greater information and understanding of the social system,[12] and developing better managerial skills and increasing the manipulation of the subjective consciousness or material opportunities available to oppressed groups. If the ruling classes are seen as benevolent or valuable in themselves, or as essential components in social stability, increasing their satisfactions and skills may also be seen as in the interest of oppressed groups, by way of a "trickle down" or "hidden-hand" effect.

Countercultural Perspective

The countercultural perspective views contemporary society and all revelant subunits as overtechnocratic and overbureaucratic (Slater, 1970). These institutional characteristics also define the individual, who generally conforms, in a Procrustean fashion, to this truncated definition. In its image of society, the countercultural perspective focuses primarily on the negative effects of social institutions and organizations on the individual. Most social change is held to result in more of the same, and not in alteration of these basically non- or anti-human characteristics. If anything, the effects of planned change, of social evolution or "progress," are considered to decrease social tolerance and initiative for creativity, individuality, and deviancy.

From this point of view, technological and social innovations overwhelmingly result in increased conformity to roles

[12] Including, especially, communication between members of scientific elites and public policy makers, e.g., "technical assistance" or "utilization of scientific knowledge."

which further remove the individual from realizing his full human potential. Desirable change is infrequently achieved because of a lack of adequate models of change and inattention to individuals' need to escape traditional patterns.

This perspective assumes that the individual is innately good, and it defines goodness in terms of internal unity, primitive union with nature, a capacity for ecstasy and joy, as well as cultural creativity and a potential for loving and fulfilling relationships. Thus, the individual is seen as basically emotional and intuitive (spiritual) rather than intellectual and technocratic (rational). Contemporary humans do not realize their goodness, which is distorted and suppressed by social institutions, whose goals and procedures are antithetical to the individual, who is treated by them as a means rather than an end.

A diagnosis of contemporary society from this perspective follows quite directly from the above conceptions of society and the individual. The individual is seen as alienated from himself and the rest of society. Because individual worth is evaluated in terms of material possessions and the ability to produce and not in terms of innate human qualities, most individuals are more concerned with protecting and enhancing possessions than with developing and sharing self with others. Conceptions of oneself are likewise fraught with concerns about marketing or hoarding an identity, relationships, and so forth (Fromm, 1947).

Social institutions no longer meet basic individual needs: for example, needs for affection, freedom, wholeness. These institutions are antihumanistic, racist, and sexist, and thereby prevent us from realizing our natural potential, individually or collectively. Public agencies as well as private corporations operate in ways that destroy people, land, and natural resources. Wedded to an achieving ethic of Protestant sacrifice, Americans glorify technical excellence and bureaucratic order. The results include a stifling of organizational innovation and fluidity, and social control of spontaneous individual creativity, emotional expression, and personal relationships. This diagnosis is applied to bureaucratized churches as well as to secular institutions; even the sacred has become profane in its nonredemptive treatment of persons.

The CC perspective heavily emphasizes individual change. Change must begin with the self and result in new personal values translated into new life styles. Life styles should include acceptance of others and full participation in a community of others. Persons must develop these new life styles by living them, not by viewing them from the outside; then they can be shared as living examples to others. Changes in self and others must be reinforced and extended through alternative organizations based on humanistic values that include racial and sexual equality, consensual decision making, and interpersonal cooperation (Steiner, 1973–74).

These three approaches to planned social change are summarized in Figure 1.

PERSPECTIVES AND PRACTICAL ISSUES

These three contemporary perspectives on planned change can be related to some familiar practical issues. The relationship between the divergent perspectives and issues wrestled with by practitioners, targets, and observers of change illumines how apparently technical matters or isolated value choices are in fact related to basic assumptions.

The Actors: Roles and Preparation

The very label "planned social change" implies the presence of intentional actors who alter social systems. Who are the actors initiating planned change? What do they do? And how are they prepared for their activities? The three perspectives tend to answer these questions differently.

The PT change agent According to the PT perspective, the actor initiating change should be a specially trained expert whose role as citizen should be subsumed or separated from his role as change agent. Political neutrality is usually seen as an important component of the role of expert.

Professional change agents thus receive formal training in applied social science, especially the study of psychology, social psychology, and sociology. Particularly important skills include system diagnosis, especially of small-group and organizational processes; force-field analyses; communication techniques; management of human interactions in groups; process facilitation; personal role clarification; and an ability to enter systems as an outside consultant. Training usually includes supervised experience in applying this knowledge to the problems of individuals, groups, organizations, and communities.

Training is largely university-based; in nonuniversity settings, it is closely related to the university system through the credentialing of its teachers, the kind of role systems employed, and standards for performance. For the most part, such training employs the typical educational model of the expert and the nonexpert, although often in freer interactive settings than is the academic norm. Once trained, these experts are expected to adhere to a set of values and procedures developed, maintained, and revised by an overtly organized reference group. The structure of this professional reference system supports the content and organization of the training received; it also provides numerous jobs and social opportunities.

The role of change agent is broadly defined as providing assistance to a social

FIGURE 1 Approaches to Planned Social Change

Key Questions	Professional-Technical	Political	Countercultural
What are its general images of society?	Complex system with functionally specialized structure Organizations and communities based on technical rationality and bureaucratic authority Made up of consensually minded persons having interdependent economic relationships and moral obligations. Conflict is dysfunctional; harmony and natural order of consensus and cooperation preferred	Society consists of many different groups, each defined by the shared interests or values of its members Competition and conflict over resources are basic processes Distribution of power among groups with different interests determinative of societal functioning	Society consists of organizations which are uniformly overtechnocratic and overbureaucratic Organizations result in individual conformity and dehumanization Basic trend of social change is more of the same
What are its general images of the individual?	Normatively committed role occupants Information processors and problem-solvers Responsive to system-controlled rewards	Powerless to meet needs by himself or herself Interdependence and group membership required to satisfy needs False consciousness frequently prevents individual from satisfying his or her needs	Innately good—capable of love, joy, and creativity More emotional and intuitive than cognitive and rational Goodness is distorted and suppressed

FIGURE 1 (Continued)

Key Questions	Professional-Technical	Political	Countercultural
What are its diagnoses of contemporary society?	Society, as managed by and represented by legitimate officials, is basically all right, although adjustments are needed. Change is inevitable. It arises from developing technology, larger scales of production, and administrative complexity. Maintenance of old bureaucratic patterns prevent adaptation to change.	State has failed in some of its regulatory functions. Power is concentrated in relatively small number of persons or organizations. Oppressed see resource allocation as unfair and elites see it as just but difficult to maintain. Laws, norms, intelligence systems, and socialization are seen as maintaining elite control: the powerless see them as oppressing them, and elites see them as not being effective enough.	Individual is alienated—evaluated in terms of material possessions and ability to produce. Society's institutions are repressive: anti-humanistic, racist, sexist, etc. Institutions operate to destroy people, land, and natural resources.
What are its priorities with regard to change?	Professionals need to plan and manage functional adaptations to change. Ongoing, incremental planned change Target of change is small groups, organizations, and social roles, attitudes and skills of individuals. Social planning at societal level Create rational, problem-solving systems	For oppressed it is altering consciousness and mobilization to achieve greater power and resources. For elites it is making their control more effective and more satisfying to exercise.	Individual change in self and life style, identity, and intimate relations Life styles centered on individuality, openness, and full acceptance of and participation in a community. Alternative organizations based fully on humanistic values and new life styles

system whose leadership expresses a desire to change. Experts who provide that assistance may be either members of the social system or outsiders. The professional usually helps the change target discover and use new information relevant to change goals, e.g., a new technology, curriculum, product, or market; or information of a process sort, e.g., concerning social relations among organizations, organizational subunits, or organizational roles and members. Specific tactics may involve analyzing a system's communication and problem-solving patterns, assisting members in using feedback and applying research findings to their situation, or developing a climate more supportive of increased communication and innovation.

The P change agent   There are more kinds of change agent roles in the political than in the professional-technical perspective. Unlike the latter, political actors do not constitute a distinct reference and interest group; they usually are seen as citizens, perhaps with certain expertise, operating out of an open and partisan political commitment.

Change agents who work full time with oppressed groups either volunteer or receive salaries that are usually well below the level of PT experts. The citizen-actor responds to the discontent of oppressed groups by helping them develop and use organizations and mobilize resources to gain the power necessary to achieve their goals.[13] Political change agents who serve elite groups, on the other hand, may be very well recompensed. They

may be elected or appointed public officials or technical advisers (of a clearly partisan nature) to such officials.[14] Their roles may involve organizing other elites, appealing directly to the public for support, controlling the ships of state, or providing political advice to occupants of steerage positions in the political system.

For the most part, political change agents are not prepared for their roles in university settings. They usually attend the university, but primarily for broad socialization and access to mobility channels, not for specific role preparation. Their preparation is not marked by academic credentials nor based on uniform standards determined by an accrediting organization. Currently, however, elite managers often look to university settings for direct aid in the management or control of the political process. A key element in the elite socialization and social control system, the Academy is seldom able to prepare effective agents of change who will serve politically oppressed groups (although this has been tried several times).

Political actors typically intern in a variety of social movement organizations, e.g., the Democratic or Republican parties, the trade union movement, Chambers of Commerce, NAACP, the Grape Boycott; in quasi-independent organizations committed to assisting the powerless to change their situation, e.g., the Industrial Areas Foundation, Southern Conference Educa-

[13] Alinsky and others argue that indigenous leaders operating from within active groups are most likely to be successful (Alinsky, 1969; Brager, 1967). This view accounts for the tactic common among community organizers to expend effort training indigenous leaders to take over roles previously held by outsiders (Kahn, 1970, Chapter 5).

[14] Technical advisers not avowedly partisan may feel they fall within the PT perspective. But providing technical advice to political actors is clearly a political act, and it clearly has partisan consequences, no matter how neutral an expert professes to be (Costello, 1971). The major outlines of partisanship, however, may be in the objective political environment rather than in the subjective consciousness of the change agent. Although intentions may vary, the consequences are still partisan.

tion Foundation, Interreligious Foundation for Community Organization, the Training and Organizing Collective of the Philadelphia Life Center; or with the powerful to consolidate their position, e.g., National Industrial Conference Board, The Brookings Institution, Systems Development Corporation.

The training of political change agents may focus on techniques of motivating oppressed people to take collective action to meet their interests, skills in analyzing social systems in terms of their power and resources and their points of vulnerability, skills in developing and operating organizations of the oppressed, and personal skills in strategy development and value clarification. Skills in social diagnosis and planning and the implementation of new political forms are also useful to political decision-makers. Tactics of negotiation, compromise, and coalition building are likewise relevant components of training for everyone.

The CC change agent   Change agents in the countercultural perspective are heavily committed to living new cultural patterns themselves and are usually identified by membership in or close relationship to communes, collectives, cooperatives, or associations with countercultural values and goals. Their role as initiators of change is defined by a personal struggle to realize new life patterns, efforts to share life patterns and skills in settings which provide for mutual growth among all participants, and the development of liberating organizations. In this perspective, the role of the actor includes as essential both the individual's "work" and "nonwork" life; in their pursuit of wholeness, many CC actors would deny even the existence of such a distinction.

CC change agents often resist salary for their efforts, and at most accept subsistence remuneration on the basis of particular roles in networks of mutual assistance. For some, roles are rooted in

tasks necessary to operate an organic homestead; for others, a food cooperative or alternative school; for still others, a commune. Preparation for those roles varies widely and generally includes: dealing with the self, e.g., personal values, physical health, and spiritual or psychological development; behavioral skills necessary to achieve new life patterns, e.g., the skills necessary in multilateral families, cooperative gardens, consciousness-raising groups; and skills in initiating and participating in organizations which support and extend new life patterns, e.g., starting a new macroanalysis seminar, developing a collective, operating a marketing cooperative.[15]

The pattern of preparation is informal apprenticeship; thus the neophyte, trainee, or disciple may enter a living commune, watch and practice with a master gardener, work under the supervision of a free-school leader, or begin the discipline of meditation with the guidance of a teacher. Generally the basis of such relationships is a teacher's commitment to share what is known as a part of an ongoing life pattern, and a learner's commitment to reciprocate with whatever skill or labor he can offer. Where such training occurs in formal organizations, it tends to be a short-term arrangement in a temporary organization, e.g., free universities, growth centers, or schools of living.

---

[15] Examples of materials used in such preparation include: *Go Ahead and Live* (Loomis, 1972), *Self Therapy* (Schiffman, 1967), *The Basic Book of Organic Gardening* (Rodale, 1971), *Light on Yoga* (Iyengar, 1966), *No More Public School* (Bennett, 1972), *Working Loose* (Anderson *et al.*, 1971), *The Community Land Trust* (R. Swann *et al.*, 1972). *Foxfire One* (Wigginton, 1972), *Whole Earth Catalog*; and periodicals like *Prevention, Communities, Alternative Life Styles, The Green Revolution, Mother Earth News*, and more.

Resources

Each of the three perspectives uses particular combinations of resources to bring about change. Although almost any resource can be used by actors within any perspective, there are consistent—and consistently different—preferences and emphases.

The PT perspective regards the key resources for change to be commitment to change by social systems managers and expertise. Commitment to change by top leadership of a target system is also viewed as an article of democratic faith in growth benefiting all, as well as an analytic projection of effective strategies. Expertise, as embodied in recognized and legitimated professionals, is of both a procedural and substantive variety, and includes diagnostic techniques in system communication, skills in problem solving and team building, and knowledge of such problem areas as education, the environment, poverty, industrial production, and governmental operations.

A closely related resource is the trust of relevant members of the system undergoing change, for it facilitates the change agent's access to information and his efforts to persuade the client to use information in new ways. When persuasion is supported by system managers it uses the organizational power structure and support system, and so increases loyalty to the system as well as the effectiveness of the change agent's efforts.

The credentials and class background, frequently race and sex, and certainly interactional and life styles of the PT change agent result in a position of relatively high status, which he can use to establish personal as well as professional linkages with the leaders of important social systems. A related resource, quite relevant to the necessary commitment of institutional managers, is money.

In the political perspective, key resources for change from the bottom are the discontent and time and energy of sizable numbers of individuals, along with the financial resources to support the organizer, establish an organization (office, telephone, etc.), and develop visibility (leaflets, advertisements, and so on). The requisite expertise is the ability to organize relatively powerless people to increase their power or to create new publics in order to further their interests. Knowledge comes in the person of someone who can build rapport with and be accountable to oppressed people, and who is willing to work at a subsistence level.

Resources for political change from the top include existing offices of legitimate power or well-developed organizations with economic, social, or cultural influence and control. Change agent skills useful in implementing those conditions include assisting already organized groups to work together or implement their powerful wills more effectively. The ability to motivate people is crucial, as are such activities as media presentation, policy formation, and the like. A personal style and social status compatible with effective social relations among elites is obviously helpful.

Countercultural resources for change include commitment to explore and realize a fuller human potential. Individuals who can invest large amounts of personal time and energy in gaining self-sufficiency and developing alternative organizations are the starting point. A key component of the necessary personal commitment is willingness to depart from traditional and popular standards of what constitutes a meaningful, successful life.

In a culture that represses efforts in that direction, the full liberation of individual creativity and consciousness is a vital source of insight and power. Individual growth experiences from encounter groups, radical therapeutic relationships, and the use of drugs, meditation, and dramatic forms help transcend the contemporary culture's boundaries of consciousness. Individuals who have attained the elements of such freedom or liberation are then able to begin collectivization of their activities through the development of consensual cultures committed to maintaining and advancing such growth. This collectivization process is reciprocal: the development of such forms provides an environment within which unliberated individuals may be helped to come to greater awareness and realization of their own potential.

The CC perspective stresses that individuals and groups concerned with change can and must develop skills that will allow them to be self-sufficient, or nearly so. The call is to lessen dependence on the dominant culture, not only in regard to its norms and life style but also in the area of economic survival; e.g., basic agricultural and building skills are essential in developing communal social forms that can be rooted in the earth. A land ethic essential for economic independence also carries with it a critique of private property, which also has its origins in the desire to live a simpler life, one more distant from technologically overdeveloped living and working structures. The redemptive theme, so common in the CC perspective, often leads to a stress on sacred meanings of land and common humanity and of sacred symbols and forms in imagining and implementing change.

Who Is Served?—Clients and Constituencies

The PT perspective frequently claims it serves a total organization or social system. Often, however, a social system is defined by, or in terms of, the interests of its decision-makers. Typically, then, the actual constituency served is middle- or high-level executives—people in power positions who seek to alter particular policies or parts (frequently middle management or lower level line officers) of the systems they manage.

Since many PT change agents operate from an academic base, they tend to assert value neutrality, argue in technical not political terms, and advocate standards of professional autonomy.[16] They may therefore see themselves as accountable only to themselves, and not to any specific public; even their claim to represent an entire system ultimately rests on *their* interpretation of that system's common interests.

The P perspective claims it serves social system subgroups that desire a greater share of social system rewards or privileges. A group with objective interests and preferred values will ask for help in organizing a movement and in devising strategy to reallocate a system's power and social rewards. The change agent—as employee or servant—is seen as specifically accountable to that interest group, and it is assumed that other people may be working with other groups. There often is self-conscious criticism within this perspective regarding whether real service is to an oppressed group or to the broader social order. Debates over system loyalties vs. partisan commitments are more vigorous when leadership comes from outside the local community or from social, economic, racial, age, or sex groupings different from the oppressed constituency.[17]

Political change agents who elect to

[16] As Benne notes, there is often a fine line between technical and political, and ". . . the ethical dimensions of problems tend to be obscured when stated by consultants who are behavioral scientists" (Benne, 1969, p. 596).

[17] A contemporary example of this debate is evident in the demands of third-world groups that leaders of change efforts in the community be from their community—geographically, ethnically, and ideologically (Karenga, 1969; Carmichael & Hamilton, 1967). Similar positions are now being debated on social research in the black community conducted by white members of the PT perspective (Billingsley, 1970; Blauner & Wellman, 1973; Merton, 1972; Thomas, 1971).

work directly with and for members of elite groups accept the elite as their basic constituency. Sometimes this is presented as service to a special-interest group in power, a group whose values are presumably congruent with the change agent's. Sometimes, however, it is explained in terms of a broader commitment to serve the entire social system by serving elites who will act in everybody's best interests. Obviously, this claim encounters some of the same solipsistic and partisan complexities as those advanced more subtly by members of the PT perspective.

The CC perspective claims everyone as its constituency and often refuses to categorize people. Frequently, however, its active constituents are relatively privileged persons—educated young whites, from middle class and upper middle class backgrounds, who have disengaged from traditional institutional membership. In fact, some counterculture critics regard its operations as serving ruling elites by siphoning capable leadership away from an active political challenge of the current order and into socially isolated, introspective searches for personal meaning and self-actualization.

On occasion, CC individuals and groups, or even whole movements, have sought to serve and influence wider social strata. By virtue of their attack on the American culture and economy, these groups have exerted leadership in the ecological movement and in the generation of hip cultures and life syle alternatives for the not-so-young and not-so-middle class (Bookchin, 1971; Loomis, 1972; Bradford & Bradford, 1973). In a number of communities where their strength and number warrant, these groups have forged political coalitions with more mainstream political groups to exercise political power and gain office and legitimate influence. By virtue of their commitment to generate new institutions, these groups have designed and implemented alternative living and schooling structures, for example, which have now begun to be introduced into mainstream systems. Though their form may be altered and perhaps operationalized, by consultants working from a PT perspective, their roots have often been in the counterculture. . . .

References

Alinsky, S. *Reveille for radicals.* New York: Random House, 1969.

Anderson, B., *et al.* (Eds.) *Working loose.* San Francisco: American Friends Service Committee, 1971.

Argyris, C. *Interpersonal competence and organizational effectiveness.* Homewood, Ill.: Dorsey Press, 1962.

Argyris, C. *Intervention theory and method.* Mass.: Addison-Wesley, 1970.

Balbus, I. D. The concept of interest in pluralist and Marxian analysis. *Politics and Society,* 1971, **1** (2), 151–177.

Benne, K. D. Some ethical problems in group and organizational consultation. In W. G. Bennis, K. D. Benne, and R. Chin (Eds.), *The planning of change,* 2nd ed. New York: Holt,

Rinehart and Winston, 1969. Pp. 595–604.

Bennett, H. *No more public school.* New York: Random House, 1972.

Bennis, W., Benne, K., & Chin R. *The planning of change,* 2nd ed. New York: Holt, Rinehart and Winston, 1969.

Billingsley, A. Black families and white social science. *Journal of Social Issues,* 1970, **26**, 127–142.

Blauner, R. *Racial oppression in America.* New York: Harper and Row, 1972.

Blauner, R., & Wellman, D. Toward the decolonization of social research. In J. Ladner (Ed.), *The death of white sociology.* New York: Vintage Books, 1973.

Bookchin, M., & Ecology Action East.

Ecology and revolutionary thought. New York: Times Change Press, 1971.

Bradford, D., & Bradford, E. A model of a middle class commune. *Communities,* 1973, 1.

Bradley, M., Danchik, L., Fager, M., & Wodetzki, T. *Unbecoming men: A men's consciousness raising group writes on oppression and themselves.* New York: Times Change Press, 1971.

Brager, G. A. The low-income nonprofessional. In G. Brager and F. Purcell (Eds.), *Community action against poverty.* New Haven: College and University Press, 1967. Pp. 163–174.

Buber, M. *Paths in Utopia.* London. Routledge and Kegan Paul, 1949.

Carmichael, S., & Hamilton, C. *Black power: The politics of liberation in America.* New York: Random House, 1967.

Chin, R., & Benne, K. General strategies for effecting change in human systems. In W. Bennis, K. Benne, and R. Chin (Eds.). *The planning of change,* 2nd ed. New York: Holt, Rinehart and Winston, 1969. Pp. 32–59.

Cloward, R., & Piven, F. *Regulating the poor: The functions of public welfare.* New York: Pantheon Books, 1971.

Coleman, J. S. Conflicting theories of social change. In G. Zaltman (Ed.), *Processes and phenomena of social change.* New York: John Wiley, 1973. Pp. 61–74.

Coser, L. *Continuities in the study of social conflict.* New York: Free Press, 1967.

Costello, T. Change in municipal government: A view from inside. *Journal of Applied Behavioral Science,* 1971, 7, 131–145.

Dahl, R. A. *Pluralist democracy in the U.S.: Conflict and consent.* Chicago: Rand McNally, 1967.

Dahrendorf, R. *Class and class conflict in industrial society.* Palo Alto, Calif.: Stanford Press, 1959.

Davis, S. A. An organic problem-solving method of organizational change. *Journal of Applied Behavioral Science,* 1967, 3, 3–21.

Durkheim, E. *The division of labor in society.* Glencoe, Ill.: Free Press, 1949.

Fairfield, R. *Communes, U.S.A.* Baltimore: Penguin Books, 1972.

Fanon, F. *Wretched of the earth.* New York: Evergreen, 1966.

Freire, P. A conversation with Paulo Freire. *Perspectives on development and social change.* 1, 9 n.d.

Fromm, E. *Man for himself.* New York: Rinehart and Co., 1947.

Fromm, E. *Sane society.* New York: Holt, Rinehart and Winston, 1955.

Gamson, W. *Power and discontent.* Homewood, Ill.: Dorsey Press, 1968.

Havelock, R. G. *The change agents' guide to innovation in education.* Englewood Cliffs, N.J.: Educational Technology Publications, 1973.

Hornstein, H., et al. *Social intervention.* New York: Free Press, 1971.

Iyengar, B. K. *Light on yoga.* New York: Schocken Books, 1966.

Jacques, E. *The changing culture of a factory.* London: Tavistock Publications, 1951.

Jones, G. N. Strategies and tactics of planned organizational change. *Human Organization,* 1965, 24 (3), 192–260.

Jordan, W. *White over black American attitudes toward the Negro 1550-1812.* Chapel Hill: University of North Carolina Press, 1968.

Kahn, S. *How people get power.* New York: McGraw-Hill, 1970.

Karenga, R. The black community and the university: A community organizer's perspective. In A. L. Robinson et al. (Eds.), *Black studies in the university: A symposium.* New Haven, Conn.: Yale University Press, 1969. Pp. 39–55.

Katz, D., & Kahn, R. *The social psychology of organization.* New York: Wiley, 1966.

Krichbaum, D. Masculinity and racism.

To appear in R. Terry and N. Sander (Eds.), In pursuit of white liberation. Grand Rapids, Mich.: Eerdmans, Fall 1974.

Lawrence, P. R., & Lorsch, J. W. Organization and environment. Homewood, Ill.: Richard D. Irwin, 1967.

Lenin, V. What is to be done. New York: International Publishers, 1943.

Likert, R. New Patterns of management. New York: McGraw-Hill, 1961.

Lippitt, R., Watson, J., & Westley, B. The dynamics of planned change. New York: Harcourt and Brace, 1958.

Loomis, M. Go ahead and live. New Canaan, Conn.: Keats, 1972.

Machiavelli, N. The prince. New York: Mentor, 1957.

March, J. G., & Simon, H. A. Organizations. New York: Wiley, 1958.

Merton, R. Insiders and outsiders: A chapter in the sociology of knowledge. In Varieties of political expression in sociology. Chicago: University of Chicago Press, 1972. Pp. 9–47.

Nearing, S., & Nearing, H. Living the good life. New York: Schocken Books, 1970.

Olmusk, K. E. Seven pure strategies of change. In J. W. Pfeiffer and J. E. Jones (Eds.) The 1972 annual handbook for group facilitators. Iowa City: University Associates 1972. Pp. 163–172.

Parsons, T. The social system. Glencoe, Ill.: The Free Press, 1951.

Peslikis, I. Resistances to consciousness. In R. Morgan (Ed.), Sisterhood is powerful New York: Vintage, 1970. Pp. 337–339.

Rhea, B. Institutional paternalism in high schools. The Urban Review, February 1968, 34, 13–15.

Rodale, R. The basic book of organic gardening New York: Ballantine Books, 1971.

Rogers, E., & Shoemaker, F. Communication of innovations. New York: Free Press, 1971.

Rothman, J. Three models of community organization practice. In F. Cox, J. Erlich, J. Rothman, and J. Tropman (Eds.), Strategies of community organization. Itasca, Ill.: Peacock Publishers, 1970. Pp. 20–36.

Schein, E. Process consultation: Its role in organizational development. Reading, Mass.: Addison-Wesley, 1969.

Schiffman, M. Self therapy: Techniques for personal growth. Menlo Park, Calif.: Self-Therapy Press, 1967.

Schutz, W. Here comes everybody. New York: Harper and Row, 1971.

Shapiro, D. On psychological liberation. Social Policy. 1972, 3, 9–15.

Slater, P. The pursuit of loneliness: American cuture at the breaking point. Boston: Beacon Press, 1970.

Sofer, C. The assessment of organizational change. Journal of Management Studies: (G. B.), 1964, 1, 128–142.

Steiner, C. Cooperation. Communities, 1973–74, 6. 40–46.

Swann, R. S., et al. The community land trust. Cambridge, Mass.: Center for Community Economic Development, 1972.

Terry, R. W. For whites only. Detroit: Detroit Industrial Mission, 1970.

Thomas, C. (Ed.) Boys no more: A black psychologist's view of community. Beverly Hills, Calif.: Glencoe Press, 1971.

Warren, R. Truth, love and social change. Chicago: Rand McNally, 1971.

Watson, G. Resistance to change. In G. Watson (Ed.), Concepts for social change. Washington, D.C.: National Training Laboratories, 1966.

Weber, M. The protestant ethic and the spirit of capitalism. New York: Charles Scribner's, 1930.

Wigginton, E. Foxfire one. New York: Doubleday, 1972.

Women: A Journal of Liberation. Consciousness-raising. Women: A Journal . . . , 1972, 2, 18–21.

Zetterberg, H. Social theory and social practice. Towata, N.J.: Bedminister Press, 1962.

5.3   SOCIAL EXPERIMENTATION AND THE CHANGING WORLD OF WORK

Neal Q. Herrick, Susan Bartholomew,
John Brandt

A central characteristic of our society today is the rapidity of its technological social and economic change. The rate of change is such that we can no longer "keep our balance"[1] through sticking to traditional ways of doing things. Rather, we must devise new and flexible ways. This means, not so much the development of specific solutions to specific problems, but the creation of institutional structures and relationships which are capable of producing timely and appropriate solutions to problems as they arise.

Increasing rates of change bring with them a greater need for coordinated solutions. Time is no longer available for one institution of society to gradually become aware of changes occurring in another institution and independently take steps responding to these changes. By the time these steps are taken, a new and different set of conditions is likely to exist and the two institutions will be as much at odds as before. The institutions to which we address ourselves in this chapter are those involved in the work and education systems: organized labor, management, educational organizations and government. We see government's role as stimulating and facilitating cooperation among the other institutions.

Edited from a paper prepared for the Fifth Yearbook of the American Vocational Association, 1975, Merle E. Strong, Editor. The present abridged version appears by permission of the authors, the American Vocational Association, and the editor of the AVA Yearbook.

Footnotes in edited portions of this paper have been deleted and remaining footnotes renumbered.

[1] "And how do we keep our balance?" inquired Tevye in *Fiddler on the Roof.* "That I can tell you in one word—Tradition!"

The major areas in which we see important needs for coordination among the institutions (and members) of the educational and work systems are:

Process. Participatory skills are more and more necessary to the effective functioning of business and industry. The educational system can provide students with these skills only by creating participatory decision making processes in the administration of its schools.

Substance. The users of the educational "product" should be involved in decisions regarding the kinds of professional and technical skills which should be taught. Industry and organized labor are in the best position to know the skills that are needed. Their involvement in the formulation of curricula should result in a more realistic allocation of educational resources.

Workforce, work-content and economic changes have brought us to the point where institutions which have been indifferent to or at odds with each other in the past must now join together to work toward common goals. Labor and management must invent cooperative arrangements in order to work toward their mutual goal of a better working environment and its by-product, increased productivity. Parents, administrators, teachers and students must work together with labor and management toward their mutual goals of a better learning environment and increased productivity (i.e., the production of graduates who possess skills needed by and valuable to both business and themselves).

This . . . [paper] will, first, mention

some workforce, work-content and economic changes. Then we will illustrate a few of the ways in which some of our work and educational institutions are already moving towards more cooperative and coordinated relationships. . . .

WORKFORCE, WORK-CONTENT AND ECONOMIC CHANGE

The cause/result relationships among workforce, work-content and economic change are far from clear. The same can be said of the relationships between changes in the workforce and changes in the educational system. No doubt the educational system is in part responding to changes in the needs of the work system by turning out people with different values and attitudes,[2] and the work system is in part changing because of the different values and attitudes of new workforce entrants. It can be said with some confidence, however, that technological advances both here and abroad are basic to all three categories of change. It can also be said that, whether the educational system is forcing changes in the work system or vice versa, the need for cooperation and coordination remains.

Changes in the workforce The values and attitudes of young workers differ from those of their leaders. This is demonstrated by the 1969 survey of working conditions done for the U.S. Department of Labor by the Survey Research Center of the University of Michigan.

. . . significantly more young workers than workers over 29 years of age express negative attitudes toward work. This was true regardless of race, sex, marital status, education, collar color, etc. . . .

We often suppose that young workers have a different set of work values than do their elders and, indeed, this appears to be quite true. But contrary to the suppositions of many older people, their values appear to be highly responsible. They placed substantially more importance on the interesting nature of the work, on their opportunity to develop their own special abilities, and on their chances for promotion. They were less concerned than their elders with being asked to do excessive amounts of work, whether or not their transportation arrangements were convenient, and whether their jobs allowed them to forget their personal problems. With regard to pay, job security, and fringe benefits, age seemed to make no difference: all age groups seemed to be equally interested in the economics of work.

It is clear from this analysis of the "satisfaction gaps" that the important difference between the dissatisfaction of young workers and that of their elders stems first, from the high value they placed on challenging work, and second, from the lack of challenge in the work they were actually required to perform.[3]

There can be little doubt that increasing levels of education have something to do with these different values and attitudes. Communications technology has given us a greater insight into how our fellow citizens work and live. In doing so, it has translated very general notions of social inequity into

[2] According to the "co-respondence principle" educational reforms become probable when the existing educational approach and its results are contradicted by changes in the functioning of work organizations. Levin, Henry M., *A Taxonomy of Educational Reforms For Changes in the Nature of Work*, Portola Institute, 1974.

[3] Harold L. Sheppard and Neal Q. Herrick, *Where Have All the Robots Gone?*, The Free Press, N.Y., 1972, pp. 115–119.

specific comparisons of offices, homes, automobiles, neighborhoods, schools and levels of social interaction. Events such as the black movement, women's liberation and gay liberation demonstrate an increasing unwillingness to accept undesirable conditions. There is a school of thought which says that young workers today, while certainly different from their elders, are no different than their elders were when they were young. A series of studies conducted on college campuses by Daniel Yankelovich, however, does not support this theory. For example, the percentage of students who did not mind the future prospect of being bossed around on the job fell from 56% in 1968 to 49% in 1969, 43% in 1970 and 36% in 1971. Yankelovich also found that the "counterculture" values held by only a minority of college students in the late 1960's have spread to about two-thirds of the college-age cohort, including many blue-collar youth. Even if today's youth were really no different from yesterday's, the attitudinal make-up of the workforce is changing rapidly simply because of the increasing proportion of workers who are young.

Work-content change The rapid sophistication of production technology in American industry has had mixed effects on the nature of jobs. It has eliminated some undesirable jobs, made some desirable jobs less so and, in some cases (e.g., continuous process technology), created new jobs which are consistent with the use of work enrichment techniques such as autonomous work groups. In terms of occupational structure, the trend is toward increases in requirements for professional and technical skills. Whether these skills will be primarily professional or primarily technical in nature is not clear. We will present two views of this matter which, while they differ in emphasis, both lead to the same conclusion: that there is an urgent need for coordination between the institutions of education and work.

U.S. Department of Labor Projections.[4] According to the U.S. Department of Labor, employment growth generally will be fastest in those occupations requiring the most education and training. For example, professional and technical occupations requiring the most education will show the fastest growth through the 1970's (see Chart 1). Personnel in these fields will be in great demand as the Nation puts greater efforts toward the country's socio-economic progress, urban renewal, transportation, harnessing the ocean, and enhancing the beauty of the land. The quest for scientific and technical knowledge is bound to grow and raise the demand for workers in scientific and technical specialties. The 1970's will see a continuing emphasis in the social sciences and medical services. By 1980 the requirements for professional, technical and kindred workers may be about two-fifths greater than 1970 employment.

In many areas of sales work, new developments in machine design and the use of new materials are requiring demonstrators to have greater technical knowledge. Repairmen must acquire even greater skills to keep the more complicated machines running smoothly. Along with the demand for greater education, the proportion of youth completing high school has increased and an ever larger proportion of high school graduates pursue higher education. This trend is expected to continue through the 1970's. In 1980, high school enrollment is expected to be 21.4 million, 7 percent above the 1970 level and college degree credit

---

[4] U.S. Department of Labor, Bureau of Labor Statistics, *Occupational Outlook Handbook*, 1972–1973 Ed., Bulletin 1700.

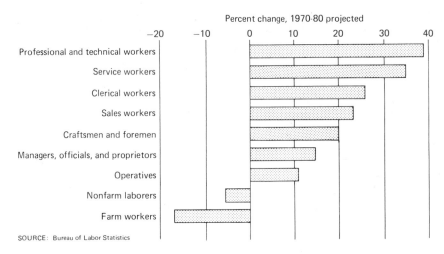

CHART 1   During the 1970's, growth will vary widely among occupations

enrollment is projected at 11.2 million, about 48 percent above the 1970 level of 7.6 million. . . .

Warnings on Over-Education. An editorial in the September 23, 1972, issue of *Business Week* addressed this problem:

> For a quarter of a century, the U.S. has channeled men and money into a frantic expansion of its colleges and universities. Now the nation has found to its dismay that the educational system is cranking out more graduates than the economy can absorb. The unemployment rate for recent college graduates is just under 8 percent, which compares with a rate of 5.6 percent for the total labor force. Moreover, there is no indication that this situation will change radically in the future.

An article in the same *Business Week* issue reported that one of every four young chemists was jobless and that U.S. law schools graduated 10,000

more people in 1972 than there were jobs. A Federal task force on higher education estimates that, by 1977, every recognized profession will have an oversupply of new graduates. This overemphasis on college not only creates an education/job imbalance but also affects the relevance of educational programs to meeting individual human needs. Among workers with comparable incomes, college experience raises expectations which can be real handicaps to attaining job satisfaction.

Economic needs may also be negatively affected. Jim O'Toole quotes Ivar Berg in arguing:

> . . . What actually happens is a process of unproductive job dislocation: More highly qualified workers bump slightly less qualified workers from their jobs. No increase in productivity occurs because the nature of the jobs is usually such that they do not require higher skills. Productivity may actually drop because the more highly qualified worker is

likely to be dissatisfied with the job. In sum, increasing the educational level of the workforce above a certain level, without concomitant changes in the structures of work to capitalize on the increased capabilities of workers, will probably have a slightly negative impact on productivity.[5]

On the other hand, there are severe shortages of technicians and assistants throughout the health and service occupations. The American Dental Association, during the spring of 1969, estimated that there was a shortage of 94,000 technicians and 15,000 assistants. Many openings for trained automobile mechanics, appliance repairmen, TV technicians, airplane mechanics, data processing personnel and secretaries exist side by side with today's unemployed and underemployed. In addition to difficulties in making the numbers match, a logistical problem arises in providing job training as part of an educational system which exists as an entity separate from the industries for which it provides the workforce. For example, equipment purchased by a school system cannot be easily updated to match the rapid technological innovations undertaken in industry.

This is not intended to be an argument for either more professional or more vocational education. We are simply

pointing out the need for coordination between the work and educational systems. Perhaps the skills required for many technical and skilled jobs are reading, writing and arithmetic. Whatever the optimal solution, it is more likely to be found and implemented if the involved institutions and their interest groups participate in developing it.

Economic change   Recent economic changes certainly affect the directions of industrial and educational reform. The shift to a service economy, for example, has important implications to the directions of changes in both the work and educational systems. The major economic change which concerns us here, however, is simply the disappearance of our technological advantage over other developed countries. The significance of this change is that it forces industrial and educational reforms to improve manpower utilization in the U.S.

International Competition.   By 1958, the U.S. began to import more low technology products than it exported. The gap by 1970 was about $7 million. Now, even such high technology products as transistor radios, typewriters and electronic calculators are being obtained largely from other developed countries. For example, in 1970 four-fifths of our radios were manufactured abroad. Of the one-fifth made in the U.S., 90% had foreign parts. In high technology products the favorable balance of trade was 4:1 in 1962 (exports of $10.2 billion and imports of $2.55 billion). In 1968 it was 2:1 (exports of $18.4 billion and imports of $9.4 billion). In 1971 the balance of trade as a whole was running at a deficit of $12 billion.

The New Service Economy.   In the years from 1960 to 1970, the workforce

[5] "The Reserve Army of The Underemployed; a Policy Agenda For The Next Decade," James O'Toole, prepared for the Center for Futures Research University of Southern California (November, 1974). It is noteworthy in this respect that Berg discovered several years ago that about 80% of American college graduates were taking jobs previously filled by people wtih less education.

has increased by about 20 million people, 17 million of these in service industries. The greatest growth has been in government. Today, one out of every six workers is employed by either Federal, State or Local governments—about 16% of the labor force. Figure 1 shows the sector breakdown:

FIGURE 1   Employment by Industry Division[6]

	1960	1970	1980 (projected)
Goods Producing Industries	37.6	33.0	31.8
Mining	1.3	.9	.6
Construction	5.3	4.7	5.3
Manufacturing	31.0	27.4	25.3
Service-Producing Industries	67.4	67.0	68.7
Transportation Comm., P.U.	7.4	6.4	5.5
Wholesale and retail trade	21.0	21.1	20.4
Finance, Ins., R.E.	4.9	5.2	4.9
Service and Miscellaneous	13.7	16.5	18.6
Government	15.4	17.8	19.4

This change from a manufacturing to a more labor intensive economy makes educational and industrial reforms leading to improved manpower utilization even more critical to our economic well being.

Exporting Jobs. Additionally, a substantial and increasing proportion of the positive side of our balance of trade consists of the return on investments abroad by American corporations. Thus, even fewer American jobs are provided by the production of exports than the balance of trade would indicate. The reduction in transportation costs and the differential in wages has made it increasingly possible for American multinational corporations to manufacture components abroad and bring them back here for assembly. This is particularly true in the auto-

[6] U.S. Department of Labor, Bureau of Labor Statistics, *Occupational Outlook Handbook*, 1972–1973 Ed., Bulletin 1700.

mobile industry. In the early 50's the U.S. produced 75% of the world's automobiles and trucks. Today the U.S. produces about 30%, although another 20%–30% are produced by American firms outside the United States.

INSTITUTIONAL RESPONSES TO CHANGE

Workforce changes suggest that people expect more challenging jobs and participatory forms of organization. Work-content changes raise a question as to whether the educational system is providing people with the substantive and participatory skills which are needed by the work system. Economic changes demand more effective utilization of our human resources if the United States is to compete effectively in the world market. Given the rapidity of workforce and work-content changes, this more effective human resources utilization requires new structures for cooperation within and among our work and educational system institutions. The inclination of some of these institutions to respond to this need is suggested by a number of events.

Government For the most part, the role of government is one of stimulating cooperation among other societal institutions. Here are some recent examples of government's willingness to perform this function with regard to the problems of labor and industry.

The Jamestown Experience. A project in the City of Jamestown, New York illustrates the role of the government in fostering cooperation between other institutions in order to deal with changes taking place in our society. A municipal joint labor-management committee has been working in Jamestown since 1971 to improve the labor relations climate in the City. At least two government agencies have provided encouragement and assistance to the project. The Economic Development Administration of the U.S. Department of Commerce provided funding for a full-time coordinator to assist the Labor-Management Committee, and the National Commission on Productivity engaged Eric Trist of the Wharton School of Finance to provide assistance to several plant-level cooperative committees in dealing with problems such as work assignments, work flow, and inspection systems. In addition, Senator Javits has been influential in the Jamestown Project's continuance and it was at the suggestion of Mayor Stan Lundeen that the Project was started. Government interest and involvement in the project has also been shown by the continuing advice and assistance provided by the Federal Mediation and Conciliation Service.

The Ohio Quality of Work Project.[7] In 1973, the State of Ohio provided funds to explore the feasibility of establishing a labor/industry controlled institution giving technical assistance to Ohio unions and businesses. This technical assistance focuses on cooperative efforts to increase worker satisfaction and productivity through improving the quality of the working environment. This institution has now initiated two formal labor/management quality of work demonstration projects, one in a goods manufacturing establishment and one in the public sector. It is now jointly sponsored by the Academy For Contemporary Problems in Columbus and by the Ohio Development Center. The Quality of Work Project plans to initiate eleven more demonstration efforts over the next two and one-half years.

Interagency Cooperation. An interagency working group, composed of representatives from the Departments of Commerce, Labor, and Health, Education and Welfare, was established in 1974 to deal with productivity and work quality issues and to coordinate the activities of the three agencies with regard to these issues. This not only demonstrates cooperation within government, but shows promise of foster-

[7] In 1973 the Governor's Business and Employment Council, chaired by George S. Dively of the Harris Corporation, formed the Ohio Quality of Work Project under the guidance of the Ohio Quality of Work Committee. This Committee was chaired by Joseph Tomasi, Director, Region 28, UAW and made up of O. Pendleton Thomas, Chairman and Chief Executive of the B. F. Goodrich Company; Everett Ware Smith, Chairman, Cleveland Trust Company; and Frank King, then President of the Ohio AFL–CIO. Mr. Tomasi is still Chairman of the Ohio Quality of Work Committee which is now being reconstructed under new sponsors.

ing cooperation among the constituencies of those agencies.

CETA. The Comprehensive Employment and Training Act of 1973 fosters cooperation between Federal and State governments and between State governments and other agencies, institutions, and governmental units. Working together these groups establish comprehensive manpower services plans.

The National Commission on Productivity and Work Quality. Public Law 93–311, approved June 8, 1974, created and funded a National Commission on Productivity and Work Quality to carry on the work begun by the President's National Commission on Productivity. The law states that the objective of the Commission shall be to "help increase the productivity of the American economy and to help improve the morale and quality of work of the American worker." Toward these ends, the Commission will encourage and assist the formation of cooperative labor-management committees to increase productivity, morale and work quality, conduct research necessary to reach its objectives, and publicize and disseminate ideas and material related to its objectives. It is hoped that the activities of the Commission will impact on the morale and working environment of the American worker, the international competitive position of the United States, the efficiency of government, and the cost of basic consumer goods and services.

Labor Changing conditions in society have brought another major institution—organized labor—to a growing awareness that solutions to problems of productivity and the quality of working life require the development of cooperative relationships with business and industry.

Labor in the United States, guided by a philosophy which has been characterized as business unionism, has traditionally concentrated on the "bread and butter" issues of wages, hours, and working conditions. This has sometimes resulted in restrictive work practices with negative effects on productivity. As far back as the 1920's, however, labor leaders recognized the need to develop cooperative—as well as adversary—relationships with management. For example, in the early 1920's, Samuel Gompers, the President of the American Federation of Labor, wrote:

> The Union is just as necessary for the newer function—cooperation—as it is for the defensive and bargaining purposes . . . Cooperation comes with maturity and development.[8]

Phil Murray, the founder of the United Steelworkers, elaborated that viewpoint in 1940.

> Power, wherever it lies, cannot in the long run be disassociated from responsibility. If the labor movement fails to develop an adequate sense of responsibility for output, the alternative will be increasing tension and bitterness over "wages, hours and working conditions," reducing the opportunity for constructive accommodation and community of interest between management and union.[9]

While these statements show an awareness on the part of organized labor of the need for cooperative relationships, until recently little progress has been made toward translating this awareness

[8] See Report, *Labor-Management Productivity Committees in American Industry,* prepared for the National Commission on Productivity and Work Quality by H. M. Douty, September, 1974.

[9] *Steel Labor,* May, 1973, pp. 12–13.

into specific arrangements. Recent years, however, have witnessed some significant activities toward this end. Two examples are particularly relevant here:

The 1971 and 1973 Steel Contracts. The 1971 agreement between the United Steelworkers of America and the steel companies called for a joint Union-Industry effort to improve productivity and promote the use of domestic steel. One of the most direct results of this provision was a Labor-Industry agreement reached on March 29, 1973. Called the Experimental Negotiating Agreement, this document is expected to have beneficial effects on the productivity and competitive position of the American steel industry. Prior to this arrangement, the three-year negotiating cycle in the steel industry was marked by strike-hedge steel inventory build-ups prior to contract expiration dates and by layoffs after accord was reached. The Experimental Negotiating Agreement aims at eliminating that destructive process by having the parties agree to forego strikes or lockouts. . . .

Management Management has also been affected by changing conditions and circumstances in the world of work. Many of the problems which are particularly appropriate for solution via cooperation have symptoms, such as reduced output or lowered efficiency, which first impact on management. The latest contracts with the Steelworkers and the Auto Workers which we cited above are examples of management's willingness to cooperate with organized labor. Instances of both informal and formal cooperation are also appearing at the plant level. As a general rule, they are efforts to achieve the common goals of increased worker satisfaction and productivity. The number of informal efforts, which usually involve union acquiescence

rather than active participation, is difficult to estimate. Formal cooperative efforts to improve the quality of the working environment, which involve written supplements to the basic contract, are an innovation which has appeared only in the past year or two.[10] . . .

Education The educational system also furnishes examples of cooperation among its participants in response to changing circumstances.

Manpower Legislation. Government has stimulated cooperation within the educational system to alleviate problems of the unemployed and disadvantaged through the Manpower Development and Training Act of 1973. This cooperation is mainly in the form of sharing financial resources, but there is evidence that educators and trainers are increasingly being given the opportunity to cooperate with the designers of such programs.

Increased Parental Involvement. Although cooperation may sometimes be lacking, there can be little doubt that the concern of parents with the educational process has reached new levels of participation. Less cooperative relationships were illustrated by parental activities in connection with school desegregation and reading list policies during the fall of 1974. These activities in Boston and West Virginia do, however, demonstrate a deep-seated desire and willingness to participate actively in fundamental decisions regarding the educational process. Constructive co-

[10] While, to the writers' knowledge, there are only four joint labor/management quality of work committees in the United States dealing with the root causes of dissatisfaction and counter productive behavior, formally established committees dealing with specific day-to-day problems in a more cooperative context have become fairly numerous, particularly in the basic steel industry.

operation between parents and educators ranges from PTA groups studying curricula changes to parent groups raising funds to support athletics and other extra-curricular activities.

Increased Student Involvement. Student demands for more participation in the design and content of education are well documented. Although there has been, as we might expect, resistance to these demands, college students now have seats on faculty senates, high school students administer judiciary boards to deal with rule infractions, and students at many levels have a voice in determining dress and discipline codes.

PITFALLS AND POTENTIAL BENEFITS

General Our analysis, then, suggests that the institutions of society are inclined to react constructively to workforce, work-content and economic change. Employers are attempting to modify the productive process to be consistent with the needs of a changing workforce. Unions are recognizing the changing needs of their members and are, in a few cases, entering into cooperative arrangements with management to meet these needs. The educational system is expanding its vocational and technical education programs to meet changing skills needs[11] and is involving students, teachers and parents in the decision-making process. Government has taken some initial steps to encourage and facilitiate cooperative institutional structures

Pitfalls Now, let us look at some of the potential pitfalls inherent in the re-

[11] Our point here is that the educational system, stimulated by government, is seeking constructive reforms. For Jim O'Toole's criticism of this particular approach, see [James O'Toole, "The Reserve Army of the Underemployed; a Policy Agenda for the Next Decade," Center for Future Research, University of Southern California, November 1974].

lationships and processes which are central to these basically constructive reactions. Then we will discuss some of the potential benefits which might accrue to individuals and to society should unions, managements, schools and governments manage to avoid these pitfalls. We would suggest that four of the major pitfalls might be termed: compromise, exploitation, imposition and discouragement.

Compromise. By compromise we mean the possibility that a cooperative relationship between management and labor in a specific plant might compromise the role of the union. Labor's basic role is one of advocacy. It protects the rights of its members and promotes their economic and psychological well-being. In the long-run, the existence of the adversary relationship is certainly in the best interest of all parties: workers, management and the union. In the short run, however, specific issues arise where what is in the best interest of the workers is not necessarily in the best interest of management. For example, collectively bargaining the share of profits which should go to capital and the share which should go to labor is necessarily —in the short run—a win/lose situation.[12] That which labor gets for wages, management cannot reinvest or pass along to its stockholders, and vice versa. Another example might be the making of certain major expenditures for occupational safety and health. While such expenditures might be to the long-range benefit of management, they might also be a short-range disadvantage and so represent a legitimate conflict of interest. These kinds of conflicts of interest are real and cannot be

[12] This is not to say that a theoretical optimum settlement does not exist from a long-range societal point of view.

ignored. A workable adversary structure must be maintained to deal with them.

The danger which we are suggesting is that the union may be drawn into the decision-making process and, having become partially responsible for production success, be handicapped in its role as a critic of management decisions. There is no easy formula for avoiding this possibility. However, basic principles should be followed. For example, when it becomes clear that no consensus can be achieved on an issue brought to the cooperative table, it should not be discussed further but should be referred to a part of the industrial relations structure which is geared to deal with adversary matters.

The union, like Caesar's wife, must be above suspicion. It is not enough to assure the integrity of the adversary relationship. It is also necessary that this integrity be clearly visible to the membership. The surface manifestations of a cooperative relationship are sometimes difficult for the rank-and-file member to distinguish from the manifestations of a sweetheart arrangement. There should, for this and for more substantive reasons, be early, substantial and continuing participation of the rank-and-file in developing and implementing policies and programs under any cooperative agreement for improving the working environment and—as a by-product—increasing productivity. Arrangements must be made for quality of work committee meetings to be open to the membership. The work of such committees must be carried out through the direct involvement of workers in shaping any changes in their working environment. If this is not done, there is no real possibility for a cooperative relationship which is constructive for all parties.

Exploitation. Should an effort to improve the working environment and increase productivity be successful, its success would be short-lived without an equitable distribution of the productivity gains between capital and labor. It is possible to avoid the danger of exploitation in a number of ways. Traditional collective bargaining may adequately distribute any gains after-the-fact. Before-the-fact productivity bargaining[13] may be a part of the solution. Arrangements which distribute gains over baseline productivity levels on a preagreed formula have been a model for providing a supportive link between improvements in the quality of work (particularly participative decision making) and economic rewards. It has not been the custom in our society, however, for management to gladly open its books to workers. And without an open book arrangement, it is difficult, if not impossible, to provide any convincing guarantees against exploitation.

Imposition. It is desirable and important that state and federal governments encourage cooperative efforts to improve the quality of education and work. It is difficult to see how substantial and widespread improvements can be achieved without some governmental involvement. The exact nature of this involvement, however, is crucial. Government should neither impose specific solutions nor avoid setting parameters based on principle. The line between government as regulator and government as catalyst is sometimes exceedingly fine. In this case, we believe that government's role should be clearly one of encourage-

[13] The term "productivity bargaining" is used here to emphasize bargaining for a share of the *results* of a total quality of work program rather than agreeing to a wage increase in return for specific contract modifications.

ment rather than regulation. The effective approaches to improving the quality of education and work varies considerably with the social structure[14] and the character of the students or workers involved. Therefore, it would be, at this time, not only difficult but counter-productive to legislate minimum standards for the non-economic learning and working environments. However, this does not deny the existence of certain principles which apply to all human beings: that is, the needs for security, equity, individuation and participation. But these needs exist in different people in different degrees (Herrick and Maccoby, 1972). One general principle which should guide the development of government programs is that they should be careful not to translate these principles to a degree of specificity which is neither general nor flexible enough to be relevant to all students and workers. In addition to providing guarantees against compromise and exploitation, while at the same time limiting themselves to reasonable degrees of specificity, governmental programs should give attention to two other principles: optionality and participation. By the principle of optionality we mean, first, that programs should not be imposed on unions, industry and educational institutions by government nor on lower levels of government by higher levels. Rather, resources and technical assistance should be offered on an optional basis. Cooperativeness cannot be enforced but, if areas of activity exist which are indeed beneficial to all parties, they can be defined and encouraged. We also mean by this principle that programs at the school and plant level should offer possibilities and opportunities to student and workers but should be careful not to impose structures which are not desired. By the principle of participation we mean that any changes in learning or work environments should be developed by the people actually involved and not unilaterally imposed by others. . . .[15]

Discouragement[16] It is clear from recorded experience to date that significant human and economic gains can be realized through improvements in the quality of work. However, anyone who has been involved in a quality of work effort can vouch for the fact that realizing these gains is not easy. There are at least as many possibilities for failure as for success, particularly since we are only in the early experimental stages of creating a social invention to deal with problems which are common to labor and management. Quality of work efforts can fail through changes in leadership, personality conflicts, mergers, economic crisis, etc. The danger here is that early and visible failure may discourage both

[14] In the workplace, technology also has a major impact on the kinds of approaches which are feasible.

[15] In his 1974 Portola Institute paper "A Taxonomy of Educational Reforms For Changes In The Nature of Work," Henry M. Levin offers an extremely useful classification of workplace reforms and the corresponding educational reforms which might facilitate them. We believe that extra care should be taken to avoid mandatory or unilateral introduction of such reforms since their chances for success are in direct proportion to their ownership by the people and institutions in the experimental schools and businesses.

[16] This section addresses itself to the "discouragement" issue as it relates to quality of work experimentation. We suppose that similar things could be said about educational experiments, but are not aware of any formal educational experiments mutually developed by parents, teachers, school administrators and students which aim at increasing security, equity, individuation and participation. Therefore, we cannot speak so confidently of the difficulties involved or of the potential benefits.

institutions and the individuals from further attempts to go through the painful trial and error process of social invention. There are two points to make here:

The early and visible efforts which are now underway or which government might stimulate in the near future should be carefully planned and assisted.

It should be recognized that some failures are not only possible but probable and that they should be examined for the lessons to be learned rather than taken as evidence that such activity cannot succeed.

The necessity to guard against discouragement is great. It is great because school and workforce problems do in fact exist and discouragement with cooperative efforts toward solutions might lead to the selection of a negative alternative by the institutions of society. This negative alternative is the adoption of repressive and regulatory measures to "get the students and the work force in hand" rather than to pursue participatory measures utilizing their potential. Given the surface attraction of the negative alternative, major failures among the experiments now in existence and the experiments proposed later on in this paper might lead to a shift away from the generally constructive positions now taken by the institutions of society.

Benefits But the possible benefits are well worth the risks. Should we successfully avoid these pitfalls, there are immense possibilities for human benefits to be gained from institutionalizing:

Parent/teacher/administration/student structures aimed at improving the quality of education.

Labor/management structures aimed at improving the quality of work.

Parent/teacher/administration/student/labor/management structures to coordinate improvements in the quality of education and work.

Should these kinds of institutionalized cooperative relationships result in increases in security, equity, individuation and participation in the school and in the workplace, substantial individual human benefits, individual economic benefits and societal benefits should follow:

Individual Human Benefits. It is possible and even probable that improvements in the quality of work which are arrived at and implemented by workers themselves may result in increased job satisfaction, increased life satisfaction, increased activeness in community and personal affairs, decreased destructive on-the-job behavior, improved mental health and improved physical health. While it has not been definitely established that these benefits automatically flow from improvements in the quality of the working environment, a large body of theoretical and empirical literature suggests that improvements in the working environment can, under certain circumstances, produce highly desirable human benefits. It is also likely that the same types of benefits may accrue to students from learning environments which are built around the principles of security, equity, individuation and participation.[17]

[17] See pp. 213–225 of *Social Character in a Mexican Village,* Eric Fromm and Michael Maccoby, Prentice-Hall, 1970, for a description of how the existence of these principles in a Mexican orphanage turned children with little chance of making it in society into constructive citizens.

Individual Economic Benefits. There are also substantial possibilities for economic gain. The possibility that increased productivity *can* result from improved working conditions raises the possibility that the worker's standard of living can be improved due both to a sharing in the productivity gains and to the depressing effect of increased productivity on inflation.

It should be noted here that the notion of increased productivity takes on different values depending on one's vantage point. If one is working in a marginal plant, increased productivity is necessary to job security. If one is working in a secure plant, a fear sometimes arises that increased productivity may result in the same work being assigned to fewer people. If one views the question of productivity from the vantage point of the international union official, there is a conflict between the desire to maintain jobs by successfully competing with other countries and the fear that increased productivity without increased demand might result in a decrease in the labor force. On the other hand, if there is no increase in productivity, many jobs might be exported to the Far East. At the level of National policy, the dilemma is resolved. This country must become more productive in order to compete with other countries or we will lose our share of the world market. Assuming that we can follow growth policies whenever productivity does increase, there are major economic benefits to be gained by workers as well as by stockholders and management.

In addition to these benefits which could result from improvements in the quality of work, increased cooperation between the worlds of education and work in developing curricula and in providing participative skills could result in a more effectively trained work-force and in resultant economic benefits to both individuals and society.[18]

Societal Benefits. In a sense, the potential societal benefits of cooperative efforts by labor, management and education to improve the quality of education and work are simply an aggregation of the benefits to individuals. Benefits to society are clearly meaningless unless they accrue to the members of society. However, it might be useful to look at certain impacts of these benefits to individuals upon the structure of society and to trace this impact back to the further individual benefits it makes possible. We would suggest that these kinds of circular benefits exist in two areas: political and economic.

Political. It has been hypothesized that more active participation by people in the school and work situations results in their more active participation in community, state and national affairs. Personal and specific successes in influencing the nature of one's environment may lead to a decrease in political cynicism and a greater willingness to participate in the political process. Certainly, it is clear that the educational and industrial organization of U.S. society is less democratic than is its political organization. It follows that harmonization of these institutions might benefit all.

Economic. The most obvious economic effect on society would be the improvement of our competitive position in the international market. A less obvious but perhaps more significant advantage is the possibility of prevent-

[18] For an excellent discussion dealing in part with this point, see Striner, Herbert E., "Continuing Education as a National Capital Investment," The W. E. Upjohn Institute for Employment Research, Mar. 1972.

ing individual malfunctions which are extremely costly to society in dollar terms. For example, should just one hypothesis (i.e., that improving the non-economic aspects of the working environment results in fewer physical malfunctions related to poor mental health) be correct even to a small degree, the implications to the availability and allocation of tax dollars are significant. Consider the physical symptoms of poor mental health and the cost of treating these symptoms. Diagnosis and treatment of an ulcer or a case of colonitis might cost several hundred dollars. Should even a minute percentage of these symptoms be quieted by improvements in the working environment, substantial dollar savings would result to both individuals and society. . . .

5.4   THE SOCIOLOGY OF INSTITUTIONS OR WHO SANK THE YELLOW SUBMARINE?
Eleven ways to avoid major mistakes in taking over a university campus and making great changes

Warren G. Bennis

One cannot expect to know what is going to happen. One can only consider himself fortunate if he can discover what has happened.—Pierre Du Pont

On December 19, 1966, I received a phone call from an assistant to President Martin Meyerson [now President of the University of Pennsylvania] at the State University of New York at Buffalo. The assistant began the conversation with almost sinful empathy: "I bet you don't know what's going on here at Buffalo, do you?" I allowed that I didn't and he proceeded to describe an academic New Jerusalem of unlimited money, a new $650-million campus, bold organizational ideas, a visionary president, a supportive chancellor and governor, the number of new faculty and administrators to be recruited, the romance of taking a mediocre upstate college and creating—well—the Berkeley of the East. Would I consider

Abridged by the author from "The Sociology of Institutions or Who Sank the Yellow Submarine?," *Psychology Today*, November 1972, pp. 112–120. Copyright © 1972 Ziff-Davis Publishing Company. Reprinted by permission of Psychology Today Magazine.

taking part in the effort? I was smitten by the verve, the *chutzpah*—and by the thought of having a hand in the transformation. S.U.N.Y. at Buffalo had been a relatively unnoticed local college founded by the 13th U.S. President, Millard Fillmore, "His Accidency." It had gained an uneven distinction between 1930 and 1962, the year it became part of the University of New York. . . .

A monumental plan to redesign Buffalo's conventional academic structure was under way. Within two months, the faculty senate had ratified the plan, which provided as follows:

1. The 90 existing departments would be restructured into seven new faculties, each with a provost as the chief academic and administrative officer. Each faculty would consist of the basic disciplines within the newly defined area, plus the relevant professional schools. (Meyerson wanted me to head the social-science disciplines that included anthropology, psychology, and—to the chagrin of the Arts and Letters Provost—philosophy and history. My domains also would include the schools of management and

social welfare.) The provosts would have ample resources and administrative leeway to create interdisciplinary programs and launch new education ventures.

2. The university would build 30 small colleges on a new campus. Each would house only 400 students with up to 600 day students as affiliates. Faculty and students would live and work together in the intimate atmosphere of these intellectual neighborhoods. Myerson hoped the small college would offset the apathy and anomie that characterize enormous campuses. In addition, they would break the stranglehold that traditional departments traditionally leave on the university. Undergraduates would not get a watered-down version of what professors taught their graduate students; they would learn directly from their teachers in a communal setting.

3. Action-research centers and councils on international studies, urban studies, and higher educational studies would unite scholars and students from the entire university (and from the outside) for work on vital issues.

Esteem The concept was impressive. Several aspects of the plan were especially attractive: the decentralization of authority, the potential of the program (if you didn't fit in with a department, you could always connect with a college, center, or council), and the clear intent to raise the self-esteem of the university, the self-esteem of the faculty and students, and the self-esteem of the Buffalo community. I was assured that with the new campus, there would be enough money to build quality on top of the university's inevitable deadwood.

I was sold. The timing seemed perfect; the new organizational design would go into effect on the same day my term of office was to begin. I arrived at Buffalo in the fall of 1967 and during 1967–1968 I recruited nine new chairmen and two deans for the faculty, and changed about 90 percent of the leadership structure in

the social-sciences area. The faculty gained 45 new full-time teachers. I spent almost three fourths of my first year in recruiting.

Buffalo raided Harvard, Yale and Princeton. Each new appointment increased enthusiasm, generated new ideas, and escalated the optimism. The tiny, crowded campus barely contained the excitement. Intellectual communities formed and flourished.

Steam The change was pervasive. Almost 75 percent of the present Buffalo faculty got their appointments under Myerson.

The newcomers were eager recruits —committed to innovation and risk-taking. The student body also was changing. By 1968, eight in 10 of the entering freshmen were from the top 10 percent of their high-school graduating classes, compared to only one in 10 a decade before. Buffalo was regarded as one of the State University's radical campuses according to *Esquire* magazine (along with Stony Brook on Long Island). Myerson's Berkeley-of-the-East approach may have had an appeal that he had not fully calculated. For one year, Buffalo was an academic Camelot. The provosts met around the president's conference table to work miracles. Occasionally I got signals that not everyone on campus took us quite as seriously as we took ourselves. One morning I found a Batman cape on my coat rack.

The anonymous critic had a point: the atmosphere was a bit heavy with omnipotent fantasy.

Although construction had not started for the living quarters on the new campus, the six human-size colleges got underway at once. Almost immediately they provoked controversy. Rumors began to circulate that course cards for College A—the unit devoted to independent study and self-evaluation—were being sold, snatched up by the students who did little or nothing and rewarded themselves with A's at the end of the semester. "Why do you think they called it 'College A'"? one cynical student asked. There were tales of credit for trips to Europe and the building of bird cages.

The master of College A regarded any impugning of its grading system as an antirevolutionary tactic. No one in the administration, including myself, wanted to take a harsh public stand against this nonsense, particularly after College A and its master became the target of vicious community attack.

Status There were other rumblings in paradise. The centers were not doing well. We learned that it was easier to break down barriers than to build bridges. For example, the Center for Higher Education did not generate new programs or attract faculty and students, as planned. The Center for International Studies began to publish a newsletter—the only substantial sign of its new status. The Center for Urban Studies undertook a series of much-needed but thoroughly conventional projects in Buffalo's inner city.

In one form or another all the faculties had problems. Many departments raised questions about the new faculty structure. I felt that the many individual accomplishments, the promising new programs, the appointment of a particularly good teacher or administrator, did not add up to a significantly changed university. We were not consolidating our gains, and I feared that they might somehow slip away. These feelings were eventually confirmed. Camelot lasted barely a thousand days.

Setting I took part in many of the crucial decisions that affected the progress of the Buffalo plan. And I now see, with all the unsettling clarity of hindsight, that we undermined many of our own best aspirations for the University. If I were asked today how to bring about change in a university setting, I would offer the following guidelines.

1. Recruit with Scrupulous Honesty

Most of the faculty who came to Buffalo shared the academic vision of its new president, Martin Meyerson.

Myerson's gift as a recruiter was his ability to transmogrify all of the highly visible and terribly real drawbacks of Buffalo and make them reappear in the guise of exhilarating challenges. Those he attracted recruited others.

Sweetener My personal recruiting at Buffalo depended on a falsely bright picture of the situation. It wasn't that I lied. But, consciously or not, I sweetened the package even when I was trying to be balanced and fair. Recruiting is a courtship ritual. The suitor displays his assets; the recruit, flattered by the attention and the promises, does not examine the assets closely. We were naive. The recruiting pitch at Buffalo depended on the future. We made little of the past and tended to deemphasize the present. Buffalo was the university of the future— of course, it would take time to catch up.

New arrivals had barely enrolled their kids in local schools before reality intruded. A labor-union dispute delayed construction of the promised new facilities. Inflation nibbled away the buying power of all the allocated construction funds at a rate of one and a half percent a month. It was easy to put up with the inconvenience of overcrowding when one was sure that the condition was temporary. But the dispute dragged on for months, and there was no room on the old campus. The situation might have been challenging if we had not led the new faculty to expect something magical. We had urged them to reveal their most creative, most imaginative educational thinking, then had assured them that their plans would receive generous support. In reality, money to staff new programs was difficult to come by. After one year, the state legislature began to pare the budget. Many new faculty members felt they had been conned. As recruiters we had not pointed out our ultimate inability to control the legislatively determined budget. We had promised a new university when our funds could provide only an architect's model.

Shock   Inadvertently, we had cooked up the classic recipe for revolution as suggested by Aaron Wildavsky: "Promise a lot; deliver a little. Teach people to believe that they will be much better off but let there be no dramatic improvement. Try a variety of small programs but marginal in impact and severely underfinanced. Avoid any attempted solution remotely comparable in size to the dimensions of the problem you are trying to solve. . . ."

The intensity of the disaffection felt by some of those I had brought to the University came to me as a shock. We had raised expectations as high as any in modern educational history. When our program met only a part of these expectations, the disillusionment that followed was predictable and widespread. The disparity between vision and reality become intolerable. No one had said a word during the seductive recruiting days about triplicate forms, resentful colleagues, and unheeded requests for help from administrative headquarters.

Support   Those who rose above the mundane annoyances provoked by university bureaucracy felt cheated in other ways. Recruits had joined our academic revolution because they shared our goal and wanted to participate. To keep such a cadre committed, an administration must keep them involved. But the warmth of our man-to-man recruiting interviews was not evident in later meetings with administrators. In fact, such meetings became fairly infrequent. The continuing evidence of personal support that might have overcome the unavoidable lack of concrete support was not forthcoming.

2. Guard Against the Crazies

Innovation is seductive. It attracts interesting people. It also attracts people who will take your ideas and distort them into something monstrous. *You* will then be identified with the monster and will have to devote precious energy to combating it. A change-oriented administrator should be damned sure about the persons he recruits, the persons who will be identified as his men or women.

A few of the persons who got administrative posts under the new administration were committed to change, but they were so irresponsible or antagonistic that they alienated more persons than they converted.

Sense   It is difficult to distinguish between agents of responsible change and those who rend all they touch. The most successful innovators often are marginal to the institution, almost in a geographical sense. They have contacts in other institutions, other areas. Their credentials are unorthodox. They are often terrible company men with little or no institutional loyalty. Change-oriented administrators must be able to distinguish the innovators, however eccentric they may be, from the crazies. An academic community can tolerate a high degree of eccentricity. But it will brutally reject an individual it suspects of masking mediocrity with a flashy commitment to innovation.

3. Build Support among Like-Minded People, Whether or Not You Recruited Them

Change-oriented administrators are particularly prone to act as though the organization came into being the day they arrived. This is an illusion, an omnipotent fantasy. There are no clean slates in established organizations. A new president can't play Noah and build the world anew with two hand-picked delegates from each academic discipline. Rhetoric about new starts is frightening to those who suspect that the new beginning is the end of their own careers. There can be no change without history, without continuity.

Stayers What I think most of us in institutions really want—and what status, money and power serve as currency for—is acceptance, affection and esteem. Institutions are more amenable to change when they preserve the esteem of all members. Given economic sufficiency, persons stay in organizations and feel satisfied in them because they are respected and feel competent. They are much freer to identify with the adaptive process and much better equipped to tolerate the high level of ambiguity that accompanies change, when these needs are needed. Unfortunately, we did not attend to those needs at Buffalo. The academic code, not the administrative one, determines appropriate behavior in the university. The president is a colleague, and he is expected to acknowledge his intellectual equals whatever their relative position on the administrative chart. Many old-guard professors took the administration's neglect as a personal snub. They were not asked for advice; they were not invited to social affairs. They suspected that we acted coolly toward them because we considered them to be second-rate academics who lacked intellectual chic and who could not cut it in Cambridge or New York. Ironically, some of the old-guard academic administrators who kept their positions *were* notoriously second-rate. We extended the appointments of several such, perhaps hoping to avoid the appearance of a purge. Among the incumbents were a couple whose educational philosophy had rigidified sometime in the early '50s. Instead of appeasing the old guard, these appointments added insult.

The old guard suspected that the new administration viewed them as an undifferentiated mass. They wondered why we kept these second-raters and overlooked a pool of potentially fine veteran candidates.

We succeeded in infusing new blood into Buffalo, but we failed to recirculate the old blood. We lost an opportunity to build loyalty among respected members of the veteran faculty. If veteran faculty members had been made to feel that they, too, had a future in the transformed university, they might have embraced the academic-reorganization plan with some enthusiasm. Instead the veteran faculty members were hurt, indignant and—finally—angry.

4. Plan for Change from a Solid Conceptual Base—Have a Clear-Cut Understanding of How To Change as Well as What To Change

Buffalo had a plan for change, but we lacked a clear concept of how change should proceed. A statement of goals is not a program.

The Buffalo reorganization lacked the coherence and forcefulness that would have guaranteed its success. The fault may have been that it was too abstract. Or perhaps it was too much a pastiche. A great many influences were evident: the late Paul Goodman and the community-of-colleges, the colleges and sense of academic tradition of Oxbridge; the unorthodoxy and informality of Black Mountain: the blurring of vocational-professional lives practiced at Antioch and Bennington; the collegiality of Santa Cruz; the college-master system of Yale. Each of these elements was both desirable and educationally fashionable, but the mix never jelled. No alchemy transformed the disparate parts into a living organism.

Students We had no coherent mechanisms for change. Instead we relied on several partially realized administrative models. The burden of change fell upon the faculty senate, which emphasized the *small-group model.* Change depended on three things: 1) participation by the persons involved, 2) trust in the persons who advocate the change, and 3) clarity about the change itself. None of these conditions was fully present at Buffalo, and, as a result, the change was imperfectly realized.

Radical students utilized a revolutionary model. The students saw an opportunity for radical educational change in the Romantic tradition—the result was the College-A controversy. The administration relied heavily on the model of successive limited comparisons, popularly known as muddling through. This is a model of most organizational decision-making. It is a noncomprehensive, nontheoretical approach. Most administrators are forced to muddle through because the decisions they are called upon to make are simply too complex to treat comprehensively—even by committees. As a result, we neglected possible outcomes, overlooked alternative solutions, and could not predict the ultimate impact of the resulting policy on values.

Sensitivity Ultimately the reorganization failed to concentrate its energies on the model that would have satisfied the ambitions of all parts of the university: an incremental-reform model. Revolution inevitably produces reaction. All power to the French people one day, and to Thermidor the next. If change is to be permanent it must be gradual. The incremental-reform model depends on a rotating nucleus of persons who continuously read the data provided by the organization and the society around it for clues that it is time to adapt. These persons are not faddists but they *are* hypersensitive to an idea whose hour has come. In a university such persons know when an idea is antithetical to the values of an academic institution and when it extends the definition of a university and makes it more viable. One cannot structure these critical nuclei, but an organization cannot guarantee continuous self-renewal without them. At Buffalo a few departments and programs developed these nuclei. Most did not.

5. Don't Settle for Rhetorical Change

We accomplished the change at Buffalo by fiat. The faculty senate announced that the president's plan had been ratified. [This was a good beginning, but only that. Ratification occurred only two months after Meyerson arrived and almost one year before the plan was implemented. The senate wasn't exactly representative and the plans were barely understood. It was basically a paper plan with virtually no commitment except to a vague and poetic vision.] Significant change does not take place that way. An organization has two structures: one on paper and another one, deep, that is a complex set of intramural relationships. A good administrator creates a good fit between the two. We allowed ourselves to be swept along by our rhetoric and neglected the much more demanding business of building new constituencies and maintaining established ones.

6. Don't Allow Those Who Are Opposed to Change To Appropriate such Basic Issues as Academic Standards

I became Academic Vice President in August of 1968. Members of the old guard soon began to accuse me of being soft on standards. I had refused to disavow some of the more flagrant abuses of self-evaluation in the new colleges and I had failed publicly to chastise faculty who subverted traditional academic practices as part of the radical revolution (although I did so unofficially).

Silence The problem of academic standards soon became a political issue. Privately we avowed our commitment to standards; publicly we were silent. The approach was notably unsuccessful. We did not want to undermine the fledgling colleges or violate the rights of radical faculty members. After "fascist," "Mc-Carthyite" is the dirtiest word you can use on a liberal campus, and none of us was eager to hear it. We allowed the least change-oriented faculty members to make the issue of standards their own. They persuaded a great majority of moderate faculty members that administration was committed to change-for-change's sake, whatever the price in academic excellence. We made a mistake that no successful revolutionary ever makes: we did not make sure that respectable people were unafraid of what was about to happen.

7. Know the Territory

A peculiar balance exists between the city of Buffalo and its one major university. Buffalo is not a university town like Princeton or Ann Arbor. The university is not powerful enough to impose its style and values on the city. Philadelphia and Los Angeles have several powerful universities that divide the city's attention and diffuse its rancor. Buffalo has a single target for its noisy anti-intellectuals. Two years ago some powerful forces in the town tried to close the university. I don't know of another campus in the country that has had to function with such constant unsympathetic pressure from the surrounding community. (The period I had in mind was the year of Kent State. From all I have heard about Meyerson's successor, he has worked hard at reviving a more sympathetic and supportive reaction to the campus.)

Meyerson barely had arrived in Buffalo when a group called "Mothers Against Meyerson" (MAM) began to petition for his removal. Their argument was that he was a Jew (a charge erroneously made against Meyerson's predecessor by an earlier group, "Mothers against Furnas") and that the campus harbored such dangerous criminal types as critic Leslie Fiedler.

Buffalo blamed the disruptions of 1970 on the "permissiveness" of the new administration. I got mail recommending that Curtis LeMay succeed Meyerson as university president. The local ex-marine who nominated LeMay believed that only the general's exotic blend of authoritarianism and right-wing values could undo the harm that we had perpetrated.

We never mastered the politics of local chauvinism. At the same time that the national press was romancing the university, one of the two local dailies was libelling her unmercifully. We devoted too little energy and imagination to public relations.

8. Appreciate Environmental Factors

Like any other human activity, change proceeds more smoothly in optimal environmental conditions. Buffalo's chief environmental problem was not its miserable weather. (Buffalo has two seasons—winter and the 4th of July. Residents recognize summer as three weeks of bad ice-skating.) The problem at Buffalo was (and still is) overcrowding. The faculty we recruited expected to move their books into futuristic offices like those promised by the architect's model of the new campus. Instead, they moved in on top of the faculty already there. The University assembled some pre-fab annexes for the overflow. Barbara Solomon, writing on the paranoia at Buffalo, noted that we pursued the life of the mind in quarters so ugly as to seem calculated. (Her article, "Life in the Yellow Submarine," appeared in a 1968 issue of *Harper's*. It pictured SUNY-Buffalo at the crest of the Meyerson dream, zany, careening, spectacularly lush, as played by the Marx Brothers in a World War II movie set of sallow, wooden barracks.)

The new University campus barely had begun to rise by the time we reached the originally proposed completion date of 1972. The University had to lease an interim campus near the new campus site. Eleven academic departments moved out to this temporary facility in the spring of 1971. The leased buildings had been designed for commercial and light-industry use. The 15-minute bus trip is a drag for students and the isolation of the interim campus is contrary to the whole spirit of the Meyerson plan.

We neglected to protect new programs from external forces. College A began an experimental program in community action that was housed off-campus because of space priorities. College A is located directly across from a parochial grammar school and a diocesan center for retarded children. Every time a Scarsdale Maoist wrote "fuck" on the wall or a braless coed played her guitar in the storefront window the residents of the neighborhood understandably reacted. Students of College A were determined to interact with their neighbors; mothers of the schoolchildren were equally determined not to interact. They picketed. The whole business snowballed, increasing the community's normally high level of outrage against the University.

9. Avoid Future Shock

Buffalo aspired to be the university of the year 2000. The future limited the campus just as the past limits the neurotic. The future insinuated itself into every attempt to deal with current issues and distorted our perception of the present. The unfinished new campus became an albatross, reminding everyone of the limited progress that was being made toward limitless goals. We put so much stock in the vision of future greatness that our disillusionment was inevitable. The problem with planning for the future is that there are no objective criteria against which to measure alternative solutions. There is not yet a contemporary reality against which to test. As a result the planner generates future shock along with valid ideas, and there's no surefire way to separate the two.

10. Allow Time To Consolidate Gains

The average tenure of an American university president is now 4.4 years and decreasing. It is impossible to transform a university in so short a time. Only a year after Meyerson assumed the Buffalo presidency, rumors began to circulate that he was leaving. Supporters of the new administration feared abandonment. Social-critic David Bazelon commented to me, "In every other university I've been to, the faculty hated the administration. Here they worry about desertion." Our proposed changes depended on continued presidential support for their success. The campus had, in effect, undergone major surgery and did not have sufficient time to heal before a series of altogether different demands, including a semester of unrest, a new president, and a major recession, were made on it.

When Meyerson finally did resign in late January 1970, it was as though someone had prematurely pulled out the stitches.

The last guideline I offer to the would-be university reformer is so basic that it might well come first.

11. Remember That Change Is Most Successful When Those Who Are Affected Are Involved in the Planning

This is a platitude of planning theory, and it is as true as it is trite. Nothing makes persons as resistant to new ideas or approaches as the feeling that change is being imposed upon them. The members of a university are unusually sensitive to individual prerogatives and to the administration's utter dependence on their support. Buffalo's academic plan was not generated popularly. Students and faculty did not contribute to its formulation. People resist change, even of a kind they basically agree with, if they are not significantly involved in the planning. A clumsier, slower, but more egalitarian approach to changing the university would have resulted in more permanent reform.

Surprise The problems surrounding innovation and change in an entrenched bureaucracy are not peculiar to universities. Every modern bureaucracy—university, government or corporation—is essentially alike and responds similarly to challenge and to crisis, with much the same explicit or implicit codes, punctilios and mystiques.

Bureaucracy is the inevitable—and therefore necessary—form for governing large and complex organizations. Essentially we must find bureaucratic means to stimulate the pursuit of truth—i.e., the true nature of the organization's problems —in a spirit of free inquiry, and under democratic methods. This calls for those virtues our universities and colleges have proved so capable of inspiring in others: an examined life, a spirit of inquiry and genuine experimentation, a life based on discovering new realities, of taking risks, suffering occasional defeats, and not fearing the surprise of the future.

The model for truly innovative and creative organizations in an era of enormous change becomes nothing less than the scientific spirit. The model for science becomes the model for all.

Assault Now, four years after the dream was born, the campus mood is dismal. Many of the visionaries are gone— those left must live with the wreckage. The spirit of change has been stamped out.

Meyerson has officially disappeared. The state considers his administration to have been the reign of an educational antipope. There is rarely mention of him or his works.

Last year the American Council on Education released its current evaluation of the nation's graduate programs. Buffalo had improved dramatically in the ACE ratings. The University proudly held a news conference at which campus officials announced that the upgrading of graduate education at Buffalo took place under the late President Furnas.

What saddens me is a suspicion that this gross assault would have been successful if we had been more effective. Meyerson wanted to transform the university, but the current administration resembles that of Meyerson's predecessor, Clifford Furnas. By all appearances, our efforts changed nothing.

EPILOGUE

I wrote the above several months after I resigned from Buffalo—an outsider, though still living in Buffalo, supported by a grant from the Twentieth Century Fund. Outsiders and expatriates adopt a more critical perspective, I suppose, than those who remain.

Perhaps this article is not "objective" truth but "exiled" truth, not especially appropriate for those presently at Buffalo. Still and all, I would hope that some external validation of their former plight will help sustain their vitality.

At the same time, I hope that this critique of the Buffalo attempts at change will provide a template of action—for myself and my new Cincinnati administration, for faculty and students as well— that will conform more closely to a humane and democratic effort at university reform. We begin with more total community support and involvement than is enjoyed by any other urban university.

Support in the Empowering and Legitimation of Change Efforts

CHAPTER SIX

Contemporary urbanized societies are often described as mass societies. Students of such societies have noted a paradox with which people in such societies are confronted. David Riesman, for example, highlights this paradox in his expression "the lonely crowd." People are more crowded, not alone in a geographic sense, but in the augmented dependence in the maintenance of life, by each of us upon "all the others," when life in urbanized society is compared with life in the agrarian and small town communities which are part of our history. And though agrarian and small town conditions of life are now irrevocably past for most of us, they still provide imaginal ideals of the "good society" for many of us.

Yet people in urbanized societies, though more crowded, are at the same time more lonely. They have less of a sense of a guaranteed and stable place or status within their social worlds. They are more mobile, experiencing more frequent uprootings from the sustaining and supporting relationships of stable neighborhoods and extended families. Most people feel and are remote from the places where decisions that affect the patterns and quality of their lives are made and they feel powerless to influence the people, whether employers, political leaders or professionals, who shape these decisions. Psychologically, it is a short distance between the feeling and condition of powerlessness to an evaluation of self as negligible and worthless, and so incapable of autonomous action and initiation of change.

The effects of life in "the lonely crowd" upon the mental health of people, upon the dissolution of common interests into a welter of conflicting interests in the political realm with the masses becoming pawns in such conflicts, and upon the reduction to meaninglessness of such normative ideas as "community" and "general welfare"—such effects have been frequently noted. Here we are concerned with its effects upon processes of conceiving and achieving changes in personal and social lives.

For agents of planned change who are committed to collaboration of all affected by a change in diagnosing, planning, implementing and evaluating it, this human condition presents excruciating difficulties. For the condition of loneliness within the midst of mechanical interdependence means that the social and personal bases for supporting collaboration between and among persons and groups are now inadequate and often nonexistent. The building of new supporting relationships which make effective participation in processes of changing possible for many in our society must be taken as a necessary part of the change process itself. We must use existing organizations as elements in the planning of change, though the nonparticipative character of decision-making in many of these must be altered. But, if planning is to involve many people affected by the changes being planned, it must go beyond existing organizations to reach and involve those who are now living, for the most part, as nonparticipative atoms in an unorganized and inarticulate mass.

In "change agent" language this task is often described as finding ways of *supporting* people, or in *building support systems* with and for people, in defining and articulating their own distinctive interests in and needs for changing and in taking action, along with others, in serving these interests and meeting these needs. *Support* is required for a number of reasons. It is required in helping people to overcome motivational barriers to taking their own needs and interests seriously, in affirming their own worth and importance in the social world, in overcoming apathy and despair. It is also required in helping people to replace false consciousness of themselves as persons and citizens—a consciousness often imposed upon them by persons and groups with greater power and prestige and a consciousness which circumscribes the legitimacy of changes which threaten existing power relationships—with a more authentic consciousness of themselves in their relations with other parts of society and as legitimate centers of influence in changing those relationships where needed. Support is also required in helping persons who have been nonparticipative in shaping their personal and social destinies to acquire and use the understandings and skills which effective participation in changing requires. These needs are probably greatest for the minorities, the poor and the oppressed within our society. But it should not be forgotten that alienation and need for support in changing are not alien to people in affluent suburbs and to professional change agents and planners as well. *Support,* as we are using the term, is a universal requirement for mature human functioning, a requirement often not readily available within the labyrinths of our mass society.

Another way of summarizing the uses of support, from the perspective of planned change, is to recognize two interrelated functions which it serves.

One function is to *empower* people, now oppressed with a feeling of power-lessness to change, to begin to assume responsibility for self-directed partici-pation in changing what needs to be changed. The other purpose is to *legitimate* people in challenging existing legitimacies in the interest of nego-tiating new and more equitable and life-affirming legitimacies in the patterning and control of their lives. The principal barrier here is a false consciousness concerning authority and authority relations.

The selections in this chapter approach the problems of diagnosing needs for support and of building required support for effective planning and chang-ing from various directions. Culbert, in "Consciousness-Raising: A Five Stage Model for Social and Organizational Change," differentiates the kinds and qualities of interpersonal and group support which persons need in perceiv-ing, articulating and pursuing alternatives to their present modes of living and working in the world. He suggests the kinds of support which change agents, professional and volunteer, need to supply to people and to help people develop for themselves, not just at the diagnostic stage but at various subsequent stages of a change project or program.

Gilbert and Eaton, in "Who Speaks for the Poor?", report data which reveal marked discrepancies between the needs for changing which profes-sional planners perceive, those which activist citizens groups perceive, and those perceived by the poor, whom both professional planners and activist leaders purport to represent and to serve. This sets a problem for both pro-fessional and volunteer change agents. It suggests a lack in the current efforts of both kinds of change agents. How do they involve themselves in empower-ing and legitimizing the poor themselves in mutually defining and articulating their own distinctive needs for changing so that they as well as "the poor" can speak authentically in the councils of planning for "the poor"? These authors do not suggest a methodology for accomplishing such empowering and legitimation by "the poor" for "the poor." But Culbert's piece and the piece by Freire in Chapter Four do suggest some elements of such a methodology.

Peattie's article, "Drama and Advocacy Planning," continues to develop the themes of empowering and legitimation in a pluralistic community con-text. She suggests an analogue between drama and political action. (See Chapter Nine, "Power and the New Politics," for further development of this analogue.) The imagery of the theatrical performance captures the "quality of emotional engagement" required in mobilizing and focusing, and thus supporting, the efforts of participants in community change programs. The analogy is further used to demonstrate the various degrees and kinds of involvement of people required in effective community change. By role dif-ferentiation between professionals, activist leaders and supporting "cast," desirable linkages among the various support systems required may be seen more clearly.

6.1 CONSCIOUSNESS-RAISING: A FIVE STAGE MODEL FOR SOCIAL AND ORGANIZATION CHANGE

Samuel A. Culbert

"Power to the People,'" the radical chant of the sixties, could well be considered the moderate maxim of the seventies. More and more people are trying to come up with alternatives and seem willing to work within the system. People seek ways of living and working which involve fewer personal compromises.

All societal roles and practices are open to suspicion. Conventional sex roles are questioned for the limitations they place on individual expressiveness. The Anglo's domination of industry and education is questioned for racist practices and elitist control. Government and the courts are suspect. Formulas and principles of welfare and taxation are challenged. No longer are conventional marriages and single careers the norm; private medicine doesn't work; the environment is deteriorating at an unacceptable rate; and all hidden forms of influence, whether from the private sector or from the government, are being viewed for the limitations they pose to individual freedom and democratic values.

Much of the critique and change results from the work of consumer and citizen's advocacy movements led by experts and lawyers. An increasing amount results from individuals and self-help groups, who through techniques of consciousness-raising, are able to see how the system conflicts with their ideals, interests and expression. The process by which individuals—sometimes on their own, usually with the support of a group —recognize conflicts between their interests and the expectations of the system,

Reprinted from *Theories of Group Process* edited by Cary L. Cooper (1975) by permission of John Wiley & Sons Ltd.

formulate alternatives that reduce the extent and the number of these compromises, and work for change, is termed consciousness-raising. One model by which this process can proceed provides the subject of this paper.

CONSCIOUSNESS-RAISING

Consciousness-raising takes place gradually with one insight paving the way for others. Usually its goals are the formulation of alternative ways for people to live and work in a social or organization system. However, it is one thing to formulate an alternative which improves our situation, and it is still another to put it into practice. Consequently, in the model I'm about to describe, alternatives we initiate which lead to our improved functioning in the system are considered but the *by-products* of consciousness-raising. It is the actions we can support others to take, based on their own ideas of what constitutes an improved situation, which are the *real products* of consciousness-raising.

Consciousness-raising has two components, the personal and the system. The personal component depends on our developing sufficient understanding of who we are naturally, that is, without our adaptations to the system, to recognize which parts of the system fail to fit our needs. The system component involves both our seeing what the system really is and how it actually works—as contrasted with how we've been conditioned to see it—and our thinking about the well-being of others who are also part of the system. Social theorists, like Paulo

Freire,[1] caution us not to accept solutions that free us from our oppression with actions that oppress others. Those we oppress will also need to escape and the pattern may never be broken. For instance, the women's movement made its most important gains only after those involved could look beyond their own oppression to see how the social structure oppressed men as well.

Most of the issues encountered in consciousness-raising have their roots in what we were conditioned to believe about our role in the social system, the social institution, or the organization that is the subject of our inquiry. Usually we began our relationships with these systems from a position of low personal power. We were marginal members who felt a strong need to establish ourselves by winning approval and acceptance from those who had power. We conformed to what we felt they expected of us and set our goals on accomplishments which we thought they would value. Had we been able to approach the system from a position of greater internal security and less exaggerated needs for external acceptance, then more of our behavior might have been more tailored to accomplishing goals which had intrinsic value and interest to us. Instead we submitted to an intense process of socialization and neglected important aspects of ourselves. Unwittingly we contributed to our own domestication in the system and supported the status quo.

Hypothetically the system to which we tailored our behavior worked well under conditions which were present when the system originated. Usually, the system evolved as our needs were articulated and undeniably recognized so that those who played key roles had to let the system change. In some systems, like

the Catholic Church in the 1960's, those in power were insufficiently responsive to the basic needs of the people and the system underwent decay. The populace determined that what they wanted was a natural expression of who they were and decided to hold out indefinitely against opposition. In contrast, in the 1970's, we see many instances of social systems, institutions, and organizations giving in to meet the demands of minorities who are no longer willing to compromise.

But large-scale change begins with our simplest feelings that something in our relationship with the system is "off." Only when we pay attention to the feelings which signal that something is off, can we hope to discover what needs to be improved. But knowing what is off does not necessarily tell us what we need to know to formulate an alternative that actually improves our situation. Oftentimes what we think is off is merely a symptom of an as yet unidentified ill. Until we develop greater understanding about ourselves, the system and our relationship to the system we are likely to make illusionary changes which remove us further from seeing what is wrong. Dealing with the surface problem makes it less likely that we will come to grips with the fundamental ill. Eventually we need a structure or a model that insures our progress is real. Of course relying on a single model can be the worst trap.

The consciousness-raising model I'm about to describe was developed to help people who work in large organizations formulate and put into practice alternatives which better fit their needs and interests than current organizational practices.[2] However, subsequent experience

[1] Freire, P. Cultural actions for freedom. *Harvard Educational Review*, Monograph series 1, 1970.

[2] The theory from which this model derived, as well as the model itself, is described in a book I wrote on its application to large organizations: *The Organization Trap and How to Get Out of It*. New York: Basic Books, 1974.

with consciousness-raising groups in a variety of settings has convinced me that this model also applies to interactions we have with just about any social system or social institution.

The model has five stages, an overview of which is portrayed in Figure 1. The outputs of each stage provide the inputs for the next, so it is important to carry out these stages in sequence. The model directs our reconsideration of the relationship we have with the social or organization system which is the focus of our inquiry. One part of this reconsideration depends on our identifying and coping with unnatural and destructive components of this system. Another part depends on our viewing and coping with the immature and self-defeating components of our own personality. A support group is necessary or we can get bogged down by our preoccupation with either part and fail to take constructive steps towards putting our relationship with the system on a higher plane of inquiry.

THE SUPPORT GROUP

Some brief comments about the characteristics and formation of the support group should prove useful in envisioning the five stages of consciousness-raising that follow. Keep in mind, however, that I intend these comments as suggestions rather than as fixed rules. When it comes to consciousness-raising, each person is different, therefore each group is different, and all procedures must remain open to modification based on the experiences of the people involved.

Composition The people who form a support group should have a common relationship to the social system or structure serving as the focus of their discussion. To include others runs the risk of having additional issues raised which,

however interesting, will diffuse the group's focus. If it's a group of married women examining their relationship to the demands of family life, then it's advisable that the group not include single women or any men. If it's a taxpayer's group examining the relationship members have to government and the economy, then it's best to include only people who are roughly in the same tax bracket. Homogeneity of composition reduces the possibility that someone will play the expert, oppressor or novice, any one of which are roles that compromise group productivity. Wherever possible the differences which exist between members' age, experience, status, etc., should have no meaning in terms of the relationships members hold to the social or organization system serving as the focus for their discussion.

Size Support groups need to be small enough for individual pictures of reality to be shared comfortably and large enough for members to construct a fairly accurate perspective on how the system under discussion sees reality. I have been in consciousness-raising groups with as few as five members. With them I enjoyed intimacy but also a troublesome feeling when one person couldn't attend a meeting that our loss was too great to continue without him. On the other hand, I've been a member of groups as large as twenty-two and, while I could always count on someone understanding exactly what I meant, it was a struggle to get a turn to talk.

Commitment It's important that group members hold a common expectation for how many sessions their group is going to have and when these will be held. I recommend that a group agree to a beginning set of three meetings with time reserved in the middle of the third to discuss whether or not group members feel there should be additional sessions

FIGURE 1 Consciousness-Raising Model for Social and Organizational Change

Stage 1: Recognizing What's "Off"

Feelings of Incoherence ⟶

Skills for

self-accepting, non-evaluative analysis

- - -

Support that

bolsters feelings of self-adequacy and encourages self-valuing of experience

⟶ Identification of Discrepancies

a. between what the system expects of us and what seems natural or consistent with our self-interests

b. between doing what comes naturally and what seems acceptable to the system

Stage 2: Understanding Ourselves and the System

Discrepancies ⟶

Skills for

"divergent problem-solving"

- - -

Support that

helps us resist convergent problem-solving and cope with the tensions which result

⟶ Increased Awareness

a. of self: our nature and ideals
b. of the system: what it is and how it works

Stage 3: Understanding Our Relationship with the System

Increased Awareness of Self and System ⟶

Skills for

explicating assumptions and determining how they were acquired

- - -

Support that

challenges existing premises, beliefs, and idiosyncratic assumptions

⟶ Increased Awareness of Our Relationship with the System

a. assumptions which underlie our goals and how we go about achieving them

b. assumptions which comprise our image of the system

c. assumptions which explain how we and the system influence one another

FIGURE 1 (continued)

Stage 4: Formulating Alternatives

Increased awareness of Self and System

Increased Awareness of Our Relationship with the System

Skills for
  seeing where existing assumptions are inconsistent with our nature, interests, and ideals

Support that
  helps us reflect on personal priorities and consider a range of alternative actions

Envisioning Alternatives

a. which change the system

b. which change our relationship to the system

Stage 5: Affecting the Lives of Others

Envisioned Alternatives

Skills for
  thinking about change in a "statespersonlike" way

Support that
  monitors change projects and helps us maintain focus when encountering resistance

Changes and Improvements in the System

a. making alternative responses to the system

b. devising alternative systems and putting them into action

c. helping others to envision their own alternatives

and, if so, how many? Having the expectation of a specified number of meetings provides members the structure they need to articulate problems that group participation is causing them and not just to drop out silently. It also gives members who are opening up a topic which cannot be resolved in a single meeting assurance that they will have another chance to complete their thoughts. If in the course of discussion the group exhausts its concerns with the system they've been discussing or interest shifts to another area, then I recommend that the group dissolve and reconstitute itself with a majority of new members. In this way old members get the benefits of fresh perspectives and new members don't have to contend with group patterns which they lack the history to appreciate.

Group roles While support groups have no leaders there are some coordination, moderator and recorder roles which need to be performed and it is best that these be traded off from meeting to meeting. We want to avoid anyone feeling overly responsible for group progress or using his or her role to avoid free and active personal involvement.

THE MODEL

Stage 1: Recognizing What's "Off"

Consciousness-raising begins with feelings that something is off in our interaction with some social or organization system. Usually these feelings are vague and we are hard pressed to specify exactly what is bothering us. Specifying what it is constitutes the output of the first stage of consciousness-raising.

The first obstacle we face in raising consciousness lies in our self-suspicions that we are making a big deal out of something minor with which we live daily. However, until we specify the *discrepancy* causing our *feeling of inco-*

herence, we can't say with confidence whether we live with it daily because it is minor or because we've been socialized to think "It can't be changed so what's the use of bothering with it?"

Analyzing what's off usually turns up a discrepancy in our relationship to the system on which we're focusing. We can discover what it is by asking ourselves some simple questions:

> In what ways could this feeling be a clue that the system expects something from me that doesn't seem natural or consistent with my self-interests?

> In what ways could this feeling be a clue that something which seems natural enough to me is considered inappropriate or inadequate by the system?

Asking ourselves these questions brings us to the next obstacle. When something is off in our relationship with an established system, we have a tendency to think that the cause can be traced back to some deficiency in us rather than in the system. We require support to overcome this intimidation and to analyze the exact nature of the conflict.

Group Support for Stage 1

When it comes to self-criticism, each of us has something deep and unique to overcome. However, within a support group, these obstacles can be at least temporarily sidestepped. First we can create a conceptual structure that helps us explicate discrepancies in relatively factual, non-judgmental terms. Reflecting on the two questions mentioned above seems to work quite nicely. These questions focus us on incompatibilities not judgements. Second, we can create a milieu of acceptance which encourages support group members not to blame themselves nor judge one another. Such a milieu develops merely by people with similar concerns acknowledging their commonality of interests. It is strengthened as members hear others describe their conflicts with the system and see that more was involved in the conflict than met the eye initially.

However, groups can reach a point where the early supportive momentum is exhausted and members talk as if greater discipline or adequacy on their parts could have avoided some of the problems which got the best of them. When this happens it's advisable to implement a small exercise that gets people back on a track of self-acceptance. For example, members can take turns relating instances where they accepted the blame or responsibility for something that went wrong only to receive a later indication that they were not at fault.

The consciousness-raising process develops momentum as members take turns converting feelings of incoherence into crisp statements of discrepancies. A discrepancy for a participant in a woman's group was between her desires to feel more in control of her body and the paternalistic treatment she receives from doctors. Her realization was sparked by feelings of anger she experienced in the waiting room of her new gynecologist. She reflected, "There's a familiar note to what I'm feeling."

As the process of articulating discrepancies gets rolling, one person's report and realizations will trigger personal insights in others. These insights need to be recorded and it saves time to have some mechanism for doing this planned in advance. Group members will use their list of discrepancies in the next stage of consciousness-raising.

Stage 2: Understanding Ourselves and the System

Recognizing discrepancies offers us an immediate opportunity to take action and set the system straight. However, if we do so, we will miss fundamental problems. Our fantasies of improvement will be circumscribed by the discrepancies which we now want to resolve. A chance to improve something fundamental as opposed to symptomatic is possible only when we delay taking corrective action and use the discrepancies we have noted to increase our understanding of ourselves —how we work and what we need—and our understanding of the system with which we're interacting—what it is and how it actually operates.

Probing for this understanding requires that we resist our usual convergent approach to problem-solving and, at least for a while, engage in a period of divergent analysis. *Convergent problem-solving* involves accepting a problem more or less as it has been stated and systematically directing our thoughts and actions towards solving it. The word convergent refers to our focus on taking steps that sequentially bring us closer to a solution. It does not refer to the number of alternative approaches considered in the process of coming up with a solution.

On the other hand, *divergent problem-solving* requires a different set of thought processes, which all of us have but which few of us can be counted on to use skillfully. They are the inductive thought processes we use when viewing a situation as if it were the symptom rather than the basic ill and then going on to inquire what ailment this symptom might signal. We use these processes when we inquire into the reasons which explain why we have a difference with someone, rather than presenting our case and arguing why our perspective is better than the other person's. In essence, these are the inductive skills which allow us to deepen the level at which problems are conceptualized and strike closer to the basic issues underlying what has been "problematized."

Group Support for Stage 2

Our support group helps us develop and use our divergent problem-solving skills.

Correspondingly, it helps us resist convergent problem-solving and cope with the tensions which result. Not only are we living with unresolved conflicts but we don't even seem to be progressing towards a resolution. Delaying action and thinking divergently requires both discipline and the anticipation of benefits.

There are any number of questions we might raise to approach a discrepancy divergently. We might ask "If this discrepancy were a symptom of a more basic conflict, what would that conflict be?" Or we might ask "What combination of human qualities and organization attributes could have produced conflicts such as the ones we've identified?" For example, consider the students who got together to discuss their relationship with a graduate program in psychology. They concerned themselves with discrepancies between their interests in having a good deal of out-of-class interaction with faculty and the non-availability of their faculty. Thinking convergently they wrote a "constructive" note to the department chairman describing this problem and asking that the situation be changed. Thinking divergently the students might have asked themselves several questions which could spark deeper understanding prior to engaging the academic system. They might have asked:

What does this situation tell us about the pressures our faculty face?
What can we learn about ourselves from the fact that we waited this long before taking action?
What does the way our faculty are conducting themselves say about the professional role we'll be taking once we get our degrees and take jobs teaching?
Have any of the ways we've been acting in relation to one another contributed to our problems with the faculty?
What assumptions are we making that prevent us from directly approaching faculty with whom we want to talk? Why haven't individual faculty members also been bothered by this problem?
etc.

Understanding developed through divergent analysis allows us to learn some of the essentials we need to know prior to thinking about a solution. We have the opportunity to upgrade the picture we hold of ourselves, both in terms of making it more realistic and in terms of making a stronger personal commitment to our ideals. We also have the opportunity to see the system, institution, or organization with which we experience discrepancies from the standpoint of its goals, priorities and assumptions about how effective operations are carried out. In this way we gain a more realistic picture of both parties involved in the conflict.

The discrepancies we submit to divergent analysis will come from the list our group generated in the first stage of consciousness-raising. Some will be discrepancies about which a large number of group members feel strongly and some will be ones with which only one or two members identify. Discrepancies with which only a few people identify usually reveal more about the individuals experiencing them than about the systems involved. While learning specific to each individual is important, it comes most easily after the group has spent some time analyzing discrepancies with which many people identify.

The group discussion proceeds most smoothly when arrangements have been made for recording what is learned from the divergent discussion. I have found it useful to have two easels with newsprint, one of which is used to record insights about the system and the other to record what is learned about the needs and interests of group members. Just how much members ought to debate differences in perception and interpretation is open to question. On one hand, we can reasonably expect defensiveness in any situation where consciousness is being raised and we may not get very far unless defenses are challenged and differences in opinion are openly discussed. On the other hand, struggling through every difference as if reality were not open to individual interpretation is unrealistic and will weaken group process. At this stage of consciousness-raising it's probably best to argue through some differences and leave others alone once it has been determined that the discussants aren't getting anyplace or what they are debating isn't all that important. Sometimes we can eliminate arguments by formulating small experiments or surveys that people can use in getting added information about a disputed issue. For instance I know a recently promoted shipping manager who was able to verify his colleagues' suspicions that this promotion was the last he would be likely to receive. He went out and surveyed all the other shipping managers in the company and saw that company history was against him.

Group members continually need to caution one another about acting precipitously. For one thing there is more we need to understand about the basis of our relationship with the system, and, for another, once we take action we usually stop searching and begin focusing convergently. In the example above, the shipping manager did not know all he needed to know in order to confront his boss intelligently. He was in danger of using the hat-in-hand approach which consistently had gotten him nowhere. His support group helped him to see this.

STAGE 3: Understanding Our Relationship with the System

Increased understanding of ourselves and of the system helps us to recognize parts of the system that suit our self-interests and to resist other parts which try to contain us. We sense a new personal freedom. However, getting carried away with this "freedom" proves to be a short term strategy for gaining control. It puts us underground, "working" the system. But eventually those who seek to influence us will discover that we've eluded them and we'll be back playing cat and dog again.

Real freedom depends on our ability to address the underlying conflicts that produce discrepancies. In order to see these conflicts we need to increase our understanding of how we've been interacting with the system. We can use what we now know about ourselves and the system to produce this understanding. We need to explicate the assumptions on which our interactions with the system are based and examine how these assumptions were formed. We'll also need to distinguish between those assumptions which are the result of our own experience and those which are the result of social conditioning.

For those assumptions which we determine to be the direct result of our experience we'll want to decide whether or not they remain applicable to current conditions. We can update our assumptions where we find conditions have changed and we can respond with renewed confidence where we find conditions are more or less the same.

The greatest opportunities for learning are found in reexamining assumptions which were acquired implicitly through our conditioning in the system. They provide us a chance to see what the system would like us to believe and to decide for ourselves whether or not this is valid. They also allow us to view in retrospect the processes used to indoctrinate us in false beliefs. Viewing these processes gives us a better handle on how we're vulnerable to external controls without knowing it.

Basically there are at least three areas of our relationship to the system where we'd do well to search out assumptions.

The first area includes the goals we hold for our interactions with the system and the means we use for achieving them. Along these lines I once listened to a group of people planning for their retirement recognize how they'd been programmed by the society to hold the goal of eventually leaving their city life and routine for an old age community in the country. They further realized that the uncertainties connected with this move caused them to have a corollary goal of parsimony. They now felt badly about having become overly-conservative spenders who deprived themselves of luxuries in their fifties so that they'd have sufficient funds for the years ahead.

The second area includes assumptions we make about the system: its purpose, values, roles in society, and, in particular, its way of viewing us. Along these lines I once listened to a group of unmarried "cohabitators" reflect on the social institution of marriage and how it impacts on their desires to have children. The learnings were diverse. One woman realized that she believed every child deserved married parents and that she was using her unmarried state as a means of hiding her own ambivalence about having children. A man from a second couple realized how his being brought up with the ethic of "children should be seen but not heard" was spoiling his relationship with the child of the woman he was living with. A third couple spent a good deal of time focusing on the legal rights of children who are born out of wedlock.

The third area involves assumptions that explain the ways we and the system influence one another. Along these lines I once listened to a group of university researchers discuss how they and the foundations which grant research monies influence one another. They realized that more often than not they were taken in by the "unimportant" modifications they thought they were making to fit their re-search proposals within the parameters of what a granting agency would fund. They also acknowledged how they sometimes reinterpret their data in order to present a valid case for why they should be awarded additional funds. Several of these researchers themselves sat on funding panels and they reflected that their own "working" of the system caused them to view other people's findings with suspicion.

Group Support for Stage 3

Support group members can help one another to explicate the assumptions they make. They can help by listening to one another talk about each of the three areas mentioned above and identifying the "as-if" and "if-then" messages contained in what they hear. For instance, in the first area members are asked to state their goals for personal success and fulfillment in relation to the system with others inquiring why these goals are personally meaningful and questioning how each speaker plans to go about accomplishing them. Each person's assumptions are recorded and later on others are asked to register their degree of identification with what they have heard. Once members have declared their connection with an assumption, then they can join the person who mentioned it in searching out when and how that assumption was formed.

Figuring out when an invalid assumption was acquired proceeds most smoothly when members trade stories about where they first acted on the assumption being examined. However, we won't always be able to track an assumption back to its origin. In instances where we can't, it may be sufficient to think of current situations in which the assumption plays a prominent role in determining how we act. In either case, we'll want to recall the people who strongly advocate the assumption, the roles they play in the system, what the assumption does for the system and the conditions under which the assumption seems to be most applicable.

Assumptions with which only one or two members identify offer special opportunities to learn about the people involved. These assumptions probably have idiosyncratic origins and may often play an important role in a person's relationships with other social systems. Whether or not constructive personal learning emerges from exploring these assumptions will depend on the trust and support that has been built up among the members of the group.

When it comes to individual learning in a group, especially where emotions are involved, I have been a longtime advocate of the simultaneous presence of support and confrontation. I'm for the type of support that accepts the person's difficulties in actively reflecting on a certain topic or on accurately hearing what has been said to him or her, not insincere support for his or her point of view. I'm for the type of confrontation that engages the person's resistance to considering what's been said and inquiring into his or her defensiveness, not confrontation aimed at getting the person to agree with what's been said. Both of these roles are difficult for a single individual to assume simultaneously, which of course is the advantage of having the help of several persons in a group.

Stage 4: Formulating Alternatives

New understanding about ourselves, about the system, and about the assumptions which link us to the system provide us what we need to know to formulate alternatives that improve our relationship to the system. We do this by noting how assumptions which have been characterizing our relationship with the system are inconsistent with that we have learned about our own needs, interests and ideals. Reflecting these inconsistencies against

what we now know about the system allows us to assess the practicality of alternatives which occur to us now.

Focusing on inconsistencies, rather than reflecting only on our nature, provides a contrast that helps us to envision alternatives. Inconsistencies stimulate thoughts about what would constitute a better situation. Basically there are two types of alternatives we might formulate: those which improve the way the system works and those which change our relationship to it. For instance, a group of nurses considered requesting permission to present their views on reforms needed in the staffing of post-operative recovery rooms to the administrative staff of their hospital. But this type of request would have reinforced their subordinate position in the medical hierarchy. Alternatively they decided to call a strike for hospital reforms with special attention to not making any demands for personal benefits that might cause others to see them as only out for themselves. In this instance they wanted treatment as professionals capable of representing the public's interest.

Overall this fourth stage of consciousness-raising involves re-examining how we've been socialized by the system. In a sense it can be likened to a self-directed process of resocialization.

Group Support for Stage 4

Group members help us spot where our relationship to the system conflicts with our self-interests and nature. They also help us reflect how these conflicts fit within the priorities of what matters to us and to conceptualize alternatives which can be put into practice without undue personal hardship. However, before group members can advise us intelligently, we have to spend some time filling out their pictures of who we are and where we want to go. With a more complete picture, they can spot when we're going off to fight a battle that doesn't need to be won and when we're involved in changing something that might cost us more than we're receiving in exchange.

While we can't tell others everything, there is much we can cover in the course of an hour by addressing ourselves to essentials. In particular we need to relate those life events and personal feelings which will help support group members to understand why the inconsistencies on which we plan to focus carry so much meaning for us. For instance, if we're someone who is interested in the public's access to coastal recreation areas, our group needs to know why we place so much importance on beaches, our history in fighting for public rights, or whatever they need to hear to appreciate why this issue grabs us the way it does.

Group members can help us to consider a broader range of alternatives than we can formulate for ourselves. For example, if an inconsistency results in our formulating an alternative that proposes a change in the system, someone in the group might ask us if we can think of an alternative that involves our changing our relationship to the system. If we can't, they might suggest one that occurs to them. They do so not because they expect us to use it but because they want to open up an entirely new avenue of possibilities for our consideration.

When it comes to our relationship to social systems there are few alternatives we can formulate that won't impact on others. Accordingly, our support group can help us think through the types of reactions we're likely to receive and think up ways to pose our alternatives so that we will evoke minimum resistance in others. When the issue is crucially important to us, and we can predict in advance that we're going to incite counterforces, our support group can help us plan how to cope with these forces and bolster us when we're under stress. Additionally, group members can help us monitor our progress. They can point out when we're making more headway than we think we are, perhaps because it is being accomplished in a slightly different form than we expected. They can also caution us not to be taken in when others whom we are trying to influence change their words but not their actions.

Stage 5: Affecting the Lives of Others

Thus far I've given the impression that consciousness-raising is something we can do on our own and doesn't necessarily involve our getting the cooperation of those whom we see as blocking us. This is true to a point, but eventually we'll do much better if others in the system develop empathy for what we are trying to achieve. To develop this empathy, we will need to approach people who see things differently and we will get furthest when we approach them from the standpoint of what's in it for them rather than from the standpoint of what's in it for us.

We must keep in mind that each person has a different view of reality and from that view most of all of his or her actions make sense. Thus, while we're ardently focusing on the problems a system creates, we can expect that there will be others who only talk about the benefits. In all likelihood these will be the very people whose cooperation we are going to need if things are to change peacefully. We will need to find a way of approaching them so that they can join us in the search for reforms.

If we go on the assumption that there is an objective reality, which will be rationally perceived by anyone who puts his or her mind to thinking things through, then we are likely to approach others by advocating a specific plan and seeking their explicit support. However, if we assume that people will resist converging on a single picture of reality, that they will proceed differently once they have grasped what is at stake, and that maximum benefits are possible only when people holding different perspectives pool their ideas of how the system can be improved, then we are better off approaching the system openendedly without advocating specific improvements. The latter approach reflects my beliefs about how to bring about change in the majority of situations. We broaden out from our parochial viewpoint to consider the well-being of all members of the system and in the process act like a statesperson might behave. Accordingly, I refer to the thinking used in this approach as "statespersonlike."

The statespersonlike approach begins after we've raised our consciousness about what's off in our relationship to a given social system and have figured out how that system is based on misassumptions about our needs and interests. We not only have a specific alternative in mind, but we also have sufficient grasp of the fundamentals to recognize alternate proposals that appropriately address our concerns.

We put this approach into action by developing a friendly dialog with people we see playing a key role in our dilemmas. In sequence: we want to point out the problems we face in our functioning in the system (not the solutions we've envisioned); we want to support these people in identifying discrepancies they experience which either are comparable to our own or are created by our experiencing of the discrepancies we have presented; and we want to acquaint them with the process of divergent problem-solving and encourage them to harvest what can be learned from the discrepancies they've conceptualized. Throughout our emphasis is on helping them identify the discrepancies which are present in their own life in the system. In doing this we need to remember that what these people learn from divergent thinking about their discrepancies is far more important than the specific phrasing they

give a discrepancy.

If in using this approach we involve ourselves in discussing specific actions, then we're likely to cross the thin line that separates a statesperson from a partisan. Consciousness is political. People are likely to become reactionary if they sense our collaborative attitude is a guise for indoctrinating them in our political beliefs. They are almost certain to feel this way if they judge the changes they are considering more likely to improve our lot than their own.

At some point we want to tactfully suggest to the people we are approaching that they begin to divergently discuss these issues with people who have similar roles in the system as themselves. Only when they are supported by a peer group of their own can we count on our discussion with them to be perceived as sufficiently fairminded so that their perspectives can be pooled with ours to create a third, more enlightened and synergistic, reality. Wherever possible we want to stay away from a modality of negotiating on the basis of "If you do this for me, I'll do this for you." We want to create an attitude of mutual cooperation. The most significant changes will come about when all parties are looking for ways to improve the overall functioning of the system and where each party can support changes which bring others closer to a more fulfilling existence in the system.

Idealistic? To be sure. But it can happen. It's the kind of tactics a group of enlightened students used in a consciousness-raising session with policemen in the spring of 1970. They did this in the aftermath of police intervention to stop unauthorized rallies protesting the United States Army's incursion into Cambodia. It is the kind of tactics I've seen human relations experts use when helping high level managers realize the consequences their assumptions about control and orderly managerial processes hold for initiation throughout the ranks of their company's workforce. And it's the kind of tactics my colleagues and I use when approaching the UCLA administration with proposals for field and laboratory courses which involve little reading.

Group Support for Stage 5

By the time we've gotten to this stage our needs for support are subtle. We need an occasional pat-on-the-back and someone who will point out that we're caught up in our own picture of things. By now we're out on our own contacting people whose viewpoints must be encountered for the system to change. Our interactions are quite complex. We are only indirectly addressing our needs for change and the very people we're talking with supportively are the ones we'd like to confront. Our support group will need to keep us directed toward long-term fundamental change as contrasted with the short-term situational change that is easiest for us to pursue. The group helps us work off the tensions which result from keeping our own ideas of how the system might be improved out of the divergent discussions we're attempting to have with those we seek to influence. Once we insert our ideas, it's we, not the people we're talking with, who are talking convergently.

To this point I have not mentioned the most powerful change tactic a support group can use. It is a tactic which we all know—banding together to overpower the opposition through a variety of mechanisms from civil disorder, to disruptive strikes, to peaceful petitions, to constructive discussions. I've avoided discussing this because it is also the riskiest tactic a group can use. It can polarize and politicize the opposition and it can produce tunnel vision and attitudes of righteousness within us. In the model I

use, it is dialog and openminded thinking that count. As a matter of principle I'm willing to sacrifice the immediate gain—but then there are always exceptions. If we can't get enough of what we need to sustain ourselves in the present, then we may feel little recourse but to indulge our desires for action. Hopefully we'll get enough nourishment from our support group to sustain our collaborative approach to meaningful change in the system.

CONCLUSION

In some ways consciousness-raising can be considered the next generation of encounter-groups and sensitivity training. It pits the human dimensions of group process against problems which have substance beyond the feelings and realities of the people discussing them. It views conflicts people have with a system as an interaction of personal needs and system structure. These are problems which cannot be solved by the creative use of emotional energy alone. Rather, these are problems which have deep substantive components requiring intellectual muscle and conceptual skills. Nevertheless, without group members to give emotional support and exercise interpersonal sensitivity, we will not develop the means of sustaining ourselves in working for fundamental and lasting change.

But change is evolutionary. Our best ideas today are just that. We can count on learning more tomorrow and this will mean new, improved visions of what is possible. Thus it's important that we not become complacent with the changes our consciousness-raising leads us to seek today. Eventually we must return to areas we have already covered and once again ask ourselves the questions which led us to see new possibilities.

6.2 WHO SPEAKS FOR THE POOR?

Neil Gilbert, Joseph W. Eaton

The "maximum feasible participation" clause in the Economic Opportunity Act of 1964 provided a chance for the poor to share in determining policy affecting them and their neighborhoods. Political attitudes regarding this decision were mixed. Liberals hoped that this innovation would engender grassroot articulation of dissatisfaction in such areas as housing, police protection, schools, and other public services. Conservatives were concerned that the frustrations of poor people would be expressed in the form of excessive demands that could not be paid for with existing tax resources.

These attitudes reflect plausible assumptions. But the reality of what the poor may want, when given a chance to register their views, is more complex. In eight Pittsburgh poverty areas, leaders who claimed to speak for their neighborhoods were vociferous in declaring popular discontent with existing local conditions. But these views were not supported by the results of a survey of the populace ostensibly represented. Irrespective of racial composition, the majority of residents in each poverty area expressed an unanticipated degree of satisfaction with the status quo in housing, police protection, schools, and other public services.

SUBSTANTIVE CITIZEN PARTICIPATION

Prior to the 1960's, federally supported social welfare programs requiring citizen involvement largely emphasized educational and administrative forms of participation. In contrast, the requirements for citizen participation in the War on Poverty and the Model Cities programs stress substantive participation in planning, policy, and decision-making positions (Piven, 1966).

Through these programs, citizen councils elected in the neighborhoods are to be responsible for developing and reviewing plans for revitalizing their areas. A movement is now underway in some localities to transform citizen councils into Neighborhood Development Corporations with legal status so they are eligible to receive federal, state, and private funds for direct operation of revitalization programs (Kotler, 1969). This emphasis on resident responsibility for re-planning neighborhoods reflects an effort to counteract the bureaucratization of urban life. Poor people, possessing neither economic nor organizational resources to protect their interests, are particularly vulnerable to administrative manipulation that disregards their personal needs (Cloward and Piven, 1965; Sjoberg, Brymer, and Farris, 1966). The citizen participation movement of the 1960's was an effort to provide the poor with control over the impersonal forces that tend to shape the urban environment.

Paralleling the development of this movement is the increasing support given an assumption that has crucial implications for the relationship between participating citizens and professionals: the assumption that those who have lived with a problem are in the best position to recognize and understand it—in the currently fashionable idiom, they can "tell it like it really is."[1]

In accordance with this assumption,

Adapted from Neil Gilbert and Joseph W. Eaton, "Who Speaks for the Poor?" Reprinted by permission of the *Journal of the American Institute of Planners*, Vol. 36, No. 6, November 1970.

Footnotes in edited portions of this paper have been deleted and remaining footnotes renumbered.

[1] Bloomberg and Rosenstock (1968) note that one of the practical reasons for resident participation is that residents "can contribute much from their own experience to the formulation of programs and projects to alleviate and reduce poverty."

the supposedly hard, cold data and intellectual abstractions of professional
planners would be modified by the direct
visceral experiences of low-income neighborhood residents. Some planners are very
certain that the "real life experience" of
the poor, as opposed to the supposedly
impersonal and unfeeling abstractions of
professionals, can provide an optimum
guide to neighborhood planning. This assumption is often defended with tenacity
by self-appointed neighborhood spokesmen, even in the absence of substantiat-
ing data.

The data presented in this study
offer a contrary view. They suggest that
assumptions concerning manifest dissatisfactions with low-income neighborhood
conditions and the ability of the poor to
"tell it like it really is" are applicable
primarily to an activist minority. If the
views expressed in this study by the majority of residents were to govern low-
income neighborhood planning, there
would be little impetus for change of the
status quo. . . .

Part of the survey [conducted in
Pittsburgh] involved a request that informants rate eleven variables pertaining
to their neighborhoods. A card with ratings along a five-point continuum from
terribly bad to very good was given to
the respondents, who were then asked:
"How would you rate (housing, schools,
and so on) in this neighborhood?" Four
of these variables were selected for
analysis in this report: public service,
housing, police protection, and schools.[2]
For purposes of clarity and economy, the
ratings were collapsed into three categories: negative (terribly bad, pretty bad);
neutral (not so bad); and positive (all
right, very good).

[2] The other variables were shopping facilities, public transportation, child care, recreation, employment opportunities, vocational
training programs, and general economic status of residents.

CITIZEN ASSESSMENT OF CONDITIONS

In the eight poverty areas, professional
planners and groups of neighborhood citizen activists had been highly critical of
conditions relating to schools, housing,
police, and other public services. Yet, in
every one of these areas, over half the
respondents rated all these conditions as
positive; in three out of four instances,
over two-thirds of the respondents rated
conditions as positive. . . . In no instance
did as many as one-third of the respondents rate a condition unsatisfactory (negative). Neutral ratings represented a small
proportion of the responses. In only two
neighborhoods did more than one-fourth
of the respondents rate any of the conditions unsatisfactory. This occurred in . . .
[the two neighborhoods] which, in comparison to the other six poverty areas,
have the largest black populations, 89
percent and 71 percent, respectively.
Other areas average less than 15 percent
black. [One of the two neighborhoods]
. . . where over one-fourth of the respondents rated all conditions unsatisfactory,
also had the longest history of profes-
sionally directed and actively sustained
community organization programs.

Further analyses of these data were
conducted controlling for the possible
effects of age and race. The results indicate a pattern similar to that described
above. Of approximately 1,200 respondents in the twenty to thirty-five age
category, 52 to 59 percent of the blacks
and 66 to 76 percent of the whites rated
the four neighborhood conditions as
positive. Negative ratings were given by
27 to 34 percent of the blacks and 13 to
21 percent of the whites in this age
category.

PROFESSIONAL ASSESSMENT
OF CONDITIONS

Conditions in Pittsburgh's low-income
neighborhoods seem to be viewed favor-

ably by those who live in them. This "people's perception" contradicts professional evaluations. During the 1960 census, trained observers gave many more negative ratings to neighborhood housing than did the majority of residents in 1967. (However, as McGimsey (1970) points out, the lack of real criteria and the questionable basis for census housing ratings have caused them to be dropped from the 1970 census.)

Yet, even if we do not consider the 1960 census figures totally accurate, the comparisons between them and our neighborhood survey are startling. In 1960, about one-third of the housing in the eight poverty neighborhoods were found either dilapidated or deteriorated according to census criteria. . . . While these poverty neighborhoods contain a little less than one-half of Pittsburgh's housing, they account for over seven-eighths of the city's dilapidated units and for over two-thirds of its deteriorated units. Any interpretation of these facts must consider that Pittsburgh is, to begin with, not nationally distinguished for good housing conditions.

With regard to schools, the conditions in poverty neighborhoods are typically rated by professionals as inadequate to meet the educational needs of the groups they serve.[3] There is no evidence

that Pittsburgh's poverty neighborhood schools are an exception, despite neighborhood respondents' predominantly favorable ratings. For example, data on conditions in the eight poverty neighborhood schools indicate that two out of the ten academic high schools serving these areas are overcrowded. The drop-out rates for these schools range from 15 to 43 percent; the median drop-out rate is approximately 29 percent (Pittsburgh Public Schools, 1968). If and when the drop-out incidence is reduced by some of the current "stay in school" programs, most of the buildings would become overcrowded.

External ratings on the quality of Pittsburgh's police are also available. A study by the International Association of Police Chiefs indicates that, in terms of patrol operations, "most of the procedures and activities observed were below standard." The organizational structure of this bureau was found to be totally outdated, with the structure of one division described as "unbelievably unreasonable." Among other shortcomings, this professional study noted the absence of an organizational unit to deal with problems of illegal or unethical conduct by officers. And, perhaps of even greater significance to low-income neighborhood residents, particular concern was expressed regarding the lack of a formal system for recording complaints against fellow officers (IAPC, 1966). The picture emerging from this study of Pittsburgh's police and the service they render is distinctly less favorable than that projected by resident ratings.[4] Since the study was conducted by a police agency, it is unlikely that the findings suffer from any preconceived bias against law enforcement organizations!

---

[3] A study of a large high school system in 1960 found that expenditures for schooling in low-income neighborhoods were less than in other areas (Sexton, 1961). These results, however, were obtained before large amounts of federal funds became available to low-income neighborhood schools through the Economic Opportunity Act of 1964 and the Elementary and Secondary Education Act of 1965. A more recent study by Kenneth A. Martyn indicates an apparent shift in the balance of expenditures in favor of low-income schools. Still, he found that upper income schools tend to be manned by higher quality teachers—measured by such criteria as education and length of experience (Hirsch,

1968). For a general statement on low-income neighborhood schools, see Sexton (1965).

[4] Also, there is general evidence that suggests residents of low-income neighborhoods receive less equitable treatment than middle class people at the hands of law enforcement officials (Reiss, 1967).

ACTIVIST ASSESSMENT OF CONDITIONS

The evidence from this study strongly indicates that resident discontent with low-income neighborhood conditions is less prevalent than it may often seem to be. On the other hand, each of the poverty areas surveyed contained small organized groups of citizens acutely dissatisfied with local conditions. One such group, for instance, the Citizens Against Slum Housing, was organized through the anti-poverty program. Its members picketed real estate agents and slumlords in efforts to get housing conditions upgraded. Another group was the Concerned Citizens. They aggressively criticized school conditions and demanded a voice in setting school board policies. In each area, neighborhood councils were working incessantly to improve the quality of local public services. Their active members, however, were few in number. Taken together, all of these groups contained probably no more than three hundred active members. They claimed to be voicing the dissatisfactions of neighborhoods containing about 250,000 residents, yet when a sample of these residents were polled, a majority evaluated local conditions favorably.

The exact meaning of these evaluations is open to interpretation. It may be that the residents are really satisfied in the sense that their wants are being adequately met. Or it may be that they are not so much satisfied as they are accepting of conditions of low-income neighborhood life; perhaps the positive ratings really mean, "conditions are as good as can be expected." In any case, what stands out is the fact that, contrary to activist intimations of serious local problems, most residents were inclined to view neighborhood conditions with equanimity.

IMPLICATIONS FOR CITIZEN PLANNING

A majority of the residents of poverty neighborhoods evidently have a low level of expectation. They express apparent satisfaction with neighborhood conditions which professional planners and citizen activists clearly view as substandard, on the basis of much supportive evidence.

Could it be that existing conditions are adequate in terms of low-income neighborhood culture and values?[5] Are the judgments of professionals and self-selected citizen spokesmen actually an imposition of middle class values, which have little relevance to the poor? Or is it that the resident ratings simply reflect an adaptation to the personal realities of a life of limited alternatives?

The discrepancy between the high level of dissatisfaction expressed by a relatively small number of self-selected neighborhood spokesmen and the apparent contentment of the majority of their neighbors raises a number of questions for community planners:

1. Can the poor fully appreciate their conditions and articulate the need for change? Or is it only an elite group of activists, "the military staff of the proletariat," as Lenin called

[5] There is considerable validity to the argument that planners often develop programs and provide services based on upper middle class values that are not always appropriate to the needs and life styles of the poor (Gans, 1962). A preliminary analysis of data collected from an attitude survey of citizens and professionals on New York's Lower East Side indicates that when asked to rate this neighborhood as a place to live, 70.5 percent of the professionals answered "poor" or "very poor" while only 37.5 percent of the indigenous staff and 34.4 percent of the community respondents agreed with this designation (Grosser, 1963).

them, who are capable of such action?[6]

2. If activist leaders differ greatly from residents in their perceptions of poverty neighborhood conditions, how does this discrepancy affect programs of citizen participation in local welfare planning?

3. How can planners who prefer to operate with popular sanction legitimately respond to activist factions if these differences between activist and majority perceptions exist? (Eaton, 1963).

For any neighborhood reform program, it is usually a small minority who define the problem. They rise up against its abuses and advocate solutions. The role of these minorities needs to be clearly recognized by planners seeking active "community support" for change. Such support is rarely given to them by a majority of the residents. It is through these minorities that planners can trigger the impulse for change.

It would be a simple matter to accept this proposition and disregard planning with the community-at-large. Indeed, this is often inadvertently the case when planners identify with activist minorities on the presumption that they represent the views and interest of the community-at-large.[7] While this may expedite the planning process and lend assurance to the planner that his democratic principles are not being violated, such action can also produce dysfunctional consequences.

Activists frequently develop into a self-sanctioning elite of citizen planners who view themselves, in fact, as a "military staff of the proletariat." This often results in an exclusiveness that inhibits participation of others in community decision-making. "Welfare colonialism," as the activists are apt to label the prior state of expert planning by technicians who sought no neighborhood sanction, is then replaced by a perhaps less onerous, but not more democratic approach in which activists monopolize the role of neighborhood spokesman. In extreme cases, citizen activists have become a new generation of "colonialists," accumulating much of the power and the prerogatives that they opposed in those who previously enjoyed this status.

Since these citizen activists often advocate programs which address themselves to certain real problems, this may be a less oppressive system than the one it replaces.[8] Indeed, while the majority of low-income neighborhood residents may view existing conditions with equanimity, they may still recognize as beneficial many of the changes advocated by

---

[6] Lenin did not view the emancipation of the working class as the responsibility of the working class itself; rather he thought this to be the task of a small, activist faction who would engineer change on the workers' behalf (Mayo, 1955).

[7] The contention that activist groups are representative of the poor is sometimes defended by pointing to neighborhood elections. To date, however, these elections have produced dismal results. Less than 2 percent of the eligible voters participated in elections held for members of the eight neighborhood councils in Pittsburgh's poverty areas (Gil-

bert, 1970). Similar evidence is found in other cities. In Philadelphia, where neighborhood elections were a relatively elaborate affair—in terms of time and money spent, less than 3 percent of the eligible residents turned out to vote (Shostak, 1966). Analyzing election processes in California, Ralph Kramer (1969) observes: "The numerous neighborhood elections and their aftermath in San Francisco and Santa Clara can best be described as *pseudo-political processes.*"

[8] The "welfare colonialist" system is run by predominantly middle class outsiders whose interests and loyalties are agency-based (Silberman, 1964).

activist spokesmen. However, there is no guarantee with this type of elitist planning that the standards of a relatively small minority of self-appointed spokesmen for the poor will not impose some unacceptable requirements on the passive majority. The new leaders are not necessarily selfless or community centered. Moreover, their formal accountability to the community-at-large is usually negligible (Gilbert, 1970; Kramer, 1969).

For example, a small group of self-proclaimed leaders in one of Pittsburgh's poverty neighborhoods was able to force the closing of a Planned Parenthood Center on the allegation that it was practicing racial genocide. Most of the group's members were men. In fact, this program was quite popular as indicated by the number of black clients who voluntarily sought out the services. In this instance, activist demands denied the community-at-large an opportunity many of its residents wanted.

While activists or indigenous spokesmen are a vital force in the citizen participation movement, their role in neighborhood planning poses a dilemma to professional planners. Professionals have an affinity for working with these people since activists are change-oriented; the activists are also more articulate than other residents of their neighborhoods; they are discontent with existing conditions and, perhaps most important, they are willing to volunteer their time and effort for a cause. Given these characteristics, it is convenient to overlook that these groups are often elite minorities who may at times advocate change in the interest of causes other than the welfare of their neighborhood and/or the broader community. The saliency of this point cannot be ignored by professional planners seeking to legitimate their activities in low-income neighborhoods through resident involvement. Currently lacking in most of these endeavors are formal mechanisms of accountability to insure that the activists' opinions and objectives are valid expressions of local sentiment. In the absence of such accountability, professional planners must attempt to assess activists' views on the basis of evidence, when it can be obtained, of who legitimately speaks for the poor.

References

Bloomberg, Warner, Jr., and Florence W. Rosenstock. (1968) "Who Can Activate the Poor—One Assessment of 'Maximum Feasible Participation.'" P. 316 in Bloomberg and Henry J. Schmandt (eds.), Poverty and Urban Policy (Beverly Hills: Sage Publications, Inc.).

Cloward, Richard A., and Frances Piven. (1965) "The Professional Bureaucracies Benefit Systems as Influence Systems." Pp. 49–50 in Murray Silberman (ed.), The Role of Government in Promoting Social Change (New York: Columbia University School of Social Work).

Eaton, Joseph W. (1963) "Community Development Ideologies," International Review of Community Development, 11, 37–50.

Gans, Herbert J. (1962) The Urban Villagers (New York: The Free Press).

Gilbert, Neil. (1970) Clients or Constituents (San Francisco: Jossey-Bass, Inc.).

Grosser, Charles F. (1963) "Middle Class Professionals . . . Lower Class Clients" (unpublished Ph.D. dissertation proposal, Columbia University).

International Association of Police Chiefs. (1966) Summary of the Principal Findings: Pittsburgh Bureau of Police Survey.

Kotler, Milton. (1969) Neighborhood Government (New York: Bobbs-Merrill).

Kramer, Ralph. (1969) *Participation of the Poor* (Englewood Cliffs: Prentice-Hall).

Mayo, H. B. (1955) *Democracy and Marxism* (New York: Oxford University Press).

McGimsey, George. (1970) "The 1970 Census: Changes and Innovations," *Journal of the American Institute of Planners*, 36 (May), 198–203.

Pittsburgh Public Schools. (1968) *A Study of School Holding Power, School Year 1966–1967* (Pittsburgh: PPS).

Piven, Frances. (1966) "Participation of Residents in Neighborhood Community Action Programs," *Social Work*, 11 (January), 74–5.

Reiss, Albert J., Jr. (1967) "Police Brutality: Answers to Key Questions," *Trans-action*, 5 (July–August), 10–19.

Sexton, Patricia C. (1965) "City Schools." Pp. 234–49 in Louis Ferman, Joyce Kornbluh, and Alan Haber (eds.), *Poverty in America* (Ann Arbor: University of Michigan Press).

Sexton, Patricia C. (1961) *Education and Income* (New York: The Viking Press).

Shostak, Arthur B. (1966) "Promoting Participation of the Poor: Philadelphia's Anti-Poverty Program," *Social Work*, 11 (January), 73–80.

Silberman, Charles E. (1964) *Crisis in Black and White* (New York: Random House).

Sjoberg, Gideon, Richard A. Brymer, and Buford Farris. (1966) "Bureaucracy and the Lower Class," *Sociology and Social Research* (April), pp. 325–37.

6.3   DRAMA AND ADVOCACY PLANNING

Lisa R. Peattie

Planners have always talked about "communities." But, in the last few years, the communities have been, to a notable degree, talking back. Recently, one of the main features of the American planning environment has been demands for "community representation" and for "community self-determination."

The emergence of these new political actors has not been uncontested. There have been challenges to the legitimacy and representativeness of the "community spokesmen" and claims that the

Reprinted by permission of the *Journal of the American Institute of Planners*, Vol. 36, No. 6, November 1970, pp. 405–410.

Author's Note: This article is adapted from a paper presented at the AAAS meeting, December 1969.

organized groups "don't really represent the whole community." A recent *New York Times* article on the trend to citizen participation in urban renewal decisions refers a little sardonically to "the influence of 'the community' as these articulate and outspoken residents are known" (Shipler, 1969). I will be arguing that these reservations and caveats are generally well taken. But I would like to go on to argue that they apply also to cases of "communities" which seem less problematic, and that the "genuineness" of the community, in the sense of its social homogeneity and social integration, is not a good criterion for political relevance.

This may have some importance since the notion of "the community" as a political force, and perhaps as a politicial entity within which resources would be aggregated and allocated, has become a central theme of American urban politics. Any public hearing on the urban renewal project has its "representatives of the community"; "community spokesmen" appear to discuss a proposed highway; a proposed Community Self Determination Act in Congress would make it possible for residents of areas within any city to organize bodies to receive funds and to carry out a variety of economic, service, and, in the broad sense, political functions in the name of the community.

I suppose that I have abetted this trend by taking part in the development of a non-profit organization to provide technical services to "low-income communities" affected by planning. It is from my experience with this organization that I would like first to comment on "community."

ADVOCATING COMMUNITY INTERESTS

The organization to which I refer, Urban Planning Aid, was founded three years ago in Cambridge, Massachusetts, by a group of professionals—a couple of architects and planners, a lawyer, a sociologist, myself—who had become convinced that the claim of some Establishment planning bodies to represent the "public interest" or the "general welfare" was in fact specious (Peattie, 1968). We believed, and still do, that the concept of a "general welfare" as a guide to policy was a mirage, that societies and cities included in fact a number of particular interests, and that any plan was actually a political instrument which represented some particular segment of these possible interests, and determined in the old phrase, who got what, when, where, and how. It seemed clear that some kinds of people got their interests better represented in the planning process than others, that the planning process favored the more

wealthy and the more powerful, and that poor people, in the absence of ways to get their interests planned for, were likely to continue to see highways routed through their neighborhoods and their aging housing demolished to make room for high-rent apartment buildings. So, we incorporated Urban Planning Aid as a non-profit organization to provide planning services to low-income communities and to advocate the interests of such communities in the planning process, much as the lawyer advocates the interest of his client in the legal framework.

The point I want to stress here is that we defined our task as that of helping low-income communities; our clients were to be "communities," not individuals, organizations, or political constituencies. I do not remember that we argued or discussed this at all; to the best of my recollection, this phraseology seemed to us all a natural one. I suppose that one question I am suggesting in this article— one which by no means do I find easy to answer—is: Why speak in the name of "the community," given what turns out, very shortly, to be the logical absurdity of doing so?

Urban Planning Aid began with two "client communities." One was a neighborhood in Cambridge slated to be traversed by an enormous highway that would displace 1,300 families and tear the social fabric by scattering long-term residents and separating people and institutions. The other was Lower Roxbury, a blighted area in Boston of predominantly black residents scheduled for clearance to build a new campus high school. The group of residents who had asked our help there wanted low and middle income housing included in the plan.

These two clients underwent rather different evolutionary change. The Cambridge group is still in existence, but has become attached to a larger coalition of citizen groups concerned with transportation planning; this coalition in effect came into being because of Urban Planning Aid's redefinition of the issue as an instance of a more general one: the class bias in favor of auto users inherent in the whole process of metropolitan transportation planning in Boston. Meanwhile, the Boston group, having won its fight for including housing in the area as well as a school, has become incorporated as a non-profit corporation and is moving into housing development.

Both of these "community groups," then, have been reasonably long-lasting and reasonably successful. They have also been reasonably legitimate, in the sense that in neither case has the position maintained been subject to question by rival definitions of the community's desires or interests. In Cambridge, not only homeowners in the path of the highway, but also city government officials have taken a strongly anti-highway position. In the Boston area under question, while some residents are more interested in building housing than others, no demand has appeared to exclude housing. But both groups have small memberships, and are skewed to greater representation of the homeowner and very long-term resident population in areas which also include a considerable number of more transient people. In Boston when we set out to assist the community group in making a survey of everyone in the area scheduled for renewal acquisitions, we soon found that there were substantial numbers of residents who had never heard of the organization, and who, even though informed that its activities were in fact serving their needs for maintaining a supply of low-cost housing in Boston, were not about to rush to join it. Indeed one might say that exactly those people whose position in the housing market was most precarious, and who might therefore be said to have the greatest interest in the issues being pushed by the community group, were also those too hard-pressed, too suspicious, and too little invested in the particular area to be joiners.

The community group was assisted not only by our organization, but also by several community organizers from social agencies. We imagined that these organizers would do the job of organizing the community and would be active in drawing non-participators into the organization so that they would take part in discussions about the area's future and what sort of building should take place there. This did not happen. At first we thought that the organizers were lazy or overburdened with other responsibilities. Then, I began to see that they knew their job: that from a certain point of view, the organization would be less effective if it continually had to incorporate, and assimilate into its internal processes, many new members. What the organization needed to be effective as a political force was: a limited group of leaders; enough supporters to fill a hall at occasional public meetings; and the absence of active local opposition.

COMMUNITY DRAMA

It was at this point that I suddenly began to see the "community" of Lower Roxbury as a dramatic performance. The community organizers were staging and directing; sometimes they edited a basically improvisational script. There were main actors, the officers and active members of the organization. And there was a supporting cast, those members of the community who could be gotten out to meetings and to public hearings and whose crowd noises at such occasions might intimidate the redevelopment authority. There were props, suggesting with some limited physical means a surrounding environment; the maps and reports our group was producing fell into this category.

Sometimes the assertion of the community as a political force may take very theatrical form indeed, as in the dramatic emergence of the organization called CAUSE, Community Assembly for a United South End.

In the South End of Boston, a large urban renewal project had been underway for some years. The project had had a sizeable component of citizen participation in the planning process—for good reason, for the first plan produced by the Redevelopment Authority had been so resoundingly defeated by local opposition that the Authority had seen no recourse but to begin again, this time eliciting citizen agreement and support (Hyman, 1969). The Authority had hired an organizer, who had managed to draw into the planning process many or most of the organized groups in the area. The plans were discussed and completed and passed by the city. But two major problems still remained unresolved. One had to do with those local people who were not involved in the planning process, mostly poor and black. The other had to do with difficulties in plan implementation. It is easier to tear buildings down than to get new housing built; thus the Authority was displacing residents before new housing could become available in the neighborhood. Indeed, doubt had arisen as to the future prospects for new housing at prices those people, mostly low-income, might afford. So there existed a potential group of leaders, not organized into the planning process, who had a potential constituency in the form of a substantial number of people with a common problem that could be translated into a grievance against the public agency. CAUSE came into being dedicated to representing the interests of these people.

But this organization was very small, consisting basically of its organizer and a small group of associates, and seemed to have great difficulty in influencing city agencies. When our planning group carried out, for the organization, an analysis of the South End plan and its implementation, matters proceeded much as before. But then the group invaded a parking lot in the area—a lot, significantly, owned by the Fire Commissioner. They blocked off the lot, threw up small shacks, erected signs demanding a halt to the execution of the Plan. Through two nights a group of people, black and white, occupied the lot, sleeping under tents and boards, sometimes drumming and singing, giving interviews to the reporters and cameramen who arrived. Sympathizers heard of the event and arrived, some with mattresses. It was a kind of political street theater, dramatizing in visual terms the demand of the participants that land be used for housing, rather than for commercial use, that planning serve "the people" rather than "the politicians," and that the people who needed housing in the South End were, many of them, poor and black.

In my own mind, I compared this "squatting" to squatter invasions of land in Latin America, and I saw that this operation was a much more theatrical one, since there was here no intent to actually hold and build on the land where the squatting took place. But at the same time, I remembered that the Latin American squatters can be quite theatrical too, with their flags, their public statements, their visual expression of the hunger for land and a home of one's own, and that the South End squatters, for all their theatricality, had a serious purpose, a real aim, in view.

In any case, the successful squatter organization changed the role of the organizers in the political process. The redevelopment authority stopped execution of the plan, and eventually established procedures for an elected urban renewal committee in the area. At the public meeting called to discuss the project, an overflow crowd acknowledged the organization by standing up when its leader spoke. The group had, in effect, acquired a kind of legitimacy, some sort of informal mandate, through its effective theater; it was now able to present itself as a spokesman for "the community."

POLITICS AS AN ECOLOGY OF THEATER

Norton Long (1958) has described the city as an "ecology of games." For some purposes, it seems to me, one might better describe it as an *ecology of dramatic performances*. For one thing, the image of a dramatic performance expresses more readily than the imagery of games the ambiguity around the question of who participates. It is a general characteristic of games that participants are sharply differentiated from non-participants and that their relations are quite formalized; if there are sides, for example, one always knows "whose side are you on," and this does not become a problem as it has in the labor-organizing processes which gave rise to the song of that name.

The image of "theater" also expresses more handily than the image of the game the quality of emotional engagement characteristic of the urban social order. For in a game one produces just enough emotional engagement necesray to maintain the game, and there is very little spillover into other activities at other times and places. One may participate in the theater in somewhat the same way, as when one goes to a good musical to relax. But we understand that there is also serious theater, theater that is intended to involve us in some more basic way and to alter our state of consciousness in such a way that it spills over into our other activities.

Some dramatic performances produced in the urban scene do have specified participants and a clear division between the players and the audience, as in traditional stage theater. Traditional planning was of this sort, complete with the public hearing in which, as Gans (1969) describes it, the attempt is made to keep the audience of citizens from "blowing" the prescripted performance by the planning actors. Other dramatic performances are much more like the audience participation productions of the Living Theatre or even like those guerilla theater actions in which the aim is to provoke bystanders into becoming part of a play which is as much the "reality" of the bystanders as the "theater" of actors.

When politics is frankly treated as theatrical and theater is treated as a political instrument, the distinction between theater and reality may become blurred indeed. One weekend at MIT we had simultaneous performances in adjacent buildings. In the Kresge Auditorium, the Living Theatre was presenting such performances as *Paradise Now* in which they try to provoke the audience into bursting through the social order as it presents itself in the normal rules of behavior in a theater. In the Student Center next door, students had organized a "sanctuary" for a deserting soldier, and the building was full of students eating and sleeping on the floor, pasting up signs, making speeches. The physical appearance and the political objectives of the two events were not dissimilar, and a number of individuals wandered back and forth participating in both.

The most explicit discussion of politics as theater is, I suppose, Abbie Hoffman's recent account of the Yippie! movement in *Revolution for the Hell of It,* though the theme surely goes back to Sorel's "Myth of the General Strike." Hoffman describes how he, Paul Krassner, and Jerry Rubin, faced with the problem of organizing to bring people to "make a statement" at the Democratic Convention, invented the Yippies! and floated the Movement as a sort of incorporeal or cinematic theater on the media. They saw themselves creating a myth— "Chicago, a festival of music, violence (Americans love to go to accidents and fires), guerilla theater, Democrats. . . . There is mass participation in the Yippie!

myth. . . . Can myths involve people to the extent that they will make the journey to a far-off Chicago? . . ." (Hoffman, 1968). Then, the drama that Hoffman calls the "Grand Central Massacre" was staged, which, of course, became the curtain-raiser for the Theater of Cruelty in the streets of Chicago.

But surely this kind of political theater or theatrical politics has nothing to do with communities? What have the freaks and radicals who were beaten by Daley's police, what has Abbie Hoffman's putting-on of the media, got to do with even what is meant usually by "community organizing," let alone what sociologists usually mean by "community"?

Let us admit, first, that the Yippies at the Siege of Chicago have, as a phenomenon, certain important similarities to the emergence of CAUSE in the South End. In both cases, a handful of individuals defined an issue they recognized as salient for a potential constituency, and by dramatizing that issue made the constituency aware of itself as a group. The dramatic form chosen was one that was open to growing participation as more and more persons identified themselves with the interest dramatized by the initiating group; not for nothing did the marchers in Chicago chant, "join us, join us," to the watching delegates. Those delegates who joined, and especially those who were then beaten by the police, found themselves "radicalized" in the process— becoming part of a kind of intellectual community of radicals. In the South End, the constituency was one based on a turf, a territory, and the issue around which CAUSE organized "the community" was a turf-located issue, the placing of low-income housing. The issues dramatized at Chicago, the issues which brought some of the delegates off the sidewalk and into the march, were less clearly turf-located issues, for they had to do with the morality of the war in Vietnam. But even here, the issues were located within national boundaries. And in any

case, the processes of organizing were much alike. Both kinds of dramatic performance tended to establish informally organized social entities: a small group of people were known as "leaders" of a much larger number of persons who had in a general sort of way expressed their support of the movement for which the leaders were the spokesmen.

But these are attempts to organize around an issue or interest one of a whole set of potential interests represented within the large and heterogeneous population of a given area. The Movement people at Chicago attempted to organize people in the United States to advocate ending the Vietnam war and political re-structuring; within the United States there were and are people committed to the war and to established party structure as well as those who are not concerned with these issues one way or another. CAUSE "organized" people in the South End who had an interest in making it possible for low-income people to remain within the urban renewal area; among inhabitants of the South End there were and are people whose interest in "up-grading" the community makes it advantageous for them to have low-income people move out, and others who do not participate either way. The need for "drama" is surely related to the need to bring together an interest group out of that background heterogeneity. One might think of the camp leader on departure day whistling and raising his banner to summon *his* little group of campers out of the crowd in Grand Central.

REAL COMMUNITIES

But is it so different in the "real" community of greater homogeneity and a high degree of internal social linkage? Some years ago I lived for a time in a working-class neighborhood (a squatter settlement) in Venezuela, a tiny "community" of less than five hundred people. The "community" was about twenty years old. The residents were not completely homogeneous, but with one exception besides ourselves they had come from various parts of Eastern Venezuela. Of the two hundred adults, a fifth had lived there less than a year at the time of the study, and another quarter had been living there only between one and five years. There was, however, a core of long-term residents; 15 percent of the adults had lived there more or less since the neighborhood came into being. Furthermore, although the residents varied in social class style from illiterate occasional laborers to an accountant with a new car, these distinctions had not become barriers to social interaction. The majority of households were linked to others by kinship. The small houses of the neighborhood were packed closely together on a small triangle of land set off by natural boundaries from the rest of the city, and coming and going in the narrow streets and shopping at the several tiny shops provided numerous occasions for social interactions. It had every likely attribute, then, of a "real community." To make the picture complete, before we came and during our stay various "community organizers" were working to "organize" this natural community into an effective entity for collaborative action.

I shall not try to describe the various issues around which organizing efforts went on (Peattie, 1968) but merely say that in several ways the situation in my tiny neighborhood was not so dissimilar from that in the South End. "Organizing" meant staging conspicuous activities in which people could join, like a clean-up campaign or the laying of a water line to make running water (at public taps) available to the residents. These efforts were described by the leaders, other participants, and non-participants as "community development," and "efforts of the community." Those leaders who had taken an active role in organizing the activities became established as "community leaders." But actually, the density of social interaction and the social networks in the neighborhoods were not, apparently, enough to insure unanimous or even general participation in the "community action." The laying of the water line, for example, was a conspicuous and immensely popular project, but perhaps 10 or at the most 20 percent of the adults participated at any time. The largest meeting I ever saw in the community called amidst terrific concern over the fact that a sewer outlet was being built on the local beach, did not exceed forty-five persons, old and young. The "community" as an entity seems as much a dramatic presentation as the more complex situations previously described.

Herbert Gans describes as "urban villagers" the Italians of Boston's pre-redevelopment West End—a highly homogeneous stable population linked by social ties, especially of kinship. Yet he says:

To begin with, the concept of the West End as a single neighborhood was foreign to the West Enders themselves. Although the area had long been known as the West End, the residents themselves divided it up into many subareas, depending in part on the ethnic group which predominated, and in part on the extent to which the tenants in one set of streets had reason or opportunity to use another.

. . .

Until the coming of redevelopment, only outsiders were likely to think of the West End as a single neighborhood. After the redevelopment was announced, the residents were drawn together by the common danger, but even so, the West End never became a cohesive neighborhood [Gans, 1962].

ACT ONE—ORGANIZATION

So wherever we look, despite the plethora of community organizing efforts, we find not organized communities but community organizations—and relating to these in various kinds of ways social networks, interest groups, territorial allegiances, ethnic identities, and other forms of social ties and group identifications. It seems that the function of the dramatic performances I have described is to link some of these social elements together into a representation of common interest and shared identity—a "community." The character and specific functions of such dramatic performances will, of course, vary with the situation to which they are addressed. A performance which is to re-confirm some established "community identity" and system of social relations can be much more formal and ritualistic, and need not require anything more of the mass of people than passive acquiescence. A performance which is to establish the legitimacy of some group of interest as a new political force must be much more vivid and should lead to participation from the floor; a successful performance should establish some theme of central concern, should attract an audience who can manifest their support in some way, and should suggest other supporters off-stage to lend the cause added legitimacy.

The legitimacy causes and leaders derived from this kind of thing is not, of course, the same kind that comes when the majority of voters in a bounded electorate choose one set of leaders over another or vote in a referendum. But it is a kind of legitimacy, and it is not made unnecessary by the electoral sort, as an elected body will find out if it cannot produce that kind of support from time to time. The Nixon government cannot just counter a mammoth peace march by pointing out that it won the last national election; it must, like the Mobe leaders, stage its dramatic show of support, if only in the form of showing a pile of telegrams on TV. A colleague and I have argued in a recent paper (Keyes and Peattie, 1970) that the elected Model

Cities Board in Boston suffered to an extraordinary degree by being committed to a planning process that made it very difficult to dramatize and attract support around particular issues, and that in the absence of this kind of action possibility, its electoral legitimacy helped little in representing "the community."

To present what are basically specific group interests as "the needs of the community" no doubt has a number of functions, not all of which are entirely clear to me. It serves to place support and to consolidate support behind the interests. It is a framework within which varying but overlapping interests can develop systems of adjustment and collaboration. At the same time, it helps to develop political accountability. It helps to generalize the specific issues, to connect them with others, and to develop them in a system of moral rationale—an ideology. It serves, indeed, much the functions of that very concept of the "general welfare" that our planning group had so forthrightly rejected.

THE ADVOCATE'S CLIENT

In any case, our advocacy planning group, Urban Planning Aid, has come to see the notion of serving "communities" as the same mirage as the traditional planner's idea of serving the "general welfare." We have come to think that we should choose as our clients community-based organizations that seem to be developing issues worth support and that seem capable of building support.

We suppose that to the extent that we see our function as that of making the planning process—and the political process—more responsive to the groups currently not well represented in our society, the groups which are for us appropriate clients will be precisely those that any onlooker can reasonably accuse of being small and "not representing the community." They will be organizing groups, building support as they develop the sense of the issue.

And, more and more, we see the process by which that is done as a dramatic one, not the planners' presentations in linear expository form which we saw at first as our main vehicle for change. Instead, although we still write reports, we also find ourselves helping to plan demonstrations and "actions" around issues. Has not theater always been a way in which men tried out and represented their views of the unrealized?

References

Gans, Herbert J. (1969) *Levittowners: Ways of Life and Politics in a New Suburban Community* (New York: Vintage Books), pp. 312–315.

Gans, Herbert J. (1962) *The Urban Villagers: Group and Class in the Life of Italian-Americans* (New York: The Free Press), p. 11.

Hoffman, Abbie. (1968) *Revolution for the Hell of It* (New York: Dial Press), p. 81.

Hyman, Herbert. (1969) "Planning with Citizens: Two Styles," *Journal of the American Institute of Planners*, 35 (March), 105–12.

Keyes, Langley, and Lisa Peattie. (1970) "Citizen Participation in Model Cities." (Unpublished.)

Long, Norton. (1958) "The Local Community as an Ecology of Games," *American Journal of Sociology*, 64 (November), 251–61.

Peattie, Lisa. (1968) "Reflections on Advocacy Planning," *Journal of the American Institute of Planners*, 34 (March), 80–7.

Shipler, David K. (1969) "Urban Renewal Giving the Poor Opportunity to Increase Power," *The New York, Times*, November 9.

"Social Structure and Social Action" (1968) In Lisa Peattie, *The View from the Barrio* (Ann Arbor: University of Michigan Press).

Interventions for Planned Change

PART THREE

PLANNING STRUCTURES AND PROCESSES

CHAPTER

Planning for change is a *multifaceted* and deeply *personal* endeavor. The search for a general integration of relevant theories and techniques, therefore, is worth the pursuit by all would-be change agents, but each change agent needs to experience the process of application and synthesis, and sort out the ebbs and flows of planned change. The selections of this chapter do *not* represent that much sought-after holistic conceptual system of planned change, but they *are* signposts for others to follow and obtain guidance as they individually go about the plannning of change.

These readings reflect the influence of the applied behavioral sciences, particularly in community planning activities over the last decade. Further, the selections recognize that planned change is both a *personal* as well as an *organizational* phenomenon; thus the major contexts within which planned change occurs are (1) an organization serving the needs of its *environment,* and (2) individuals (*clients* and *planners*) serving their personal needs and interacting to identify mutually derived objectives and the means for their achievement. Each of the selected readings contributes a partial understanding of these major contexts; and importantly, these readings represent building blocks or elements for identifying *structure* among the essential *processes* of planned organizational and community change.

The opening reading of the chapter by Corey suggests that the complexities of planned community change require ordering and analysis in order to achieve better understanding and more effective application. The notion of personal constructs is used as a means for identifying structure among selected elements of recent community planning practice. Drawing upon the influence of organization development and transactional behavior in community planning, the major components of this recent tradition in planned community change are discussed and differentiated; included are the *environment* of the planning effort, and both *knowledge structures* and *action structures* that are essential to the realization of planned community change. The case is made that great variations and differentiations exist among community planning structures; such discrimination can help the client change agent and the consultant change agent alike to more effectively strategize and plan interventions. While Corey's piece addresses planning *structures*, the dynamics of planning *processes* are left to the remaining readings.

G. K. Jayaram explicates and guides the reader through the operation of the *Open Systems Planning* process. It is a technique both for appreciation and instrumentation. The core of this planning process is in the delineation of client-participants' values as various change interventions are planned collaboratively with a consultant. André Delbecq and Andrew Van de Ven also set forth a useful planning process approach, the *Program Planning Model*. These authors work from the guidance suggested by small group theory, and they proffer the "nominal group" meeting format for the effective initiation of a program development process. Similar to Jayaram's Open Systems Planning, the Program Planning Model also is a sociological model; further it enables the reader to extend the citizen participation discussion of Corey, in that it demonstrates the necessity of identifying key actors and the essential reference groups that need to be involved in each successive phase of the program planning process.

The chapter excerpt by John Friedmann is included in order to remind the reader that the "transactive style" of planning is essential to the continuous need to bridge "the widening gulf in communication between technical planners and their clients." The transactive planning style has been at the core of the organization development tradition of community planning, and this piece details its essential elements and draws the reader's attention to the major implications of this recent planning style. Thus, this selection serves as a reminder to the planned change agent that he is in continual need of re-education if he expects to change "knowledge into action through an unbroken sequence of interpersonal relations."

Finally, the last reading selection of the chapter, by Herbert Shepard, picks up and expands the theme of planned change at the individual level. To realize the potential of being effective community change agents, both citizens and professionals need to be in tune with themselves in order to get in tune with their communities; Shepard's *life planning process* offers an opportunity for doing just such a tuning exercise. Importantly, the life planning process is a learning outlook that enables one to relate environment and purpose; this is significant to each change agent because purpose is the catalyst for the planning of change.

7.1 STRUCTURES IN THE PLANNING OF COMMUNITY CHANGE: A PERSONAL CONSTRUCT

Kenneth E. Corey

The point of this statement is to share with the reader a series of selected conceptual structures that have been found to be personally useful in the doing and facilitating of planned community change. The structures are presented as a potential aid for others as they attempt to identify structure in the range of fundamental ideas underlying the planning of community change.

The strategy employed here is to construct a personal structure for use in better understanding and taking action in the planning of community change. Having set out this one example of a personal planned community change structure, it is intended that the reader will be stimulated to formulate his own construct. Toward this end, the reader is directed to the writings of Jerome Bruner on *the importance of structure in learning* (1960 , pp. 17–18); D. Bannister and Fay Fransella on *personal construct theory* (1971); John Friedmann and Barclay Hudson on the *organization development (OD) tradition in community planning* (1974). Particularly useful is John Friedmann's *model of transactive planning;* the elements of this model have been used in organizing the personal construct that follows.

SOME KNOWLEDGE STRUCTURES: CITIZEN PARTICIPATION VARIATIONS

The client citizen participant can perform the role of community change agent to a greater or lesser degree. It is useful for the change agent to be able to identify his position among a range of role options; thereby the citizen change agent can make more effective decisions designed to maximize his objectives. Sherry Arnstein has provided us with a practical construct that can aid in our sorting out processes (Arnstein, 1969). See Figure 1. Her "Ladder of Citizen Participation" distinguishes between degrees of participation ranging from the high rung of "citizen control" to the low rung of outright citizen "manipulation." The rungs of "manipulation" and "therapy" therefore are contrivances of nonparticipation; the aim of such "participation" is to educate or to cure the participant (Burke, 1968, p. 288–89). The rungs of "informing," "consultation," and "placation" form a category of token participation where the citizen may be involved, but he lacks the clout to insure that his involvement and advice will mean change. The highest rungs of the participation ladder include "partnership," "delegated power," and "citizen control"; at these levels the citizens are either coequal or dominant in the planning decisions (Burke, 1968, p. 292). Arnstein concludes that while her ladder is a simplification, "it helps to illustrate the point that so many have missed—that there are significant graduations of citizen participation" (p. 217).

Of course, there are even more complex variations associated with citizen participation structures. Citizen participation is one of several methods available to solve the problems associated with improving the delivery of public services. The rationale for citizen participation in the improvement of service delivery "is that when service recipients choose people like themselves for positions that influence service delivery decisions, they are guaranteed access and accountability" (Gilbert, 1972, p. 27). Thus, in this context, citizen participation is a way to attempt to change planning decisions that affect the delivery of services.

Within a social policy context, Jon

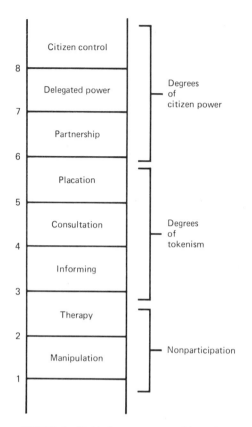

FIGURE 1 Eight Rungs on a Ladder of Citizen Participation (Reprinted by permission from Sherry R. Arnstein, "A Ladder of Citizen Participation," *Journal of the American Institute of Planners*, Vol. 35, No. 4, July 1969).

Van Til and Sally Bould Van Til used a multidimensional taxonomy to develop a sophisticated typology of citizen participation: (1) "elite coalition" involves the interaction of community elites with the administrative process; (2) "citizen advice" involves the interaction of both elites and nonelites in administrative matters; (3) "client participation" is a result of nonelites participating in administration; (4) when nonelites are involved with both political and administrative matters, the resulting type of citizen participation is "grass-roots participation";

(5) "pluralistic participation" is the outcome when both elites and nonelites interact with political and administrative concerns; and (6) the participation of only elites in political and administrative issues produces the "politics of reform" (Van Til and Van Til, 1970). Thus, citizen participation in its many complexities can be construed so as to reveal structure and order. But, the citizen participant client is only one element of the transactive style of community planning, the professional advocate is the other.

SOME KNOWLEDGE STRUCTURES: ADVOCATE PLANNING VARIATIONS

Similar to the citizen participant, the professional advocate in planning has demonstrated many forms and variations. "A Ladder for Advocacy Planning" has been constructed by Ronald Caines (see Figure 2); it illustrates the various impact levels available to the advocate planner (Caines, 1970, p. 10). Caines asserts that much of the practice of advocacy has occurred at the low impact level of *project planning*. Project results affect change on behalf of the advocate's client, but rarely beyond. In a hierarchical relationship, project-level plans are dependent on *program planning*; this rung of advocacy is intermediate in its degree of change impact, and therefore program planning represents a higher order objective to be pursued by the advocate. In turn, programs are creatures of *policy planning*; therefore, this, the highest level of impact, represents the ultimate planning level for the change-oriented advocate to pursue. In other words, advocacy at the policy planning levels is likely to result in "more bang for the buck." Systemic and institutional change potential is greatest at the policy rung of the advocacy planning ladder, and the lower one descends on the ladder, the more the change effort is likely to be limited, incremental, and

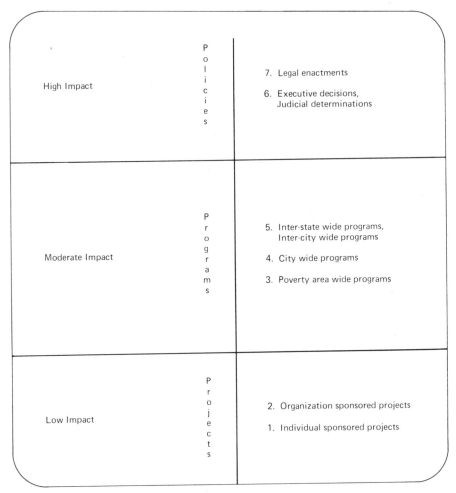

FIGURE 2   "A Ladder for Advocacy Planning," from Caines, *Advocacy for the 'Seventies Will Aim at Public Policies*, AIP Newsletter, January 1970, Vol. 5, No. 1. Reprinted by permission of the American Institute of Planners, Washington, D.C.

reformist. The observant reader might want to extend his thinking beyond that suggested by Caines' ladder; as one contemplates the implications of decategorization (Mogulof, 1973), it becomes clearer that the policy-program-project hierarchical set can occur all along *each* of the geographic scales of community planning. Thus, irrespective of whether the advocate plans at the neighborhood, city, regional, state, or national scale, he is well advised to concentrate his change efforts more toward the policy rung than

toward the project rung.

In addition to advocacy variations by planning level, one also can distinguish different types or styles of advocate planning (Corey, 1972). By juxtaposing three polar dimensions, it is possible to identify six discrete types of advocate planning. The polar dimensions are (1) whether the advocate planner has a *direct* or an *indirect* relationship to a client; (2) whether the advocate planning is done by staff *internal* or *external* to an elite institutional base; and (3) whether the purpose of the advocate planning is more *educative* or more *liberating*. While many more than six combinations may be derived from these dimensions, the following types of advocate planning have been practiced and are evident from analysis of the literature:

1. Nondirected-Internal Advocate Planning

This advocacy type finds the professional planner working within an establishment or elite institution and attempting to plan in support of a perceived constituency or so as to promote his own ideology. This is a form of planning *for* people. Marshall Kaplan has written of this type of advocacy as it was practiced in Oakland, California Model Cities Planning (Kaplan, 1969).

2. Directed-Internal Advocate Planning

The professional planner operates from within an institutional base and plans on behalf of organized interests that are autonomous and outside the institution. This is a form of planning *with* people. Paul Buckwalter has written on the development of this form of advocacy as it was practiced in the Community Development Committee of the Cincinnatti Community Chest and Council (Buckwalter, 1972).

3. Nondirected-External Advocate Planning

Under this form of advocacy the professional plans from an organizational base that is nonelitist; this is a clientless type of advocacy where the planner promotes his own personal ideology. This is a form of planning *by* and *for* the planner; in situations where the advocate planner attaches himself without invitation to a cause of a constituency, this can be classed as a form of planning *for* people. Paul

Davidoff and his Suburban Action Institute colleagues have practiced and written on this, an ideological form of advocacy planning (Davidoff, Davidoff, and Gold, 1970).

4. Directed-External Advocate Planning

This type of advocacy has the professional planner providing technical planning in the service of a client. The planner and the client are organizationally independent and usually linked by a formal contractual relationship. This is a form of planning *with* people. Earl Blecher has researched and written of this type of advocacy, particularly as practiced by the Architects' Renewal Committee of Harlem, and Urban Planning Aid in Massachusetts (Blecher, 1971).

5. Educational Advocate Planning

The primary function of this form of advocacy is to teach; particularly this has meant the instruction of nonelites on the procedures of planning, such that they might be in a better position to counter plans not of their making. This is a form of bringing planning *to* people. William Bunge and his Detroit Geographical Expedition colleagues have advanced this form of advocacy to a high degree (Horvath, 1971).

6. Indigenous-Liberation Advocate Planning

This type of advocacy is largely theoretical to date. Simply, it is residents planning and advocating for themselves and their community. This is a form of planning *by* people. The Dayton, Ohio, West Side Model Cities planning effort practiced this type of advocacy planning, and Robert Goodman has called for an advanced form of this brand of advocacy, especially as it might affect systemic poltical-economic change (Goodman, 1971).

Thus, there are *many* advocacy plannings, both as to level and as to type. One must take great care in making blanket statements about advocacy planning, since it comes in so many shapes and variations. More importantly, as one attempts to sort out his own role as an advocate, such frameworks can enable him to achieve a clearer self-understanding.

SOME ACTION STRUCTURES: INTERVENTION AND CONFLICT

Community change agents need to have the capacity for intervention in change processes (also see Friedmann, 1973, p. 188); community conflict situations offer the potential for intervention to produce change. After the analysis of hundreds of community conflicts, the Community Crisis Intervention Center of Washington University has found that five basic intervenor roles always applied. The Center differentiated the roles on the basis of the intervenor's: organizational and fiscal base; relationship with the conflicting parties; and skills in the conflict situation. Figure 3 illustrates the five intervenor roles "in terms of a typical pattern of conflict between an IN party (established institution, organization, or agency) and an OUT party (clients, employees, citizens' pressure groups, or petitioners for inclusion)" (Community Crisis Intervention Center, 1973, p. 2). The *activist* role sees the actor working closely with the OUT party; conversely the IN party attracts a *reactivist* role in support of its cause. The activist and reactivist take on the goals of the group for which they apply their skills; these include public speaking, organization and strategizing.

The community *advocate* role is usually consultative to, but not a member of, one of the conflicting parties. Often the IN advocate has management skills and the OUT advocate has community organizing skills. Strategy timing and planning is a special skill of the advocate. The *mediator* role is one of an independent third party assisting the conflicting parties to arrive at a mutually satisfying settlement through bargaining. The *researcher* is the broadest and most general of the intervenor roles; its function is to offer an objective analysis of all the conflicting interests. The intervention can take the form of publicizing research findings or testifying at a formal hearing. Finally, the *enforcer* role is often performed by the police, the courts, a resource controller, or an arbitrator; the role represents the ultimate coercive power; it can impose conditions on both of the conflicting parties. Thus the power of the enforcer role cuts across each of the parties and all of the other roles in a community dispute.

Community change agents and agencies have not only a range of intervention roles available, but a conflict situation also suggests variations in the potential resolution of a controversy. The three decision models discussed by Mumphrey, Seley, and Wolpert (1971) set out a range of strategies for planning conflict interventions. Using the case of planning the location of controversial public facilities, the authors set out several planning options beyond the traditional least-cost approach that has so often been used in highway and urban redevelopment planning. By failing to anticipate opposition to a planned physical facility, the costs, both human and economic, can be quite high in the long run. Decision models are available that incorporate project opposition into the solution. The more short run approach is to meet the demands of the most powerful opposition; through such side payments the risk of conflict can be reduced; this approach is *political placation*. There is a longer run approach that is essentially *welfare distri-*

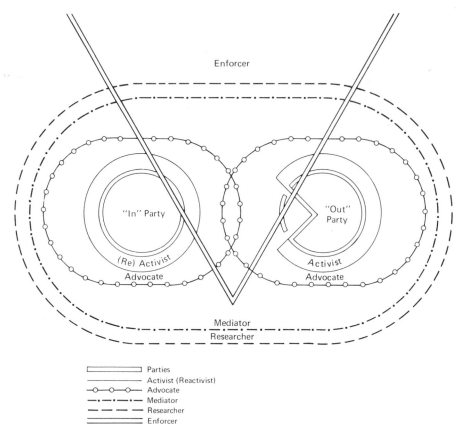

FIGURE 3   Intervenor Roles (From James H. Laue, Alana Cohen and Gerald Cormick, "Intervenor Roles: A Review," *Crisis and Change*, III (Fall 1973), 4–5.)

bution in its intent. It consists of granting concessions and side payments to the less powerful and the most at-risk groups in a planning controversy. The planned result is to compensate those most adversely impacted by a noxious facility, and thereby achieve greater equity and minimize unnecessary politicization of relatively powerless groups by granting benefits rather than imposing punishments.

As in the structures of citizen participation and advocacy planning, planned intervention in conflict situations also exhibits variations and strategy options. Again, these perceived constructs do suggest structure in the complex business of

translating planning knowledge into *planned* action.

SOME ACTION STRUCTURES: LATENT FUNCTIONS, LIMITING OBJECTIVES AND HUMANIZING

In situations where "expert knowledge is joined to action" (Friedmann, 1973, p. 190), and where thoughtful reflection on the results of planned community change has occurred, a number of useful learnings are available for our action constructs. After studying comprehensive planning and coordination strategies as operated in nine U.S. cities, Roland

Warren concludes that it is necessary to understand the latent functions[1] that result from the application of such strategies. With special reference to Model Cities planning, he summarizes his analysis by identifying the following latent functions that result from the local comprehensive planning coordination strategy:

It strengthens existing local agencies; it tends to reduce competition; it provides funds for agency expansion; it defines the poverty problem in terms of needed services which the existing agencies can offer; it gives the agencies a major role in channeling the efforts which go into its solution; it gives the aura of massive change efforts with little threat to the status quo; and it provides stimulus and funds for employment. These functions form a vital part of the social dynamics under which the strategy is preserved and elaborated. (Warren, 1973, p. 362).

Despite the reactive trend suggested by these conclusions, Warren found little evidence that these latent functions were deliberately intended. This knowledge is a strong challenge to change agents to be sensitive to, and go beyond the obvious manifest functions of program planning and to pursue effective community change by planning for likely and anticipated implicit consequences of planned action.

Effective action can be realized by means of planned strategies and disciplined implementation. When the national-level citizen advocate organization

[1] Latent functions are unintended and unrecognized consequences of social beliefs or social practices; manifest functions, conversely, are both intended and recognized. Robert Merton has defined these functions, and they are used in Roland L. Warren, "Comprehensive Planning and Coordination: Some Functional Aspects," *Social Problems*, 20 (Winter 1973), p. 360.

Common Cause was initiated, it set out eight rules for accomplishing its change (Gardner, 1971, p. 8):

1. Citizen action is a full-time, sustained, and continuing effort.
2. Accomplishing intended change requires a channelling of energy and resources; the rule is to "limit the number of targets and hit them hard!"
3. Professional-level skill must be developed by citizen change agents as they attempt to impact government processes.
4. Form alliances; citizen groups of similar purpose sometimes need to set up ad hoc arrangements to work together on a specific objective.
5. The change problem and solution must be dramatized and communicated to the public in order to arouse and channel public interest.
6. Rather than recruiting vast numbers of members, the citizen change organization needs to develop a group of dedicated workers that multiplies its impact by outreach into the wider community.
7. The citizen organization should develop allies within the target institution that it is planning to change.
8. "Organize for action"; many groups talk "action," but are organized more for discussion, education, or research.

After three years of following this action strategy, Common Cause Chairman John Gardner assessed its effectiveness by concluding that "limiting our targets is the best strategy for winning battles." Along with the disciplined focusing of organization energies on a few Board-selected issues,

it is crucial, of course, that the members have a voice in the selection of issues. That is why we have a member-elected Board. That is why it takes only 20 signatures to get on the ballot by petition. That is why we regularly probe membership issue priorities through the use of a referendum (Gardner, 1974, p. 7).

Thus, after thoughtful planning, implementation, and evaluation, a strategy of systematic action that was guided by citizen-generated issues has proved to be an effective action structure. Does this knowledge hold action implications for other community change organizations? At other levels of community scale? For change efforts by economically and educationally deprived communities?

Friedmann and Hudson have observed that OD community planning emphasizes the "human side of planning" (1974, p. 13). Such an emphasis suggests yet another organizing structure; a structure that also manifests a varying range of change-agent behavior, along with implications for construing planned action. Humanistic beliefs and practices have received a great deal of popular and mass-media attention over the last decade, so much so that this phenomenon can be termed a "movement"—the humanism movement. This movement is concerned with understanding one's self in order to be able to better interact and function with others, and in the process, call upon the interrelatedness of one's mind, feelings, and behavior. This movement is dominated by professionals interested in group process and change. Many humanistic professionals are associated with the fields of psychology, law, the policy sciences, medicine, and urban planning.

Mario Fantini recently expressed serious concerns about some of the trends and the direction of the humanism movement. He observed that significant segments of the humanists have become distorted by overemphasizing the self-indulgent side of the movement, and thereby isolating the heavily middle-class movement from the harsh environments faced daily by the nation's poor, the Black, the Spanish-speaking, and the native American Indian (Fantini, 1974). He asserts that:

until we learn how to change these environments, until they can be converted into settings that support human dignity, we are settling for a compromise with the very objectives of the humanistic movement (1974, p. 402).

Further, he points the way by calling for the humanism movement to expand its framework by associating itself with humanistic individuals throughout those walks of life that are devoted "to changing the negative conditions under which so many of our fellow human beings now live" (1974, p. 402).

Thus, for our purposes here, Fantini cautions that humanism is far from a panacea. As practiced, humanism can become overly inward-looking. But potentially, it could become a force for systematic change, particularly as it might stimulate *action* on society's problems of "slums, poverty, disease, and inequality."

CONCLUSION

As we conclude this personal construct, it is helpful to use the conflict-resolution decision strategies of Mumphrey, Seley, and Wolpert as descriptive models for summarizing the realities of the recent practice of OD community planning. To the "least-cost" approaches of redevelopment and highway planning have been added the "placation" approaches of the Community Action and Model Cities Programs. But in the implementation of these incremental methods of reform may exist some latent forces for fundamental community change. For, as we have shown above, our constructs of variation have many forms when applied to selected structures of transactive planning, including its environments, its knowledge systems, and its action systems. Not all of these variations are reactive forces against change. In other words, so much of the literature concludes that citizen participation and advocacy in planning have failed, but other interpretations can conclude that the evidence is as mixed as the variety of forms of participation and advocacy that have been practiced. A number of authors have envisioned and called for new institutional and behavioral forms. As these evangelists have the opportunity to test further their strategies it may well be that the self-transformational characteristics of the transactive style of OD community planning *could* generate the latent forces for equitable and liberating change. For instance, the Van Tils conclude:

that the experience with citizen participation in recent social policy demonstrates the critical importance of the development of new institutional forms that will represent the interests of the poor and will build those interests into the larger political and social structure such that these purposes can be achieved. It is growing too late to paper over class conflicts and subcultural differences with the explanation that participation will not work. The crisis of our times is too immediate, and its potential for social chaos is great (pp. 321–322).

This plea for change suggests the adoption of a "social welfare" approach. In quite complementary conclusions to those of the Van Tils, both Fantini and Friedmann would have much more humanizing and transactive behavior—particularly at the participation-advocacy interface of the citizen and the planner. America is characterized as a society that is increasingly "non-participant" in its behavior; this is coupled with a rising level of ignorance and self-serving attitudes, often at the expense of its least powerful groups. It is within this context that Friedmann concludes:

The basic structural problem of the American guidance system is its rising level of ignorance. Reason has become unhinged from action. . . . To re-establish the essential linkage, society needs a heightened learning capacity (1973, pp. 192–193).

What then, are the change options? What alterations are possible in the existing field of forces? As a result of the above discussion, we have been able to list planning structures and array change forces in a manner so as to suggest personal significance. For me, these structures suggest the following:

There is a context and tradition for the planning of community change; it is labelled organizational development (OD) community planning.

The OD tradition in planning is implemented by *change agents;* they are characterized: by developing a sense of *self awareness,* by knowledge of *organizational behavior and change process,* by a *transactive style of interacting with others* in an organizational change situation (e.g., clients, target agencies, support groups, community constituencies, and so on), and by a *humanistic value system.*

Change occurs at *many levels* and at *many scales;* the one segment of the environment over which I have the most control is *me.*

To be an *effective* change agent therefore, I should strive to *enable* myself and others to recognize forces in the environment, to *understand* the consequences of intervening among those forces, and to provide the necessary support to take planned *action.*

In my pursuit of *knowledge* toward the end of taking effective *action,* I am not without some guidance. The OD tradition of community planning has evolved, and it has generated a complex mass of experience.

I can attempt to harness the latent energy of that experience by seeking a *structure* to the underlying fundamental ideals of planned community change.

My individual structuring is enabled by both the logical guidance of *personal construct theory* and the *structures* (e.g., ladders, models, types, styles) *of others.*

My planned community change knowledge is advanced as a direct result of that structuring and clarifying effort, such that I can *associate my personal behavior* with each of the knowledge and action structures.

Thus, armed with the principles of OD

planning and supported by the perception of my own location on the various planned change structures, I am better able to *chart desired changes and more humanistic directions.*

In the future, should I find my planned change behavior serving nonhumanistic and reactive ends, this approach will *prevent me from blaming my ignorance.*

How do you perceive your community environment? What are its major elements? What are its forces for and against change? Is there order and pattern to those forces? Where are you relative to those patterns; where do you want to be? Where do you want your community to be? What are you going to do about it?

References

Arnstein, Sherry R. (1969) "A Ladder of Citizen Participation," *Journal of the American Institute of Planners,* XXXV (July): 216–224.

Arnstein, Sherry R. (1972) "Maximum Feasible Manipulation," *Public Administrative Review,* XXXII (September): 377–402.

Bannister, D., and Fransella, Fay. (1971) *Inquiring Man: The Theory of Personal Constructs* (Harmondsworth, Middlesex: Penguin Books Ltd.).

Bennis, Warren G., Benne, Kenneth D., and Chin, Robert (Ed.) (1969) *The Planning of Change.* Second Edition (New York: Holt, Rinehart and Winston).

Blecher, Earl M. (1971) *Advocacy Planning for Urban Development: With Analysis of Six Demonstration Programs* (New York: Praeger Publishers).

Bruner, Jerome S. (1960) *The Process of Education* (Cambridge, Massachusetts: Harvard University Press).

Buckwalter, Paul. (1972) "The Case of Inside-Directed Advocacy Planning" (Unpublished Master's Thesis University of Cincinnati).

Burke, Edmund M. (1968) "Citizen Participation Strategies," *Journal of the American Institute of Planners,* XXXIV (September): 287–294.

Caines, Ronald M. (1970) "Advocacy for the 'Seventies' Will Aim at Public Policies," *AIP Newsletter,* 5 (January): 10–11.

Community Crisis Intervention Center, Washington University. (1973) "Intervenor Roles: A Review," *Crisis and Change,* III (Fall): 4–5.

Corey, Kenneth E. (1972) "Advocacy in Planning: A Reflective Analysis," *Antipode: A Radical Journal of Geography,* 4 (July): 46–63.

Davidoff, Paul. (1965) "Advocacy and Pluralism in Planning," *Journal of the American Institute of Planners,* XXXI (November): 331–338.

Davidoff, Paul, Davidoff, Linda, and

Gold, Neil Newton. (1970) "Suburban Action: Advocate Planning for an Open Society," *Journal of the American Institute of Planners*, XXXVI (January): 12–21.

Denbow, Stefania A., and Nutt, Thomas E. (1973) "The Current State of Planning Education," *Journal of the American Institute of Planners*, XXXVIII (May): 203–209.

Fantini, Mario. (1974) "Humanizing the Humanism Movement," *Phi Delta Kappan*, LV (February): 400–402.

Friedmann, John. (1973) *Retracking America: A Theory of Transactive Planning* (Garden City, New York: Anchor Press/Doubleday).

Friedmann, John, and Hudson, Barclay. (1974) "Knowledge and Action: A Guide to Planning Theory," *Journal of the American Institute of Planners*, XXXIX (January): 2–16.

Gardner, John W. (1974) "Limiting Our Targets Is the Best Strategy For Winning Battles," *Common Cause*, 4 (February): 7.

Gardner, John W. (1971) "We Have Learned Some Rules for Effective Action," *Common Cause*, 1 (September): 8.

Gilbert, Neil. (1972) "Assessing Service Delivery Methods," *Welfare Review*, 10 (May/June): 25–33.

Goodman, Robert. (1971) *After the Planners* (New York: Simon and Schuster).

Horvath, Ronald J. (1971) "The 'Detroit Geographical Expedition and Institute' Experience," *Antipode: A Radical Journal of Geography*, 3 (November): 73–85.

Kaplan, Marshall. (1969) "The Role of the Planner in Urban Areas," *Citizen Participation in Urban Development*, Volume 11—Cases and Programs, Edited by Hans B. C. Spiegel (Washington, D.C.: NTL Institute for Applied Behavorial Science): 255–273.

Mazziotti, Donald F. (1974) "The Underlying Assumptions of Advocacy Planning: Pluralism and Reform," *Journal of the American Institute of Planners*, XXXIX (January): 38–48.

Mogulof, Melvin B. (1973) *Special Revenue Sharing in Support of the Public Social Services* (Washington, D.C.: The Urban Institute).

Mumphrey, Anthony J., Jr., Seley, John E., and Wolpert, Julian. (1971) "A Decision Model for Locating Controversial Facilities," *Journal of the American Institute of Planners*, XXXVI (November): 397–402.

Van Til, Jon, and Van Til, Sally Bould. (1970) "Citizen Participation in Social Policy: The End of the Cycle?" *Social Problems*, 17 (Winter): 313–323.

Warren, Roland L. (1973) "Comprehensive Planning and Coordination: Some Functional Aspects," *Social Problems*, 20 (Winter): 355–364.

7.2 OPEN SYSTEMS PLANNING

G. K. Jayaram

Open Systems Planning (OSP) entails the identification and delineation of the (person-task-process-environment) dynamics. In other words, the model highlights the vital need to understand the external and internal environments (of the system), the basic core socio-technical process/processes (of the system), the dynamic equilibrium in which the transactions exist between and amongst the internal and external domains as well as across the boundaries (of the system) and the extension of all these three dimensions into the future through both the (relatively) subjective and objective filters of the planning group assembled to work through the model. This can only be done in a "community of trust," which emphasizes the prerequisites of sharing and trusting processes. If the OSP exercise is not imbued with a considerable degree of trust, the product would be mere superficialities or, worse, distortions in a game of political oneupmanship. Even without the games of power, it would still be a shell without spirit or substance, a mere symbol without any significance.

These features evidence that this model harvests the benefit of learning from all the earlier phases and attempts to combine the best of the heritage. It is, in other words, not an idiosyncratic special tool, but a first faltering step at the integration of the learnings from the major contributions of the past.

The process of open systems planning* consists of the following steps:

1. Creation of the "Present Scenario:"
   a. External domains of the environment—expectations and interactions.
   b. Internal identity, expectations and interactions;
   c. Transactions across the boundaries of the system.

* The description of the workshop model which follows is adopted from the manuscript written by the author under the title "Major Field Statement" in 1970 and another manuscript in 1972 at UCLA. Changes and modifications from the earlier versions appear here, as a result of four years of usage of the model in consulting practice in diverse types of organizations. The coauthor of the model is Mr. Charles Krone; however, the responsibility for the commissions or omissions in this and earlier descriptions of the model rest entirely with the author.

2. Creation of "Realistic Future Scenario" (under a, b & c of (1) above).
3. Creation of "Idealistic Future Scenario" (IFS) under a, b, & c of (1) above.
4. Sharing of IFS's, comparison of (1), (2) & (3) and identification of broad areas of consensus, controversy and total disagreement about future.
5. Temporal (time-based) planning of action programs for the areas identified earlier.

The above five steps are described in what follows. Interspersed through the description are examples or notes from personal consulting experience relevant at that particular point.

DESCRIPTION

1. Creation of "Present Scenario"

(a) External The group as a whole is asked to concentrate on a concrete socio-technical system central to all the members; e.g., the factory or the ship or the school or the hospital, and enumerate all the *expectations* coming on that system from the external environment. [Figure 1].

Note: The rationale behind the choice of 'System' for focus should be that it should reflect common stakes for all the subsystems of the group.

Note: The exercise starts with looking at the external environment and *not* with an analysis of the internal milieu. This is a deliberate choice dictated both by concepts and experience. Conceptually, the crucial insights involved in thinking of one's system as part of many larger systems with simultaneous multiple membership and engaged in a dynamic process of give and take with the environmental domains are most valuable starting points for holistic analysis. Experience with the model indicates that the 'view of the navel'—the delineation of the internal being difficult and seductive at the same time—permits a group to wallow in the egocentric, ptolemaic pursuit of one's own tail. It is tougher to turn from inside to outside than the other way around. Besides, the habit pattern, which is the exclusive attention to the internal system, needs to be broken.

Note: Part of the 'technology' of this process consists of writing in pictures and words the stream of what is being expressed by the group on newsprint sheets in different colored crayons and pasting all these data on the walls of the room. The consultant may act as the synthesizer and recorder of data at times and may encourage the group to do so at other times. As high a degree of creativity as the group can muster should be evoked in this whole process, including use of recording materials, writing, use of idioms —metaphors (the system's own mythology, language, symbols and rituals).

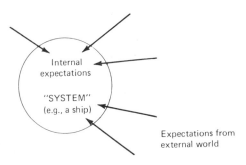

FIGURE 1

This is an unstructured, open-ended process. The consultant acts as recorder. He encourages participation from all around the room at random. He deliberately encourages metaphorical phrases for the expectations so that the scenario may come alive for the members.

When this process is done sufficiently, according to the discretion of the group and the consultant, the group is asked to classify the expectations according to the sources from which they are *perceived to* emanate—i.e., domains of expectation (reference groups/role senders, etc.).

In other words, the first question is, "What is expected of this system?" The second question is, "Who expects this?"

This process of classification by domains may make the client group realize that there are many relevant domains left out from the earlier data and/or that there are many expectations felt for which no source is traceable and/or there are some obvious domains whose expectations are not clear.

At this stage, they may also begin to perceive shared expectations among many domains, unshared ones, contradictory ones. They may begin to glimpse the dynamic interaction among the variables in between the domains.

All these perceptions may persuade them to redo the first scenario with greater sophistication and insight a second time around.

Note: This step by itself may have the following constructive results:

(a) This may be the first time the different functionaries are sharing in a real (and not gamey) sense, their individual perceptions about the world 'out there'. This can be a revealing 'ah ha' experience if the group members are open to change from one another.

Example: One of the early groups who experienced this process had their first major breakthrough at this stage. Two different departmental heads sharing their perceptions of the external expectations, realized together that each had come to view the other as at best dumb, at worst an enemy, because each saw the other doing things contrary to one's own perceptions of the pressure from outside. Each one realized here for the first time that it was a different (and contradictory) perception of the expectations from the top management outside that led each, in a loyalty to the system, to do what he or she did. The sense of relief and unity in the room was electric.

(b) Internal environment—its identity and core processes The objective of this step is for the group to identify and represent the real picture of their system from its center to its peripheries in all its complexity and richness. The step can be partially similar in the questions asked to the step gone through earlier in the case of the external environment— i.e., the internal expectations, domains, interactions and values.

Members of the group are encouraged to range, in their search from intra- and inter-personal to inter-subsystemic expectations. (Needless to say, the discretion of the consultant is to be exercised in narrowing or broadening the band of search, depending on the political climate in the group, the stage of cohesiveness, interpersonal-intergroup trust, structural and functional needs of the system, etc.)

Note: This step deserves a special note since client groups seem to experience great difficulty in responding to the questions at this stage. The real question which is being asked here is a search for identity—systematic or organizational identity. This can be conceived both as content and process, i.e., identity, and core process or processes which express that identity. It is this crucial and intimate nature of this question that seems to cause the blocks in the creativity of the group response. In fact, in contrast to this, the earlier step of delineating the external environment is done relatively easily since it is more distant, seemingly less threatening and amenable to greater objectivity. The pains surrounding the attempt to create the internal scenario reminds one of the ancient Indian saying: "The shadow is the darkest underneath the candle"—self-perception and awareness

is difficult at the organizational and institutional level as much as at the individual personality level.

To facilitate the creative process, the consultant may suggest such questions as: "What would you give up if you had to give up 90% of what you are, as a system?" He may also use such conceptual categories as activities, interactions and sentiments to help the group analyse the internal milieu. He may ask the same set of questions as were asked about the external environment. He may also encourage them to identify where the 'tension tendons' or energy of the system lie. The purpose of the intervention should not be to escape the rigour of the question, but to approach it from various sides like approaching a fortress, looking for a natural entry into the 'systemic imperatives'. This may be different for different systems.

Example: The plant management of a large plant in Southern California struggled for an interminable amount of time with this question. They wondered aloud whether they should describe the organizational chart or departmental set-up or functions or profit centers or cost centers. The traditional pictures paraded as 'the organization' in front of outsiders were considered and discarded as lacking 'soul'. None seemed to capture where the energy of the system lay. At long last, they began a search of what internal domains seemed to matter. What they came up with were a set of dichotomies or 'tension bipolarities' such as young vs. old, women vs. men, Black vs. white, mechanics vs. non-mechanics, crafts vs. unskilled, etc. This was their breakthrough towards opening the doors of data on what the internal life of the system was like for the insiders.

This stage may reveal the host of borderline expectations, which cannot be easily labeled "internal" or "external." The individual himself is always a part of his own environment and is partly responsible for it (Menninger). This is equally true for the system. The group may go through similar insights, as in the case of external domains, in the case of internal subsystems. In addition, they may begin to glimpse transactions across the boundaries between the internal parts and the external domains, the degree of permeability across different parts of the boundary and the complex networks of relationships among variables in all the dimensions.

(c) The consultant now responds to the feeling of overwhelming complexity by introducing the notion of value systems underlying the expectations. (Incidentally, none of these terms, "value systems" included, need be elaborated upon in their technical context; instead, their colloquial meanings would suffice to produce effective process.)

The group is asked the question, "Why does who expect what?" The value systems perceived to be prevalent in each domain leading to expectations are traced and recorded, again with emphasis on striking anecdotes, phrases, etc. Similar delineation of the nuances of the value systems in the internal world is done, starting from each one's personal values as reflected in the organizational context.

Note: Invariably at this stage of the process, there develops in the group a deep sense of gloom. Approximately a day long search has taken place to weave the present scenario of the system's outside and inside. A pervasive feeling of helplessness and uncontrollability about the system's destiny is manifest at this point. This may get expressed in various overt or covert ways, including projection of sense of failure to the consultant. The group (or some members) may turn with varying degrees of hostility and rejection on the consultant and say: "So what! Big deal. We knew all of this before we started" or "Now that we know how bad it all is, what have you done to help us get through it? Nothing!" If this deep gloom and reaction is reminiscent of similar phenomena in T-groups or therapeutic interventions, it is not a coincidence but the evidence of isomorphic existential realities at different systemic levels and is conceptually warranted. One can only suggest (to the consultant) to stay with it—to hang in there and let the group do the same, eschewing the temptation to fly from the pain of the overwhelming complexity of the scenario and a perception of one's finite capacity to deal with it.

2. Creation of "Realistic Future Scenarios"

The group is now asked: "Suppose there was no deliberate intervention for any kind of change. What would the system scenario be in some indeterminate future?" (If the curve from past to present is projected on to the future [same slope] (where would the system be at some point in the future?)

Calling this *"The Realistic Future Scenario,"* the group is asked to go through the same steps as in the creation of the present scenario, ending again with the projection, to their logical consequences, of their present value systems.

Note: The purpose in introducing this step is as follows: The seeds of the future may be with us at the present moment; but it is almost universally true that it is difficult to perceive the future or the futures that are inherent or emerging from the present. Some reasons for this myopia may be obvious and some subtle. It may be part of the human condition to suffer "the tyranny of the eternal yesterday" (Weber). The yesterdays are never so dead that their ghosts won't haunt to prevent the unborn tomorrows to cast their prenatal shadows. Also the capacity to 'separate the wheat from the chaff' in the present—the mere fad from the deeper step-function or quantum change, the peripheral from the central—is surely lacking in most groups (including Social Sciences). Hence the attempt to project the scenario to a point in the future may help as a start for the distinguishing of what may be here to stay from what may be sure to pass. Also it may bring to the surface suppressed feelings (positive or negative) about present trends. This may energize action about those trends.

This step in experience, has proved to be of varying importance for different groups.

3. Creation of "Idealistic Future Scenarios"

At the third stage, the group is asked the question: "Suppose you made change interventions, what *alternative futures* would you wish *to create?*" or "If you had the power to change anything in the earlier scenarios, *what* would you like to change and *how* would the scenario look when changed?"

For this process the group is asked to split into dyads or triads—with the choice of membership of each group either made from within the group or by the consultant (if he has, by now, special conceptual constructs about the nature of the group and feels optimal to prescribe certain composition in each group).

Note: This is the stage to dream unfettered by realities—temporarily at least. It is to be noted that the question does *not* include "how or why would you make changes?" Self-conscious creativity is encouraged in the small subgroups. The consultant can float around or leave the process uninterrupted. It is to be expected that individuals will bring forth their biases, which may hail from their func-

tional specializations, political orientations, socio-economic backgrounds, cultural-ethnic factors or idiosyncratic personality features. It is valuable to encourage such subjective creation and discussion in the subgroup.

4. Sharing of IFS's

(a) Now, all the small groups are invited to gather back in one large group and present to one another their *idealistic future scenarios.*

In this process, the groups may be reminded to perceive *all the relevant dimensions* of the causal texture of the environment—socio-technical, socio-psychological, politico-legal, economic, ecological, etc., and the impact of the changes in these dimensions on their future designs. Each individual is to ask himself and others the question: "If the suggested changes were to take place, how would they affect anything and/or everything else (in terms of quality and quantity)?" Again, the choice of introducing the appropriate degree of complexity into the process is left to the discretion of the consultant and the group—the reading of the pulse of the group.

(b) All the previous scenarios are placed in front of the group. The question is: "What are the variances you see between (a) the present and the idealistic futures, (b) the realistic and idealistic futures and why. Speculate. "Can you do anything about absorbing the variance with sufficient lead time? If so, what? If not, why not?" The list of questions at this stage, with the wealth of data and the possible absorption of the client-consultant system into the process, is only limited by the limits of collective comprehension and imagination.

(c) As a natural product of the two steps described above in (a) and (b), the group is asked to identify *three sets of issues* for the future.

(i)   areas of broad concurrence or consensus among the group (as evidenced in the above steps including the Future Scenarios), called "the Yes list" (i.e., "we are all agreed");

(ii)   areas of uncertainty, partial agreement or controversy (the reasons for which may be lack of data in the group or lack of conviction or willingness or values to face those issues), called "the maybe list" (i.e., "we are doubtful");

(iii)   areas of intense disagreement (the reasons ranging all over the broad—philosophical, contextual or emotional—bases), called "The Yes-No" list.

5. Temporal Planning

The group is asked at this final stage facing the three lists: "What would you do about each item on each list in three time dimensions:

(i)   tomorrow;
(ii)   six months from now;
(iii)   two years from now."

The group has to decide on the choice of change interventions they would/could/should make. Here again, the heart of the process is the delineation of values underlying each choice of intervention—why to intervene at all? What kind of intervention and why? Where to intervene and why there? Why proceed towards that particular future?

The nature of action steps would differ in the case of the three lists. The "yes-list" may invite concrete planning and implementation process of the details of each issue, since issues have been identified and consensus reached. In the case of the "Yes-No" list, processes of unearthing the causes of the sharp disagreements

may be at any of the following five levels: ideology, values, strategy, operation, tactics.[1] The "maybe" list may need further research on issues or participation of relevant people in the data search or clarification. The action steps here may include such processes as the replication of open systems planning at other levels of the system and/or information gathering processes. As the final and important step, the group decides on the follow-up schedule to (a) share the flow of action steps and (b) update the scenarios.

FEATURES TO KNOW ABOUT THE PROCESS

1.   OSP is effective as an iterative process. Since the data (both facts and values) are distributed all over the open system, the exercise (in its data-gathering function) can be used laterally and vertically all over the organization.

2.   The primary or initial group to walk through the model preferably should be the formal planning group of the organization. Without the feeling that the group has the power and legitimacy to perform the task, the power of the model in its execution is decreased. However, this group may decide the need for particular other groups or individuals to participate in a similar process.

3.   There is vital need to follow up on this process at regular frequency. It becomes in a sense like the board on which the movement of stocks is indicated in the Stock Exchange. Only here the changes to be posted are a lot more complex, a lot less certain, but equally (or more) unpredictable—hence the great need to prepare the framework and up-

[1] From G. K. Jayaram, "Conflict Resolution: Some Concepts" and "Fact-Value Analysis: A Method for Conflict Resolution." (Unpublished monographs.)

date it regularly. Some issues may recur at different points of time at different intensities or new issues may enter the picture, changing the scenarios substantially. The issues may arise in the external or the internal or some combination of both.

4. There needs to exist, as a precondition for an effective open systems planning process, a degree of trust which permits open communication of positive and negative interpersonal aspects. This has been mentioned before (p. 276). The design implication of this feature is thusly: The intervener may diagnose mutually with the client group (by whatever diagnostic means available or preferable in the context, e.g., depth interviews, survey questionnaires, observation of group meetings, etc.) the level of mutual trust in the group. He may then decide on a 'team-building exercise' as a prerequisite before OSP *or* he may decide that an adequately open expression exists in the group for the sharing of cognitive-affect data needed in OSP.

Figure 2 indicates that an alternating between the interpersonal openness processes team-building and systemic openness processes like OSP may be advisable. At no level (individual, interpersonal, group or system) should it be assumed that a one-shot process suffices 'to hold the glue' forever. Like hunger and thirst and sex at the individual level, the systemic needs at the process and content levels require responses at regular frequencies.

There need be no anxiety to get all the data in one shot, since this is an iterative design, involving successively larger or smaller chunks of organizational space in the spatio-temporal dimensions.

5. The consulting resources would do well to possess considerable skills (diagnostic and training skills) at the process, structure and cognitive (conceptual) content levels.

6. The model is useful in any kind of system ranging from family through organizations (industrial and non-industrial), communities, etc.

7. Finally, a note on the time duration of the workshop:

Note: The group would work for an initial one- and one-half days. The steps that would be completed in this period are 'the present scenario', the realistic future scenario', and 'the idealistic future scenario'. There would be a specific contract suggested right at the start to the effect that as they work through these steps, the group would deliberately list 'areas of incomplete knowledge' in any domain, internal or external. At the end of 1½ days, the group takes the responsibility to research, by whatever means necessary and feasible, these items of incomplete knowledge. The time allotted would be one week. This would also be the time for individual reflection on what has transpired in the initial sessions. At the end of the week, the group gathers for the second and final one- and one-half days of work. They will start out by sharing both their research and their reflections with one another. The products of the earlier sessions would be modified, if needed, according to new data. This will be for 2–3 hours. Then the group would start on the last phase of the model —'the temporal planning.'

Hence the actual time needed for OSP is three days, but this duration is cut in two allowing for a very valuable week of research and reflection.

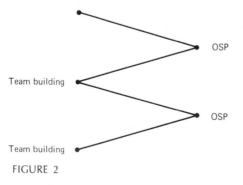

OSP

Team building

OSP

Team building

FIGURE 2

FINAL COMMENTS

This design is a technique for appreciation and for instrumentation. It helps the client-system evolve, from within its own self (and in collaboration with a consultant at the initial stages), the Scenarios of its present world and its probable future worlds. Both the internal and external textures in each of these temporal dimensions can be delineated, with great richness of detail and as organized complexities. The client creates his own crystal ball, develops eyes that can gaze into the ball and looks into change, if necessary, to know, at all cost, in order to be prepared for the holocaust—or the utopia.

At successive stations in the process, the client comes to evoke the underlying value systems in his internal environment and attempts to empathize with the value systems of the domains relevant to him in the external environment. This process will be seen by the client to involve considerable fact-search and feeling-search, not only among the particular group involved in this process, but also in other relevant groups.

This data search and a gradual filling of the canvas—the creation of the three scenarios—at its minimum, is a data-generating technique and at its best, an active intervention for change.

7.3 A GROUP PROCESS MODEL FOR PROBLEM IDENTIFICATION AND PROGRAM PLANNING[1]

André L. Delbecq, Andrew H. Van de Ven

The purpose of this paper is to present a group process model for situations . . . which planning groups can use for (a) identifying strategic problems and (b) developing appropriate and innovative pro-grams to solve them. The model was originally developed from social-psychological studies of decision-conferences and studies of program planning in an (Office of Economic Opportunity) Community Action Agency. The model, which we abbreviate as PPM (Program Planning Model), has been used by the authors in a wide variety of organization change and task force situations—in business, industry, government, and education.

PPM is not a rationalistic econo-logical model for system planning. It is, rather, a socio-logical model suggesting a planning sequence which seeks to provide an orderly process of structuring the decision making at different phases of planning.[2] In developing the model, we were particularly concerned with situa-

This paper is an edited version of a paper published in the *Journal of Applied Behavioral Science*, No. 4, 1971, pp. 466–492. Reproduced by permission of Nat'l Training Laboratories.

[1] This research was supported by funds granted to the Matrix Management Project in the Graduate School of Business at The University of Wisconsin by the National Aeronautics and Space Administration; and by funds granted to the Institute for Research on Poverty, The University of Wisconsin, by the Office of Economic Opportunity. The authors are grateful to the following persons who directly participated in discussion of the model: Fremont A. Shull, Alan Filley, Andrew J. Grimes. Footnotes in edited portions of this paper have been deleted and remaining footnotes renumbered.

[2] The terms "econo-logical" and "socio-logical" are taken from the decision-making studies reported in James D. Thompson and Arthur Tuden (1959).

tions where a variety of groups, fragmented in terms of vested interests, rhetorical and ideological concepts, and differentiated expertise, needed to be brought together in order for a program to emerge or change to take place. Modern decision theory clearly indicated that different problem-solving phases and different types of problems called for different group processes (Delbecq, 1967). It did not, however, provide guidelines for interfacing divided groups involved in the vortex of large-scale planning situations. . . .

THE PPM PROCESS OUTLINED

PPM divides program planning and development into five phases. While these phases are compatible with the "scientific method," PPM suggests specific group techniques and specific roles for different interest groups at different phases in the process.[3] The entire process may be briefly summarized as follows:

Phase I: *Problem Exploration*
  Involvement of client or consumer groups
  Involvement of first-line supervisors
Phase II: *Knowledge Exploration*
  Involvement of external scientific personnel
  Involvement of internal and external organizational specialists
Phase III: *Priority Development*
  Involvement of resource controllers
  Involvement of key administrators
Phase IV: *Program Development*
  Involvement of line administrators
  Involvement of technical specialists
Phase V: *Program Evaluation*
  Involvement of client or consumer groups
  Involvement of staff and administrative personnel

---

[3] For a treatment of problem-solving phases in small groups, see Bales and Strodtbeck (1967).

We can now proceed to discuss each phase in appropriate detail.

PHASE I: PROBLEM EXPLORATION

Phase I begins with the identification of a cross section of client or consumer groups divided according to age, geography, technical applications, or whatever client or user categories are in keeping with the nature of the service or product in question. The heart of the process is a problem exploration meeting which is conducted according to the following format. . . . [See Figure 1.]

Theoretical Defense of Phase I

Use of nominal groups to increase creativity One of the objectives of PPM is to facilitate, in the greatest degree possible, innovation and creativity in program planning. The Phase I PPM format is based on research which shows that creativity can often be facilitated by following specific group processes. While research supports the desirability of involving certain types of creative individuals in later phases (Scott, 1965), Phase I emphasizes our agreement with Victor Thompson and Smithburg (1968) on the need to structure group processes. They write: "Mystical, charismatic personality qualities have been greatly overemphasized in the discussion of creativity and discovery in comparison to . . . structural rather than personality variables."

The overriding imposed process in Phase I is the use of the nominal group technique in the early part of the meetings. In recent years, a number of major research studies substantiate the superiority of *nominal groups* (groups in which individuals work in the presence of one another but do not interact) as compared with conventional "brainstorming" groups.[4] This research indicates that interacting groups produce a smaller number of problem dimensions, fewer high quality suggestions, and a smaller number of different kinds of solutions than groups in which members were constrained from interaction during the generation of critical problem variables (Campbell, 1968; Dunnette, Campbell & Jaastad, 1963; Leader, 1967; Taylor, Berry, & Block, 1958; Vroom, Grant, & Cotton, 1969). Since the use of nominal groups is not characteristic of most meeting formats, a word of explanation for the overriding superiority of nominal groups in the struc-

[4] A complete treatment of the empirical research and the social-psychological dynamics of both nominal and interacting groups is available in Andrew H. Van de Ven and André L. Delbecq, "Nominal versus interacting groups for committee decision-making effectiveness," *J. Acad. of Mgmt.* June 1971, 14 (2).

ture of PPM is in order. The following factors seem to explain the superiority of the nominal technique for the generation of problem dimensions and appropriate solutions (though in Phase I of PPM we are not concerned with solutions).

There seems to be little question that interacting groups inhibit the performance of their members (Taylor et al., 1958). Despite elaborate attempts (e.g., "brainstorming") at freeing individuals to speak spontaneously and fully share their ideas, people seem comfortable in sharing only fairly well-developed ideas with the group, particularly in a newly formed group.

The second explanation relates to the tendency of interacting groups to focus on a particular train of thought. Interacting groups often "fall into a rut" by concentrating on and elaborating a single problem dimension. Individuals find it more comfortable to react to some-

---

FIGURE 1   Outline of Phase I Meeting—Program Planning Model

I. Selection of Client or Consumer Sample
    (Divided according to age, geography, technical application, or other appropriate categories)
II. Meeting with Clients or Consumer Groups to explore problem dimensions
    A. Introduction (10 minutes)
        1. Welcome
        2. Expression of organization(s)' interest in clients' problems
        3. Indication that focus is on problems, not solutions
        4. Explanation of "personal" vs. "organizational" problems
    B. Directions for small-group participation
        1. Assign clients to small groups of 6 to 9
        2. Instruct them in nominal group format
            a. Listing "personal" problem dimensions on 5" x 7" cards (15 minutes)
            b. Listing "organizational" problem dimensions on 5" x 7" cards (15 minutes)
        3. Provide flip chart and recorder for round-robin sharing of individually noted items
            a. Items from individual cards (first organizational, then personal)
            b. New items suggested by process
    C. Fifteen-minute break
    D. Interacting group discussion of each item on flip chart in serial fashion for clarification, elaboration, and/or defense, but not for collapsing or condensing items
    E. Nominal group voting on 3" x 5" cards for top five priority items on both "personal" and "organizationtal" lists
    F. General Session—discussion of tabulated votes from each small group
    G. Explanation of PPM and election of representative(s) for Phase II

one else's idea than to generate their own ideas. This is especially limiting since early ideas which become the focus of the group's attention often contain obvious rather than subtle problem dimensions (Dunnette et al., 1963; Osborn, 1957; Taylor et al., 1958).

It is also necessary for participants to become fully and thoroughly enmeshed in the problem. The tension created by the nominal group situation, in which other members at the table are industriously writing, maximizes social facilitation-tension which is important for individuals' full involvement in the task at hand. "Creations and discovery are much more likely when there is a personal commitment to searching for a solution" (Victor Thompson & Smithburg, 1968).

The nominal group process also avoids evaluation of any particular problem dimension and the distraction of elaborating comments, while problem dimensions are being generated. This is congruent with Maier's (1963) research on creative groups.

Finally, the round-robin procedure, coupled with the separation of "personal" from "organizational" problems, increases the tendency of individuals to begin sharing risky problem dimensions with other members of the group (issues that involve increasing degrees of self-disclosure). The round-robin procedure of each member's offering a single idea allows secure personality types who are greater risk-takers to engage in early self-disclosure. This modeling by the more secure members of the group makes it easier for less secure members to take their turn and suggest risky problem dimensions, particularly "personal" problems which they might hesitate to bring before the group in an interacting situation (Culbert, 1968). Experience also suggests that clients or consumers will avoid identifying "personal" dimensions dealing with social-emotional problem dimensions unless stimulated by

a separate category beyond the "organizational" category.[5]

Other Benefits

Interfacing clients and professionals
The process specified for Phase I contains a number of other benefits in addition to the facilitation of innovation suggested by the above discussion of creativity in nominal groups.

One of the critical issues in program development is the interfacing of client or consumer with professional personnel. Authors dealing with organizational innovation stress the need for such interfacing, but mechanisms for the facilitation of this boundary relationship are seldom discussed. The process specified in Phase I has two special benefits for the total program planning process in relating professionals and nonprofessionals. The first benefit relates to the value of focusing attention on client needs as the starting point for program development. Such an approach is quite consistent with a number of evolving perspectives on organization programming. It is congruent with the "new marketing concept" in industrial organizations which stresses the need for consumer panels or market research as a basis for product development. It is likewise consistent with the new emphasis on involvement of the clients of a social agency as a basis for planning programs. Contemporary literature is replete with instances where social agency professionals have planned client services which do not meet real needs of the clientèle.

---

[5] For example, in a meeting exploring services for elderly persons, "organizational" or "outside" problems such as cost of drugs, transportation, and so on were easily mentioned. Only when groups of elderly were asked as separate individuals to list "personal" problems did areas such as fear of death, loneliness, preoccupation with sickness, feeling disliked by younger people, and other critical social-emotional issues come out.

The second benefit of Phase I relates to the interaction dynamics of professionals and clients. Getting professionals to react to client statements is a tricky business. The experience of OEO and political agencies has been that the interfacing of client groups with professional or political groups has often resulted in "maximum feasible *mis*understanding" (Moynihan, 1969) rather than maximum feasible participation. Indeed, the literature would suggest that low-status clientèle interfaced with high-status professionals will often be forced into a rather passive and subordinate position by the professional staff (Delbecq, 1968)[6]. . . .

Further, militant representatives of clients or customers often confront professionals with rhetoric which alienates the professional or political resource controller. As Lipsky (1968) has pointed out, militant client leaders are often obliged to substitute rhetorical and psychological rewards for material benefits to appear charismatic. As a result militant consumer or clientèle representatives often master the art of overstatement, which pleases constituents but interferes with problem solving. The nominal group technique focuses the attention of client and consumer groups on real problems, thus helping to avoid emphasis on psychological and ideological statements by formal leaders. Our own experience has been that rhetorical leaders are not able to dominate problem-centered discussion by consumers or clients in nominal group situations. As a result, the output from Phase I provides a summary of critical problem dimensions in comfortable terms to which professionals in Phase II and resource controllers in Phase III can respond. In a similar fashion, the technique avoids dominant focus on the personalities of the organizational representatives leading the meeting.

[6] *See also* references [Arnstein (1969), Lipsky (1968), Mogulof (1969), and Warren (1969)].

Finally, the organization may tap several reference client or consumer groups, so that it does not focus its response on a particular group which claims to speak for a charged, faction-ridden constituency.

Avoiding semantics and producing richness The round-robin aspect of listing problem dimensions also lessens argumentation over semantics and facilitates increased balance in participation. Verbally skilled members are precluded from easily monopolizing the group with arguments over wording. The listing of all problem dimensions also increases qualitative richness, which, in turn, adds to the tension which is the catalyst (or precursor) of change.

Creating tension and facilitating change A central issue in getting a new program underway is the development of sufficient tension in professional organizations to justify new change programs. The nominal group process provides both quantitative data in the sense of voted-upon priorities and qualitative data in terms of a rich, descriptive discussion of the problem. The qualitative data flow from the discussion which follows the nominal group activity, in which members often provide critical incidents or personal anecdotes. The combined qualitative and quantitative data encourage professional reaction to real client needs. That is to say, the data from Phase I, together with the presence of representatives from the Phase I meeting in Phase II, create a situation in which professionals cannot easily ignore client priorities established in the first phase. Furthermore, both the priorities which the group votes upon and the qualitative incidents become news for public media, where this type of pressure is appropriate. News releases, summary memoranda, and internal reports can all evolve from the consumer- or client-centered meetings in Phase I as mechanisms for eliciting the tension which must underlie change by the sponsoring organization.[7]

Expediency in terms of time expenditure While they are not always appropriate substitutes for quantified survey research, Phase I processes are easily activated. Since it can be activated in a single evening for a large number of clients or consumers, the process is a minimal but effective mechanism for increasing the focus of the program planners on real client or consumer problems. Further, if Phase I is elaborated by means of survey research, the items which emerge in Phase I become an important base for the development of survey research instruments.

Summary of the Benefits of Phase I

Phase I, then, is a deliberate, structured process which seeks to accomplish the following objectives: (a) to facilitate problem definition by a rich input of problem dimensions through nominal group techniques; (b) to focus attention on those items which have the highest priority in the clients' or consumers' perspective; (c) to avoid reaching toward a limited few "leaders" or a single client group to create the definition of the clientèle or consumer problem, but rather to react to multiple reference groups and representative clients; (d) to force professional members to react to the realities of client perceptions rather than to their own theoretical or professional biases; (e) to create sufficient tension to assure responsiveness on the part of the professional organization to clients or consumers; (f) to provide a mechanism for the interfacing of both clients and professionals in a manner which avoids mutually frustrating semantic hangups; and

[7] For a discussion of the role of tension in fostering organizational change, *see* Dalton (1969).

(g) to increase the legitimation of later program proposals by early involvement of client or consumer groups.

PHASE II: KNOWLEDGE EXPLORATION

Phase II begins with the identification of external scientific and organizational experts whose discipline and functional skills relate to the priority items which evolved in Phase I. Combined with internal functional experts from the principal organization(s) who will be responsible for the implementation of the planning program, this group of knowledge resource persons (hereafter referred to as "specialists") is invited to engage in a problem-solving meeting following processes somewhat similar to the Phase I format.

In preparation for the Phase II meeting, the problem items developed in Phase I are divided into major and minor categories.[8] A large visual display of these problem categories, together with an indication of the priority vote, is presented to the knowledge resource panel. Once again, the organization representative opens the meeting by stating the interest of his organization in developing an adequate program to deal with the priority problems of clients or consumers which emerged in the Phase I meeting. He then discusses the character of the Phase I meeting and thoroughly reviews the display of problem items. He is careful not to interpret the items analytically but he does provide a qualitative description of problems which underlie the items by repeating the anecdotes and vignettes which client or consumer groups had mentioned in the earlier meeting. To assist in

[8] The development of this classification system is undertaken by a staff member of the sponsoring organization. If there are grey areas of dispute with respect to this taxonomy, the reclassification of items can be tested against a panel of people who were present at the earliest Phase I meeting.

this descriptive clarification, he asks for the help of the client or consumer representatives who were elected in Phase I to be present at the Phase II meeting.

Following this review of problem dimensions, he directly defines the role of the "specialists" present. He indicates that they were invited as "idea men," not as "representatives" of their particular home organizations. He states that the purpose of the Phase II meeting is to identify alternative solution components and resources for the priority items which emerged in the Phase I meeting.* In this breakdown, first he asks for help in developing a list of solution components and resources *presently available* within organizations they are familiar with which can· be adapted to, or which already directly relate in their present form to, the problem dimensions. Second, he asks them to recommend *new* types of solution components and resources which could be developed as partial or complete solutions to the problem dimensions. . . .

Following a break, each group engages in a discussion of the various existing and new solution components and resources which can be incorporated in the program to deal with the priority problem items. The purpose of this discussion is to determine the most reasonable and adequate combination of solution components and resources for each priority problem. At the conclusion of this discussion, each group of specialists presents to the total assembly the list of solution components and resources which it feels must be part of the final program.

* "Component" in this case means an element or part of a solution program. "Resource" means a person, organizational unit, or funding source. For example, a problem priority identified in an OEO Phase I meeting was "lack of available medical services in geographically dispersed low-income neighborhoods in the country." In this case a solution component listed was "develop a mobile medical clinic." A resource listed was "use university medical interns."

Theoretical Defense of Phase II

It is not necessary to repeat the discussion of nominal groups and their advantages for this particular phase of the PPM process. There are, however, a number of unique problems specific to the character of the Phase II meeting which can be minimized by the use of the nominal group technique.

A problem encountered prior to the use of nominal group techniques was a tendency for knowledge resource persons to fall into the role of defending programs which their organizations were presently engaged in relative to the priority problem categories suggested by clients or consumers, rather than creatively exploring the development of new types of programs. In community groups in particular, agency and university specialists seemed to feel that it was necessary to justify the adequacy of present endeavors dealing with problem categories during Phase II meetings rather than explore the development of new types or recombinations of solution components and resources which could be part of a new program. The Phase II combination of the verbal role definition calling for specialists to be "idea men," not representatives,[9] together with the nominal technique asking for both existing and possible new solution components and resources, greatly decreases this tendency for specialists to defend or proselytize for present program structures.

At the same time, listing both "existing" and "new" components and resources forces program planners to consider pooling resources and approaches to problems. It is aimed at avoidance of unnecessary duplication of resources and

[9] The importance of verbal role definitions and research on their effect is treated in Delbecq (1964).

at encouragement of collaborative programs across organizations.

The actual participation of knowledge resource persons in the PPM process should be discussed. Research on change programs indicates that a critical feature in achieving change is the cognitive remapping of problem situations. (Dalton, 1969). Unless existing problems can be perceived through new types of conceptual lenses, the probability of innovative programs of solution remains limited. Therefore, the use of external knowledge specialists is an attempt to maximize the probability of reconceptualization of problem sets, making use of the differentiated conceptual lenses of these experts. In this respect, the juxtaposition of pure

scientific personnel and applied organizational specialists is particularly important.

Research indicates that there are two types of creativity. One type is concerned with seeing critical causal elements or dimensions of problems; the other type is the ability to synthesize these elements into appropriate and feasible solution patterns (Gordon & Morse, 1968). The use of both pure and applied specialists in tandem is an attempt to maximize the probability of both types of creativity's being included in the evolution of solution programs.

The use of differentiated age groups is also important since the character of creativity of younger and older scientists is shown to be quite different. The former

---

FIGURE 2   Outline of Phase II Meeting—Program Planning Model

  I. Selection of Knowledge Resource Panel
     Involvement of external scientific personnel
     Involvement of internal and external organizational specialists
 II. Meeting with Knowledge "Specialists" to explore solution components and needed resources
    A. Introduction
       1. Welcome
       2. Emphasis on the fact that the meeting's focus is upon priority problems of consumers or clients
       3. Review of Phase I
          a. Visual display of critical problems and priorities
          b. Nonanalytical elaboration of examples with assistance of client or consumer representatives from Phase I
       4. Role definition that asks specialists to be "idea" men, not "representatives" of programs or organizations
    B. Directions for small-group participation
       1. Assign specialists to small groups of 6 to 9 providing for a cross section of age, scientific and organizational affiliation and functional expertise
       2. Instruct specialists in nominal group format on each side of the 5" x 7" cards, and ask specialists to list critical solution components and resources under "existing" and "new" headings (30–45 minutes)
       3. Provide a flip chart and person to serve as recorder for round-robin sharing of individually noted solution components and resources (a separate sheet for each priority problem)
    C. Interacting group discussion in which each small group develops a package of solution components and resources for priority problems
    D. Report of each small group in general session. (Recorders make a master list of solution components and resources.)
    E. Nominal group voting on 3" x 5" cards on those solution components and resources absolutely essential for an effective program to solve priority items
    F. Explanation of PPM and election of representatives for Phase III

tend to reconceptuualize problems while the latter tend to be much more attuned to questions of feasibility and implementational relevance (Pelz & Andrews, 1966, Chap. 10 & 11).

Finally, by reaching outside the sponsoring organization, the Phase II procedure avoids provincial viewpoints. It is improbable that such a cross section of specialists will tend to step into the solution program out of one common psychological set, while an organizational group might well do so.[10] Indeed, the research by Utterback (1971) indicates that successful change programs obtain more than 50 per cent of the information about technical means to solve a problem outside the sponsoring organization.

At the end of Phase II, the existence of the essentials of an appropriate solution program agreed upon by a cross section of specialists adds greatly to the ease of crossing the boundary to resource controllers. The fact that the essential elements of the proposed solution program have been investigated by (and endorsed across) a number of interdisciplinary experts lends an aura of legitimacy to the program. In conveying this fact, the role of the representatives from Phase II is very critical in Phase III. These representatives of the specialist group provide expert-witness testimony; they are able to cast in appropriate social science or physical science terminology the justification of program components and resources which are part of the solution strategies voted upon as essential program elements.

Summary of the Benefits of Phase II

Phase II, then, is a deliberate, structured process which seeks to accomplish the following objectives: (a) to reconcep-

tualize priority problems from Phase I in terms of essential solution components and resources through use of scientific and organizational expertise; (b) to focus on new combinations of solution components and resources, avoiding defensive discussions of existing programs; (c) to activate differentiated types of creative insight by interdisciplinary and cross-generational group composition; (d) to call attention to existing but untapped solution components and resources as well as the need for new components and resources; (e) to provide a legitimate "scientific" endorsement of essential program components and resources for an adequate solution to priority problems.

PHASE III: PRIORITY DEVELOPMENT[11]

The description of the two prior phases of PPM has emphasized the *process* appriate for the particular meeting involved. In Phase III, the process for the meeting

[10] Pelz and Andrews (1966) include a discussion of calcification of viewpoints in a specialist team in Chap. 13; *see also* Dalton (1969, pp. 21–30) for a discussion of the need for new interpersonal ties in change programs.

[11] There are several important caveats which need to be made at this point. First, PPM is not a model for protest. That is, it presumes a degree of openness to client or consumer needs on the part of resource controllers. In cases where there is extreme polarization of positions, the intermediate degree of tension which PPM generates will be inadequate. Second, we have deliberately not incorporated budgeting and financial constraints into the process. Budgeting overlays and techniques for dealing with funding issues are sufficiently complex in themselves that we are incorporating budget issues in a later paper. In addition, the later paper juxtaposes the PPM process with the structure of an organization whose primary mandate is concerned with developmental and experimental work (as often performed by a planning agency) as cpposed to ongoing operating line work (as often performed by a social referral agency). *See* André L. Delbecq and Andrew H. Van de Ven, The generic character of program management: A theoretical perspective. Madison, Wisconsin: The Univer. of Wisconsin, Graduate School of Business. Unpublished manuscript, March 1971.

is not so significant as the timing of the meeting relative to the total PPM sequence.[12]

Phase III calls for a meeting—in which key resource controllers and key administrators participate, together with representatives from Phases I and II—to review the priorities and critical solution elements of the emerging program. The critical timing of the meeting can be justified as follows.

Klein (1967) describes resistance to programs as often being a function of the way change is introduced. He notes that most planners run into trouble when the agents of change have done all their planning *before* introducing their ideas to those who will be affected and who control resources. When this happens, "the innovators have usually developed a considerable investment in their plans and are often far more committed to defending them than to attempting to understand objections to them. They are not prepared to repeat with newcomers the long process of planning which finally led them to their conclusions" (Klein, 1967, p. 29). Klein goes on to note that attention to critics of an innovation plan can serve three useful functions:

First, . . . [critics] are most likely to perceive and point out any real threats to the well-being of the system which may be unanticipated consequences of the projected changes. Second, they are especially likely to react against any change that might reduce the integrity of the system.

[12] Indeed, research indicates nominal techniques are most applicable for generating information, while interacting groups are appropriate for evaluating information. In this sense, Phases I and II are the nominal preparation for Phase III. (*See* Vroom, Grant, & Cotton, 1969 for discussion of generation vs. evaluation.) To avoid rhetorical cleavage, provide focus, and create balance, therefore, greater attention to visuals (referred to below) is important.

Third, they are sensitive to any indication that those seeking to produce change fail to understand or identify with core values of the system they seek to influence (Klein, 1967, p. 31).

The essential contribution of our *Phase III is that it seeks to obtain responses from potential critics* of the program who are in a position to withhold resources or to negate appropriate involvement of functional administrative units in the implementation of the program, *while program proponents are still flexible.*

In the Phase III meeting, the outputs from the prior two phases are presented to the line administrators and resource controllers.[13] The format of the presentation is straightforward: the same list of critical problems and priorities from Phase I and the output from Phase II—the outline of agreed-upon solution components and resources—are presented to the key line administration and resource controllers. Of necessity, this represents the adumbration of a program

[13] The extent to which separate client or consumer representatives are invited to attend Phase III meetings is dependent on the extent to which resource control groups (often policy boards) include client or user groups in their membership. Increasingly, policy groups have so structured their board membership that proportional representation of clients is automatically assured when Phase III review before resource controllers takes place. Where this is not the case, the Phase III meeting should include proportional representation of client or consumers together with resource control board members and key administrators. Because of the difficulties of client or consumer members in holding their own during the verbal give-and-take of such meetings, the word *proportional* should be underscored. Token representation is not satisfactory. For the remainder of the discussion of Phase III, the proportional representation of client or consumer members will be assumed.

proposal rather than the presentation of specifics. The timing of Phase III is such that by meeting date there should be sufficient content in both problem analysis and solution analysis to provide appropriate focused discussion for resource controllers and administrators. At the same time, those individuals who will be charged later with the responsibility of developing the details of the program proposal have not yet become closed-minded nor have they made decisions on all the specifics of the proposed program. As a result, program sponsors will still be in a position to respond flexibly to the type of realistic adjustments which administrators and resource controllers are likely to suggest.

It is not an unusual occurrence for meaningful programs to be vetoed by resource controllers or administrators due to rather minor implementational issues. In other words, the essence of the program may be quite acceptable, while minor matters of program implementation often may not be satisfactory. What one seeks, then, in Phase III is a review of the types of reservations or qualifications that resource controllers and key administrators may have, and the adjustments required in order for the program proposal to be fully endorsed and supported. The structure of Phases I and II is such that neither the clients nor knowledge specialists are likely to attend to system and administrative constraints which those present in Phase III will be attuned to. The juxtaposition of client or consumer representatives from the Phase I meeting, knowledge resource persons from the Phase II meeting, and administrators and resource controllers spurs bargaining and negotiation in Phase III, so that within the content of the final program proposal the essential concerns of each of these reference groups can be included. The essential process caveat is that proponents of the program elements from Phases I and II must define their roles in such a way

that they are open to inputs of resource controllers and administrators and view them as relevant new problem dimensions to be incorporated in the final program, rather than as hostile "attacks" from an audience critical of the elements which evolved in the prior two phases. A detailed process guideline for the structuring of this discussion is suggested in the elaboration of bargaining strategy by Delbecq (1967).

Summary of the Benefits of Phase III

Phase III, then, represents an important but frequently overlooked phase of program development. It provides a step prior to "calcification" of thinking by program proponents, in which the general outline of a program plan containing both problem definition and critical solution elements is reviewed, so that administrative and resource controller concerns are incorporated in a manner that "buys insurance" relative to future endorsement and support of the program proposal. Following modifications, the output of Phase III should be a "go ahead" signal.

PHASE IV: PROGRAM DEVELOPMENT

Phase IV of the PPM model is simply a necessary step like that in conventional program evolution. In Phase IV, working from the input of the earlier three phases, technical specialists and line administrators who are sponsors of the program develop a finalized, specific program proposal. The essential matter here is to ensure that those specialists responsible for developing the details of the program remain sensitive to critical elements developed in prior phases.

PHASE V: PROGRAM EVALUATION

Phase V brings representatives from each of the constituent groups involved in

Phases I, II, and III together for a final time, to complete one cycle of the PPM process.[14] The need for this last meeting is based on several probable events: that a good deal of time will have elapsed between the initiation of Phase I and this final meeting prior to activation of the program; that some of the élan associated with involvement in the PPM process will have faded due to the extended time span; that some critical concern may have been overlooked in the technical development of the program; and finally, that a number of necessary compromises will have occurred in each phase so that cooperation, at least potentially, may be eroded by the feeling that the solution program is not "perfect." Phase V is structured to deal with the above developments in a manner which both reinvolves critical personnel and deals with honest hesitations about the technical plan in a constructive rather than destructive manner.

The Phase V meeting begins with a report from technical specialists of the details of the program to be implemented in the near future, but focuses this report in a specific fashion. Each critical feature of the detailed plan of action is overtly related to the input from prior phases. That is to say, it is not simply a report from technical specialists of their program plan, but rather a unified statement of program plans which seeks to operationalize the specific critical elements that emerged in earlier meetings. In this sense, the orientation of the meeting must show a clear linkage between the final plan and the problem priorities, solution and resource elements, and administrative and controller concerns raised in earlier phases. This manner of presentation (a) refreshes memories of earlier meetings and (b) directly connects planning de-

[14] In modified form the PPM cycle can be repeated, using the evaluation data prescribed in Phase V as the starting point.

tails to prior critical elements. As such, it is an important mechanism for rekindling enthusiasm lost during the long planning cycle.

The matter of hesitations about "imperfections" remains to be considered. Since it is doubtful that any operationalization of a program will totally satisfy every representative, a portion of the Phase V process, therefore, focuses on reviewing control and evaluation measures which will test whether or not the final program proposal incorporates earlier critical dimensions. If it is felt that the final program deviates from earlier expectations, there are two types of compromises possible: (1) a change in some detail of the finalized program proposal, or (2) further evaluation to determine whether a minority objection proves to be a valid weakness in the program. Generally speaking, Type 1 changes are made when a majority of the representatives at the Phase V meeting agree. This still leaves open the possibility that a recalcitrant minority will withdraw support. In this sense the Type 2 compromise offers a safety valve. By focusing the attention of minority members on the Type 2 compromise, individuals who retain reservations about the program against the majority judgment of the meeting still have recourse. Using a Type 2 compromise, disputation about selective details of the program can be dealt with by incorporating control and evaluation measures which test the relative effectiveness or ineffectiveness of the questioned program component.

Phase V, therefore, is a meeting designed to question whether the specialists' technical translation of the outputs of Phases I, II, and III as set forth in the final program proposal is an adequate interpretation of earlier discussions. If so, how will this adequacy be measured? Some adjustments where inadequacy is predicted may be forthcoming in the meeting. In addition, to avoid a stalemate at this late phase of program development, unresolved issues about adequacy can be handled by including in the evaluation design specific measures that will provide answers about the disputed matter for later program planning and adjustment.

Summary of the Benefits of Phase V

Phase V, then, seeks to accomplish the following objectives: (a) to reinvolve client or consumer representatives, knowledge resource people, and resource controllers and administrators by structuring the review of the technical proposal around critical concerns developed in prior phases; (b) to examine the extent to which the technical program plan honors earlier concerns by focusing upon evaluation designs; (c) to allow an opportunity for majority-approved last-minute adjustments; (d) to provide an outlet for minority reservations in the form of careful control measures to determine whether such reservations are justified; and thus (e) through the above processes, to refocus and rekindle interest in the change program.

SOME CONCLUDING REMARKS

We feel that PPM as a group process model is an insightful conceptualization of program planning. It both highlights critical issues and provides a guideline for developing innovative solution strategies where clients or consumers, specialists, resource controllers, and administrators must be interfaced. It further suggests group processes and agenda formats which guide each phase of program evolution.

Finally, the general character of the process is consistent with current research on creativity, organization change, and social planning.[15]

The authors . . . [have prepared] a detailed description of the application of PPM in social service planning and health planning organizations in a . . . [recently published] book.[16] From this and a number of other applications of PPM they are convinced of its practicality and power, but also convinced that considerable skill is required to activate the process. While a treatment of the requisite skills is a subject in the . . . book, briefly, the authors' experience suggests that practitioners often need previous training in order to (1) cognitively internalize the planning process as a discrete series of workable phases, (2) integrate the target reference groups in each phase, and (3) apply the appropriate group roles and processes necessary in each phase of the planning process.

The failure of many program planning endeavors in comprehensive health planning, urban planning, educational planning, new products development, and venture management attests that whatever approach to change is utilized, sophisticated attention to the issues which PPM seeks to cope with is required.

---

[15] Once again, however, we hasten to add that PPM is a model for change, not for protest or confrontation, where groups are severely polarized.

[16] *See* André L. Delbecq . . . [Andrew H. Van de Ven, and David H. Gustafson, *Group Techniques for Program Planning*. Glencoe, Ill.: Scott, Foresman, 1975.]

References

Arnstein, Sherry R. A ladder of citizen participation. *J. Amer. Inst. of Planners*, July 1969, 35 (4), 216.

Bales, R. F., & Strodtbeck, F. L. Phases in group problem solving. In M. Alexis and C. Z. Wilson, *Organizational decision making*. Englewood Cliffs, N.J.: Prentice-Hall, 1967. Pp. 122–133.

Campbell, J. P. Individual versus group problem solving in an industrial sample.

J. appl. Psychol., 1968, *52* (3), 205–210.

Culbert, S. A. Trainer self-disclosure and member growth in two t groups. *J. appl. Behav Sci.,* 1968, *4* (1) 47–74.

Dalton, G. W. Influence and organizational change. Paper presented at the Conference on Organizational Behavioral Models, College of Business Administration, Kent State Univer., May 16, 1969. Pp. 7–13.

Delbecq, A. L. Leadership styles in managerial conferences. *J. Acad. of Mgmt.* December 1964, *7* (4), 225–268.

Delbecq, A. L. The management of decision-making within the firm: Three strategies for three types of decision-making. *J. Acad. of Mgmt.* December 1967, *10* (4), 329–339.

Delbecq, A. L. The myth of the indigenous community leader. *J. Acad. of Mgmt.* March 1968, *11* (1), 11–26.

Dunnette, M. D., Campbell, J., & Jaastad, Kay. The effect of group participation on brainstorming effectiveness for two industrial samples. *J. appl. Psychol.,* 1963, *47* (1) 30–37.

Gordon, G., & Morse, E. V. Creative potential and organizational structure. *Academy of Management Proceedings of 28th Annual Meeting,* Chicago, Illinois, December 1968.

Klein, D. C. Some notes on the dynamics of resistance to change: The defender role. In G. Watson (Ed.), *Concepts for social change.* Washington, D.C.: Cooperative Project for Educational Development, National Training Laboratories, NEA, 1967.

Leader, A. H. Creativity in management. Paper read at 10th Annual Midwest Academy of Management Conference, held at Northwestern Univer., Evanston, Illinois, April 7–8, 1967.

Lipsky, M. Radical decentralization: A response to American planning dilemmas. Reprint #28. Madison, Wis.: The Institute for Research on Poverty, Univer. of Wisconsin, 1968.

Maier, N. R. F. *Problem-solving discus-*

sions and conferences. New York: McGraw-Hill, 1963. Pp. 247–249.

Mogulof, M. Coalition to adversary—Citizen participation in three federal programs. *J. Amer. Inst. of Planners,* July 1969, *35* (4), 225–245.

Moynihan, D. P. *Maximum feasible misunderstanding: Community action in the war on poverty.* New York: The Free Press, 1969.

Osborn, A. F. *Applied imagination.* New York: Scribners, 1957.

Pelz, D. C., & Andrews, F. M. *Scientists in organizations.* New York: Wiley, 1966. Chap. 10 & 11.

Scott, W. E. The creative individual. *J. Acad. of Mgmt.* September 1965, *8* (3).

Taylor, D. W., Berry, P. C., & Block, C. H. Does group participation when using brainstorming facilitate or inhibit creative thinking? *Admin. Sci. Q.,* 1958, *3,* 23–47.

Thompson, James D., & Tuden, A. Strategies, structures and processes of organizational decision. In J. Thompson, P. Hammond, R. Hawkes, & A. Tuden, *Comparative studies in administration.* Pittsburgh, Pa.: Univer. of Pittsburgh Press, 1959.

Thompson, Victor A. Bureaucracy and innovation. *Admin. Sci. Q.,* June 1965, *10* (1), 1–21.

Thompson, Victor A., & Smithburg, D. W. A proposal for the study of innovation in organization. Unpublished paper, Univer. of Alabama, Huntsville, 1968.

Utterback, J. M. The process of technological innovation within a firm. *J. Acad. of Mgmt.* March 1971, *14* (1), 75–88.

Vroom, V. H., Grant, L. D., & Cotton, T. S. The consequences of social interaction in group problem solving. *Organization Behav. & Human Performance,* 1969, *4,* 77–95.

Warren, R. Z. Model cities first round—politics, planning and participation. *J. Amer. Inst. of Planners,* July 1969, *35* (4), 24–56.

7.4 RETRACKING AMERICA: A THEORY OF TRANSACTIVE PLANNING

John Friedmann

THE TRANSACTIVE STYLE OF PLANNING

Bridging the Communications Gap

Transactive planning changes knowledge into action through an unbroken sequence of interpersonal relations. As a particular style of planning, it can be applied to both allocation and innovation. This chapter states the principal conditions for transactive planning and explores its major implications.

Transactive planning is a response to the widening gulf in communication between technical planners and their clients. To simplify the discussion, let us assume that planners as well as clients are individual persons rather than institutions, and that clients generate streams of action on which they wish to be advised. . . .

The barriers to effective communication between those who have access primarily to processed knowledge and those whose knowledge rests chiefly on personal experience are rising. We have seen that this problem is not unique to America; it is found to some extent in all societies that seek the help of technical experts. Messages may be exchanged, but the relevant meanings are not effectively communicated. As a result, the linkage of knowledge with action is often weak or nonexistent. This is true even where planning forms part of the client system itself; even there, actions tend to proceed

largely on the basis of acquired routines and the personal knowledge of the decision makers. Planners talk primarily to other planners, and their counsel falls on unresponsive ears. As we shall see, however, the establishment of a more satisfactory form of communication is not simply a matter of translating the abstract and highly symbolic language of the planner into the simpler and more experience-related vocabulary of the client. The real solution involves a restructuring of the basic relationship between planner and client.

Each has a different method of knowing: the planner works chiefly with processed knowledge abstracted from the world and manipulated according to certain postulates of theory and scientific method; his client works primarily from the personal knowledge he draws directly from experience. Although personal knowledge is much richer in content and in its ability to differentiate among the minutiae of daily life, it is less systematized and orderly than processed knowledge. It is also less capable of being generalized and, therefore, is applicable only to situations where the environment has not been subject to substantial change. The "rule of thumb" by which practical people orient their actions is useful only so long as the context of action remains the same. Processed knowledge, on the other hand, implies a theory about some aspect of the world. Limited in scope, it offers a general explanation for the behavior of a small number of variables operating under a specified set of constraints.

The difficulties of relating these two methods of knowing to each other reside not only in their different foci of attention and degrees of practical relevance (processed knowledge suppresses the operational detail that may be of critical importance to clients), but also in language. The planner's language is conceptual and mathematical, consciously drained of the lifeblood of human intercourse in its striving for scientific objectivity. It is intended to present the results of his research in ways that will enable others, chiefly other planners, to verify each statement in terms of its logic, consistency with empirical observation, and theoretical coherence. Most planners prefer communicating their ideas in documents complete with charts, tables, graphs, and maps, as well as long appendices containing complex mathematical derivations and statistical analyses. The concepts, models, and theories to which these documents refer are often unfamiliar to the clients to whom they are supposedly addressed.

The language of clients lacks the formal restrictions that hedge in planning documents. It, too, employs a jargon to speed communications, but the jargon will be experience- rather than concept-related. Client language is less precise than the language of planners, and it may encompass congeries of facts and events that, even though they form a meaningful whole in terms of practice, are unrelated at the level of theory. Planners may therefore seize upon a favorite term from their client's specialized vocabulary and subject it to such rigorous analysis that what originally might have been a meaningful expression to the client is given back to him as a series of different but theoretically related concepts that reflect a processed reality. . . .

The language of clients—so difficult to incorporate into the formalized vocabulary of the planner—is tied to specific operational contexts. Its meanings shift with changes in the context, and its manner of expression is frequently as important as the actual words employed. This

is probably the reason why planners prefer written to verbal communications, and why the latter tend to be in the form of highly stylized presentations. Tone of voice, emphasis, subtle changes in grammatical structure and word sequence, so important in the face-to-face communications of action-oriented persons, are consistently de-emphasized by planners. Whereas planners' formal communications could be translated by a computer into a foreign language without substantial loss of meaning, a tape-recorded conversation among clients could not. . . .

The mutual dependence of planner and client, coupled with a relative inability to exchange meaningful messages, leads to ambiguous and stereotyped attitudes that do little to solve the basic problem. Speaking among themselves, planners say: "Ours is clearly a superior form of knowledge that enables us to gain incisive insights into conditions of structured complexity. As members of a professional elite, we are able to achieve a greater rationality than our clients. Effective problem-solving lies in the widespread use of processed knowledge." But they also admire the practical successes of their clients and secretly deplore their own inability to score in the same game.

The clients, on the other hand, in the sheltering environment of their own groups, counter the planners' claims: "Experience clearly counts most. Ours is a superior kind of knowledge, tested under fire. Planners are impractical dreamers who know more and more about less and less. Nothing of what they know can be applied. Problems get solved because we are in charge." But they also admire the planners' knowledge of things that are not visible to the unaided eye and so transcend the possibilities of knowledge grounded in experience.

What can be done to overcome these barriers to effective communication between planners and clients? The traditional means, an exchange of formal documents, has not proved spectacularly successful in the past. Strangely enough, most planners are probably still unaware of this. . . .

All these questions converge upon a single answer. If the communication gap between planner and client is to be closed, a continuing series of personal and primarily verbal transactions between them is needed, through which processed knowledge is fused with personal knowledge and both are fused with action.

Transactive Planning as the Life of Dialogue

In transactive planning, two levels of communication have to be distinguished. The first is the level of person-centered communication. It presumes a relationship that is applicable to all forms of human intercourse. This I shall call the life of dialogue. The second is the level of subject-matter-related communication, which is sustained by the primary relation of dialogue and cannot be understood independently of it. Both levels are indispensable to planning. Where they become dissociated, thought is reduced to theorems and action to pure energy.

The life of dialogue always occurs as a relationship between two persons, a You and an I. Its characteristic features may be briefly stated:

1. *Dialogue presumes a relationship that is grounded in the authenticity of the person and accepts his "otherness" as a basis for meaningful communication.* In the life of dialogue, each person seeks to address the other directly. To be authentic means to discover yourself through dialogue with many others. And therefore we can say: The life of dialogue engenders a process of mutual self-discovery. At each stage in the process, you attempt to integrate discoveries about yourself into the already existing structure of your

personality, thereby changing and expanding it. To do this well, you must have found an inner security based on a consciousness of what you have become and are yet capable of becoming; a basic confidence in your ability to integrate new learning; and, finally, a willingness to open yourself to others.

Opening yourself to another implies an acceptance of the other in his radical difference from yourself. The life of dialogue is not possible between two persons who hide behind their many masks and are therefore incapable of growing and extending their knowledge about themselves. It requires an openness that confirms the other in all the differences of his being. It is precisely this that makes changes in self possible. Through dialogue, you accept the freedom of the other to choose himself.

2. *Dialogue presumes a relation in which thinking, moral judgment, feeling, and empathy are fused in authentic acts of being.* The authentic person is an indivisible whole. Nevertheless, four states of his being can be distinguished. The permanent dissociation of these may lead to a warping and even to the destruction of the person. Intellect alone is barren; moral judgment alone is self-righteous; feeling alone is destructive; and empathy alone is unresponsive. These four states of being must be held in mutual tension so that each may regulate the others. The point of intersection among them may be called the center of the fully integrated person, whose thought is tempered by moral judgment, whose judgment is tempered by feeling, and whose feeling is tempered by empathy.

Where these four states are brought into conjunction, speech becomes simply an extension of being, and the meanings of speech are backed up by the person as a whole: they can be taken on good faith. This does not always make them right, however. The learning person in the life of dialogue can make mistakes, he may be torn by inner doubts and conflicts, and he may be incapable of expressing himself integrally, leaving his meanings ambiguous and only partially articulated. Nevertheless, the standards of his speech are based not upon the extremes of truth, morality, feeling, and empathy taken each alone, but on the values that result from the conjunction of these states.

3. *Dialogue presumes a relation in which conflict is accepted.* The acceptance of the other in the plenitude of his being as a person different from yourself implies that the relationship cannot always be harmonious. Conflict arises out of your different ways of looking at the world, your different feelings about the world, and your different ways of judging the world. It may also arise from a failure to make your meanings clear within the context of the other's perceptions and feelings. But conflict can be overcome by a mutual desire to continue in the life of dialogue. This is the basis for resolving conflict at the level of interpersonal relations.

4. *Dialogue presumes a relationship of total communication in which gestures and other modes of expression are as vital to meaning as the substance of what is being said.* Everything you say and everything you do—or fail to do—carries a message to the perceptive other. Dialogue is a web of meanings from which not a single strand can be separated. Where gesture and speech convey contradictory meanings, the authenticity of dialogue is put in doubt. Such contradictory behavior is, by itself, no proof of lack of authenticity, but it gives rise to a suspicion of bad faith.

5. *Dialogue presumes a relation of shared interests and commitments.* The life of dialogue cannot be sustained unless there is a sense of partaking in the interests of the other. Mutual participation in a matter of common concern is not a precondition of authentic dialogue;

it may evolve through dialogue. Where it fails to evolve, the dialogue is interrupted.

We sometimes use one another to advance different interests. To the extent that this occurs, dialogue becomes an instrument to subordinate the other to your will. Presenting yourself to the other according to the demands of the situation is an inescapable part of dialogue, but "using" the other for interests that are not shared destroys any possibility of sustaining it. The life of dialogue is a relation of equality between two persons. It must not be perverted into an instrumental relationship.

6. *Dialogue presumes a relationship of reciprocity and mutual obligation.* Though dialogue is possible only between two persons who are free to choose themselves, this freedom is by no means unlimited. Dialogue is a contractual relationship. In accepting the other in his radical difference, you also assume responsibility for the consequences of this relationship. The act of "accepting" implies an act of "giving." The other "gives" or "entrusts" himself to you as a person, as you entrust yourself in turn. This exchange need not be balanced equally: no records are or can be kept. Nevertheless, a one-sided giving cannot continue for long. To the extent that you are willing to "accept" the other, your obligations to him will increase, and you must be willing to give at least a part of yourself in return.

7. *Dialogue presumes a relationship that unfolds in real time.* Dialogue takes place in the "here and now" even as it relates what has gone before to what is yet to come. It is therefore a time-binding relationship capable of infinite evolution. Nevertheless, it cannot escape the constraints of a given situation and must ultimately become relevant to the particular conditions of each participant's life. Storytelling is not dialogue; dreams are not dialogue. You cannot crawl out of time; dialogue is not a route of escape.

Dialogue brings you back into time and into the conditions of your being here.

As described, the life of dialogue suggests an intimacy that most people associate with the relationship between husband and wife, parents and children, and close friends. In the circle of this extended family, non-utilitarian, person-centered relationships predominate. Outside its magic circle, relationships are expected to rest on a working, professional basis, to be centered on specific roles rather than persons—a form of behavior that carefully isolates intellectual and technical contributions from their matrix of moral judgments and feelings and presumes purely utilitarian transactions, in which no sharing need occur.

But this conception is basically wrong. The world of planning need not be qualitatively set apart from the world of non-utilitarian relationships. On the contrary, the impersonal, professional style of communication has been notoriously unsuccessful in joining knowledge to action.

It is true, of course, that one cannot maintain deep personal relationships with everyone one meets. But a person-centered relationship can be sustained at varying degrees of intensity and over periods of time that extend from only a few minutes to an entire life. Looking back at the requirements of dialogue, we see that the conditions are applicable to any relationship. We can be open and alert to the other, whoever he may be. We can accept him as a person different from ourselves without being threatening or feeling threatened in turn. We can try to hold our intellectual, moral, affective, and empathetic states of being in mutual tension. We can accept conflict as an inevitable part of dialogue and not its termination. We can look for the patterns of shared interests. And we can concentrate the life of dialogue on the here and now.

An attitude favorable to dialogue tends to call forth on the part of the other a desire to engage in it. Some persons are more difficult to reach than others, but in most cases, the response to an attempted dialogue is dialogue.

Transactive planning is carried on the ground swell of dialogue. When I prepared the memorandum for the Chilean Government, the basis for dialogue had not yet been established. Later, all this changed. In recruiting the advisory staffs, emphasis was given to the personal qualities of each advisor—his ability to be a person (not a role-playing professional alone), to establish direct relations with others that would not be perceived as threatening, to be sensitive to the needs of others, and to learn quickly from complex, novel situations. Technical qualifications were also considered important, but they carried less weight.

At the start, the newly recruited advisor spent from six months to a year learning about the multi-faceted situation in which he had been placed and establishing relations of dialogue with a few key persons in the offices to which he was assigned. Although his formal role was not eliminated, it was so loosely structured that the advisor was able to emerge as a person. And once a relationship of this kind had been established, transactive planning could begin in earnest.

The Process of Mutual Learning

Planners are forever coming up against new situations, but they confront them with knowledge that is little more than an aid to rapid and effective learning. Their theories, hypotheses, conceptual schemes, and analytical methods are useful only for converting the raw data of observation into general statements about reality. The validity of these statements is limited to a set of specified conditions. But the problems on which planners work —whether the design for a new town, a program for harnessing the waters of a river, or a policy for the development of scientific capabilities—must be studied in the fullness of historical circumstances. The number of variables that must be considered is substantially greater than those included in the analytical models of scientific work.

The planner's special skill, therefore, lies in his ability to be a rapid learner. His is an intelligence that is trained in the uses of processed knowledge for the purpose of acquiring new knowledge about reality. He comes equipped to bring order into a seemingly chaotic universe of data and sense impressions, to reduce this to a structure of relative simplicity, to isolate the processes responsible for the emergence and maintenance of the structure, to probe its propensities for change, and to locate the points of potentially effective intervention. Regardless of his specific procedure, the planner makes substantial use of analytical techniques in his work. The greater his virtuosity in this regard, the greater his pride in the results obtained. As I have said, his interests as a professional often get the better of his interest in serving his client. . . .

In mutual learning, planner and client each learn from the other—the planner from the client's personal knowledge, the client from the planner's technical expertise. In this process, the knowledge of both undergoes a major change. A common image of the situation evolves through dialogue; a new understanding of the possibilities for change is discovered. And in accord with this new knowledge, the client will be predisposed to act.[1]

---

[1] There are problems so technical that the authority of experts will be accepted at face value. These problems are usually close to the operational level, such as the design specifications of a bridge. Mutual learning is not applicable to these cases. It is useful

The Tao of Transactive Planning

Planners are often inspired by a wish to change existing reality. This almost compulsive desire stands in direct relationship to their inability to influence the requisite behavior to produce a change. The head of a large technical assistance operation once exclaimed in my presence, pounding his fist on the table: "We have to show controlled impatience." It was not clear to me then, nor is it clear to me now, why impatience was called for. He had neither the power nor the responsibility to act. His job was simply to advise the government, not to replace it.

This incident has remained with me over the years. It reflects, I think, a complete lack of understanding of the essential tasks of planning. Clearly, the man was eager to step into the driver's seat. Lack of sufficient progress, according to his lights, was due entirely to the laziness, corruption, recalcitrance, decadence, cupidity, political irresponsibility, and irrationality of the guidance institutions of the country to which he had been called. He knew what needed to be done, and he had told his clients how to do it. Why did they not follow his advice?

His model of the planning process was exceedingly simplistic. The planner plans; the client buys the plans and uses all the means at his disposal to see them carried out. If planning follows a transactive style, however, a different, more complex model has to be considered (Figure 1). The Taoist philosophy of wu-wei—doing nothing—would seem to be more appropriate to this model than controlled impatience.

The Tao says: *All things go through their own transformations.*—All systems obey their own laws of internal change. These laws cannot be arbitrarily reversed

---

only where the personal knowledge of the client is an important component of any solution that may be offered.

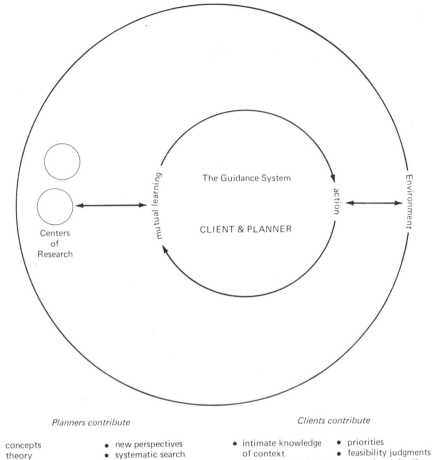

Planners contribute

- concepts
- theory
- analysis
- processed knowledge
- new perspectives
- systematic search procedures

Clients contribute

- intimate knowledge of context
- realistic alternatives
- norms
- priorities
- feasibility judgments
- operational details

FIGURE 1   A Model of Transactive Planning

without causing substantial harm to the system. Both the maintenance and the change of a system are the result of processes that relate the system's elements to one another. A good deal of system behavior is regulated automatically, but sometimes there is insufficient change, or the change is not the kind we would like, or changes are too rapid, causing the system to fall into disorder. If the planner wants to rectify any of these conditions, he must concentrate upon the processes of maintenance and transformation in order to see how to accelerate, decelerate, or contain them; occasionally a new process should be introduced or a process that has lost its vital functions should be discarded. To change a process means to act upon the sources that generate the lawful behavior of the system. But both planner and client must respect the laws of transformation and be mindful of their limited abilities to control the flow of events.

The same principle applies to mutual learning. Learning cannot be imposed; it obeys the laws by which a structure of thinking, feeling, and valuing is changed. The planner may learn rapidly. But the more he assimilates his client's knowledge, the greater the complexity of which he is aware. To change the reasons why people act the way they do and produce the results they do, one must respect the processes by which they learn. Anxieties have little influence upon the outcome. Students do not learn because their teachers want them to. They learn only when they are ready to accept the new perceptions and to make new images their own.

The Tao says: *Truly, a great cutter does not cut.*—Knowing the laws of transformation, the planner need not slash wildly into the tangle of social relationships, tearing out whole living tissues here and grafting others there, piling control upon control to make the process bend to his will. He will use the "natural" forces at work in society to produce the desired results. This means selective intervention and methods of indirect or field control. A knowledge of the consequences of strategic intervention is essential to the art of planning.

Similarly, the planner involved in mutual learning will not start by destroying the world view of his client. He will withhold his judgments, respecting his client's freedom and autonomy. To begin a restructuring of the client's field of cognition, the planner must discover within that field itself the points that provide an opening. What are the client's interests? What are the inconsistencies in his way of thinking and feeling? What are his secret doubts? What aspects of his knowledge are not supported by the values he affirms? It is through a process of selective focusing at such critical points that the planner can achieve the transformation and expansion of his client's learning.

The Tao says: *Tao invariably does nothing, yet there is nothing that is not done.*—Under conditions of mutual learning, the planner appears to be doing nothing: he learns, and, learning, he imparts new knowledge. As perceptions and images are changed, so is the behavior that flows from them. Time is necessary for changes in behavior to occur. In the natural course of things, little appears to happen, yet everything happens in due time. Persons change, institutions change, the environment for action changes. The ideas of the learner take root, are themselves transformed, and pass into action, affecting the behavior of society.

The Tao says: *The most yielding of things outruns the most unyielding.*—Mutual learning cannot be compelled; the planner cannot accelerate the processes of understanding and behavior change. Time is needed; listening is needed.˙ If the planner listens carefully and long enough, his own thoughts may eventually be given back to him as the ideas of others. Only then can the planner truly be said to have succeeded in his task.

The future cannot be conquered by the present; compulsion destroys the generative forces in society. The planner must learn to yield when necessary, but also to persuade. Dialogue is essential to learning. Through dialogue, mutual learning occurs; and through mutual learning changes are brought about in the collective behavior of society.

The Tao says: *To give life, but not to own, to achieve but not to cherish, to lead but not to be master—that is the mystic virtue.*—This is the most important, and also the most difficult of the five teachings of the Tao. It says: let everyone be free to choose himself, do not desire what is not your own, do not hold back on what you know. As a teacher, fade into the background and let the student speak; as a student, take new learning and use it to advantage. But when there are neither teachers nor students, as in mutual learning, the property of learning is held in common trust: no one is master, each has something to give and something to receive. From period to period, you pass to higher levels of understanding. Do not cherish them. Keep your mind open to what is yet to come.

If the processed knowledge of planners is serviceable only insofar as it is used as an instrument for learning; if learning cannot be imparted to others except through dialogue; and if dialogue creates a process in which each partner has as much to give as to receive, then the Tao provides good counsel.

Transactive Planning in the Context of Society

American society needs a heightened capacity for learning about itself and, to make what it learns effective in guiding its own development, a way to transform learning into appropriate actions. This implies that we must find a way to join scientific and technical intelligence with personal knowledge at the critical points for social intervention. I have argued that

transactive planning is the most appropriate method for achieving this linkage.

The transactive style is not, admittedly, applicable to every situation where expert knowledge is joined to action. It is inappropriate, for instance, *where expertise carries sufficient authority to act without the benefit of mutual learning.* The mechanic, the airplane pilot, or the surgeon is each prepared to do his job without elaborate discussion with his clients. There is no need for dialogue. Few questions will be asked and fewer answered. Nor are situations of mutual learning between expert and client common in highly stratified societies, where technical expertise enjoys high social esteem and clients unhesitatingly accept its judgments simply because they are offered under a prestigious professional label. In all other situations, however, the transactive style is essential to the ultimate success of planning. And this holds true with particular force in American society today. . . .

7.5   LIFE PLANNING

Herbert A. Shepard

Life planning is planning life-worth-living. The choices you make today create your future, as well as your here-and-now. And you have some freedom of choice, today, and tomorrow as well. We are only slowly emerging from an era of deterministic science, when it was assumed that today's choices are completely the product of yesterday's choices, and the very notion of choice a quaint illusion.

Reprinted by permission of the editors and publisher from H. A. Shepard. "Life Planning." In K. Benne, L. Bradford, J. Gibb, and R. Lippitt, (Eds.) *Laboratory Method of Changing and Learning: Theory and Application.* Palo Alto, Calif.: Science and Behavior Books, 1975.

The psychologists assured us that life after the age of five was merely an unfolding of a personality set in early childhood. And our culture demands of each of us so many promises and contracts that most of us seem to have signed away our future choices. We seal our fates.

Many people see their futures as fated in another way. They think of the future as something that happens to them. When they are asked to draw a line representing the way they think about their total lives—from the beginning in the past to the end in the future—they can portray certain aspects of their past but are unable to map the future. The past can be re-interpreted, but it cannot be managed. Only the future is manageable, but these people have great difficulty in thinking about it that way.

Some people plan their careers, and invest their energies in bringing about certain career achievements. Unfortunately, when people plan only their careers, the other aspects of their lives are unanticipated and sometimes unhappy consequences of their career choices. When these people draw their life lines, they draw only career lines.

Life planning is a self-confrontation. It is the induction of an identity crisis and a destination crisis for yourself. It requires the reexamination of basic values and assumptions. Many of us are enslaved to beliefs and fears that turn us into instruments used for some purpose outside ourselves. One therapist greets new patients with the question: "Why haven't you committed suicide?" The answers often lie outside the person and his joy in life, or lack of it: responsibilities to family, God and country, or even to the life insurance company. And if a married couple is asked: "Why haven't you divorced?", the answers are often outside their joy in each other, or lack of it: family responsibilities or social embarrassment.

Yet Fritz Perls' Gestalt Prayer[1] counsels:

I am not in this world to live up to your expectations
And you are not in this world to live up to mine.
You are you and I am I
And if by chance we find each other
It's beautiful.
If not, it can't be helped.

Who am I and who are you? The first answers that come to mind are usually "marketing" answers. They describe what makes you or me a respect-

---

[1] Frederick S. Perls, *Gestalt Therapy Verbatim*. Utah: Real People Press, 1969.

able commodity: title, profession, memberships, loyalties, skills, hobbies, roles as parent, spouse or manager. The answers that come later take us beyond the boundaries of such socially prescribed selves and precipitate an identity crisis.

Who *should* you be? Our culture provides us with many reasons for being that lie outside ourselves, with many images of what we should be. The self-confrontations of life planning involve the unravelling or deeply, often automatically, held assumptions about shoulds and oughts, goods, and bads. A dictator concerned only with the maintenance of his own power would value such qualities in the citizenry as loyalty, respect for authority, law and order, unselfishness, humility and competitiveness. When you perform well, whom are you trying to please? When you are winning, is it ever at the cost of something more important? Is having a fine reputation at all like being trapped? Is being independent ever lonely? Is the greatest risk not risking?

On the subject of what one ought to be, Kahlil Gibran had this story to tell.

It was in the garden of a madhouse that I met a youth with a face pale and lovely and full of wonder.
And I sat beside him upon the bench, and I said, "Why are you here?"
And he looked at me in astonishment, and he said, "It is an unseemly question, yet I will answer you. My father would make of me a reproduction of himself; so also would my uncle.
My mother would have me the image of her illustrious father.
My sister would hold up her seafaring husband as the perfect example for me to follow. My brother thinks I should be like him, a fine athlete.
"And my teachers also, the doctor of philosophy, and the music-master, and the logician, they too were determined,

and each would have me but a reflection of his own face in a mirror.

"Therefore, I came to this place. I find it more sane here. At least I can be myself."

Then of a sudden he turned to me and he said, "But tell me, were you also driven to this place by education and good counsel?" And I answered, "No, I am a visitor."

And he said, "Oh, you are one of those who live in the madhouse on the other side of the wall."[2]

The location of the madhouse is less important than whether either the inmate or the visitor has learned to make his own life worth celebrating. What were those moments when you rejoiced in life, when you were fully alive, and living fully, and experiencing fulfillment? You're likely to find that many of them were quite "simple," and had little to do with the way you spend most of your time. If you can identify the conditions under which your life is fulfilling, you can set about creating those conditions.

Easier said than done. A basic fact of life—that it is to be lived fully—is difficult to grasp. Lyndon Johnson's widow, reflecting on their last years together, commented:

To be close to death gives you a new awareness of the preciousness of life, and the extreme tenuousness of it. You must live every day to the fullest, as though you had a short supply—because you do. I said that glibly for years, but I didn't know how intensely one should live.[3]

Some people can apprehend the preciousness of life by writing their own obituaries, focusing on activities and feelings, and writing the obituary twice: once

[2] Kahlil Gibran, "The Madman" in *The Wanderer*. New York: Knopf, 1932.

[3] Ladybird Johnson, *TIME*, May 21, 1973, p. 41.

as an extrapolation of present life style, and again as one would wish it to be. But many others find this rather direct way of facing the question, "What shall I do with the time I have left?'" too threatening to be taken seriously.

What are the conditions under which it is possible to rejoice in life? Perhaps one can learn from infants. An infant rejoices when it can affect its environment in ways that please it. It rejoices in loving and playful interaction with other beings. And it rejoices in the functioning of its own body. These three sources of fulfillment, translated into adult words, can be called autonomy, resonance and tone.

As used here, autonomy refers to your ability to create a world worth living in for yourself. Typically, the autonomous person has many skills useful to himself and society, continually develops his physical, emotional and intellectual capacities, can relate in many ways to others, is proactive and foresighted, imaginative and realistic, takes responsibility for his choices and their consequences, is open to new experience and learns from it. But the essence of autonomy is not in what one's resources are, but how they are used, the purpose they serve: namely, the creation and maintenance of a world worth living in. Thus, autonomy differs from related terms like power, skills, achievement, independence or wealth, which may become ends in themselves, or may be used to create a world for oneself that is not worth living in. The characteristics of such a world and of autonomy are not the same for every person. Robert Frost described the meaning of autonomy in the poet's world.

The reason artists show so little interest
In public freedom is because the freedom
They've come to feel the need of is a kind
No one can give them—they can scarce attain—
The freedom of their own material:

So, never at a loss in simile,
They can command the exact affinity
Of anything they are confronted with.
This perfect moment of unbafflement,
When no man's name and no noun's adjective
But summons out of nowhere like a jinni.
We know not what we owe this moment to.
It may be wine, but much more likely love—
Possibly just well-being in the body,
Or respite from the thought of rivalry.
It's what my father must mean by departure,
Freedom to flash off into wild connections.
Once having known it, nothing else will do.
Our days all pass awaiting its return.[4]

The second source of fulfillment is resonance, a relationship with other beings which is empathic, responsive, mutually stimulating and expansive for all those involved. The term can describe a person's relationship with other environments as well. Resonance differs from the common meaning of love, which is usually understood to be an exchange relationship rather than a resonance relationship. Freya Stark describes the essence of resonance in the following passage.

For it must be remembered that silence can be dead or living, and the two kinds must be distinguished. And perhaps the poles of being are in the distinction—the one an end and a downfall and a destruction, and the other a part of that which has neither beginning nor end; and even in the humblest instance there is a difference in the silence of these two.

There is, for instance, regrettably often a noticeable blank in the wedded silence, when a couple have been married a long time. One sees them in restaurants or on cruises—middle-aged, averted faces that turn toward each other with no light in their eyes and drop words of such astonishing triviality that one wonders how the air consents to carry them: surely the sort of conversation Sartre was thinking of when he described Hell as one prolonged domestic scene.

Yet if a young creature were to ask for advice whether to say yes or no to the man or woman she or he thought of marrying, one might do worse than ask: 'Are you happy to be silent together?' That companionship is the living silence—a relaxation that finds speech superfluous, an atmosphere of well-being where nothing needs to be explained, a part of that current which can make not only men but most living things happy to be together. It is, I like to imagine, the stream that flows beneath all differences of language and carries each one of us from those cindery beginnings toward our undiscovered end.[5]

The third source of fulfillment, tone, is an alertness of all the senses and organs. The meaning we attach to the term "muscle tone" captures the quality referred to as the tone of the whole organism—sensory, mental, emotional, muscular, etc. The concept of tone differs from the concept of health. Health is usually defined as the absence of disease, and mental health is usually regarded as something different from physical health. Tone is a psychophysiological concept: anxiety is as much its enemy as drugs. Lowen expresses this idea as follows:

A person experiences the reality of the world only through his body. . . . If the body is relatively unalive, a person's impressions and responses are dimin-

[4] Robert Frost, "How Hard It Is to Keep from Being King When It's in You and in the Situation," in *The Poetry of Robert Frost*, Holt, Rinehart, and Winston, New York, 1969, p. 453.

[5] Freya Stark, "On Silence," *Holiday Magazine*, December, 1965.

ished. The more alive the body is, the more vividly does he perceive reality and the more actively does he respond to it. We have all experienced the fact that when we feel particularly good and alive, we perceive the world more sharply. . . . The aliveness of the body denotes its capacity for feeling. In the absence of feeling the body goes 'dead' insofar as its ability to be impressed by or respond to situations is concerned. The emotionally dead person is turned inward: thoughts and fantasies replace feeling and action; images compensate for the loss of reality. . . . It is the body that melts with love, freezes with fear, trembles in anger, and reaches for warmth and contact. Apart from the body these words are poetic images. Experienced in the body, they have a reality that gives meaning to existence.[6]

When autonomy, resonance and tone are all high, we rejoice in life. This is a peak experience, and as Frost says, "Once having known it, nothing else will do." The three are closely interwined: if autonomy is used in ways that reduce resonance, it will not produce a world worth living in; low tone will adversely affect resonance and autonomy. Treating them as separate aspects of life-worth-living may have some value in the life planning process for persons who have been spending all their energies on work and neglecting their relationships with others or their own bodies; or for persons who only feel strong when they are going against others and don't know that it is possible to be strong when going with others; or for persons who overeat at the expense of tone and resonance; or for persons with many resources, persons who possess the elements making for autonomy, but have experienced little fulfillment.

[6] Alexander Lowen, *The Betrayal of the Body*, Macmillan, New York, 1967, pp. 5–6.

How does the infant's delighting in its experience of autonomy become transformed into the adult's striving for status or winning over others? How does the infant's joy in resonance become transformed into the adult's view of love as a commodity and commodities as substitutes for love? How does the infant's joy in its own body become transformed into emotional deadness? Perhaps it is because our socializing institutions demand that the child give up his search for autonomy in exchange for packages of pseudo-romance. Whatever the telling events in the process of socialization are, many people "grow up" having learned "truths" that blind them to life. Such distorting values are reflected in the following excerpt from a paper examining the relevance of Taoist and Buddhist philosophy to modern man in modern organization.

The second piece of advice is: Observe the cormorant in the fishing fleet. You know how cormorants are used for fishing. The technique involves a man in a rowboat with about half a dozen or so cormorants, each with a ring around the neck. As the bird spots a fish, it would dive into the water and unerringly come up with it. Because of the ring, the larger fish are not swallowed but held in the throat. The fisherman picks up the bird and squeezes out the fish through the mouth. The bird then dives for another and the cycle repeats itself.

To come back to the second piece of advice from the neo-Taoist to the American worker. Observe the cormorant, he would say. Why is it that of all the different animals, the cormorant has been chosen to slave away day and night for the fisherman. Were the bird not greedy for fish, or not efficient in catching it, or not readily trained, would society have created an industry to exploit the bird? Would the ingenious device of a ring around its neck, and the simple procedure of squeezing the bird's neck to force it to regurgitate the fish have been devised? Of course not.

Greed, talent, and capacity for learning then are the basis of exploitation. The more you are able to moderate and/or hide them from society, the greater will be your chances of escaping the fate of the cormorant.

. . . it is necessary to remember that the institutions of society are geared to make society prosper, not necessarily to minimizing suffering on your part. It is for this reason among others, that the schools tend to drum into your mind the high desirability of those characteristics that tend to make society prosper—namely, ambition, progress and success. These in turn are to be valued in terms of society's objectives. All of them gradually but surely increase your greed and make a cormorant out of you.[7]

One need not view the fate of the cormorant as gloomily as does Siu to recognize that he provides a novel perspective on some attributes—ambition, talent, and capacity for learning—which are prized in our culture. Life planning is essentially an invitation to explore new perspectives from which to view past experience, one's current life, and future alternatives. As Siu implies, the value system we inherited is not necessarily designed to make life worth living.

The discovery and creation of perspectives that deepen our appreciation of ourselves in the universe is the fourth aspects of life-worth-living. It is akin to resonance, as suggested by the terminology William O. Douglas used to describe what is meant here by perspective:

Man is whole when he is in tune with the winds, the stars and the hills as well as with his neighbors. Being in

tune with the apartment or the community is part of the secret. Being in tune with the universe is the whole secret.[8]

In everyday experience, being in tune with the universe, or having an adequate perspective means seeing problems from above rather than from underneath, means not getting locked in to one end or the other of a presumed polarization, means being free in your situation rather than dependent on it, means owning your behavior rather than claiming someone else's behavior "caused" yours.

Life planning is a quest, and it is also a continuous part of life-worth-living. And while the life planning process and outlook described here may help you to live more fully, it will not protect you from pain. Developing towards higher levels of autonomy, resonance, tone and perspective faces you with all the awkwardness, mistakes, and painful choices involved in any learning. Living more fully means investing yourself more fully in the creation of your experience: and anything you invest yourself in to the point that it can bring you great joy can also bring you great grief by its loss.

AN APPENDIX

If you ask a person why he is in his present job, he is quite likely to tell you how he got into it rather than how he is using it in the accomplishment of his purpose. Life planning is learning to see the environment through the eyes of your purpose, and the principal work of life planning is the creation of purpose. You become what you think. "A man defines himself by his project."[9]

Logically, career planning is a part of life planning. But psychologically and culturally, the two are often separated. For some, work or career or profession is

[7] Ralph Gildi Siu, "Work and Serenity," *Journal of Occupational Mental Health*, 1, 1, 1971, p. 5.

[8] William O. Douglas, Associate Justice, U.S. Supreme Court.

[9] R. D. Laing and G. O. Cooper, *Reason and Violence*, Tavistock, London, 1964, p. 61.

the sole source of self esteem, the only justification for being permitted to exist. For others, it is not felt to be a part of life at all, and life planning refers to the time outside of work, when they can live a little.

Life planning is to make life more whole, to make living a good Gestalt, so that the parts of one's life are mutually enriching. Work belongs in life, along with love, laughter, prayer and all the other elements of human experience.

Life planning has several aspects: arousal of motivation, freeing of imagination, generation of data about oneself, identification of themes in the data, formulation of purpose, and development of action plans. Many vehicles are available for taking this trip, and the ones noted below are examples.

1. Draw Your Life Line

Draw a line that represents ways you have of thinking about your life. Maybe it will be a straight sloping line drawn between the coordinates of chronological age and maturity. Maybe it will be a chart of your educational and work life. Maybe it will be two lines, one representing your career, the other the rest of your life. Maybe it will be jagged, with lots of peaks and valleys. Maybe it won't be a line at all, but a string of pictures, or something that looks like a tree, or a map. Maybe it will be several lines, each concerned with a different aspect of your life.

Make it a complete life line: beginning with your birth and ending with your death. Put a mark on it to show where you are right now. Let yourself play with the future part of the line. Be sure to bring the line to an end: the decision on how long to live is best made by yourself, and you can change your mind about it tomorrow.

When you have completed your drawing, its meaning is apparent only to yourself. If you explain to some others what you tried to portray, their questions and comments may lead you to discover additional meanings, and you can also gain perspective on your own life by learning how others represent theirs.

2. Identity Search

The next steps are explorations of the space between the "now" mark on your line and the future end of the line, beginning with the now mark: your current identity. Find as many answers as you can to the question "Who am I?" The first answers that occur to you will probably be the roles you take: your occupation, your family roles, your memberships, etc. Then explore the many other sides of yourself: adjectives that describe some aspect of you and your life: personality traits, beliefs, skills, attitudes, habits; impulses and inhibitions; dreams, wishes, fears and regrets; the kinds of relationships you form with other people; the things you like about yourself and the things you don't; the things you're not; the other people who are part of your life.

If you are in the company of someone who knows you, ask her or him to make a list of answers to the question "Who are you?" to provide you with additional data for your identity search. Now look over your list item by item, and spend some time assessing the importance of that item to your sense of yourself. Suppose it were suddenly removed, how would you feel? You may find that some are so important that if they were taken away you'd be lost and terrified; you may find some whose disappearance would be a relief.

Then review the list again, marking those aspects of your identity you want to maintain, and perhaps enhance, in the future, and those aspects you want to rid yourself of. Add any new identities you want to become.

The identity search is enriched by being shared with others; for example, some of the items on their lists probably belong on yours too.

3. Write Your Obituary

After exploring the now mark on your life line in this way, move to the future end of the line and look back over your whole life, especially the part you haven't lived yet. Write your obituary, covering as many aspects of your life as you can, and concentrating on the part between the now mark and the future end of the line. Write about the way your life will probably turn out if you continue in your current life patterns and trends. If you don't make any major shift in life style, priorities, values, etc., what will your obituary say? After you've written it and shared it with the others, you can think about any changes you want to make in it.

4. Newspaper Clippings

The next steps are explorations of the space between now and the future end of the line. Take the Sunday edition of a large metropolitan newspaper and clip out items that intrigue you. They may be news items of a political, or educational, or scientific, or sports, or cultural nature; or travel advertisements and descriptions of other countries; or cartoons and pictures; or business and real estate opportunities; or jobs and occupations; things offered for sale; perhaps a portion of someone's obituary.

Paste the clippings on a large sheet of paper and share them with others. See what patterns you can find in the things that interested you.

5. Fantasy Day

Somewhere in the space between now and the end of the line, create a special day for yourself. Give your fantasy free rein: don't ask whether you can afford to do what you want to do in that day; don't ask whether all those things could be fitted into one day. Just plan a day that you would love to have.

After you've lived that day in fantasy, and shared what you dare about it with others, look at it more critically. Did you build into the day any wishes or dreams that you want to take seriously and turn into plans? Many people suppress and altogether forget youthful dreams and wishes when they become "responsible adults." Dreams that were unattainable when you were younger may no longer be out of reach. See if you can recapture some of your wishes. Are they still attractive? Are they realizable?

6. A Way of Life

Take a larger segment of the line between now and the end, perhaps a year, and describe a life style you'd like to try. Again, don't be too "realistic." Take the segment from far enough in the future that you'd have time to do something about the obstacles that stand in the way of spending such a year. And after you've written and shared it, think about whether you mean any of it seriously enough to start planning.

7. A Review of Highs

What can you learn from your past that you can use in creating your future? If you can identify the conditions under which your life was fulfilling, you may be able to re-create those conditions.

Think back to the times when you felt best about yourself and your life. Some of them may have been brief moments, peak experiences. Some of them may have been projects that took years to accomplish. Some may have been work, some pure play. Some may have been solitary experiences, others full of people.

Write a paragraph about each one, describing it in as much detail as you can. Give yourself lots of time to recapture these highs: a whole evening, or a weekend. After you've described a number of them (try to find at least ten), go back over them in search of patterns. What strengths did you display or develop in each of the experiences? What did you contribute to the creation of the experiences? What were the sources of your satisfaction in each experience? Ask others to help you with this analysis: they are likely to see strengths that were too obvious for you to see yourself.

8. Psychological Tests

Through the use of psychological tests, you can generate more data about your identity and your potentials. For example, the Thematic Apperception Test can give you a new perspective on your needs for achievement, influence and intimacy. FIRO-B reflects your needs in the areas of control, affection and inclusion. The Strong Interest inventory tells you how your patterns of interests, likes and dislikes match those of people who have been successful in various occupations.

9. Getting It All Together

By now you have amassed so much information about yourself that it will take some time and thought to assimilate it and comprehend it. As you look through it all, you will find the same set of messages, in different words and contexts, many times. You may also find some seeming contradictions and paradoxes. Some of these may be artifacts of the method used in generating the data: for example, the product of a particular mood you were in during one of the exercises. But often the paradoxes contain the possibility of discoveries about yourself that can be important to you in creating your future. A person with whom you have good rapport can be helpful to you in the process of sorting it all out and getting it all together.

10. Purpose and Themes

When you have identified some of the themes that you want to be central in your life, try to formulate a statement of mission or purpose that organizes the themes into a good Gestalt, a wholeness that is satisfying to you. Your purpose may evolve logically and obviously from your study of the data; it may have emerged clearly in the process of generating the data; or it may continue to elude you and then appear as a flash of insight. It may also be that you cannot formulate a purpose until you have made some further explorations.

11. Your Partners in Life

If you have a partner or partners in life, you should probably have been together throughout the process described above. But partners do not build identical life plans, nor plan to do everything together. The partners are separate beings who have created a third being, the couple, and the welfare of the couple is not served by imprisoning the partners within it. The couple should reserve itself those areas of mutuality which are fulfilling for both partners, and the partners need to discover what those are and can be. Beyond that, the value of the gift of being or having a partner is in serving as resources to each other in creating the life that the other is seeking.

Education
and Re-Education

CHAPTER

This chapter is the heart of the normative re-educative approach to planned change. The selection of articles to appear was difficult and, to a large degree, arbitrary, because of the large number of articles, books, and pamphlets available. There is a burgeoning set of articles, collections of articles, hand-books, and volumes on the theory, research, approaches, and techniques of the laboratory education or normative re-educative strategies of planned change. "The Laboratory Method of Changing and Learning: Theory and Application" (Palo Alto, California: Science and Behavior Books, 1975), by Benne, Bradford, Gibb, and Lippitt, is an extensive survey and his bibliographies of other publications on the differentiated aspects of personal growth, T-groups, laboratory education designs, small group processes, and Organizational Development. The uses of survey research and evaluation research and training are omitted from this chapter because they are increasingly technical and voluminous. The emphasis here is on the processes underlying the normative re-educative approaches.

It is a pleasure to reintroduce Lewin through Benne's article, "The Processes of Re-Education: An Assessment of Kurt Lewin's Views." Practitioners of planned change and applied behavioral scientists have long pointed to Lewin's role in the development of the field. By reviewing some of the original work by Lewin and Grabbe published in 1945, Benne shows the present continuity and modifications down to the seventies. For those concerned with their own intellectual rootage, this paper supplements the attributions typically made to Kurt Lewin's role and contributions as a social psychologist to an applied social science, namely the use of the small group, and force field analysis.

"Process Consultation" by Edgar Schein captures the concrete uniqueness of the set of activities on the part of the consultant which help the client to perceive, understand, and act upon the process events which occur in the client's environment. The client, that is, the manager in a work group, or the teacher-counselor with students, unfreezes values and perceptions, develops new diagnostic stances and skills, and creates new action structures in working with the processes in the work group or the school. Community mental health consultation (Caplan, "Types of Mental Health Consultation," in *The Planning of Change*, 2d Edition, 1969) has pioneered a parallel approach. In "Explorations in Consulting-Client Relationships," by Chris Argyris, the style of working and values as a consultant are contrasted with those of the organization. The consultants' ability to role-model a style for the clients was seriously hindered by the consultants' own needs and defensiveness.

Franklin, in "Toward the Style of the Community Change Educator," proposes that the community be viewed as a client system or systems learning to cope with or manage change. He contrasts the role of community change educator with the role of advocate. The place of a team in community change is often necessary due to the complex systems of groups in a community.

8.1 THE PROCESSES OF RE-EDUCATION: AN ASSESSMENT OF KURT LEWIN'S VIEWS

Kenneth D. Benne

Kurt Lewin was an inveterately hopeful man. Yet this hope was more than a general temperamental stance toward life and experience. It drew its substance from several deep value commitments. One of these was to science, not as a body of knowledge but as a way of life. Science, for Lewin, "is the eternal at-

This essay is a shortened version of a paper read at the celebration of the 25th anniversary of the Connecticut State Workshop on Intergroup Relations conducted at New Britain, Connecticut, in the summer of 1946. It was here that the T-group was discovered or invented. Staff members were Kurt Lewin, Kenneth D. Benne, Leland P. Bradford, Ronald Lippitt, Morton Deutsch, Murray Hurwitz, and Melvin Seeman.

tempt to go beyond what is regarded as scientifically accessible at any specific time." "To proceed beyond the limitations of a given level of knowledge, the researcher, as a rule, has to break down methodological taboos which condemn as 'unscientific' or 'illogical' the very methods or concepts which later on prove to be basic for the next major progress." Lewin, following the lead of one of his philosophy teachers, Ernst Cassirer, saw science as an adventuring into poorly known yet important areas of experience and an inventing of ways to gain dependable knowledge of those hitherto unknown or vaguely known areas. He had ventured early in his Berlin days to bring the study of human will and emotion into the range of psychological experimentation. In doing this, he had struggled "against a prevalent attitude which placed volition, emotion and sentiments in the 'poetic realm' of beautiful words, a realm to which nothing corresponds which could be regarded as 'existing' in the sense in which the scientist uses the term. . . . Although every psychologist had to deal with these facts realistically in his private life, they were banned from the realm of 'facts' in the scientific sense."[1]

This same commitment to the spirit of science as a human enterprise, as intrepid inquiry, in which current scientific taboos are overcome through bold theorizing and creative research designs and methods, had led Lewin, in his Iowa days, to collaborate with Ronald Lippitt and Ralph White in bringing small group processes into the ambit of experimental inquiry. Lewin was a theorizer and researcher. But he saw theory not alone as a way into significant inquiry and research but as a practical guide to reconstructive work in social practice and action as well.

Lewin was thus a moralist as well as a scientist. But he was decidedly not a moralistic moralist, in the sense of one who seeks to impose the principles of any established moral tradition upon the realities of contemporary conduct in order to control it within the confines of that tradition. His was rather a morality of reality-orientation toward confronting contemporary situations in their tensions and conflicts, a morality of focusing the cooperative human intelligences of those within those situations upon inventing ways of managing and improving them. The values to which he was most basic-

ally committed were thus methodological values, combining values inherent in scientific and democratic processes and methods.

Lewin's hope for cooperative action research as a way for human beings to solve their problems and manage their dilemmas represents best this dynamic fusion of democratic and scientific values. In a real sense, the whole Connecticut workshop was a project in cooperative action research. Ronald Lippitt's book on the workshop makes this clear.[2]

Kurt Lewin was moved by fears as well as by hopes. He was a Jew who had been driven out of his homeland by anti-Semitism become an article of official state policy in Hitler's Third Reich. His mother died in a Nazi gas chamber. He found strong currents of anti-Semitism, of racism, of ethnocentrism in his adopted country, the United States. He felt the contradictions between America's professed democratic commitment to the nurture of self-directing personalities and the self-hatred and self-rejection which persons within oppressed minorities avoided or overcame only with great effort and suffering. He saw democratic institutions eroded by the perpetuation of racial injustice and threatened by mounting and unresolved intergroup conflicts. He feared that the seeds of totalism might grow to destroy democracy in the United States and in the world unless the forces of research, education and action could be united in the eliminating of social injustice and minority self-hatred and in the wise resolution of intergroup conflicts. Kurt's fears reinforced the vigor of his efforts to serve his hopes and commitments.

The lure of learning answers to unanswered questions was a passion in Lewin, the man, the scientist, and the moralist. My fondest memories of Kurt

[1] All quotations from K. Lewin, "Cassirer's Philosophy of Science and Social Science," in Paul A. Schlipp (ed.), *The Philosophy of Ernst Cassirer* (New York: Tudor, 1949).

[2] R. Lippitt, *Training in Community Relations* (New York: Harper's, 1949).

in the Connecticut workshop are of his deep engagement in discussing the problems which participants laid before him. He was prepared to learn along with anyone—he seemed to be unusually free of status consciousness. He listened and questioned avidly. From time to time he would raise a finger of his right hand and say "Ah ha! Could it be this way?" And he would then propose a new conceptualization of the problem which more often than not opened up a new way of seeing it and new avenues toward solution. The lure of unanswered questions and of finding data which might lead toward better diagnoses and prognoses was strong in Kurt and in those who collaborated with him.

One central theme running through the concerns and curiosities of the mature Lewin and exemplified in the New Britain workshop is the theme of re-education. Through what processes do men and women alter, replace or transcend patterns of thinking, valuation, volition, overt behavior by which they have previously managed and justified their lives into patterns of thinking, valuation, volition, and action which are better oriented to the realities and actualities of contemporary existence, personal and social, and which are at once more personally fulfilling and socially appropriate? The processes are more complex than those of learning anew as any action leader, therapist, or teacher of adults knows from experience. They involve not extrinsic additions of knowledge or behavorial repertoire to the self or person but changes in the self, and the working through of self-supported resistances to such changes. And, since self-patterns are sustained by norms and relationships in the groups to which a person belongs or aspires to belong, effective re-education of a person requires changes in his environing society and culture as well.

About a year before the Connecticut workshop, Lewin, along with Paul Grabbe, formulated ten general observations on re-education.[3] These principles of re-education were not simple derivations from Lewin's field theoretical perspective on human conduct. They grew out of his attempt to interpret, out of that perspective, reports of a number of projects in re-education as various as Alcoholics Anonymous, a training program for police officers in intergroup prejudice, and a successful attempt to change a stereotype of older workers in an industrial organization.

What I propose to do is to assess these Lewinian generalizations in the light of the knowledge and know-how concerning re-education accumulated, in the twenty-five years of experience and experimentation with training, since their original publication. My assessment will, of course, reflect the limitations of my knowledge of these cumulative experiences in training and my own theoretical and value orientation.

Lewin's analysis assumed that effective re-education must affect the person being re-educated in three ways. The person's *cognitive* structure must be altered. And for Lewin this structure included the person's modes of perception, his ways of seeing his physical and social worlds, as well as the facts, concepts, expectations, and beliefs with which a person thinks about the possibilities of action and the consequences of action in his phenomenal world. But re-education must involve the person in modifying his *valences* and *values* as well as his cognitive structures. *Valences* and *values* include not alone his principles of what he should and should not do or consider doing—which along with his cognitive views of himself and his world are represented by his beliefs. They include also

[3] K. Lewin and P. Grabbe, "Conduct, Knowledge and Acceptance of New Values," *The Journal of Social Issues*, Vol. I, No. 3, August 1945.

his attractions and aversions to his and other groups and their standards, his feelings in regard to status differences and authority, and his reactions to various sources of approval and disapproval of himself. Re-education finally must affect a person's motoric actions, his repertoire of behavioral skills, and the degree of a person's conscious control of his bodily and social movements.

The complexities of re-educative processes arise out of the fact that they must involve correlative changes in various aspects of the person—his cognitive-perceptual structure, his valuative—moral and volitional—structure, and his motoric patterns for coping with his world(s). And changes in these various aspects of the person are governed by different laws and relationships. Thus re-education runs into contradictions and dilemmas. For example, a person's learning facts which run counter to his stereotypic attitudes toward members of an outgroup may actually lead to denial of this knowledge and increased guilt and more frantic defense of his stereotypes unless his valences and values are opened up, explored, and altered. And changed stereotypes may leave the person awkward in dealing with members of the outgroup, if his motoric skills have not been brought into line with his new cognitive and value orientation. This awkwardness may evoke responses in his trying to deal with members of the outgroup in new ways which reconfirm him in his old stereotypes or lead him to immobilization because of augmented inner conflicts. Re-educative experiences must be redesigned with the multi-faceted aspects of behavorial change in mind and designed further to help persons become aware of and responsible for the dilemmas and contradictions which arise out of this inescapable complexity. I believe that experiences with re-education since Lewin's formulation have confirmed his assumption that the "whole person" must

somehow be involved in processes of effective re-education.

Lewin's principles dealt with the complex interrelationships between changes in cognitive-perceptual orientation and value orientation. He did not deal with the involvement of motoric changes in their interrelationships with the other two. Experimentation with body movement and with behavioral conditioning in achieving behavioral change has thrived during the quarter of a century since Lewin wrote. And some of my supplementation of his principles of re-education arises from this fact.

1. Lewin stated his first principle as "The processes governing the acquisition of the normal and the abnormal are fundamentally alike." This principle breaks cognitively through the wall that has traditionally separated dealing re-educatively with persons manifesting "abnormal" behavior and with those who are seen as "normal" behaviorally. Behavioral abnormalities have been classified as pathological or as criminally or quasi-criminally deviant. Special personnel with special training, working in special settings with special techniques, have been developed to deal in segregated fashion with the therapy of the pathologically abnormal and rehabilitatively with the criminally deviant. "Education" for "the normal" has been sharply separated conceptually and institutionally from "therapy" for the pathological and "rehabilitation" for the deviant.

The wall between "education" on the one hand and "therapy" and "rehabilitation" on the other has been breached on many fronts—in mental health, in prison reform, and in converging movements between education and therapy. But the resistance to thinking about and dealing with re-education of persons as they are, normal and abnormal, and in the same processes is still powerful in the thinking and practice of most people. Probably, this is related generally to the persistence of class theoretical thinking as over against field theoretical thinking in the management of human affairs, a distinction with which Lewin, the philosopher of science, was much concerned. For people whose ways of thinking are class-theoretical, classifications devised as artifacts, as abstract tools of thought, not as representations of reality, "abnormal" and "normal" people, for example, are given the status of realities, with class membership constituting a difference of kind or substance for the individuals in the class. Field theoretical thinking about people and the processes of their re-education keeps a focus on the reality of concrete persons in their actual manifold relationships and situations and does not let abstract classifications of persons prescribe the mode or manner of their differential treatment. I see field theoretical thinking as highly desirable in contemporary analyses and management of human affairs. This Lewinian construction of a way of thinking about thinking seems to me both more conducive to the fuller actualization of humane values and to effectiveness in our policies and practices of education and re-education.

Controversies about what is "therapy" and what is "education" have dogged the development and extension of T-group practices since their inception. Actually, the lines between the two have become blurred in a number of ways, and rightly so in my opinion. Educational programs are slowly escaping the fetters of their traditional exclusive preoccupation with cognitive development and are taking responsibility for affective and volitional development as well. As this happens, expressive behavior which might once have been considered abnormal in educational settings is becoming legitimized as relevant to the idiosyncratic development of persons. In fact, we have discovered that behavioral manifestations in intensive group experiences which might once have been coded as pathological, and so to be avoided and repressed, are actually aspects, even necessary aspects, of processes of personal growth and self-discovery. The lines between the pathological and the growthful in behavior still need to be drawn. But training experiences, along with extensions from therapeutic practice into preventive mental health education, have shown that the lines are not easy to draw. As they are drawn, I hope they will be taken as practical judgments of re-education that persons require from time to time in their careers, not as a restoration of nonfunctional distinctions between the "normal" and "abnormal" which Lewin's first principle of re-education wisely repudiates.

2. The theory and practice of training is only beginning to catch up with Lewin's second principle—"The re-educative process has to fulfill a task which is essentially equivalent to a change in culture." Counseling and therapy have traditionally sought to facilitate changes in persons with little or no assumption of responsibility for facilitating changes in the cultural environment in which persons function outside the counseling or therapeutic setting. This tends to place the entire burden of behavioral adjustment or adaptation upon the individual. Changes in the cultural environment, which was involved in the dysfunctional behavior which brought the person to counseling or therapy, have not been focused upon in the re-educative process, which is ordinarily carried on in a specially designed setting apart from the social and cultural involvements of the person's ongoing life. There is now a tendency to involve significant other persons and their common culture in the process of reexamination, reevaluation, and commitment to change, along with the person who has felt the environmental stress most deeply—as in therapy for a family in place of or as adjunct to therapy for an individual family member; treatment of disturbed individuals in their home and work settings, not in

segregated situations, and so forth. In training, work with what Gibb has called embedded groups—work staffs, entire organizations, whole families—has come to supplement or to replace cultural island training of persons drawn away from their home settings. This involves changes in culture that are ideally consonant with and supportive of changes in personal knowledge, value orientation, or motoric skill achieved through training.

At the same time as organizational development and community development approaches to personal-social-cultural changing have come into being and spread, personal growth training in settings designedly abstracted from the outside roles and institutional involvements of participants have been developing in various laboratory programs and growth centers. These seem to focus on personal re-education with little or no assumption of responsibility for changes in the culture, outside the center, in which persons live and function most of their lives. Do the successes claimed for such programs contradict Lewin's second principle of re-education?

I do not think that they do. A counterculture has grown up in the United States (and outside as well) with norms that are markedly different from those of established culture. This counterculture has found social embodiment in communes of various sorts, in Hippie gatherings, in various associations of drop-outs from established institutional life. The manifestations of counterculture are often closer to the norms cultivated and in various degree internalized by participants in personal growth laboratories and centers—living in the moment, suspicion of deferred gratification, guidance of the choices of life by feelings, authenticity of personal expression as the prime virtue, and so on.

What we are seeing in certain developments in the training field is not an abrogation of the principle that effective personal re-education involves correlative changes in culture. It is rather a difference in the subculture of our national culture for which training is being conducted. It may be more accurate to say that community and organizational development streams in human relations training are more hopeful about the possibilities of reconstructing and humanizing established organizations and institutions than are those who train for participation in the counterculture. Trainers who see training for personal growth without reference to correlative training for social and cultural change as a way of changing established culture are, I think, denying the reality embodied in Lewin's second principle of re-education.

3. "Even extensive first hand experience does not automatically create correct concepts (knowledge)." Lewin leveled his third principle against re-educators who, aware that lectures and other abstract ways of transmitting knowledge are of little avail in changing the orientations or conduct of learners, see experience as such as the way to personal changing, including cognitive changes toward correct knowledge, which are required by effective re-education. He pointed out that thousands of years of human experiences with falling bodies did not bring men to a correct theory of gravity. What was required was specially constructed man-made experiences, experiments, designed to reach an adequate explanation of the phenomena of falling objects, in order to achieve a correct theory. Lewin was convinced that re-educative experiences must incorporate the spirit of experimental inquiry and, insofar as possible, the form of experimentation, if correct knowledge is to be the result. I believe that Lewin is correct. It is important to recognize that the principle opens to question the effectiveness of traditional classroom practices which seek to induce students to learn about the results of other people's in-

quiries and do not involve them in processes of inquiry in areas where their own beliefs are recognized by them to be vague, conflicting, or somehow in doubt. It is important to recognize also that the principle equally throws doubt upon the effectiveness of training where trainers and participants confuse having an exciting and moving experience with the achievement of adequate and transferrable learnings (cognitive changes).

In training, it takes time and effort for a group to learn a method of experimental inquiry where their own feelings, perceptions, commitments, and behaviors are the data to be processed in the inquiry. But this is the goal of responsible training. At least, experiences which have not been prehypothesized need to be reflected upon and conceptualized *post factum,* if valid learnings are to issue from the training process.

Actually this principle supports Lewin's advocacy of action research as a format for integrating personal re-education and social change into the same process. Action research when it is most valid achieves the form of field experimentation.

4. "Social action no less than physical action is steered by perception." The world in which we act is the world as we perceive it. Changes in knowledge or changes in beliefs and value orientation will not result in action changes unless changed perceptions of self and situation are achieved.

Developments in the training field since Lewin's day have reconfirmed this principle. And much of the development of training technology has been focused on ways of inducing people to entertain, try out and perhaps to adopt ways of perceiving themselves and their situations which are alternative to their habitual ways of perceiving. Openness to new knowledge and new valuations usually follows rather than precedes changes in perception. Habitual perceptions are chal-

lenged by open exchange of feedback between members of a group as they share their different responses to the "same" events. If a member attaches positive valence to other members of the group or to the group as a whole, he can accept different perceptions of other members as genuine phenomenological alternatives to his own ways of perceiving self and world. And he may then try to perceive and feel the world as others in his group perceive and feel it. In the process, his own perceptual frames may be modified or at least recognized as belonging to him and operating as one among many other constructions of social reality.

It is, I think, true that the most impressive developments in training technologies have been focused upon the inducing of perceptual change—more powerful forms of feedback, including the uses of audio and videotape, extending awareness of previously unnoticed processes and feelings, bodily and otherwise, as in Gestalt therapy, training in listening and in observation, psychodrama and fantasy experiences, experiences with the arts, and so on. These illustrate ways of cleansing, opening and refining the doors of perception, which have been developed over the years by practitioners and theorists of re-education. Lewin may have been a lonely phenomenologist among re-educators when he enunciated this principle twenty-five years ago. Most re-educators have become phenomenologists today.

5. "As a rule the possession of correct knowledge does not suffice to rectify false perceptions." This principle underlines the relative independence of processes of perception from processes of cognition and valuation in the organization of the person, a point already emphasized. Lewin did not recognize so fully as most trainers do today the close linkage between social perception and self-perception. Dynamically, I tend to see others in a way to support and main-

tain my image of myself. And I perceive myself in a certain way in order to justify myself to myself and to others. Only as the need to justify myself is reduced, as in a supportive, acceptant, loving social environment, can I freely experiment with alternative perceptions of myself and in turn with alternative perceptions of other people. Changes in self-perception and in social perception come about through "experimentation" in interpersonal relations at precognitive levels of experience.

6. "Incorrect stereotypes (prejudices) are functionally equivalent to wrong concepts (theories)." All of us who have studied prejudices in ourselves and others know how incorrect stereotypes can persist as ways of explaining the motivations and behavior of persons against the weight of evidence to the contrary. The story of the man who believed he was dead illustrates the point. His friends and his psychiatrist pointed out evidences to indicate that he was alive but the belief persisted. Finally, his psychiatrist got the man to admit that dead men don't bleed and gained his permission to prick his finger with a pin. When the blood came, the man, astonished, said, "Doctor, I was wrong. Dead men do bleed."

What Lewin was underlining here with respect to re-education of incorrect stereotypes was the inadequacy of experience as such to change a person's or group's theories of the world. Specially designed experiments which people design and carry out for themselves are required to instate new more adequate concepts in the place of those which they have held habitually. One condition of experimentation is for the experimenter to accept the fact of alternative conceptualizations of some event. The experimenter can then arrange experiences to furnish evidence for or against the alternative hypotheses in trying to determine which of the alternatives most adequately explains the evidence. In recognizing that an incorrect stereotype is functionally equivalent to a theory in his mental organization, the experimenter must develop and accept an ambivalence in himself toward the adequacy of his stereotype. Without ambivalence, the person sees no need to submit his stereotypes to an experimental testing.

Ambivalence toward one's habitual ways of explaining social events usually comes when consensual validation toward social events breaks down. Other people whose views he prizes explain the same event in ways different from his own. If he can acknowledge his ambivalence toward the stereotype, he can become active in gathering and evaluating evidence to disconfirm or confirm the stereotype or its alternative. Changes in stereotypes will ordinarily not occur until the person is involved as a self-experimenter with his own and alternative ways of explaining his social world. The self-experimenter must have an appropriate laboratory in which to work, both as a support to his persistence in arduous processes of self-inquiry and to furnish the data which the testing of his alternative hypotheses requires.

7. "Changes in sentiments do not necessarily follow changes in cognitive structures." Just as some of Lewin's earlier principles have urged the relative independence of processes of changing cognition and processes of changing perception, this principle stresses the relative independence of processes of cognitive change and changes in value orientation, action-ideology, or sentiment.

Lewin was quite aware that many re-educative attempts reach only the official system of values and do not involve the person in becoming aware of his own action-ideology, often nonconscious, which actually shapes his personal decisions and actions. Such superficial re-education may result in merely heightening the discrepancy between the superego (the way I ought to feel) and the ego (the way I actually do feel). The individual develops a guilty conscience. Such a discrepancy leads to a state of high emotional tension but seldom to appropriate conduct. It may postpone transgressions from the official ideology but it is likely to make the transgressions more violent when they do occur.

Subsequent training experience seems to bear out one factor of great importance in facilitating a person's reconsideration and reconstruction of his action-ideology, his sentiments or his value system. This is the degree and depth to which an individual becomes involved in seeing and accepting a problem with respect to the adequacy of his operating values. Lacking this involvement, no objective fact is likely to reach the status of a fact for the individual, no value alternative is likely to reach the status of a genuine alternative for the individual, and therefore come to influence his social conduct.

8. "A change in action-ideology, a real acceptance of a changed set of facts and values, a change in the perceived social world—all three are but different expressions of the same process."

It was a part of Lewin's great contribution to an understanding of re-education to emphasize the intimate connection between the development of a value system by a person and his growth into membership in a group. An individual becomes socialized through internalizing the normative culture of the groups to which he comes to belong. His value system is his own putting together, perhaps in a unique way, the various internalized normative outlooks of the significant associations which have contributed to the building of his social self—family, religion, age group, sex group, ethnic group, racial group, and so forth. Re-education, as it affects action-ideology, value orientation, perception of self and social world, is a process of re-socialization or, as Lewin tended to prefer, a process of re-enculturation. Re-education of persons thus requires their involvement in new

groups with norms that contrast in significant ways with those of the groups to which a person has previously belonged. The norms of the re-educative group must, as Lewin pointed out again and again, be those which support and require members to engage in experimental inquiry into their own socialization as it affects their present functioning and their development into the future. The norms of re-educative groups are thus not accidental. They are the norms of the social research community—openness of communication, willingness to face problems and to become involved in their solution, willingness to furnish data to facilitate own and other's inquiries, willingness to submit ambivalences and moot points to an empirical test, and so on. The material dealt with in the re-educative group is, of course, personal and social material. It is inquired into not alone in the interest of gaining more valid and dependable knowledge of interpersonal and social transactions in general but in the interest of rendering contemporary personal and social action more informed, more on target, more in line with clarified and chosen values, and in the further interest of narrowing the gap between internal intention and outer consequences in processes of decision and action.

Lewin's views of re-education helped the staff at New Britain to project out of their experience there the T-group as the prototype of the re-educative group. The T-group, as it developed, tended to focus on inquiry into interpersonal relationships between members and into the idiosyncratic aspects of member selves as they revealed themselves in T-group transactions. The typical T-group, whatever that may be, did not ordinarily explore directly the social selves of members, the effects of significant membership and reference groups upon members and their attempts to deal with each other in fruitful processes of inquiry and experimental action.

Max Birnbaum and I have been developing laboratory groups, which we call clarification groups, in which members are encouraged to inquire into their social selves.[4] The effects of memberships on action-ideology, value orientation, social perception, stereotypy are explored openly and directly. We like to think that this variation in laboratory training, which supplements rather than supplants T-groups and consultation with groups and group interfaces embedded within organizations and communities, is in line with Lewin's central interest in improving community and intergroup relations.

Lewin was quite aware of one dilemma which faces all re-educators. The principle of voluntarism, of free choice by persons to engage in self and social inquiry, is an important element in effective re-education. Yet the urgency of unsolved human problems leads all of us at times to force people into programs and processes of re-education. The maintenance of the principle of voluntarism is very difficult in field experiments in which entire social systems—schools, industries, community agencies—become involved. Lewin put the dilemma in this way—"How can free acceptance of a new system of values be brought about, if the person who is to be educated is, in the nature of things, likely to be hostile to the new values and loyal to the old?"

This, I believe, is a real dilemma. There is no neat solution to it. Training experience has indicated that two operating attitudes or stances of re-educators are very important in managing the dilemma. The first is an attitude of respect for resistance and a commitment to utilize the resources of the resistant in shaping plans for experimental action and its evaluation. The second is to seek ways of helping hostile rejectors to recognize that

[4] See Max Birnbaum, "The Clarification Group," chapter 15, in Benne, Bradford, Gibb, and R. Lippitt (Eds.), *The Laboratory Method of Changing and Learning* (Palo Alto, Calif.: Science and Behavior Books, 1975).

their stance of total rejection usually masks a genuine ambivalence and conflict within themselves. If they can accept this ambivalence within themselves, they are accepting the existence of a problem to be inquired into and so become candidates for voluntary involvement in the processes of its resolution.

9. "Acceptance of the new set of values and beliefs cannot usually be brought about item by item."

Lewin here points out the inescapable fact that a value system is a system. It must have an integrity of its own if it is to perform its function of helping persons maintain their identity and whole-heartedness in the choices which their conflicted environment thrusts upon them. Introducing new particular values which are not coherent with other values in the person's outlook on self and world may augument the inner conflict and compartmentalization, the reduction of which is a part of the motivation that brings persons into a process of re-education.

I think that many trainers, coming as many do out of indoctrination in social science which, however dubiously, claims value neutrality, avoid facing up directly to the dimension of inquiry into value orientation which is a necessary aspect of effective re-education. They may encourage participants to clarify feelings, to apply and test new concepts, and to practice skills of inquiry. They may avoid direct confrontation of differences among participants and themselves with respect to beliefs and ideologies. A piecemeal approach may be quite appropriate to skill development, expression of feelings, and even to conceptual clarification. It is, and here I agree with Lewin, inappropriate in the reconstruction of a value orientation. Some of us, in the training profession, have done some work in training for value inquiry. More work needs to be done.

10. "The individual accepts the new system of values and beliefs by accept-

ing belongingness in a group." This insight of Lewin's into the indispensability of groups as media of effective re-education and its basis in the nature of human socialization has already been emphasized. This fact of life is resisted by many persons made impatient by the urgency of recognized needs for behavioral change in various areas of pressing social issue. They frequently try to bypass the group participation which is required for behavioral changes—put it on TV, write more popular books on psychiatry and applied social science, pass a law, require people to change their behavior. I am not against any of these as aspects of programs of social change. But, taken as adequate means for the humanization and personalization of relationships in our bureaucratized mass society and culture in which loneliness, alienation, personal confusion, impotence are the lot of many if not most people, the counsel seems a counsel of despair not of hope. The counsel of hope seems to me to involve reconstruction of our organized life of social research, of education, and of social action. And the reconstruction will come only as collaboration between researchers, educators, and actionists comes to replace the self-segregation and autistic hostility which now tend to characterize their relationships. This was Kurt Lewin's vision of a re-educative society and it is one in which I gladly share.

Lewin and Grabbe's wise discussion of the implications of his tenth principle are worth quoting at length.

When re-education involves the relinquishment of standards which are contrary to the standards of society at large (as in the case of delinquency, minority prejudices, alcoholism), the feeling of group belongingness seems to be greatly heightened if the members feel free to express openly the very sentiments which are to be dislodged through re-education.

This might be viewed as another example of the seeming contradictions inherent in the process of re-education. Expression of prejudices against minorities or the breaking of rules of parliamentary procedures may in themselves be contrary to the desired goal. Yet a feeling of complete freedom and a heightened group identification are frequently more important at a particular stage of re-education than learning not to break specific rules.

This principle of in-grouping makes understandable why complete acceptance of previously rejected facts can be achieved best through the discovery of these facts by the group members themselves. . . . Then, and frequently only then, do the facts become really *their* facts (as against other people's facts). An individual will believe facts he himself has discovered in the same way that he believes in himself or in his group. The importance of this fact-finding process for the group by the group itself has been recently emphasized with reference to re-education in several fields. . . . It can be surmised that the extent to which social research is translated into social action depends on the degree to which those who carry out this action are made a part of the fact-finding on which the action is to be based.

Re-education influences conduct only when the new system of values and beliefs dominates the individual's perception. The acceptance of the new system is linked with the acceptance of a specific group, a particular role, a definite source of authority as new points of reference. It is basic for re-education that this linkage between acceptance of new facts or values and acceptance of certain groups or roles is very intimate and that the second frequently is a prerequisite for the first. This explains the great difficulty of changing beliefs and values in a piecemeal fashion. This linkage is a main factor behind resistance to re-education, but can also be made a powerful means for successful re-education.[5]

I would like now to comment briefly on an omission from Lewin's principles of re-education of which he was quite aware. You will recall that Lewin recognized three dimensions to effective re-education—cognitive and perceptual structures, values and valences, and motoric action—the individual's control over his physical and social movements. It was the third dimension which Lewin chose not to conceptualize. And it is the place of physical and social movements in processes of re-education which has become most controverted in the field of training and re-education generally in recent years.

I recognize three developments in which the motoric dimension of behavioral change has been focused upon and made the object of research and experimentation. The first arose within the Lewinian training movement itself. This was the attempt to define human relations skills and to devise opportunities for people to practice these skills for themselves with feedback near to the time of performance—both through simulation under laboratory conditions and through field practice under reality conditions. This development thrived as an adjunct to T-group experience in early laboratory designs. Then as the T-group, often under the ambiguous name of sensitivity training, tended to be taken as the complete process of re-education by some trainers and by many participants, interest in skill practice as an important part of re-education declined. Lately, new interest in structured experiences in human relations training has been manifested, and a number of guidebooks for trainers and groups have been published, outlining skill practice exercises which have been developed and tested over the years in the emerging training profession. I

⁵ Lewin and Grabbe, op. cit.

think this revised interest is a healthy one and should be encouraged. Let me suggest two cautions. First, "putting participants through" exercises before they have, in Lewinian language, been unfrozen, before they have seen reasons to change their concepts, perceptions, ideologies, or skill will likely leave little lasting deposit in their behavioral repertoire. Or it may leave them with new bags of tricks which are not integrated with altered and better integrated values, concepts, or perceptions and so can be utilized only mechanically rather than organically in their life and work.

Second, I tend to distrust prescriptions by trainers which do not grow out of a joint diagnosis by trainers and participants of their needs for skill development. If they are used openly and frankly as a tool for furnishing diagnostic data to trainers and participants, such use may avoid the timing error of putting the cart before the horse.

The second use of movement as an aid to re-education has arisen within the field of applied humanistic psychology, to which, in one sense, Lewinian psychology belongs. But these developments draw heavily on the more organismic psychologies of Wilhelm Reich and Fritz Perls, among others. These uses of movement draw heavily upon tactile and kinesthetic perception as a corrective to the more socialized and moralized visual and auditory perceptions and their chief tools of expression and communication—words. Experiences in nonverbal movement help to open up people to awareness of conflicts and discrepancies within themselves and between themselves and others in their social world. I believe that dissimulation and self-delusion is more difficult in tactile and kinesthetic perceptions than in verbalized reports of what people see and hear. And I have found nonverbal movements a useful tool to extend awareness to ordinarily nonconscious bodily processes, feelings, and emotional states. "Movement" can be effectively designed into overall programs and processes of re-education. I have two cautions which I would make about the use of experiences in nonverbal movement in training. First, it may increase the dependence of participants upon the trainer who knows the powerful technology which the participants do not know. It may thus, unwittingly, fail to develop the autonomy of participants in assuming more intelligent control of their own continuing socialization in the society in which they live. Second, the hesitation to verbalize the meaning of nonverbal experiences may militate against the conceptualization of the meanings of the experience which is a necessary part of transfer of learnings beyond the laboratory. For words are the tools of valid conceptualization as well as tools of obfuscation and self-delusion as they are often used.

The third emphasis on motoric action in re-education comes out of behavior therapy and is based on the rather strict behavioristic psychology, particularly of Skinner. I do not doubt the evidence of behavioral changes accomplished through reconditioning processes. I have grave doubts about the effects of such re-education upon the "inner" processes of valuing, conceptualizing, willing, which, on their own assumptions, behavior therapists do not take into account in their experimentation or in the evaluation of its results. I have more faith in re-education which helps persons bring their inner and outer behavior into more integral relationships through a process in which participants play a responsible part as researchers, educators, deciders of and for themselves.

My reassessment of Lewin's views of re-education has, I hope, convinced you, as it has convinced me, of their continuing fruitfulness in guiding continuing developments in the training field and in applied social science more generally.

8.2 PROCESS CONSULTATION

Edgar Schein

Managers often sense that all is not well or that things could be better, and yet do not have the tools with which to translate their vague feelings into concrete action steps. The kind of consultation I will attempt to describe . . . deals with problems of this sort. Process consultation does not assume that the manager or the organization knows what is wrong, or what is needed, or what the consultant should do. All that is required for the process to begin constructively is some *intent* on the part of someone in the organization to improve the ways things

From Edgar H. Schein, *Process Consultation: Its Role in Organization Development* (Reading, Mass.: Addison-Wesley Publishing Company, 1969), pp. 4–9.

are going. The consultation process itself then helps the manager to define diagnostic steps which lead ultimately to action programs or concrete changes.

Process consultation is a difficult concept to describe simply and clearly. It does not lend itself to a simple definition to be followed by a few illustrations. Instead, I will . . . give some perspective by contrasting P-C with more traditional consultation models.

HOW IS PROCESS CONSULTATION DIFFERENT FROM OTHER CONSULTATION?

We do not have in the field of management a neat typology of consultation processes, but a few models can be identified from the literature . . . and from my own experience in watching consultants work.

The Purchase Model

The most prevalent model of consultation is certainly the "purchase of expert information or an expert service." The buyer, an individual manager or some group in the organization, defines a need —something he wishes to know or some activity he wishes carried out—and, if he doesn't feel the organization itself has the time or capability, he will look to a consultant to fill the need. For example: (1) A manager may wish to know how a particular group of consumers feel, or how to design a plant efficiently, or how to design an accounting system which fully utilizes a computer's capability. (2) The manager may wish to find out how he could more effectively organize some group. This would require some surveying of their activities, attitudes, and work habits. (3) A manager may wish to institute a morale survey procedure for his production units, or an analysis of the quality of some complex product. In the first of the above examples, the manager desires *information;* in the latter two examples, he wishes to *purchase a service* from the consultant. In each of these cases there is an assumption that the manager knows what kind of information or what kind of service he is looking for. The success of the consultation then depends upon:

1. whether the manager has correctly diagnosed his own needs;
2. whether he has correctly communicated these needs to the consultant.
3. whether he has accurately assessed the capability of the consultant to provide the right kind of information or service; and
4. whether he has thought through the consequences of having the consultant gather information, and/or

the consequences of implementing changes which may be recommended by the consultant.

The frequent dissatisfaction voiced by managers with the quality of the services they feel they receive from their consultants is easily explainable when one considers how many things have to go right for the purchase model to work.

Process consultation, in contrast, involves the manager and the consultant in a period of *joint* diagnosis. The process consultant is willing to come into an organization without a clear mission or clear need, because of an underlying assumption that most organizations could probably be more effective than they are if they could identify what processes (work flow, interpersonal relations, communications, intergroup relations, etc.) need improvement. A closely related assumption is that no organizational form is perfect, that every organizational form has strengths and weaknesses. The process consultant would urge any manager with whom he is working not to leap into an action program, particularly if it involves any kind of changes in organizational structure, until the organization itself has done a thorough diagnosis and assessment of the strengths and weaknesses of the present structure.

The importance of *joint* diagnosis derives from the fact that the consultant can seldom learn enough about the organization to really know what a better course of action would be for that *particular group* of people with their *particular sets* of traditions, styles, and personalities. However, the consultant can help the manager to become a sufficiently good diagnostician himself, and can provide enough alternatives, to enable the manager to solve the problem. This last point highlights another assumption underlying P-C: problems will stay solved longer and be solved more effectively if the organization solves its own problems; the consultant has a role in teaching diagnostic and problem-solving skills, but he should not work on the actual concrete problem himself.

The Doctor–Patient Model

Another traditionally popular model of consultation is that of doctor–patient. One or more executives in the organization decide to bring in a consultant or team of consultants to "look them over," much as a patient might go to his doctor for an annual physical. The consultants are supposed to find out what is wrong with which part of the organization, and then, like a physician recommend a program of therapy. Often the manager singles out some unit of the organization where he is having difficulty or where performance has fallen off, and asks the consultant to determine "what is wrong with our—— department."

As most readers will recognize from their own experience, in spite of the popularity of this model it is fraught with difficulties. One of the most obvious difficulties is that the organizational unit which is defined as the patient may be reluctant to reveal the kinds of information which the consultant is likely to need in order to make his diagnosis. In fact, it is quite predictable that on questionnaires and in interviews systematic distortions will occur. The direction of distortion will depend upon the company climate. If the climate is one of mistrust and insecurity, the respondent is likely to hide any damaging information from the consultant because he fears that his boss will punish him for revealing problems; if the climate is one of high trust, the respondent is likely to view contact with the consultant as an opportunity to gripe, leading to exaggeration of problems. Unless the consultant spends considerable time *observing* the department, he is not likely to get an accurate picture.

An equally great difficulty in the doctor–patient model is that the patient is sometimes unwilling to believe the diagnosis or accept the prescription offered by the consultant. I suspect most companies have drawers full of reports by consultants, each loaded with diagnoses and recommendations which are either not understood or not accepted by the "patient." What is wrong, of course, is that the doctor, the consultant, has not built up a common diagnostic frame of reference with the patient, his client. If the consultant does all the diagnosis while the client-manager waits passively for a prescription, it is predictable that a communication gulf will arise which will make the prescription seem irrelevant and/or unpalatable.

Process consultation, in contrast, focuses on joint diagnosis and the passing on to the client of diagnostic skills. The consultant may recognize early in his work what some of the problems are in the organization and how they might be solved. He does not advance them prematurely, however, for two reasons. One, he may be wrong and may damage his relationship with the client by a hasty diagnosis which turns out to be wrong. Two, he recognizes that even if he is right, the client is likely to be defensive, to not listen to the diagnosis, to misunderstand what the consultant is saying, and to argue with it.

It is a key assumption underlying P-C that the client must learn to see the problem for himself, to share in the diagnosis, and to be *actively involved* in generating a remedy. The process consultant may play a key role in helping to sharpen the diagnosis and in providing alternative remedies which may not have occurred to the client. But he encourages the client to make the ultimate decision as to what remedy to apply. Again, the consultant does this on the assumption that if he teaches the client to diagnose and remedy situations, problems will be solved more permanently and the client will be able to solve new problems as they arise.

It should be emphasized that the process consultant may or may not be expert in solving the particular problem which is uncovered. The important point in P-C is that such expertise is less relevant than are the skills of involving the client in self-diagnosis and helping him to find a remedy which fits his particular situation and his unique set of needs. The process consultant must be an expert in how to diagnose and how to develop a helping relationship. He does not need to find an expert resource in those areas, finance, and the like. If problems are uncovered in specific areas like these, the process consultant would help the client to find an expert resource in those areas, but he would *also* help the client to think through how best to get help from such an expert.

ASSUMPTIONS UNDERLYING PROCESS CONSULTATION

Let me pull together here the assumptions stated thus far. I have said that P-C assumes that:

1. Managers often do not know what is wrong and need special help in diagnosing what their problems actually are.
2. Managers often do not know what kinds of help consultants can give to them; they need to be helped to know what kind of help to seek.
3. Most managers have a constructive intent to improve things but need help in identifying what to improve and how to improve it.
4. Most organizations can be more effective if they learn to diagnose their own strengths and weaknesses. No organizational form is perfect; hence every form of organization will have some weaknesses for which compensatory mechanisms need to be found.

5. A consultant could probably not, without exhaustive and time-consuming study, learn enough about the culture of the organization to suggest reliable new courses of action. Therefore, he must work jointly with members of the organization who *do* know the culture intimately from having lived within it.
6. The client must learn to see the problem for himself, to share in the diagnosis, and to be actively involved in generating a remedy. One of the process consultant's roles is to provide new and challenging alternatives for the client to consider. Decision-making about these alternatives must, however, remain in the hands of the client.
7. It is of prime importance that the process consultant be expert in how to *diagnose* and how to *establish effective helping relationships* with clients. Effective P-C involves the passing on of both these skills.

DEFINITION OF PROCESS CONSULTATION

With these assumptions in mind, we can attempt to formulate a more precise definition of P-C.

P-C is a set of activities on the part of the consultant which help the client to perceive, understand, and act upon process events which occur in the client's environment.

The process consultant seeks to give the client "insight" into what is going on around him, within him, and between him and other people. The events to be observed and learned from are primarily the various human actions which occur in the normal flow of work, in the conduct of meetings, and in formal or informal encounters between members of the organization. Of particular relevance are the client's own actions and their impact on other people.

It should be noted that this definition brings in several new concepts and assumptions, relating in general to what one looks for in making one's *diagnosis*. The important elements to study in an organization are the human processes which occur. A good diagnosis of an organizational problem may go beyond an analysis of such processes but it cannot afford to ignore them. By implication, the process consultant is primarily an expert on processes at the individual, interpersonal, and intergroup levels. His expertise may go beyond these areas, but it must at the minimum include them. Improvement in organizational effectiveness will occur through effective problem finding in the human process area, which in turn will depend upon the ability of man-

agers to learn diagnostic skills through exposure to P-C.

I am not contending that focusing on human processes is the *only* path to increasing organizational effectiveness. Obviously there is room in most organizations for improved production, financial, marketing, and other processes. I am arguing, however, that the various functions which make up an organization are always mediated by the interactions of people, so that the organization can never escape its human processes. . . . As long as organizations are networks of people, there will be processes occurring between them. Therefore, it is obvious that the better understood and better diagnosed these processes are, the greater will be the chances of finding solutions to technical problems which will be accepted and used by the members of the organization.

8.3   EXPLORATIONS IN CONSULTING-CLIENT RELATIONSHIPS

Chris Argyris

I should like to explore the role of the consultant based upon an analysis of two cases of a particular consultant group. Obviously one cannot generalize very much from such restricted data. This descriptive and exploratory report has as its objective the delineation of some issues and the generation of hypotheses. It marks the first stage of a long-range program whose ultimate goal is the development of appropriate models to understand the client-consultant relationship

Chris Argyris, "Explorations in Consulting-Client Relationships." Reproduced by permission of the Society for Applied Anthropology from *Human Organization*, 20 (3), 1961.

and its impact on organizational change and development.

THE NATURE OF THE DATA AVAILABLE

The consultants studied have had at least several years of experience as a team offering consulting advice to any unit within the corporation which requests it. Typically, they make notes of all their activities during each day in the field. These notes vary greatly in detail and scope. Although the policy followed is to record one's notes as soon as possible, there are times when there is a delay of several days.

I was given access to all the personal notes of all the consultants. Also, all the files were open for my use and study. According to my count, I read over three thousand pages of notes and research reports. I was given the freedom to interview anyone that I wished on the team or at the plants. Because of the exploratory nature of the study, I limited my interviews and discussions to the consultants. Although I had the complete cooperation of everyone, the nature of the data available does not permit us to reach any conclusions. The most that we can do is to raise questions for further research and indulge in some hypothesizing as to what might have happened if the consultants and the clients behaved differently.

I have selected two cases from the files which I believe best illustrate the problems which I wish to discuss. The selection is, therefore, *not* a random one. It is specifically loaded in the difficulties which consultants face. Consequently, the reader should not infer that the material accurately represents the competence, activities, and successes of the consultants.

THE VALUES OF THE CONSULTANT GROUP

If we are to ascertain the effectiveness of the consultants, it is important to learn their objectives. What are they offering the client? Once having ascertained their objectives, then we may explore the degree to which they are able to achieve them. We may hypothesize that the consultants' effectiveness will tend to increase as the degree to which they achieve their objective increases.

The consultants studied offered professional assistance in the field of human relations. They view their overall objective as helping an organization solve its problems in such a way that it becomes more competent in solving the same or a similar class of problems without the

continued help of the consultants. Thus we can ask at the end of the paper if the clients have resolved their problems in such a way that they no longer need the consultants.

There is another dimension along which insights can be obtained regarding the effectiveness of the consultants. They believe that there is a hierarchy of values whose fulfillment will tend to enhance the effectiveness of human relationships within organizations. These values are particularly relevant to our study. They may be outlined as follows.

1. Two important and interrelated components of administrative competence may be described as technical, intellective competence and interpersonal competence. Both levels of competence are important. If either or both is low, or if either is significantly higher than the other, administrative difficulties will tend to arise.[1]
2. Interpersonal competence, the consultants believe, tends to increase as the executive:
   a. becomes more aware of himself and of his impact upon others.
   b. solves human problems in such a way that the same or a similar class of problems do not recur.
3. These two components of interpersonal competence will tend to increase as executives are able in their relationships to:
   a. give and receive feedback about self and others so as to create minimal defensiveness in self and others.
   b. own, and to help others own their feelings, values and attitudes.
   c. remain open to new values and

[1] Empirical research will be required to define the point at which interpersonal competence is low or the point where the gap between the two is too large.

attitudes and help others to experience the same.

d. experiment with new values and attitudes and help others to do the same.[2]

From the above we may hypothesize that the consultants will perceive that they are achieving their objective as the clients begin to give and receive feedback with minimal defensiveness, to own their feelings, etc. But, as we shall see in a moment, in order for the consultants to be of help to the client along these dimensions they (the consultants) must behave according to these values. The consultants must behave *genuinely* which we may define as behaving in accordance with one's values.[3] But to behave genuinely is not enough. It is important to behave genuinely in such a way that others (in this case the clients) have freedom to behave genuinely. Whenever human relationships are established where genuineness is possible on the part of *both* parties, they may be defined as *authentic*. Individuals cannot be authentic; authenticity is a property of interpersonal relationships. In our terms, the consultant hopes to influence his client to learn to establish more authentic relationships within the firm. In order to accomplish this, the consultant must also strive to establish authentic relationships in his relations with the client.

THE DILEMMA OF THE CONSULTANT

Formal organizational strategy tends to reward communication, openness, experimentation on the rational level. It tends to penalize openness, levelling, and experimentation on the interpersonal and emotional levels.[4] This, in turn, tends to decrease the participants' interpersonal competence within the organization.[5]

The emphasis upon rationality tends to create an organizational culture in which feelings are considered to be "bad," "immature," "irrational," and many times irrelevant. For example, in a recent study of a top management group (N = 18), all but one reported that:

. . . personal feelings should be kept out of group meetings.

. . . if people did become emotional it would be the leader's responsibility to bring them back to the facts being discussed.

. . . if the personal feelings continued the leader should call off the meeting and talk to the individuals involved separately.[6]

The point I am trying to make is that it is not possible for this type of consultant to help an organization deal

---

[2] The major activities of the consultant group reside in the area of increasing interpersonal effectiveness within the organization. Because the consultants focus in this area it should not be interpreted to mean that the consultants do not feel that there are other areas which are as relevant to administrative competence and organizational development. The consultants recognize the importance of environmental and organizational factors and do include these in their studies whenever they feel they are relevant to the solution of the problem.

[3] The concept of genuineness is, I believe, similar to and most certainly stimulated by Dr. Carl Roger's concept of congruence.

[4] Chris Argyris, *Personality and Organization,* Harper & Row, Publishers, New York, 1957.

[5] The degree to which each of these generalization holds in real life is a matter of empirical study. I am predicting, however, that the overall trend would be in the direction implied in the propositions.

[6] Chris Argyris, "Toward a Theory of Authentic Relationships," mimeographed report, Yale University, Fall, 1960.

with its interpersonal difficulties and with those organizational problems that have an interpersonal base without helping the clients to deal with feelings and emotions. Yet these are the very factors that the clients would tend to find painful, and which they have "learned" to consider as signs of "immaturity" and "incompetence."

A consultant therefore, who wishes to help an organization learn to solve its own interpersonal difficulties is faced with a serious dilemma. He believes that in order for him to be of help he may have to ask the client to consider values that are fundamentally different from those upon which the organization, its controls, and his leadership pattern are based. For example, instead of considering feelings and emotions as irrelevant in administration (as is the case of most of industry) he sees them as being central to the resolution of human problems and the enhancement of openness, accurate information flow, trust, and an attitude of experimentation and risk taking.[7]

As such, the consultant will probably be threatening to the members of the organization. Quite understandably, the members will tend to question seriously the necessity for the reduction of hostility, tension, interpersonal rivalries, etc. They may be even more skeptical about the consultant's assumption that openness, trust, feedback, experimentation, etc., if increased, will tend to alleviate significantly some of the problems that they have come to perceive as part of organizational life.

One of the best ways a client has to test the effectiveness of the consultant's ideas is to see if his "product" works. In most cases the client has to wait until the consultant is finished before be can make such a judgment. However, in the case of the consultant offering to increase the effectiveness of the human relation-

[7] Ibid.

ships, the client can actually begin to test the validity of the consultant's approach from the outset of the relationship. If the consultant's views of effective human relationship are valid and effective, the client reasons, I should be able to evaluate the consultant by seeing if he (the consultant) uses them while attempting to help the organization change and develop. If the consultant does not use his views to stimulate effective changes, why should the client adopt them in his relationships within the organization? Moreover, the client can increase the difficulty of the test which the consultant has to pass by simply increasing the forcefulness with which he apparently adheres to his ideas and "rejects" the consultant's. If, as the consultant attempts to help the client change, he does not behave consistently with his ideas and values then why should the client use these ideas and values?

The consultant is in a very difficult position. If he behaves according to his ideas and values, he stands a good chance of being a threat to the client. He could be asked to leave. If he decides to behave even temporarily in accordance with the client's values, he may be accepted but he runs a serious risk of failing to change and develop.

CASE A

Let us begin with the consultants feeding back their results of a systematic interview-questionnaire diagnosis to the top management of plant A. The comments emphasized such findings as: 1) the employees report a barrier between themselves and the management, 2) the employees feel uninformed, and consequently 3) tend to feel confused and "left out" while at the same time, 4) they fear to communicate upward their feelings of mistrust. These findings were digested by the top management for several weeks before they invited the consultants to the plant for further consultations. A meeting was held where the results were again discussed.

Two of the consultants reported their impressions about the meeting:

Consultant A

This meeting was interesting in that the plant manager was neither outspoken nor defensive. We reviewed some of the highlights of the findings and certain members of the management committee discussed these in the meeting in his office. The meeting did not have too much spark until one of the young technical men started to express resentment in terms of being critical, partly of the accuracy of our findings, and partly of the fact that some of their employees were disloyal in the type of comments they made. Otherwise, most of the management committee seemed to be accepting the findings in the report, although admittedly they were not very vocal in expressing suggestions as to how to bring improvements.

Consultant B

At this meeting the newest department head was most angrily defensive about the report. His clear expression made it possible to focus the issues, openly face the fact that the report was a "hot potato," and also that necessity which fully justifies management actions could produce some unwanted results.

The meeting ended with the issue of what to do next up in the air. No one quite knew how the plant manager felt. There was an assumption that he would make a decision, but he did not make any.

The Consultants Do Not Behave According to Their Values

The consultants as well as many of the subordinates reported that they felt frustrated and had a sense of incompleteness as a result of the plant manager's silence. However, this frustration and concern was not communicated. They were not being open or leveling. Instead someone asked if the results should be fed back to the next lower level of management. The discussion was guarded and most looked toward the plant manager for his views. He decided, and the subordinates "agreed," that it would be best to give only a summary or "light" report of the findings.

This was done. The consultants attended the meeting where the data were fed back to the lower management in a summary form. They reported that,

. . . the reaction of the supervisors at this point is that the survey had not accomplished very much.

However, added the consultants, the supervisors were not too disappointed because,

. . . their expectations had not been too high that any public reporting of the data would be any more explicit than it was.

Here we see the consultants exposed to a situation where they chose not to behave according to their values. The plant manager, they reasoned, was not ready to discuss his feelings about the report, no less his interpersonal impact upon those at the meeting.

The Impact of the Consultants' Behavior

The immediate "payoff" for the consultants is that they are still in the "good graces" of the plant manager. But this is obtained at a cost. The first part of the cost is that the plant manager has living evidence that under stress the consultants do not tend to behave in accordance with their values. On the contrary, they use the values of the client system. Why then should he change? A second part of the cost is that those present at the meeting also see that the consultants behave in accordance with the values of the client-system. Understandably, they may also have questions about the validity and practicality of the consultants' values. Moreover, they can also interpret the consultants' actions as being submissive toward the plant manager. If this is the case, they may reason, the plant manager may have the consultants under his control. Perhaps they had best be careful in "leveling" with the consultants. Finally we note from the consultants' reports that the subordinates who viewed the feedback at a separate meeting concluded that "nothing had changed or would come of the research." Therefore, as some suggested later on, they concluded that the consultants might be "on the top management side" or at least certainly associated with the status quo.

To summarize, the costs for the consultants of going along with the client-system values seem to be fourfold. All the members of the client system may begin to have decreased confidence in the consultants and especially in the values that they represent. Second, the subordinates may begin to view the consultants as agents of the plant manager. Third, the consultants, unknowingly let themselves and their research create an administrative situation in which the client-system values and the status quo are reenforced. Fourth, the clients may have learned that if enough pressure is placed upon the consultants they can be manipulated to change their values. This conclusion may make the clients feel more secure in that they can "control" the consultants. However, this "control" can also act to increase deeper fears and insecurities because it is not comforting to know that one's consultant can be as nongenuine as the client he is attempting to help.

Another alternative action for the consultants would have been to behave in accordance with their values. They

could have told the plant manager during the meeting that they felt a sense of frustration and incompleteness. They might have asked the group if others felt as they did. Finally, they could have, again at the group meeting (or later in private if necessary) predicted for the plant manager some of the impacts outlined above. This could help him to see more clearly his impact upon the organization and prevent the reenforcement of the feelings of being left out, mistrusted, etc., reported in the diagnostic survey. More about this in the final section.

The Client-System Values Become Reenforced

Returning to the consultants, their notes suggest that they were aware of not behaving according to their values. However, they reported, this was necessary if they were to be asked to remain in the organization. They also reported that since they did not upset the plant manager they were in a better position to be of help to him.

The consultants held a meeting with the plant manager. They reported that they were able to convince the plant manager, "that a job lay ahead to develop the subordinates" especially in "leveling," "openness," "interpersonal impact," etc. Note that the plant manager was not told that he also may need such help. Moreover, the consultants suggested the establishment of a "steering committee" to help plan the laboratory.

The plant manager agreed. A Steering Committee was created whose task it was to examine the survey results to explore what ought to be done for organization improvement. As a result of the committee's meetings a decision was reached to hold a three-day workshop program where the survey results would be studied in detail by all the management to stimulate self-analysis.

The planning of the meetings was

masterminded by one of the consultants. He wrote that he felt he had to engineer the programs since the committee lacked the concept of a "laboratory" program. He continued that he:

. . . is able to move them in the direction of the laboratory design.

The consultant being quite secure and extremely competent also noted,

. . . in this respect our meeting had been almost comic. I had insisted that the program was the Committee's or the management's and that my role was only to help them design it. However, I consistently felt that I should be designing the program since they didn't know how to. Of course, this eventually worked out into my doing so.

Thus we see that, in order to take some action, the consultants again had to behave in ways which reflect the values of the client system. They influenced the plant manager to approve training which he and few others in the client-system fully understood. Moreover, they created a Steering Committee to give the subordinates a greater feeling of participation. Yet they admittedly manipulated the members to go in the direction that they (the consultants) desired. All this was done in order "to get results."

This need, on the part of the consultants, to "get on the with job" is exactly what the clients desire. They can use it to manipulate the consultant to become responsible for planning and carrying out the change programs. The dependent relationship that the client has with the top management, he (the client) now creates with the consultant.

An example for the consultant's report that illustrates the points being made is:

Members of the Steering Committee made it clear [to the consultant] they felt some pressure to get going, the pressure coming partly from their own feelings of frustration about lack of decision, and in part because they thought management was breathing down their necks with respect to some proposals. The comment was made in a joking manner that we'd better get something going in order to have something to submit to the manager. The time of the next committee meeting was set up at this time and I was invited to attend.

In this example, the committee tries to communicate their sense of frustration and urgency to the consultant. However, they also imply to the consultant that, along with them, *he* is now responsible for the success or failure of the project. If the consultant accepts the responsibility, he has unwittingly placed himself in a traditional leadership position within the group. Under these conditions, the consultant soon begins to feel that he *is* responsible for doing the creative thinking about what the committee ought to discuss during the next meeting.

Apparently this is what happens. The consultant, after listening to the above, develops an excellent list of questions which, as he states,

It seems to me the committee should give attention to.

For example:

What is the plant manager's image of the desired direction which the company should go?

How are the goals used by the people at headquarters, to whom the plant manager reports, department heads and superintendents, operating management, and non-management?

How much motivation is there to carry them out?

How about people's skills for carrying them out effectively?

What is required for movement toward these goals:

By the management group.

The work force?

What obstacles can be anticipated?

Action plans:

Communicating the committee's report and recommendations to the manager.

The manager cutting the rest of the management group in communicating the plan to the non-management group.

The first event in the improvement program.

These are important questions. However, in defining them as an agenda for the clients, the consultant becomes responsible for the group's diagnosis. In taking the initiative, the consultant again influences the clients to become dependent upon him. Such a requirement is congruent with the client's expectations and values, but not with the consultant's.

One wonders what would have happened if the consultant asked the group members why they were telling him about their failures and pressures. If, as he feels, this is an attempt by the clients to induce him to internalize their pressures and anxieties, he might profitably raise the issue. This would be an excellent opportunity for the committee to begin to become aware that they will seriously impair the consultant's potential contribution if they try to make him behave according to their values. If he is to be of help, he ought not to be controlled by the very values which are the cause of their problems. Assuming these problems are worked through, then the consultant can help the group to develop its own list of questions. In doing so he places the emphasis upon the clients developing their own questions. He shows, by his actions, that he believes 1) clients can, through such activity, learn much about one another, their organizations, and the requirements of effective group problem solving, 2) that it is the group

members who will have to take the action and thus should participate in the diagnosis, 3) which, in turn, would begin the process of decreasing the clients' dependence upon the consultant.

Returning to our case, the consultants actually planned and held several different types of short laboratories. The attendees reported positive feelings about the programs. Generally they reported that they had been helped to understand one another's job, as well as to set the ground work for some concrete changes to be made in the practices as well as the organization of work. The data available suggested that some of these changes were carried out and other changes were planned and also carried out.

Although the men reported new and enlarged awareness about the difficulties of their fellow managers in getting the job done, the data suggested that this behavior did not change very much. Also, there was evidence that the enthusiasm for change was highest when the consultants were present. This sign of dependence of the clients upon the consultants did not disturb the plant manager. Indeed, he reported satisfaction that concrete tasks of important value to the plant were being accomplished.

The plant manager had no reason to be disappointed in the process by which these jobs were being done. It was the same one that he used in his relationships with the subordinates. The fact that the manager had established dependent relationships with the consultants did not displease him as long as actions were being taken. The consultants are now being perceived by the plant manager as resource people to be used by his subordinates in order to accomplish specific tasks. Little thought is being given to the original objective of helping the clients examine their basic values and interpersonal relationships. It is interesting to note that the consultants were lauded by the plant manager to their (the consultants') superior because:

> . . . they were not forcing themselves upon the plant and letting themselves be used as the plant members saw fit.

One of the consultants was not content with the compliment. He wrote:

> While this compliment sounds encouraging, I still have some feelings of uneasiness about the relationship. I think the main source of it now is that when I call the plant manager he is usually, in fact, almost always tied up at a meeting. Although I ask that he call me back he seldom does so. One day—I arranged an appointment with him to review how things were going. However, although I was there for a full half day, I was able to spend only approximately forty-five minutes with him, and this between telephone calls and other forms of interruption.

This is an excellent illustration of the human relationships which are typical of the client system. One possible reason is that the need for the consultant is now not as great. The plant manager may feel that he has received as much help as he can from the consultant. Another possibility is that, since the consultants have been incorporated and become so much a part of the client system, they no longer can put into use the skills and knowledge that they have regarding opening and facilitating effective change. Moreover, if the client can no longer see much difference between the consultants and the other members of the client system, there is no major reason to show any high interest in them. Finally, from research in clinical psychology and psychotherapy, we may hypothesize that a client can decrease his confidence in the consultant if he feels that he can manipulate the consultant to accept his (the client's) values and goals. A client will

probably not respect an individual who, in the face of stress, takes on the values and norms of the client culture. That is the very reason the client needs help.

We continue to describe other events. They would primarily illustrate that the consultants had achieved great success in helping the organization accomplish certain specific tasks. However, the success does not seem as great in the area of interpersonal effectiveness. The consultants began their relationships with a strategy to behave according to the values of the client system until they had achieved acceptance by the top management and helped the clients to accomplish specific work tasks. This did indeed win compliments. However, it also created a chain reaction where the plant manager and the other clients induced the consultants to behave according to the client-system values. The consultants were never able to break away from this chain reaction. Although they were able to help some of the clients to explore their values, the impact was never very great. In short, they became "accepted" by becoming *a part* of the client system. They were not accepted as consultants with a set of different values whose effectiveness the client-system ought to explore seriously.

CASE B

The second case begins with the consultants' explorations at a particular plant. Upon conducting a reconnaissance, the consultants concluded that, since the management group was relatively free of suspicion of consultants, the latter might be able to create a program which would help "to free" the clients (management and employees) in such a way as to release their potential. Moreover, because the organization was relatively small, they might be able to offer a two-pronged tailor-made program which could help achieve the management's objectives. The first prong was an

. . . emphasis on organization improvement rather than crisis or criticism.

The consultants believed that such an emphasis would steer away from the plant's history of difficult problems and relations thereby decreasing the clients' defensiveness and simultaneously emphasizing progress to be made in the future. In the opinion of the consultants such a strategy would lead to minimal client resistance. In the consultants' opinion this would make it easier for the clients to accept the idea of an organization improvement project.

The second prong was the consultants' desire to help the top management: 1) to

get [their] people to take a responsible lead in this work so that it is not just [top management's] program,

2) to prove that their objective is a desirable change, 3) that they had confidence in the organization, 4) that they are not criticizing, that they are seeking consulting help to build for the future, and 5) that they are not trying to import "any packaged program."

It is interesting to note a contradiction in the consultants' behavior. On the one hand, there is the consultants' desire to help the plant manager make this *his* program so that *his* people would, in time, make it *their* program. On the other hand, is the fact that the consultants develop the prognosis with little or no participation from the clients. Assuming that the prognosis is valid, and assuming that it is accepted by the management, then one can predict that the plant manager will tend to develop a dependency relationship with the consultants. The plant manager will tend to feel that the program is not his but the consultants', to the extent that he accepts what they tell

him they think he ought to do. One may also hypothesize that, if the above happens, it will decrease the probability that the subordinates will feel this is their program.

Another example of how the consultants tend to control the relationship with the client is when they decide unilaterally that the plant manager

. . . might consider improving upward communication: to signal ways he wants to operate.

Since the consultants believe the problems lay at the top, it would be necessary, they reason, to reassure the plant manager of his effectiveness and give him a chance to talk out his problems and ideas. Thus, once the top jobs are clarified as to scope and duties, it would be possible to reach out for new ideas.

If this strategy is valid, then the plant manager will be moved in the right direction *because of the consultants' prognostic* skills. But, the problem of the plant manager is to improve his own prognostic skills. A way for him to become more effective and simultaneously to decrease his need for the consultants would be for them to help him learn how to diagnose as effectively as they do.

THE PROJECTED SURVEY

The consultants recommended to the plant manager that a survey program be conducted to help the management people

. . . dig out and clarify their own goals and then find ways to attain them.

They also pointed out that,

. . . the consultants would act as if they were outside consultants. . . . All data would be for the local plant only. None would be communicated to higher authorities without clearance with the authorities at the local level.

The plant manager accepted the project. He suggested that the consultants explain it to Mr. Brown, an "old timer," who, according to the plant manager, feels hurt because he expected to become a plant manager but never made it. The plant manager also suggested that the projected survey be discussed with the top management Committee (hereafter known as the committee). The consultants agreed.

Mr. Brown apparently resisted the consultants and their program. He questioned if the people would tell the truth. The consultants decided not to help Mr. Brown explore his fears toward them, research, and the past. Rather they attempted to allay his fears by pointing out,

That they were not interested in looking backward, in studying the mistakes of previous managers or in studying the plant's morale, but rather that the focus would be on the future.

One may question the effectiveness of asking Mr. Brown to forget fears which are related to the past by assuring him that the consultants will do so. The consultants note, among themselves,

At the end of the meeting, Mr. Brown appeared to understand what the consultants were going to do from the point of view of the procedures involved in the survey. There is no evidence of support for the idea . . . the notion of organization improvement was not accepted or even understood by Mr. Brown.

Nor did they communicate to him their impression that in their opinion he is,

. . . an incessant talker, oblivious to listener reaction and very insensitive to his own needs and power.

This diagnosis may be correct. But is it not equally correct that one reason that the consultants did not "level" with Brown (a value which they hold) was because they were responding to their own needs? The consultants probably felt that it was best not to "level" with Mr. Brown lest this explode their projected survey.

The following day, the consultants held their meeting with the committee. They were introduced by the plant manager who told his subordinates: 1) that he wanted the consultants to be of help,

2) emphasized that he believes there is potential gain in having an outside group observe and lend assistance, and 3) by being particularly careful to say that, in his opinion, there was not necessarily anything wrong at the plant, but under the best of circumstances one can look for ways to do a better job.

How helpful is this introduction of the plant manager to the consultants and to the clients? How is this project going to become the subordinates' if they come to a meeting where 1) they are told to accept the consultants, 2) they sense the plant manager's defensiveness when he says that the consultants are not looking for anything to criticize, and 3) that they are told the organization is not doing an effective job? How helpful is this approach if everyone concerned feels that there *is* something wrong? If there are not weaknesses why hold the survey? Will not this approach be perceived by the subordinates as more of the top management

. . . diplomatic talk that is always going on?

If so, what will be their view of the consultants if this management nonauthenticity is sanctioned by them? Is this not an opportunity to test the consultants to see if they really mean that "openness" is a good thing? If so, then the consultants tend to enhance the difficulties since they not only refrain from exploring the problem above but they sanction it by taking the same approach. They emphasize that they are not interested in the past, that they are not making a checkup of employee morale, and that they are interested in the future and how the consultants might help the management better to achieve their goals for the future.

If the consultants want the subordinates to make this their project, then why do they not find out if the subordinates want the same? Moreover, how will they be perceived by the subordinates when the findings are released and the majority of them deal with their morale? Is the consultants' strategy more of a response to the plant manager's anxieties about getting the project accepted, than a logically thought through plan which takes into account the total management group?

The consultants reported that the committee attitude appeared, on the surface, excellent, and that almost immediate joviality

. . . was used to mask feelings and keep conflict from becoming overt.

Here is an incisive hypothesis but the consultants do not explore its possible validity with the clients. The consultants also note that the committee does not function as a decision-making body. The consultants would not think of resisting the plant manager's proposal with the possible exception of Mr. Brown.

Why are these hypotheses not checked? One reason may be that the consultants want to refrain from doing anything which will upset the committee and doom the survey. Another may be that they believe that they ought not to begin to confront the committee until after the survey when the consultants will know much more about the clients. Finally, it may be that the consultants, temporarily acting as researchers, do not want to disturb the situation. However, subsequent data will show that the consultants continue this strategy after the survey is completed.

One interesting situation occurred during the survey. One manager reported to the plant manager that his people were worried over the possibility of holding a survey. Instead of helping the plant manager to resolve the issue, the consultants met with the reluctant group. They told them the same information that they gave the committee. Apparently (and we shall see later, only temporarily) the reluctant group "accepted" the survey. One wonders, for example, what might happen if, instead of doing the above, the consultant stated to the group.

I am told that you are concerned about the survey. It makes us feel good that you raise these concerns openly. What kinds of information do you wish from me? How can I be of help to you?

The consultant might also ask if the group could help him to understand the degree to which their concerns are shared by others. If so, what hunches they may have to deal with the problem.

THE RESULTS OF THE SURVEY

As in the previous case, a carefully planned systematic questionnaire and interview study was conducted. After feeding back the results to the plant manager the consultants suggested a series of courses of action that were indicated from the survey.

1. There is evidence of resignation if not a feeling of helplessness on the part of management.
2. Steps need to be taken to galvanize or stimulate the organization to new levels of spirit and enthusiasm.
3. Mr. Brown ought to be changed because the problems that his behavior cause could prevent the organization from carrying out any proposals that it evolves.
4. The number of levels of manage-

ment need to be reexamined to see if they are all necessary.

5. To help the management look more creatively at what they can do both as individuals and as members of a team. Also to get them to feel that they *do* have the power, influence, and responsibility for getting it done.

In presenting the prognosis the consultants helped to focus the plant manager's attention on the steps that they felt were necessary if the organization was to improve. They were apparently most anxious to induce the plant manager to do something with Mr. Brown, who they felt was a thorn in the organization's as well as the consultants' side.

A meeting was then held with the committee to feed back the results. With the exception of Mr. Brown, the committee did not resist the results. Mr. Brown raised questions about the validity of the study and according to the consultant made a bit of a nuisance of himself. One of the consultants

. . . purposely took a seat next to Mr. Brown in order to restrain him from talking a great deal by putting his hand on Mr. Brown's arm or otherwise diverting his attention.

Although there was no overt disagreement by other committee members, the consultants left the meeting questioning the committee's probable degree of commitment to work through the results. Perhaps if the consultants would not view Mr. Brown's behavior as a thorn but as stemming from a person who is so anxious that he breaks the barriers of secrecy and tells the consultants how he (and perhaps others) feel, the consultants might have utilized his charges about the research to learn more about the other members' feelings. Such a step would also help the consultants begin to reach one of the objectives that they define as cru-

cial; namely, to help the committee work through their reluctance to be open.

Upon the return to the organization for further discussion with the committee the consultants explored plans which the plant manager might consider to cope with Mr. Brown. The plans became quite detailed to the point where the consultants considered suggesting a new organizational position for Mr. Brown; one which would, in effect, greatly decrease his power and control. From the consultants' viewpoint, this action was necessary if the plant was to progress.

Perhaps this was the case. However, if the plant manager accepted the plans, the consultants would make the plant manager more dependent upon them because one of the plant manager's basic problems was that he needed to become an effective diagnostician of such difficult situations. In filtering out the alternatives and presenting those with greatest merit, the consultants were preventing the plant manager from learning more about these crucial steps in the decision-making process. If the plant manager agreed with the consultants, then he would surely tend to increase his dependence upon them. Yet, the consultants believed that they must help the plant manager overcome his dependence upon them. Moreover, the consultants wished that the committee be less dependent on the plant manager. But, why should the committee believe the consultants' view that dependence is bad when they see that their boss is being made dependent upon the consultants?

Returning to Mr. Brown, the plant manager accepted the consultants' recommendations. As soon as Mr. Brown left for a vacation the plant manager announced to the management the realignment of duties which radically changed Mr. Brown's duties. Exactly why this decision was made after Mr. Brown left is not clear. One can only hypothesize that the plant manager must have felt quite uncomfortable in making the decision and thus waited until Mr. Brown left. Whatever the reason, it seems that the consultants should have helped the plant manager to explore the impact of the decision. To be sure, the survey results suggest that the management group is not particularly in favor of Mr. Brown. But to demote a man in this way is to provide living evidence to the management that the plant manager and the consultants are not able to be open when making difficult decisions. What guarantee do any of the managers have that their jobs might not be changed in the same way someday when they are on vacation?

As one might predict, upon his return to the plant Mr. Brown was astounded to hear the news of the change. He became depressed and hostile. From then on Mr. Brown evidenced increased hostility toward the plant manager. Mr. Brown became more withdrawn but made one final attempt to be open with his hostile feelings. He refused to listen and resisted. The consultants dealt with this defensiveness by suggesting if Mr. Brown did not cooperate, the consultants might be forced to leave the organization. Mr. Brown reacted with "violent hostility." No other comments exist about the meeting. The consultants noted, however, that since that meeting Mr. Brown promised the plant manager to cooperate until his retirement.

Thus Mr. Brown was neutralized and the consultants felt an important obstacle was removed.

THE DECREASE IN MANAGEMENT INTEREST

However, it was not long before a new problem seemed to arise. The committees created to work through the survey results and suggest concrete action were, for the most part, ineffective. At the same time, the plant manager reported to the consultants that

. . . plant people are looking upon [them] as spies.

One employee even asked

. . . is it a good idea to have them around so much?

Apparently, the consultants did not take any action to explore these rumors. About a month later, the plant manager visited the consultants and reported "discouragement with the program." He said it has slowed down for various reasons: a main one being that less time was being spent by the consultants at the plant. He stated that he was looking for some new ideas because of the loss of momentum in the program.

The consultants diagnosed the decrease in interest as

. . . caused by the fact that these [management] groups could not come up with any more problems and did not see any responsibility beyond problem definition.

The consultants apparently do not believe that they might be partially responsible for the lack of responsibility. After all, *they do* condone behavior on the part of the plant manager which is unilateral and punitive (Mr. Brown's case). Also, it *is* the consultants and the plant manager who want the study. Why should the shop feel responsible for something that they never really accepted?

According to the consultants, the few departments which needed help least were holding the more effective meetings. The poorer departments did not seem to be motivated to hold further meetings. After some visits by the consultants, the meetings were begun again. However, the consultants reported that there was not as much openness as they had hoped for.

After one meeting, a member told one of the consultants that the group wondered why he attended the meetings and wished they knew what they planned to do with his observations. They feared he might report upwards. The consultant reported that he was

. . . too confused after this meeting, because he was beginning to question whether his own behavior, as practiced in the meetings, was appropriate.

This is not an easy conclusion to contemplate and it illustrates the internal security of the consultant. One wishes that he would consider discussing his feelings with the management group. If he is able to be open with them about their relationship, would not this provide the clients with a rich living experience of how useful it is to explore one's inadequacies with a group of peers which provides a supportive climate? How is it possible for the consultants to expect the clients "to level" if they find it difficult to do so?

A NEW CHANGE PROGRAM

Apparently, the consultants decided not to discuss their problems with their clients (e.g., being perceived as spies, etc.). Instead they decided that the next step should be a new workshop program.

In the meantime the plant manager again told the consultants that he was discouraged in the way the departmental meetings were dwindling. Perhaps, this would be an ideal moment for the consultants to invite the plant manager to become more aware of his dependency upon the consultants. It may also help the consultants to become more aware of their role in the problem. Moreover, if the plant manager experiences "the experts" raising questions about their effec-

tiveness, he may begin to feel less anxiety about discussing his own difficulties.

Instead the consultants suggested that the plant manager might raise the question with the department heads as to whether or not they wished to continue. The plant manager replied that although he wished them to continue, he did not wish to legislate the group meetings.

The consultants reported that their impression was that the plant manager was attempting to get them to return to the plant and rejuvenate the program. For reasons not mentioned, the consultants do not use this ideal opportunity to explore their views of the plant manager's dependence upon them. Instead they suggest that they meet with some of the plant people to design a new program.

The consultants decided that a new training program might be useful because:

The consultants after this meeting discussed between themselves the merits of continuing versus discontinuing the group meeting. It appeared that most groups were by now under a good deal of tension. They could not seem to see clearly any responsibility beyond problem definition and felt they had exhausted problem defining. If they could not move to the next phase of exploring solutions and taking action, it might be well to discontinue the meetings. After several days of consideration, the consultants decided that the two problems that were a contribution to the problem of group movement were: 1) Inadequate understanding of the objectives of the program (the objectives had been becoming clearer since the survey) and 2) Lack of skilled leadership in meetings (group functions were not being performed). The notion at this point was that if the groups could be helped to continue meeting, a number of desirable consequences could be achieved. First, plant problems would continue to get worked on a lower level; second, groups and individuals would get greater sensitivity to problems of group functioning, and third, the desire of top management, especially the manager, to move groups toward a better understanding of the goal of greater self-determination at lower levels would be pursued.

A program was evolved by the consultants with the overall objective of developing within the plant an atmosphere in which all members 1) feel a greater responsibility for influencing the future of the organization, and 2) feel they can influence this future constructively.

In a way the program is ironic. The men are going to be induced to become more responsible yet they never really have been offered an opportunity to truly develop any program to enhance the clients' feelings of self-responsibility if the clients have almost nothing to say regarding their perceived need for the program, and the program, and the kind of human experience it shall be?

One can predict that if the program is composed of many experiences that involve the clients, and if these experiences are deeply meaningful to them, then they may increase their motivation. If this happens, one can predict further, however, that the "charge" given to them by the program will tend to wear off and a new program will be needed. If such is the case, then the consulting relationship has succeeded in shifting the dependence of the clients from their boss to the consultants.

DISCUSSION AND CONCLUSIONS

First, we must emphasize that the study is limited to those consulting relationships designed to increase the effective-

ness of human interpersonal relationships within the organization. A consultant operating at this level tends to find himself in a major dilemma. It appears that if he tends to go along with the traditional values implicit in the formal organizational structure, he tends to set off a chain of events that have varying consequences. On the one hand, he does not tend to be very threatening to the client system. He is usually liked and accepted as "being one of the boys" and "part of the culture."

It also appears that the unintended consequences of this strategy are that the consultant soon finds that he has worked himself into the role of planning, creating, and implementing change. Moreover, he behaves toward the clients in the same way as the clients tend to behave toward their subordinates, i.e., in a directing, controlling manner. This relationship is usually well known by the subordinates. They, in fact, tend to use and go along with the consultant in this relationship because they can control him and protect themselves. For example, they gladly take on the reciprocal role of being dependent upon the consultant. This leads to the consultant becoming primarily responsible for change that may occur. Under these conditions changes *are* made in the organization. However, the quality and usefulness of these changes is largely a result of the consultants' ingenuity. Thus, the organization has become dependent upon the consultants.

In traditional consulting practice, consultants who permitted themselves to get into such a position would probably be evaluated quite highly. After all, they have been able to get the organization to make progress in clearly defined and observable ways. Moreover, management acknowledges their value in helping to achieve certain crucial objectives. It may be argued that, given the realities of organizational life and the "human encounter" in which the consultants are immersed, this is probably as well as one can expect the consultants to perform. However, as we have seen, the success tends to be short lived and relegated primarily to certain non-human changes in interpersonal relationships and basic values which were originally planned never materialize.

A. The Marginal Role of the Consultants

In an attempt to help us to begin to understand the complexity of the consulting role it might be useful to explore it more systematically. What follows is an attempt to relate aspects of the consultative process to certain basic psycho-social concepts. However, appropriate examples will be used from the data available.

To the extent that the client's present value system is different from the one the consultants represent, the consultant places himself in a marginal position because he will work in a system whose values and norms are different from those of his own team. To make matters more difficult, most client systems are usually composed of two sub-systems. On the one hand, is the group which desires to see their organization change. In most cases this sub-system is composed of those in management who invited the consultants. On the other hand, are all those who are either not aware of a necessity for change, or disagree as to the proper direction for change, or resist any attempt at change. To the extent that any one or a combination of these factors exists, the consultant will find himself confronted with another set of factors that will tend to reinforce and magnify the role of a "marginal man."

From the research on the role of "marginal man" it is possible to infer that the consultant will tend to experience the following kinds of problems.

1. Although he accepts the management's request to conduct diagnoses of the employees' world, the employees may choose not to inform him about the very problems he is supposed to help resolve.

In the cases above, no lower-level employees are included in the study. However, there are numerous examples where the lower-level supervisors tend to withhold information. For example, in Case A the lower-level supervisors were not willing to discuss the difficulties which they felt with the leadership pattern of the top management echelons. They also resisted talking about the question, "How am I doing?" which was a question in which top management was most interested. Similarly, in Case B the supervisors had some serious questions about the role of the home office in the life of their organization. However, they did not feel free to discuss them openly with the top management. (They did discuss them, however, with the consultants.)

2. Although the consultant is asked by management to help them, they may not inform him of their informal activities, especially those that they keep from one another. Usually, these are the activities that are the sources of many organizational problems.

It is difficult to cite examples of this condition because our raw data came primarily from the consultants' reports. However, there are a few examples that can be used where the top management withheld important information from the consultants. In Case A the management group met informally for four hours to discuss one of the consultants' questionnaires without inviting him to participate. Later the consultant learned that the management group never accepted phase X of his plan although for many months they acted as if they accepted it. In Case B the plant manager communicated confidential survey data about an employee to people outside the organization.

3. The consultant could experience frustration and conflict if he is asked by

members in either sub-culture to participate in activities that the other does not sanction. To the extent that he feels "required" to comply the consultant will tend to increase the probabilities of jeopardizing his position in the organization.

According to the consultants they experienced conflict numerous times when top management asked them to make evaluations of subordinates. They felt the subordinates would not approve these discussions. Equally conflicting, but not as numerous, were times when the subordinates attempt "to pump" the consultants as to what they were learning from the "Top Brass."

4. The consultant will tend to experience conflict and frustration to the extent that the two — sub — cultures fluctuate in their decisions, norms, etc. For example, he might feel that management ought to make up its mind on a particular policy so that he can provide consistent replies when asked by the employees. He may also feel that the employee attitudes about certain things do keep vacillating, and he is therefore unable to make a valid report to the management (which may be the employees' objective).

5. The consultant will tend to experience conflict and frustration to the extent that his values are incongruent with the clients'.

The major portion of the paper is taken up with examples of the differences in values between the consultant and the clients. Whereas the former emphasizes openness, self-awareness, self-acceptance, and emotionality, the latter emphasized diplomacy, subordination, dependence and rationality. These basic differences forced the consultant into continual conflict choice situations. In most cases, we have seen, the consultant's values were subordinated to the clients'. The former became increasingly nonauthentic which

pleased the clients but prevented the consultant from providing the degree of help which he is capable.

To summarize, the consulting relationship is influenced greatly by several complex factors. They are: 1) the discrepancy between the consultant's values and those of the clients, 2) the division of the organization into those who are aware of and/or wish, and those who are unaware of and/or do not wish, to bring about effective change, and 3) the division between those who invited the consultant "to straddle" a series of overlapping, conflicting, and at times antagonistic, sub-cultures.

This marginal status can lead to many difficulties for the consultant. If he attempts to behave simultaneously in accordance with the requirements of both sub-cultures, he will find himself in constant conflict since the demands are antagonistic. Moreover, he will tend to be perceived by those in the sub-culture, at best, as being ambivalent and unsure. At worst, the consultant will be perceived as a hypocrite and a man "playing both sides against one another." If he values one sub-culture over the other, then his behavior will be perceived as "management-dominated," or "employee-dominated," depending upon which sub-culture he values most and who is doing the judging.

Finally, each situation will tend to be new for the consultant. Consequently even with a high degree of training and experience his behavior will not tend to be efficient (e.g., follow the shortest path to the goal). There will be much exploratory, trial-and-error behavior. Errors and false steps will be made at the very time that he is being most cautious. Frustration and conflict will occur as well as feelings of ambivalence. These, in turn, will tend to lead the consultant to vacillate, to shift his ground, his strategy. He may be easily influenced and easily led especially by those representatives of the sub-culture that he values. His resistance to suggestion from the same group will tend to be low.[8]

B. The Emphasis upon the Process of Development

The consultants upon whom we are focusing have an additional problem that confronts them continually. In many consulting relationships, the ends are considered more important than the means. If a marketing consultant comes up with a bright idea or an organization specialist suggests a more effective organizational structure, either not much attention is paid to the interpersonal processes involved in achieving these ends or strategies are developed and executed that "sell," "persuade," "pressure," "motivate," the employees to accept these changes.

A consultant who is interested in helping the organization achieve its needs in such a way that it can continue to do so with decreasing "outside" aid must give attention to the processes by which the new plans are developed, introduced, and made part of the organization. He will tend to invite a much greater degree of participation on the part of the clients in all the phases of the program. Such participation, if it is not to become bogged down, will have to be based on effective interpersonal and group relationships. At the core of such relationships are such factors as openness, the capacity to create minimal defensiveness in oneself and in others, listening with minimum distortion, etc. In order to succeed in their work these consultants must therefore be interested in the *processes* or means for development as well as the ends. For ex-

[8] The analysis of the impact of a new situation on behavior is drawn from Roger Barker, Beatrice A. Wright, and Mollie R. Gonick, *Adjustment to Physical Handicap and Illness,* Social Science Research Council, Bulletin 55, 1946, pp. 1–44.

ample, it is not very worthwhile to use covert or diplomatic approaches to get the clients to see that they are not open or that they are diplomatic in their relationships. It does not seem effective to help the clients become aware of their defenses if, in the process, the consultants behave defensively. Thus we find that the consultant strives to create a process for change which requires the very values that he is supposed to help the organization to overcome.

It is extremely difficult, however, for the consultant, to be open when he is operating under the difficulties and ambiguities of a new situation compounded by being in a marginal role. All this is doubly compounded by the fact that his job depends upon not upsetting the clients whose basic problems are that they work in a system that sanctions non-authenticity and deplores authenticity. How is the consultant expected to behave according to his values and, at the same time, survive in a world in which these values may lead to failure? To make matters more difficult, he is on the client's payroll. Thus his job could be placed in jeopardy if he risks confronting the clients by questioning their values.

One implication is that management may need to learn to create a climate where the consultant can feel free and encouraged to express his beliefs, especially different ideas about the process of effective organizational change. Unless this is done, the consultant, quite understandably, out of fear of his own position and in need for acceptance, soon takes on the values already held by the organization that he is trying to help. At this point, he tends to lose the very qualities that would make him valuable to the organization.

Along with line management's helping to develop a climate where the consultants are helped to express their uniqueness, certain organizational changes might be considered organizationally to reinforce the consultants in their effective assistance. Specific recommendations for defining the nature of such a relationship go beyond the scope of this study. However, in other organizations, consultants have developed effective relationships where the following kinds of conditions existed. The consultants:

1. May never become part of line management.
2. Have their own professional salary scale as do medical directors.
3. May never be fired for focusing on such processes as openness and authenticity but,
4. May be dismissed if they are judged by their professional colleagues to be incompetent, and
5. May be dismissed as a part of the organization to the extent that it is coercing their behavior against their better judgment.

In addition, line management could optimize its return on the investment of the kind of consulting assistance discussed in this report if it would change its policy from asking for such assistance only when trouble is imminent or has already erupted to a more preventative philosophy of conducting their organizational diagnoses when the pressure "to put out a fire" is not at its peak. Under pressure of resolving a "hot issue," individuals tend to become more anxious, feel greater tension, see fewer alternatives, manifest less patience, become less effective at problem solving. Their organizational defensiveness becomes more pronounced, and they demand more urgent solutions. Under these conditions it is difficult indeed to solve effectively important long-range organizational issues. One can imagine the difficulty if these issues are rooted in human relations, human actions, and human effectiveness. Under these conditions, the consultants, who would be the first to admit the infancy of their pro-

fession, cannot be expected to do the effective job the management desires.

At this point some readers have asked, why is it dysfunctional for the consultant to accept temporarily the values of the client-system? For example, is it not advisable for a consultant to suppress his feelings if he believes that the client is "not ready" to explore his interpersonal relationships. Why should not the consultant continue providing help to achieve the tasks with the hope that he will return to the interpersonal relationships later on? There are several reasons that might be worth exploring.

1.   The two cases suggest that it is difficult for the consultants to help the clients to behave more openly if the consultants do not do so. The more the consultant is willing not to be open and to level, the more reason he gives the client to continue to lack genuineness. Every human interaction between client and consultant that is not authentic helps to build a norm of non-authenticness. If most of the client's interactions initially are non-authentic, then the norm of the non-authenticness (which already exists in the organization) becomes embedded in the client-consultant relationship. As these norms are reinforced it will tend to be difficult for the consultant to switch values and it will place the client in a strong conflict situation.

2.   There are limits to the consultant's openness. If he believes that the members of the client system are psychologically too disturbed to deal with interpersonal relationship (and if some of the organization's problems are related to these interpersonal relationships) then the consultant may find it appropriate to recommend that the executives consider some form of therapy. If the client, after careful explanation and exploration, decides against therapy, the consultant may wish seriously to consider leaving. Otherwise, these interpersonal relationships will eventually embroil him, the executives,

and others in the organization in great difficulties which he will be unable to cope with since the client has said they were "off limits." If, however, the consultant believes that the client is not that defensive and that he can accept help in this area, even though at first it may be painful to the client, he should strive to provide help.

Some ask if the consultant does not run the risk of terminating the relationship if he upsets the client. The answer is yes he does run that risk. But, if he succumbs to this fear, then the client has control over the consultant. It is this fear of breaking off the relationship which probably makes the subordinates suppress their feelings. If the consultant can communicate that he does not fear terminating the relationship, then he helps the client to face up to his impact and responsibilities.

I do not, therefore, mean to imply that openness is an all-or-nothing phenomenon. Needless to say, the consultant will have to be cautious in his feedback until he ascertains the degree of receptivity of the client. I am suggesting, however, that, in an organization, the consultant may not have available to him as much time as he would wish to make a proper diagnosis, nor as much freedom to postpone being open. For example, in an individual therapeutic session, the therapist may be able to judge his openness primarily by the patient's response. In an organization, however, it is not so easy. If the key executive, for example, was more defensive and less aware than the subordinates then the consultant's "patient waiting" for the opportune moment may be perceived by the subordinates as the executive controlling the consultant. The reader may recall that this is what occurred in Case A during the first feedback session.

In several instances where I have sensed that the defensiveness of the key executive is significantly greater than the others, I have found it helpful to work

with him personally before the relationship expands to the remainder of the organization. Under these conditions, I was able to move more slowly without developing the problems discussed above.

The defensiveness of the clients, however, is not the only relevant factor. The consultant's defensiveness is equally crucial. If he tends to be easily threatened by the hostility that understandably would flow from the confrontation of the client with his feelings, then he will not tend to see the appropriate moment for intervention, nor will he intervene in a way to optimize the possibilities for learning. He should strive to utilize his own values when he gives feedback. His feedback should be, as much as possible, descriptive of the situation as he sees it. He should minimize making evaluations. For example, the reader may recall that the consultants felt that Mr. Brown talked too much. There are several alternatives open to them for intervention. One is for the consultants to describe to Mr. Brown the impact he is having upon the group without evaluating it as good or bad. More important, however, they could hypothesize that Mr. Brown's talkativeness was not "too much." Rather they could view it diagnostically as Mr. Brown's attempt to deal with anxiousness about what the consultants were doing to him and to the others. If they could have raised this question (e.g., "Perhaps you feel we are meddling and not very helpful") this might have released the others to support that part of Mr. Brown's position which most of them felt was valid. The group support might have influenced Mr. Brown to reduce the intensity of his need to fight the consultants.

In short, the appropriate time for the consultant to focus on interpersonal issues is when they become a problem. More specifically, the consultant should focus on interpersonal issues when he believes 1) that these are operating to block the client from achieving his stated objectives and 2) that the client, by not being genuine is beginning to prevent the consultant from providing the skills and assistance for which he was hired.

It should be evident by now that there are many factors operating on the consultant, influencing him away from being effective. This leads to the final recommendation. Client systems may have to recognize that they have certain responsibilities which they must fulfill if the consultant is to optimize his—and therefore eventually help the client's—genuineness. A consultant is first a human being. Although he has much knowledge about human behavior he too can be influenced by pressures, conflicts, frustrations, and non-authenticity in an organization. This suggests that the clients should strive to minimize these, or at least to encourage the consultant continually to raise the questions even though in doing so the clients should strive to mini-

mize those situations where they are knowingly being non-authentic with the consultant.

Typically many consultants hide these responsibilities from the clients. Indeed, some even prevent them from coming to the client's awareness. As long as the client (unknowingly or knowingly) turns over his responsibility to the consultant, then a strong dependency relationship is established between the client and the consultant. In my own experience, many consultants prefer the dependency relationship not only for the increased "billing time." Less discussed, and perhaps equally important, is the consultant's deep anxiety to face himself and to see what he is *really* doing to the client system. Perhaps, the best sign of the strength in these consultants is their willingness to face themselves and their practice and to learn from this experience.

8.4 TOWARD THE STYLE OF THE COMMUNITY CHANGE EDUCATOR

Richard Franklin

The change agent does not, of course, function in isolation from events and environments. He comes on the scene because of conditions necessitating change. As Edgar Schein has said, "Technological change, which is proceeding at an incredible rate, creates problems of ob-

This essay is excerpted from a paper originally presented at the 10th Annual National Adult Education Research Seminar, Feb. 10, 1969, Toronto, Canada. Reproduced by special permission from NTL/Learning Resources Corp., NTL Institute for Applied Behavioral Science, "Toward the Style of the Community Change Educator," Richard Franklin, pp. 1–23, 1969.

References and footnotes in deleted portions of this essay have been omitted; remaining references and footnotes have been renumbered.

solescence. Social and political changes occurring through the world create a constant demand for new services and the expansion of presently existing ones."[1] Schein might have added that these changes are not occurring "someplace out there." They take place on streets and country roads where people live, in city hall, the slum and suburbia.

Yet the forces for change often originate outside the community in which they are most strongly felt. External and impersonal—even global—dynamics impinge on the community. While the mechanical cotton picker, for example, was

[1] Schein, E. H. *Organizational Psychology.* Englewood Cliffs, N.J.: Prentice-Hall, 1965, p. 16.

not developed or manufactured in an Alabama cotton field, its impact is felt there—as well as in Chicago, Philadelphia and other swelling inner cities to which unemployed farm hands have been migrating since its invention. Congress initiated the Interstate highway system, which today slices through towns and cities and rural neighborhoods everywhere in the nation, linking collectives of people and institutions like splices in an unending cable. Some changes thus superimposed are unwelcome and accompanied by unintended consequences. Some, like the highways, bring both plus and minus values. But even though the changes come from without, local choices still remain.

Aside from forces bearing in upon it, the community has its own internal disequilibria at work in the form of purposes, pains, conflicts, needs, traditions. The pressure for community change can be both locally and nationally propelled, such as the drive for racial equality. This issue is more personal, less macroculture. It offers a high potential for generating social energy for local action and reaction. The factors involved, notwithstanding, may be no less tension-ridden or resistant to human management than the more macrocosmic forces.

Whether a response to external forces or intrinsic dynamics or both, community change is fairly certain to encompass problems common to one or more organized groups. Such groups increasingly feel inadequate, or actually lack the skill and experience to carry through a program of intentional, planned change.[2] Since intervention by a change agent can

be crucial, he himself becomes a vector in the change program.

The kind of vector he becomes depends upon his *behavior pattern* or *style*. This is expressed in (a) his methods of interacting with his client system (an individual, group, or multi-group); (b) his underlying purpose; and (c) his philosophy of what constitutes "help." His means of entry into the problematical situation and the intensity and extensiveness of his involvement with its cast of characters are also significant. . . .

The change agents I have known seem to have these characteristics in common:

1. They are trying to use themselves and their skills as intervenors to foster intentional change within a social or natural environment.
2. They are seldom in "power" positions, but depend on "influence" (knowledge, persuasion, personal interaction, charisma, experience, diagnostic skills) to affect change.
3. They customarily get paid for their efforts.

Although these helping professionals may or may not reside in the community or organizational system with which they work, they in any case do have a continuing relationship with their clients. . . . They have various degrees of identity with their immediate region but work with organized groups to which they are not necessarily formally connected.

They almost universally find that resistance to community change is lively beyond all rational explanation. Barriers to change—ignorance, intergroup tension, fear, resignation, contentment with the old and orthodox, disparity of power or influence, lack of funds or energy, divergent goals, dysfunctional attitudes—which caused the problem in the first place, persist vigorously. While the change agent needs to know all he possibly can about

---

[2] One analysis of community change appears in Roland L. Warren's *Types of Purposive Social Change at the Community Level*, Waltham, Mass.: Florence Heller Graduate School for Advanced Studies in Social Welfare, Brandeis University, 1965, in which he discusses particularly "collaborative," "campaign," and "contest" change strategies.

the conditions both impeding and supporting change, the central consideration here is the change agent's behavior. . . .

COMMUNITY CHANGE EDUCATOR

The term Community Change Educator derives from the terms "community consultant," "change agent," and "adult educator." As a helping style it, in my view, is the most distinctive and effective of the quintet.* It may also be the most empirically grounded, owing much to the thinking and investigation of such leaders in applied behavioral science as Carl Rogers, Jack Gibb, and Ronald Lippitt.[3]

A distinctive mark of this style is concentration by the Community Change Educator (CCE) on a group-intergroup configuration, rather than on the individual, as the medium of change. Central, too, is a desire to help those comprising the client system learn the how and why of change or development. He takes initiative in generating a learning environment for change. Aims and means merge in this focus. Substance and process, decisions and decision making, people and problems, "soft" feelings and "hard" data all interpenetrate. Above all, human occupants of a social milieu are perceived as more crucial to that environment than its physical aspects or man-invented artifacts. Interaction between

---

* [Editors' note: In a deleted portion of this essay, Franklin describes four other community change agent styles with which he contrasts the CCE style; they are: Advocate, Instructor, Servitor, and Paterfamilias.]

[3] C. R. Rogers' works, e.g., *On Becoming a Person,* Boston: Houghton Mifflin, 1961, are widely known. A classic study is R. Lippitt et al., *The Dynamics of Planned Change,* New York: Harcourt, Brace, 1958. Succinct and sharp is J. R. Gibb's "Is Help Helpful?" *Association Forum,* National Council of YMCA, February, 1964.

---

agent and client becomes highly emphasized, since such interaction is seen as paramount in a partnership to activate the problem-solving process. The climate is one of openness to mutual influence and growth.

This style is based in part on trainer behavior in community leadership laboratories and related types of experiential laboratories. However, it can be transferred to non-training settings. Some laboratory practitioners see the T (Training) Group as a microcosmic community. I suggest the reverse: that the community can be viewed as a "macrolab," in the sense that the community constitutes a client system or systems learning to cope with or manage change. The CCE comprehends both cognitive and emotional data in the situation as integral to the change process, relates collaboratively with the client, helps enlarge the number of available options, and perceives the decision for change as the responsibility of the client group. . . .

We need to probe more extensively the CCE's pattern of behavior, his relationships with the client system, his perceptions. It will also be relevant to look at the change agent's own group. While it appears impossible to catalog segments of conduct or the skills of a change agent (or any other professional, for that matter), some dimensions of attitude and action can be sorted out.

To begin, we can suggest that the CCE is a blend of scientist and poet. The scientist in the CCE strives to describe reality and "tell it like it is." He is able to sort fact from fancy. He values experimentation. The poet in him, on the other hand, tries to see truth beyond the fact. He is creative; he seeks to discover the new amidst the old and see fresh mixes of familiar ingredients. He senses human potential—in this case the potentiality of persons and groups to go beyond their current level of productivity or satisfaction. The Advocate* can be poet. The Instructor* can be scientist. But I see the CCE as more likely to blend the experimental tradition of scientist with the creative tradition of art in dealing with human relationships. He will exhibit detachment, yet his warmth will come through. His clients will come to see what he sees—their potential for growth in independence, their ability to choose wisely for themselves, their emerging capacity to work in concert.

There is another dimension: empathy vs. kindredness. . . . Many change agents tend to be like those with whom they work. They have grown up in the same subculture. They share the same traditions, perspectives, biases, and responses as their clients. As a result, the role of the change agent becomes blurred. He, in effect, is part of the group. Almost a tribal identification with the client system prevails, and his impact is greatly undercut. Traditions are not examined, folkways questioned, nor significant social change goals established. . . .

Empathy is a more appropriate characteristic for the CCE. It encompasses positive feeling for the client group and an understanding of client difficulties. Still, the CCE retains a delicate detachment from the group, a marginality that allows him to be *with* but not *of*. He is accepted as trustworthy across class, interest, and ethnic boundaries, yet a part of him stays uncommitted to the client-as-is and committed instead to the client's capacity for development.

To establish a change environment, a tension needs to prevail between the CCE's vision and values and those of the client system. The helping relationship as an interaction between two perspectives becomes the base for stimulating a creative tension for change. Such a style—marginal, empathic—is not calculated to

* See Editors' Note on page 354.

gain blind devotion. It is apt to entail high-risk behavior. The agent cannot always meet client expectations; he may be seen at times as too progressive or as disloyal to the "Establishment." But to try to be close to a group, yet not be its captive, is always risky. The key lies in how flexible agent and client can be and whether they come to trust one another sufficiently to tolerate differences in means and aims. Inevitably the CCE will "lose a few." His successful change relationships, hopefully, will give him the confidence, security, and energy to ride out the failures.

Earlier I isolated an Advocate style as ultimately malfunctional. Does this mean, then, that the CCE promotes nothing, stands for nothing, teaches nothing? Not quite. A change agent with the Advocate style is committed to his fixed solution to a problem. The agent with the CCE style is committed to helping people learn to cope with the intricacies of group/community problem solving and decision making. He is a *generalist* in terms of the problem, a *specialist* in terms of the process. He is also an advocate of human growth, of healthy interdependence, of community wholeness. Most of all, he is discontented with the status quo and believes the educational approach is the optimal way to bring about intelligent community change.

Much has been written about *social action* processes.[4] A core component of the CCE's helping behavior is the way he interacts with the client group in the process of making the choices necessary for resolving problems. His function, as we have seen, is not to take over the problem. His is much more of a diagnostic stance, an "exploring with" the client.

[4] One publication on this theme is Richard and Paula Franklin's *Urban Decision Making—The Findings from a Conference,* Washington, D.C.: NTL Institute, 1967.

This begins with defining and redefining the problem through interaction. It continues through the analysis, the creative search for workable solutions, the critical testing of these options against situational reality and the ultimate goal. He does not choose *for* the group, nor does he implement the action decided upon. He helps delineate what the client needs to know throughout the process and helps the client obtain such knowledge or skill from available sources, including himself. The CCE is more likely to understand the dynamics of the process than client system members. He can help them to examine these dynamics, to modify interpersonal blocks and to retain affective strengths, to utilize latent resources of talent, to learn by examining their experiences.

The *problem* is not the sole consideration for the CCE. He is aware of the client system's *process* of development. He remains as sensitive to the organic life of the group as to its chosen target, for these are intertwined. The group that has not dealt with its internal conflict issues, for instance, may not be able to generate thrust toward concerted action.

There are methods by which to analyze a social system's developmental process. One that can help the CCE and his client system measure growth is provided by Jack Gibb, who lists "modal concerns" of development and pinpoints early-later changes as a system resolves these concerns. A few such signs of development include movement from distrust to trust, caution strategy to functional feedback, competition to goal integration, dependence to participative interdependence.[5] Though Gibb's model deals only with the small group, I believe a case can be made that it applies generally to interlocking intergroup systems (organizations, communities).

Whatever the nature of his client, therefore, the CCE explicitly behaves in ways he hopes will help it to develop. He uses himself to help the client system mature as it strives to resolve its problems. His reward is greater understanding of his own role and the professional pleasure of helping the client system develop. The CCE-client relationship thus evolves into a mutual adventure, from which both grow as "partners-in-charge." In the course of one analysis, Jack Gibb asked the disturbing question: Is help helpful?[6] I believe the Community Change Educator ultimately stands a good chance of being truly *helpful*.

THE TEAM CONCEPT

A final dimension to explore is the impossibility of one change agent behaving in all the ways described. Many social change needs call for a team of change agents. If the client system is large, subparts such as small learning groups in a leadership laboratory, or a spectrum of study-action committees in a community development undertaking, may require concurrent help from several CCEs. In community arenas, conflict often develops between factions. The climate at the interface may become so voltage-charged that one side will not trust a consultant who also works with "the enemy." Here a team of CCEs, each working with a different faction, can become a third party. At certain stages such a team may comprise the major link between conflicting groups, the primary arc of communication in a ruptured set of relation-

[5] Gibb, J. R., "Climate for Trust Formation," chapter in L. P. Bradford, J. R. Gibb, and K. D. Benne (Eds.), *T-Group Theory and Laboratory Method*, New York: Wiley, 1965.

[6] Gibb, J. R., "Is Help Helpful?" op. cit.

ships, the only centripetal force able to prime the process of healing.[7]

In some cases the client group is relatively powerless in efforts to work out issues involving more potent segments of the community. The CCE may have no choice at first but to help his client develop sufficient "clout" (through wider participation, more internal cohesion, better cross-group linkages, more effective planning skills) to confront more potent groups on a basis of parity.[8] Such a confrontation may then be eased if a teammate has been consulting with the "strong side" in ways that help it see the need to share power interdependently. (Some conflict situations, as between blacks and whites or poor and affluent, may not in every case benefit from a team. There still is much we do not know about conflict management.)

There is also the matter of competencies and personal attributes. One CCE may be more poet and his colleague more scientist. One may excel in helping groups to analyze problem situations and establish attainable goals, another in encouraging clients to place more validity in their own experiences and desires; one in sparking an innovative working climate, another in knowing where to turn for relevant data. The team makes possible multiple interventions into the life of the client system.

Obviously, not all change organizations have funds to sponsor more than one change agent to a client on a continuing basis. There remains, though, the alternative of forming *ad hoc* teams at

crucial points in the change process, colleagues who come to help for a day or a week. . . . Some of the most effective work with clients that I have seen has occurred when four to a dozen CCEs formed a temporary helping team. By working closely with one another and with the client system, they established a living demonstration of interdependent collaboration.

THE AGENT'S OWN GROUP: THE CHANGE AGENCY

Since few change agents find it possible to consult with organizations or communities as self-employed entrepreneurs, the change agency is an overriding consideration. The nature of his sponsoring organization has a strong influence upon the change agent's approach to his role. If the agency itself is centered on a single problem (disease prevention, for example) it probably *advocates* a solution. It wishes to work only with clients interested in that problem and willing to accept the agency's solution. Since the agency's view is apt to be geographically all-encompassing—global, national or state—its program seldom takes local variations into account. The more the change agent in the field is able to adopt the style of the CCE the farther he may be departing from his organization's policy. . . .

The helping relationship is influenced by the agency to which the agent belongs. The same influences are perceived differently and dealt with differently by various change agents, depending on their individual internal dynamics and basic helping styles. Clearly, certain relationships with his own sponsoring organization must be present or possible if the agent is to behave in the CCE style. . . .

There is a growing backlog of criti-

[7] The mediative "third party" concept was discussed at a 1968 University of Michigan conference on interracial tensions by Floyd Mann, research/faculty member of the University of Michigan's Institute of Social Research.

[8] The question of "clout" and "parity" are taken up in Franklin and Franklin, op. cit., Chapter 6, "Two Decision-Making Strategies."

cal social problems and challenges facing us. We must connect our knowledge to the people in the problems and internalize our experience and our research to move from understanding to action. The Community Change Educator is one who can provide aid to such a process.

Yet I do not view the CCE as the latest in a passing parade of religious, military, executive, or scientific saviors. He can perhaps begin a new tradition of helping people realize their potentialities, keep their dreams alive, and expand their patience for the uncertain adventure of community living. The CCE style does not lend itself to heroics. At best, the only monument that may mark his work is the more "competent community."[9]

[9] A term borrowed from Hans Spiegel, Urbanologist at Columbia University.

POWER
AND THE NEW POLITICS

CHAPTER NINE

"Mankind falling suddenly out of love with its own destiny" is how Teilhard de Chardin put it. Falling suddenly out of control of its own destiny is still another aspect of what seems to have happened. As a reaction against helplessness, alienation, confusion, and oppression. As a response to affluence, to cultivated and refined aspirations ignited by a society and a generation which lacked no material need but were haunted by a longing to make things better. Better justice. More equity. Fuller lives. Self-actualization. Liberation of blacks, women, chicanos, Indians. Liberation for everybody. Power to the people.

The confluence of a new leisure class, soaring federal rhetoric, the media, the works of Dr. Martin Luther King, Jr., and God knows what else has created a new political artistry—with as many variants as contemporary art and in some cases, as short-lived—an artistry with a fuller understanding and demonstration of power than we have witnessed since the incredibly successful American Revolution.

The "new politics" defies description or instant analysis. Only historians, later on, will be able to show us its patterns and designs, its coherences and contours. We still lack that historical aerial view. What we hear and discern now is not one voice or vehicle but a confusing jim-jangle of chords: an *a capella* choir here, a closely harmonized brass quintet there, a loud raucous atonal gang in the balcony using their bodies or kazoos, a flower child whispering clean songs of desire. When they write—or, more likely, "get interviewed," the language and rhetoric are all over the lot. Pungent. Obscene.

Funny. Cosmically antic. Autonomously generated jargon, understood possibly by the "true believers" but guaranteed (it seems purposely so) to turn off "the others." The "book" is more often than not impossibly awkward, adolescent or embarrassingly abstract, like a teenager who tries to talk like Hegel writes. But the *performance*, when it works, is inspired.

In this chapter we've attempted to let the analysts and exemplars of the "new politics" speak for themselves. They need no interpretation or intellectual exegeses. While passion and commitment carry the weight of ideas far longer than one would have expected, the fact is that the logic of linear writing cannot contain the velocity of direct action. Despite the occasional references to Marxist-Leninist dialectics, their style, both verbally and "in action," bears little if any resemblance to the Marxists' "logic of the next step."

They owe more to Cage and Cronkheit than they would care to admit; but their obsessive self-consciousness illuminates their actions only up to a tolerable point, making them feel like cultural orphans—even at advanced ages —free from the knowledge of more subtle chains than Marx ever dreamed of.

Listen to Saul Alinsky, the man who says:

A fundamental difference between liberals and radicals is to be found in the issue of power. Liberals fear power or its application. . . . Radicals precipitate the social crisis by action—by using power. (From *Reveille for Radicals*, New York: Vintage Books, 1969, pp. 21–22).

For example, I have emphasized and re-emphasized that tactics means you do what you can with what you've got, and that power in the main has always gravitated towards those who have money and those whom people follow. The resources of the Have-Nots are (1) no money and (2) lots of people. All right, let's start from there. People can show their power by voting. What else? Well, they have physical bodies. How can they use them? Now a melange of ideas begins to appear. Use the power of the law by making the establishment obey its own rules. Go outside the experience of the enemy, stay inside the experience of your people. Emphasize tactics that your people will enjoy. The threat is usually more terrifying than the tactic itself. Once all these rules and principles are festering in your imagination they grow into a synthesis.

I suggested that we might buy one hundred seats for one of Rochester's symphony concerts. We would select a concert in which the music was relatively quiet. The hundred blacks who would be given the tickets would first be treated to a three-hour pre-concert dinner in the community, in which they would be fed nothing but baked beans, and lots of them; then the people would go to the symphony hall—with obvious consequences. Imagine the scene when the action began! The concert would be over before the first movement! (If this be a Freudian slip—so be it!). (From *Rules for Radicals*, New York: Vintage Books, 1972, pp. 138–139).

Listen:

This synthesis, which constitutes the foundation for a radical concept of planning, is part and parcel of the emerging pattern of our time. We presently live under a world view consisting of the maintenance of a mass technocratic society governed by the myth of an objective consciousness, through the demands of the rational-comprehensive model, with emphasis on an accommodating economic growth. The paradigm rising to challenge this present concept of reality is based on systems change and the realization of a decentralized communal society which facilitates human development by fostering an appreciation of an ecological ethic based on the evolutionary process: spontaneity and experimentation. . . . [See Grabow and Heskin in readings that follow.]

And listen:

Though people at Sanctum call their businesses "co-ops," most are in fact *collectives,* in which decision making and all the roles of work are shared democratically. They are training centers, preparing people for a different sensibility of work. All cooperate in collecting the voluntary 2 percent community tax, which nets several thousand dollars each month. These funds are disbursed to community groups, to seed new projects, by a loose community council, drawn from the co-ops, which meets weekly in some confusion and talks and smokes its way to consensus. . . .

Their truer sophistication is experiential. I can hardly speak of their lives here, but in this domain of co-operative work they've undertaken an audacious and perhaps profound self-education. Inwardly they're learning to live in a democratic family; outwardly, as more farms are linked into town enterprises and they work on a credit union committed to capitalize larger community ventures, they are learning to build complex models of a new social order, increasingly comprehensive. For all their clumsy romanticism, they are pragmatic and shrewd, after working through these lean years. Pursuing a gradual infiltration of civic government, in the recent city elections they got two aldermen in, barely missed another, and got a seat on the building permit appeals board. It is not hard to see in this a rehearsal for play on a grander scale. . . . [See Rossman in this chapter.]

And again:

The relationship between females and males in this and virtually every society has been a power relationship—of males over females. The current women's movement, a revitalization of earlier feminist movements, seeks to end or reverse this power relationship. As such feminists are concerned with analyzing the nature of male power and the condition of women and developing organizations and vehicles for change that are consistent with feminist principles. . . . [See Polk in this chapter.]

That's a small, maybe not even representative, sample of the writing. Whatever else one can say about it, one thing is clear and puts to rest Alinsky's avowed concern with "boredom": it's a helluva lot more interesting than your usual case studies or analyses of "planned organizational change." And more incoherent. But we doubt that revolutions were ever as coherent as Crane Brinton made them out to be.

What these and other readings tell us about the "new politics" are:

1. They're not new at all. Alinsky has been at it for at least 30 years,

and he borrowed some of his ideas from the creative indulgences of the Chicago "mob." The so-called "new politics" is neither new, and at times, isn't politics. (His excremental demonstrations were either fantasies or ineffective politics.) What makes it seem new is that the media and a new critical mass have consigned old revolutionary tactics to a new status which, in our times, cries out for labeling. Hence, we say "new politics," an omnibus term that includes everything from the genius of Dr. Martin Luther King's ad hoc tactics to the adventurous hi-jinks that would have made Marx wince.

2. There is an overall concern with "system," with structure, with locating the ills of society not in individuals but in the social fabric and norms which govern behavior and shape a reality which inevitably blinds "the people" to injustice and inequity. They take very seriously the Marxist idea that the most oppressed people are the last to know it.

3. The "new politics" is a "power play." Rightly concerned with and unashamedly involved with power: "It is not hard to see in this a rehearsal for a play on a grander scale." So it is theater, the creation of just enough distance between the reality and the image so that the audience can laugh and cry but not so much distance that the connection between the present reality and the symbolism of liberation will be lost. Closing the gap but allowing the discrepancies between the false consciousness of the present and the future liberation of the soul to sink in, to hurt enough. Enough to lead to action.

4. The "new politics" is kaleidoscopic, protean, erratic, impossible to pin down. Like "theater," we have witnessed flops and failures, political artists and political hacks. To make matters even more complicated—but still not losing its connection to theater—we have seen great political artistry work in one place and fail somewhere else. Montgomery, Alabama, isn't Chicago; Rochester isn't even Buffalo. (FIGHT was eminently successful in Rochester while its sister organization in Buffalo, CAUSE, was far less successful. Both Alinsky-inspired, both with excellent leadership, practically simultaneous movements.) Who knows why? Possibly the next generation of historians can tell us. Possibly. All we know for sure is that there are occasions when we must wait until things are almost over before discovering what has been occurring. We still have a long wait.

5. One generalization we hazard to make. The "new politics" attempts, unself-consciously, to change the audience's perception of reality. Instead of asking what reality is, the "new politics" jolts and shocks us by giving matters a subversive phenomenological twist, italicizing the following question: Under what circumstances do we think things are real? The trick, then, is not only to create "happenings" where multiple perceptions can be spontaneously generated, but when innocent adversaries can be drawn into starring roles, unwitting change agents who help the advocates of the new politics create new meanings without knowing they're "on stage." Martin Luther King, Jr., had practically given up on the Selma campaign until he heard, from an aide, about Sheriff Bull Connor beating up a black protestor before the cameras. He smiled and said: "We've won." Bull Connor participating

in the pageant of King's revolution is only one example of the theater of action, the new politics, the generation of energy through the creative act which lights up the prism of multiple realities.

New politics is theater, the theater of arousal; evoking new realities, realities that imply a contrast to our feeling and the pseudo or false reality we have come to take for granted. All of the "new politics"—at least that which has been effective—shocks, jolts us as we careen from one reality to another. (For a deliberate use of theater in the process of planning, see Lisa Peattie in Chapter Six, this volume.)

The readings represented here cannot possibly provide the full range of the radical voices that make up the "new politics." This is not intended as an apology but an explanation. There's simply too much; and of the available supply, there is a lot of "junk." A good deal of it seems to be frustratingly immune to conventional forms of language. Our authors do the best they can and their writing, whether one agrees with them or not, appealed to us either because of its representativeness (Grabow and Heskin, for example, whose egregious jargon will undoubtedly leave you alternately angry and hopeful, like a parent who patiently awaits the end of a long word from her six-year-old, or Rossman, who has always turned out subversively winsome prose). Slater, McClusky, and to a lesser extent, Polk, were selected not as exemplars or practitioners as such—though they may be out in the streets at this very moment—but because of their conceptual bite and their daring to order, to make sense out of these jumble of voices, the new and noisy and messy chorus of kazoos.

9.1 ALTERNATIVE TO THE STATUS QUO: EDUCATION AT SANCTUM

Michael Rossman

Recently I was invited to lecture at a large state university. I'll call it Sanctum because I want to talk about a free university that grew up next to it, and I've seen too much damage done to places of delicate growth by being exposed to public view. I had visited Sanctum often between 1966 and 1970 because it was an

exemplary campus, displaying clearly the typical development of student activism in political, social, and educational affairs, and then of countercommunity. Returning in 1973 after three years, I felt as if I were stepping into a time-warp mixing elements of three decades.

The most archaic note was the eruption of energy one night in a giant dorm complex; waterfights, tussling tugs of war, hours of clamoring chaos. The cops arrived with truncheons at the ready, paranoid with years of political riot; then they relaxed,   somewhat   sheepishly,   and watched the play. It was like the panty-raids of the fifties, only students now are not so obsessively deprived of sex. I didn't find it as depressingly innocuous as did some of my friends, who recognize such lettings-off of steam as essential safety-valves to maintain the ultimate tranquility of an institution designed to repress and mold the energies of young people. Were I an administrator of the state, I would be disquieted by periodic outbreaks of Dionysian spirit, whatever their guise, for they testify to an unquenched vitality that can move unpredictably to new urges.

That possibility has been quickly forgotten on campuses where students seem again in a mood to accept the institution numbly. At Sanctum as elsewhere, the late sixties agitation for educational reform seems to have produced little change in the curriculum, structure, and processes of formal education. In a certain fringe of classes the process is looser, a bit affective; some departments permit students to design an occasional course, but the changes are largely cosmetic. Throughout higher education the old power relationships remain basically the same. Students have little control over their own learning in the small, let alone the large. Bureaucratic control continues to centralize. Faculty find their reform efforts stifled by colleagues—or channeled through the offices of administrators who have little commitment to innovation but who are attentive to anything that smacks of processing more degrees for less money.

The pockets of educational experiment that do exist tend to be marginal. They don't affect the larger institution: they bind the energy of an adventurous few. Minorities, women, professors, and staff employees have grown organized enough to play formal parts in the instituitions' lower power processes, but each group seems to be looking out for its own interests, conceived in narrow, traditional terms—better wages, more positions. So

far they have no effect on the assumptions of institutionalized education.

Many campuses harbor exceptions to these generalizations. But the overall institutional climate within which students define themselves is static and depressing. It engenders little excitement, vitality, or commitment. What wonder students again see themselves as passive and apathetic? One friend who has had recent contact with colleges believes that most of the faculty and students who retain the wit and will to try new means in their commitment to change have left the campuses, finding them barren places to work and learn.

Given all this, I was surprised to find at Sanctum in 1973 a situation much like that of the mid-sixties, when the currents of reform began stirring in higher education. Six thousand students had signed a petition against the "termination" of a professor who had grown too loose for the chancellor to entertain. A small group of malcontents had been agitating to abolish the foreign language requirement; to change the rules governing student discipline, which exposed them to double and arbitrary jeopardies; and to have some say concerning the uses of buildings built with student fees. Activism on such issues is a decade old and has been unsuccessful; here it was recapitulating its beginnings, each issue taken separately on its naive merits, without a broader ideological perspective. Yet, evidently it had meaning for more students than the few who sparked it, for their full slate of candidates swept into power in the recent student government elections.

I met with the victors on my last night there—bread and wine in the student government offices. They wanted to consult about starting what they called variously a free school or a learning exchange. "Huh?" I said.

"You know, a way to get people who

wanna teach something and people who wanna learn together, and involve people from the community in it and all."

"We used to call that idea a free university," I said, as gently as I could: "There was one here a few years back but it folded. Tell me more about what you have in mind." They tried. It took me a while to adjust my expectations and to recognize that they didn't know much more.

I marveled at how quickly the learning of the previous student generation had vanished with them from the campus, leaving these people to begin from scratch. Their group process was as primitive, most of the talking being done by the president-elect, a young man of earnest vigor and good will, benignly recreating the traditional power game among people who had barely begun the evolutions of personality which undergird truly collective work. I suggested they research the previous free university's positive features, and the institutional realities that dissolved it, before deciding on a form. I reminded them that some of its organizers were still in town—a resource they had not thought to tap because of the psychic distance that now separated them from the campus; and I wished them good luck. Then I went off to join my friends, the former organizers of that free university, at their restaurant in town.

To understand what happened to that free university, we must look back at the context within which it grew and, apparently, faded. When I first saw Sanctum, in 1966, it seemed monotonous and apathetic, a standard large campus. The next spring a few activists claimed a table in the cafeteria as a base, and a tentative antiwar demonstration developed. By 1968 many students were involved in action to open things up for blacks on campus, and some were turning their attention to the neglected problem of student government. Student discontent with education was becoming overt, and by 1969 it became an organizing thrust for educational reform. By then the campus was alive with action against dorm rules and Dow recruiters. Even the fraternity boys were wearing peace pins, and older activists took over student government with a progressive program.

Side by side with departmental organizing, a group of undergraduates founded the free university, with some 30 courses, mostly in new culture and politics, taught by students and a few adventurous professors. In 1970 thousands of students, fraternity-led, trashed the campus in protest of computer construction for war use, and the student government transformed itself into a voluntary organization, free to spend its small funds as it would.

In 1968 campus political activists banded together to form the first commune in town. By 1970, when the free university was already dissolving, there were 15 communes off-campus, the core of a loose countercommunity of some 400 people, most of whom had grown up involved in the campus actions. The focus of their energies was just then turning from campus to town, and they were forming their first cooperative businesses —a restaurant, a crafts shop. The next year the student government, in the full development of a consciousness tended for five years, voted some thousands of dollars to help seed more cooperative retail services in town.

When I came back to Sanctum—the countercommunity, not the university— in mid-1973, I found an evolution no one would be prepared for who believed the media myth about the death of the student movement. True, the streets have been empty since we found that when we turn out en masse and angry they will kill us without compunction. But meanwhile our lives have been moving on.

Sanctum now boasts an economic network of 38 enterprises—food, clothing, construction, records, auto repair—in a total net of some hundred groups working also in media, politics, the schools, and so on.

Though people at Sanctum call their businesses "co-ops," most are in fact *collectives,* in which decision making and all the roles of work are shared democratically. They are training centers, preparing people for a different sensibility of work. All cooperate in collecting the voluntary 2 percent community tax, which nets several thousand dollars each month. These funds are disbursed to community groups, to seed new projects, by a loose community council, drawn from the co-ops, which meets weekly in some confusion and talks and smokes its way to consensus.

What is growing in Sanctum is at once primitive and rudimentary, sophisticated and powerful. From some angles it is hard to take seriously this bunch of grown-up children playing at fantasy and living on the skinny. At best their enterprise is marginal: together their co-ops support some 200 people working in them for wages of 80 cents to $2 an hour, out of a countercommunity of some 3,000 now. But collectively, they do $3 million of retail business a year, in a town of 100,000. They're just waking to the fact that they have clout at the bank.

Their truer sophistication is experiential. I can hardly speak of their lives here, but in this domain of cooperative work they've undertaken an audacious and perhaps profound self-education. Inwardly they're learning to live in a democratic family; outwardly, as more farms are linked into town enterprises and they work on a credit union committed to capitalize larger community ventures, they are learning to build complex models of a new social order, increasingly comprehensive. For all their clumsy romanticism,

they are pragmatic and shrewd, after working through these lean years. Pursuing a gradual infiltration of civic government, in the recent city elections they got two aldermen in, barely missed another, and got a seat on the building permit appeals board. It is not hard to see in this a rehearsal for play on a grander scale.

Meanwhile, the political sympathies they learned on campus have not faded, for all that demonstrations are lacking. In fact, they've deepened and become amalgamated with spiritual concerns. They're expressed in the day-to-day of the women's movement, in long-developed cooperation with black organizers, in the meat market started in "Okietown," in the organic food store where mothers and Chicanos and longhairs swirl while old ladies poke at the peaches and ask to have the community tax explained.

The question of what happened to the free university can now be answered. The experiment that bore that title lasted less than two years on campus. Most broadly put, it tried to compete with the university on the university's terms, and lost. It offered new material, some chance to reconstruct the relationships of learning, and no bureaucracy. But its customers were in effect prisoners of the larger institution, obligated to satisfy its requirements before their own. Those who could not or would not do this soon left. As for the rest, when the punishment of grades loomed, the voluntary course languished. Innovative and substantive courses taught by frustrated professors or graduate students were welcomed into credit legitimacy—to be silently axed later—and departments broadened the options for a few student-designed courses of "independent study." Sapped by co-optation and attrition, the free university as a whole dissolved; and after completing a canonical cycle of experience, its organizers moved on to the more fruitful ground of the town.

In a deeper sense the free university persisted and is flourishing in the community of Sanctum. Its original curriculum had courses in new politics and economics, new culture, life-style, and consciousness. Yet its people were reaching an understanding of education that saw the artifice of courses as inadequate and recognized studenthood as an act of the whole being in a total social fabric. In the town now we see the tangible conjunction of that curriculum and this understanding, in a community of learners.

I watched them at the restaurant that evening. Two years earlier I'd sat on bare crates in a wrecked-out building shell, while they met yet again to coordinate their planning for the complex of businesses that would share the space. This night I sat on well-crafted benches— products of the woodshop which grew and moved uptown—in cubbies graceful with plants and hangings. I remembered them late in their campaign to take over student government. They would stumble home to dens decorated in psychedelic play, but they slowly realized the profound effects of environment on learning and action. The growth of their awareness and their art was reflected not only in the restaurant but in the food store opening naturally into it, and in the way they solved the traffic flow between the meeting room and bookstore.

A waiter brought us salad and told us about their research on the problem of nutrition at peoples' prices, their progress in developing a net of organic farmers who would directly supply them. As they left, people drifted to our table from the kitchen and the bike shop in back to tussle with the current problem. Finances were sound at last; wages were over two bucks an hour and rising, even after the community tax; tips were collectively shared; and no personal crises were pending in the loose family of 30 who handled the restaurant itself. But it

was turnover time again: the last of the restaurant's original core of organizers had learned what they could from the work and were ready to move on, and a number of recent escapees from the campus had joined the crew. How could responsibility best be taken, they all wondered, for carrying on the ethos of work that had developed there?

The coffee cups multiplied on our table, as the feminist meeting below broke up and came to ask advice on hustling the community council for a grant to train two of their people to lead women's sex therapy groups. I went downstairs. In the reading room I found Robin, a quiet, brilliant organizer who, in the years since I'd seen him, had taken to Christ and to working through Sanctum's churches. As he discussed mysticism with a local Maoist, I realized how naturally the many streams of a Sanctum's learning intermingled in this classroom they had made.

In Sanctum now they study the dynamics of social collectivity; the transformation and maturation of personal identity; the reconstruction of industry and service, government, agriculture and parenting, technology and economics; the social uses of art and theology; the nature of their sexuality. They puzzle out the mechanics of history even as they shape it. All this and more, in an integrated educational praxis that drapes a thin living tissue of learning around a skeleton of evolving alternative institutions.

If you ask what happened to educational reform, one important answer is that many who tried it on campus left to lead other lives of learning. From the perspective of Sanctum, which is a survival school, the original free university model seems much closer to institutionalized higher education than it once did. Sanctum's people don't think of it primarily as an educational *institution*, as much from modesty as from the absence of language to describe it as such. No one would claim its curriculum to be adequate or its process accomplished. Yet it deserves to be taken seriously as an alternative institution of higher education, one that changes roughly at the same rate at which its people grow. The university, on the other hand, changes ever so slowly and still behaves as if our understanding of society and people and education were not evolving radically.

And so we have two institutions that try, with quite different means and perspectives, to educate people in the skills and knowledge society needs. They approach studenthood, for example, from very different directions. Most people accept the (old) institution's definition of what a student is: essentially one who is passive, dependent, and powerless. To secure a niche in a highly organized and exploitive economic order, one eats what one is fed. One accepts others' definitions of what is useful and meaningful; one adapts to a bureaucratized environment, satisfying its requirements in order to gain small private patches of freedom; one relates to authority in a framework of (ultimately economic) punishment and reward, and to one's peers in competitive isolation; for years one uses small fractions of the self on small fractions of projects beyond comprehension. Whatever the catalog says, this is what a college education teaches, and it prepares its graduates to go on doing precisely the same things for the rest of their lives in the institutions that wait to welcome them.

The contrasting definition of students—people perpetually learning to control their environment and realize themselves—is scarcely new. To some extent this state is inalienable: even the universities' most docile students glimpse it. Were the processes of higher education too inflexible to allow a certain minority the chance to implement their true studenthood more richly—albeit still privately and selfishly—colleges would not have endured as they have. But my respect and love are aroused more strongly by those who dare more than just "independent study," those who, while taking the best the institution offers, also learn through first-hand and collective experience what it means to be an active shaper of society, a true citizen rather than a subject.

In this light I see as exemplary the university education of my friends at Sanctum who came together in small bands to puzzle out what needed to be done for a more-than-material survival. In order to discover this and learn how to put their discovery to work, they had to reverse their conditioning: they had to learn to work together and voluntarily, in democratic groups; to engage their passions on a large social scale, as well as privately; to understand and direct the generation of culture, rather than merely to endure it.

I recall their experience with cinema. Stoned and horsing before the slow-motion lens of a Bolex, on the lawn of the first commune in town, they caught fire from a film buff and started a tidy business, importing the best experimental films to show on the cheap in hustled halls. They learned to do offset graphics and blitz advertising, outclassing the belated competition from university and town theaters. They thought of art as expanding consciousness, and tried to judge the political impact of the radical pure images they were bringing to an innocent audience. When the time was right, film benefits bankrolled their campaign for student government, and their practical mastery of propaganda paid off at the polls. Meanwhile, others managed to bring pressure that created a place in a university department for a cinema curriculum grown from this experience, giving them a toehold for future operations on the student mind and university pocketbook.

Their college was a model of the

dominant institutions of our society, and they used it to study the structure and processes of power in a bureaucracy. They also experimented with a tickle here and a push there, learning to manipulate these systems over time to get space and resources for growth.

It's easy to dismiss their accomplishment by observing that four years' earnest effort by several hundred people resulted at best in freeing a piddling few thousand official dollars for seed funds, and left no significant structural or spiritual mark on the ongoing processes of the institution. But it's a mistake of scale to see them only as mice in a stainless-steel warehouse. Their most important product was themselves, not simply as individuals but also as a loose collectivity. And now, very few years after choosing to leave the campus, they plainly continue to do all they were learning to do in school. From tending new family through working collectively to gain economic and civic strength, progressing with no lesson plan and through failure, they apply and extend the lessons of their true studenthood, they dare to take the responsibility of constructing their reality. And as their activity in college schooled them to attempt and tend a small community within the larger society, so this Sanctum is in turn their school, a free university whose education is more intense and whole and various and open to the broader world. Sometimes I think it a mirage, this marginal, stumbling enterprise; sometimes I think it a kindergarten of what hope we have.

From this perspective the opportunities for a college education are not so limited and routine as most of those now enduring one have been led to believe. The best possibilities require that people learn to work cooperatively and autonomously for a common good and learn to control the conditions that affect their lives by this work. However rigorous or barren an institutional terrain appears, such things are possible for those who choose to see them. And if the attempt seems outwardly a failure, as the current reform efforts of students may prove on the Sanctum campus, still this is necessary learning too.

For we do not know whether our universities and other institutions can be brought to change enough, and rapidly enough, for our just survival. Each group of people who move independently to transform them are testing this out, are learning for themselves and for us all what works and what does not.

This education may well be the most important in America, and it is crucial that it proceed within the university as without. . . .

I have suggested that new town may come to compete with old gown as a teacher, with a self-consciousness and purpose that town could never muster. Well before this the countercommunity may begin to play the university and town off against each other, politically and economically: perhaps the right hand will push to get university lands added to the municipal tax base while the left hand organizes university support to restructure city government. By 1976 Sanctum will surely have long since begun to investigate such rich possibilities. Nothing suggests that the dynamics of higher education will be less interesting in this decade than they were in the sixties.

9.2   HALF SLAVE, HALF FREE

Philip Slater

THE OLD CULTURE AND THE NEW

There are an almost infinite number of polarities by means of which one can differentiate between the two cultures. The old culture, when forced to choose, tends to give preference to property rights over personal rights, technological requirements over human needs, competition over cooperation, violence over sexuality, concentration over distribution, the producer over the consumer, means over ends, secrecy over openness, social forms over personal expression, striving over gratification, Oedipal love over communal love, and so on. The new counter-culture tends to reverse all of these priorities.

Now it is important to recognize that these differences cannot be resolved by some sort of compromise or "golden mean" position. Every cultural system is a dynamic whole, resting on processes that must be accelerative to be self-sustaining. Change must therefore affect the motivational roots of a society or it is not change at all. An attempt to introduce some isolated element into such a system produces cultural redefinition and absorption of the novel element if the culture is strong, and deculturation if it is susceptible. As Margaret Mead points out, to introduce cloth garments into a grass- or bark-clad population, without simultaneously introducing closets, soap, sewing, and furniture, merely transforms a neat and attractive tribe into a dirty and slovenly one. Cloth is part of a complex

cultural pattern that includes storing, cleaning, mending, and protecting—just as the automobile is part of a system that includes fueling, maintenance, and repair. A fish with the lungs of a land mammal still will not survive out of water.

Imagine, for example, that we are cooperation purists attempting to remove the invidious element from a foot race. We decide, first of all, that we will award no prize to the winner, or else prizes to everyone. This, we discover, brings no reduction in competitiveness. Spectators and participants alike are still preoccupied with who won and how fast he ran relative to someone else now or in the past. We then decide to eliminate even *announcing* the winner. To our dismay we discover that our efforts have generated some new cultural forms: the runners have taken to wearing more conspicuous identifying clothing—bright-colored trunks or shirts, or names emblazoned in iridescent letters—and underground printed programs have appeared with names, physical descriptions, and other information facilitating this identification. In despair we decide to have the runners run one at a time and we keep no time records. But now we find that the sale of stopwatches has become a booming enterprise, that the underground printed programs have expanded to include voluminous statistics on past time records of participants, and that private "timing services," comparable to the rating services of the televsion industry, have grown up to provide definitive and instantaneous results for spectators willing to pay a nominal sum (thus does artificial deprivation facilitate enterprise).

At this point we are obliged to elminate the start and finish lines—an innovation which arouses angry protest from both spectators and participants, who have evinced only mild grumbling over our previous efforts. "What kind of a race can it be if people begin and end wherever they like? Who will be interested in it?" To mollify their complaints and combat dwindling attendance, we reintroduce the practice of having everyone run at the same time. Before long we observe that the runners have evolved the practice of all starting to run at about the same time (although we disallow beginning at the same place), and that all of the races are being run on the circular track. The races get longer and longer, and the underground printed programs now record statistics on how many laps were run by a given runner in a given race. All races have now become longevity contests, and one goes to them equipped with a picnic basket. The newer fields, in fact, do not have bleachers, but only tables at which drinks are served, with scattered observation windows through which the curious look from time to time and report to their tables the latest news on which runners are still going. Time passes, and we are increasingly subjected to newspaper attacks concerning the corrupt state into which our efforts have fallen. With great trepidation, and in the face of enormous opposition from the ideologically apathetic masses, we inaugurate a cultural revolution and make further drastic alterations in racing rules. Runners begin and end at a signal, but there is no track, merely an open field. A runner must change direction every thirty seconds, and if he runs parallel with another runner for more than fifteen seconds he is disqualified. At first attendance falls off badly, but after a time spectators become interested in how many runners can survive a thirty-minute race without being eliminated for a breach of these rules. Soon specific groups become so skilled at not running parallel that none of them are ever disqualified. In the meantime they begin to run a little more slowly and to elaborate intricate patterns

of synchronizing their direction changes. The more gifted groups become virtuosi at moving parallel until the last split second and then diverging. The thirty-second rule becomes unnecessary as direction changes are voluntarily frequent, but the fifteen-second rule becomes a five-second one. The motions of the runners become more and more elegant, and a vast outpouring of books and articles descends from and upon the university (ever a dirty bird) to establish definitive distinctions between the race and the dance.

The first half of this parable is a reasonably accurate representation of what most liberal reform amounts to: opportunities for the existing system to flex its muscles and exercise its self-maintaining capabilities. Poverty programs put very little money into the hands of the poor because middle-class hands are so much more gifted at grasping money— they know better where it is, how to apply for it, how to divert it, how to concentrate it. That is what being middle class means, just as a race means competition. No matter how much we try to change things it somehow ends as merely a more complex, intricate, bizarre, and interesting version of what existed before. A heavily graduated income tax somehow ends by making the rich richer and the poor poorer. "Highway beautification" somehow turns into rural blight, and so on.

But there is a limit to the amount of change a system can absorb, and the second half of the parable suggests that if we persist in our efforts and finally attack the system at its motivational roots we may indeed be successful. In any case there is no such thing as "compromise": we are either strong enough to lever the train onto a new track or it stays on the old one or it is derailed.

Thus it becomes important to discern the core motivational logic behind the old and the new cultures. Knowing this would make rational change possible

—would unlock the door that leads most directly from the old to the new.* For a prolonged, unplanned collision will nullify both cultures, like bright pigments combining into gray. The transition must be as deft as possible if we are to minimize the destructive chaos that inevitably accompanies significant cultural transformations.

The core of the old culture is scarcity. Everything in it rests upon the assumption that the world does not contain the wherewithal to satisfy the needs of its human inhabitants. From this it follows that people must compete with one another for these scarce resources—lie, swindle, steal, and kill, if necessary. These basic assumptions create the danger of a "war of all against all" and must be buttressed by a series of counternorms which attempt to qualify and restrain the intensity of the struggle. Those who can take the largest share of the scarce resources are said to be "successful," and if they do it without violating the counternorms they are said to have character and moral fibre.

The key flaw in the old culture is, of course, the fact that the scarcity is spurious—man-made in the case of bodily gratification and man-allowed or man-maintained in the case of material goods. It now exists only for the purpose of maintaining the system that depends upon it, and its artificiality becomes more palpable each day. Americans continually find themselves in the position of having killed someone to avoid sharing a meal which turns out to be too large to eat alone.

* This of course makes the assumption that some kind of drastic change is either desirable or inevitable. I do not believe our society can long continue on its old premises without destroying itself and everything else. Nor do I believe it can contain or resist the gathering forces of change without committing suicide in the process.

The new culture is based on the assumption that important human needs are easily satisfied and that the resources for doing so are plentiful. Competition is unnecessary and the only danger to humans is human aggression. There is no reason outside of human perversity for peace not to reign and for life not to be spent in the cultivation of joy and beauty. Those who can do this in the face of the old culture's ubiquity are considered "beautiful."

The flaw in the new culture is the fact that the old culture has suceeded in hiding the cornucopia of satisfactions that the new assumes—that a certain amount of work is required to release the bounty that exists from the restraints under which it is now placed. Whereas the flaw in the old culture has caused it to begin to decompose, the flaw in the new culture has produced a profound schism in its ranks—a schism between activist and dropout approaches to the culture as it now exists. We will return to this problem a little later.

It is important to recognize the internal logic of the old culture, however absurd its premise. If one assumes scarcity, then the knowledge that others want the same things that we have leads with some logic to preparations for defense, and ultimately (since the best defense is offense), for attack. The same assumption leads to a high value being placed on the ability to postpone gratification (since there is not enough to go around). The expression of feelings is a luxury, since it might alert the scarce resources to the fact that the hunter is near.

The high value placed on restraint and coldness generates in turn another norm: that of "good taste." One can best understand the meaning of such a norm by examining what is common to those acts considered to be in violation of it, and on this basis the meaning of "good taste" is very clear. "Good taste" means tasteless in the literal sense. Any act or product which contains too much stimulus value is considered to be "in bad taste" by old-culture adherents. Since gratification is viewed as a scarce commodity, arousal is dangerous. Clothes must be drab and inconspicuous, colors of low intensity, smells nonexistent ("if it weren't for bad taste there wouldn't be no taste at all"). Sounds should be quiet, words should lack affect. Four-letter words are always in bad taste because they have high stimulus value. Satire is in bad taste if it arouses political passions or creates images that are too vivid or exciting. All direct references to sexuality are in bad taste until proven innocent, since sexual arousal is the most feared result of all. The lines in old-culture homes, furnishings, and public buildings are hard and utilitarian. Since auditory overstimulation is more familiarly painful than its visual counterpart, brilliant, intense, vibrant colors are called "loud," and the preferred colors for old-culture homes are dull and listless. Stimulation in any form leaves old-culture Americans with a "bad taste" in their mouths. This taste is the taste of desire—a reminder that life in the here-and-now contains many pleasures to distract them from the carrot dangling beyond their reach. Too much stimulation makes the carrot hard to see. Good taste is a taste for carrots.

In the past decade, however, this pattern has undergone a merciless assault from the new culture. For if we assume that gratification is easy and resources plentiful, stimulation is no longer to be feared. Psychedelic colors, amplified sound, erotic books and films, bright and elaborate clothing, spicy food, "intense" (i.e., Anglo-Saxon) words, angry and irreverent satire—all go counter to the old pattern of understimulation. Long hair and beards provide a more "tactile" appearance than the bland, shaven-and-shorn, geometric lines of the fifties. Even

Edward Hall's accusation that America is a land of "olfactory blandness" (a statement any traveler will confirm) must now be qualified a little, as the smells of coffee shops, foreign cooking, and incense combine to breathe a modicum of sensation even into the olfactory sphere. (Hall is right, however, in the sense that when America is filled with intense color, music, and ornament, deodorants will be the old culture's last-ditch holdouts. It is no accident that hostility to hippies so often focuses on their olfactory humanity.) The old culture turned the volume down on emotional experience in order to concentrate on its dreams of glory, but the new culture has turned it up again.

New-culture adherents, in fact, often display symptoms of *under*sensitivity to stimuli. They say "Wow!" in response to almost everything, but in voices utterly devoid of either tension or affect. They seem in general to be more certain that desire can be gratified than that it can be aroused.

This phenomenon probably owes much to early child-rearing conditions. Under ordinary circumstances a mother responds to her child's needs when they are expressed powerfully enough to distract her from other cares and activities. Mothers who overrespond to the Spockian challenge, however, often try to anticipate the child's needs. Before arousal has proceeded very far they hover about and try several possible satisfactions. Since we tend to use these early parental responses as models for the way we treat our own impulses in adulthood, some new-culture adherents find themselves moving toward gratification before need arousal is clear or compelling. Like their mothers they are not altogether clear which need they are feeling. To make matters worse they are caught in the dilemma that spontaneity automatically evaporates the moment it becomes an ideology. It is a paradox of the modern condition that only those who oppose complete libidinal freedom are capable of ever achieving it.

Another logical consequence of scarcity assumptions is structured inequality. If there is not enough to go around then those who have more will find ways to prolong their advantage, and even legitimate it through various devices. The law itself, although philosophically committed to equality, is· fundamentally a social device for maintaining structured systems of inequality (defining as crimes, for example, only those forms of theft and violence in which lower class persons engage). One of the major thrusts of the new culture, on the other hand, is equality: since the good things of life are plentiful, everyone should share them: rich and poor, black and white, female and male.

It is a central characteristic of the old culture that means habitually become ends, and ends means. Instead of people working in order to obtain goods in order to be happy, for example, we find that people should be made happy in order to work better in order to obtain more goods, and so on. Inequality, originally a consequence of scarcity, is now a means of creating artificial scarcities. For in the old culture, as we have seen, the manufacture of scarcity is the principal activity. Hostile comments of old-culture adherents toward new-culture forms ("people won't want to work if they can get things for nothing," "people won't want to get married if they can get it free") often reveal this preoccupation. Scarcity, the presumably undesired but unavoidable foundation for the whole old-culture edifice, has now become its most treasured and sacred value, and to maintain this value in the midst of plenty it has been necessary to establish invidiousness as the foremost criterion of worth. Old-culture Americans are peculiarly drawn to anything that seems to be the exclusive

possession of some group or other, and find it difficult to enjoy anything they themselves have unless they can be sure that there are people to whom this pleasure is denied. For those in power even life itself derives its value invidiously: amid the emptiness and anesthesia of a power-oriented career many officials derive reassurance of their vitality from their proximity to the possibility of blowing up the world.

The centrality of invidiousness offers a strong barrier to the diffusion of social justice and equality. But it provides a *raison d'être* for the advertising industry, whose primary function is to manufacture illusions of scarcity. In a society engorged to the point of strangulation with useless and joyless products, advertisements show people calamitously running out of their food or beer, avidly hoarding potato chips, stealing each other's cigarettes, guiltily borrowing each other's deodorants, and so on. In a land of plenty there is little to fight over, but in the world of advertising images men and women will fight before changing their brand, in a kind of parody of the Vietnam War.

The fact that property takes precedence over human life in the old culture also follows logically from scarcity assumptions. If possessions are scarce relative to people they come to have more value than people. This is especially true of people with few possessions, who come to be considered so worthless as to be subhuman and hence eligible for extermination. Many possessions, on the other hand, entitle the owner to a status somewhat more than human. But as a society becomes more affluent these priorities begin to change—human life increases in value and property decreases. New-culture adherents challenge the high relative value placed on property, although the old priority still permeates the society's normative structure. It is still considered permissible, for example, to kill someone who is stealing your property under certain conditions. This is especially true if that person is without property himself—a wealthy kleptomaniac (in contrast to a poor black looter) would probably be worth a murder trial if killed while stealing.*

A recent sign of the shift in values was the *Pueblo* courtmartial. While the Navy, standing firmly behind old-culture priorities, argued that the Commander of the spy ship should have sacrificed the lives of ninety men to prevent the loss of "expensive equipment" to the enemy, the public at large supported his having put human life first. Much of the intense legal upheaval visible today—expressed most noticeably in the glare of publicity that now attaches to the activities of the U.S. Supreme Court—derives from the attempt to adapt an old-legal system to the changing priorities that render it obsolete.

It would not be difficult to show how the other characteristics of the old culture are based on the same scarcity assumptions, or to trace out in detail the derivation of the new culture from the premise that life's satisfactions exist in abundance and sufficiency for all. Let us instead look more closely at the relationship that the new culture bears to the old—the continuities and discontinuities that it offers—and explore some of the contradictions it holds within itself.

First of all it should be stressed that affluence and economic security are not in themselves responsible for the new culture. The rich, like the poor, have always been with us to some degree, but the new culture has not. What is significant in the new culture is not a celebration of

* A more trivial example can be found in the old culture's handling of noise control. Police are called to prevent distraction by the joyous noises of laughter and song, but not to stop the harsh and abrasive roar of power saws, air hammers, power mowers, snow blowers, and other baneful machines.

economic affluence but a rejection of its foundation. The new culture is concerned with rejecting the artificial scarcities upon which material abundance is based. It argues that instead of throwing away one's body so that one can accumulate material artifacts, one should throw away the artifacts and enjoy one's body. The new culture is not merely blindly reactive, however, but embodies a sociological consciousness. In this consciousness lies the key insight that possessions actually generate scarcity. The more emotion one invests in them the more chances for significant gratification are lost—the more committed to them one becomes the more deprived one feels, like a thirsty man drinking salt water. To accumulate possessions is to deliver pieces of oneself to dead things. Possessions can absorb an emotional cathexis, but unlike personal relationships they feed nothing back. Americans have combined the proliferation of possessions with the disruption, circumscription, and trivialization of most personal relationships. An alcoholic becomes malnourished because drinking obliterates his hunger. Americans become unhappy and vicious because their preoccupation with amassing possessions obliterates their loneliness. This is why production in America seems to be on such an endless upward spiral: every time we buy something we deepen our emotional deprivation and hence our need to buy something. This is good for business, of course, but those who profit most from this process are just as trapped in the general deprivation as everyone else. The new-culture adherents are thus not merely affluent—they are trying to substitute an adequate emotional diet for a crippling addiction.

The new culture is nevertheless a product of the old, not merely a rejection of it. It picks up themes latent or dormant or subordinate in the old and magnifies them. The hippie movement, for example, is brimming with nostalgia—a nostalgia peculiarly American and shared by old-culture adherents. This nostalgia embraces the Old West, Amerindian culture, the wilderness, the simple life, the utopian community—all venerable American traditions. But for the old culture they represent a subordinate, ancillary aspect of the culture, appropriate for recreational occasions or fantasy representation—a kind of pastoral relief from everyday striving—whereas for the new culture they are dominant themes. The new culture's passion for memorabilia, paradoxically, causes uneasiness in old-culture adherents, whose future-oriented invidiousness leads to a desire to sever themselves from the past. Yet for the most part it is a question of the new culture making the old culture's secondary themes primary, rather than simply seeking to discard the old culture's primary theme. Even the notion of "dropping out" is an important American tradition —neither the United States itself nor its populous suburb would exist were this not so.

Americans have always been deeply ambivalent about the issue of social involvement. On the one hand they are suspicious of it and share deep romantic fantasies of withdrawal to a simple pastoral or even sylvan life. On the other hand they are much given to acting out grandiose fantasies of taking society by storm, through the achievement of wealth, power, or fame. This ambivalence has led to many strange institutions—the suburb and the automobile being the most obvious. But note that both fantasies express the viewpoint of an outsider. Americans have a profound tendency to feel like outsiders—they wonder where the action is and wander about in search of it (this puts an enormous burden on celebrities, who are supposed to know, but in fact feel just as doubtful as everyone else). Americans have created a society in which they are automatically nobodies, since no one has any stable place or enduring connection. The village idiot

of earlier times was less a "nobody" in this sense than the mobile junior executive or academic. An American has to "make a place for himself" because he does not have one.

Since the society rests on scarcity assumptions, involvement in it has always meant competitive involvement, and, curiously enough, the theme of bucolic withdrawal has often associated itself with that of cooperative, communal life. So consistently, in fact, have intentional communities established themselves in the wilderness that one can only infer that society as we know it makes cooperative life impossible.

Be that as it may, it is important to remember that the New England colonies grew out of utopian communes, so that the dropout tradition is not only old but extremely important to our history. Like so many of the more successful nineteenth century utopian communities (Oneida and Amana, for example) the puritans became corrupted by involvement in successful economic enterprise and the communal aspect was eroded away—another example of a system being destroyed by what it attempts to ignore. The new culture is thus a kind of reform movement, attempting to revive a decayed tradition once important to our civilization.

In stressing these continuities between the new culture and the American past, I do not mean to imply a process unique to our society. One of the most basic characteristics of all successful social systems—indeed, perhaps all living matter as well—is that they include devices that serve to keep alive alternatives that are antithetical to their dominant emphases, as a kind of hedge against change. These latent alternatives usually perist in some encapsulated and imprisoned form ("break glass in case of fire"), such as myths, festivals, or specialized roles. Fanatics continually try to expunge these circumscribed contradictions, but when they succeed it is often fatal to the society. For, as Lewis Mumford once pointed out, it is the "laxity, corruption, and disorder" in a system that makes it viable, considering the contradictory needs that all social systems must satisfy.[1] Such latent alternatives are priceless treasures and must be carefully guarded against loss. For a new cultural pattern does not emerge out of nothing—the seed must already be there, like the magic tricks of wizards and witches in folklore, who can make an ocean out of a drop of water, a palace out of a stone, a forest out of blade of grass, but nothing out of nothing. Many peoples keep alive a tradition of a golden age, in which a totally different social structure existed. The Judeo-Christian God, patriarchal and omnipotent, has served in matrifocal cultures to keep alive the concept of a strong and protective paternal figure in the absence of real-life examples. Jesters kept alive a wide variety of behavior patterns amid the stilted and restrictive formality of royal courts. The specialized effeminate roles that one finds in many warrior cultures are not merely a refuge for those who fail to succeed in the dominant pattern—they are also a living reminder that the rigid "protest masculinity" that prevails is not the only conceivable kind of behavior for a male. And conversely, the warrior ethos is maintained in a peaceful society or era by means of a military cadre or reserve system.

These phenomena are equivalent to (and in literate cultures tend increasingly to be replaced by) written records of social practices. They are like a box of seldom-used tools, or a trunk of old costumes awaiting the proper period-play. Suddenly the environment changes, the tolerated eccentric becomes a prophet,

[1] Lewis Mumford, "The Fallacy of Systems," *Saturday Review of Literature*, XXXII, October 1949; Gideon Sjoberg, "Contradictory Functional Requirements of Social Systems," *Journal of Conflict Resolution*, IV, 1960, pp. 198–208.

the clown a dancing-master, the doll an idol, the idol a doll. The elements have not changed, only the arrangement and the emphases have changed. Every revolution is in part a revival.

Sometimes societal ambivalence is so marked that the latent pattern is retained in a form almost as elaborated as the dominant one. Our society, for example, is one of the most mobile (geographically, at least) ever known; yet, unlike other nomadic cultures it makes little allowance for this fact in its patterns of material accumulation. Our homes are furnished as if we intended to spend the rest of our lives in them, instead of moving every few years. This perhaps represents merely a kind of technological neurosis—a yearning for stability expressed in a technological failure to adapt. Should Americans ever settle down, however, they will find little to do in the way of readjusting their household furnishing habits.

Ultimately it seems inevitable that Americans must either abandon their nomadic habits (which seems unlikely) or moderate their tendency to invest their libido exclusively in material possessions (an addiction upon which the economy relies rather heavily). The new culture is of course pushing hard to realize the second alternative, and if it is successful one might anticipate a trend toward more simply furnished dwellings in which all but the most portable and decorative items are permanent installations. In such a case we might like or dislike a sofa or bed or dresser, but would have no more personal involvement with it than we now do with a stove, furnace, or garage. We would possess, cathect, feel as a part of us, only a few truly personal and portable items.

This tendency of human societies to keep alternative patterns alive has many biological analogues. One of these is *neoteny*—the evolutionary process in which foetal or juvenile characteristics are retained in the adult animal. Body characteristics that have long had only transitional relevance are exploited in response to altered environmental circumstances (thus many human features resemble foetal traits of apes). I have not chosen this example at random, for much of the new culture is implicitly and explicitly "neotenous" in a cultural sense: behavior, values, and life-styles formerly seen as appropriate only to childhood are being retained into adulthood as a counterforce to the old culture.

I pointed out earlier, for example, that children are taught a set of values in earliest childhood—cooperation, sharing, equalitarianism—which they begin to unlearn as they enter school, wherein competition, invidiousness, status differentiation, and ethnocentrism prevail. By the time they enter adult life children are expected to have largely abandoned the value assumptions with which their social lives began. But for affluent, protected, middle-class children this process is slowed down, while intellectual development is speeded up, so that the earlier childhood values can become integrated into a conscious, adult value system around social justice. The same is true of other characteristics of childhood: spontaneity, hedonism, candor, playfulness, use of the senses for pleasure rather than utility, and so on. The protective, child-oriented, middle-class family allows the child to preserve some of these qualities longer than is possible under more austere conditions, and his intellectual precocity makes it possible for him to integrate them into an ideological system with which he can confront the corrosive, life-abusing tendencies of the old culture.

When these neotenous characteristics become manifest to old-culture adherents the effect is painfully disturbing, for they vibrate feelings and attitudes that are very old and very deep, although long and harshly stifled. Old-culture adherents have learned to reject all this, but since

the learning antedated intellectual maturity they have no coherent ideological framework within which such a rejection can be consciously understood and thoughtfully endorsed. They are deeply attracted and acutely revolted at the same time. They can neither resist their fascination nor control their antipathy. This is exemplified by the extravagant curiosity that hippie communes attract, and by the harassment that so often extinguishes them.[2] It is usually necessary in such situations for the rote-learned abhorrence to discharge itself in persecutory activity before the more positive responses can be released. This was true in the case of the early Christians in Rome, with whom contemporary hippies are often compared (both were communal, utopian, mystical, dropouts, unwashed; both were viewed as dangerous, masochistic, ostentatious, the cause of their own troubles; both existed in societies in which the exclusive pursuit of material advantages had reached some kind of dead end), and seems equally true today. The absorption of the persecution is part of the process through which the latent values that the oppressed group protects and nurtures are expropriated by the majority and released into the mainstream of the culture.

Up to this point we have (rather awkwardly) discussed the new culture as if it were an integrated, monolithic pattern, which is certainly very far from the case. There are many varied and contradictory streams feeding the new culture, and some of these deserve particular attention, since they provide the raw material for future axes of conflict.

The most glaring split in the new culture is that which separates militant activism from the traits we generally associate with the hippie movement. The first strand stresses political confronta-

[2] See, for example, Robert Houriet, "Life and Death of a Commune Called Oz," *New York Times Magazine,* February 16, 1969.

tion, revolutionary action, radical commitment to the process of changing the basic structure of modern industrial society. The second involves a renunciation of that society in favor of the cultivation of inner experience and pleasing internal feeling-states. Heightening of sensory receptivity, commitment to the immediate present, and tranquil acceptance of the physical environment are sought in contradistinction to old-culture ways, in which the larger part of one's immediate experience is overlooked or grayed out by the preoccupation with utility, future goals, and external mastery. Since, in the old culture, experience is classified before it is felt, conceptualization tends here to be forsworn altogether. There is also much emphasis on aesthetic expression and an overarching belief in the power of love.

This division is a crude one, and there are, of course, many areas of overlap. Both value systems share an antipathy to the old culture, both share beliefs in sexual freedom and personal autonomy. Some groups (the Yippies, in particular) have tried with some success to bridge the gap in a variety of interesting ways. But there is nonetheless an inherent contradiction between them. Militant activism is task-oriented, and hence partakes of certain old-culture traits such as postponement of gratification, preoccupation with power, and so on. To be a competent revolutionary one must possess a certain tolerance for the "Protestant Ethic" virtues, and the activists' moral code is a stern one indeed. The hippie ethic, on the other hand, is a "salvation now" approach. It is thus more radical, since it remains relatively uncontaminated with old-culture values. It is also far less realistic, since it ignores the fact that the existing culture provides a totally antagonistic milieu in which the hippie movement must try to survive in a state of highly vulnerable parasitic dependence. The activists can reasonably say that the flower

people are absurd to pretend that the revolution has already occurred, for such pretense leads only to severe victimization by the old culture. The flower people can reasonably retort that a revolution based to so great a degree on old-culture premises is lost before it is begun, for even if the militants are victorious they will have been corrupted by the process of winning.

The dilemma is a very real one and arises whenever radical change is sought. For every social system attempts to exercise the most rigid control over the mechanisms by which it can be altered—defining some as legitimate and others as criminal or disloyal. When we examine the characteristics of legitimate and nonlegitimate techniques, however, we find that the "legitimate" ones involve a course of action requiring a sustained commitment to the core assumptions of the culture. In other words, if the individual follows the "legitimate" pathway there is a very good chance that his initial radical intent will be eroded in the process. If he feels that some fundamental change in the system is required, then, he has a choice between following a path that subverts his goal or one that leads him to be jailed as a criminal or traitor.

This process is not a Machiavellian invention of American capitalists, but rather a mechanism which all viable social systems must evolve spontaneously in order to protect themselves from instability. When the system as it stands is no longer viable, however, the mechanism must be exposed for the swindle that it is; otherwise the needed radical changes will be rendered ineffectual.

The key to the mechanism is the powerful human reluctance to admit that an achieved goal was not worth the unpleasant experience required to achieve it.[3] This is the basic principle underlying

[3] Leon Festinger, *A Theory of Cognitive Dissonance* (Stanford, Calif.: Stanford University Press, 1965).

initiation rituals: "if I had to suffer so much pain and humiliation to get into this club it must be a wonderful organization." The evidence of thousands of years is that the mechanism works extremely well. Up to some point, for example, war leaders can count on high casualties to increase popular commitment to military adventures.

Thus when a political leader says to a militant, "why don't you run for political office (get a haircut, dress conservatively, make deals, do the dirty work for your elders) and try to change the system in that way"—or the teacher says to the student, "wait until you have your Ph.D. (M.D., LL.B.) and then you can criticize our program," or the white man says to the black man, "when you begin to act like us you'll receive the same opportunities we do"—there is a serious subterfuge involved (however unconscious it may be) in that the protester, if he accepts the condition, will in most cases be automatically converted by it to his opponent's point of view.

The dilemma of the radical, then, is that he is likely to be corrupted if he fights the *status quo* on its own terms, but is not permitted to fight it in any other way. The real significance of the New Left is that it has discovered, in the politics of confrontation, as near a solution to this dilemma as can be found: it is always a bit problematic whether the acts of the new militants are "within the system" or not, and substantial headway can be made in the resulting confusion.

Yet even here the problem remains: if an activist devotes his life to altering the power structure, will he not become like old-culture adherents—utilitarian, invidious, scarcity-oriented, future-centered, and so on? Having made the world safe for flower people will he be likely to relinquish it to them? "You tell me it's the institution," object the Beatles, "you'd

better free your mind instead." But what if all the freed minds are in jail?

The dilemma is particularly clear for blacks. Some blacks are much absorbed in rediscovering and celebrating those characteristics which seem most distinctively black and in sharpest contrast to white Western culture: black expressiveness, creativity, sensuality, and spontaneity being opposed to white constrictedness, rigidity, frigidity, bustle, and hypocrisy. For these blacks, to make too great a commitment to the power game is to forsake one's blackness. Power is a white hangup. Yet the absence of power places rather severe limits on the ability of blacks to realize their blackness or anything else.

There is no way to resolve this dilemma, and indeed, it is probably better left unresolved. In a revolutionary situation one needs discipline and unity of purpose, which, however, leads to all kinds of abuses when the goal is won. Discipline and unity become ends in themselves (after the old-culture pattern) and the victory becomes an empty one. It is therefore of great importance to have the envisioned revolutionary goals embodied in a group culture of some kind, with which the acts of those in power can be compared. In the meantime the old culture is subject to a two-pronged attack: a direct assault from activists—unmasking its life-destroying proclivities, its corruption, its futility and pointlessness, its failure to achieve any of its objectives—and an indirect assault by the expansion of expressive countercultures beyond a tolerable (i.e., freak) size.

Closely related to the activist-hippie division is the conflict over the proper role of aggression in the new culture. Violence is a major theme in the old culture and most new-culture adherents view human aggression with deep suspicion. Nonviolence has been the dominant trend in both the activist and hippie segments of the new culture until recently. But more and more activists have become impatient with the capacity of the old culture to strike the second cheek with even more enthusiam than the first, and have endorsed violence under certain conditions as a necessary evil.

For the activists the issue has been practical rather than ideological: most serious and thoughtful activists have only a tactical commitment to violence. For the dropout ideologues, however, aggression poses a difficult problem: if they seek to minimize the artificial constriction of emotional expression, how can they be consistently loving and pacific? This logical dilemma is usually resolved by ignoring it: the love cult typically represses aggressive feelings ruthlessly—the body is paramount only so long as it is a loving body.

At the moment the old culture is so fanatically absorbed in violence that it does the work for everyone. If the new culture should prevail, however, the problem of human aggression would probably be its principal bone of contention. Faced with the persistence of aggressiveness (even in the absence of the old culture's exaggerated violence-inducing institutions), the love cult will be forced to reexamine its premises, and opt for some combination of expression and restraint that will restore human aggression to its rightful place as a natural, though secondary, human emotion.

A third split in the new culture is the conflict between individualism and collectivism. On this question the new culture talks out of both sides of its mouth, one moment pitting ideals of cooperation and community against old-culture competitiveness, the next moment espousing the old culture in its most extreme form with exhortations to "do your own thing." I am not arguing that individualism need be totally extirpated in order to make community possible, but new-culture enterprises often collapse because of a dogmatic unwillingness to subordinate the whim of the individual to the needs of the group. This problem is rarely faced honestly by new-culture adherents, who seem unaware of the conservatism involved in their attachment to individualistic principles.

It is always disastrous to attempt to eliminate any structural principle altogether; but if the balance between individualistic and collective emphases in America is not altered, everything in the new culture will be perverted and caricatured into simply another bizarre old-culture product. There must be continuities between the old and the new, but these cannot extend to the relative weights assigned to core motivational principles. The new culture seeks to create a tolerable society within the context of persistent American strivings—utopianism, the pursuit of happiness. But nothing will change until individualism is assigned a subordinate place in the American value system—for individualism lies at the core of the old culture, and a prepotent individualism is not a viable foundation for any society in a nuclear age.

9.3   BEYOND THE CARROT AND THE STICK: LIBERATION AND POWER WITHOUT CONTROL[1]

John E. McClusky

INTRODUCTION

It is a truism to say that the exercise of power and influence are at the heart of politics. In both theory and research, political scientists have devoted extensive attention to its study. Nevertheless, basic aspects of power relations remain relatively unexplored and poorly understood by political scientists. This is particularly true of power relations which do not adversely affect the target or compliant party. The present investigation is aimed at improving our understanding of power relations in which the influencing party

(A) elicits important, beneficial changes in the target (B).[2]

[1] This manuscript is a substantially abbreviated version of a paper of the same title presented at the Midwest Political Science Association Meetings on May 2, 1975 in Chicago. For a fuller treatment of the ideas as well as illustrative and supportive evidence of this essay, see the latter. Also, for an elaboration of three elements of the theory presented here—1) exemplary power; 2) non-controlling power; and 3) intrinsically reward compliance—see our companion essay, "Power without Control: Exemplary Power and Intrinsic Rewards," presented at the American Political Science Association Meetings, September 5, 1975. The data on which this exploration is based are essentially of two types: historical evidence from sources such as Castro's guerrilla movement, Gandhi's movement for Indian independence, and segments of the women's movement today; and, social science research on leadership, social facilitation, identification, and related phenomena. The writing of these manuscripts has been supported by a fellowship grant (F-73-344) from the National Endowment for the Humanities and by a University of Iowa Old Gold Fellowship.

[2] The usage of "power" in this essay follows several leading definitions and is elaborated below in fn. 15. Here it is sufficient to note that Bachrach and Baratz in an earlier work, *Power and Poverty: Theory and Practice* (New York: Oxford, 1970), Dahl in his early work, e.g., *Modern Political Analysis* (Englewood Cliffs, N.J.: Prentice-Hall, 1963), and Lasswell and Kaplan, *Power and Society* (New Haven: Yale University Press, 1950), among others, stipulated that power denotes *coercive or adverse* influence. (Interestingly, throughout the early debate about the distribution of power in local and national communities, pluralists such as Dahl and their critics such as Bachrach often agreed on this definitional point). By contrast, Dahl in his recent work, "Power," in *International Encyclopedia of the Social Sciences* (1968), pp. 405–415, De Jouvenel, Easton, Friedrich, Frey, and other political scientists as well as most social psychologists who study power do *not* stipulate that it is *coercive*. We do not so stipulate, either. Such a stipulation is no longer common practice in the literature, if it ever was. More importantly, to restrict the meaning of power to coercive influence seems not only arbitrary but confusing. It is not congruent with its usage in ordinary language. There power is more often a core word in the political vocabulary with a much broader meaning at best ambiguous with regard to coercion. In our technical language, therefore, it might be less confusing to use the term, coercion, to refer to coercive influence, and to use power as the more inclusive term denoting the entire set of phenomena in which people elicit desired responses or changes from others. The significant differences among the ways in which people elicit changes in terms of their legitimacy, coerciveness, and adversity for the target can appropriately be noted by terms such as authority, persuasion, coercion, force, domination, leadership, etc.

Such an understanding is vital for any A who wants to liberate B, e.g., assist B to increase his or her awareness, efficacy, and self-esteem. A may be an individual or organization; a teacher, therapist, community organizer, political leader, or participant in a liberation movement. Such an understanding is also vital for B. E.g., it can help B determine if the influencing party's professed intent to assist or liberate him or her is likely, in fact, to produce the changes B desires.

We offer a theory to describe *and* explain power relations in terms of such changes. We suggest a scheme to systematically describe the *changes in B elicited by compliance with A*. In our scheme B's changes are analyzed along the following continuous dimensions: (1) powerlessness/efficacy; (2) self-degradation/self-esteem; (3) dependence/independence; (4) hopelessness/aspiration; (5) igorance/awareness; and (6) insecure/secure identity.[3] We use the term *liberat-* *ing* power to denote those relations eliciting significant change in a *positive* direction on several of B's dimensions (e.g., toward greater efficacy, independence, and awareness). *Debilitating* power denotes those relations eliciting significant change in a *negative* direction on several such dimensions.[4]

---

[3] The meaning of some of the dimensions, such as the fourth and fifth, is self-evident. Others require elaboration. B's powerlessness/efficacy refers to how much B's behavior can determine the occurrence of the outcomes he or she seeks. This is based somewhat upon Seeman's definition of powerlessness widely used in studies of alienation. See Melvin Seeman, "The Meaning of Alienation," in Ada W. Finifter, *Alienation and The Social System* (New York: Wiley and Sons, 1972), p. 46. However, our usage departs from Seeman's and others by emphasizing B's *competence* at tasks or activities (including his/her ability to influence others) more than B's *perception* of that competence. In other words, we focus upon the *performance* aspects of B's "powerlessness/efficacy" more than purely phenomenological approaches do.

B's "self-degradation/self-esteem" refers to how much B respects or values him or herself; how worthy B thinks he or she is. And B's "dependence/independence" refers to how *autonomous* or self-determining he or she is, especially in relating with others and choosing alternatives in action. It does *not* mean "iso- lation or lack of relationship to others." B can be independent while engaging in numerous relationships including an enduring one with A, who influences B through exemplary power and other non-coercive means. This usage follows that of Martin Buber, in which a person can be independent or autonomous while fully engaged in interhuman, even communal life. In fact, each partner must be autonomous for a truly mutual, interhuman relation to flourish; and such relations, in turn, are at the heart of community. See Martin Buber, "Distance and Relation," *The Knowledge of Man* (New York: Harper and Row, 1965).

Finally, B's "insecure/secure identity" refers to how secure, firm, or strong B's awareness of self is. How well does B know who and what he or she is? For our discussion of identity, see below, fn. 24. Our six-fold set of B's dimensions does not exhaust those which might be affected by compliance with A. But each of them does seem salient to our ordinary meaning of liberation, which is the change we are attempting to describe.

[4] Of course, many power relations result in opposing changes in B along these dimensions. E.g., through compliance with A, B can typically *gain* efficacy (competence at some valued task) by *losing* independence (freedom from A who restricts B's access to resources needed to accomplish the task). We explicitly limit the use of the terms "liberating" and "debilitating" power to those relations in which B's changes do not significantly counter-balance each other along these dimensions. This limitation not only maintains precision as to the kind of power relation to which our terms refer in the phenomenal world, but also avoids prematurely assessing the relative weight of the dimensions or their inter-relations. We see no reason, for instance,

We employ the terms, "liberating" and "debilitating," because we view human liberation in part as a process in which people exhibit changes along these dimensions. No one would deny that to be "liberated" is to be emancipated or freed in some sense. Beyond this vague generalization, however, differences in meaning occur. Our usage emphasizes the positive rather than negative meanings of liberation. To be liberated is to be freed to do, be, or become what one can; i.e., to develop one's potential, explore, express, and realize one's self.[5]

We suggest that such liberation centers around changes in a person's self-identity, independence (autonomy), and basic efficacy or competence as a striving, achieving human being. In turn, other dimensions in our scheme of liberat-

ing change (awareness, aspiration, and self-esteem) are related to these.[6]

We also suggest a core hypothesis to explain the variance between liberating and debilitating power. The more a power relation exhibits the following conditions, the more likely it is liberating instead of debilitating: (1) A's *enabling* and *confirming* B in obtaining B's compliance; (2) A's *exercising exemplary* power (i.e., setting an example or demonstrating a course of action *without* promising a reward in return for compliance or threatening a punishment for non-compliance); (3) A's *abstaining from controlling* B's access to rewards; and (4) B's perceiving that the performance of the act A urges is *intrinsically rewarding*, independent of any extrinsic benefits accruing to B by means of compliance.

These four characteristics are *not necessary* conditions for a liberating power relation. Surely relations occur in which A elicits changes in B toward greater self-esteem, efficacy, etc. without their presence.[7] Nor are they exhaustive of

to attach weights *a priori* to the various dimensions. Is a change in self-esteem always three times as important as a change in efficacy? Such comparative evaluations can only be made, if at all, on the basis of observations of each power relation in the empirical world.

[5] To be able to exercise such freedom requires, in turn, the existence of negative freedom *from* conditions that oppress or restrict people (whether they be economic, political, cultural, or some other). When we talk of national, racial, ethnic, and sexual "liberation" movements we are referring to the struggle of some broad collective to emancipate itself from these restrictive conditions at a macro-level in society. At the same time, we would argue that leaders of many of these movements are also hoping to elicit liberating changes in their individual adherents at the micro-level. And the latter, in turn, partly understand and experience their participation in a movement in terms of such personal changes. They may partly evaluate their movement in terms of how successfully it promotes their self-esteem, autonomy, and basic human competencies.

[6] In this regard we echo the view of many social and humanistic psychologists, including French, Kahn, and Rogers, who elucidate an integral relation among a person's self-identity, self-esteem, autonomy, and numerous more specific attitudes and patterns of overt behavior. See, e.g., John R. P. French, Jr. and Robert L. Kahn, "A Programmatic Approach to Studying the Industrial Environment and Mental Health," in *The Journal of Social Issues*, xviii, no. 3 (July, 1962), pp. 1–47. See also, Nevitt Sanford, *Self and Society* (New York: Atherton Press, 1966), ch. 1. Our discussion of liberation is similar though not identical to the latter's discussion on human development.

[7] E.g., A may get B to perform some task both consider demeaning, by threatening to punish B if he or she doesn't do it. In the process of compliance, however, B may unexpectedly gain critical training at some generalized skill which increases his or her efficacy at a wide range of tasks, as well as his or her awareness, self-confidence and consequently, self-esteem.

the conditions conducive to liberating power. Nevertheless, both social research and everyday observation of power relations lead us to assert that a relation in which all four conditions are present is likely to be liberating to B. The presence of the first condition, A's enabling and confirming B, e.g., appears to be particularly pivotal in this regard.[8]

Obviously this core hypothesis would require vast amounts of research including experimental and statistical control to verify in a strict sense.[9] What follows

[8] See below, pp. 390–391 for an elaboration of this claim.

None of the propositions in this paragraph deny the fact that in natural social situations B often exhibits liberating changes without their being intentionally elicited by A—without some actor directly influencing B to do so. Sometimes, in fact, B exhibits such changes as a negative counter to others' abortive attempts to keep him or her from engaging in liberating action. Thus, during the civil rights movement in the South, law enforcement agents often tried to induce compliance from activists by measures which backfired, actually triggering further liberating behavior and attitudes on the activists' part. E.g., being jailed was considered a "merit badge" rather than a deterrent to many participants at certain stages in the movement.

History is replete with such ironic dialectics between social control agents and their adversaries, a fact which receives central attention in the theories of liberation/revolution offered by Sartre and Fanon, among others. For an exposition and critique of Sartre's theory in this regard, see John E. McClusky, *A Dilemma of Existential Political Theory: Reconciling Freedom and Cohesion* (unpublished PhD dissertation, University of California, Berkeley: 1971), pp. 81–89; 212–220.

[9] Among other things, one would have to collect data from a large sample of power relations varying along the continuum from purely liberating to debilitating and see if they differ in accord with our hypothesis as to the presence of these four conditions. Just as obviously a theory of this scope lends itself to a variety of empirical tests.

is not such a verification, for our theory is in the exploratory stage. The evidence we employ is intended to illustrate and support its main concepts and propositions, not verify them.

Other theories have recognized that power relations can be liberating for B. In traditional political theory this was recognized by scholars such as Plato, Sir Thomas More, Rousseau, and Marx who prescribed utopian communities (no matter how different they were in terms of hierarchy, citizen participation, and basic public values). Plato's philosopher-king, More's phylark, Rousseau's grand legislator and sovereign people expressing the general will, and Marx's communist revolutionary all exercised liberating power in their respective utopian communities.[10]

And in contemporary studies of power, Cartwright, Emmet, Etzioni, and Friedrich are among the many scholars who recognize something akin to liberat-

[10] Despite this similarity, in other respects our theory is quite dissimilar from these traditional ones. We recognize that power relations vary from pure domination by A over B to pure freedom for B to choose whether or not to comply, unrestricted by A's controlling in any way B's access to rewards. This point is *at best* ambiguous regarding Plato's philosopher-king and Rousseau's sovereign people expressing the general will. Rousseau's classic conception that obedience to the general will can "force one to be free" is *not* the kind of freedom to which we refer. Some objection might be raised that the notion of power hardly figures in Plato's theory, but that seems unsound. The term, "power," may not be used, but the governance and direction of the polis is a central concern in Plato's theorizing and this activity clearly involves the exercise of power. Obviously, Plato faced this fact himself, and altered his prescription for controlling the exercise of power in government accordingly as he moved from *The Republic* to *The Laws*. See, for example, Sheldon Wolin, *Politics and Vision* (Boston: Little, Brown, 1960), ch. 2.

ing power. Cartwright's reference to "benevolent power" and Emmet's concept of "aedificatory power" (in which A strengthens and inspires B) are similar though not identical to liberating power. So are Etzioni's concept of "normative power" and Friedrich's "consenual power."[11]

However, none of these scholars attempts to describe and explain liberating power in the manner we do. First, our schematic description of power relations allows us to more systematically identify their emancipating consequences for B as well as adverse ones. Second, our explanatory hypothesis about the differences between liberating and debilitating power relations allows us to see beyond the "carrot and stick" (reward/punishment) conception held by many political scientists.[12] In the latter conception, the primary if not exclusive method of exercising power is the control of rewards. A obtains B's compliance by promising

[11] See Dorwin Cartwright, *Studies in Social Power* (Ann Arbor: University of Michigan Press, 1959), pp. 11–12; Dorothy Emmet, *Function, Purpose, and Power* (London: Macmillan, 1958), ch. 8; Amitai Etzioni, *A Sociological Reader on Complex Organizations* (New York: Holt, Rinehart, and Winston, 1969), p. 66; and Carl Friedrich, "Political Leadership and the Problem of Charismatic Power," *Journal of Politics*, 23 (February, 1961), p. 7. Friedrich's concept of "initiating leadership" on p. 21 in that article is similar to our concept of "exemplary leadership."

[12] Lest we cause undue alarm among some of its long-standing proponents, we are not proposing to throw the "carrot/stick" conception of power on the scrap heap of discarded social theories. We would agree that numerous power relations are adequately described by that conception and its emphasis upon A's controlling B's access to rewards as the primary means of gaining B's compliance. Nevertheless, it does not adequately describe *all* power relations, and one type which frequently exhibits features counter to the carrot/stick conception is liberating power.

rewards in return for compliance and/or threatening punishment for non-compliance. Such a conception underlies reinforcement, bargaining, exchange, and related theories proliferating in our discipline.

Our explanatory hypothesis refers to two critical facts about power often overlooked by this "carrot/stick" conception. One is that A sometimes exercises power without controlling in any way B's access to rewards. Rather, A simply shares rewards with B or shares information B needs to more effectively pursue rewards, *without* assurance of B's compliance in return. One of the most common ways this operates is by A setting an example or demonstrating a course of action to B without promising a reward or threatening a punishment. This method of influence we refer to as "exemplary power."

A second fact this "carrot and stick" conception overlooks is that B's compliance is sometimes *intrinsically rewarding*. B perceives that the acts A urges upon him or her are ones whose very performance is highly charged, rewarding, and possibly self-actualizing to B. B may be doing something he or she would not otherwise do, but it actualizes self-esteem, efficacy, and freedom. It is highly valuable in itself. This major motive for compliance is beyond the purview of the "carrot/stick" conception of power. In that conception the act B is urged to perform is seen itself only as a *means* to the attainment of some extrinsic benefit or the avoidance of some extrinsic punishment. The very concept of A's *promising* a reward *in return for B's compliance* entails this. However, when the reward to B is the value of performing the complying act itself, then A need not promise anything in return.

The "carrot/stick" conception of power actually manifests itself far beyond the confines of reinforcement, bargaining, and related theories. It is the view found in most schemes for classifying methods of power or influence. Such schemes either expressly exclude methods which do not involve controlling rewards and punishments or use language implying that such control is involved in all methods. Two of the most widely used schemes, those of Etzioni and Parsons, illustrate this point. Neither of these scholars would normally be considered reinforcement or bargaining theorists.

In Etzioni's typology the various methods of exercising power are described in terms of the "manipulation and allocation of rewards and punishments" for the "control" of the complaint party. This is as true of his category of "normative or identitive" power as it is of "utilitarian or remunerative" and "coercive" power. Likewise, Parsons' typology of methods of influence is based on A's obtaining compliance from B through the use of various *"presumptive conditional outputs"* in the form of "positive or negative sanctions."[13]

[13]Amitai Etzioni, *Reader on Complex Organizations*, pp. 61–62; and "Organizational Control Structure," in James March, ed. *Handbook of Organizations*, p. 651. Talcott Parsons, "On the Concept of Political Power," in *Politics and Social Structure* (Figure 1, "paradigm of sanctions"). My italics. Not all typologies are limited to such "carrot/stick" methods of influence. One which expressly includes other methods is Dorwin Cartwright's and Alvin Zander's in *Group Dynamics* (New York: Knopf, 1968), p. 220. Elsewhere we have traced the prevalence of this "carrot/stick" conception of power in social science to two factors: the theoretical legacy of Machiavelli, Hobbes, and Weber; and, certain patterns in American political culture and structure. See McClusky, "Power without Control," pp. 4–6; and, the extended version of this article presented at the Midwest Political Science Association Meetings, May 2, 1975, pp. 6–7.

LIBERATING AND DEBILITATING POWER

We have chosen to introduce our theory by means of the "paradigmatic" case.[14] That is, we will illustrate the theory by reference to one of the most conspicuous cases of liberating power in recent American history; namely, Martin Luther King, Jr.'s leadership of black people in the civil rights movement, particularly when he emerged in Montgomery, Alabama in 1955. Few power relations come closer to approximating our hypothesis in undiluted form than that between King and the Montgomery movement's participants. It resulted in well-documented changes among those participants that were extraordinarily liberating. It exhibited an unusually high incidence of the four conditions we hypothesize to be strongly associated with liberating power.

Before we describe this extraordinary relationship, let us first be sure we are describing the exercise of power at all. According to the most widely used definitions of the concept, Martin Luther King was exercising power in Montgomery. Whether one defines power/influence as Dahl does, "A getting B to do something B would not otherwise do," as Schopler has, "A's ability to elicit desired responses from B," as Etzioni, Shils, and others

[14] We are *not* using Kuhn's notion of "paradigm" offered in *The Structure of Scientific Revolution* (Chicago: University of Chicago Press, 1963). It has several technical dimensions distinguishing it from the meaning given in ordinary language. We follow the latter: a "paradigmatic" case is one which stands as a model or example of the set of phenomena our theory intends to describe and explain. By analyzing that case one can observe those phenomena about as clearly and distinctly as is possible. This is the primary reason the "paradigmatic" case is employed to illustrate the explanatory and descriptive value of any theory, whether it be in the physical or social sciences.

do, "A's getting B to change in ways congruent with A's intent," or more broadly as Morgenthau does, "any changes in B which can at least partially be attributable to the actions of A (the 'causative agent')," it characterizes many of King's relations to black people in Montgomery and elsewhere.[15]

Martin Luther King frequently got these people to do things they would not otherwise do. In fact, in Montgomery he amazed most people (including himself and his associates) in obtaining the pace and level of compliance he did. When he urged them, blacks engaged in countless acts similar to those others had previously urged but failed to elicit. Where others had unsuccessfully attempted to organize boycotts, King and his associates organized a bus boycott that was approximately 95% effective for an entire year. Thousands of black people organized and operated their own substitute taxi service

[15] Robert Dahl, *Modern Political Analysis*, p. 40; John Schopler, in *Advances in Experimental Social Psychology*, p. 185; Amitai Etzioni, *Reader on Complex Organizations*, p. 60; Herbert Goldhamer and Edward Shils, "Types of Power and Status," *American Journal of Sociology*, 45 (September, 1939), p. 171; and Hans Morgenthau, *Politics Among Nations* (New York: Knopf, 1964). The definitions we have given do not follow these sources verbatim except in the case of Dahl. Many other leading definitions of power or related terms adhere closely to these. They all refer, additionally, to a causal relation of some kind between A and B (A is "eliciting" or "getting B to do" something; "changes in B are partly attributable to A's action").

We employ these leading definitions throughout the essay to demonstrate that our analysis of power does not hinge upon some esoteric or limited meaning of the concept. Although Dahl's definition may be the most restrictive in this regard, they all denote a set of phenomena by which "A gets B to do what A wants." This is as useful a definition of power for our purposes as any, expressing what underlies the others.

throughout this period. They developed the Montgomery Improvement Association (M.I.A.) to act upon their long-suffered grievances. And they became a politically organized *community* for the first time. The black population of Montgomery had been divided into factions prior to the boycott and King's leadership.[16] But now the "hoodlums" and parishioners were working and celebrating together in a collective struggle. The mass meetings of the M.I.A. were characterized by a profound outpouring and sharing of emotion among black people which contributed to their morale, communication, and unity. They were now a politicized, efficacious movement where they had been a powerless, divided mass.[17]

Clearly, these changes (elicited to a significant extent by King) were extrinsically rewarding for black people. They were means to greater independence from the white power structure and to redressing specific grievances. But these changes were also intrinsically valuable. They were changes whose very adoption disclosed self-worth, dignity, and efficacy. Simply engaging in such acts of protest and independence from the white power structure was a novel, highly charged, and rewarding experience. A mass meeting celebrating the end of the Montgomery struggle was a "peak experience" illustrative of this. Lerone Bennett, Jr. recalls the event:

[16] William Robert Miller, *Martin Luther King, Jr.* (New York: Avon, 1968), p. 51. King's ability to work well with various factions and not be identified with any one of them contributed to his being selected to lead the boycott by its organizers.

[17] Lerone Bennett, Jr., "When the Man and the Hour Are Met," in C. Eric Lincoln, *Martin Luther King, Jr.: A Profile* (New York: Hill and Wang, 1970), p. 18. The emotionalism was not something King originally intended to elicit, but he altered his intentions after it emerged and he realized its value.

The Reverend Robert Graetz . . . decided that night to read the scripture according to Paul; 'When I was a child, I spoke as a child, I understood as a child.' At this point, there was a vast uproar. All over the floor now, men and women were on their feet, waving handkerchiefs and weeping. It was only with great difficulty that Graetz completed the sentence. '. . . But when I became a man, I put away childish things.'[18]

In this event, thousands of people who complied with King shared a spontaneous, public affirmation of their profound change in self-identity, courage, and esteem. As a co-leader in the Montgomery boycott reported, "The struggle . . . was won, really, at the point where King, and through him, the Negro population cast off fear, saying with their spirit and, most importantly, with their bodies, that they were ready to *lose* everything in order to win."[19]

Such changes in the targets exemplify the liberating power relation. We have suggested that these changes can be systematically analyzed along several continuous dimensions, including powerlessness/efficacy, dependence/independence, and self-degradation/self-esteem. Both behavioral and attitudinal indicators can be employed to measure the target's changes from a point prior to entering into a power relation until a point after the relation has endured for some time.[20] Of

course, not all changes will be as dramatic and conspicuous as those King helped to elicit in the boycott. And measuring such changes in natural social settings can be complicated in any case.

If we select just one dimension, B's dependence/independence, the complications in measuring a target's change are easily illuminated. We must look not only at changes in B's degree of independence from A, but also from other actors in his or her life space. A would not be liberating B very much if his or her power induced B to become much more dependent upon a third party (C) than B was upon A to begin with—all other things being equal, such as C's and A's benevolence toward B. In liberation movements a leader such as King is helping Bs rise vis-à-vis Cs (e.g., members of local white power structures) who have been oppressing them. A enters the conflict as a benevolent power agent who is likely to help Bs overcome some of their dependence upon Cs. Bs are motivated to comply with As partially as a means to improving their relationship to Cs.[21]

---

[18] *Ibid.*, p. 31.

[19] *Ibid.*, p. 29.

[20] This obviously requires the collection of *pre*-event data. When studying power relations in movements as well publicized as the Montgomery boycott, an abundance of documentary sources are available from which to collect data. These include news reports, historical records, newsreels, video-tapes, and personal narratives by the participants before, during, and after the occurrence of the power relation. Survey research on attitudes exhibited prior to the power relation by the population from which the participants emerged will often be available as well. This ought to correct gross inaccuracies about participants' pre-event attitudes (and behaviors) that are reported in news accounts. And, through interviews and other means one can tap participants' and observers' recollections of the power relation (including the pre-event behavior and attitudes of the participants) although the validity of data gathered by this means must be checked against other sources.

[21] Of course, sometimes followers become more *dependent* on their leaders while they collectively struggle to become more *independent* of their common adversary or oppressor. Such ambiguities are among the dilemmas of liberationist and revolutionary politics which political theorists and actors have argued about for centuries. This particular ambiguity is a central concern for such contemporary political/social theorists as Arendt, Buber, Camus, Merleau-Ponty, and Sartre. Our scheme for analyzing the target's

As the case of King's liberating power indicates, some of the evidence of B's independence from A or C is not difficult to assess in natural social settings. *Behavioral* evidence is indicated by such things as the degree to which B overtly challenges A or C, initiates activities on his or her own, sustains activities beyond their perceived request, or even acts against their perceived wishes. The changes we have noted in those who complied with King demonstrated an exceptional increase in independence from the white power structure. But those people also exhibited independence toward one another and King. Open debate and disagreement were common features of the movement under King's leadership. This was evident in executive sessions, mass meetings, and personal encounters. Moreover, while King and his associates began the Montgomery movement by urging a boycott only, the mass membership used the M.I.A. as a vehicle for the expression and attempted solution of a much more extensive range of grievances.[22]

Attitudinal evidence of B's independence can also be gathered in natural social settings. A major indicator would be the extent to which Bs identify themselves exclusively as subordinate to A or the collective to which A belongs. To what extent do they remain unique, individual beings in their awareness? The extreme of subordination is exemplified by the totalitarian personalities described by Arendt, Buber, and others.[23] These personalities view themselves as first and foremost "Nazis" carrying out the orders of the Party or Fuehrer. Their total identity is wrapped up in their collective role. They are submerged in it.

Evidence regarding the degree to which a person identifies as a subordinate can be drawn from a variety of sources including self-reports in interviews and public, even recorded communications. These include what we call "self-identifying acts."[24] Such acts are an ordinary

---

changes along several dimensions (including independence/dependence) would allow the investigator to make comparisons across movements and between leader-follower relationships within the same movement as to how "liberating" they are for their participants.

At the same time, our description of "liberating power" is not derived specifically from such political movements but is meant to help us understand all kinds of power relations in terms of the liberating and debilitating changes they elicit in their targets. For example, it allows us to examine helping relations such as psychiatric counseling with regard to our six dimensions of liberating change and the four conditions we hypothesize to be associated with it. Often professionals in such helping relations cloak the elements of dominance and manipulation in their interaction with clients by describing it in the language of medicine and helping. (See, for example, Murray Edelman, "The Political Language of the Helping Professions," in *Politics and Society*, v. 4, no. 3 (1974).

[22] Through the M.I.A. these ministers and the black community "agreed on a six-point, long-range constructive program which would include (1) the founding of a 'Negro' bank, (2) a credit union, (3) expansion of the voter-education clinics, (4) establishment of institutes for training in non-violent action, (5) taking on some of the work of the NAACP which had been outlawed in the State of Alabama, and (6) providing economic assistance to those who were fired from their jobs for participating in the boycott." Miller, *Martin Luther King, Jr.*, p. 65.

[23] For an exposition of the phenomenological accounts of extreme subordination to a "total" collective, see John E. McClusky, *A Dilemma of Existentialist Theory*, pp. 228–234.

[24] The term, "self-identity," has varied meanings. We use it to refer to any identification of the self, particularly awareness of "who" and "what" the self is. It is distinctly more than "self-image," if the latter refers to viewing oneself as a bearer of attributes, such as being an occupant of certain roles. The

part of political life and a significant aspect of protest behavior, intended to disclose the performer's identity. In liberation movements they may disclose their performer's new freedom, efficacy, and self-esteem. The slogans of liberation movements are frequently uttered as self-identifying acts, such as "sisterhood is powerful," "Ain't I a Woman," "Black is beautiful," and "I am a Man." By analyzing such acts, one can gather data about how independent the performer is from those with whom he or she complies, including leaders in his or her movement.

From data of this kind we can only expect to make rough and approximate measurements of changes in B's independence and other dimensions elicited by A's exercise of power. Numerous scholars have offered schemes for measuring A's power over B. Typical categories include: (1) the "domain" of A's power, i.e., the number of people from whom A can elicit desired changes; (2) the

"scope," i.e., the number of issues about which A can elicit changes in a particular person; and (3) the "range of states of B" (items of a particular person's behavior, decisions, attitudes, etc.) affected by A's influence.[25]

Our exploration intimates that significant variations in the amount of power A exercises over B remain to be studied. The possible depth, intensity, and duration of the changes A elicits in B, for example, have hardly been noticed. Observing B's changes along the six dimensions we have enumerated is particularly useful in probing these deeper, more enduring affects of power. To illustrate, the conversion experience in which B may reintegrate his or her personality around a newly emerging self-identity is tapped by our dimension, insecure/secure identity. It is likely to be affected most in those power relations in which B identifies strongly with and is highly loyal to A, such as a charismatic one. It and other dimensions help us to observe and measure significant variations among charismatic relationships as to how liberating or debilitating they are for the followers. These variations are often overlooked in studies of charismatic leadership. Dorothy Emmet believes this neglect is due to the influence of Weber's account of "charismatic authority" in the social sciences. In Emmet's words:

I cannot help thinking there is something rather Teutonic, suggesting the Fuehrer-Prinzip, about this [Weber's] description. The alternative to bureacratic authority, working by rule and rote, is described as a romanticized kind of personal authority inspiring blind obedience in devoted followers. But is there not a

---

latter is self-categorization or typing, whether it be in terms of socio-economic, biological, psychological, or other attributes. By contrast, we are interested in self-understanding of "who" one is as well as "what" one is. Following the existentialist perspective, one discloses to others and oneself "who" one is through the evolving series of actions one performs. These actions are one's continuing choice of a specific way to be at every moment in life. In this sense, *every* act one performs discloses one's identity, not just the set we have termed, "self-identifying." Finally, the content of B's identity which A calls B to disclose is an important variable in a liberating power relationship. How "open" or "closed" is it? Does it entail, that is, a self-developing identity for B—one B continues to shape for him or herself—or an identity A rigidly imposes on B? Is it more like King calling people to assert that they are free, self-respecting folk who can say "I am a Man"? Or, is it like Hitler calling Germans to be good Nazis who are loyal to the party and "obey orders"?

[25] For a discussion of "range" and "domain," see Cartwright and Zander, *Group Dynamics*, p. 216; for a discussion of "scope," see Dahl, "Power," in *International Encyclopedia of the Social Sciences*, pp. 405–415.

real distinction between the kind of personal leader who exercises a kind of hypnotic power and is content to dominate people, and the kind of charismatist who is able to strengthen the will power of the people he influences, so that they make their own best effort in their own way?[26]

Our analysis of liberating power reinforces Emmet's contention. There are important differences between the power of a Hitler, on the one hand, and Martin Luther King or Cesar Chavez, on the other. Yet all of them fit equally within Weber's conception of "charismatic authority." According to that conception, charismatic leaders are perceived by their followers as endowed with "extraordinary and personal gifts of grace." Their followers are "absolutely personally devoted and personally confident" in their "qualities of personal leadership."[27] As Tucker states, such leaders consequently appear to their followers to be persons in whom "the promise or hope of salvation—deliverance from distress—" is embodied.[28]

But none of this results, necessarily, in the follower's total obedience and subservience, contrary to Weber. Perhaps he misunderstood how varied followers' attitudes can be when they exhibit "devotion born of distress and enthusiasm."[29] Independent judgment and action are common among such followers. In the first place, as Parsons, Tucker, and others

argue, such leadership is virtually always innovative and engaged in bringing about major change in society, tending to diverge from customary ways of thinking and acting. It is therefore novel, unpredictable, and raises questions in followers' minds. Particularly in modern liberation or revolutionary movements, a considerable amount of disagreement is typical among leaders and followers.

Secondly, any careful examination of the interactions between certain charismatic leaders and followers will produce abundant evidence of the latter's independence, self-confidence, etc. Such evidence is found among people who believed in Martin Luther King's charisma. Their meetings with him were often marked by debates and disagreements in which he did not simply dominate. Such disagreements were even voiced at the most critical junctures of mass demonstrations. Surely King's relationship to several early black power advocates such as Carmichael and McKissick illustrates this.[30] In the words of a major participant in the Selma campaign, "King made mistakes," he was "human" and "down to earth," yet people "believed in King's charisma," "felt his extraordinary presence" when he entered a room amidst clamorous meetings, and in many cases "wanted to touch his 'robes' " as did the followers of Jesus.[31]

Evidence from several other charismatic leaders indicates the same point: the policy discussions and deliberations within some charismatic movements are frequently more open and wide-ranging

[26] Dorothy Emmet, *Function, Purpose, and Power*, pp. 233–234. For a somewhat related critique focusing on other problems with Weber's account of charisma, see Friedrich, "Political Leadership and the Problem of Charismatic Power," *Journal of Politics*, 23 (February, 1961), pp. 3–24.

[27] Max Weber, *Politics As a Vocation* (Philadelphia: Fortress Press, 1965), p. 3.

[28] Robert C. Tucker, "Theory of Charismatic Leadership," *Daedalus*, 97 (Summer, 1968), p. 742.

[29] Quoted in Dorothy Emmet, *Function, Purpose, and Power*, p. 233.

[30] Miller, *Martin Luther King, Jr.*, pp. 252–260.

[31] Ernest Bradford, Selma minister, interview of July 7, 1973, in Lincoln, Neb. Similar statements about King's charisma, replete with deific descriptions, were made by quite different people in other interviews, including a white, middle-aged, lower-middle class woman from Chicago. All of them were directly influenced by King in various situations.

than those which occur within many bureaucracies, whether they be military units or White House staff. Perhaps we need to rethink the differences between bureaucratic and charismatic authority regarding the type of obedience they elicit. At least Weber's description of charisma—and that of many contemporary scholars such as Levy and Willner— is mistaken in positing that it elicits hypnotic and spell-bound subservience.[32]

CONDITIONS CONDUCIVE TO LIBERATING POWER

1. A Enables and Confirms B in Seeking B's Compliance

In addition to offering a scheme for describing and measuring the changes A elicits in B, we have suggested the hypothesis that those changes are very likely to be liberating in a power relation exhibiting four conditions. One is that As *enable* and *confirm* Bs in seeking their compliance.

In getting Bs to adopt changes they desire, As *enable* Bs when they help Bs: (1) obtain goals more effectively than they otherwise would; (2) pursue goals they would not otherwise pursue; or (3) act out values more effectively or affirmatively than otherwise. Martin Luther King's actions in Montgomery illustrate this. His influence attempts toward black

people as well as others (including white adversaries and federal authorities) enabled the former to acquire new social opportunities and conditions, such as riding integrated busses and eliminating daily humiliation from drivers and passengers. It also enabled them to behave in new, independent, and efficacious ways as well as adopt new attitudes, such as self-esteem, courage, and political awareness.[33]

Likewise, A *confirms* B when A's actions indicate to B that their beliefs about who and what B is correspond. As Bennis has stated, in this interaction "there is mutual recognition of B, and the validity of B's self-image is confirmed."[34] To illustrate, a child who does something intending to aggravate her parents is disconfirmed if they respond with

---

[32] This could be said to varying degrees about followers of Chavez, Gandhi, Jesus, and Lenin, to mention a few, as well as King. Contrary to Willner, their relationship need not "involve abdication of choice and judgment." Ruth Ann Willner, *Charismatic Political Leadership: A Theory* (Princeton: Center of International Studies, 1968), p. 6. Contrary to Levy, "the fact that the leader says a given thing is right makes it right" does not always hold. Marion Levy, Jr., *Modernization and Structure of Societies* (Princeton: 1966), p. 350.

[33] James Baldwin poignantly and humorously depicts these changes in an account of a Montgomery bus ride after the boycott was victorious. See Baldwin, "The Dangerous Road Before Martin Luther King," in *Harper's Magazine* (February 1961). Actually, it appears that the relationship between A's *enabling* and *liberating* B is an analytic and necessary, not empirical and contingent one. As we use the terms, to say that A "enables" B entails among other things that A "aids B to more effectively pursue his or her goals and/or act out his or her values," both of which are entailed, in turn, in the concept of "efficacy." Consequently, to "enable" a person is by definition to "help them increase their efficacy," one of the dimensions of liberating change in our scheme.

The relationship between the other conditions we have identified as being conducive to liberating power, on the one hand, and dimensions of liberating change in B, on the other, seems in most cases to be empirical rather than analytic. E.g., This is certainly the case with regard to the exercise of exemplary power. See below, pp. 397–401.

[34] Warren Bennis, "Some Interpersonal Aspects of Self-Confirmation," in Bennis, Edgar Schein, *et al., Interpersonal Dynamics: Essays and Readings on Human Interaction.* (Homewood, Ill.: Dorsey, 1968), p. 219.

calm indifference or warmth. The child thinks her act is irritating, but when no one responds appropriately, she does not know whether what she thinks she is doing in the everyday social world is in fact occurring there. The child's sense of reality and of effective agency in the world are eroded by such disconfirming relations. Conversely, the more parents and others respond in ways appropriate to the intent of her actions, the more her sense of efficacy and reality are confirmed.

Clearly, confirmation is an important factor in the development of personal identity and security, as a host of psychologists who have investigated these processes concur.[35] For this reason and others presented in our essay, we suggest that the *combined* effect of one person confirming as well as enabling another is especially conducive to the latter's liberation. Its effect on the latter's efficacy, self-esteem, secure identity, and awareness is likely to be particularly significant.

If we examine the process by which one person *confirms* others when influencing them, we can better understand this effect. The influence agent may confirm targets in several ways, including: (1) urging others to perform acts disclosing self-identities they deeply value; (2) validating that identity by the message he or she communicates to them; and (3) validating it by the style in which he or she communicates the message.

Martin Luther King exemplified all of these methods of confirmation in his exercise of power among Montgomery blacks (and millions of other people). To begin with, in urging them to adopt changes in themselves and their social conditions, King was calling them to an identity they highly valued. For allegiant blacks and whites he urged actions revealing their own values. His "I Have A Dream" speech is only the most publicized instance of this, where he crystallized and confirmed beliefs shared by millions of people. For blacks, especially, he urged the performance of acts which frequently expressed an identity they covertly valued, but most other authorities had disconfirmed.

This is a particularly crucial point for understanding liberation movements and liberating power. Many black people had suffered deep *dis*confirmation of their basic needs and aspirations throughout their lives. Then King and similar actors entered their world and helped them develop an identity emancipated from the humiliating one given them by whites and often reinforced by their own black leaders. Suddenly, in 1955 Montgomery citizens were being urged to act out an identity as free, courageous, efficacious people with pride and dignity. King was relating in deeply confirming ways to them. In such power relations, the targets are "emancipated" through compliance.

---

[35] These include Bennis, Erikson, R. D. Laing, Carl Rogers, and Kurt Wolff. For example, see Bennis, *Ibid.*; Ronald David Laing, *The Divided Self* (London: Tavistock Publications, 1960) and *The Self and Others* (London: Tavistock, 1961); and Carl Rogers, *On Becoming a Person* (Boston: Houghton, Mifflin, 1961). Bennis claims that "under conditions providing consistent social confirmation of all aspects of the self, a strong and integrated identity will develop and be sustained." He asserts that at least "two kinds of beliefs must be *socially* validated and confirmed if an individual's self-image or identity is to remain secure: 1, beliefs about the self, about who and what we are; and 2, beliefs about the nature of social reality." *Interpersonal Dynamics*, p. 219. Erikson suggests that identity crises result when other people or society are willing to recognize a person only as something he or she cannot or does not want to be.

For a summary of the literature on the role of confirmation in the development of personal identity and security, see Carl Rogers, "Some Characteristics of a Helping Relationship" in Bennis, *Interpersonal Dynamics*, pp. 309–324.

No trivial and ordinary confirmation is occurring here. Rather, King is confirming the central, primitive aspects of others. As Buber noted, there is a "wish of every man to be confirmed as what he is, even as what he can become . . ."[36] Such basic wishes were languishing unfulfilled among Southern blacks, according to studies of the civil rights movement as well as general opinion surveys. For example, Gallup polls taken during the 1950s highlighted the disjunction between blacks' self-perceptions and aspirations, on the one hand, and the identity given them by Southern whites, on the other.[37] Similar disconfirmed self-identities were documented in studies of the motives inducing people to join the Black Muslim movement.[38]

Just as the actions King urged these people to perform validated their identities, so did the message he communicated. From the moment he was selected to lead the Montgomery boycott until the eve of his assassination, he spoke directly to their aspirations. He began the address initiating the boycott by reviewing the long history of abuses blacks had experienced:

We are here this evening to say to those who have mistreated us so long that we are tired of being segregated and humiliated, tired of being kicked around by the brutal feet of oppression. [He closed the address by saying] If you will protest courageously and yet with dignity and Christian love, when the history books are written in future generations, the historians will have to pause and say, 'there lived a great people—black people —who injected new meaning and dignity into the veins of civilization.' This is our challenge and our overwhelming responsibility.[39]

Abernathy summarized this quality of King's by saying, "It's his ability to communicate, to place in words the longings, the dreams, the hopes, and the aspirations of an oppressed people"—and, it might be added, others who were not directly oppressed—that made King unique among black leaders and orators.[40]

Additionally, the *style* by which one person communicates to others may confirm them in a way purely cognitive and instrumental elements of the message do not. In this regard the particular words and phrases a person uses in preference to others with similar denotations—"the allusions, metaphors, similes, and other symbol-laden words"—is a critical variable.[41] Many participants and observers of the black movement considered Martin Luther King a genius at using these stylistic elements. Supporting our hypothesis, they attribute part of his liberating power to this skill. The "I Have A Dream" ad-

[36] *The Knowledge of Man*, p. 68. He is probably the most influential forerunner to contemporary psychologists in the study of confirmation.

[37] Taken at the time of King's early activism, these polls determined that the "most distasteful" aspect of Southern society for the Negro was the "use of derogatory racial terms when referring to Negroes, and the assumption of superiority on the part of the Southern white"; in short, not treating us as "being human." J. M. Fenton, *In Your Opinion* (Boston: Little, Brown, 1960), p. 167. These convictions were publicly expressed in many civil rights and poor people's demonstrations, some of which have already been noted above.

[38] E. E. Essien-Udom, *Black Nationalism: A Search for Identity in America* (New York: Dell, 1964), p. 95.

[39] Marcus H. Boulware, *The Oratory of Negro Leaders: 1900–1968* (Westport, Conn.: Negro University Press, 1969), pp. 246–247.

[40] *Ibid.*, p. 257. Whether or not King uniquely excelled at this need not be investigated here. Surely Malcolm X and other leaders in the movement exhibited similar ability.

[41] These stylistic elements have been investigated in relation to charismatic leadership by Willner, *Charismatic Political Leadership*, p. 105.

dress is illustrative. A leading biographer of King gives the following account:

> At the foot of the Lincoln monument, King began by saying 'Five score years ago, a great American in whose symbolic shadow we stand today signed the Emancipation Proclamation . . . But one hundred years later, the Negro is not free.' He likened the Constitution and the Declaration of Independence to a promissory note which, in the case of the Negro has not been cashed but has been stamped 'insufficient funds'. He could hardly have chosen a more apt figure of speech in the context of the affluent society, and his hearers interrupted with cheers. And cheered again the next sentence, 'But we refuse to believe that the bank of justice is bankrupt.'[42]

King continued by drawing upon basic documents of the land which blacks and whites professed alike; he drew upon democratic platitudes from civics texts and a patriotic song familiar to the heterogeneous audience, "Let Freedom Ring." And after sharing his dream, he declared that when it came to pass, "both blacks and whites, people of all religions, will have been emancipated, and like those black folk liberated by Lincoln's decree they will sing, 'Free at last, free at last; thank God Almighty, we're free at last.'"[43]

If King's symbol-laden expressions confirmed others, so did his use of rhetorical devices such as repetitions, rhythms, and tonal inflections.[44]

In fact, King was tapping deeply ingrained experiences and traditions of the black American culture with this ora-

torical style. It was authentic to him, because it was the oral tradition of the black Baptist preacher with which he grew up and was trained. As an early Montgomery associate tells us, he fused this oratorical style and image with that of Gandhi, thereby turning the black religious tradition and faith in the church into a potent social and political movement, "overlaying all with Negro songs and symbols that bypassed cerebral centers and exploded in the well of the Negro psyche." In sum, "it was a huge achievement."[45]

Obviously, differences in communicative styles are significant in explaining actors' relative success at confirming and enabling others. One can compare communicative acts (e.g., addresses) for such differences. Ideally one could control such variables as topic, length, and audience to see if more confirming speakers exhibit performance styles more attuned to their audience. Observers of the March on Washington noted that Martin Luther King's moving "dream" address was distinguished from others given at the same occasion in this regard. And surely the enabling and confirming persuasion of charismatic leaders such as Castro and F.D.R. can be distinguished along these lines as well.[46]

What other factors besides these persuasive capacities account for differences in people's ability to confirm others? One factor is empathic understanding. Martin Buber has elucidated this association:

> The capacity for confirming and being confirmed depends on 'imagining the real'. It means that I imagine to myself what another man is at this very moment wishing, feeling, perceiving, thinking, and not as a detached content but in his very

---

[42] Miller, *Martin Luther King, Jr.,* p. 176.

[43] *Ibid.,* p. 178.

[44] The "Dream" address and many others King gave were exemplary in this regard, as well. E.g., see reports and records of his addresses in *Ibid.*; and Boulware, *Oratory of Negro Leaders.*

[45] Bennett, in Lincoln, *M.L. King, Jr.: A Profile,* p. 25.

[46] E.g., for an analysis of Roosevelt's oratory, see Willner, Op. Cit., p. 103ff.

reality, i.e., as a living process in this man.[47]

Two additional factors are genuineness and trust. A representative piece of research bearing on these relationships is that of Halkides. Her study directly focused on the association between a counselor's attitudes and behavior toward a client and the latter's "constructive personality change" in a therapeutic relationship.[48] Despite differences between a therapeutic relation and one between a leader and follower in a political movement, they share much that is germaine to this inquiry. For instance, Halkides' concept of "constructive personality change" in the client is similar to ours of "liberating change" in a target. She found a remarkable correlation between the client's constructive personality change and the counselor's manifestation of empathic understanding and genuineness.[49]

If we turn from therapy to political leadership, the association among empathic understanding, genuineness, and confirmation holds true in Martin Luther King's case. The evidence we have gathered from people who complied with King indicates a common belief that he exhibited exceptional genuineness, trustworthiness, and understanding, far beyond that of many leaders. In fact, his trustworthiness was virtually absolute in their minds.[50]

2. A Exercises Exemplary Power as a Method of Gaining B's Compliance

If A's trustworthiness and genuineness in B's eyes affect his or her ability to confirm B, they also affect his or her ability to exercise *exemplary power*. This denotes a specific method of influence whereby A sets an example or demonstrates a course of action as the means of obtaining B's compliance, without promising a reward or threatening a punishment. It is a common method, yet often overlooked (especially in theories emphasizing conditional responses—"carrots and sticks"—as the method of exercising influence).[51]

We contend that a liberating as compared to debilitating power relation is much more likely to exhibit this method. Trustworthiness and genuineness are only two of many variables affecting how successfully A exercises exemplary power toward B. Other variables include the degree to which B perceives that A is a credible agent for setting an example, and, the degree to which B positively identifies with A.[52]

B can infer information about several of these variables from the way A attempts to set an example. This is dramatically exhibited in liberation movements where A may be urging B to do things the latter feels are impossible or too costly to attempt. Among other things, in setting an example as the method of influencing B, A will be more likely to suc-

---

[47] *The Knowledge of Man*, p. 70.

[48] G. Halkides, *An Experimental Study of Four Conditions Necessary for Therapeutic Change* (unpublished PhD dissertation, University of Chicago, 1958).

[49] These counselor attitudes were significantly associated at the .001 level with the therapeutic cases involving the most constructive personality change.

[50] Highly diverse people "believed in him" and "knew he was genuine." He was "down to earth," "one of us," "shared in our lives," "loved to stop and play pool with us," etc. A Selma participant spontaneously re-

marked to this author before the question had been raised, "there was never any question about King's trust. It did not even occur to us to distrust King." Ernest Bradford, Selma minister, interview of July 7, 1973 in Lincoln, Neb.

[51] See McClusky, "Power without Control," pp. 23–24, for the distinction between exemplary power and related phenomena such as imitation and behavioral contagion.

[52] We have analyzed a list of these variables in *Ibid.*, pp. 45–67.

ceed if he or she accepts equivalent or greater risks than B will if the latter complies. In the vernacular, "A must lay his body on the line." In liberation leadership A may take greater risks than B by initiating or organizing certain activities, thereby attracting the attention of social control agencies or the retaliation of private citizens.

The acts of Martin Luther King and his associates epitomize this. King was arrested and jailed numerous times, physically assaulted, stabbed nearly fatally in the chest, his home bombed while his family was inside, his life and that of his family frequently threatened, and he was assassinated in the prime of life. Through such exemplary courage and sacrifice, the potential risks and dangers to those whose compliance he seeks may seem by contrast much lighter and easier to bear. As James Baldwin commented, King "suffered with people, and thus, he helped them to suffer."[53] Of course, the same thing can be said of numerous exemplary leaders, including many prophets and martyrs, military and revolutionary heroes.

In any case, such risks and sacrifices cement a person's credibility and trustworthiness in others' eyes. In this respect, exemplary power can be understood as "persuasion by deed." Because of such exemplary actions, an individual's attempts at verbal persuasion take on added credibility, authenticity, and attraction to those whose compliance is sought. Exemplary power and persuasion therefore reinforce each other as methods of influence for many leaders.

A typical illustration of this reinforcement is provided by Hoebel's description of the Eskimo headman. This leader's authority "resides in his superior skill as a hunter, which is compounded of his

outstanding energy, his technical proficiency, and a personality that evokes favorable responses from the members of his community." As a hunter, "he is first out on the ice in the morning. . . . Experience has demonstrated that the times and places he chooses for the hunt bring consistently better returns. . . . He rarely commands or explicitly orders behavior. Rather, he leads by suggestion and example."[54] Hoebel asserts that such leadership is the common pattern among "simple, nomadic, food-gathering peoples."[55]

In our analysis the "exemplary leader" is one who exercises exemplary power as a generalized method of influence across many activities and relationships. It refers to people who embody and act out goals or values others share; and, typically, demonstrate courses of action and strategies for pursuing shared goals which elicit others' cooperation. A central variable associated with effectiveness at such leadership is a person's general life-style. Castro with his spartan life marked by guerrilla heroism and revolutionary labor in the sugar cane fields, Gandhi with his "ahimsa," Chavez with his devout, sacrificial living, Mao with the guerrilla heroism of the long march and other feats—all stand as models of the values of their respective movements.[56]

[53] Baldwin, "The Dangerous Road Before Martin Luther King," in *Harper's Magazine* (February, 1961).

[54] E. Adamson Hoebel, "Authority in Primitive Societies," *Nomos,* p. 226.

[55] *Ibid.,* p. 233.

[56] Obviously, exemplary power is a type of authority, as the latter is commonly defined. Whether one follows Bachrach and Baratz, Morton Fried, David Easton, Bertrand de Jouvenal, D. S. McIntosh, or almost any other contemporary scholar, "authority" is viewed as "legitimate" power or influence. "Legitimacy" refers to the compliant party's perception that compliance with the influencing party is "right and proper," for whatever reasons. As Bachrach and Baratz put it, in a situation involving authority, "B complies because he recognizes that the command is reasonable in terms of his own values, not be-

And Martin Luther King's general life-style was a model for his movement, as well. When he was chosen by executive committee election and by the devotion of rank-and-file members to be the primary leader of the civil rights movement, he made a personal decision to act as a symbol for its struggle.[57] When he spoke of courageous, dignified black people struggling for freedom and justice, yet being compassionate even to their enemies, he lived this paradox in his daily encounters. It was exhibited in part through his strategy of personally leading people to confront the Jim Clarks and Bull Connors of the land in dramatic, ingenious encounters which crystallized the conflict of the black and poor against the power structure. Performing such deeds that captivate public imagination is an important component of exemplary leadership.

How does A's exercise of exemplary power motivate B to adopt the desired change or response? In social psychological terms, one way is by overcoming B's inhibitions to adopt the response. A's initial action (setting an example) may induce this change in the latter for several reasons. For instance, when B observes A's example it may alter B's belief in: (1) the extent of the risks involved in adopt-

ing the response A desires; (2) the chances of attaining the goal they share (which A wants B to pursue); (3) the personal relevance of some goal or action A wants B to adopt; and/or (4) the value of the goal or action.

In liberation movements, A's example alters B's beliefs so as to overcome B's inhibition to adopt a change in countless ways. It occurs when a small nucleus of feminists open a cooperative health clinic and others follow suit by joining or by organizing their own after observing the self-esteem, efficacy, medical competence, and political awareness that can develop from such efforts. It occurs when Chavez organizes farm workers in California and others join the movement after observing the self-esteem, solidarity, and more tangible economic benefits it promotes. And it occurs when Martin Luther King or Jesse Jackson organizes a Poor People's Campaign, a voting rights drive, an Operation Breadbasket and P.U.S.H.

Another way in which A's setting an example can motivate B's compliance is by directing B's attention to specific strategies in an ambiguous situation. In social psychology this is referred to as "selective attention"—a process whereby "diverse interests and grievances in a collective are fused in a specific situation."[58] This occurs when independent truckers in one location shut down their operation, setting an example to truckers located elsewhere of ways to capture the attention of the media and government to articulate their demands. And it occurs when Martin Luther King, by sheer force of his personal example, defuses an armed, angry crowd in an event which came to be known in the movement as "the parable of the porch."

cause he fears deprivation. . . ." *Power and Poverty: Theory and Practice*, p. 33. In a situation involving exemplary power, as we define it, B clearly *does* view compliance as reasonable in terms of his/her own values, although the "command" dimension to the relation is missing. More generally, a power relation exhibiting the four conditions we hypothesize to be conducive to eliciting liberating changes in B will be an authority relation, as well. *However*, a liberating power relation itself need not be an authority relation, because it refers eliciting particular changes in B, which may occur in the absence of the four conditions we analyze in this essay.

[57] Bennett, in Lincoln, *M.L. King, Jr.: A Profile*, p. 24.

[58] For a more extensive analysis of these social psychological processes by which A's exercise of exemplary power motivates B to adopt the intended change, see McClusky, "Power without Control," pp. 31–45.

The "parable" took place on the night of January 30, 1956. King's Montgomery home was bombed while Coretta and their daughter were inside. Martin was addressing a mass meeting at the time, and when he arrived home:

The house was ringed by an angry Negro crowd armed with guns, knives. . . . King stood on the front porch for a moment studying the crowd. At his side were the mayor and other city officials, their faces graven with anxiety and apprehension. It was clear to almost everyone that Montgomery was on the verge of a blood bath. . . . Shouts, threats, curses rent the air.[59]

Dr. King's deep baritone voice rang out over the crowd. "Don't get panicky! Don't do anything panicky at all! If you have weapons, take them home; if you don't have them, please do not seek to get them. We cannot solve this problem through retaliatory violence. . . . We must love our white brothers no matter what they do to us. We must make them know that we love them. Jesus still cries out in words that echo across the centuries: 'Love your enemies, bless them that curse you; pray for them that despitefully use you.' This is what we must live by. We must meet hate with love."

The crowd had fallen silent. "I did not start this boycott," he continued. "I was asked by you to serve as your spokesman. I want it to be known the length and breadth of the land that if I am stopped, this movement will not stop. What we are doing is just, and God is with us."

"God bless you, son!" a woman shouted. Cries of "amen" could be heard as the crowd drifted away.[60]

In this action King clearly fastened the ambivalent and opposing moods of the crowd onto a specific behavior and attitude he sought. In fact, he directed most of them to a course of action diametrically opposed to that which they were on the verge of committing. But the latter was only one of many strategies available to express the diverse grievances and interests of the crowd. Through his own example King diverted them to the strategy he desperately hoped they would pursue. Participants and scholars of the movement concur as to the efficacy of this act:

This movement changed the course of the protest and made King a living symbol. He and other members of the boycott directorate had spoken before of love and forgiveness. But now, *seeing the idea in action*, fleshed out by pain, paid for by anguish, millions were touched, if not converted. . . . King now became leader, not only by election, but also by the acclamations of committed hearts.[61]

King's liberating power is replete with instances of this. The events which triggered the sit-in and freedom ride stage of the black movement are illustrative. King's leadership and strategy in the Montgomery boycott were the examples which explicitly catalyzed the participants in the first sit-in.[62] And once the latter were launched, their actions

[59] Bennett, *Op Cit.*, p. 22.
[60] Miller, *Martin Luther King, Jr.*, p. 57.

[61] Bennett, *Ibid.*, p. 23.
[62] Ezell Blair, Jr. and Joseph McNeil, roommates at a college in Greensboro, North Carolina, began the first sit-in on February 1, 1960 at a lunch counter in that city. They explicitly were prompted to this action by reading the 'comic book' narrative of King's efforts in *Martin Luther King and the Montgomery Story*, a Fellowship of Reconciliation publication. Within two weeks the mass media coverage of their sit-in had triggered similar actions in ten North Carolina towns as well as schools in South Carolina, Tennessee and Virginia. Throughout these campaigns, the protestors looked to Martin Luther King as their symbolic leader. For a detailed account of these events, see Miller, *Martin Luther King, Jr.*, pp. 98–103.

stood as an example along with King to thousands of others engaging in similar campaigns across the South. As often happens in situations where diffuse goals are shared among an otherwise unorganized aggregate, exemplary power can catalyze a chain reaction of examples. The net effect can be of vast proportions far beyond the impact of any single party or act of influence.

Apart from the personalized leadership of simple societies such as the Eskimo or the heroic leadership of exemplars such as King, Castro, or Jesus, the exercise of exemplary power is also operating in more mundane leadership settings. A more general examination of these processes as well as other forms of exemplary power distinct from leadership has led us to conclude that it is a much more prevalent phenomenon than people nurtured in the "carrot and stick" conception of power realize.[63]

3. A Abstains from Controlling B's Access to Rewards

Our examination of exemplary power takes us beyond the prevailing view of the exercise of power as the *control* of rewards and punishments. We are beyond the conception exemplified by Etzioni's and Parsons' "carrot and stick" typologies of power/influence or by Dahl's recent formulation that power relations involve a "controlling and a responding unit."[64]

We recognize a critical fact others often neglect: power relations vary greatly as to how much A *controls* B's access to rewards. This control bears directly on how free B is. At one extreme are power

relations of absolute control, such as master over slave. In these one party *monopolizes* the other's access to all rewards, including life, health, livelihood, physical freedom, and other values.

At the other extreme are power relations in which A does *not* control B's access to the rewards involved. The case of Martin Luther King or the Eskimo headman exercising exemplary power represents the latter. King enables others to achieve goals he shares with them, such as freeing themselves from poverty and racism, powerlessness and despair. But he does not control their access to goals in the way the master controls the slave's continued access to life. In such cases, the target's freedom is not curtailed at all. To the contrary, it is frequently expanded in the sense that King's influence activates whole new realms of opportunity, experience, and strategy for the party, be they poor Montgomery blacks or students emboldened to launch freedom rides.

There are several variables determining where on the control continuum between pure domination and pure freedom a power relation fits.[65] One is the degree to which A *tries* to restrict B's access to rewards in seeking the latter's compliance. Another is the degree to which B perceives that A *does* control his or her access; in other words, the degree to which B believes access to those rewards is exclusively restricted to complying with A. A third variable is the degree to which the rewards are things whose access *can* be controlled, and, in particular, are within A's ability to control.

Let us illustrate these variables with reference to Martin Luther King's power relation to black people in Montgomery. He rarely threatened them with punishment for non-compliance. It was against his entire philosophy of life and social

---

[63] See McClusky, "Power without Control," pp. 22–31; and 71–72.

[64] See above, p. 386, for our analysis of these typologies; and, Dahl, "Power," in *International Encyclopedia of the Social Sciences*, p. 407.

[65] We have analyzed each of these extensively in "Power without Control," pp. 8–21.

action; against the norms of the movement he led; and, therefore, would have been self-defeating. He certainly would not have been an exemplary, catalytic leader in that movement if he had gone around threatening its members.[66]

But a person can try to control others' access to rewards in various ways besides threatening to deprive them (punish). He can *promise rewards only in return for compliance*. Of course, Martin Luther King sometimes appealed to rewards people might gain by complying with him. But that is quite different from promising them in return for compliance. The rewards King could appeal to were for the most part not resources he had at his disposal to "hand out" the way a government official or businessperson might hand out contracts or jobs. Millions of people complied with King and adopted thousands of changes he desired. But the rewards they perceived for doing so were not resources he controlled.

Instead, some of those rewards were tangible goals such as voting rights, the elimination of poverty, or equal employment opportunities. Such goals could only be obtained after prolonged effort and the action of many private and/or public agencies outside King's control. More de-

[66] He did threaten punishment for non-compliance against his opponents in the civil rights struggles, such as Southern power elites. But even this was within the broader strategy of reconciliation and compassion toward them, including attempts to persuade them through appeals to tangible rewards, conscience, and values the opposing sides might share. At times blacks who complied with King may have *perceived* threats of punishment for non-compliance even though King did not make them or intend for anyone else to do so. E.g., They might have thought they would lose influence or status in the black community or organizations with which they strongly identified if they did not comply.

cisively, the most enduring rewards—and those King most emphasized—were things such as increased self-esteem, efficacy, political awareness, freedom, and a community of love. These could only be attained, if at all, by people's extended efforts far beyond complying with King's specific influence attempts. Nobody could control such rewards in return for another's compliance. And Martin Luther King did not mislead anyone into thinking he could do so. Nor did he lead them to think they could be quickly attained if people would only comply with him. Listen, for example, to a typical statement he made presenting the rewards of one of his major campaigns:

to create the kind of awareness in people that will make it impossible for them to be enslaved or abused, and create for them the kind of democratic structures which will enable them to deal continually with the problems of slum life.[67]

Consequently, at times the exercise of power may not involve promising rewards in return for compliance as much as unconditionally sharing rewards or pointing out ways to pursue them. This is typically done by A setting an example providing B with information about attaining rewards. By doing so, A allows B to retain his or her freedom in the power relation. This is one of the reasons we hypothesize that such unconditional methods of influence are likely to characterize liberating power relations much more than debilitating ones.

CONCLUSION

We have attempted to improve our understanding of power relations in which A elicits important, beneficial changes in B. To do this we have gone beyond the

[67] Miller, *Martin Luther King, Jr.*, p. 248.

reward/punishment theories of power. As Harsanyi noted long ago, the latter are mistaken in forgetting that it is possible for A to modify B's behavior by giving B, "with no strings attached," something he or she needs in order to accomplish some objective.[68] It is just such methods of power we have emphasized.

We have hypothesized that liberating power relations are much more likely than debilitating ones to exhibit four conditions. The fourth—intrinsic reward —has received the least attention here. Often the act, attitude, or condition A wants B to adopt is itself intrinsically valuable to B, quite independent of any extrinsic benefits which may accrue to B by means of it. Metaphorically, B perceives that the reward lies in revelling in the rainbow itself, rather than peeking over his or her shoulder for the pot of gold at its end.

This is a potent motive A can tap in gaining B's compliance. Liberating leaders such as Martin Luther King are constantly tapping it. We have noted this in the Montgomery movement, where King was urging people to engage in "peak experiences" such as protesting against the white power structure for the first time, assembling at mass meetings to pour their feelings and hopes out together, or organizing their own transport and other services. Through these activities they grew to proclaim that "they had given up their childish ways and become men." Such intrinsically rewarding experiences play a major role in a person's development of self-esteem, efficacy, self-confidence, and aspiration. The relevance of such rewards for eliciting liberating changes in a power relation can hardly be overemphasized.[69]

In closing, some of the policy implications of this theory have been unravelled elsewhere.[70] Our theory is intended to raise specific questions for any parties in a power relation in which liberating change is a goal. Do they abstain from restricting their partners' access to rewards? Do they enable and confirm others in seeking their compliance, or disable and disconfirm them? Do they use methods which set examples to others, unconditionally sharing information or rewards? And, do they urge people to adopt changes which are intrinsically rewarding, perhaps realizing new self-worth, creativity, or efficacy?

When we begin taking such questions seriously, we open up new possibilities for the liberating effects of power. Such possibilities are especially vital today to remind us that power results in "We Shall Overcome" as well as "Watergate."

---

[68] J. C. Harsanyi, "Measurement of social power, opportunity costs, and the theory of two person bargaining games," *Behavioral Science*, 7.

[69] For our further exploration of intrinsic rewards as motives for compliance, see "Power without Control," pp. 64–67. And for a discussion of exemplary power as a causal relation, see the fuller version of this essay referred to in footnote number one above.

[70] See e.g., Florence Howe, John McClusky, and Elizabeth Wilson, "Hierarchy, Power, and Women in Educational Policy-Making," (Institute for Educational Leadership, George Washington University: 1975) for an application of our theory to the women's movement.

9.4   MALE POWER AND THE WOMEN'S MOVEMENT

Barbara Bovee Polk

The relationship between females and males in this and virtually every society has been a power relationship—of males over females. The current women's moment, a revitalization of earlier feminist movements, seeks to end or reverse this power relationship. As such, feminists are concerned with analyzing the nature of male power and the condition of women and developing organizations and vehicles for change that are consistent with feminist principles. . . .

THE CONTEMPORARY CONDITION OF WOMEN

I see four major approaches to understanding the contemporary condition of women: analyses in terms of sex roles, differences between feminine and masculine culture, male-female power relationships, and economic relationships.* Because the purpose of this paper is not to discuss the conflict and factions within the movement, I present a "modal" analysis of each viewpoint rather than ideal types. Extreme positions within each viewpoint are largely omitted and perspectives overlap to some degree, for in practice, most feminists subscribe to some combination of two or more perspectives.

From Barbara Bovee Polk "Male Power and the Women's Movement, *The Journal of Applied Behavioral Science*, Volume 10, Number 3, 1974, p. 415–431. The present abridged paper appears by permission of the author and National Training Laboratories Institute.
    * A basic tenet of the women's movement is that no one woman can speak for it. This paper expresses my own perspective on the movement, and it is limited by my own experiences, understanding, and biases. It must be read as such. . . .

Although I refer to groups or writings which seem to me to fit a particular approach, it should be kept in mind that in no case is it possible to provide a "pure" example.

Sex-role socialization   Drawing on social-psychological analysis, this approach views the contemporary oppression of women as the result of the inculcation of socially defined sex roles. This approach is the basic one adopted by most academic social scientists, including Alice Rossi, Cynthia Epstein, and Jessie Bernard, as well as other well-known feminists such as Gloria Steinem, Betty Friedan, Carolyn Bird, and Germaine Greer. It is also the basic orientation of such national groups as the National Organization for Women, Women's Equity Action League, and the Women's Political Caucus. For recent examples of the sex-role perspective, see Chafetz' . . . (1974) and the . . . Safilios-Rothschild's reader (1972).

The main components of this analysis are:

1. Each society *arbitrarily* views a wide variety of personality characteristics, interests, and behaviors as the virtually exclusive domain of one sex or the other. The fact that societies vary in their definition of feminine and masculine roles is proof that sex roles are based on social rather than on biological factors.
2. The parceling up of human characteristics into "feminine"and "masculine" deprives all of full humanness.
3. Sex roles are systematically inculcated in individuals, beginning at birth, by parents, the educational

system, peers, the media, and religious institutions, and are supported by the social sciences and the economic, political, and legal structures of society. Individuals learn appropriate roles through models and differential reinforcement.

4. Sex roles form the core of an individual's identity. Because self-evaluation is closely linked to sex ("That's a good girl/boy") and to adequacy of sex-role performance, the propriety of the role to which one was socialized becomes difficult to dislodge in adulthood, even when it is seen as dysfunctional. In addition, individuals often link concepts of their adequacy in *sex roles* to their adequacy in *sexual* interactions and vice versa. Thus, a threat to one's role definition is perceived as a threat to one's sexual identity. Such threats are a major mechanism for psychologically locking people into traditional roles.

5. Sex roles are basic roles and thus modify expectations in virtually all other roles. Differential expectations by sex in other roles lead to differential perception of the same behavior in a woman and a man (a businessman is strong-willed; a business woman, rigid). Differential expectations and selective perception limit the extent to which individuals can step outside their sex roles and are major mechanisms for the maintenance of sex roles.

6. Female and male roles form a role system in which the expectations for and behaviors of each sex have implications for the definitions of and behaviors of the other sex. (A man can't be a "gentleman" if a woman will not let him hold the door for her.)

7. The male role has higher status. This status is directly rewarding and provides access to other highly valued statuses and rewards: however, male status also places heavy pressures on men to maintain that status.

8. Males have power over females because of role definitions. "Being powerful" is itself a part of the masculine role definition. In addition, the "rationality" assigned to the male role gives men access to positions of expertise as well as credibility, even when they are not experts.

Conflicting cultures approach This approach focuses on value differences rather than role differences between the sexes. It points out that women who talk only in terms of role differences may seek a solution to their oppression by emulating male roles. The cultural approach is therefore a more overtly feminist analysis, focusing on the positive aspects of feminine culture. Examples of this approach include Firestone (1970), Burris (1971), and Solanas (1968), although the latter is quite different from the view presented here. The main ideas behind this approach follow.

1. Just as roles are dichotomized by sex, so are values. "Masculine" values include competitiveness, aggressiveness, independence, and rationality; "feminine" values include their counterparts: cooperativeness, passivity, dependence, and emotionality. These values are not inherent as male or female (according to most versions of this analysis) but are socially assigned and derived from sex-role definitions. *All* are important qualities of humanness.

2. Masculine values have higher status and constitute the dominant and visible culture of the society. They inform the structure of personal,

political, and economic relationships and provide the standard for adulthood and normality (cf. de Beauvoir's [1953] discussion of woman as "the Other").

3. Women are oppressed and devalued because they embody an alternative culture. (In one version of this analysis [Burris, 1971], men are seen as colonizing women's bodies in order to subordinate an alien value system, much as men colonized the land and peoples of other civilizations.)

4. Men are socialized almost exclusively to the masculine value system, but women receive dual socialization because of the dominance of male institutions and because they must comprehend masculine values in order to survive (the slave syndrome). Dual socialization tempts women to try assimilation into the masculine culture, but it also gives women insight into the artificiality of the value dichotomization.

5. Masculine values are highly responsible for the crisis in our society. Competitiveness pits human against human and results in racism, sexism, and colonialism, as well as the rape of the natural environment in the pursuit of economic power. Aggressiveness leads to war. Exaggerated independence inhibits society's ability to solve common problems by failing to recognize the fundamental interdependence among humans and between humans and the physical environment. Excessive rationality is linked to the building of a run-away technological and scientific system incapable of recognizing and granting legitimacy to human needs and feelings.

Power analysis This perspective does not deny the importance of sex roles and cultural differences in bringing about and maintaining the oppression of women, but it views them as symptomatic of the primary problem, which is the domination of females by males. Thus, it is more concerned with focusing on the mechanisms of male power than on its origins; e.g., Millet (1970) and Chesler (1972). Its major tenets may be summarized as follows:

1. Men have power and privilege by virtue of their sex. They may and do oppress women in personal relationships, in groups, and on the job.

2. It is in men's interest to maintain that power and privilege. There is status in the ability to oppress someone else, regardless of the oppression one suffers oneself. In addition, power over women in personal relationships gives men what they want, whether that be sex, smiles, chores, admiration, increased leisure, or control itself.

3. Men occupy and actively exclude women from positions of economic and political power in society. Those positions give men a heavily disproportionate share of the rewards of society, especially economic rewards.

4. Marriage is an institution of personal and sexual slavery for women, who are duped into marrying by the love ethic or economic necessity.

5. Although most males are also oppressed by the system under which we live, they are not oppressed, as females are, *because* of their sex.

6. Feminine roles and cultural values are the product of oppression. Idealization of them is dysfunctional to change.

7. Males have greater behaviorial and economic options, including the option of oppressing women. Where individuals have wider options, they are responsible for their choices. In this way, men are responsible, in-

dividually and collectively, for their oppression of women.

8. Men oppress women through the use of brute force, by restricting options and selectively reinforcing women within these options, through control of resources and major institutions, and through expertise and access to the media.

Socialist perspective This approach holds that the oppression of women is only one aspect of the destructiveness of a generally oppressive economic system and therefore contends that socialism is a prerequisite to feminism. As the basis for outlining this viewpoint, I am using the general orientation of The Socialist Worker's Party and the International Socialists, as discussed with me in conversation, and the writings of Reed (1969). Although I have chosen to use the viewpoint of socialist organizations heavily dominated by males (thus they are not feminist organizations), women in these groups often form formal or informal caucuses on feminist issues. Closely related are the analyses of the unaffiliated, all-female socialist groups, although these groups generally disagree with the following analysis by affirming the need for an independent women's movement. Their approach is represented by Mitchell (1971). Simone de Beauvoir's work, *The Second Sex*, fits primarily into this category, although the work is so broad that it incorporates the main ideas from all analyses presented here. That de Beauvoir identifies with the socialist perspective on the women's movement as presented here is clear in her autobiography, *Force of Circumstances* (1965).

1. The oppression of women originated in the concept of private property. Women were defined as property largely because of their ability to reproduce, thereby providing new workers as well as heirs for the elite. Because private property is the institution on which capitalism is founded, the oppression of women is fundamentally linked to capitalist structures and is necessary to their continuation.

2. Sexism is functional to capitalism because it enables capitalists to buy two workers for the price of one. A man is paid a wage; his wife, who is unpaid, provides the necessary services for him to perform his job (even if she, too, has a job).

3. Women provide a cheap reserve labor force for capitalists, thereby holding down wages and increasing profits.

4. Although the rebellion of women against their roles is contrary to the interests of capitalism, an independent women's movement is not, for it separates one oppressed group from others and forestalls a coalition which could overthrow the system.

5. Equality for women is impossible until capitalism is replaced by socialism. . . .

APPROACHES TO CHANGE—
A NEW SOCIETY

Surrounded by male power, from sources which overlap and reinforce one another, women find that they must totally transform society to achieve their goal of freedom from oppression. As a result, strategies for change are many and diverse, giving the women's movement the appearance of a lack of direction. However, no one tactic is intended to accomplish the entire task. Groups choose targets and activities partly on the basis of their analyses of women's oppression, partly on the basis of available opportunities for action, and partly according to the personal dispositions of any particular group or collective of women. There is, then, no easy one-to-one match between the perspectives of the participants and the activities of the movement, which I briefly review in the following section.

De- or Resocialization of Oneself

Self-change is important for all perspectives, though in the socialist approach, it is seen as effected through social action. To the extent that sex-role definitions, value systems, and the power which is based on them are socialized characteristics, each of us to some extent participates in those definitions. The most prevalent activity in the women's movement, therefore, has been the small consciousness-raising or rap group in which women piece together an understanding of their oppression and challenge their assumptions about themselves, other women, and men. Within these groups, women find that their experiences, private fears, and self-doubts are not unique but common to many other women and related to their social conditioning. Personal experience thus becomes a basis for political analysis and action.

Most groups focus on building solidarity and support among members, replacing the distrust and dislike of other women with which many enter these groups. In addition, most groups raise questions about appropriate routes to liberation, challenge the notion that liberation means imitating male roles and values, and debate the extent to which individual freedom is possible in the absence of general structural change in the society. In this way, women begin to redefine and change themselves and build a basis for initiating larger changes.

Changing Personal Interactions and Micro-Role Systems

New definitions are useless if not put into action. All perspectives encourage actions to redefine personal relationships and micro-role systems, although they vary to some extent in the kinds of actions they favor. The sex-role analysis focuses heavily on individual change of personal relationships and the broadening of individual life options. The cultural perspective emphasizes decreasing dependence on emotional support from males and substituting strong alliances among women. The power perspective favors direct confrontation with males in all interactions—on the job, in the street, and in personal relationships.

Since, in a sex-role system, definitions are upheld and reinforced by both role actors, when a woman moves outside of traditional definitions, she forces a change in complementary roles. For example, the rap group is often important in providing support for married women seeking more egalitarian sharing of housework and child care, or attempting to return to school, take a job, or resume a career; and for single women attempting to deal with the restrictiveness of a father or boyfriend. Through an analysis of the costs and rewards to both parties in a relationship, the group helps its members find ways of decreasing the rewards (increasing the costs) for male resistance to such changes, while increasing their rewards for more egalitarian behavior.

The support function of women's groups is a step toward substituting women for men as a basic reference group. This process reduces women's reliance on the kinds of rewards they receive from men. Approval and emotional support is instead sought within the group. In this way, a new set of sisterly relationships are formed, which, for some groups, involves mutual economic support in living communes and sexual gratification in lesbian relationships, making women largely self-sufficient and males almost irrelevant.

Still, almost all women must relate to men in less personal interactions. The power analysts, in particular, help each other develop strategies for confronting rather than ignoring street hassles, for confronting and changing condescending comments and gestures in work and other settings, and for challenging the "servant chores" (making coffee, buying presents, dusting the office, providing a sympathetic ear to the boss) which are a part of many female occupations.

Learning karate and other forms of self-defense as well as engaging in sports activities is one popular feminist strategy for combatting the physical power men have over women. Many women believe that if they develop their strength and learn to understand, use, and have confidence in their bodies, they will be less likely to be attacked physically and more able to defend themselves in the event of an attack. As men are aware that women are able to fight back, the attacker–victim role relationship should become less frequent.

In the attempt to change others through personal interaction and micro-role system change, women undermine several sources of male power. Normative power is further reduced by destroying traditional male roles through withholding cooperation, making them irrelevant, or challenging them directly. To the extent that women provide a support group for one another, they reduce the power of males to define women's options and control their behavior through rewards. Self-defense techniques reduce the threat of brute force. These small-scale attempts at change gradually produce new bases for more egalitarian interaction than traditional practices.

Resocialization of Others

The second most prevalent activity of the women's movement has been use of or attacks on the media in order to extend the resocialization process beyond the boundaries of the movement. These activities have been engaged in primarily by women who use the sex-role perspective, which emphasizes socialization. The cultural approach and the power analysis both caution against dependence on media and media change as main tools of the movement, since the media are dominated by men. As a result, they warn, attempts by women to convey their ideas through the media will tend to distort the message in a way that ridicules or discredits the movement.

Those who use the media view it as a way of reaching and changing women who have not been exposed to rap groups. By publishing books, magazines, and articles, by speaking, producing radio and TV programs, by being interviewed or holding demonstrations covered by the media, women in the movement extend their insights to those outside it. In this way, countless women who do not identify with the movement begin to reevaluate and change their lives.

Women's access to the media also helps reshape men's understanding of the female condition. For those who believe that change can come about through convincing men of the disadvantages of their roles or of masculine values, the media provide a major vehicle for reaching and changing men. Communicating with men in this way provides the beginnings of social legitimation for legal changes and lays the groundwork for a new value system in society.

Much attention is also focused on the socialization of children. A number of groups are publishing feminist books for children and compiling lists of children's literature offering a positive image of women. *Ms.* magazine has even published a children's record, containing liberated songs. In addition, several women's groups throughout the country have formed feminist child care centers or cooperatives.

Some academic women are concerned with building a social science that defines females as full participants in society and creates and supports new definitions of women. This attempt, however, has little support among many active feminists, who point out that the social sciences are male-dominated in membership, substance, and style, thus forcing academic women to work under non- or antifeminist constraints. I myself believe that the most exciting social-psychological analyses in the past five years have taken place in feminist groups. To the extent that this thinking has filtered into academic meetings and writing, it has been a grossly watered down and devitalized version of feminist thought (my own work not excepted). Thus the movement puts little faith in the social sciences' provision of a basis for new images of women and society.

Changing Male Dominance of Institutions

So far, the approaches to change with which I have dealt focus heavily on undermining male normative and cultural power and substituting female group support for male approval. However, these approaches are limited by male control of social institutions, against which women have few resources. The main tactics we employ are legal action, direct action and moral pressure, and skill building.

Growing out of the civil rights movement, several legal changes in the past decade open new options to women. Under law, public accommodations must be available to women, and discrimination in hiring or pay on the basis of sex is illegal in any business or educational institution. These changes formally open the possibilities for women to travel freely, gain skills, and obtain economic and positional resources. However, none of these laws are adequately enforced. It has been incumbent upon women to identify discrimination and file suits or complaints with federal, state, or local

agencies. This technique is currently in wide use by university women, who are filing complaints against institutions with HEW. In addition, local movement groups give support and advice to individuals seeking redress of employment or pay discrimination cases and rent and loan discrimination.

Another attempt at law enforcement is a current project, coordinated through NOW, to challenge the renewal of TV and radio station FCC licenses on grounds of sexism (discrimination in employment and failure to provide fair and adequate service to a segment of the public).

Women seek to change as well as enforce laws. Campaigns, rallies and marches in support of legalized abortion, welfare rights, and child care attempt to influence public opinion and bring public pressure to bear on legislators. This tactic is especially favored by socialist groups. In addition, ad hoc groups of women have pressured politicians for new laws—the Equal Rights Amendment, laws on the treatment of female criminals, changes in marriage and divorce law, laws and procedures governing rape cases, etc.

Direct action includes sit-ins, economic boycotts, moral pressure, and attempts to form women's unions. Sit-ins and boycotts are used to draw attention to illegal and unjust institutional practices as well as to affect the economic position of those against whom they are directed. Groups employing these tactics often negotiate directly over their demands. In addition, these approaches sometimes speed up investigatory or legal action by providing adverse publicity and forcing a business or organization to defend itself publicly.

An example of successful moral pressure is the project of two Wayne State University women who analyzed the Detroit public school system's textbooks, using the latter's own guidelines on treatment of minority groups. As a result of their efforts, Detroit school guidelines now explicitly include females with other groups that must be portrayed fairly in school texts—an incentive for authors and publishers to produce such books.

Attempts to form women's unions in order to collectivize and institutionalize women's power to bargain for better working conditions, equitable pay, and job definitions which allow for promotion are underway in many parts of the country. They are also necessary because unions have been notoriously insensitive to the needs of women. (In Detroit, some UAW leaders crossed picket lines for the first time in their lives when their female staff went on strike.) Some women are organizing unions that cut across occupational types or place of employment and are attempting to pull employed women and housewives into one union, with demands that include pay for housework. Women's unions are most strongly promoted by groups using a power analysis.

A final, and less direct, way of changing institutions is through skill building. Women's lack of power in institutions stems partly from a lack of knowledge, skills, and confidence. Many feminist projects are devoted to building women's personal and collective resources to enable them to challenge institutional power. Some groups, convinced that all individuals are capable of any activity given the opportunity to learn and practice, build speaking and writing skills by seeking opportunities for all members to engage in those activities and by assigning members to fill speaking engagements by lot rather than by degree of competence.

Some professional women are actively recruiting women into their ranks. At Wayne State University and elsewhere, women law students accompany recruiters to college campuses, talking to women about careers in law and providing information about the field, entrance requirements, and preparation for Law Board exams. Women from other professions speak at high schools and on college campuses to encourage young women to consider new career opportunities. Within professions, women are beginning to form support groups or caucuses or to change the focus of existing women's professional organizations to consider the roles of women and ways in which they can implement feminine values within their occupations. The entrance of women into prestigious fields such as law, medicine, business, and education not only gives females a basis for power within those institutions but also begins the process of building female expertise as a counter to male expertise, and in some cases begins the systematic introduction of feminine values into institutional structures.

Building Alternative Institutions

Partly as a result of the cultural analysis, which argues that the institutions of society are corrupted by their weddedness to masculine values, and partly for reasons of sheer survival, many women are engaged in building alternative institutions that incorporate feminist values and can thereby serve as models for institutions in a new society. In fact, the women's movement itself may be seen in this light. *The New Woman's Survival Catalogue* (Grimstad & Rennie, 1973) is an excellent resource for locating feminist institutions in the U.S. It also contains information on organizations, publications, and other activities discussed elsewhere in this paper.

The numerous women's self-help medical clinics primarily aim to break down male monopoly on basic medical information. They provide women with information about their bodies that enables them to stay healthy, know when something is wrong, know how to communicate with—and if necessary how to challenge—their doctors or seek alternative care. These clinics operate on the assumption that women lose control of their bodies partly through ignorance. They strive to reduce the distinctions between patients, aides, nurses, technicians, and doctors by teaching each other how to do breast and vaginal self-examinations and basic laboratory tests, and by sharing information on such topics as menopause and nutrition. Self-help groups also collect lists of doctors who are nonchauvinist and those whom women should avoid. Gradually these groups are beginning to negotiate with doctors, hospitals, and clinics for changes in the treatment of female patients, and more radically, in the structure of the medical professions.

In the field of law, a group of female lawyers in San Francisco is using its expertise to train women in law. If a client wishes, she may work in the office, including the preparation of her own legal brief in lieu of some or all of her legal fees. The approach incorporates feminist values into the practice of law by reducing mystification of the law and monopolization of expertise. Status relationships are also equalized as lawyers frequently answer phones and type letters while clients prepare legal briefs.

Another alternative institution is the commune. Although the communal movement is not feminist, many women have seen its potential for providing an alternative to the nuclear family, which power analysts in particular view as a primary oppressive institution. Communes offer women who are already married an opportunity to reduce the sex-role pressures of the nuclear family by sharing work and home roles among several adults; single women find mixed or all-female communes a way of meeting social and economic needs and reducing the pressure on them to marry; single mothers have found that collective living with others in the same position eases child care and economic problems. An important component of all these communal styles is that they increase support among women, who live together rather than in isolated homes, and reduce their dependence on males. Hence they are alternatives especially favored by women using a cultural or power approach.

In the process of working for a feminist revolution, the women's movement has attempted to structure itself around its values for a new society. Since women have been placed in a largely powerless role in society, they are especially sensitive to the degradations associated with powerlessness. Therefore, in seeking change, the movement has sought organizational techniques which do not subject women to oppression within or without the movement. Most groups have been reluctant to recruit actively, depending instead on women coming to the movement when they become aware of their own opposition as women. As mentioned earlier, the media provide indirect recruitment, but most women avoid pressuring or coercing individuals with their views. . . .

References

Beauvoir, S. de. *The second sex.* Trans. by H. M. Parshey. New York: Alfred A. Knopf, 1953; first published in 1949.
Beauvoir, S. de. *Force of circumstances.* London: Andre Deutsch, 1965.
Burris, B., in agreement with K. Barry, Barry T. Moon, J. DeLor, J. Parent, and C. Stadelman. *The fourth world manifesto: An angry response to an imperialist venture against the women's liberation movement.* New Haven, Conn.: Advocate Press, 1971.
Chafetz, J. S. *Masculine/feminine or human?* Itasca, Ill.: F. E. Peacock Publishers, 1974.
Chesler, P. *Women and madness.* New

York: Doubleday & Company, 1972.

Firestone, S. *The dialectic of sex*. New York: William Morrow, 1970.

Grimstad, K., & Rennie, S. (Eds.) *The new woman's survival catalogue*. New York: Coward, McCann and Geoghegan/Berkeley Publishing Corporation, 1973.

Millett, K. *Sexual politics*. Garden City, L.I., N.Y.: Doubleday & Co., 1970.

Mitchell, J. *Woman's estate*. New York: Random House, 1971.

Reed, E. *Problems of women's liberation: A Marxist approach*. New York: Merit Publishers, 1969.

Safilios-Rothschild, C. (Ed.) *Toward a sociology of women*. Lexington, Mass.: Xerox College Publishing, 1972.

Solanas, V. *The scum manifesto*. New York: Olympia, 1968.

9.5 FOUNDATIONS FOR A RADICAL CONCEPT OF PLANNING

Stephen Grabow, Allan Heskin

Not only the goals of planning, but its internal structure as well needs changing. At present, it perpetuates elitist, centralizing, and change-resistant tendencies. A new paradigm rising to challenge the "rational-comprehensive" model of modern planning is based on systems change and the realization of a decentralized communal society that facilitates human development in the context of an ecological ethic by evolutionary social experimentation.* Planning in the radical sense is the facilitation of this change through a dialectical synthesis of rational action and spontaneity. . . .

Reprinted by permission of the *Journal of the American Institute of Planners*, Vol. 39, No. 2, March 1973.

Footnotes in edited portions of this paper have been deleted and remaining footnotes renumbered.

* [Editors' Note: Compare Grabow and Heskin's approach with the more conventional views of planning represented by the selections included in Chapter Seven of this volume.]

MODERN PLANNING

At the core of modern planning, of our only existing concept of planning, is the "rational-comprehensive" model: the establishment of an objectively defined set of goals; the statement of all possible alternate courses of action to attain these goals; the evaluation of those courses of action in terms of their efficiency; the selection of that alternative which most nearly optimizes the set of goals; and finally, the assessment of that action, once implemented, in terms of its actual effects upon the overall structure.

While many planners follow this structure and even try to extend its applications[1] it is well known that the rational-comprehensive model itself is an unattainable "ideal" (Bolan, 1967). Nevertheless, almost all current theory is an attempt to modify the model in order to cope with both "political reality" and the perceived limits of human ra-

[1] For example, see articles in May 1965 issue of the *Journal of the American Institute of Planners*."

tionality.[2] These attempts do not change its internal structure at all because they do not question the fundamental assumptions upon which it is based.

The distinctive feature of the rational-comprehensive model, in its original and "modified" forms, assumes knowing in advance the probable outcome of any course of social action (that is, it is predictive). Both modern planning and its technique—the rational-comprehensive model—exist within the context of objective consciousness: "a state of consciousness cleansed of all subjective distortion (and) all personal involvement." (Roszak, 1969: 208). The predictive nature of the rational-comprehensive model calls for this objective state of mind, one which evaluates alternative futures by objective means. This objectivity, this attempt at being rationally comprehensive, is at the heart of our critique of modern planning.

CRITIQUE OF MODERN PLANNING

Modern planning, objective planning, has elitist, centralizing, and change-resistant tendencies.

1. Modern planning is elitist in that it sets the ostensible "planner", the rationally comprehensive advisor, apart from the world he or she is to "plan." It sets up what Theodore Roszak calls an "invidious hierarchy":

As soon as two human beings relate in detachment as observer to be observed,

[2] For example, some well-known modifications include: describing the structure to be nonlinear; correlating action with governmental policy formulation; encouraging "citizen participation" in the formulation of goals; and integrating "intelligence systems" and computer-aided techniques within the process of generating and assessing alternate courses of action. See also: "Bounded Rationality" in Herbert Simon (1959); Charles Lindblom (1959); and Amitai Etzioni (1972).

as soon as the observer claims to be aware of nothing more than the behavioral surface of the observed, an invidious hierarchy is established which reduces the observed to a lower status. (1969: 222).

In *I and thou,* Martin Buber captured this critique in his distinction between *using* the world ("I-It") and *relating* to the world ("I-Thou"). Planning as it exists today calls only for the use or manipulation of others, of nature, of the world; it foregoes a meaningful relationship *with* the world.

2. Modern planning is centralizing. The outcome of the attempt to know in advance results in preordained behaviorism or self-fulfilling prophecy, whether consciously—as the philosopher Herbert Marcuse (1969) would have us believe —or unconsciously—as the psychoanalyst Erich Fromm (1967) would have us believe. Modern planning, planning in the objective, manipulative sense, requires the monitoring and control of all observed activity. This type of control necessitates centralized authority. Again, Roszak provides us with an explanation:

. . . the social environment—the body politic—must be brought as completely under centralized, deliberate control as the physical body has been brought under the domination of the cerebrum. Unless the order of things is readily apparent to a command and control center—in the individual, it is the forebrain; in society, it will be the technocracy—and available for manipulation, it cannot be respected as order at all. (1969: 226).

3. Modern planning is change-resistant. The final result of the attempt to know in advance, to control outcome, is the eventual elimination of all but preprogramed social change. Unpredictable change is uncontrollable and is considered synonymous with undesirable change. All attempts are made to suppress it. But history has taught us that significant

change is always unique, unpredictable and unrepeatable: change is an open-ended creative process; in the rational-comprehensive model, it is precisely the creative sources of social change that are not and cannot be taken into account (Dunn, 1971: 125).[3]

PERCEPTIONS OF DUALITY

From this critique of modern planning, several dichotomies suggest themselves: elitism versus anarchy, manipulating versus relating, centralization versus decentralization, control versus chaos, programing versus creativity, objectivity versus subjectivity, and rationality versus irrationality. In the original debate over planning, these or similar dichotomized issues were presented. In 1959, John Friedmann stated that this debate was now closed:

We no longer ask: Is planning possible? Can planning be reconciled with a democratic ideology? But: How may existing planning practice be improved? The problem of planning has become a problem of procedure and method. (1959)

From our perspective, Friedmann spoke too soon. In the crisis of the 1960's the debate has been reopened.[4] There are today two principal methods for resolving this new debate, most simply stated as the

[3] While Dunn and others have been able to get at the core of modern planning in their critique of its internal inconsistencies and malfunctioning, our critique goes further: we maintain that, even if modern planning *could* work on its own terms, it is incompatible with human freedom. For a convincing discussion of why planning *can't* work as it is presently conceived, see Dunn (1971); and Haran Ozbekhan (1969:47–155).

[4] It should be noted that Friedmann himself is in the forefront of this new debate. See this development in Friedmann (1966) and (1969) and (forthcoming 1973).

dichotomy between planned action and spontaneity. These two methods grow out of different perceptions of duality: dominance and balance. A third view, dialectic, constitutes the foundation for a more radical perception of duality than either of these two. . . . [The] . . . third view, *dialectic,* sees the entities not as related opposites but as components of the same thing—only their immediate context causes them to appear contradictory. The dialectic acknowledges an unbearable tension, an incongruity in the context of presently perceived reality, and gives rise to forces which are wholly at odds with existence as we know it to be. It aspires to go beyond our present notions of "reality," redefining the meaning of existence in such a way that the contradictions between the specific instances of the duality disappear; everything is seen as a manifestation of the same thing. The process by which this transcendent state is attained is synthesis.[5] It is our intention in this essay to attempt that synthesis.

THE NEW PARADIGM

This synthesis, which constitutes the foundation for a radical concept of planning, is part and parcel of the emerging pattern of our time. We presently live under a world view consisting of the maintenance of a mass technocratic society governed by the myth of an objective consciousness, through the demands of the rational-comprehensive model, with emphasis on an accommodating economic growth. The paradigm rising to challenge this present concept of reality is based on *systems change and the realization of a decentralized communal society which facilitates human development by foster-*

[5] For a particularly vivid visual impression of dialectical synthesis, see M. C. Escher (1971), especially his woodcut "Dag en Nacht," p. 11.

ing an appreciation of an ecological ethic based on the evolutionary process: spontaneity and experimentation.

SYSTEMS CHANGE

The new paradigm recognizes the fragile nature of the present view of reality. It recognizes that when anomaly arises to seriously question the efficacy of the dominant world view, societies seek a new world view, a new reality, which deals with the anomaly and ends the crisis.[6] It also recognizes that societies to date have not looked upon this process of "paradigm shift" as being existential in nature and in the interest of human development: such change has been resisted. We believe that there is sufficient anomaly to demand revolutionary change. We further believe that the new paradigm must itself recognize the process of paradigm shift as a good and necessary component in the human learning process. Only in this way can society serve the *present* needs of both individuals and the world based on an understanding of the past and an open future.

[6] See Thomas Kuhn's description of the rise and fall of scientific paradigms in his *The Structure of Scientific Revolutions* (1962). He traces the emergence and inevitable disintegration of competing explanations of the perceived universe: the competition for attention among alternate views; the arrival of consensus upon one view; the articulation and extension of that view to cover all perceptions of reality; the emergence of a phenomenon which calls the view into question; and the crisis in which alternate views again compete for attention to resolve the anomaly. It is by calling into question the principles of validation by which consensus comes about, as well as articulating the inevitability of the cycle, that Kuhn effects a profound loss of innocence.

THE DECENTRALIZED SOCIETY

Decentralization is necessary to reduce the scale of joint activity. Mass society is alienating—its byword is efficiency. The byword of efficiency is control. If people are to be free—not, in the words of C. Wright Mills (1959), just "cheerful robots"—they must be free to form their own unity with the world. As Erwin Gutkind has said:

Where is the firm basis on which we can build a new social structure? There are only two starting points—the individual human being and the unity of the world. Everything in between is of doubtful value. . . . artificial, a man-made incident of history—leaders, States, frontiers. All the abstract concepts attached to them are obstacles to the emergence of man into the full light of self-respectability and independence, of world consciousness and intimate social contact (1953: 20–21)

From this basis, society must be reorganized so that the maximum number of decisions possible can be within the effective reach of as many people as possible. Decisions affecting the mass can be made with the consent of the mass by *temporary* organizations[7] called together by the mass: in our view organizational continuity is the first step to tyranny.

The collective is the primary organized unit of this society. The Canyon Collective speaks to the oft-asked question of the desirable size and organizing principle of these decentralized units:

Size is a question of politics and social relations, not administration. The collective should not be bigger than a band. The basic idea is to reproduce the collective, not expand it. The strength of the collective lies in its social organiza-

[7] For a complete presentation of this idea, see Warren Bennis and Philip Slater (1968).

tion, not its numbers. The difference between expansion and reproduction is the difference between adding and multiplying; the first bases its strength on numbers and the second on relationships between people. (Canyon Collective, 1970: 9)

Decentralization is ecologically sound: complex, diversified organisms survive; specialized organisms perish.[8] The tendency of mass society is to cause the grouping of fewer and fewer units (that is, metropolitan centers) and by the weight of its very size prevent flexibility and demand conformity. However, the evolutionary future of human beings is bound up with the ability of their social organizations to cope with an ever-changing environment. Civilizations survive or perish in accord with this ability. Innovation and experimentation in social organization is therefore necessary for human development. Mass society inhibits social experimentation. The City—the locus of mass society—having served its purpose in the evolution of the demand for change, is no longer useful in its present form and only inhibits further evolution.[9]

THE COMMUNAL SOCIETY

The decentralized society is communal. By communal we mean socialist and "utopian": the organization of society and the division of labor to the advantage of all.[10] Our present society also professes this ideal. It promises that this ideal society will be achieved through competition. In recent years, a partial

[8] See especially Peter Kropotkin's presentation of the ecological basis of decentralization in his *Mutual Aid*.

[9] For a more complete presentation of this idea, by an urban historian, see Erwin Gutlind, *The Twilgiht of Cities* (1952) and his *The Expanding Environment* (1953).

[10] Buber describes such a society in *Paths in Utopia* (1968: 14, 80).

"balance" between the notions of competition and cooperation has been sought under the title of the "Welfare State." Its promise, however, has not been kept.[11]

In the dialectics of competition and cooperation, competition is seen as the frustration of cooperation. Our present society, then, is seen as artificially creating and nurturing this frustration to encourage competition (Slater, 1970). The denial of the material benefits of society by virture of sex, race, or class; the exploitation and the accumulation of capital by some while others are forced to do alienating labor; the measuring of progress, achievement, and success in terms of power—all are manifestations of this artificial frustration that festers like a sore in our humanity.

Human conflict and struggle are, of course, inevitable as part of the "pain of being human" (Marcuse, 1969). They may even be psychologically necessary for human development (Maslow, 1968). But, the communal society does not nurture and enlarge this conflict. It rather is a society in which the struggles of human beings are devoted to resolving conflict between man and himself, man and man, and man and nature, to attaining symbiosis: living together for the mutual benefit of all. Most of all, a communal society is not a society which finds the value of togetherness only in a fight against an external and terrifying "them." (Laing, 1967: 91–94). . . .

THE FACILITATION OF HUMAN DEVELOPMENT

Human development consists of social and economic development and should be contrasted to the present emphasis on

[11] See Michael Harrington's *The Other America*, the Report of the Kerner Commission, or the Pentagon Papers.

economic growth. As René Dubos notes, "All societies influenced by western civilization are at present committed to the gospel of growth" (1968: 191). This desire for growth, sold to the people by the promise of economic well-being, has proven a hollow victory: the emphasis on economic growth has resulted in the alienation of individuals from themselves and from each other—as Marx claimed,[12] and from their environment—as Dubos claims (1968: 191–193).

Combining the ideas of both Marx and Dubos, we perceive that society must look not only to the attainment of a minimum *quality* of life but to the setting of a maximum quantity as well. If indeed the phenomenological world is finite, then setting the maximum has taken on the importance of attaining the minimum.

A major factor in the acceptance of the growth drive is the western concept of death. The fear of death and the concomitant desire for "extended" life has placed an almost unbearable pressure on the world.[13] It is ironic that the drive for extended life should result in so much death.

We accept a view of humanity which includes a desire for disequilibrium as well as a desire for equilibrium: in other words, individuals desire to risk their lives as well as to survive,[14] as Albert Camus has tried to tell us in many ways.[15] The present dominance in our society of the survival drive—sublimated into the drive

for status—over the risk-taking drive may mean more than an "escape from freedom." It may mean the end of survival. The attainment of maximum equilibrium and minimum disequilibrium may mean total disequilibrium. Some level of economic well-being is necessary for people to exercise choice between survival and risk, but once attained, continued economic growth seems only to prevent further development of the individual.

THE CONTEXT OF AN ECOLOGICAL ETHIC

The ecological ethic is simply stated as the merging of the development of the individual with the unity of the world.[16] While many writers have described it in part, it is not a wholly intellectual concept. Because of this, no one person, or group of persons, can realistically claim a special relationship to it. Each of us is born with knowledge of it.[17] Societies to date have mutilated that knowledge and have not allowed it to mature. Carl Rogers describes this knowledge as an "organismic value system,"[18] and Abraham Maslow describes the mature state as self-actualization.[19] Martin Buber describes it as an "I-Thou" relationship with all that surrounds the individual—whether "thou" be a person, a cat, or a

[12] See, for example, "The Meaning of Human Requirement," Karl Marx, *Economic and Philosophic Manuscripts of 1884* (1964).

[13] See, for example, Norman O. Brown, *Life Against Death* (1959), especially pp. 105–109.

[14] See, for example, Edgar Dunn (1971: 177–180).

[15] The existentialism of this quality is described in Albert Camus, *The Stranger* (1946) and *The Rebel* (1956).

[16] For the only comprehensive presentation of this concept in the West, see Pierre Teilhard de Chardin, *The Phenomenon of Man* (1965). The introduction by Julian Huxley is an essential part of the presentation.

[17] Trigant Burrow speaks of this as the "preconscious foundations of human experience" in this book of the same title (1964).

[18] See, for example, Carl Rogers, *Person to Person: The Problem of Being Human* (1967).

[19] See, for example, Abraham Maslow, *Toward a Psychology of Being* (1968).

tree.[20] He also noted the difficulty one encounters in attempting a full description: as one approaches the true relationship, words fail, concepts disintegrate. Its totality is more than we have learned to rationally communicate. The science of Loren Eisley approaches that description but only metaphorically.[21] In the evolution of human consciousness, it appears as a merging of the unconscious, the self-conscious, and the object-conscious parts of the individual psyche.[22] Marx referred to it as the "species essence."

The ethic is being increasingly restated in many ways and in many forms. It encompasses the ecology "movement" itself as well as the themes of peace, love, and freedom. It is expressed in a growing awareness and interest in eastern theology and philosophy, such as described in the work of Alan Watts (1968). It finds expression in a striving for higher "synergy" described by Hampden-Turner (1970: 54–56).[23] and finally, in an attempt to evolve an ecological theory of value described by Arthur and Stephanie Pearl (1971).

Although on numerous occasions in this essay we have referred to the development of the individual, it should now be understood that the emerging paradigm is not "individualistic" in nature.[24] In stating that the ecological ethic is the merging of the development of the individual with the unity of the world, we are stressing that people do not exist alone but rather, with each other, with nature and with the entire world. Society, no matter what the scale, socializes every individual; the ethic calls for a society that allows the "organismic value system" within the individual to mature rather than to be suppressed. It calls for human development on a scale not experienced to date. The fulfillment of the ethic requires "planning"—in a radical sense—of the nonrepressive society.

Modern planning has as its major theme the desire of man to control his own destiny. But the emerging paradigm is not man-centered. Consequently, the major theme of radical planning is every individual's organic desire to merge with the unity of the world. One is no longer striving to be master, only an equal par-

---

[20] See, for example, Martin Buber, *I and Thou*. In this translation by Walter Kauffman, the word "you" is preferred to the archaic "thou" by which Buber really meant "HE is here now"—an essentially mystical translation.

[21] See, for example, Loren Eisley, *The Immense Journey* (1956).

[22] This is based on a "triad" theory, with modified correspondence to Jung's concept of the "collective unconscious," the "personal conscious," and the "personal unconscious." This is outlined in his "The Structure and Dynamics of the Psyche" (1927/1941) in vol. 8 of the collected works. See Carl G. Jung, *Memories, Dreams and Reflections*, edited and recorded by Aniella Jaffe (1961), especially pp. 324–326. This integration of the parts of the pysche paves the way for more possibilities of consciousness, what Maslow has called: ". . . transpersonal, transhuman, centered in the cosmos rather than in human needs and interest, going beyond humanness, identity, self-actualization, and the like." (Maslow, 1968: iv).

[23] See, for example, Charles Hampden-Turner, *Radical Man* (1970), especially Chapter 3: "A Model of Psycho-Social Development," pp. 54–56.

[24] In the introduction to *The Phenomenon of Man*, Julian Huxley writes: "A developed human being . . . is not merely a more highly individualized individual. He has crossed the threshold of self-consciousness to a new mode . . . and as a result has achieved some degree of conscious integration—integration of the self with the outer world of men and nature, integration of the separate elements of the self with each other. He is a person, an organism which has transcended individuality in personality." (Teilhard de Chardin 1965: 19).

ticipant in the totality of the world. Lincoln said: "As I would not be a slave, so I would not be a master." Instead of controlling the flow of history, one attempts to join that flow.

SYNTHESIS

In the process of dialectical synthesis, the two components critical to integration of contradictions in reality are consciousness and action. We have identified that consciousness as the organic unfolding of an ecological ethic, but what remains seems to be the question of appropriate *action*.[25] In relationship between consciousness and action, further synthesis is imperative. Each is related to and dependent upon the other. To value one over the other is to suggest a lesson of history: the incompleteness of all "revolutions" to date.

The action component of the emerging paradigm is an "existential leap" out of anomaly and crises, out of duality and contradiction. In Montgomery, Alabama, 1955, Rosa Parks, a black seamstress, sat down in the front of a bus in a seat reserved for whites and made that leap: she denied objective reality. Martin Luther King describes the moment:

So every rational explanation breaks down at some point. There is something about the protest that is suprarational: it

cannot be explained without a divine dimension. Some may call it a principle of concentration, with Alfred N. Whitehead; or a process of integration, with Henry N. Wieman; or Being-itself, with Paul Tillich; or a personal God. Whatever the name, some extra-human force labors to create a harmony out of the discords of the universe. There is a creative power that works to pull down mountains of evil and level hilltops of injustice. (1958: 69–70)

In the deep regions of "dialectic" there is this question: Do the material conditions of society determine consciousness—as Marx would have it—or does consciousness determine the material conditions of society—as Hegel would have it? Neither answer alone, it would seem, tells us much about Mrs. Parks. She was, as Dr. King says:

anchored to that seat by the accumulated indignities of days gone by and the boundless aspirations of generations yet unborn. She was a victim of both the forces of history and the forces of destiny. She had been tracked down by the Zeitgeist—the spirit of the time. (1958:70)

What of this leap? Of the synthesis of rational action and spontaneity? We have yet to describe the way in which we can all sit down, as it were, in the front seat of the bus.

EVOLUTIONARY EXPERIMENTATION

The action component of the emerging paradigm we have chosen to call "evolutionary experimentation."[26] It is called

[25] Richard Flack's notes in "Strategies for Radical Social Change" (1971: 7–14), that the failure of Marxist Socialism was the failure of the working class to achieve that appropriate consciousness. Along with Marcuse, Roszak, and others, he makes a strong case for the "belated" emergence of that appropriate consciousness. But the problem now seems to be the question of appropriate "action" (e.g., "the long march").

[26] We are indebted to Edgar Dunn (1971) for this term and for parts of its meaning.

evolutionary because it borrows much from what we know of biological evolution.[27] Biological evolution is a revolutionary process: these revolutions are called "mutations." The history of biological evolutionary processes is the history of the successes and failures of these mutations.[28] Social evolution is the history of successful and unsuccessful attempts at social mutation. Humans have the ability to mutate—to change reality—not only in the sense of extending a trend but in the sense of a radical shift, one which, although it learns from the past, is wholly new.[29] To date, most have thought it impossible to plan revolution. If one uses "plan" to mean "predict," we would agree. But if one uses "plan" to mean "facilitate," we would disagree. The process of evolutionary experimentation, in full cognizance of the nature of change, is the engagement in social experimentation, the attempt of mutation, as a means of facilitating social evolution. In this sense, as Huxley says: "man discovers that he is nothing else than evolution become conscious of itself" (in Teilhard de Chardin, 1965: 221).

We see evolutionary experimentation as having three components: the ethic, social experimentation, and learning.

1. The ethic—the ecological—is the only constant in the process, although it appears to be changing as it unfolds and our knowledge of its implications increases.

2. To experiment is to act, to act without the necessity of certainty or probability of result: to take risks, but always with the purpose of learning. Experimentation in the social world rather than in the closed world of the laboratory entails a realization that situations rarely, if ever, reoccur: life is constantly in flux.[30] However, one is not attempting to deduce "rules" from the experiment but rather, to acquire a facility to deal with complexity—to learn.

3. Learning includes the concepts of understanding, evaluation, and reformulation. Understanding means recognizing the present, the past, and the nature of change. Evaluation means recognizing the present, the past, and the nature of change. Evaluation means deciding whether experimentation has brought us closer to or taken us away from the ethic. Reformulation is the reintegration of the individual's knowledge (or the group's knowledge) with that of society's into greater complexity. It is reformulation, as opposed to addition: it is, to acknowledge a concept from eastern philosophy, "karmic."

. . .

RADICAL PLANNING

What we mean by planning is a *synthesis* of rational action and spontaneity: evolu-

[27] We use the term "borrows" because biology and social evolution have a number of significant dissimilarities. See Dunn (1971), pp. 105–109.

[28] Also see Thomas Kuhn (1962) for a general description of a similar process in regards to the rules of science itself.

[29] Also see Thomas Kuhn (1962) for a discussion of "normal" versus "extraordinary" science.

[30] Henri Bergson described this "flux" in relation to personality growth: "Each of its moments is something new added to what was before. We may go further: it is not only something new, but something unforseeable." See his *Creative Evolution* (1944: 8).

tionary social experimentation within the context of an ecological ethic.[31]

In this radical definition of planning, who is the planner? In our view, the planner is active: a radical agent of change. He or she is not, as are so many of today's professionals, a creature of divided loyalty, one who owes as much or more to the profession as to the people. Instead, the job is to facilitate social experimentation *by* the people. The radical planner is a nonprofessional professional: no longer one with a property right entitled "planning," but rather an educator and at the same time a student of the ecological ethic as revealed in the consciousness of the people. Such an individual strives for self-actualization of one-self and of the others with whom one lives. Finally, he or she is not apart

from the people: the "planner" is one of us, or all of us.

The emerging paradigm will be realized by any, and the many, means necessary. This recognizes the need for experimentation, and it recognizes the manifold activity which makes up a unified revolution.[32] Change must take place in all realms: social, economic, technological and scientific, educational, religious, cultural, sexual, and political. It is no longer productive to argue which should come first. It is no longer productive to claim the right way to make a revolution. The answer will not be found in either the seizure of power or in the destruction of all power. We are all part of the same process in the evolution of human consciousness. The revolution is where you are, and it what *we* are becoming: consciousness and action merge. Martin Buber was perhaps more eloquent:

Just as I do not believe in Marx's "gestation" of the new form, so I do not believe either in Bakunin's virgin birth from the womb of revolution. But I do believe in the meeting of idea and fate in the creative hour. (1958: 138)

---

[31] Marcuse calls this: "the union of the new sensibility with a new rationality: The imagination becomes productive if it becomes the mediator between sensibility on the one hand, and theoretical as well as practical reason on the other, and in this harmony of faculties . . . guides the reconstruction of society" (*An Essay on Liberation*, 1969: 37–38). Only in this sense are the basic problems of planning, as Roszak says, "questions of social philosophy and aesthetics" (1969: 230), or as Shulamith Firestone would have it: "The merging of art with reality." See, for example, *The Dialectic of Sex* (1971).

[32] The only limit we see is the ecological ethic itself, which seems to suggest that while an act may be necessary for the survival of humanity, it may not be necessary for humanity to survive.

References

Bennis, Warren, and Philip Slater (1968) *The Temporary Society*. New York: Harper and Row.

Bergson, Henri (1944) *Creative Evolution*. New York: Modern Library.

Bolan, Richard (1967) "Emerging Views of Planning," *Journal of the American Institute of Planners* 33, no. 4 (July).

Brown, Norman O. (1959) *Life Against Death: The Psychoanalytic Meaning of History*. New York: Vintage.

Buber, Martin (1968) *Paths in Utopia*. Boston: Beacon.

——— (1970) *I and Thou*. New York: Scribner's.

Burrow, Trigant (1964) *Preconscious Foundations of Human Experience*. New York: Basic Books.

Camus, Albert (1946) *The Stranger*. New York: Vintage. (1956) *The Rebel*. New York: Vintage.

Canyon Collective (1970) "Communalism."

de Chardin, Pierre Teilhard (1965) *The Phenomenon of Man.* New York: Harper and Row.

Dubos, René (1968) *So Human and Animal.* New York: Scribners.

Dunn, Edgar (1971) *Economic and Social Development: A Social Learning Process.* Baltimore, Md.: The Johns Hopkins Press.

Eisley, Loren (1956) *The Immense Journey.* New York: Vintage.

Escher, M. C. (1971) *The Graphic Works.* New York: Ballantine.

Etzioni, Amitai (1967) "Mixed Scanning: A Third Approach to Decision-Making," *Public Administration Review* 27 (Dec.).

Firestone, Shulamith (1971) *The Dialectic of Sex: The Case for Feminist Revolution.* New York: Bantam.

Flacks, Richard (1971) "Strategies for Radical Social Change," *Social Policy* (March/Apr.).

Friedmann, John (1959) "The Study and Practice of Planning," *International Social Science Journal* 11, No. 3:327–339.

——— (1966) "Innovative Planning: The Chilean Case," *The Journal of the American Institute of Planners* 35, no. 5 (Sept.)

——— (forthcoming 1973) *Transactive Analysis.* Garden City. N.Y.: Doubleday.

Fromm, Erich (1967) *Escape from Freedom.* New York: Avon.

——— (1970) *The Crisis of Psychoanalysis.* Greenwich, Conn.: Fawcett.

Gatkind, Erwin (1952) *The Twilight of Cities.* London: Watts.

——— (1953) *Community and Environment.* London: Watts.

——— (1953a) *The Expanding Environment: The End of Cities—The Rise of Communities.* London: Freedom Press.

Hampden-Turner, Charles (1970) *Radical Man.* Garden City, N.Y.: Anchor Books.

Harrington, Michael (1959) *Toward a Democratic Left: A Radical Program for a Majority.* Baltimore, Md.: Penguin.

Jung, Carl G. (1961) *Memories, Dreams and Reflections.* Aniella Jaffe, ed. New York: Vintage.

King, Martin Luther, Jr. (1958) *Stride Toward Freedom: The Montgomery Story.* New York: Harper and Row.

Kropotkin, Peter (1955) *Mutual Aid.* Boston, Sargent Press.

Kuhn, Thomas (1962) *The Structure of Scientific Revolutions.* Chicago: University of Chicago Press.

Laing, R. D. (1967) *The Politics of Experience.* New York: Dell.

Lindblom, Charles (1959) "The Science of Muddling Through," *Public Administration Review* 19 (Sept.)

Marcuse, Herbert (1966) *One-Dimensional Man.* Boston. Beacon.

——— (1969) *An Essay on Liberation.* Boston: Beacon.

Marx, Karl (1964) *Economic and Philosophical Manuscripts of 1884.* New York: International.

Maslow, Abraham (1968) *Toward a Psychology of Being.* Princeton, N.J.: Van Nostrand.

Mills, C. Wright (1959) *The Sociological Imagination.* London: Oxford.

Montagu, Ashley (1962) *The Humanization of Man.* New York: Grove Press.

Ozbekhan, Hasam (1969) "Towards a General Theory of Planning," in Erich Jantsch, *Perspectives of Planning.* Paris: Organization for Economic Cooperation and Development, pp. 47–155.

Pearl, Arthur and Stephanis (1971) "Toward an Ecological Theory of Value," *Social Policy* (May/June).

Rogers, Carl (1967) *Person to Person: The Problem of Being Human.* Walnut Creek, Calif.: Real People.

Roszak, Theodore (1969) *The Making of a Counter Culture.* Garden City, N.Y.: Anchor Books.

Simon, Herbert (1959) *Models of Man.*

Slater, Philip (1970) *The Pursuit of Loneliness.* Boston: Beacon.

Watts, Alan (1968) *The Book: On the Taboo Against Knowing Who You Are.* New York: Collier.

Values
and Goals

PART
FOUR

Finding Direction in Planned Change

CHAPTER TEN

Whatever else planning may mean, it signifies an anticipation of some future state of affairs and the confirmation of a vision of that future in the present in order to motivate, guide, and direct present action. A planner's present situation always includes a time perspective forward—a future different from the present, yet populated with more or less clearly delineated agents and counteragents, objects to be avoided, objects to be embraced, means to empower avoidance or embracing, and some context of interrelated factors and forces, human and nonhuman, benign, hostile, or neutral. Man as planner must climb out of his involvement in present transactions to look beyond the horizon of the present and to bring back a vision of the future to modify the tempo, quality, and direction of his present transactions.

It is the fact of change in the internal and external conditions of human life that makes planning important and necessary to time-bound men and women, choosing and acting of necessity within the medium of history. And it is the fact of change that makes planning difficult for time-bound men and women. If the future were to be like the present, there would be no need to give thought to preparing for it. Yet, since the future will be different from the present, men do not know how far to trust their present anticipations of it in preparing to meet and cope with it. All human planning is planning for change and requires judgments about the proper balance between investment of energy and resources in the pursuit or avoidance of consequences we can now anticipate and the massing of free and uncommitted energy and resources for coping with unanticipated consequences.

Kenneth Boulding has illuminated the predicament of men in attempting to plan the future of the social systems in and through which they live in his distinction between "evolutionary systems" and "mechanical systems."

One thing we can say about man's future with a great deal of confidence is that it will be more or less surprising. This phenomenon of surprise is not something which arises merely out of man's ignorance, though ignorance can contribute to what might be called unnecessary surprises. There is, however, something fundamental in the nature of our evolutionary system which makes exact foreknowledge about it impossible, and as social systems are in a large measure evolutionary in character, they participate in the property of containing ineradicable surprises.[1]

Mechanical systems have no surprise in them since time as a significant variable has been eliminated from them in the sense that they have no past or future and the present is a purely arbitrary point. The traditional lure among scientific students and planners of human affairs toward interpreting social systems as mechanical systems may rest on some inherent preference for a world of no surprise among scientific men. Yet system breaks which result in more or less sudden changes in the defining characteristics of the system itself seem to characterize the temporal careers of all human systems. And human planners must plan with the possibilities of system breaks somewhere within their field of consciousness.

We have spoken so far of the predicament of human planning in general. Yet planning always occurs within some time-bounded historical situation. What characteristics of the present historical situation have given new point and poignancy to men's efforts to find confident direction in planning for the future?

A radical increase in the rate of change in the conditions of life has thrown the problem of direction finding and planning into new perspective. Concentration of energy and resources in basic and applied research has resulted in a continuing revolution in the means and conditions of work, play, education, and family and community living. Men have found the established institutions and wisdoms from the past less and less dependable as guides to the effective and humane management of new knowledges and technologies in the conduct of life. Men in a slowly changing culture could validly assume that the ecological contours of their future life would be substantially similar to those of their past. Changes to be planned for could be seen as confinable and manageable within the patterns of a viable tradition out of the past. Modern men have been betrayed by tradition direction. They face both the hopes and terrors of an unknown future more directly than past men did, bereft of security in the guidance of traditional forms and wisdoms.

---

[1] Kenneth E. Boulding, "Expecting the Unexpected: The Uncertain Future of Knowledge and Technology," Edgar L. Morphet and Charles O. Ryan (eds.), *Prospective Changes in Society by 1980* (Denver, Colo.: July 1966).

Finding direction for the future by projecting the forms and values of a traditional culture upon that future has been further undermined by the omnipresent fact of intercultural contact, confrontation, and mixing within nations and between nations. The development of vast networks of interdependence, the spread of mass media of communication, reduced security in spatial and political boundaries between cultures, due to space-destroying means of transportation and other related factors, have brought about uneasy contact and confrontation between traditionally segregated nations, classes, races, and subcultures. As we seek new bases for an interdependent future across these cleavages of culture by projecting the traditions of any one cultural tradition, the futility of this way of defining the future for purposes of planning becomes more and more apparent to modern men. If there is to be a common future, it must be constructed and reconstructed by men in a way to lead beyond the present maze of disparate and conflicting traditions. The outlines of the task have become clearer than the means for achieving it.

A third feature of contemporary man's struggles to find viable directions into his future is a widespread decline of confidence in a presiding Providence which will automatically and without human attention bring the plural and conflicting plans and actions of individual men and groups of men into the service of commonly valuable purposes. Confidence in some pre-established ordering principle within history—a principle which men can depend upon to bring meaningful and moral order out of the confusion and chaos of diverse and conflicting individual and group decidings and strivings—has taken many forms in the history of human affairs. The principle has been conceived theistically and naturalistically, personally and impersonally, immanently and transcendentally, pessimistically and optimistically. And it has been given many names—the Will of God, Fate, the Nature of Stoics and Taoists, the "Unseen Hand" of Adam Smith and the free-market mechanism of the classical economists, the Idea of Progress in Western liberalism, the historical inevitability of socialism in Marxism. One may recognize the common function which these versions of a superhuman directing principle have played in the direction of human affairs and in setting limits to human responsibility in planning man's future, without denying the differences which adherence to one version or another has made in the organization and deployment of human energies and resources. The effect of this confidence has been to narrow the range of human responsibility for finding and giving direction to the course of human history. Decline of confidence means a widening of man's responsibility for designing and inventing his own future. If there is to be an ordering principle in human planning, a principle attentive to the conservation and augmentation of human values, men must find, or better construct and apply, the principle through their own collective intelligence and volition.

In this human condition, it is not surprising that a new "discipline" of "futuristics" has emerged recently. The aim of "futuristics" is to help men and women find and keep direction in their efforts to envision and build a viable future for man on earth. Elise Boulding, in "Learning to Image the Future," offers a constructive critique of contemporary "futuristics" and envisions a way of imaging the future which incorporates the transcendence that human hope requires, which is egalitarian rather than elitist, and which is transnational rather than nationalistic in its scope. She also projects the kind of educational processes which men and women will require in learning to image a future for man and models of which, she argues, have already emerged in the contemporary scene.

Margaret Mead works out of a similar value commitment in "The Future as the Basis for Establishing a Shared Culture." She is impressed by the fragmentation, "the agglomeration of partly dissociated, historically divergent and conceptually incongruent patterns" of culture and subculture which now block men and women in their search for a better future for mankind. Imaginatively, Miss Mead envisions a focus upon a future to be jointly built as the basis for uniting young and old, men and women, people of various nationalities and religions, scholarly and nonscholarly, in going beyond the fragmentation of culture which now divides them into the construction of a shared culture. The future, unlike the past, is always newborn. To involve all living persons in constructing the future is to release and facilitate change and growth all around. Mead's method of grappling with the future is prophetic, in the sense that she is concerned not primarily with predicting but rather with invoking and shaping the future in the service of an overarching value—"shared culture."

The changes which contemporary men and women are undergoing, and, insofar as they can summon the directed energy and wit, changes which they help to shape and direct, extend not only to human institutions but to the organization of human persons as well. What kind of persons will the future require and elicit? Robert Jay Lifton sketches the shape of the persons who are now emerging in "Toward a Protean Style of Self-Processing." This Protean style is the personal counterpart of the temporary human systems which Bennis, Slater, and others have seen as characteristic of a postbureaucratic society. John Dewey once identified the ultimate devotion of persons who live in and with change and who assume responsibility for directing it as commitment to the process of intelligent self-remaking. If Lifton is empirically correct, contemporary society is now developing "Protean" persons with such a devotion. Lifton is not unaware of aberrations of the Protean style which contemporary life is also spawning in his recognition of a "plastic" style, characterized by "repeated change of 'color' or appearance without serious depth of immersion anywhere" and a "shedding" style characterized by "intense immersion followed by equally intense rejection." Thus the Protean style is still *human* and so beset by dilemmas of value commitment.

10.1 LEARNING TO IMAGE THE FUTURE

Elise Boulding

The intimate relationship between the reconstruction of education and the reconstruction of society has come out frequently in the preceding chapters. The capacity of a society to generate creative images of the future, that will act back on the present and draw it toward the envisioned tomorrow, is simultaneously reflected in and fostered by its educational institutions. It is in these institutions that the battle between the past and the future is fought. On the one hand children are prepared for the maintenance of existing structures through training in the social and technical skills familiar to the adult generation. They may even be trained to meet long-past crises, just as nations train soldiers to fight old wars. At the same time they must be prepared to adapt to, and even to create, new institutions and new possibilities for humankind. While the rhetoric of education all lies in the direction of creating new futures, the actuality lies much more in the re-creation of the past.

The rise of futuristics as an intellectual discipline is forcing education to re-examine its rhetoric and its reality. As the professional futurist moves in, the educator is waking up and saying, "Hey, the future is my business too! This is what I work with!" It is good that he does so since this is his best protection against an excessively technocratic futurism, which simply treats the future as a problem to be solved. The technocrat-cum-

planner tends to see the educational system as a powerful tool to assist him in shaping the future he is blueprinting. If education is to be more than a complex piece of software for implementing certain types of futures in a technological society, a more indepth understanding of the dynamics of imaging the future, and the role of education in it, is required. . . .

We are discussing here a complex set of three-way interactions between society, the imaged future, and society's learning communities. Each of the three acts on the other two. In order to understand this interaction we need to examine (1) the nature of the imaging process, (2) the politics of imaging the future in a period of redistribution of social power, (3) the reservoir of human knowledge on which we draw in the imaging process, and (4) the changing character of the learning communities.

IMAGING THE FUTURE

While the idea of envisioning the future is as old as human society, and in fact marks humankind off from other animal species, the specific term "image of the future" has come into usage rather recently. The scholar who has dealt the most delicately and sensitively with the concept is Fred Polak, one of the first of the post–World War II European futurists. Writing in the bleak aftermath of Nazism when it looked as if the future was closing off for Europe, he probed searchingly into the history of the West to try to identify the ground of past visions, and their effects on the societies that held them. *Was* there a relationship between man's imaging capacity and the future itself? *Did* the envisioned future act back upon the groping present,

Originally published as "Futurism as a Galvanizer of Education," in N. Shimahara (Ed.), *Educational Reconstruction* (Columbus, Ohio: Charles Merrill Pub. Co., 1972).

References in the deleted parts of this essay have been removed and the remaining references renumbered.

and draw it surely towards itself? And if this was indeed the case, what were the features of the image itself that gave it such power over the present?

In Polak's book, *The Image of the Future*,[1] he traces the relationship between prevailing images of the future and the ensuing future of succeeding periods of Judaeo-Christian society, getting a running start in Mesopotamia. His hypothesis that the image of the future acts as a time bomb going off in the future itself is amply demonstrated in this book. This time-bomb characteristic of the image stems from its combination of two elements, the eschatological and the utopian.

The *eschatological, or transcendent, is the element which enables the visionary to breach the bonds of the cultural present and mentally encompass the possibility of a totally other type of society, not dependent on what human beings are capable of realizing.* While transcendence refers to the supernatural dimension, there is a theoretically unspecified interaction between the known and the conviction concerning the eventually attainable imagined other.

The *totally other* is, of course, in fact not conceivable by man, but this term (an exact translation of the Dutch) is used without modification because it emphasizes the notion of discontinuity as a key aspect of dynamic social change. Kenneth Boulding's discussion of "Expecting the Unexpected"[2] points up the dilemma underlying the concept of discontinuity.[3] It is clear, however, that a society with an eschatological outlook, one which conceives the possibility, even the desirability, of drastic social change, is very different from the society that seeks familiar tomorrows.

The second element in the ideal-type image of the future is the humanistic utopian, or immanent, element which designates men as the copartners with nature (or God) in the shaping of The Other in the Here-and-Now. Polak suggests that the Judaic image of the future was an ideal embodiment of these twin elements. The Judaic conception of the Covenant, a unique bonding between man and the supernatural,[4] held man responsible for creating the new Zion out of the dusty materials of the planet Earth. Paradise was to be nowhere but here. But man had instructions, and he had to listen carefully to get them right. If he didn't listen, the deal was off—the covenant broken. It was the character of the instructions that set a handful of nomads apart from their fellow tribes in Syriac-Palestine.

This delicately balanced conception of the relationship between immanence and transcendence, man and the supernatural, has never lasted for long, though it has reappeared from time to time in the history of the West. The pendulum has swung back and forth. Either God was taking care of everything and man had but to go along with it (St. Augustine), or everything was up to man and he'd better get with it (Comte). Furthermore, societies have alternated between

---

[1] Fred L. Polak, *The Image of the Future*, Elise Boulding (tr.) (New York: Oceana, 1961); abridgement by Elise Boulding to be published by Elsivier in 1972.

[2] Kenneth E. Boulding, "Expecting the Unexpected: The Uncertain Future of Knowledge and Technology," in *Prospective Change in Society by 1980 Including Some Implications for Education*, reports prepared for the first Area Conference, Designing Education for the Future, Edgar L. Morphet and Charles O. Ryan (eds.) (Denver: 1966), pp. 199–215.

[3] See also Peter F. Drucker, *The Age of Discontinuity* (New York: Harper & Row, 1968).

[4] The supernatural, which is used in several different ways by Polak, may in general be thought of as a kind of governor on the total ecosystem of the earth, standing outside that system even while partaking of it.

optimistic and pessimistic views of the nature of reality and man. Four modes of imaging the future emerge from various combinations of attitudes to the basic categories of Seinmüssen (that which must be) and Seinsollen (that which ought to be):

1. *Essence optimism combined with influence optimism:* the world is good and man can make it even better.
2. *Essence optimism combined with influence pessimism:* the world is good but it goes of itself and man cannot alter the course of events.
3. *Essence pessimism combined with influence optimism:* the world is bad but man can make it better.
4. *Essence pessimism combined with influence pessimism:* the world is bad and there isn't a damn thing man can do about it.

Influence optimism can be further divided into direct and indirect influence optimisim, depending on whether man is perceived as running the show or acting in partnership with the supernatural.[5] Clearly, a society suffering from both essence and influence pessimism is not generating any dynamic images of the future, and the social paralysis engendered by the lack of positive images of the future will lead to the death of that society, according to Polak. The most dynamic society is the one with both essence and influence optimism, and if the image has eschatological elements with a sense of the possibilities of breakthrough to a to-

---

[5] Questions may be raised concerning the nature of relationships between man and the supernatural which are not dealt with in Polak's theory. This relationship is formally specified as nonhierarchical, but the specification is exceedingly fuzzy given the difference between the dimension "human" and the dimension "supernatural."

tally new order, this adds to the dynamism. These eschatological elements always present a danger to any society, however, in that there is a tendency to spiritualize the other reality and come to think of it as realizable only in heaven, or in an after-life, and not in this world. This is what happened to Christianity. The ever-deferred paradise, conceived as imminent in Jesus' time, was finally thought to be not for this world at all.

Out of the turbulence of the Middle Ages, when conflicting modes of viewing the future were doing battle with each other both inside and outside the church, came the great surges of influence optimism that characterized the Renaissance. From that time on the utopian and eschatological streams diverged more and more as the church retreated in the face of increasing confidence in man's capacity to shape his own destiny, with the aid of science. In the end only the pentecostal and adventist sects kept intact the concept of "the peaceable kingdom" as coming on earth, and the rest of the Christian church settled for a spiritualized kingdom within man or located at a comfortable remove in outer space.

Two sets of discoveries released the pent-up energy of the Middle Ages for utopian construction of possible future societies: scientific discoveries that opened up the possibilities of using nature as a tool to shape the environment, and voyagers' discoveries of exotically other cultural patterns which revealed that human society was highly malleable. The sixteen, seventeen and eighteen hundreds produced a heady array of "futures." These ranged from classical-style Platonic utopias such as Bacon's *New Atlantis,* which drew on a prevision of future scientific and technological developments to outline a kind of universal communism, through romantic, satirical, and rollicking utopias which combined sharp critique of the times with glimpses of an upside-down, right-side-up society—Rousseau, Rabelais,

DeFoe, Swift, Fenelon, Holberg[6]—and on to the socialist utopias of Owen, Saint-Simon, and Fourier.[7] This is the point at which social scientists got into the utopia-writing business, and Comte and Marx each constructed utopian future societies based on "natural law," though Marx vehemently attacked the concept of utopism itself.[8]

Utopian writing about the future interacted with social experimentation and the more popular imagination to create social innovations in every sphere from the economic (the trade union movement, profit sharing, social security, scientific management) through the political (parliamentary democracy, universal suffrage) to the social (universal education, child welfare practices, women's "emancipation," New Towns, social planning).[9] As Polak says, most features of social design in contemporary Western society were first figments of a utopia-writer's imagination.

[6] Rousseau, *Confessions*; Rabelais, *L'Abbaye de Theleme*; Defoe, "Essays of Projects"; Swift, *Gulliver's Travels*; Fenelon, *Les Adventures de Telemaque*; Holberg, *The Underground Journey of Nicholas Klim.*

[7] Owen, *Signs of the Times, or the Approach of the Millenium* and *Book of the New Moral World*; Saint-Simon, *De la Reorganisation de la Société Europeene*; Fourier, *The Social Destiny of Man, Theory of the Four Movements*, and *The Passions of the Human Soul.*

[8] There is some danger of overemphasizing the role that contact with other people's "differentnesses" has in generating a sense of transcendence. Such contact may simply extend the range of an invading culture's manipulative abilities rather than stimulate the envisioning of totally new kinds of social structures. If there were a direct correspondence between contact with other cultures and transcendence generation, the West would not now stand accused of having done so much harm to the world.

[9] Frank E. Manuel (ed.), *Utopias and Utopian Thought* (Boston: Beacon, 1967).

Somewhere in the 1800s, however, something began happening to the "other space" and the "other time" of utopian fantasy. It began in Germany, home of the universalistic utopians Lessing (1730) and Kant (1785), in such works as Fichte's *Geschlossene Handelsstaat* (1800), which designs a specific future for a specific country—Germany. From this time on nationalism and an orientation toward the immediate future began eroding the creative imaging powers of the utopist. The sense that man can breach time and create the totally other is gone.

It is Polak's contention that the capacity to image the future is a core capacity in any culture that is manifested in every aspect of that culture. Therefore the decline in the ability to envision totally other "realities," the compressing of the mental perceptions of time and space into the here and now, will be revealed not only in the literature of an era, but also in its art, architecture, poetry and music, in its science and philosophy, and in its religion. Polak in fact documents this decline in imaging capacity in science, philosophy, and religion in the twentieth century. The predominantly Orwellian tone of twentieth century science fiction is presented as the most damaging evidence of all concerning the diseased futurism of the present. Prometheus is re-bound, tied up in knots by his own science and technology and fear of the future he had thought to master. What went wrong?

The cultural lag in ability to generate new visions appropriate to the complex knowledge structure of a hyperindustrialized society has been examined at length in contemporary social science literature. The rate of change itself is usually seen as the culprit. Whether or not the human imagination can adapt itself to reconceptualizing reality as fast as reality changes in this century of exponential growth curves is a subject for debate. An element usually left out of the debate, however, is the disappearance of the eschatological sense of a totally other order of reality. The divorce of utopia from eschatology which characterized the Enlightenment appeared as a liberation of human thought at the time; but Polak points out that the utopian and eschatological modes are symbiotic, and either without the other goes into decline. Once the eschatological otherness of utopian images of the future was weeded out, utopias themselves came to be conceived as more and more static images of a boring, end-state of man. The true utopia is not static, however, but historically relative.[10]

The historical evolution of utopias is a part of the battle between past and future mentioned earlier, and it is in the setting of the learning community that much of this battle takes place. In tracing the decline of the imaging capacity Polak faults the university severely (as many others have done). In criticizing the standarization of learning and of mass output of students at the expense of nurturing a creative minority who can dream dreams and re-create society, however, he is guilty by implication of looking back to older models of the *universitas* in a society where few were educated. We can't go back. We live on a small, densely populated planet, and we want education for everyone. How do we regenerate our utopianizing capacity?

Polak emphasizes that it is the *eschatological* component of our thinking that has declined in every sector of society, including the educational. In the high mass-consumption societies of the West, we sit like so many spoiled children, with all our splintered and lifeless utopias

[10] Elise Boulding, "Futuristics and the Imaging Capacity of the West," in *Human Futuristics.* Magoroh Maruyama and James A. Dator (eds.) (Honolulu: University of Hawaii, Social Science Research Institute, 1971), pp. 29–53.

scattered around us like so many broken toys. It is not future shock[11] that is hurting us. We know that there will be more and better toys next year. What is hurting is that it is the day after Christmas, and we have lost our sense of the transcendent. What we can make, break, and fix is all there is. It is this loss of the sense of transcendence that has weakened our imaging capacity. Is the loss reparable? Can the learning community do anything about it?

THE POLITICS OF IMAGING

Talk about the sense of the transcendent smacks of elitist thinking. We think of it as a concept belonging exclusively to the province of the philosopher and the theologian, dreaming away in cloister or ivory tower. This leads to the question, are we the imagemakers, anyway? And for whom are the images? These are crucial questions in the libertarian age. Historically, the image makers have always been the intellectual elite. Whether or not they included "something for the masses" in their images of the future, they did their image making *for* society, not with it. There have been two parallel traditions of dealing with the masses in imaging the future in the Christian West. One has made use of an equalitarian model of the social structure, the other of a stratified model. Plato's *Republic* serves as the prototype of the stratified model, and reappears in Dante's *DeMonarchia,* Jean Bodin's *La Republique,* Bacon's *New Atlantis,* Campanella's *City of the Sun,* and—in a subtle way—in Skinner's *Walden II.*

An early version of the equalitarian model is found in the Old Testament books of the Prophets, where an image of simple tribal patterns of nomadic days

[11] Alvin Toffler, *Future Shock* (New York: Random House, 1970).

is held up in contrast to the wicked city which draws lines between rich and poor. Equalitarian utopias are scarce before the Middle Ages, however. If they were written, the church probably suppressed them. In the twelfth century Joachim de Fiore ignored the interests of the ecclesiastical hierarchy and wrote of the coming of a radical new age on earth in which all men should be holy and equal, and the church would fade away. Three centuries later Thomas More's *Utopia* appeared as the first secular equalitarian utopia and became the prototype for all the modern equalitarian utopias. Karl Marx translated the equalitarian ideal into the industrial setting.

While both equalitarian and stratified models have reappeared again and again in utopian images of the future, our accumulated historical experience seems to tell us that only a hierarchically structured multiclass society has viability over time. (Melvin Tumin, Kingsley Davis and Wilbert Moore laid out the pros and cons of this hypothesis in their famous debate in 1953.[12]) It is startling, therefore, to realize in surveying the actual experiments in alternative communities, often based on a literary utopia, that the models in which people invest their lives are predominantly the equalitarian models. The willingness to invest one's own life-energy in these historically "unworkable" equalitarian models has increased dramatically in the past two decades.

The politics of imaging is complex. Primitive Christian communism and sophisticated ecclesiastical hierarchy have alternated inputs into the secular social structures of the West for two thousand years now. The industrial and technological revolutions, which concentrated social power in new ways while destroying once functional feudal distribution systems, generated a new set of social inequities and also a constant flow of ideas about ways to remove them. The socialist utopists—Owen, Saint-Simon, Fourier—all contributed to the lessening of the inequities, and to the development of educational and welfare reforms in the name of an equalitarian ideal. Still, these utopists were all intellectual elitists working on behalf of, not with, the masses.

Today, the real polarization in society (as has often been noted) is not between the radical and the reactionary, but between the radical and the liberal.

Futurists are on the whole in the liberal tradition, and are in the business of imaging futures for people they know very little about. (This is equally true of many radicals.) However, it is not fair to lump all futurists together under one label, since there are substantially different approaches and value systems represented among them.

Within social science, futurism has taken various forms, including social planning in specialized and general systems-type planning, the development of special techniques such as brainstorming for inventing new futures, and the development of a variety of conceptual tools for predicting the future *à la* Kahn and Wiener, Helmer, etc. Straddling the social and engineering sciences are the evolutionary nucleators such as Mead, Platt, and Doxiades. The ecological futurists range from Ward and Boulding, who offer a spaceship earth vision of the future, through social geographers and ecologists to whole-earth romanticists and pre-Raphaelite Aquarians. Finally there are the revolutionary futurists, some political, some nonpolitical, some militant, some gentle, and all dedicated to a completely

[12] Kingsley Davis and Wilbert E. Moore, "Some Principles of Stratification," *American Sociological Review, 10* (April, 1945), pp. 242–49; Melvin Tumin, "Some Principles of Stratification: A Critical Analysis," *American Sociological Review, 18* (August, 1953), pp. 387–97. The Tumin article contains comments by Kingsley Davis and Wilbert E. Moore.

new society for man—and there are the science fiction writers.

Most social science futurists are utopians. This means that they are operating on the premise that everything depends on humankind's evolving capacities as social artisans. Since humankind hasn't done too well so far, this leads the utopist to an elitist position, putting his superior capacities at the disposal of the as yet inarticulate masses. The utopian tradition is by and large the elitist liberal tradition, which takes seriously the responsibility of modifying social structures and removing inequities on behalf of those who suffer from them.

The libertarian radical futurists are operating on different premises. In the tradition of the politicized peasant chiliasts who followed on the heels of Joachim de Fiore in the Middle Ages, they believe in the possibility of a radical break in history. The concept of conscientization of the masses involves the conviction that there is something radically Other in every human being which can be awakened, and which once awakened represents a new kind of force in history which will lead to a totally new kind of society. The libertarian radical therefore refuses to do a band-aid job on existing structures, and he refuses to do the thinking of the masses for them. (I am using the term "libertarian radical" here to distinguish him from the authoritarian radical, who in fact does impose his thinking on the masses, and is not a true radical at all but only an angry, impatient elitist liberal who wants to do his thing right away.)

It is this burning sense of what conscientization can do for the mass of humankind that enables the libertarian radical to have confidence in the imaging process of the masses, and to work in the direction of coparticipation in the creation of images of the future (as well as in the creation of actual futures). Mao Tse-Tung and Paulo Freire arrive at these convictions along different routes, but they both base their work as evolutionaries on this process of coparticipation in imaging. Freire calls it dialogic education; the teacher-student learns from the students-teachers and then reflects back to them what he has learned from them, with the additional insights and clarity he can provide.[13] Freire recognizes that Mao Tse-Tung is talking about the same thing when he says "we must teach in the masses clearly what we have received from them confusedly."[14] Freire distinguishes this dialogic approach very sharply from the authoritarian approach of the pseudoradical, in which the revolutionary decides what is best for the masses and then tells them. The traditional conception of the public school and university hardly fits this dialogue-with-the-masses approach. The learning community concept, however, does.

This is not the place to go into a discussion of the whole question of the possibility of a nonhierarchical society. The possibility of the learning community providing a nonhierarchial network of relationships within the larger society and generating images of possible futures within that society that draw on the life experiences and dreams of a great diversity of previously inarticulate social groups is an exciting one. It depends, however, on an eschatological view of humankind and history which is uncomfortable for today's liberal.

THE CULTURAL RESERVOIR OF IMAGE-MATERIAL

Coparticipation in the development of images of the future on the part of diverse

[13] Paulo Freire, *Pedagogy of the Oppressed* (New York: Herder, 1971).
[14] Freire, *Pedagogy of Oppressed*, p. 82n.

groups within a national society enriches the reservoir of image material, but still leaves out a vast array of cultural experience in human history. It is at this point that we become the most conscious that the universitas is not a universitas at all, but only a very ethnocentric community of scholars turned inward to the West, making occasional libations to other cultural traditions. Futurists are the worst offenders of all in this regard.

Their global ethnocentrism is an unintended by-product of an honest effort to think about the planet as a whole. To describe the macroproblems of the planet within the frame of reference of a particular Western sequence of experience, however, is about as appropriate as for the Australian bushman to describe the problems of the planet in terms of his own experience of desert life. The Australian bushman has a very sophisticated technology of environmental utilization, given the resources he has available. He knows how to find food and water and how to deal with distance, time, space, and heat in very remarkable ways. His knowledge, however, is useful in a very limited range of settings. Our knowledge covers more settings, but our cognitive map of the planetary sociosphere is still very inadequate.

This is serious, because the resources available to us for social change are limited by the thought models used to describe and label them. The intellectual reality constructs of the scientific subculture of the West make quite a few resources unavailable to us, including large chunks of human experience codified in non-Western historical records, and the possibility of living in multidimensional time. On the whole we think of ourselves as being "locked in" to a high technology society with the only imagined exits involving an unthinkable return to the past. The feeling of being locked in is a result of the acceptance of a peculiarly Western

unilinear theory of development that postulates such a tight interlocking of physical technology and social patterns (the urbanization-industrialization-based media network theory of development) that we are convinced we can only go where urban-based technology will take us.

The Data Banks of History

Here is where history as a social resource can help free us. Complex communications networks have evolved in the absence of urbanization, as the horseback empire of Ghengis Khan demonstrates; this empire undertook the first mapping of the kingdoms of Europe when the local princes could not even find their way to each other's castles.[15] Pluralism and decentralized control is possible even with large-scale administrative systems of empire, as the millet system of the Ottoman Empire demonstrated, allowing a variety of religions and political subsystems to exist within an over-all Moslem administrative structure. A passion for learning can exist without a large-scale planned educational technology, as the sudden flourishing of lay teachers of the three R's outside the cathedral schools of the medieval European church demonstrated, once people got the idea that knowing how to read was advantageous.[16] A passion for experimentation with the building of new societies can exist without governmental subsidy by monarchies or parliaments, as the countless adventurous bands of Hittites, Celts, Phoenicians, Greeks, and other Mediterranean people showed in the second millenium BC, in organizing

[15] Michael Prawdin, *The Mongol Empire: Its Rise and Legacy* (New York: Free Press, 1940, 1967).

[16] Philippe Aries, *Centuries of Childhood* (New York: Knopf, 1962), 2 vols.

do-it-yourself utopian expeditions all around the Mediterranean.[17]

A passion for experimenting with forms of household organizations and kin patterning is endemic in human civilization, and the storied variants in primitive tribes are only a tiny fraction of the arrangements that have been tried. The 200-person communes of the European middle ages make our young people's counterculture experiments seem tame.[18] Humankind has developed many patterns for dealing with varying population densities over the past 10,000 years; and 7000 years of experience with urbanism is no small heritage to draw on. Almost any kind of family or communal experiment that is being tried today has been tried over and over again under varying conditions—nomadic, settled rural, settled urban, seasonal migration, utopian colonization.

In short, the innovative spirit was not born in the West, and is not dependent on modern technology. Furthermore, there is no one-to-one correspondence between environmental resources and culture, any more than between technological resources and culture. Tightly packed and environmentally deprived Japan and the Netherlands would never have made it if they had depended on physical resources. Their chief resource was social ingenuity. Assuming that we are all potentially as ingenious as the Japanese or the Dutch, we are free to borrow social technology from India, Japan, China and elsewhere—technologies that were developed in totally different contexts but which can be adapted. Our main problem is to inventory all the existing social technologies so we know

what we have to draw on. This we have not done because we think that what we have is all there is. The BLTMT[19] is a millstone around the neck of the West. There is nothing inherently wrong in projecting Basic Long-Term Multiform Trends, as long as we include all the forms—but a reading of futurist literature only gives us the Western variants.

Why this emphasis on borrowing from other social technologies? Are we really so badly off in the urban West, apart from some impending mineral shortages that can be solved by a combination of consumer education and new scientific discoveries? Maldistribution of existing resources is after all a soluble problem. Development theory tells us that the increase in individual rationality and social competence that modern urbanization makes possible will lead to a society both more equalitarian and more affluent than the one we have now.

THE MYTHOLOGY OF COMPETENCE

In spite of the comforting doctrines of development theory, we are ambivalent on this question of competence. We think we have it, yet we fear we don't. Our fear of being locked in by current technologies indicates our uncertainty about our competence. There is good reason for this uncertainty. On the one hand, although we have been able to develop very complex large-scale systems of administration of physical and social resources in Europe and North America, there seems to be some evidence in the United States at least that at this moment we are unable to do anything but elaborate on present patterns. We may

[17] C. D. Darlington, *Evolution of Man and Society* (New York: Simon & Schuster, 1969).

[18] Marc Bloch, *Feudal Society* (Chicago: University of Chicago, 1961).

[19] Kahn and Wiener were among the first to make use of this terminology. See Kahn and Wiener, *The Year 2000* (New York: Macmillan, 1967).

not be able to deal with structurally generated inequities because we cannot address ourselves to structural change. A paper by Roland Warren analyzes the participation of community decision organizations in the Model Cities Program and concludes that all the rhetoric about a redistribution of decision-making power among the peoples to be served by the Model Cities Program led to nothing but a reinforcement of existing structures.[20] After three years of major and well funded effort, nothing had changed. There were a variety of reasons for this failure, but one important one was a complete inability on the part of the persons involved to question habitual structures and behaviors. By leaning on a mythology of competence, they could avoid examining alternatives. . . .

THE CHANGING CHARACTER
OF LEARNING COMMUNITIES

By using the term "learning communities" for educational institutions, I have already built my own image of the future for education into this chapter. There seems to be some convergence among both educators and futurists on the notion of increased flexibility of organization of learning facilities and of teaching-learning relationships in the future. Billy Rojas' Delphi Survey on Alternative Educational Futures[21] indicates a surprising consensus on the part of futurist-oriented educators concerning the disappearance by 1980 of traditional curricula, teaching methods, and attendance requirements in the public schools at least of the more progressive states.

[20] Roland L. Warren, "The Sociology of Knowledge and the Problems of the Inner Cities," *Social Science Quarterly*, in press.

[21] Billy Rojas, "Delphi Survey—Alternative Educational Futures" (Pippa Passes, Ky.: Alice Lloyd College, Futuristics Curriculum Project, 1971).

It is further widely held that community people and paraprofessionals will outnumber teachers in the schools by this date. There is a similar consensus on the disappearance of conventional academic departments and degree requirements in the universities. By 1985, many educators believe that "college departments at most state universities will become task-oriented rather than academically centered as at present. A 'department of environment' might be established, for instance, to eliminate pollution in a four-county area. When the task is accomplished, the department would phase out, its members regrouping in other departments."[22] Students will collect modular credits for short-term academic experience, and cash them in like trading stamps for a diploma when the necessary number have been acquired.[23]

In general, the changes envisioned represent a freeing up of existing structures, but no real change in the conception of the university. Even the relatively radical statement "25 percent of colleges and universities [will be] governed by postbureaucratic administrations of type described by Warren Bennis,"[24] still assumes a recognizable campus structure. It is hard to get away from the banking conception of education, to use Freire's terminology, in which students become the vaults and the teachers the depositors.

[22] Rojas, "Delphi Survey."

[23] This is already a pattern, of course. Students who dropped out in the early sixties as freshmen and sophomores are now, ten years later, returning to the campuses to collect enough credits for a B.A. They are taking a strictly utilitarian attitude towards this enterprise, doing the "shit work" uncomplainingly because they want the accreditation to upgrade their job opportunities. Often these returnees have done rather well in salaried jobs in the past few years, but are bored with their work.

[24] Rojas, "Delphi Survey."

Even postbureaucratic administrations cannot administer co-intentional communities. The development on a large scale of learning collectives pursuing co-intentionality in education is not yet within our capacity to imagine. And yet it may come about sooner than we think.

The rate of experimentation with nonhierarchical communal enterprises in economic production, scientific research, and information network development, as well as in educational ventures, is very high. The character of these enterprises can sometimes be identified by the use of the label "collective" in the name, but more often they have to be visited in order to discover this. The style of these enterprises is informal, provisional, task-oriented, and network-oriented. They form and reform according to perceived tasks and perceived colleagues in given enterprises, and are continually "in touch" through a network which is as ad hoc as the groups, and yet is building up in a recognizable communal infrastructure that is transnational in character.

These collectives are enormously diverse in style and activity focus, but they give us important clues about future patterns of living, learning, working, and playing. The ones I will mention here all have a common orientation to the production of new knowledge which will be useful in the creation of a new society. That is, they all seek to be agents of social change. That is not in itself so unusual. But in addition they all choose to incorporate into their own communal structures the features of the radically new society as they are beginning to understand it. This means that they usually include both intellectuals and nonintellectuals in their group, and also include people of all age groups from grandparents to teen-agers, with one important group being young parents with small babies. Their principle of functioning is that everyone in the community has inputs to make of equal importance with

everyone else, but in order to ensure this each member must teach the others what he knows best how to do. Thus, internationally known intellectuals will be seen baking bread and running mimeograph machines, and teen-agers will be sent out to speak in settings where "people of reputation" are expected to sit on the platform. At its best this kind of equalitarianism helps each member of the community to reach his highest level of potential functioning, and in place of the traditional superstar model of creativity which measures that creativity in the number of publications, etc., produced, a new communal style of creativity emerges that needs different measures, but can be identified in the continuous acts of shaping new social patterns. . . .

One of the major theoreticians of the new transnational, nonhierarchical, nonorganization collectives is Anthony Judge, Associate Executive Secretary of the Union of International Organizations in Brussels. He is in a unique position to observe the dynamics of the emergence of new transnational networks, and has developed an interesting model for transnational nonhierarchical systems. He also has a theory of nonorganizations appropriate to the fluidity of the ever-forming and re-forming collectives: all groups should be ad hoc and stay "potential organizations," constructing information and communication systems through the careful development of mailing lists and by-passing the membership approach, constitution, and so on, entirely. This avoids cluttering the social scene with superannuated organizations determined to live forever. Not a bad approach for universities!

The value of this type of fluidity eludes many in the older generation of scholars, businessmen, and activists, who set great store by the institutional "base of operations" they may have spent years building. Such people feel that the short lifespan of many collectives demonstrates definitively their lack of social viability. The possibility that the stability and permanence may be here in the networks themselves, rather than in particular organizational bases, is not easily accepted by persons equally committed to social change but operating with a more institution-based model for bringing about change. The *Source Catalogue* and its contemporaries, the *Whole Earth Catalogue,* the *Big Rock Candy Mountain,* and various directories of social change movements, all illustrate the network principle of action.

The Introduction to the *Source Catalogue* encapsulates this whole approach:

Sharing is at the heart of revolutionary activity, and the sharing of information is primary in the struggle to return control of America to its people. Information is a source of power to determine our own lives and the culture of our communities. We need information about our movement, its resources, projects, skills, and dreams in order to build the support networks needed to liberate this country and ourselves. . . .

The Source Collective's beginnings were with the Educational Liberation Front (ELF) Bus—a project-information center and Movement media-bookmobile that traveled 20,000 miles visiting fifty campus communities in 1969 and 1970. After a year's experience, it was obvious that we had collected too much material for one bus to pass on. From this realization came *Source,* whose original idea of one catalog quickly expanded to the idea of thirteen 100 to 200 page catalogs, each covering a different area of the Movement.[25]

The learning communities of tomorrow are already here. They are new creatures entirely, and will not simply replace our existing learning institutions. They will grow side by side with them, modifying the character of all other institutions and social groupings and breaking down many social barriers of age, status, and affluence to which we have been long accustomed. The importance of existing institutions of learning will be lessened in a society which has increasing numbers of ELF buses driving around the country plugging people into networks.

While the new learning communities won't replace schools and universities, they will modify them. Co-intentional learning will be rediscovered, and within our more formal institutions many co-intentional groups of faculty and students will be formed, working in a new way with old skills. What kind of imaging of the future can we expect from more communally oriented educational groups? At present, the futurist on the university campus sets a high value on his capacity to dream up radically different alternatives for society by special techniques for jogging people loose from their mental ruts.[26]

One significant limitation upon brainstorming is the point made by Barnett that "the expectation of change always envisages limits upon its operations. Change is expected only between certain minimal and maximal boundaries."[27] Barnett cites the example of the Samoans who set a high value on innovations in design, but the range of total variation is so narrow that the untrained Western eye has difficulty in detecting differences between one design and another, whether in textiles, songs, or

[25] *Source Catalogue,* "Communications: An Organizing Tool" (Chicago: Swallow Press, 1971).

[26] Alex Osborn, *Applied Imagination,* 3rd ed. (New York: Scribner's, 1963); William J. J. Gordon, *Synectics* (New York: Collier, 1961).

[27] H. G. Barnett, *Innovation: The Basis of Cultural Change* (New York: McGraw-Hill, 1953).

dances. Whether the range is wide or narrow, the cultural limits are firmly set. In short, the proverbial man from Mars might not be very impressed with the alternative futures dreamed up by the wildest of blue sky imagineers. While this kind of limitation operates on all human fantasizing, it operates much more strongly in a technique-oriented setting such as brainstorming than it does for the lone fantasist.

Neither brainstorming nor a sophisticated projection of future trends, then, will break us out of our technological trap. The sense for the totally other, the capacity for transcendence that Polak has said is seriouly weakened in our society, will not recover via that route.

It is precisely in the learning communities that the capacity for transcendence is being reborn. They are building "fear-free unhassled envelopes of free space deep within the heartlands of the dominant culture" through "learning based on love."[28] In a bureaucratic society that appears to be destroying children and adults alike, these intentional learning groups feel that they are rescue operations for the human race.

There is a specific reason why the capacity for otherness is fostered in these educational settings, and it relates to the general direction that educational theory and practice has taken in recent decades. Stages of cognitive development have come in for a great deal of attention. The body of research dealing with emotional development, and particularly the interplay between experiences of human warmth in the family and other settings and the development of cognitive skills,[29]

has had much less attention. That which has had least attention of all is the challenge of orchestrating different modes of knowing in order to allow for an integration of the cognitive and affective aspects of life experience.[30] In particular the spiritual-intuitive mode of knowing that draws on a special capacity to listen for what Peter Berger calls "signals of transcendence" has been ignored.[31] Imagine children being encouraged to sit and listen for signals of transcendence in a public school classroom! It is the discovery of the fruits of training in that kind of listening which has delighted many young people in their exploration of Eastern religions. That coin of that kind of knowledge is easily debased, however, when not carefully related to the development of cognitive and affective capacities. Gandhi's education for *Satyagraha* combines training in these three modes of knowing in a unique way that deserves much more attention.[32] There are traditions in the Christian church that draw on a combination of these three modes too. The tendency of the church to become separated from the world, and particularly for the lovers of God within the church to separate themselves further in monastic movements has usually led to a wildly imbalanced development of the spiritual-intuitive at the expense of the other modes of apprehending reality.

[28] Salli Rasberry and Robert Greenway (eds.), *Rasberry Exercises: How to Start Your Own School . . . and Make a Book* (Box 357, Albion, Calif.: The Freestone Publishing Company, 1970), p. 26.
[29] Bonnie Barrett Stretch, "The Rise of the Free School," *Saturday Review* (June 20, 1970), pp. 76–77.
[30] W. Ron Jones with Julia Cheever and Jerry Ficklin, *Finding Community: A Guide to Community Research and Action* (Palo Alto, Calif.: James E. Freel, 1971); P. S. Holzman, "The Relation of Assimilation Tendencies in Visual, Auditory, and Kinaesthetic Time-Error to Cognitive Attitudes of Leveling and Sharpening," *Journal of Personality*, 22 (1954), pp. 375–94.
[31] Peter L. Berger, *A Rumour of Angels* (New York: Doubleday, 1969).
[32] Elise Boulding, "The Child As Shaper of the Future" (unpublished "think piece," January 1972).

The Benedictines have succeeded better than others in avoiding this imbalance.

Intentional learning communities today are exploring the nature of that balance, and developing ways of learning that will foster it. They are making mistakes, but that is because they are trying to do something which we have systematically avoided doing in recent centuries; and it will take time to discover how to do it.

The only way to understand the excitement, joy, and willingness to commit one's life totally to intentional community while by-passing many of the comforts that technological society offers that characterizes the members of these intentional learning communities is to recognize that they are in fact tapping this missing dimension of transcendence in modern life. Where others despair, they see visions of an awakened society—and they feel themselves to be coparticipants in the awakening.

Technocratic futurism cannot be the galvanizer of education. All that this kind of futurism can provide is some skills to do better what educators are already trying to do. That which will galvanize education is the sense of The Other. The signals are there. Are we listening?

10.2   THE FUTURE AS THE BASIS FOR ESTABLISHING A SHARED CULTURE

Margaret Mead

1. THE PRESENT SITUATION

The world today is struggling with many kinds of disjuncture. Some derive from the progressive fragmentation of what was once a whole—as higher education has broken down into a mass of separate specialties. Some have come about with the development of world views that parallel and often contradict older and displaced—but not replaced—ways of viewing the world. Others result from a juxtaposition of vastly different and extremely incongruent world views within the national and also the world-wide context provided by our contemporary press and television coverage. Within the framework of the United Nations we have balloting for representatives both from

Margaret Mead, "The Future as the Basis for Establishing a Shared Culture," reprinted by permission of *Daedalus,* Journal of the American Academy of Arts and Sciences, Boston, Massachusetts. Winter 1965, *Science and Culture.*

countries with many hundreds of years of high civilization and from countries just emerging from a primitive way of life. Still others are the effect of changing rates in the production of knowledge which bring about unexpected discrepancies between the young and the old. In a sense, these different kinds of disjuncture can also be seen as related to the very diverse ways in which the emergent, changing world is experienced by people of different ages—particularly young children—who are differently placed in the world, the nation, and the community.

Discussion of this tremendous fragmentation and of the agglomerations of partly dissociated, historically divergent, and conceptually incongruent patterns has been conducted, too often, in a narrow or a piecemeal fashion which takes into account only certain problems as they affect certain groups. The recent "two cultures" discussion is an example of such an approach, in which neither the arts nor the social sciences are included in what is essentially a lament about the state of communication within a small sector of the English-speaking world, whose members for various reasons of contemporary position or achievement think of themselves as an elite. In another context it is demanded that children's textbooks should portray "realistically" the conditions in which many American children live, because the conventional house pictured in advertisements and schoolbooks is unreal to the underprivileged children who live in cabins and coldwater flats and tenements. Even though the aim was to rectify the consequences of social and economic fragmentation at one level, a literal response to this demand would result in further fragmentation of our culture at another level. Wherever we turn, we find piecemeal statements, each of which can be regarded as a separate and partial definition of the basic problem of disjuncture, and piecemeal attempts at solution, each of which, because of the narrowness of the context in which it is made, produces new and still more complicated difficulties.

Yet these partial definitions and attempts at solution point in the same direction. We are becoming acutely aware that we need to build a culture within which there is better communication—a culture within which interrelated ideas and assumptions are sufficiently widely shared so that specialists can talk with specialists in other fields, specialists can talk with laymen, laymen can ask questions of specialists and the least educated can participate, at the level of political choice, in decisions made necessary by scientific or philosophical processes which are new, complex, and abstruse.

Models for intercommunication of this kind—poorly documented but made vividly real through the treatment given them by historians—already exist, in the past, within our own tradition. One model, of which various uses have been made, is the Greek city, where the most erudite man and the simplest man could enjoy the same performance of a tragedy.

Another, in which there has been a recent upsurge of interest, is medieval Europe, where the thinker and the knight, the churchman, the craftsman, and the serf could read a view of the world from the mosaic on the wall, the painting above the altar, or the carving in the portico, and all of them, however far apart their stations in life, could communicate within one framework of meaning. But such models are not limited to the distant past. Even much more recently, in Victorian England, a poet's words could be read and enjoyed by people of many different backgrounds, when he wrote:

Yet I doubt not thro' the ages one increasing purpose runs,
And the thoughts of men are widen'd with the process of suns.[1]

Whether or not the integration of culture which we construct retrospectively for these golden ages existed in actuality is an important question scientifically. But thinking about models, the question of actuality is less important. For the daydream and the vision, whether it was constructed by a prophet looking toward a new time or by a scholar working retrospectively, can still serve as a model of the future. Men may never, in fact, have attained the integration which some scholars believe characterized fifth-century Athens. Even so, their vision provides a challenging picture of what might be attained by modern men who have so many more possibilities for thinking about and for controlling the direction in which their culture will move.

However, all these models—as well as the simpler model of the pioneering American farmer, dressed in homespun, reared on the King James version of the Bible, and sustained by simple foods and simple virtues—share one peculiarity. In

[1] Alfred Lord Tennyson, "Locksley Hall" (1842).

each case the means of integration is a corpus of materials from the past. The epic poems of Homer, the Confucian classics, the Jewish and the Christian Scriptures—each of these, in giving the scholar and the man in the street, the playwright and the politician access to an articulate statement of a world view, has been a source of integration. But the community of understanding of what was newly created—the poem, the play, the set of laws, the sculpture, the system of education, the style of landscape, the song—still depended on something which had been completed in the past. Today there is a continuing complaint that we have no such source of integration, and many of the measures which, it is suggested, would give a new kind of order to our thinking are designed to provide just such a body of materials. There is, for example, the proposal to teach college students the history of science as a way of giving all of them access to the scientific view of the world. Or there is the related proposal to teach all students evolution, particularly the existing body of knowledge about the evolution of man and culture, as a way of providing a kind of unity within which all specialists, no matter how specialized, would have a common set of referents.

But such suggestions place too much reliance on the past and necessarily depend on a long time span within which to build a common, shared view of the world. In the present crisis, the need to establish a shared body of assumptions is a very pressing one—too pressing to wait for the slow process of educating a small elite group in a few places in the world. The danger of nuclear disaster, which will remain with us even if all stockpiled bombs are destroyed, has created a hothouse atmosphere of crisis which forces a more rapid solution to our problems and at the same time wilts any solution which does not reflect this sense of urgency. For there is not only a genuine need for rapid solutions but also a growing restiveness among those who seek a solution. This restiveness in turn may well become a condition within which hasty, inadequate solutions are attempted—such as the substitution of slum pictures for ideal suburban middle class pictures in slum children's textbooks—within too narrow a context. Speed in working out new solutions is essential if new and disastrous fragmentations are not to occur—but we also need an appropriate framework.

Measures taken at the college level to establish mutual understanding between the natural scientist and the humanist, the social scientist and the administrator, men trained in the law and men trained in the behavioral sciences, have a double drawback. The cumulative effect of these measures would be too slow and, in addition, they would be inadequate in that their hope lies in establishing a corpus based on something which already exists—a theory of history, a history of science, or an account of evolution as it is now known. Given the changing state of knowledge in the modern world, any such historically based body of materials becomes in part out of date before it has been well organized and widely taught. Furthermore, it would be betrayed and diluted and corrupted by those who did the teaching, as they would inevitably have to draw on their own admittedly fragmented education to convey what was to be learned. One effect of this fragmentation can be seen in attempts to express forms of new knowledge in imagery which cannot contain it, because the imagery is shaped to an earlier view of the world. In a recent sermon, for example, the Bishop of Woolwich presented a picture of dazzling contemporaneity in disavowing the possibility of belief in the corporeal ascension of Christ; but, then, in proclaiming a new version of the Scriptures, he used the image of the sovereignty of Christ—an outmoded image in the terms in which he was speaking.

In the last hundred years men of science have fought uneasily with the problem of their own religious belief, and men of God have hardened their earlier visions into concrete images to confront a science they have not understood. Natural scientists have elaborated their hierarchical views of "true" science into an inability to understand the nature of the sciences of human behavior, welcoming studies of fragmented aspects of human behavior, or an inappropriate reduction in the number of variables. Human scientists have destroyed the delicacy and intricacy of their subject matter in coarse-grained attempts to imitate the experimental methods of Newtonian physics instead of developing new methods of including unanalyzable components in simulations or in developing new methods of validating the analysis of unique and complex historical events. As a result we lack the capacity to teach and the capacity to learn from a corpus based on the past. The success of any such venture would be comparably endangered by the past learning of the teachers and the past learning of the students, whose minds would already be formed by eighteen years of exposure to an internally inconsistent, contradictory, half-articulated, muddled view of the world.

But there is still another serious drawback to most current proposals for establishing mutual understanding. This is, in general, their lack of inclusiveness. Whether an approach to past knowledge is narrowly limited to the English-speaking world or includes the whole Euro-American tradition, whether it begins with the Greeks or extends backward in time to include the Paleolithic, any approach through the past can begin only with one sector of the world's culture. Inevitably, because of the historical separation of peoples and the diversity of the world's cultures throughout history, any one view of any one part of human tradi-

tion, based in the past, excludes other parts and, by emphasizing one aspect of human life, limits access to other aspects.

In the newly emerging nations we can see clearly the consequences of the efforts made by colonial educators to give to distant peoples a share in English or French or Dutch or Belgian or Spanish culture. Ironically, the more fully the colonial educators were willing to have some members at least of an African or an Asian society share in their traditions and their classics, the more keenly those who were so educated felt excluded from participation in the culture as a whole. For the classical European scholar, Africa existed mainly in very specialized historical contexts, and for centuries European students were concerned only with those parts of Africa or Asia which were ethnocentrically relevant to Greek or Roman civilization or the early Christian church. Throughout these centuries, peoples without a written tradition and peoples with a separate written tradition (the Chinese, for example, or the Javanese) lived a life to which no one in Europe was related. With the widening of the European world in the fifteenth and sixteenth centuries, Europeans treated the peoples whom they "discovered" essentially as peoples without a past, except as the European connoisseur came to appreciate their monuments and archeological ruins, or, later, as European students selectively used the histories of other peoples to illustrate their own conceptions of human history. Consequently, the greater degree of participation felt by the member of one of these more recently contacted societies in a French or an English view of the development of civilization, the more he also felt that his own cultural history was excluded from the history of man.

It is true that some heroic attempts have been made to correct for this colonial bias. Looking at a synchronic table of events, a child anywhere in the world may sit and ponder what the Chinese or the ancient canoe-sailing Hawaiians were doing when William the Conqueror landed in England. But almost inevitably this carefully constructed synchrony—with parallel columns of events for different parts of the world—is undone, on the one hand, by the recognition that the New World and the Old, the Asian mainland and the Pacific islands were *not* part of a consciously connected whole in A.D. 1066, and, on the other hand, by the implications of the date and the dating form, which carry the stamp of one tradition and one religious group within that tradition. It is all but impossible to write about the human past—the movements of early man, the building of the earliest known cities, the spread of artifacts and art forms, the development of styles of prophecy or symbolism—without emphasizing how the spirit of man has flowered at different times in different places and, time and again, in splendid isolation. Even in this century, the efforts to integrate the histories of the world's great living traditions have led, in the end, to a renewed preoccupation with each of these as an entity with its own long history.

Today, however, if we are to construct the beginning of a shared culture, using every superior instrument at our command and with full consciousness both of the hazards and the possibilities, we can stipulate certain properties which this still nonexistent corpus must have.

It must be equally suitable for all peoples from whatever traditions their present ways of living spring, and it must not give undue advantage to those peoples anywhere in the world whose traditions have been carried by a longer or a more fully formulated literacy. While those who come from a culture with a Shakespeare or a Dante will themselves be the richer, communications should not be so laden with allusions to Shakespeare or Dante that those who lack such a heritage cannot participate. Nor should the wealth of perceptual verbal detail in distinguishing colors, characteristic of the Dusun of Borneo or the Hanunóo of the Philippines, be used to make less differentiated systems seem crude. The possession of a script for a generation, a century, or a millennium must be allowed for in ways that will make it possible for all peoples to start their intercommunication on a relatively equal basis. No single geographical location, no traditional view of the universe, no special set of figures of speech, by which one tradition but not another has been informed, can provide an adequate base. It must be such that everyone, everywhere can start afresh, as a young child does, with a mind ready to meet ideas uncompromised by partial learning. It must be cast in a form that does not depend on years of previous learning—the fragmented learning already acquired by the college student or the student in the high school, the *lycée,* or the *Gymnasium.* Instead, it must be cast in a form that is appropriate for small children—for children whose fathers are shepherds, rubber tappers in jungles, forgotten sharecroppers, sailors or fishermen, miners or members of the dispossessed urban proletariat, as well as for the children whose forebears have read one of the world's scripts for many generations.

If this body of materials on which a new, shared culture is to be based is to include all the peoples of the world, then the peoples of the world must also contribute to it in ways that are qualitatively similar. If it is to escape from the weight of discrepant centuries, the products of civilization included within it must be chosen with the greatest care. The works of art must be universal in their appeal and examples of artistic endeavor whose processes are universally available—painting, drawing, carving, dancing, and singing in forms that are universally comprehensible. Only after a matrix of shared understanding has been developed will the way be prepared for the inclusion of specific, culturally separate traditions. But from the first it must have the character of a living tradition, so it will be free of the static qualities of older culures, with texts that have become the test of truth and forms so rigid that experimentation has become impossible. And it must have the qualities of a natural language, polished and pruned and capable of expansion by the efforts of many kinds of different calibres, redundant and sufficiently flexible so it will meet the needs of teacher and pupil, parent and child, friend and friend, master and apprentice, lawyer and client, statesman and audience, scientist and humanist in their different modes of communication. It is through use in all the complexity of relationships like these that a natural language is built and given form and content by many kinds of human beings, becomes a medium of communication that can be learned by every child, however slight its natural ability. This projected corpus should not be confused with present day *popular culture*, produced commercially with contempt for its consumers. Instead, by involving the best minds, the most sensitive and gifted artists and poets and scientists, the new shared culture should have something of the quality of the periods of folk tradition out of which great art has repeatedly sprung.

A body of materials having these characteristics must bear the imprint of growth and use. Yet it is needed now, in this century, for children who are already born and for men who either will preserve the world for a new generation to grow up in or who, in failing to do so, will doom the newly interconnected peoples of the world to destruction by means of the very mechanisms which have made a world community a possibility. The most immediate problem, then, is that of producing, almost overnight, a corpus which expresses and makes possible new processes of growth.

We believe that the existing state of our knowledge about the processes of consciousness is such that it is necessary for us only to ask the right questions in order to direct our thinking toward answers. Today engineering and the technology of applied physical science have outstripped other applied sciences because in these fields searching questions have been asked urgently, sharply, and insistently. This paper is an attempt to ask questions, set up a series of specifications, and illustrate the order of answer for which we should be looking. There will be better ways of formulating these questions, all of which have to do with communication, and better ways of meeting the criteria which will make answers possible. In fact, it is my assumption that the creation of a body of materials which will serve our needs will depend on the contribution and the participation of all those who will also further its growth, that is, people in every walk of life, in every part of the globe, speaking every language and seeing the universe in the whole range of forms conceived by man.

2. THE FUTURE AS A SETTING

I would propose that we consider the future as the appropriate setting for our shared world-wide culture, for the future is least compromised by partial and discrepant views. And I would choose the new future over the far future, so as to avoid as completely as possible new confusions based on partial but avowed totalistic projections born of the ideologies of certainty, like Marxism and Leninism, or the recurrent scientific dogmatisms about the possibilities of space travel, the state of the atmosphere, or the appearance of new mutations. But men's divergent dreams of eternity might be left undisturbed, providing they did not include some immediate apocalyptic moment for the destruction of the world.

Looking toward the future, we would start to build from the unknown. In many cases, of course, this would be knowledge very newly attained. What we would build on, then, would be the known attributes of the universe, our solar system, and the place of our earth within this system; the known processes of our present knowledge, from which we shall proceed to learn more; the known treasures of man's plastic and graphic genius as a basis for experience out of which future artists may paint and carve, musicians compose, and poets speak; the known state of instrumentation, including both the kinds of instrumentation which have already been developed (for example, communication satellites) and those which are ready to be developed; the known numbers of human beings, speaking a known number of languages, and living in lands with known amounts of fertile soil, fresh water, and irreplaceable natural resources; the known forms of organizing men into functioning groups; and the known state of modern weaponry, with its known capacity to destroy all life.

These various kinds of knowledge would be viewed as beginnings, instead of as ends—as young, growing forms of knowledge, instead of as finished products to be catalogued, diagrammed, and preserved in the pages of encyclopedias. All statements would take the form: "We know that there are at least X number of stars" (or people in Asia, or developed forms of transportation, or forms of political organization). Each such statement would be phrased as a starting point—a point from which to move onward. In this sense, the great artistic productions of all civilizations could be included, not as the splendid fruit of one or another civilization, but on new terms, as points of departure for the imagination.

The frenetic, foolhardly shipping of original works of art around the world in ships and planes, however fragile they may be, can be looked upon as a precursor of this kind of change—as tales of flying saucers preceded man's first actual ventures into space. It is as if we already dimly recognized that if we are to survive, we must share all we have, at whatever cost, so that men everywhere can move toward some as yet undefined taking-off point into the future.

But if we can achieve a new kind of consciousness of what we are aiming at, we do not need actually to move these priceless objects as if they were figures in a dream. We can, instead, take thought how, with our modern techniques, we can make the whole of an art style available, not merely single, symbolic examples, torn from their settings. Young painters and poets and musicians, dancers and architects can, today, be given access to all that is known about color and form, perspective and rhythm, technique and the development of style, the relationships of form and style and material, and the interrelationships of art forms as these have been developed in some place, at some time. We have all the necesssary techniques to do this. We can photograph in color, train magnifying cameras on the inaccessible details of domes and towers, record a poet reciting his own poetry, film an artist as he paints, and use film and sound to transport people from any one part to any other part of the world to participate in the uncovering of an ancient site or the first viewing of a new dance form. We can, in fact, come out of the "manuscript stage" for all the arts, for process as well as product, and make the whole available simultaneously to a young generation so they can move ahead together and congruently into the future. Given access to the range of the world's art, young artists can see in a new light those special activities and art objects to which they themselves are immediately related, wherever they are.

Working always within the modest limits of one generation—the next twenty-five years—and without tempting the massive consequences of miscalculation, we can include the known aspects of the universe in which our continuing experimental ventures into space will be conducted and the principles, the tools, and the materials with which these ventures are beginning. Children all over the world can be given accurate, tangible models of what we now know about the solar system, models of the earth, showing how it is affected by the large scale patterning of weather, and models showing how life on earth may be affected by events in the solar system and beyond. Presented with a clear sense of the expanding limits of our knowledge, models such as these would prepare children everywhere to participate in discoveries we know must come and to anticipate new aspects of what is as yet unknown.

Within these same limits, we can bring together our existing knowledge of the world's multitudes—beginning with those who are living now and moving out toward those who will be living twenty-five years from now. The world is well mapped, and we know within a few millions, how many people there are, where they are, and who they are. We know—or have the means of knowing—a great deal about the world's peoples. We know about the world's food supplies and can relate our knowledge to the state of those who have been well nourished and those who have been poorly fed. We know about the world's health and can relate our knowledge to the state of those who have been exposed to ancient plagues and those who are exposed to "modern" ambiguous viruses. We can picture the ways of living of those who, as children, were reared in tents, in wattle and daub houses, in houses made of mud bricks, in tenements and apartment houses, in peasant houses that have survived unchanged through hundreds of years of occupancy and in the new small houses of modern suburbs, in the anonymity of urban housing, in isolated villages, and in the crowded shacks of refugee settlements. We can define the kinds of societies, all of them contemporary, in which human loyalties are restricted to a few hundred persons, all of them known to one another, and others in which essential loyalties are expanded to include thousands or millions or even hundreds of millions of persons, only a few of them known to one another face to face. In the past we could, at best, give children some idea of the world's multitudes through books, printed words and meager illustrations. Today we have the resources to give children everywhere living experience of the whole contemporary world. And every child, everywhere in the world, can start with that knowledge and grow into its complexity. In this way, plans for population control, flood control, control of man's inroads on nature, plans for protecting human health and for developing a world food supply, and plans for sharing a world communication system can all become plans in which citizens participate in informed decisions.

None of this knowledge will in any sense be ultimate. We do not know what form knowledge itself will take twenty-five years from now, but we do know what its sources must be in present knowledge and, ordering what we now know, we can create a ground plan for the future on which all the peoples of the earth can build.

Because it must be learned by very young children and by the children of very simple parents, this body of knowledge and experience must be expressed in clear and simple terms, using every graphic device available to us and relying more on models than on words, for in many languages appropriate words are lacking. The newer and fresher the forms of presentation are, the greater will be the possibility of success, for, as in the new mathematics teaching, all teachers—those coming out of old traditions and having long experience with special conventions and those newly aware of the possibilities of formal teaching—will have to learn what they are to teach as something new. Furthermore, parents will be caught up in the process, in one sense as the pupils of their children, discovering that they can reorder their own knowledge and keep the pace, and in another sense as supplementary teachers, widening the scope of teaching and learning. Knowledge arranged for comprehensibility by a young child is knowledge accessible to all, and the task of arranging it will necessarily fall upon the clearest minds in every field of the humanities, the sciences, the arts, engineering, and politics.

There is, however, one very immediate question. How are we to meet the problem of shared contribution? How are we to ensure that this corpus is not in the end a simplified version of modern western—essentially Euro-American—scientific and philosophic thought and of art forms and processes, however widely selected, interpreted within the western tradition? Is there any endeavor which can draw on the capacities not only of those who are specially trained but also those with untapped resources—the uneducated in Euro-American countries and the adult and wise in old, exotic cultures and newly emerging ones?

A first answer can be found, I think, in activities in which every country can have a stake and persons of every age and level of sophistication can take part. One such activity would be the fashioning of a new set of communication devices—like the visual devices used by very simple peoples to construct messages or to guide travelers on their way, but now raised to the level of world-wide intelligibility.

In recent years there has been extensive discussion of the need for a systematic development of what are now called glyphs, that is, graphic representations, each of which stands for an idea: male, female, water, poison, danger, stop, go, etc. Hundreds of glyphs are used in different parts of the world—as road signs, for example—but too often with ambiguous or contradictory meanings as one moves from one region to another. What is needed, internationally, is a set of glyphs which does not refer to any single phonological system or to any specific cultural system of images but will, instead, form a system of visual signs with universally recognized referents. But up to the present no sustained effort has been made to explore the minimum number that would be needed or to make a selection that would carry clear and unequivocal meaning for the peoples of the world, speaking all languages, living in all climates, and exposed to very different symbol systems. A project for the exploration of glyph forms and for experimentation with the adequacy of different forms has been authorized by the United Nations Committee for International Cooperation Year (1965—the twentieth anniversary of the founding of the United Nations). This is designed as an activity in which adults and children, artists and engineers, logicians and semanticists, linguists and historians—all those in fact, who have an interest in doing so—can take part. For the wider the range of persons and the larger the number of cultures included in this exploration, the richer and the more fully representative will be the harvest from which a selection of glyphs can be made for international use.

Since meaning is associated with each glyph as a unit and glyphs cannot be combined syntactically, they can be used by the speakers of any language. But considerable experimentation will be necessary to avoid ambiguity which may lead to confusion or the adoption of forms which are already culturally loaded. The variety of meanings which may already be associated with certain forms can be illustrated by the sign + (which, in different connections, can be the sign for addition or indicates a positive number, can stand for "north" or indicate a crossroad, and, very slightly modified, can indicate a deceased person in a genealogy, a specifically Christian derivation, or stand for the Christian sign of the cross) or the sign O (which, in different connections, may stand for circumference or for 360°, for the full moon, for an annual plant, for degrees of arc or temperature, for an individual, especially female, organism, and, very slightly modified, can stand for zero or, in our alphabet, the letter O).

Work on glyphs can lead to work on other forms of international communication. In an interconnected world we shall need a world language—a second language which could be learned by every people but which would in no sense replace their native tongue. Contemporary studies of natural languages have increased our understanding of the reasons why consciously constructed languages do not serve the very complex purposes of general communication. Most important is the fact that an artificial language, lacking the imprint of many different kinds of minds and differently organized capacities for response, lacks the redundancy necessary in a language all human beings can learn.

Without making any premature choice, we can state some of the criteria for such a secondary world language. It must be a natural language, chosen from among known living languages, but not from among those which are, today, politically controversial. Many nations would have to contribute to the final choice, but this choice would depend also on the outcome of systematic experiments with children's speech, machine simula-

tion, experiments with mechanical translation, and so on. In addition, it would be essential to consider certain characteristics related to the current historical situation. Politically, it should be the language of a state too small to threaten other states. In order to allow for a rapid development of diverse written styles, it must be a language with a long tradition of use in written forms. To permit rapid learning, it must be a language whose phonetic system can be easily learned by speakers of other languages, and one which can be easily rendered into a phonetic script and translated without special difficulty into existing traditional scripts. It should come from the kind of population in which there is a wide diversity of roles and occupations and among whom a large number of teachers can be found, some of whom are already familiar with one or another of the great widespread languages of the world. Using modern methods of language teaching, the task of creating a world-wide body of readers and speakers could be accomplished within five years and the language itself would change in the process of this world-wide learning.

Once a secondary world language is chosen, the body of knowledge with which we shall start the next twenty-five years can be translated into it from preliminary statements in the great languages, taking the stamp of these languages as divergent subtleties of thought, present in one language and absent in another, are channeled in and new vocabulary is created to deal with new ideas.

One important effect of a secondary world language would be to protect the more localized languages from being swamped by those few which are rapidly spreading over the world. Plans have been advanced to make possible the learning and use of any one of the five or seven most widespread languages as a second language. Fully implemented, this would divide the world community into two classes of citizens—those for whom one of these languages was a mother tongue and those for whom it was a second language—and it would exacerbate already existing problems arising from differences in the quality of communication—rapid and idiomatic among native speakers and slower, more formal and less spontaneous among those who have learned English, French, or Russian later. In contrast, one shared second language, used on a world-wide scale, would tend to equalize the quality of world communication and, at the same time, would protect the local diversity of all other languages.

Another important aspect of a shared culture would be the articulate inclusion of the experience of those who travel to study, work, explore, or enjoy other countries. One of the most intractable elements in our present isolating cultures is the interlocking of a landscape—a landscape with mountains or a desert, jungle or tundra, rushing cataracts or slow flowing rivers, arched over by a sky in which the Dipper or the Southern Cross dominates—and a view of man. The beauty of face and movement of those who have never left their mountains or their island is partly the imprint on the human form of a complex relationship to the scale and the proportions, the seasonal rhythms and the natural style of one special part of the world. The experiences of those who have been bred to one physical environment cannot be patched together like the pieces of a patchwork quilt. But we can build on the acute and vivid experiences of those who, reared in a culture which has deeply incorporated its environment, respond intensely to some newly discovered environment—the response of the countryman to the city, the response of the city dweller to open country, the response of the immigrant to the sweep of an untouched landscape and of the traveler to a sudden vista into the past of a whole people. In the past, the visual impact of discovery was recorded retrospectively in painting and in literature. Today, films can record the more immediate response of the observer, looking with fresh eyes at the world of the nomadic Bushman or the people beneath the mountain wall of New Guinea, at the palaces in Crete or the summer palace in Peking.

We can give children a sense of movement, actually experienced or experienced only in some leap of the imagination. In the next twenty-five years we shall certainly not explore deep space, but the experience of movement can link a generation in a common sense of anticipation. As a beginning, we can give children a sense of different actual relationships to the physical environments of the whole earth, made articulate through the recorded responses of those who have moved from one environment to another. Through art, music, and film, we can give children access to the ways others have experienced their own green valleys and other valleys, also green. We can develop in small children the capacity to wonder and to look through other eyes at the familiar fir trees rimming their horizon or the sea breaking on their island's shore.

In the past, these have been the experiences of those who could afford to travel and those who had access, through the arts, to the perceptions of a poet like Wordsworth in *The Prelude*, or a young scientist like Darwin on his Pacific voyage, or painters like Catlin or Gauguin. With today's technology, these need no longer be the special experiences of the privileged and the educated elite. The spur to action may be the desire for literacy in the emerging nations or a new concern for the culturally deprived in older industrialized countries. And quite different styles of motivation can give urgency to the effort to bring the experience of some to bear on the experience of all.

Looking to the future, the immediacy

of motivation is itself part of the experience. It may be an assertive desire to throw off a colonial past or a remorseful attempt to atone for long neglect. It may be the ecumenical spirit in which the Pope can say: "No pilgrim, no matter how far, religiously and geographically, may be the country from which he comes, will be any longer a stranger to this Rome. . . ."[2] It may be the belief that it is possible to remake a society, as when Martin Luther King said:

I have a dream today . . . I have a dream that one day every valley shall be exalted, every hill and mountain shall be made low. The rough places will be made plain, and the crooked places will be made straight. And the glory of the Lord shall be revealed, and all flesh shall see it together. This is our hope. This is the faith that I go back to the South with. With this faith we will be able to hew out of the mountain of despair a stone of hope.[3]

Or it may be the belief, expressed by U Thant, that men can work toward a world society:

Let us look inward for a moment on this Human Rights Day, and recognize that no one, no individual, no nation, and indeed no ideology has a monopoly of rightness, freedom or dignity. And let us translate this recognition into action so as to sustain the fullness and freedom of simple human relations leading to ever widening areas of understanding and agreement. Let us, on this day, echo the wish Rabindranath Tagore stated in these memorable words, so that our world may be truly a world

Where the mind is without fear and the head is held high;

Where knowledge is free;

Where the world has not been broken up into fragments by narrow domestic walls;

Where words come out of the depth of truth;

Where tireless striving stretches its arms toward perfection. . . .[4]

There are also other ways in which experience can more consciously be brought to bear in developing a shared understanding. All traditions, developing slowly over centuries, are shaped by the biological nature of man—the differences in temperament and constitution among men and the processes of maturation, parenthood, and aging which are essential parts of our humanity. The conscious inclusion of the whole life process in our thinking can, in turn, alter the learning process, which in a changing world has become deeply disruptive as each elder generation has been left behind while the next has been taught an imperfect version of the new. One effect of this has been to alienate and undermine the faith of parents and grandparents as they have seen their children's minds moving away from them and as their own beliefs, unshared, have become inflexible and distorted.

The policy in most of today's world is to educate the next—the new—generation, setting aside the older generation in the mistaken hope that, as older men and women are passed over, their outmoded forms of knowledge will do no harm. Instead, we pay a double price in the alienation of the new generation from their earliest and deepest experiences as little children and in the world by an older generation who still exercise actual power—hoarding some resources and

2 *The New York Times*, May 18, 1964.

3 From the speech by the Rev. Martin Luther King at the March on Washington, *New York Post Magazine*, September 1, 1963, p. 5.

4 From the Human Rights Day Message by (then) Acting Secretary-General U Thant, December 8, 1961 (United Nations Press Release SG/1078 HRD/11 [December 6, 1961]).

wasting others, building to an outmoded scale, voting against measures the necessity of which is not understood, supporting reactionary leaders, and driving an equally inflexible opposition toward violence. Yet this lamentable outcome is unnecessary, as the generation break itself is unnecessary.

In the past the transmission of the whole body of knowledge within a slowly changing society has provided for continuity. Today we need to create an educational style which will provide for continuity and openness even within rapid change. Essentially this means an educational style in which members of different generations are involved in the process of learning. One way of assuring this is through a kind of education in which new things are taught to mothers and young children together. The mothers, however schooled, usually are less affected by contemporary styles of education than the fathers. In some countries they have had no schooling; in others, girls are warned away from science and mathematics or even from looking at the stars. So they come to the task of rearing their small children fresher than those who have been trained to teach or to administer. Child rearing, in the past fifty years, has been presented as almost entirely a matter of molding the emotional life of the child, modulating the effects of demands for cleanliness and obedience to permit more spontaneity, and of preserving an environment in which there is good nutrition and low infection danger. At the same time, we have taken out of the hands of mothers the *education* even of young children. So we have no existing rationale in which mother, child, and teacher are related within the learning process. What we need now, in every part of the world, is a new kind of school for mothers and little children in which mothers learn to teach children what neither the mothers nor the children know.

At the same time, grandparents who, perforce, have learned a great deal about the world which has gone whirling past them and in which, however outmoded they are declared to be, they have had to maintain themselves, can be brought back into the teaching process. Where patience, experience, and wisdom are part of what must be incorporated, they have a special contribution to make. Mothers of young children, lacking a fixed relationship to the growing body of knowledge about the world, provide freshness of approach; but older people embody the experience that can be transformed into later learnings. The meticulous respect for materials, coming from long experience with hand work, the exacting attention to detail, coming from work with a whole object rather than some incomplete part, and the patient acceptance of the nature of a task have a continuing relevance to work, whatever it may be. So also, the disciplined experience of working with human beings can be transformed to fit the new situations which arise when democracy replaces hierarchy and the discipline of political parties that of the clan and the tribe.

We have been living through a period in which the old have been recklessly discarded and disallowed, and this very disallowance resonates—as a way of life which has been repressed rather than transformed—in the movements of unaccountably stubborn reaction from which no civilization in our present world is exempt. Grandparents and great-grandparents—even those who are driven from their land to die in concentration camps and those who voluntarily settle themselves in modern, comfortable Golden Age clubs—live on in the conceptions of the children whose parents' lives they shaped. Given an opportunity to participate meaningfully in new knowledge, new skills, and new styles of life, the elderly can embody the changing world in such a way that their grandchildren—and all children of the youngest generation—are given a mandate to be part of the new and yet maintain human ties with the past which, however phrased, is part of our humanity. The more rapid the rate of change and the newer the corpus of knowledge which the world may come to share, the more urgently necessary it is to include the old—to transform our conception of the whole process of aging so their wisdom and experience can be assets in our new relation to the future.

Then we may ask, are such plans as these sufficiently open ended? In seeking to make equally available to the peoples of the world newly organized ways of moving into the immediate future, in a universe in which our knowledge is rapidly expanding, there is always the danger that the idea of a shared body of knowledge may be transformed into some kind of universal blueprint. In allowing this to happen we would, of course, defeat our own purpose. The danger is acute enough so that we must build a continuing wariness and questioning into the planning itself; otherwise even the best plan may result in a closed instead of an open ended system.

This means that we must be open ended in our planning as well as in our plans, recognizing that this will involve certain kinds of conscious restriction as well as conscious questioning. For example, we must insist that a world language be kept as a second language, resolutely refusing to consider it as a first language, in order to protect and assure the diversity of thought which accompanies the use of different mother tongues. We should also guard against a too early learning of the world language, so that the language of infancy—which also becomes the language of love and poetry and religion—may be protected against acquiring a too common stamp. We must insist on the inclusion of peoples from all over the world in any specific piece of planning—as in the development of

an international system of glyphs—as a way of assuring a growing and an unpredictable corpus. We must be willing to forego, in large-scale planning, some kinds of apparent efficiency. If we are willing, instead, to include numerous steps and to conceive of each step somewhat differently, we are more likely, in the end, to develop new interrelationships, unforeseeable at any early stage. A more conscious inclusion of women and of the grandparental generation in learning and teaching will carry with it the extraordinary differences in existing interrelations between the minds and in the understanding of the two sexes and different age groups.

We can also take advantage of what has been learned through the use of cybernetic models, and equip this whole forward movement of culture which we are launching with a system of multiple self-corrective devices. For example, criteria could be established for reviewing the kinds of divergences that were occurring in vocabulary and conceptualizations as an idea fanned out around the world. Similarly, the rate and type of incorporation of special developments in particular parts of the world could be monitored, and cases of dilution or distortion examined and corrected. Overemphasis on one part of knowledge, on one sensory modality, on the shells men live in rather than the life they live there, on sanitation rather than beauty, on length of life rather than quality of life lived, could be listened for and watched for, and corrective measures taken speedily.

A special area of concern would be intercommunication among all those whose specializations tend to isolate them from one another, scientist from administrator, poet from statesman, citizen voter from the highly skilled specialist who must carry out his mandate using calculations which the voter cannot make, but within a system of values clearly enough stated so that both may share them. By attending to the origins of some new communication—whether a political, a technical, or an artistic innovation—the functioning of the communication process could be monitored. Special sensing organs could be established which would observe, record, and correct so that what otherwise might become a blundering, linear, and unmanageable avalanche could be shaped into a process delicately responsive to change in itself.

But always the surest guarantee of change and growth is the inclusion of living persons in every stage of an activity. Their lives, their experience, and their continuing response—even their resistances—infuse with life any plan which, if living participants are excluded, lies on the drawing board and loses its reality. Plans for the future can become old before they are lived, but the future itself is always newborn and, like any newborn thing, is open to every kind of living experience.

10.3   TOWARD A PROTEAN STYLE OF SELF-PROCESS

Robert Jay Lifton

There is a widespread inclination these days to interpret man, not in terms of what he actually is or might be, but of what he has left behind or survived. We speak of man as postmodern, postindustrial, post-historic, post-civilized, post-identity, post-economic, post-materialist, post-technocratic, and so on. There are great pitfalls in thus naming the present (or, by implication, the future) after what is presumed to no longer exist. Still we feel a certain resonance from such terminology, precisely because our sense of survivorhood pervades our deepest image of our selves and our fate. Perceptions of holocaust, past or anticipated, suffuse our social imagination, and we experience a profound loss of faith in the very structure of our culture —not so much in this symbol or that, but in its entire intricate web of words, images, rituals, institutions, and material objects.

Originally published as "Transformations," in *Tradition and Revolution* (Toronto, Macmillan Co. of Canada, Ltd., 1971). Reprinted by permission of Robert Jay Lifton and International Creative Management. Copyright © 1971 by Robert Jay Lifton.

Survivors can be numbed and incapacitated by the extremity of their experience. But they can also be energized. Hence the struggles for transformation we witness everywhere. To deserve the name, transformations must connect with the past while going beyond mere survival of that past in the creation of new forms and modes. The process is both psychological and historical, and at the same time prominently aesthetic, very much a matter of sensibility. . . . The very problems of the categories may then illuminate something about present efforts to confront our strange and partly unimaginable psychological landscape.

The concept of Protean man, in its emphasis upon change and flux, avoids such traditional terms as character and personality, as these suggest relative fixity and permanence. Erikson's concept of identity has been, among other things, an effort to get away from a principle of fixity. I have been using the term "self-process" to convey still more specifically a sense of fluidity and transformation. For it is quite possible that the image of personal identity, particularly as it suggests stability and sameness, derives from a vision of traditional culture in which man's relationship to his institutions and symbols are still relatively intact, hardly the case today. And if we understand the self to be the person's symbol of his own organism, then self-process refers to the continuous psychic re-creation of that symbol.

I want to stress that I came to this emphasis upon a Protean style of self-process while working in cultures outside of my own—with Chinese who had experienced various forms of personal and social upheaval, and with post–World War II Japanese youth—and then found related (though of course not identical) psychological trends occurring in Europe and the United States as well. I came to the conclusion that something rather general was taking place, that, despite very important cultural differences, a universally shared style of self-process was emerging. I see this pattern as derived from a three-way interplay responsible for the behavior of all human groups. There is, first, the psychobiological potential common to all mankind, or the universal dimension; second, those traits given special emphasis or style in a particular cultural tradition, the cultural or national-character emphasis; and third, that element related to modern (and especially contemporary) historical forces, the historical dimension. This third factor, ignored in most psychological work, is, in my judgment, becoming increasingly important in shaping self-process. In other words, shared aspects of contemporary historical experience enable Chinese, Japanese, and American self-process to take on striking points of convergence.

I would stress here two general historical developments as being of special importance for creating Protean man. The first of these is the worldwide sense of what I called *historical*, or *psychohistorical dislocation*, the break in the sense of connection men have long felt with vital and nourishing symbols of their

cultural traditions—symbols revolving around family, idea systems, religions, and the life cycle in general. In our contemporary world, one perceives these traditional symbols as irrelevant, burdensome, or even inactivating, and yet one cannot avoid carrying them within, or having one's self-process profoundly affected by them.

The second large historical tendency is the *flooding of imagery* produced by the extraordinary flow of postmodern cultural influences over mass communication networks—of enormous importance but also greatly neglected in psychological studies. These cross readily over local and national boundaries, and permit each individual to be touched by everything, but at the same time cause him to be overwhelmed by superficial messages and undigested cultural elements, by headlines and by endless partial alternatives in every sphere of life. In other words everything becomes available to everyone in greater or lesser depth. These alternatives, moreover, can be shared simultaneously—if not as courses of action, at least in the form of significant inner imagery.

There is a third historical factor, related to the other two: the technological revolution, and especially the development of ultimate weaponry of mass destruction, which I must keep coming back to as a central theme in both my ethical concerns and my interpretation of what is happening to contemporary man.

We know from Greek mythology that Proteus was able to change his shape with relative ease—from wild boar to lion to dragon to fire to flood. But what he did find difficult, and would not do unless seized and chained, was to commit himself to a single form, the form most his own, and carry out his function of prophecy. We can say the same of Protean man, but we must keep in mind his possibilities as well as his difficulties.

The Protean style of self-process, then, is characterized by an interminable series of experiments and explorations—some shallow, some profound—each of which may be readily abandoned in favor of still new psychological quests. The pattern in many ways resembles what Erik Erikson has called "identity diffusion" or "identity confusion," and the impaired psychological functioning which those terms suggest can be very much present. But I would stress that the Protean style is by no means pathological as such, and, in fact, may well be one of the functional patterns of our day. It extends to all areas of human experience—to political as well as sexual behavior, to the holding and promulgating of ideas and to the general organization of lives.

I would like to suggest a few illustrations of the Protean style, drawn mostly from American and European literature and art, though reflecting similar patterns I have encountered in research interviews and in psychotherapy.

In contemporary American literature, Saul Bellow is notable for the Protean men he has created. In *The Adventures of Augie March,* one of his earlier novels, we meet a picaresque hero with a notable talent for adapting himself to divergent social worlds. Augie himself says: "I touched all sides, and nobody knew where I belonged. I had no good idea of that myself." And a perceptive young English critic, Tony Tanner, tells us: "Augie indeed celebrates the self, but he can find nothing to do with it." Tanner goes on to describe another of Bellow's Protean heroes, Herzog, as "a representative modern intelligence, swamped with ideas, metaphysics, and values, and surrounded by messy facts. It labours to cope with them all."

There are many other representatives of the Protean style in the work of contemporary novelists: in the constant internal and external motion of "Beat Generation" writings, such as Jack Kerouac's *On the Road;* in the novels of

a gifted successor to that generation, J. P. Donleavy, particularly *The Ginger Man;* and of course in the work of European novelists such as Günter Grass, whose *The Tin Drum* is a breathtaking evocation of prewar Polish-German, wartime German, and postwar German environments, in which the protagonist combines Protean adaptability with a kind of perpetual physical–mental "strike" against any change at all. Also very much in this genre is the work of John Barth and Kurt Vonnegut.

In the visual arts, one of the most important postwar movements has been aptly named Action Painting to convey its stress upon process rather than fixed completion. And a more recent and related movement in sculpture, Kinetic Art, goes further. According to Jean Tinguely, one of its leading practitioners, "Artists are putting themselves in rhythm with their time, in contact with their epic, especially with permanent and perpetual movement." As revolutionary as any style or approach is the stress upon innovation per se which now dominates painting. I have frequently heard artists, themselves considered radical innovators, complain bitterly of the current standards dictating that "innovation is all," and of a turnover in art movements so rapid as to discharge the idea of holding still long enough to develop a particular style.

John Cage, the composer, is an extreme exponent of the Protean style, both in his music and in his sense of all of us as listeners. He concluded a letter to the *Village Voice* with this sentence: "Nowadays, everything happens at once and our souls are conveniently electronic, omniattentive." The comment is McLuhan-like, but what I wish to stress particularly is the idea of omniattention—the sense of contemporary man as having the possibility of "receiving" and "taking in" everything. In attending, as in being, nothing is "off limits."

To be sure, one can observe in contemporary man a tendency which seems to be precisely the opposite of the Protean style. I refer to the closing off of identity or constriction of self-process, to a straight-and-narrow specialization in psychological as well as in intellectual life, and to reluctance to let in any "extraneous" influences. But I would emphasize that where this kind of constricted or "one-dimensional" self-process exists, it has an essentially reactive and compensatory quality. In this it differs from earlier characterological styles it may seem to resemble (such as the "inner-directed" man described by Riesman, and still earlier patterns in traditional society). For these were direct out-growths of societies which then existed, and in harmony with those societies, while at the present time a constricted self-process requires continuous psychological work to fend off Protean influences which are always abroad.

Protean man has a particular relationship to the holding of ideas which has, I believe, great significance for the politics, religion, and general intellectual life of the future. The increasing difficulty faced by representatives of thought systems—by religions, academic specialties, or social movements—is not to get prospective converts to doubt previous ideas but rather to hold people to a *sustained* belief in *any* set of convictions. Until relatively recently, no more than one major ideological shift was likely to occur in a lifetime, and that one would be long remembered as a significant individual turning point accompanied by profound soul-searching and conflict. But today it is not unusual to encounter several such shifts, accomplished relatively painlessly, within a year or even a month. Among many groups, the rarity is a man who has gone through life holding firmly to a single ideological vision.

In one sense, this tendency is related to "the end of ideology" spoken of by Daniel Bell, since Protean man is incapable of enduring an unquestioning allegiance to the large ideologies and utopian thought of the nineteenth and early twentieth centuries, at least in their pristine forms. One must be cautious about speaking of the end of anything, however, especially ideology, and one also encounters in Protean man what I would call strong ideological hunger.

Intimately bound up with his flux in emotions and beliefs is a profound inner sense of absurdity, which finds expression in a tone of mockery. The sense and the tone are related to a perception of surrounding activities and beliefs as profoundly strange and inappropriate. They stem from a breakdown in the relationship between inner and outer worlds—that is, in the sense of symbolic integrity—and are part of the pattern of psychohistorical dislocation mentioned earlier. For if we take Cassirer and Langer seriously and view man as primarily a symbol-forming organism, we must recognize that he has constant need of a meaningful inner formulation of self and world in which his own actions, and even his impulses, have some kind of "fit" with the "outside" as he perceives it.

The sense of absurdity, of course, has a considerable modern tradition, and has been discussed by such writers as Camus as a function of man's spiritual homelessness and inability to find meaning in traditional belief systems. But absurdity and mockery have taken much more extreme form in the post–World War II world, and have in fact become a prominent part of a universal life style.

In American life, absurdity and mockery are everywhere. Perhaps their most vivid expression can be found in such areas as Pop Art and the more general burgeoning of "pop culture." Important here is the complex stance of the pop artist (and his cultural successors) toward the objects he depicts. On the one hand he embraces the materials of the everyday world, celebrates and even exalts them—boldly asserting his creative return to representational art (in active rebellion against the previously reigning nonobjective school), and his psychological return to the "real world" of *things*. On the other hand, everything he touches he mocks. "Thingness" is pressed to the point of caricature. He is indeed artistically reborn as he moves freely among the physical and symbolic materials of his environment, but mockery is his birth certificate and his passport. This kind of duality of approach is formalized in the stated "duplicity" of Camp, a poorly defined aesthetic in which (among other things) all varieties of mockery converge under the guiding influence of the homosexual's subversion of a heterosexual world.

Also relevant are a group of expressions in current slang. Some of these come originally from jazz and black experience, some from youth culture, but they tend to pervade all of society—and they change rapidly. The "dry mock" has replaced the dry wit; one refers to a segment of life experience as a "bit," "bag," "caper," "game," (or "con game"), "scene," "show" or "scenario"; and one seeks to "make the scene" (or "make it"), "beat the system" or "pull it off"—or else one "cools it" ("plays it cool"), resorts to the "put-on," "cops out," or "splits." The thing to be experienced, in other words, is too absurd to be taken at its face value; one must either keep most of the self aloof from it, or if not one must lubricate the encounter with mockery.

A similar spirit seems to pervade literature and social action alike. What is best termed a "literature of mockery" has come to dominate fiction and other forms of writing on an international scale. In this country the divergent group of novelists known as "black humorists" also fit into the general category—related as they are to a trend in the American literary consciousness which R. W. B. Lewis has called a "savagely comical apocalypse" or a "new kind of ironic literary form and disturbing vision, the joining of the dark threat of apocalypse with the nervous detonations of satiric laughter." For it is precisely death itself, and particularly threats of the contemporary apocalypse, that Protean man ultimately mocks. Men are not so much afraid of dying as they are of dying inappropriately, prematurely, under absurd circumstances. The spirit of mockery and absurdity have much to do with this fear.

A related characteristic of Protean man can be called "suspicion of counterfeit nurturance." Involved here is a severe conflict around dependency, a core problem of Protean man. I came to the idea several years ago while working with survivors of the atomic bomb in Hiroshima. I found that these survivors both felt themselves in need of special help, and resented whatever help was offered them because they equated it with weakness and inferiority. In considering the matter more generally, I found this equation of nurturance with a threat to autonomy to be a major theme of contemporary life. The breakdown of arrangements for mutual care in traditional institutions leads Protean man to seek out replacements wherever he can find them. The large organizations (government, business, academic, etc.) to which he turns, and which contemporary society more and more holds out as a substitute for traditional institutions, present an ambivalent threat to his autonomy in one way; and the intense individual relationships in which he seeks to anchor himself, in another. Both, therefore, are likely to be perceived as counterfeit. But the obverse side of this tendency is an expanding sensitivity to the unauthentic, which may be just beginning to exert its general creative force on man's behalf.

Technology   (and   technique   in

general), together with science, has special significance for Protean man. Technical achievement of any kind can be strongly embraced to combat inner tendencies toward diffusion, and to transcend feelings of absurdity and conflicts over counterfeit nurturance and inauthenticity. (A number of young American veterans of the Vietnam War have told me how they stifled profound inner doubts about that war and their own role in it by devoting themselves totally—in some cases almost fanatically—to the operation of their technical equipment. There is much of the same pattern in the over-all American "operation" in Vietnam.) The image of science itself, however, as the ultimate power behind technology and, to a considerable extent, behind contemporary thought in general, becomes much more difficult to cope with. Only in certain underdeveloped countries (and perhaps no longer even there) can one find, in relatively pure form, those expectations of scientific–utopian deliverance from all human want and conflict which were characteristic of eighteenth and nineteenth century Western thought. Protean man retains much of this utopian imagery, but he finds it increasingly undermined by massive disillusionment. More and more he calls forth the other side of the God–devil polarity generally applied to science, and sees it as a puryevor of total destructiveness.

He seeks modes of knowing outside the scientific, as Roszak and a number of others have begun to point out. But the encounter between contemporary or Protean man and science has not yet really been grasped, and has certainly not yet been resolved. We should not be too quick to assume that Protean man simply rejects science or technology outright. His more fundamental attitude is experimental and questioning. The strong attraction of many young artists toward various elements of contemporary tech-

nology can be understood as an effort to transform that technology from dead matter to vital imaginative force. But this confrontation with science and technology, suffused as it must be with flux and mockery, tends to be sporadic and unpredictable. It epitomizes the more general search for inner forms that "take hold" within people instead of "holding them down," that make contact with fundamental images at what might be called the "formative zone" of the psyche.

Protean man is not free of guilt. He suffers from it considerably, but often without awareness of what is causing his suffering. For his is a form of hidden guilt: a vague but persistent kind of self-condemnation related to the symbolic disharmonies I have described, a sense of having no outlet for his loyalties and no symbolic structure for his achievements. This is the guilt of social breakdown, and it includes various forms of historical and racial guilt experienced by whole nations and peoples, both by the privileged and the abused. But it may be quite misleading to speak of the classical "superego," of internalization of clearly defined criteria of right and wrong transmitted within a particular culture by parents to their children. Where standards for good and evil are not only less than clearly defined but relatively open, then these too must be re-created if they are to be meaningful. Hence there is in Protean man a diminution of clear feelings of evil or sinfulness but often a nagging sense of unworthiness all the more troublesome for its lack of clear origin.

There are similarly vague constellations of anxiety and resentment. Viewing himself as in a sense betrayed by his entire culture, looking upon its offerings and controls with considerable distrust, Protean man is likely to feel simultaneously engulfed and abandoned. He can neither find a specific cause for his anxiety nor a consistent target for his anger. But causes and targets exist for him, even if they too tend to be in flux. Moreover, just as he needs his relative freedom from the *classical* form of superego—a kind of symbolic fatherlessness—for his creative experiments, so does he make use of his fear and his anger.

Following upon all that I have said are radical impairments to the symbolism of transition within the life cycle—the *rites de passage* surrounding birth, entry into adulthood, marriage, and death. Whatever rites remain seem shallow, inappropriate, fragmentary. Protean man cannot take them seriously, and often seeks to improvise new ones with whatever contemporary materials he has available. Perhaps the central impairment here is that of symbolic immortality—of the universal need for imagery of connection predating, and extending beyond, the individual life span, whether the idiom of this immortality is biological (living on through children and grandchildren), theological (through a life after death), natural (*in nature itself which outlasts all*), or creative (through what man makes and does). I have suggested elsewhere that this *sense* of immortality is a fundamental component of ordinary psychic life, and that it is now profoundly threatened: by simple historical velocity, which subverts the idioms (notably the theological) in which it has traditionally been maintained; and, of particular importance to Protean man, by the existence of nuclear (or other ultimate) weapons, which, even without being used, call into question all modes of immortality. (Who can be certain of living on through children and grandchildren, through creative work, teachings, or kindnesses?)

Protean man is left with two paths to symbolic immortality which he tries to cultivate, sometimes pleasurably and sometimes desperately. One is the natural mode we have mentioned. His attraction to nature and concern at its desecration has to do with an unconscious sense that,

in whatever holocaust, at least nature will endure—though such are the dimensions of our present weapons and pollutions that he cannot be certain even of "experiential transcendence"—of seeking a sense of immortality in the way that mystics always have, through psychic experience of such great intensity that time and death are, in effect, eliminated. This, I believe, is the larger meaning of the drug revolution, of Protean man's hunger for chemical aids to expanding consciousness. Many, after experimenting with drugs, turn to other activities, mystical or prosaic, for similar kinds of experience, suggesting that expanded consciousness—some form of personal transformation—takes precedence over drugs as such. And indeed all revolutionary upheavals may be thought of, at bottom, as innovations and transformations in the struggle for immortality, and as producing new combinations of old modes. . . .

We are survivors, then, but more than *mere* survivors. There is fierce energy and a powerful forward thrust to our transformations. Yet some pressing questions remain about the agent of these transformations, about the entity I have called Protean man. The questions lead quickly to neglected areas of psychology and history, and the answers given here are meant to do no more than suggest ways of thinking about these areas.

First, is Protean man only a *young man*? Is he simply a part of "youth culture"? I believe he is most vividly Protean when young, but it is much too simple—and in my view, wrong—to think of him as exclusively young. We all live in the midst of the currents I have described: no one is immune from Protean influences. It is tempting for those who wish to hold to pristine individual-psychological perspectives to view the Protean process as merely an expression of the "psychology of adolescence"—but to do so is to negate precisely the psychological transformations most central to contemporary experience.

Is he a *new* man? Hasn't he appeared in previous historical epochs? One can find historical predecessors during periods when times were also "out of joint": there seems to be a correlation between radical historical change and the emergence of a Protean-like figure. Cases in point are the Renaissance in the West and the Meiji Restoration in Japan. But there are new historical elements that intensify the process manyfold: the extent to which traditional symbols have broken down (in the Renaissance, for instance, the medieval cosmology being rejected still had great force, while today there is a sense in which the psychic underpinning of society has disappeared); the unprecedented mass-media explosion; and the existence of ultimate weaponry (earlier theological ideas about the end of the world were themselves part of that theological structure, as opposed to the unstructured absurdity associated with imagery of massive death from nuclear weapons). Thus both the extent and intensity of Protean influences make Protean man virtually a new man.

What, if anything, in Protean man is stable? Does he not require something more than continuous flux? He does indeed, and here we do well to distinguish three different versions of the Protean style. There is first a shallow plasticity, repeated change of "color" or appearance without serious depth of immersion anywhere—a style more accurately termed plastic than Protean. A second pattern is that of intense immersion followed by equally intense rejection, so that one ends up almost where one began, with virtually nothing—or what might be called the "shedding style." Finally there is what I would view as the more genuinely Protean style, the one most consistent with patterns of transformation, in which there is immersion, resurfacing,

and reimmersion, with retention of certain aspects of each of the elements or experiences in which one has been immersed, so that there is an accruing of inner forms and a constant recombining of psychic elements. Islands of stability, moreover, enhance the process by contributing energy and confidence to the explorations. These islands of stability can vary—family or group arrangements for some, special intellectual or ethical or professional commitments for others, and for still others an aesthetic style of expression that pervades all. There can even be an element of constancy in the commitment to flux itself, in the continuous re-creation and recombination of forms. We have not yet learned the full possibilities for living and creating within the Protean style—and it is likely that artists, with their struggles toward form and transformation, will continue to anticipate more general social and political possibilities.

These issues have particular force for those of us who write, teach, or create in any form, for those directly concerned with the transmission and revitalization of culture. The extent of our loss of faith in received dogma is such that we simply cannot inwardly "receive" that dogma any longer. So much so that for some time, as the Protean process evolves, we may not be able to pursue our intellectual and creative disciplines with the traditional comfort of an authoritative system of ideas dominating each. We may have to live, intellectually and symbolically, with greater uncertainty and greater imaginative associativeness than we have been used to doing. The feeling of crisis that now exists in all fields may thus give way to new combinations of sustained duress and associative possibility. And those who appear to be the most iconoclastic critics of traditional forms—in the various radical caucuses and intellectual and professional communes—may turn out to perform a very conservative function as well. For what many of these groups seek is a significant connection with the techniques and intellectual–creative traditions of a particular area of work while at the same time setting forth a fundamental critique of existing practices and assumptions.

We may not, then, be so much in a postmodern, postindustrial, or postcivilized era as in a pre- or early Protean one. Focusing only on Protean excess, terrified and attracted by the psychic revolution suggested by the Protean style, all too many succumb to the illusion that it can be "nipped in the bud." For although the transformations it holds out to us can cause all kinds of difficulties and founder at times in their own confusions, they can be eliminated neither by violence nor fiat. Some of the absurdity of our situation has been personified by Samuel Beckett, through his character, Molloy: "My life, my life, now I speak of it as something over, now as of a joke which still goes on, and it is neither, for at the same time it is over and it goes on, and is there any tense for that?" Everything, in other words, is threatened. Nothing is certain. Everything is before us.

SOME VALUE DILEMMAS
of THE CHANGE AGENT

CHAPTER

Value considerations have appeared in discussions of planned change and the change-agent role throughout this volume, even where the focus of the discussion has been upon historical, cognitive, or technological matters. In fact, the differentiation of planned change from other modes of human change is grounded in a cluster of value commitments on the part of the agent of planned change—a commitment to collaborative ways of working, a commitment to the basing of plans for change upon valid knowledge and information, and a commitment to reducing power differentials among men and groups of men as a distorting influence upon the determination of the tempo and direction of justifiable changes in human life. We have tried to be open about the value commitments of our enterprise throughout our discussion. What more needs to be said?

In the first place, the meaning of these overarching value commitments is frequently not clear in the complex and confused situations in which the change agent functions. Value considerations present themselves intertwined with cognitive and technical considerations, and it is often difficult to sort out the value component of decisions and judgments from other components when it needs most to be confronted in its own right. Confrontations of value differences and conflicts are often freighted with subjectivity and emotional heat as compared with confrontations of differences in cognitive and technical matters. And most of us are unsure of our ability to handle our subjectivity and emotional heat constructively. As a result, we tend to avoid value confrontations. This tendency is highly prevalent in behavioral-science

467

types—and many change agents are behavioral scientists. For scientists have frequently been indoctrinated in a value-free ideal of science. In addition to the basically human difficulties in handling value confrontations constructively, behavioral scientists often suffer additional feelings of shame and guilt for being involved in value commitments at all, if these are, by definition, unscientific.

In addition, the conditions of society and culture, which were examined in the last chapter as placing processes of goal setting and direction finding in a radically new light, also load the value judgments and choices of change agents, where, behaviorally, values and value orientations function and perchance grow and develop, with new and wider responsibilities as indeed the choices of all men are now similarly loaded. We now know that we are no longer choosing wisely when we choose within the framework of assumed and unexamined traditions of belief and practice. We are literally legislating the future for ourselves and for others as we choose and act upon our choices. Since our value orientations are at least partial determinants of our choices, responsibility requires that we become clear about and responsible for our actual as well as our professed ideal values as they function or fail to function in the choices we make as change agents.

The purpose of this chapter is to illuminate some of the contexts in which value clarification and responsibility are required of change agents and, by extension, of behavioral scientists in their functioning as researchers as well as in their practitioner and policy-influencing functions. There is, thus, a wide spectrum of social interventions where the intention of the interveners is to influence the direction, tempo, and quality of social change. The intervention may be a micro-intervention as in processes of training and of organizational and community consultation. Or the intervention may be a macro-intervention as in processes of policy-determination with respect to such national issues as population control or such international issues as technical assistance and modernization. And there are various social interventions which fall between these two extremes. Warwick and Kelman, in the first reading in this chapter, make the correct point that the authors of *The Planning of Change* have been centrally concerned with a narrow range of social interventions. They have focused on micro-interventions where change agent–client system relationships are more or less clearly defined. In such interventions, collaboration between change agent and client system in setting change goals and in deciding on change strategies and methods is more easily achieved than in the making and implementation of national and transnational policies. The implication of this emphasis for Warwick and Kelman seems to be that the approach of the authors of *The Planning of Change* to the ethical dilemmas of change agents is not adequate to the diffuse and anomic situations in which the planning and implementation of macro-interventions are typically carried on today. We are not entirely convinced of this inadequacy.

But we do appreciate the clarity of the analysis which Warwick and Kelman have made of the ethical dilemmas involved in such macro-issues as population policy, modernization, economic policy, and environmental manipulation. Their demonstration that in change programs, ethical as well as technical and cognitive considerations are unavoidably involved in goal setting, in target definition, in choice of means, and in assessment of consequences is masterly and convincing.

We have no doubt that Warwick and Kelman describe accurately the sources of values to which policy-makers typically turn in formulating value orientations for the justification and guidance of their policy-making. These sources are cultural and religious traditions. If our argument in Chapter Eleven is correct, these sources are now inadequate. Tradition-direction has failed contemporary man. To turn to the past for ethical justification of plans and actions is to deepen and rigidify cleavages among culture groups internationally and among subculture groups within national cultures. Such turning to the past for ethical guidance and justification actually thwarts the building of shared culture which Margaret Mead and other futurists see as a necessity in our fragmented social world.

Those who place their hope in a future-orientation place their bets on *the creation by people of new shared values* in processes of planning which today necessarily involve the management and resolution of value conflicts as Warwick and Kelman make abundantly clear. The emphasis of change agents shifts, in this view, from *a priori* justification of plans and actions in terms of traditional values to the construction of conditions which support people out of differing and conflicting traditions in creating new shared values as an integral part of the process of planning, implementing, and assessing social interventions. This means an emphasis upon the values and ethical guidelines inherent in a methodology of joint inquiry and reconstruction. Warwick and Kelman are not devoid of methodological commitments. They demonstrate a methodology in the analysis they provide. It is a methodology of raising the consciousness of social interveners concerning the ethical dimension of their work and of clarifying the value conflicts in which interveners are unavoidably involved. These are important methodological values. But their methodology seems not to extend to the ways in which interveners and those affected by their interventions can work through their value conflicts toward a widening area of shared value affirmations. Such value affirmation will no doubt draw upon the traditional values which conflicting parties bring to their confrontation. But the shared affirmation of value will have been created anew.

In the second reading of this chapter, Benne proposes a moral orientation for change agents which incorporates the future-oriented and methodological value stance sketched above. Although he uses the language of "laboratory method," we like to believe that his viewpoint is applicable to the choices and work of social interveners, whatever the scope of their intervention. It places great emphasis on mutual re-education as an integral part of ethically defensible programs of changing. But, in our world, we believe, parties to the various value-conflicts which beset us must re-educate each other or perish.

11.1 ETHICAL ISSUES IN SOCIAL INTERVENTION

Donald P. Warwick, Herbert C. Kelman

Social intervention is any act, planned or unplanned, that alters the characteristics of another individual or the pattern of relationships between individuals. The range of acts covered in this definition is intentionally broad. It includes such macro phenomena as national planning, military intervention in the affairs of other nations, population policy, and technical assistance. It also applies to psychotherapy, sensitivity training, neighborhood action programs, experimentation with human subjects, and other micro changes. The concept of social intervention seems more helpful in considering the ethics of social change than the concept of "planned change," which tends to exclude from ethical review a host of activities with serious personal, social, and political implications.

The existing literature on planned

Originally published in *Processes and Phenomena of Social Change,* edited by Gerald Zaltman (New York: John Wiley & Sons, Inc., 1973). Copyright © 1973 John Wiley & Sons. Reprinted by permission of John Wiley & Sons, Inc.

The authors are grateful to the Center for the Study of Development and Social Change, Cambridge, Massachusetts, for organizing a discussion of an earlier draft of this chapter. We wish to thank especially James Lamb, Director, Denis Goulet, William Frain, and David Robinson for their helpful criticisms.

change (e.g., Lippitt, Watson, and Westley, 1958; Bennis, Benne, and Chin. 1969) confines itself to a relatively narrow range of interventions. The usual paradigm is concerned with micro efforts such as organizational development or community action programs. An organized attempt by a business corporation to improve communication, morale, and productivity in its U.S. plant is considered planned change; a decision by the same company to build a new plant in Guatemala is not. In fact, the greater the scale and impact of social intervention, the less likely it is to be called planned change. One reason is that models of planned change place heavy emphasis on the role of the change agent, often a social science consultant. In many cases of macro change, it is extremely difficult to fit the facts of the situation into a paradigm involving change agents and client systems. The decision by the General Motors Corporation to build an automobile plant in Oshawa, Ontario, was undoubtedly the result of complex deliberations within the corporation and then further negotiations with the Canadian and U.S. governments. No single change agent was involved, and it would be hard to find a "client" for the action. Yet the result was a major intervention with critical effects on the Canadian economy and, some would argue, on Canadian political autonomy (cf. Levitt, 1970).

A second and very different example

further illustrates the need for a broader focus in viewing the ethics of social change. It is now clear that psychoanalysis, which began as a theory of personality and a system of psychotherapy, has had a marked impact on morality and self-conception in Western societies (Seeley, 1967; Rieff, 1961, 1966). In many cases guilt about the presence of strong sexual impulses has been replaced by shame about their absence. Repression has become the secular equivalent of sin, mental health the substitute for salvation. Judged by its effects, psychoanalysis would certainly qualify as one of the cardinal social interventions of the century. Yet by the usual standards it would not meet the test of planned change, nor could Freud properly be considered a change agent in producing these larger effects.

A focus on social intervention, more broadly defined, allows for ethical evaluation of institutional structures and practices with critical social effects, as well as of situations with more readily identifiable change agents. We can thus explore the ethical implications of government policies or intellectual traditions, for example, even though these are not explicitly geared toward producing social change and are not associated with a single individual or agency. The major focus of our discussion, however, will be on deliberate interventions. In many cases the difference between deliberate and nondeliberate intervention is itself the central issue in an ethical evaluation. Insofar as an intervention remains nondeliberate, it is relatively easy to ignore its effects. A heightened awareness of the consequences of social intervention is at the heart of ethical responsibility and concern.

The moral questions raised by social intervention are as old as human society: What are the ends of men? Of the various "goods" known to man, which should be pursued above the others? What are the rights of men and societies?

What abridgments of human freedom are necessary for the common good? And, most difficult, what criteria should be used to choose among alternative ends and means?

VALUE PREFERENCES AND VALUE CONFLICTS

One can distinguish four aspects of any social intervention that raise major ethical issues: (1) the choice of goals to which the change effort is directed; (2) the definition of the target of change; (3) the choice of means used to implement the intervention; and (4) the assessment of the consequences of the intervention. At each of these steps, the ethical issues that arise may involve conflicting values—questions about what values are to be maximized at the expense of what other values. (We define values as individual or shared conceptions of the desirable, that is, "goods" considered worth pursuing.)

Thus values determine the choice of goals to which a change effort is directed. On the one hand, the intervention is designed to maximize a particular set of values. For example, a government may undertake a massive literacy program with the avowed intention of increasing the freedom of its citizens. On the other hand, those setting the goals of an intervention are also concerned with minimizing the loss in certain other values. These imperiled values thus serve as criteria of tolerable and intolerable costs in a given intervention. Under pressures of rapid demographic growth and limited resources, for example, a government might contemplate a set of coercive population control measures, such as involuntary sterilization, to reduce fertility. The benefit to be promoted by this program would be the common welfare or, in extreme cases, even the physical survival of the country. At the same time the policy makers might be concerned about the effects of this program on two other values: freedom and justice. These values would be seen as social goods to be preserved—benefits that should not fall below some minimal threshold. Values may influence the choice of goals not only in such explicit, conscious ways but also in a covert way. This may happen, as we shall see, when a change program departs from a value-based but unquestioned definition of a "problem."

The definition of the target of change is often based on just this kind of implicit, unexamined conception of where the problem lies. For example, a change effort designed to improve the conditions of an economically disadvantaged group —such as the black population in the United States—may be geared primarily toward changing institutional arrangements that have led to the systematic exclusion of this group from the economic life of the country, or toward reducing the educational, environmental, or psychological "deficiencies" of the disadvantaged group itself. The choice between these two primary targets of change may well depend on one's value perspective: a focus on removing systemic barriers is more reflective of the values of the disadvantaged group itself, whereas a focus on removing deficiencies suggests the values of the more established segments of the society.

Third, values play a central role in an ethical evaluation of the means chosen to implement a given intervention. Questions about the morality of coercion, manipulation, deception, persuasion, and other methods of inducing change typically involve a conflict between the values of individual freedom and self-determination, on the one hand, and such values as social welfare, economic progress, or equal opportunity, on the other. For example, to what extent and under what conditions is a government justified in imposing limits on the freedom to pro-

create for the sake of presumed long-run improvements in the quality of life?

Finally, conflicting values enter into assessment of the consequences of a social intervention. One of the consequences of industrialization, for example, may be a weakening of traditional authority structures or family bonds. To what extent one is willing to risk these consequences depends on his commitment to such traditional values relative to those values that industrialization is designed to enhance. In other words, our assessment of the consequences of an intervention depends on what values we are willing or unwilling to sacrifice in the interest of social change.

Before examining some of the ethical problems that may arise at each of these four points in the change process, and the value conflicts from which they derive, we shall consider some more general procedural issues that must be faced in any effort at applied ethics. These refer to the procedures to be followed in deriving the values that apply in a social intervention, in determining whose values should be given what weight, and in adjudicating value conflicts.

The Derivation and Content of Values

An analysis of the ethics of social intervention presumes some notion of what values should apply and how they are to be derived. The problem is simplified, of course, if the analyst simply accepts the values held out by the initiators of the change. Hence, if a government agency says that it undertook a population program in order to promote the general welfare, and that it also considered the costs of the program for individual freedom, the analyst might confine his attention to the values of freedom and welfare. Few students of ethics, however, would be content to let the individual or group initiating a change be the sole judge of the relevant values at stake. The human bent toward selective perception and self-deception, not to mention the protection of vested political interests, is simply too great to justify this approach. In the example cited, the concerned observer might also wish to examine the effects of the population program on other values, such as justice, dignity, or the self-esteem of minority groups. By leaving the definition of the ethical situation to the sponsor of a program one abdicates his own moral judgment.

Ultimately the choice of values as well as their application depends on one's final court of ethical appeal. The bases for choosing and using values are varied and often incompatible. Gustafson (1970, pp. 169–170) discusses a number of the different bases that may underlie such choices. For some, especially in the Judaic and Christian traditions, an appeal is made to revelation. The salient values are those contained in scripture. Others, especially members of the Catholic Church, have looked to "natural law" as a basis for moral values. Many outside this religious tradition show a similar belief in the capacity of human reason to arrive at self-evident moral truths. Still others hope to derive a framework of values on an inductive basis through an examination of ethnographic reports and other materials from the social sciences. For their part, social scientists often work with value frameworks derived from their theories of man and society. Lasswell and Kaplan (1950), for example, propose a set of eight values thought to cover a wide variety of human situations. At the opposite end of the spectrum are the cultural relativists who hold that value analysis should be founded on an understanding of the rights and obligations prevailing within a single society, rather than on general paradigms.

In practice the situation is not as hopelessly eclectic as this diversity of approaches would suggest. Closer analysis of the *results* of these positions reveals considerable overlap, often obscured by differing terminology. The most salient values suggested by natural law theories are very similar to those derived from revelation. The notions of freedom, justice, love, and the common good are likely to appear in any general ethical theory, and they usually have their counterparts in social scientific theories. Even the cultural relativists often approach value analysis with a set of categories not unlike those of classical ethics. Still, the task of laying out the content and derivation of values remains a fundamental challenge in any discussion of ethics. Let us consider an example illustrating ways in which this challenge can be met.

The example comes from *The Cruel Choice* by Denis Goulet (1971), a recent work on the ethics of economic and social development. Goulet asks if it is possible to identify "any common values which all societies desire and which development claims to foster" (p. 87). He concludes:

. . . three such values can be recognized as goals sought by all individuals and societies. These are proper universalizable goals inasmuch as their forms and modalities can vary in different times and places. Nevertheless, these goals relate to fundamental human needs capable of finding expression in all cultural matrices at all times (p. 87).

The first of these is *life sustenance.* The nurture of life is everywhere treasured by sane men. . . . All objects that satisfy men's basic requirements for food, shelter, healing, or survival can be called life-sustaining "goods". . . .

A second universal component of the good life is *esteem*—what Everett Hagen calls every man's sense that he is a being of worth, that he is respected, that others are not using him as a tool to attain their purposes without regard for his own purposes. All men and all societies seek esteem, although they may call it identity, dignity, respect, honor, or recognition . . . (p. 89).

A third trans-cultural component of the good life, valued by developed and non-developed societies alike, is *freedom.* Countless meanings attach to this troublesome word. At the very least it signifies an expanded range of choices for societies and their members, together with the minimization of constraints (external, though not necessarily internal) in the pursuit of some perceived good (p. 91).

Though few would contest the ethical desirability of these three values, certain questions could be raised about the process by which they were derived. In the passages cited and elsewhere Goulet indicates that he used two basic criteria: (1) universality—the degree to which a value represents "goals sought by all individuals and societies"; and (2) the frequency with which "development" claims to foster this value. Presumably, a value would qualify for inclusion by the second criterion if it appeared with some regularity in statements of development goals. One might ask, first, why the author accepts the essentially statistical approach implied in this criterion. Furthermore, assuming that the criterion refers to statements in the existing literature, one might ask why he confined his attention to present possibilities. If a broader criterion had been used, additional values might have been included, such as justice, power, beauty, and affection. In short, the nature of the operative values in any change effort depends on the procedures used in deriving these values. Deliberate attention to these procedures therefore is an important step in an ethical evaluation. . . .

Whose Values Should Be Given What Weight?

Another fundamental procedural question concerns the weights assigned to different, and often competing, sets of values. Dis-

cussions of national population policy sharply raise the issue of whose values should prevail. The Population Task Force of the Institute of Society, Ethics, and the Life Sciences (1971)[1] addressed this question in its report:

The American ethical, legal and political tradition is rich in the elaboration of basic values which have been present since the beginning. That is why it is possible to speak of an American tradition, one which also joins the mainstream of the western tradition as a whole. The United States is also constituted of many different racial, ethnic, class, religious and professional groups, each with value perspectives special (if not necessarily unique) to themselves.

The formation of a population policy must take account of these realities, not only because a traditional commitment to pluralism requires it, but also because any population policy formulated in ignorance of these realities will stand in dire political jeopardy (p. 65).

The report goes on to show variations in cultural values and definitions of the "population problem" among blacks, Spanish-speaking Americans, American Indians, feminist groups, the New Left, the major religious groups, economic groups, and population specialists. Blacks, for example, show a fear of physical or cultural genocide, and a positive concern for group survival and power. Spanish-American culture seems to place a stronger emphasis on family ties and children than U.S. society as a whole. The New Left is suspicious that the current emphasis on population and pollution may be an evasion of more basic problems such as poverty and war. Thus even at the national level the decisions about social interven-

[1] Donald Warwick was a member of the Task Force and a co-author of its final report.

tion must weight the claims and concerns of diverse groups within the society.

The problem of "whose values" becomes even more complex in international programs of development or technical assistance. Such programs are often planned and carried out by individuals and agencies external to the society in which changes are introduced. Because of the real possibility that the values of the change agents may deviate from those of the local population, the question of whose values determine the goals, targets, and means of change takes on special importance. The issue is not only whose interests are being served by the program, but whose conceptual framework generates the definition of the problem and the setting of goals. The latter problem persists even when representatives of the local society are fully involved in the planning and execution of the change program, since these representatives—often trained abroad—may themselves have adopted the conceptual framework of the external agency.

Images of the "ideal person" to which change efforts should be directed provide a good illustration of the possible effects of competing values on the way in which development is conceptualized. Western writers have often described the ideal person (from the point of view of development) as one who possesses those personality traits and attitudes conducive to rapid economic growth and/or political effectiveness. For example, Alex Inkeles (1966) includes the following characteristics in his list of attitudes of "modern man": a disposition to accept new ideas and try new methods; a readiness to form and hold opinions over a broad range of problems and issues; a democratic orientation to opinions; a time sense oriented more to the present and future than to the past; and a sense of personal efficacy. He concludes:

I have pointed to a set of qualities of mind that I call modern, which I believe have much to recommend them. They are not compatible in all respects with qualities that are widespread in traditional cultures, but I believe that they are qualities men can adopt without coming into conflict, in most cases, with what is best in their cultural tradition and spiritual heritage. I believe they represent some of the best things in the modernization process. But whether we view them as positive or negative, we must recognize these as qualities that are fostered by modern institutions, qualities that in many ways are required of the citizens of modern societies (pp. 149–150).

The set of modern attitudes identified by Inkeles derives, at least in part, from an empirical analysis: these are the attitudes found to be held by individuals, in several societies, who have had experience with "modernizing institutions" such as the factory. Nevertheless, Inkeles' statement reflects, to a considerable extent, his personal judgment and is thus undoubtedly influenced by his own values, rooted in his particular cultural experiences. First, the statement makes certain empirical assumptions that are by no means inevitable. There is certainly empirical support for the proposition that the qualities listed are conducive to economic growth and good citizenship, but the support is not overwhelming, and, in any event, it does not demonstrate that these are the only qualities consistent with development. The statement also assumes that these qualities are usually consistent "with what is best" in various cultural traditions—an assumption for which it would be exceedingly difficult to muster empirical support. Even if the empirical assumptions were entirely correct, however, the decision to promote the modern attitudes identified by Inkeles would constitute a value judgment. These attitudes may indeed facilitate economic and political modernization, but, as Inkeles points out, "they are not compatible in all respects with qualities that are widespread in traditional cultures." It is not a foregone conclusion that the requirements of modernization must be given priority over the protection of traditional values and, indeed, it can be argued that any effort to change personality and basic orientations for instrumental reasons is ethically questionable.

To point out that Inkeles' statement is influenced by his personal and cultural values does not constitute a criticism of that statement. Indeed, it is our position that such statements inevitably reflect value judgments and priorities, even when they are partly based on empirical evidence. Recognition of this fact sensitizes us to the need of asking *whose* values are reflected in a given statement and of giving proper weight to competing points of view. Since the writings of social scientists often provide the conceptual frameworks for development programs, it is particularly important to scrutinize them in these terms.

We shall have more to say about the ethical implications of whose values are reflected in a social intervention—or in the conceptual frameworks that underlie it—in later sections, particularly when we discuss the choice of goals for change efforts.

The Resolution of Value Conflicts

Deliberate attention to the content and derivation of values and to the different groups whose values are engaged by a given action often reveals value conflicts. Different values held within the same group and differences in value priorities set by different groups may present incompatible claims. Perhaps the most difficult challenge for ethical analysis is in providing some approximate guidelines for adjudicating such competing claims.

Consider the case of population pol-icy. Advocates of a noninterventionist policy typically base their arguments on the value of freedom. In this view legal or other limits on procreative behavior place unwarranted restrictions on the liberty of couples to determine their own family size. Those who favor strong population control measures, on the other hand, usually depart from the values of welfare and survival. If population is allowed to grow unchecked, they argue, the resulting numbers of people will pollute the environment, consume an unreasonable proportion of the world's natural resources, and possibly even threaten the survival of the human species. The critical question is the optimum balance between freedom and welfare (including survival). *How much* freedom, in other words, ought to be sacrificed in the interests of welfare?

Similar questions arise in debates over the preservation of traditional cultures in programs of national development. On the one side is a body of opinion holding that agents of "modernization" have no right whatsoever to tamper with traditional beliefs and practices. The arguments offered to support this view include the need for cultural diversity, the right of all peoples to determine their own destinies, and the importance of traditional values as a matrix for the development of self-identity and self-esteem. At the opposite extreme are those who feel that traditional values are by definition obstacles to development and must therefore be changed as rapidly and efficiently as possible. Again the question concerns the most desirable trade-offs between conflicting values: How much traditional culture ought to be sacrificed for the sake of modernization? . . .

In discussing the procedures to be followed in resolving value conflicts—as well as those in deriving the values to be applied to social intervention and in considering the competing values of different groups—we have provided no answers to the ethical questions that arise in social intervention. We have merely identified some of the analytical steps that an ethical evaluation calls for. These steps do not eliminate the need for value judgments, but they make such judgments more conscious and deliberate. With these procedural issues in mind, we shall now turn to some of the ethical questions raised by each of the four aspects of social intervention that we distinguished earlier: the choice of goals, the definition of the target, the choice of means, and the assessment of consequences.

CHOICE OF GOALS

Social scientists and others writing about social change are always making assumptions—explicitly or implicitly—about the nature and the end-points of the changes that are necessary and desirable. These assumptions are influenced not only by the values that the individual writer brings to his research, but also by the interests and orientations that surround the issue of social change in his own society, whatever its political coloration or level of development may be. Gunnar Myrdal (1968), writing about development, points out:

> ... quite apart from any formal or informal pressures from the authorities or from public opinion, the individual scientist is himself usually deeply engaged in these momentous events. As an American, a European, or a national of one of the underdeveloped countries, he is bound to be anything but indifferent to the theoretical and practical findings of his research. This must have an influence on his inclinations in research and on how he presents his results to the public—unless he exercises the utmost care to avoid a biased view (pp. 10–11).

We would go further to argue that, even with utmost care, a biased view cannot be avoided. It can be counteracted only insofar as it is made explicit and confronted with analyses based on alternative perspectives.

Our own perspective on social change places it in the context of a worldwide revolution of human rights, which has set into motion powerful forces toward political independence, economic development, and social reform, both in the developing world and within industrialized countries. Given this perspective, we would start the process of delineating goals for social intervention by asking how the challenge posed by this revolution can best be met. What can be done to facilitate social change and to increase the likelihood that it will move in constructive directions? What kinds of institutional arrangements would improve the living conditions of the masses of the population, would be consistent with their needs for security and dignity, and would broaden the base of participation in social, political, and economic affairs? What conditions are conducive to a population's sense of political legitimacy, its feeling of national identity, and its readiness for involvement in citizenship responsibilities, economic enterprises, and social planning? What techniques of change would minimize the use of violence, the brutalization of the active and passive participants in the change process, and the predisposition to govern by coercion and repression? How can social intervention be introduced without destroying the existing culture patterns that provide meaning and stability to a people, while at the same time helping to build the new patterns and values that a changing society requires if it is to remain human? (Kelman, 1968, p. 63).

This list of questions—and the goals for social intervention that it implies—is clearly based on certain value assump-

tions. It presupposes not only the desirability of social change, but also a preference for certain kinds of change over
others. Thus, for example, it assumes that
social institutions must be judged in terms
of their consistency with human needs,
and it favors institutional arrangements
that encourage participation, legitimacy,
nonviolence, and respect for traditional
values.

The statement implies a rough ordering of priorities. It suggests that, in choosing goals for intervention, a major criterion be the concrete needs of individuals rather than some abstract notion of
what is good for society. It clearly regards changes that involve violence, coercion, or the destruction of traditional
values as unacceptable except under the
most compelling circumstances. The application of these criteria to a specific
situation, however, requires some difficult
judgments. How does one determine
which of various alternative policies is
most consistent with the concrete needs
of individuals, or what circumstances are
sufficiently compelling to justify changes
that involve varying degrees of violence,
coercion, or destruction of traditional
values? Different analysts agreeing on
these priorities may nonetheless disagree
in their specific applications of them.

Beyond such differences in the application of these criteria to concrete interventions, it is also unlikely that everyone will agree with the delineation of
goals and priorities implied in the foregoing statement. We would like to believe that these goals are consistent with
basic and universal human needs and that
they are widely shared over different population groupings and cultures. Yet we
are also cognizant of the very real possibility that our ordering of priorities reflects, in some important ways, our own
cultural and ideological biases and that—
even when it deviates from the governing
ideology of our society—it is influenced
by our own relatively favored positions

within the society and our society's favored position within the international
system. Thus, before basing the choice of
goals for intervention on such a statement, one must recognize that it represents one perspective, which has to be
confronted with those derived from other
relevant points of view.

Recognizing that the choice of goals
for intervention is determined by the
value perspective of the chooser—which
is not necessarily shared by all interested
parties—is the first and a frequently
neglected step in an ethical analysis of
social intervention. The goals to be pursued in social change are by no means
self-evident. They depend very much on
what one considers a desirable outcome
and what costs in terms of other values
he is prepared to bear for the achievement of this outcome—a complex judgment about which there may be considerable disagreement.

The role of cultural and ideological
biases in the choice of goals is often ignored because the change effort may have
a hierarchy of values built into its very
definition. These values may simply be
taken for granted without questioning
their source and their possibly controversial nature. A clear example of such covert
ideological influence is seen in definitions
of national development and modernization. The word *development*, whether
used in botany, psychology, or economics,
implies an unfolding toward some terminal state. Typically this state, whether it
be adulthood, maturity, or an ideal economic system, is also considered desirable. By implication, a "more developed"
nation is seen as better in some sense
than a "less developed" nation. In the
1950s the dominant models of national
development took as their implicit end-
points the economic and political systems
of the Western industrial nations. Within
this teleological framework primary emphasis was given to economic values.
Works such as *The Stages of Economic*

Growth (Rostow, 1960) argued, in effect, that the ultimate measure of political and social institutions was their contribution as "preconditions" for economic growth. From an ethical standpoint the most serious problem with these models was that value judgments were slipped into seemingly value-free definitions of historical processes. Statements about goals for change deemed desirable from a particular value perspective were often presented as empirical statements about the conditions for a universal process of development.

The same problem arises with the more recent concept of *modernization*. At first glance this too seems like an ideologically neutral term solidly anchored in scientific theory and data. Closer analysis reveals a definite but elusive set of value assumptions. Specifically, this concept contains value-based notions of what *will* happen and what *should* happen in social change, with substantial overlap between the two. At the level of what will happen, the concept of modernization often includes two types of predictive assumptions: those implying the historical inevitability of certain trends, such as secularization; and those specifying given conditions, including a particular set of societal values, as necessary prerequisites for "modernity." Not surprisingly, the conditions portrayed as necessary or inevitable have strong ideological overtones and often resemble the idealized social system in the writer's own society. Such predictions can become self-fulfilling prophecies when they are treated as fact by some political leaders and translated into policy.

Similarly, the concept of modernization contains explicit or implicit notions of what *should* happen in social change. Most definitions do not include everything modern (in the dictionary sense of contemporary or up-to-date) as part of the end-state of modernity. Air pollution, biological warfare, and other products of a technological civilization are generally omitted (cf. Smith, 1965). In practice the choice of contents for modernity is influenced by what a writer considers ethically desirable. Such latent choices of goals are especially troublesome because they are masked by connotations of scientific rigor and historical inevitability. In other words, when terms like modernization or development are used as if they represented empirical descriptions of generic, natural processes, it is too easy to ignore the particular historical experiences and ideological preferences that enter into one's formulation of these processes.

In recognizing the role of his own value preferences, the change agent (or the social scientist who conceptualizes the process of social change) does not abandon his values or attempt to neutralize them. It is neither possible nor desirable to do so. Rather, awareness of his own value perspective allows him to bring other perspectives to bear on the choice of goals and to reduce the likelihood of imposing his own values on the population in whose lives he is intervening. This process of relating one's own values to those of others in the choice of goals for intervention—without either abandoning or imposing his own values—can often be aided by a distinction between general goals and specific institutional arrangements designed to give expression to these goals. It may be possible to identify certain broad, basic end-points that are widely shared across different cultures and ideological systems—at least among groups and individuals operating within a broadly humanistic framework. These groups or individuals may at the same time disagree about the specific political, social, and economic institutions that they regard as most conducive to the realization of these ends. Thus one may be able to define the goals for intervention in more or less universal terms, while recognizing that these goals may be achieved through a variety of specific arrangements and that different cultures and ideologies may differ sharply in their preferences for these arrangements. . . .

In the area of individual welfare, [for example,] there is probably little disagreement about the value of eliminating disease, teaching literacy, and protecting men against such natural disasters as earthquakes and floods. There is greater disagreement about the society's obligation to meet the welfare needs of its individual citizens, particularly about the institutional arrangements best suited to accomplish this end.

There is probably even less consensus on what constitutes personal well-being and individual freedom—on the definition of the "ideal man" to which social change ought to be directed. The choice of goals in this area depends on one's view of what is good for man, of what is happiness, and of how individuals should relate to the state and the surrounding society. We have already mentioned that the instrumental view, which describes the ideal man as one whose personality characteristics and attitudes are most conducive to rapid economic and political development (perhaps of a particular variety) is open to challenge on ethical grounds. Economic and political processes should be designed to serve individuals rather than to be served by them. Moreover, when an outside change agent propounds such a view, he may be imposing his own values on others, in that the personality traits and attitudes that he regards as conducive to economic growth and political effectiveness may be those fostered by the particular economic and political institutions that characterize his own society. We would therefore prefer to define the psychological goals of development in terms of a broader conception of man's needs as he interacts with his physical, interpersonal, and social environment. Thus we would emphasize such personality characteristics as personal efficacy, self-utilization, and self-development in our formulation of broad goals for social change. The specific meaning of these characteristics no doubt varies across different cultures and ideologies. It remains to be seen whether there is cross-cultural agreement about these general characteristics themselves and about the broader conception of human needs to which they are linked. . . .

The problem of competing interests and values in the goal-setting process is complicated by the fact that the change agents and those to whom the change effort is directed usually represent different segments of the population. In national programs, the government officials and social engineers who initiate and carry out the intervention and the policy-makers and social scientists who provide the conceptual frameworks on which it is based usually come from the more established, affluent, and highly educated segments of the society; the target population usually consists of poorer and less educated segments, minority groups, or groups that are for various reasons (e.g., age, health, addiction, or criminality) in a dependent status. In international programs, the leadership and conceptual framework (whether Western or Marxist) usually come from the more powerful, industrialized nations, whereas the change is directed at developing countries. Thus, in both cases, the change agent is in some sense an "outsider" to the target population—in terms of social class, or national affiliation, or both. Moreover, he is usually not a disinterested outsider: social change programs may have important implications for the wealth, power, and status of his own group. The problem is further exacerbated by the fact that the agents and the targets of change usually represent groups that are not only different, but different along a power dimension. The change agents come from the more powerful classes and nations, the targets from the less powerful ones. . . .

Despite the ambiguities that often remain when an outside, more powerful change agent involves representatives of the less powerful target population in the change effort, such involvement constitutes the best protection against the imposition of foreign values. Thus in an ethical evaluation of a social intervention, one would want to consider such criteria as these: To what extent do those who are affected by the intervention participate in the choice of goals? What efforts are being made to have their interests represented in the setting of priorities, and to bring their perspectives to bear on the definition of the problem and the range of choices entertained? To what extent does the process enhance the power of the target population and provide them with countervailing mechanisms of protection against arbitrary and self-serving uses of power by the change agents?

DEFINITION OF TARGET

Social intervention usually begins as an effort to solve a problem. A decision to undertake a program of organizational development, for example, may spring from a concern about poor communication, intraorganizational conflicts, or underutilization of employee abilities. The adoption of population controls may be an effort to deal with the problem of scarce resources or that of preserving the quality of life. In every case, identification of "the problem" represents, in large part, a value judgment. What we consider to be problematic—to fall short of some ideal state and to require action—depends very much on our particular view of the ideal state. Moreover, it depends on the perspective from which we make this evaluation. For example, in the face

of demonstrations, riots, or other forms of social unrest, different groups are likely to cite different problems as requiring social intervention: those who identify with the status quo are likely to see the problem as a breakdown of social order; whereas those who identify with the protesters are more likely to see the problem as a breakdown of social justice.

Identification of the problem has important ethical implications because it determines selection of the target to which change efforts are directed. *Where* one intervenes depends on where he—given his value preferences and perspectives—perceives the problem to lie. Thus in the example of reactions to protest, those who see the problem as a breakdown of social order are likely to define the protesters as the proper targets of change. They may use a variety of means, ranging from more stringent social controls, through persuasion and education, to efforts at placating the protesters and giving them a stake in the system. Whatever the means, however, this is the wrong target from the point of view of those who see the problem as failure in social justice and who want to direct change efforts to the existing institutions and policies. In their view, interventions designed to reduce the protesters' ability or motivation to protest merely perpetuate injustices and serve the interests of the advantaged segments of the population at the expense of the disadvantaged. In short, who and what is being targeted for change may have important consequences for the competing interests of different groups and for the fate of such core values as justice and freedom.

Definition of the target is the center of one of the unending debates in economic planning. Many economists, especially those on the political left, hold that the most effective avenue to economic growth lies in massive changes of unjust or archaic social structures, such as land tenure systems. David McClelland and his associates, on the other hand, lean more toward changing individuals and their motives. Specifically, McClelland has launched a series of programs designed to increase achievement motivation (McClelland and Winter, 1969).

The decision to move to one side or another in this debate rests partly on theoretical convictions about economic development, partly on related value-judgments about appropriate strategies of change. The preference for working with individuals typically grows out of a conviction that economic growth is best achieved through private initiative or entrepreneurship. The major barrier to entrepreneurship is seen as an inadequate supply of individuals who are willing to innovate and take financial risks. The solution is to change the motivational structure of relevant members of society, such as businessmen, to provide the missing ingredient.

Without challenging the empirical evidence supporting the individual approach, one could question the value premises on which it rests. Clearly McClelland regards the basic "problem" as the individual. A Marxist critic might argue that this assumption represents an affirmation of the capitalist structures surrounding the individual. A decision to train the individual to perform better within the system implies an ethical acceptance of that system. Moreover, the critic might continue, by tracing the problem of poverty to individual motivation. McClelland is, at least by implication, exonerating society as a whole from blame for misery and injustice. The ethical critique could, of course, be turned around and applied to the Marxist position; critics might, for example, consider the premises on which that position rests to be inconsistent with the freedom and self-development of the individual. In either event, assumptions about "the prob-

lem" of development and the varying definitions of the target of change that these generate flow from value judgments and in turn have important value implications. . . .

Social sicentists play a major role in identifying, or at least articulating, the problems to which change efforts are to be directed and thus in defining the targets for social intervention. A good example is provided by research on various forms of social deviance. Much of this research has focused on "the deviant behaviour itself and on the characteristics of the individuals and groups that manifest it and the families and neighbourhoods in which it is prevalent, rather than on the systemic processes out of which it emerges" (Kelman, 1970, p. 82). Many reasons for this emphasis can be cited. In part it grows out of the "social problems" tradition, which has fostered among social scientists a commitment to help troubled individuals and groups. In part it is due to the fact that research on social deviance is often sponsored by agencies whose mission includes the control of deviant behavior and reflects the sponsors' problem-definition. Research on the characteristics of deviant populations is perfectly legitimate in and of itself, but it raises ethical questions insofar as it provides the dominant framework for conceptualizing deviance as a social phenomenon and thus for setting social policy.

By focusing on the carriers of deviant behaviour, social research has reinforced the widespread tendency to explain such behaviour more often in terms of the pathology of the deviant individuals, families, and communities, than in terms of such properties of the larger social system as the distribution of power, resources, and opportunities. The policy implications that such research yields are more likely to serve the interests of the status quo than those of social change. The research points more readily to ways of controlling or at best preventing deviant behaviour than it does to ways of restructuring the social realities that are indexed by this behaviour. The control and certainly the prevention of many kinds of social deviance are worthy social goals, yet they are more reflective of the concerns of those segments of the society that have a vested interest in maintaining the established order than of the poor, the disadvantaged, and the minority groups from whose ranks the deviants are most often drawn (Kelman, 1970, p. 83).

In short, research on social deviance has often derived from and contributed to a definition of the problem in terms of the characteristics of the deviant. In keeping with this problem-definition, the deviant individuals and communities, rather than the institutional arrangements and policies conducive to social deviance, have commonly been singled out as the targets for intervention. This particular way of identifying the problem and defining the target for change tends to reflect the concerns of the more established segments of the population and has potential consequences for the competing interests of different groups within the society.

This example illustrates some of the ethical implications of social science research. Far from being ethically neutral, the models with which social scientists work may play a major role in determining the problems and targets for social intervention. In defining their research problems, choosing their models, and communicating their findings, therefore, social scientists have a responsibility to consider the consequences for the populations affected. More broadly, they have the responsibility to assure that all segments of the population have the opportunity to participate in the research enter-

prise, which influences the definition of the problems for intervention, and have access to the research findings, which influence the setting of policy.

CHOICE OF MEANS

The most difficult ethical choices in deliberate social intervention usually concern the selection of means. Is it ever morally justified, for instance, to force individuals to accept a program under the threat of death, physical harm, or other severe deprivation? What ethical problems are posed by manipulating the environment so that people are more likely to choose one alternative than others? Should a change program make full use of group pressures for conformity, or attempt to tamper with basic attitudes and motives? These are real questions in most change programs, and there are no easy answers.

It is possible however, to clarify some of the issues at stake by relating the various means to the value of freedom. Warwick (1971a, pp. 14–15) has defined freedom as the capacity, the opportunity, and the incentive to make reflective choices and to act on these choices. An individual is thus free when:

1. The structure of the environment provides him with options for choice.
2. He is not coerced by others or forced by circumstances to elect only certain possibilities among those of which he is aware.
3. He is, in fact, aware of the options in the environment and possesses knowledge about the characteristics and consequences of each. Though such knowledge may be less than complete, there must be enough to permit rational deliberation.
4. He is psychologically able to weigh the alternatives and their conse-

quences. In practice this means not only the possession of information but the ability to use it in coming to a decision.

5. Having weighed the relative merits of the alternatives, he can choose among them. Rollo May (1969) has argued that one of the pathologies of modern existence is an inability to choose—a deficiency of will. A person who cannot pass from deliberation to choice must be considered less than free.

6. Having chosen an alternative, he is able to act on it. Among the conditions which may prevent him from doing so is a lack of knowledge about how to implement his choice, anxiety about acting at all, or a low level of confidence in his abilities, even when he has sufficient knowledge to act.

This discussion of freedom suggests a typology of means used in implementing social interventions. At the "least free" end is coercion, a situation in which a person is forced to do something that he does not want to do, or to avoid doing something that he does want to do. Next comes manipulation, then persuasion, and finally, at the "most free" end, facilitation.

Coercion

In simple terms, coercion takes place when one person or group forces another person or group to act or refrain from acting under the threat of severe deprivation. Philosophers have added many qualifications to this definition, but basically coercion arises in two situations: (1) an actor *wants* to perform a certain action or in the normal course of events *would* perform this action, but he is constrained from doing so by physical means or the threat of severe deprivation; and (2) an actor desires *not* to perform a certain action or normally *would not* carry out this action, but he actually does so because of physical compulsion or threats by another party. It is difficult to arrive at a precise definition of "threat" or "deprivation," but basically they refer to the loss of highly valued goods, such as one's life, means of livelihood, or the well-being of relatives. Coercion should be distinguished from compliance occurring within the framework of legitimate authority. In a certain sense tax laws may be coercive in that they cause people to behave in a way that they would prefer not to behave and do so under the threat of penalties. However, to the degree that such individuals comply with the law out of a belief that it is right to do so, in that the law is rooted in consensual processes, their behavior would not be coerced.

Coercion forms an integral part of many programs of social intervention. Some clear examples are the nationalization of a foreign-owned petroleum refinery or the outright confiscation of land in agrarian reform programs. In both cases the government's action is immediately backed by the use of physical force—those who do not comply may be evicted or jailed. The acceptance of the government's legitimate right to carry out such interventions is usually minimal. Other examples hover at the borders of coercion, manipulation, and persuasion. It has been proposed, for instance, that governments try to limit population by levying higher taxes against families with more than two or three children, or by depriving them of social benefits such as free education, welfare, or medical coverage. Such programs could be considered coercive if the threatened deprivation involved highly valued goods or the threat of great hardship, and if those affected would not accept the legal or moral legitimacy of the interventions. If the rewards and punishments at stake were relatively moderate, on the other hand, the means of intervention could be considered either manipulative or persuasive, according to the circumstances.

Is coercion ever ethically justified in social intervention and, if so, under what conditions? Though it is beyond the scope of this chapter to attempt an answer to this tangled question, we can point out two broad conditions commonly invoked to defend coercive methods. The first is a grave threat to basic societal values. Thus highly coercive population control programs are frequently recommended on the grounds that excessive fertility jeopardizes the continued survival of the human race or the material welfare of a nation's citizens. The second justification is the need for prompt and positive action to accomplish the goals of a change program, even when there is no threat to such values as physical survival. This argument is typical of revolutionary governments bent upon executing major reforms in a short period of time. The two arguments are related in the sense that a failure to show swift results might create a drastic loss in basic values such as the legitimacy or credibility of the government.

In the first case an ethical justification of coercion requires the change agent to demonstrate, rather than assume, the threat to basic values. The population field is punctuated with dire predictions of disaster offered to the public with little supporting evidence. The legal concept of "clear and present danger" would seem to be an appropriate test of any proposal for coercion. Even then, however, it may not be justified. In the second case the defense of coercion usually rests on personal evaluations of the system in question. In gross terms, those who favor a given regime will generally support its use of coercion to promote rapid change; those who oppose it will reject its coercive methods. For example, much of Denis Goulet's book on the ethics of development is a plea for voluntarism,

participation, and respect for individual dignity and esteem. Yet he writes:

> . . . China's campaign to make intellectuals work in factories and fields is no arbitrary manipulation of a class. On the contrary; it is an effort to instill in professional men populist values which they might otherwise disdain: respect for manual labor, direct contact with primary materials, symbiosis with physical tools. Such mobilization builds up inter-class solidarity and thereby constitutes a profoundly ethical strategy of human resource development (1971, p. 116).

Quite clearly Goulet is selective in his endorsement of coercion. For unexplained reasons these methods are "profoundly ethical" in China but immoral in other settings.

Since the justification of coercive tactics often rests on the legitimacy of those who use them, determinations of legitimacy become an important part of ethical analysis. The legitimacy of a regime, in Western democratic tradition, is evidenced by the fact that its major officials have been duly elected, but there are other ways of establishing that a regime is representative of the population and governs with its consent. Even if the regime is seen as generally legitimate, however, some of its specific policies and programs may be considered illegitimate by various segments of the population, because they exceed the regime's range of legitimate authority, or because they are discriminatory, or because they violate certain basic values. Ethical evaluations become even more difficult when coercive interventions are introduced by revolutionary movements whose claim to legitimacy has not yet been established. In such a case, an observer would be more inclined to justify coercive tactics to the extent that he sees the movement as representative of wide segments of the population and feels that their tactics are directed at power-wielders who themselves are illegitimate and oppressive.

Environmental Manipulation

Individual freedom has two core components: the availability of options in the environment, and the person's capacity to know, weigh, choose, and act on these alternatives. Manipulation is a deliberate act of changing either the structure of the alternatives in the environment (environmental manipulation) or personal qualities affecting choice without the knowledge of the person involved (psychic manipulation). The cardinal feature of this process is that it maintains the semblance of freedom while modifying the framework within which choices are made. No physical compulsion or threats of deprivation are applied, and the individual may be no more than dimly aware that he or the environment has been changed. Somewhat different ethical considerations are raised by environmental and psychic manipulation.

The term "environmental manipulation," though it carries sinister overtones, applies to a broad range of activities generally regarded as necessary and desirable. These include city planning; governmental intervention in the economy through means such as taxation and control of interest rates; the construction of roads, dams, or railroads; and the addition of new consumer goods to the market. In each case a deliberate attempt is made to alter the structure of opportunities through addition, subtraction, or other modification. And yet few challenge the ethics of these changes, though they may question their wisdom.

Other forms of environmental control arouse greater moral concern. Limitations on the freedom of the news media are widely attacked as abhorrent to a democracy. Job discrimination, ethnic quotas in universities, and other restrictions on the equality of opportunity are similarly condemned. Thus even the public at large draws a distinction between justifiable control of opportunities.

But what are the limits of justifiable manipulation? And what ethical calculus should be used to establish these limits? Is it morally justified for one group of men to attempt to shape an entire cultural environment in the interest of promoting happiness and survival? In *Beyond Freedom and Dignity* B. F. Skinner (1971) makes precisely such a proposal:

Physical and biological technologies have alleviated pestilence and famine and many painful, dangerous, and exhausting features of daily life, and behavioral technology can begin to alleviate other kinds of ills. In the analysis of human behavior it is just possible that we are slightly beyond Newton's position in the analysis of light, for we are beginning to make technological applications. There are wonderful possibilities—and all the more wonderful because traditional approaches have been so ineffective (pp. 213–214).

The responsibility for implementing control of the entire population "must be delegated to specialists—to police, priests, owners, teachers, therapists, and so on, with their specialized reinforcers and their codified contingencies" (p. 155). In Skinner's world view there is no place for freedom and dignity. These are outmoded concepts standing in the way of progress and survival, the supreme values. His only concession to freedom is that the controller should be a member of the culture that is to be controlled. The ultimate aim, however, is to get the culture to control itself (p. 172).

Skinner's proposals raise many more questions about manipulation than can be handled in this chapter. For example, a fundamental issue—with serious ethical implications—concerns the scientific foundation on which Skinner builds his elaborate scheme (cf. Chomsky, 1971).

Perhaps the key question is who decides what controls are to be instituted. Even Skinner, with all of his confidence in the morality (or at least amorality) of behavior technology, admits that decisions about the precise shape of the new environment are not self-evident. "Who is to construct the controlling environment, and to what end? Autonomous man presumably controls himself in accordance with a built-in set of values; he works for what he finds good. But what will the putative controller find good and will it be good for those he controls? Answers to questions of this sort are said, of course, to call for value-judgments" (p. 22). Indeed they do, but Skinner does not tell us, except by implication, what these value judgments are. Above all else he favors the "survival of a culture," but he provides few clues about what this culture should contain. At root Skinner's book is an apologia for a disembodied technology of behavior change which could be used equally well to design an efficient concentration camp or a utopian commune built on love. As he puts it: "Such a technology is ethically neutral. It can be used by a villain or saint. There is nothing in a methodology which determines the values governing its use" (p. 150). This statement is true only if one accepts the premise that man is an organism whose behavior is governed by environmental "reinforcers," and rejects any notion of inherent rights to human freedom and dignity. This seems to be Skinner's basic ethical stance.

Related ethical issues are seen in behavior (or action) therapies. Unlike "insight" therapies, which concentrate on changing motives, perceptions, and other psychic qualities, behavior therapy aims at treating symptoms. If a patient has a phobia the therapist uses desensitization methods to reduce his anxiety. The techniques involved are identical to those suggested by Skinner for the design of cultures. They are based on the prin-ciple of selective reinforcement, through which desired behaviors are rewarded and undesired behaviors are punished, and they emphasize *specific acts* rather than global personality characteristics. Environmental manipulation is thus a key to the success of these therapies.

Skill at manipulation, anathema to insight therapy, is the moral prize beyond purchase of the actionists, whose title to exercise control is as certain to them as their responsibility for healing is clear. To them, successful manipulation is not merely a useful tactic but a moral imperative which they must satisfy to have the right to offer help at all. Therapeutic intervention in the patient's life is the goal and *raison d'être* for their activity (London, 1969, pp. 64–65).

From an ethical standpoint the principal difference between Skinner's macromanipulation and behavior therapy lies in the degree to which the individuals affected may control the process. Though there are vague murmurings in Skinner's book about "participation by those affected," his basic model is one of total control by an elite of culture designers. By contrast, in behavior therapy the patient seeks help with a problem and is free to terminate the relationship at any time. In other words, though the therapy process involves careful manipulation of his behavior, he usually knows what is happening and can exercise a fair degree of control over the process. Further questions could be raised about the efficacy and the ethics of behavior therapy, but on the scale of freedom used here it comes out relatively well. . . .

In sum, the ethical issues involved in any attempt at environmental intervention are usually complex. If human freedom and dignity are taken as critical values, there is reason for concern with deliberate attempts to manipulate one person's environment to serve the needs of another. The value of freedom requires not only the availability of options for choice at a given point in time, but an awareness of major changes in the structure of these alternatives. Complete awareness of these changes and their causes, however, is obviously impossible. There is also the danger of a strong conservative bias in defending the environment of choice within which we happen to find ourselves. Most of us, after all, are not aware of the origins of our present options for choice. Why, then, should we have a right to know when it is being changed? In other words, *how much* awareness of the structure of our present environment and of modifications in this environment is necessary for human freedom and dignity? And, assuming that this awareness will always be less than complete, who should have the right to tamper with the environment without our knowledge and what conditions should govern such intervention? Some thought has been given to criteria for an ethical evaluation of environmental manipulation. For example, manipulation would seem more acceptable to the extent that the people affected participate in the process, their entry and exit remain voluntary, and their range of choices is broadened rather than narrowed; and to the extent that the manipulators are not also the primary beneficiaries of the manipulation, are reciprocally vulnerable in the situation, and are accountable to public agencies. On the whole, however, ethical thought on all of these questions remains very limited.

Psychic Manipulation

Even with a constant environment of choice, freedom can be affected through the manipulation of its psychological components: knowledge of the alternatives and their consequences; motives; and the ability to reason, choose and implement one's choices. Recent decades have seen dramatic developments in the techniques of psychic manipulation. These include "insight" therapies, the modification of brain functioning through surgery, chemicals, or electrical stimulation; hypnosis; sensitivity training; and programs of attitude change (cf. London, 1969). The emergence of behavior control technology raises fundamental questions about the nature of man and the baseline assumptions about man for ethical analysis.

The ethical questions raised by psychic manipulation are similar to those presented by environmental control and the criteria for ethical evaluation are applicable. In many interventions of this type, however, particular attention must be paid to moral problems of deception and incomplete knowledge of effects.

The success of many programs of psychic change rests heavily on the skillful use of deception. For example, in an attitude change experiment the research subject usually enters the situation knowing that something will happen to him. However, knowledge of the precise nature of the experimental manipulation might destroy the phenomenon that the experiment is designed to observe, and might create expectancy effects (Rosenthal, 1966). Hence a prime challenge for the experimenter is to entice the person into the experiment without revealing critical features of its design. The moral problems posed by deceptive methods have received increasing attention in recent years, as they apply to both laboratory experiments (cf. Kelman, 1968; 1972) and other research situations (cf. Warwick, 1971b). The constituencies affected include not only the researcher and the research subject, but others in the social science professions and often the public at large. Kelman (1972) has written:

Deception presents special problems when it is used in an experiment that is stressful, unpleasant, or potentially harmful to the subject, in the sense that it may create self-doubts, lower his self-esteem, reveal some of his weaknesses, or create temporary conflict, frustration, or anxiety. By deceiving the subject about the nature of the experiment, the experimenter deprives him of the freedom to decide whether or not he wants to be exposed to these potentially disturbing experiences. . . . The use of deception presents ethical problems even when the experiment does not entail potential harm or discomfort for the subject. Deception violates the respect to which all fellow humans are entitled and the trust that is basic to all interpersonal relationships. Such violations are doubly disturbing since they contribute, in this age of mass society, to the already powerful tendencies to manufacture realities and manipulate populations. Furthermore, by undermining the basis of trust in the relationship between investigator and subject, deception makes it increasingly difficult for social scientists to carry out their work in the future (p. 997).

Similar issues arise in all efforts at psychic manipulation.

In other situations the most serious ethical problem is not outright deception but the participant's incomplete or distorted knowledge of the effects of an intervention. Many individuals enter sensitivity training sessions (T-groups), for example, to learn more about their impact on others in a group. Though such learning may well take place, much more *may* happen. The unsuspecting participant sometimes finds that the group process releases violent impulses or even pathological reactions in himself and others. He may be subjected to harsh personal attacks for his feelings and idiosyncrasies, or engage in such attacks on others. Moreover,

The T-group may foster a concept that anything goes regardless of consequences. Instead of creating interpersonal

awareness it may foster personal narcissism. If an individual says anything he wishes, then he may come to assume that just because he feels like expressing himself is justification enough to do so. This may preclude effective communication, for he then ignores whether the other person is receptive to his message, and he ignores the effect of his message on the other person. Communication may not be seen as an interpersonal event but merely as the opportunity to express oneself (Gottschalk and Pattison, 1969, p. 835).

Effects of this sort are scarcely evident in such phrases as "learning about group processes." Of course, properly structured and well-supervised sensitivity training may also bring unexpected benefits. The basic ethical question, however, concerns the right of the participant to be informed of potential dangers in a group experience. The same observation would apply to other forms of psychic manipulation, including brain stimulation or drug experiments. It is all too easy for the experimenter or change agent to present only the probable benefits without mentioning harmful side-effects.

Often the change agent is himself unaware of the fact that he is engaged in manipulative efforts or at least of the ethical implications of these efforts. He may be convinced that all he is doing is conveying information or providing a setting in which self-generated change processes are allowed to emerge, failing to recognize the situational and structural factors that enhance his power over the client and the subtle ways in which he communicates his expectations of him. Even if he is aware of his manipulative efforts, he may be so convinced that what he is doing is good for the client that he fails to recognize the ethical ambiguity of the control he exercises (cf. Kelman, 1968, Chapter I). Such dangerous blind spots among change agents, which preclude their even raising the ethical questions, are particularly likely to arise in psychic manipulation with its often subtle effects.

Persuasion

The technique of persuasion is a form of interpersonal influence in which one person tries to change the attitudes or behavior of another by means of argument, reasoning, or, in certain cases, structured listening. In the laboratory, as well as in the mass media, persuasion is usually a one-way process. In interpersonal relations in natural settings it is generally a mutual process, with the various participants trying to persuade one another. Persuasion is frequently used as a means of social intervention in the mass media and, at the one-to-one level, in insight therapies. Persuasion initially may seem highly consistent with the value of freedom—almost its exemplification. The communication process appears to be carried out in the open, all parties are free to consider the arguments and then to reject or accept them, and no coercion is practiced. Quite clearly, when compared with outright coercion or the more gross forms of manipulation, persuasion emerges as a relatively free method of intervention. But at the same time its seeming openness may sometimes mask covert and far-reaching efforts at personality change.

Insight therapies such as psychoanalysis would generally be regarded as persuasive means of attitude and behavior change. Through such therapy the individual is led to a better understanding of the source of his complaints—why he thinks, acts, and feels the way he does. The guiding assumption is that self-knowledge will take him a long way toward dealing with the problems. The techniques used to promote understanding are generally nondirective, and the client is urged to assume major responsibility for talking during the therapy sessions.

In principle, at least, insight therapy shows a high degree of respect for the patient's freedom. He does most of the talking, the therapist does not impose his values, and the process can be ended at any time. However, closer analysis reveals numerous opportunities for covert influence. Many patients, for example, report feelings of guilt over violations of sexual standards. Following the moral traditions of psychoanalysis, most forms of insight therapy view the guilt feelings, rather than the sexual behavior, as the problem to be solved. Under the guise of moral neutrality the therapist encourages the patient to understand why he feels guilty, and to see that such feelings are irrational (and therefore unjustified). Similarly, by deftly steering the conversation in certain directions through probes and nods of assent, the therapist can lead the patient toward "desirable" attitudes on moral or other matters. And, as Peggy London (1964) observes, even the attitude of moral neutrality in psychotherapy is an ethical stance:

> It is, from the therapist's side, a libertarian position, regardless of how the client sees it (indeed, in some ways he may justly see it as insidious). Expressed in a variety of ways, this position is currently in vogue among psychotherapists of quite dissimilar orientations. Some of the concepts that serve to legitimize and popularize moral neutrality are "democracy," "self-realization" or "actualization," and "existence." All these concepts are oriented towards people's freedom to do as they please (pp. 13–14).

It is hard to escape the conclusion that the therapist, like the confessor, is an active agent of moral suasion. The ethical problem posed by psychotherapy, however, is that the values guiding the influence process are hidden behind global notions such as "mental health," "self-actualization," and "normality." The problem is mitigated to the extent that the therapist recognizes that he is bringing his own values into the relationship and labels those values properly for the patient. "Among other things, such a recognition would allow the patient, to a limited extent, to 'talk back' to the therapist, to argue about the appropriateness of the values that the therapist is introducing" (Kelman, 1968, pp. 25–26).

When we move from persuasion in the one-to-one context to efforts at mass persuasion, the question of who has the opportunity and the capacity to mount a persuasion campaign takes on central importance. Since such opportunities and capacities are not equally distributed in any society, this question is fraught with ethical implications. It arises, for example, in the debate over the impact of modernization on traditional values, to which we alluded earlier. In this connection, after defending the need for cultural diversity, Denis Goulet (1971) writes:

Development economists often ask what they should do about local customs which get in development's way. No sensitive change agent is blind to the traumatic effects of the "bull-in-the-china-closet" approach to local customs. Nevertheless, persuasive campaigns are sometimes necessary, even if they are unpopular (p. 270).

The question is, Who should be responsible for deciding *when* and *where* persuasive campaigns are necessary? Should the interested parties from a community be involved in the decision about *whether* a campaign should be launched, and not only in the later stages of the intervention? Furthermore, how can illiterate villagers argue on an equal plane with sophisticated national planners armed with charts, statistics, debating skills, and prestige? Those in power usually are in a much better position to launch a persuasion campaign and to carry it out effectively. Thus, even though persuasion itself may be more consistent than other means of intervention with the principles of democratic dialogue and popular participation, it often occurs in a context where some are more equal than others.

Facilitation

Some strategies of intervention may simply be designed to make it easier for an individual to implement his own choice or satisfy his own desires. An underlying assumption in these strategies is that the person has some sense of what he wants to do and lacks only the means to do it. Though facilitation, like persuasion, seems highly consistent with freedom, it too can move close to the borders of manipulation.

Consider an example from the field of family planning—a common form of social intervention. At some level, vague or specific, a woman is concerned about the size of her family. A local family planning service becomes aware of her concern, and tries to devise a strategy of assistance. The following would be among the possibilities of facilitation, running from the least to the most manipulative:

1. The woman is highly informed about the possibilities of contraception, and strongly motivated to limit her family size. Moreover, she has a specific form of contraception in mind (the pill) and is lacking only the means to obtain it. A change program which provided a regular supply of contraceptive pills would be an example of almost pure facilitation.
2. The woman is generally aware of the possibilities of contraception, and strongly motivated to limit her family size, but cannot decide which

contraceptive method would be best in her case. A change program is set up to (a) provide counseling on the advantages and disadvantages of various methods of family planning; (b) assist the woman in coming to a decision about the means most appropriate in her case; and (c) provide the materials or services necessary to implement her choice. In this case facilitation would be mixed with some degree of manipulation or persuasion.

3. The woman is strongly motivated to limit her family size but is totally uninformed about the possibilities of contraception. The clinic recommends a single method—the intra-uterine device—without explaining its relative merits in comparison with other methods. This strategy would also involve facilitation, but with even stronger elements of manipulation and persuasion than in the previous case.

4. The woman vaguely feels that she has too many children, but she is not strongly motivated to reduce her family size and possesses no information on contraception. The clinic arranges for visits to her home with the purpose of increasing her level of motivation. Once the vague concern is translated into a concrete intention to practice contraception, the woman is provided free transportation to a local family planning clinic. For purposes of this example we will leave open what happens there. Though facilitation is clearly involved in the later stages of this program, in its origins it is basically a form of either manipulation or persuasion. That is, it requires that motivation be channeled before actual facilitation can take place.

The ethical problems of intervention increase as one moves from more or less

"pure" facilitation to cases in which facilitation occurs as the last stage of a manipulative or persuasive strategy. But ethical questions can be raised even about seemingly pure facilitation. The most vexing problem is that the selective reinforcement of an individual's desires, even when these are sharply focused and based on adequate information, can be carried out for someone else's purposes. Here we face a critical question about the ethics of planned change: is it right for party A to assist party B to attain B's own desires when the reason for this assistance is that B's actions will serve A's interests? In other words, does any kind of facilitation also involve elements of environmental manipulation through the principle of selective reinforcement? For example, survey data suggest that many poor blacks and Mexican-Americans in the United States are desirous of family planning services. But racist groups would also like to see these minorities reduce their fertility. If the government decides to provide voluntary family planning services to these and other poor families, is it serving the interests of racism or the freedom of the families in question? Although it is sometimes possible to determine that a given intervention leans more one way than the other, it is often impossible to say whose interests are served most by a change program. . . .

ASSESSMENT OF CONSEQUENCES

A final set of ethical concerns arises from the consequences of a change program—both its products and its by-products. The following are among the questions that might be raised in a specific case: Who benefits from the change, both in the short and the long run? Who suffers? How does the change affect the distribution of power in the society, say between elites and masses or between competing social groups? What is its impact on the physical environment? What social values does it enhance and which does it weaken? Does the program create a lasting dependency on the change agent or on some other sponsor? What will be its short-term and long-term effect on the personalities of those involved? Many of these questions can be grouped under the headings of *direct* and *indirect* consequences.

Direct Consequences

Certain effects flow immediately from the substance or contents of the change. The direct effect of an abortion is to terminate the life of a fetus. A direct effect of the agrarian reform program introduced by Peru in 1969 was to place a certain amount of land in the hands of a certain number of small farmers. An ethical analysis of these effects would relate them to the set of basic values used as criteria for assessing the intervention. This general procedure was followed by the Population Task Force of the Institute for Society. Ethics, and the Life Sciences (1971) in its examination of specific proposals for population policy. The core values used in its report, as noted earlier, were freedom, justice, security/survival, and welfare. Among the specific proposals examined in the light of these values were voluntarist policies, such as providing free birth control information and materials, and penalty programs, including those that would limit social benefits (education, welfare, maternity care) to families with less than *N* children.

In brief, the Task Force concluded that voluntarist policies had the great advantage of either enhancing or at least maintaining freedom, and in certain cases of promoting the general welfare. At the same time there was some concern that, under conditions of rapid population growth and preferences for large families, voluntarist policies alone might jeopardize the general welfare and possibly survival. Also, questions of justice could be raised one group in the society was growing

at a much faster rate than others. The major ethical drawback of penalty programs, on the other hand, was their possible injustice to those affected. The primary impact of measures such as the withdrawal of educational benefits would be precisely on those who needed them most—the poor. Considerations of justice would also arise if, as is likely, society or the family turned its wrath on the poor creature whose birth order happened to be $N + 1$.

Indirect Consequences

Almost any change program will have an impact on areas of society and personality beyond its immediate intentions or scope of influence. These indirect effects must form part of any serious ethical evaluation. To carry out such an evaluation one must have a guiding theory of change—how one part of a system affects another. To put the point another way, it is a form of ethical irresponsibility to tamper with individual personality or social relationships without knowing or at least considering the by-products and side-effects of the change. Unfortunately, many efforts at social intervention completely ignore these "systems effects," or discover them only too late. Among the most common unanticipated effects are the destruction or weakening of integrative values in the society; change in the balance between aspirations and achievement; and strengthening the power of one group at the expense of another.

One of the latent consequences of many programs of modernization is to undercut or challenge existing values and norms, particularly in rural areas. The introduction of a new road, building of an industrial plant, teaching literacy, or even selling transistor radios may expose the isolated villager to a variety of new stimuli that challenge his traditional world-view. Though the direct effects of such programs often serve the values of welfare, justice, and freedom, the indirect effects may generate abundant confusion and a search for new alternatives. Similarly, quasi-coercive population policies can affect societal values in subtle ways.

A careful analysis of proposals for population control must also pay heed to their unanticipated consequences in areas of life seemingly remote from population. It is quite possible, for example, that one of the side effects of a semicoercive penalty program administered by the federal government would be an increase in political corruption. Some may find it more palatable to bribe local enforcement officials than to limit their procreative behavior. Similarly, in cases where the moral or even political legitimacy of a program was seriously questioned by large segments of the population, a by-product of its implementation might be increased cynicism about government in general. . . . One could also question the advisability of incentive programs which, in effect, bribe people not to have children. Though this practice may successfully reduce family size, its long-term effect may be the encouragement of the same commercial mentality in other spheres of life. . . . Before experimenting with financial incentive programs, therefore, it would be prudent to ask if there are certain goods which we would rather not have bought and sold on the open market, such as one's body, one's vote, and one's personal liberty (Warwick, 1971a, pp. 20–21).

Another common side-effect of change involves a shift in the balance between individual aspirations and the opportunities for achieving them. The delicate ethical question in this case concerns the degree to which a change agent is justified in tampering with aspirations. The dilemma is often severe. On the one hand, to do nothing implies an endorsement of the status quo. On the other hand, in raising aspirations to stir up motivation for change, a program may overshoot its mark. The unintended result may be a rise in frustration.

Questions of this type could be raised about the innovative method of literacy instruction developed by Paulo Freire (1971). His approach, which he calls *conscientização*, attempts to develop not only an ability to read but also a heightened consciousness of one's position in society and the forces shaping his destiny. Freire's method makes use of words that are relevant to personal and local concerns and that are charged with political meaning. The apparent success of this approach in Northeast Brazil and elsewhere raises an interesting ethical problem. To the degree that an individual not only learns to read, but develops a critical consciousness of his position in the social structure, one could argue that his freedom has been enhanced. But a change in critical consciousness and political aspirations without a corresponding modification of the social environment may also be a source of profound frustration. Where collective action to change the system is impossible, because of either strong political repression or other barriers to organization, the net effect may be short-term enthusiasm followed by long-term depression. In fact, the experience of having been stimulated and then frustrated may lead to a lower probability of future action than existed before the intervention. One must thus ask if it is morally justifiable to raise political aspirations without at the same time ensuring that there are opportunities for implementing these aspirations. . . .

SUMMARY AND CONCLUSIONS

Social intervention may impinge on human rights and values in many ways— through the ends served by the change, the targets at which it is directed, the means chosen to implement it, and its direct or indirect consequences. At its core, ethical responsibility requires a full consideration of the process and probable consequences of intervention in the light of a set of guiding values. This essay suggests that it is not an easy matter to exercise such responsibility, partly because of ambiguity about which values should apply, partly because of difficulties in assessing the impact of an intervention on the values chosen. The discussion also underscores the intimate connection between ethics and an empirical understanding of social influence. Often moral judgment rests heavily on a prediction about how a specific intervention will affect individuals and groups. Although our knowledge of the processes and effects of social change is still at a rudimentary level, existing theory and research can be of considerable help in arriving at informed decisions. In the end, the search for an ethics of social intervention recalls Plato's comment that "in the world of knowledge the idea of good appears last of all, and is seen only with an effort."

References

Bennis, W. G., Benne, K. D., and Chin, R. (Eds.) *The Planning of Change* (2d ed.) New York: Holt, Rinehart and Winston, 1969.

Blake, J. Population policy for Americans: Is the government being misled? *Science,* 164, 1969, 522–529.

Callahan, D. Population limitation and manipulation of familial roles. Unpublished essay, Institute of Society, Ethics, and the Life Sciences, Hastings-on-Hudson, N.Y., 1971.

Chomsky, N. The case against B. F. Skinner. *New York Review,* December 30, 1971, pp. 18–24.

Freire, P. *Pedagogy of the oppressed.* New York: Herder and Herder, 1971.

Gottschalk, L. A., and Pattison, E. M. Psychiatric perspectives on T-groups and the laboratory movement: An overview, *American Journal of Psychiatry,* 126, 823–840.

Goulet, D. *The cruel choice.* New York: Atheneum, 1971.

Gustafson, J. M. Basic ethical issues in the bio-medical fields. *Soundings,* 1970, 53 (2), 151–180.

Inkeles, A. The modernization of man. *The dynamics of growth.* New York: Basic Books, 1966. pp. 138–150.

Kelman, H. C. *A time to speak: On human values and social research.* San Francisco: Jossey-Bass, 1968.

Kelman, H. C. The relevance of social research to social issues: Promises and pitfalls. In P. Hadmos (Ed.), *The sociology of sociology* (The Sociological Review: Monograph No. 16). Keele: University of Keele, 1970. pp. 77–99.

Kelman, H. C. The rights of the subject in social research: An analysis in terms of relative power and legitimacy. *American Psychologist,* 1972, Vol. 27, pp., 989–1016.

LaPalombara, J. Public administration and political change: A theoretical overview. In C. Press and A. Arian, *Empathy and ideology: Aspects of administrative innovation.* Chicago: Rand McNally, 1966. pp. 72–107.

Lasswell, H., and Kaplan, A. *Power and society.* New Haven: Yale University Press, 1950.

Levitt, K. *Silent surrender: The multinational corporation in Canada.* Toronto: Macmillan of Canada, 1970.

Lippitt, R., Watson, J., and Westley, B. *The dynamics of planned change.* New York: Harcourt, Brace, 1958.

London, P. *The modes and morals of psychotherapy.* New York: Holt, Rinehart and Winston, 1964.

London, P. *Behavior control.* New York: Harper & Row, 1969.

May, R. *Love and will.* New York: Norton, 1969.

McClelland, D. C., and Winter, D. *Motivating economic achievement.* New York: Macmillan, 1969.

Myrdal, G. *Asian drama, Vol. 3.* New York: Pantheon, 1968.

Population Task Force of the Institute of Society, Ethics, and the Life Sciences. *Ethics, population, and the American tradition.* A study prepared for the Commission on Population Growth and the American Future by the Institute of Society, Ethics, and the Life Sciences, Hastings-on-Hudson, N.Y., 1971.

Rieff, P. *Freud: The mind of the moralist.* Garden City, N.Y.: Doubleday (Anchor Books), 1961.

Rieff, P. *The triumph of the therapeutic.* New York: Harper & Row, 1966.

Rosenthal, R. *Experimenter effects in behavioral research.* New York: Appleton-Century-Crofts, 1966.

Rostow, W. W. *The stages of economic growth.* New York: Cambridge University Press, 1960.

Seeley, J. *The Americanization of the unconsicous.* New York: Science House, 1967.

Skinner, B. F. *Beyond freedom and dignity.* New York: Knopf, 1971.

Smith, W. C. *Modernization in a traditional society.* New York: Asia Publishing House, 1965.

Warwick, D. P. Freedom and population policy. In Population Task Force, *Ethics, population and the American tradition.* Institute of Society, Ethics, and the Life Sciences, Hastings-on-Hudson, N.Y., 1971. (a)

Warwick, D. P. Tearoom trade: A case study of ends and means in social research. Unpublished paper, York University, Toronto, 1971. (b)

11.2   THE MORAL ORIENTATION OF LABORATORY METHODS OF EDUCATION AND CHANGING

Kenneth D. Benne

The laboratory method of learning and changing is by no means devoid of values. Nor do its proponents function without value commitments. The method incorporates values from the orientations of science, of democracy and of the processes of giving and receiving help, as already noted. Those who practice laboratory method share certain moral commit-

Reprinted by permission of the editor and the publisher from K. D. Benne, "The Moral Orientation of Laboratory Methods of Education and Changing." In Benne, Bradford, Gibb and Lippitt (Eds.), *The Laboratory Method of Changing and Learning: Theory and Application.* Palo Alto, Calif.: Science and Behavior Books, 1975.

ments. And yet they differ widely in the ultimate values they espouse as persons, the disciplines and professions through which they make a living and practice a vocation, and the life styles they express and enact. At any rate, this moral community in difference is an ideal among laboratory educators, an ideal sought, if not always attained, in their working relationships. And it is also an ideal, we believe, which laboratory educators, implicitly or explicitly, invite their clients to adopt as a standard at least provisionally, and to evaluate, whether the context be one of training, consultation or applied research.

Laboratory educators typically work with persons and human systems caught up in confusions and conflicts. And ordinarily these conflicts involve differences in values among contending "parties," whatever other clashing or dissonant factors may be involved. Conflicts often lead to polarization, in some degree, between and among contending or hostilely segregated parties. The "normal" behavior to be expected of those related to the conflict, as polarization deepens, is to take sides, to become partisan advocates of the purposes, rights and virtues of one side as over against those of the other(s).

Those who, like laboratory educators, try to avoid the role of partisan advocate in relation to the conflicts they are working with are not infrequently seen by those involved in the conflict as uncommitted people, as dehumanized persons or as witting or unwitting stooges for one side of the conflict or another, most often as stooges for the "establishment," or as some combination of these far from savory roles and characters. Can laboratory educators maintain commitment to certain values at stake in a conflicted human situation and still maintain openness and objectivity in and toward it? And, if they can, should they? We will consider the question of possibility first and deal with the question of desirability later.

Actually, more than one kind of values are at stake in any conflicted human situation. One kind of values may be called *substantive* values. A community, for example, may be divided and in conflict over the legalization of the sale and use of marijuana. Substantive positions develop around the issue. Advocates of the removal of all legal restrictions on sale and use mass evidence and arguments concerning the harmlessness or the beneficence of marijuana, concerning the disrespect for law which maintenance of unenforceable laws, which try to regulate relatively harmless personal tastes, engenders, concerning the inequity and injustice of making criminals out of purveyors and users of marijuana as over against the legalization of the sale and use of alcohol and tobacco, which may be equally or more harmful to health, etc. Advocates of the maintenance of legal restrictions and sanctions mass evidence and arguments concerning the unproved harmlessness of marijuana, concerning the connection of its use with "graduation" to addiction to harmful drugs by the users, concerning alleged character deterioration associated with the use of drugs, etc. Advocates of various intermediate positions usually emerge.

Another kind of values at stake in such a situation may be called *methodological* values. These have to do with the ways in which such conflicts should be settled in making and remaking decisions or policies which are valid and mutually acceptable, at least ideally, to all parties to the conflict. There may be concern with the quality of the evidence used in settling the issue, its validity and its reliability. There may be concern with the inference processes by which meanings for action are derived from the evidence by various partisans. The human effects of the means of persuasion used—coercion, group pressures against the expression of minority opinions, exploitation of anxieties and fears, etc.—may be an object of concern. The quality of communication, of listening, of empathy between contending parties may be examined and pointed out as important in affecting the quality of the settlement reached. Concern may be generated that parties to the conflict do not learn anything from the conflict, do not invest imagination in creating solutions integrative of the substantive values in conflict and embodying new values created in the exchange, that energy is invested only in trying to impose rigid, prepared positions, one upon the other and destroying, not strengthening, whatever moral community has existed among the parties. And *advocates* of appropriate, relevant and creative methodologies to be applied in and to controverted situations may and do appear along with *advocates* of various substantive positions.

Practitioners of laboratory method are *methodological advocates* with respect to the proper ways of settling confused, controverted, conflicted human situations. They work on the assumption that there is a close interconnection between the human quality of the means used by people in resolving issues and the human quality of the resolution attained. It is not true that they do not have substantive values with respect to the ends of human action. The assumption is rather that they, along with all other persons, have such values. It is further assumed that persons involved now differ in their ultimate value orientations and will probably continue to do so. But laboratory practitioners do believe that differences in value orientation need not be a blemish upon and a threat to learningful common deliberation and action if commitment to the use of methodologies which respect differences and employ them to enrich and improve common action can be attained and maintained by all parties in and through conflict situations.

The best safeguard to the continuation and enhancement of personal and sub-group differences within a society may well be the cultivation of common commitment to appropriate methodologies for dealing with social difficulties and issues. These must be methodologies which incorporate respect for differences, which build upon the expectation of open expression of articulated differences by all parties in the arena of public deliberation, which *require* the imaginative weaving of differences into the fabric of common policies and decisions reached, and which *conceive* of conflict resolution as potentially a process of mutual and desirable learning, re-education and change for all of those involved.

This is, of course, not a description of the way in which conflicts are typically resolved in contemporary society, whether at the personal, interpersonal, intergroup or international levels of human organization. It is rather a normative position about effective and desirable conflict resolution. The fact that moral commitments are often interpreted in terms of steadfast and unchanging substantive commitments to socially inherited and frequently unexamined or allegedly unexaminable value orientations does not lead validly to the conclusion that such an interpretation of moral commitments is morally right or viable for our historical period. It does set a vast re-educative task for those who define moral commitments in terms of the utilization of methods of conflict resolution which are designed to lead to intelligent and mutually acceptable resolutions to particular controverted situations and to a general building, strengthening and widening of moral community in difference among the contending parties. This is the re-educative task to which proponents of laboratory method are committed.

Actually, every human person has both a substantive and a methodological character. He possesses more or less integrated and consciously criticized value orientations with respect to the ends and objects of human life and action. But he possesses also more or less integrated and consciously criticized value orientations concerning the ways in which he should deal with conflicts in himself, between himself and others, and between the group(s) to which he belongs and other groups. If the function of laboratory methods of learning and changing is to challenge and support persons and groups in examining their "methodological characters" and in refining and improving these toward greater relevance to and power in the choices and decisions with which contemporary life confronts people, this does not mean that the goal is to deprive people or groups of variegated substantive commitments or to destroy their commitments to differing personal ends in living. Improved methodological characters should rather lead men and women to develop various ultimately unique substantive orientations which are yet more reality oriented, more tuned to the demands of contemporary living, and more open to continuing re-education through exchanges and transactions with others.

Many cultural anthropologists speak of their way of learning cultures different from their own as participant observation. This implies that each anthropologist as a person is at once a participant and an observer. By extension, as each person becomes his own functioning anthropologist, he develops himself both as an observer and as a participant. As participant he enacts the substantive values which he has come to hold through his past processes of enculturation. As observer, he attends and responds to the different values and behaviors which others around him are enacting and in the same process becomes an observer and critic of his own behaviors and value orientations. And as he pursues his processes of observant participation he may hope to improve his skills, understandings and commitments, both as observer and critic of and as participant in human life. This is another way of describing the interactive growth in methodological and substantive characters which the laboratory educator seeks to develop for himself and which he encourages others with whom he works to develop for themselves.

As already noted, the laboratory method derives its moral orientation from the value orientations of science, democracy and of the "pedagogical" process, conceived of as a process of reciprocal giving and receiving of help in facilitating growth and learning within and between persons. To make sense of this derivation, "science" must be seen as, most

basically, a process of inquiry into situations marked by conflicting knowledge claims. The goal of inquiry is to test variant knowledge claims and to attain validated and verified knowledge with respect to whatever confused or conflicted matters of fact the inquiry is addressed. The values of science operate as an ethic of investigative conduct in the individual scientist and as norms of proper investigative conduct within the scientific group or community. Scientists cannot know in advance the outcome of a genuine inquiry. They can best guarantee the validity of the outcome by attending to the methods and processes by which the inquiry is pursued.

Similarly, democracy may be seen basically as a process by which persons and groups who differ in interests and orientations, seek, through exchange, deliberation and joint experimental actions, to attain uncoerced bases of common action to guide and control their common and public life. It is important that democracy not be identified with the political and economic institutions of any particular polity, American or otherwise, although this is a continual temptation in polarized conflicts among groups as each seeks to justify and exalt the rightness of its traditional culture and, as a consequence, to exempt inadequate features of that tradition from open and internal examination and reconstructive criticism. We are using democracy as John Dewey once used the term "democratic" to characterize any society or group which is committed to becoming aware of and responsible for the effects of its actions upon the life and growth of persons affected by them. And this includes, of course, persons within the society as well as persons outside. Such a society or group strives to become more of a moral community, and less a collectivity in Martin Buber's meanings of those terms. As in the case of the scientific community of inquiry, a democratic community can not know in advance whether its decisions and policies will actually enhance the life of various persons involved. It must expect "mistakes," surprises, unanticipated consequences. But it pays attention to the methods it employs in making its decisions and policies in terms of open communication and of full participation of interested persons and groups in its processes of deciding as the best guarantee of avoiding moral and political "mistakes" and of learning and self-correction through surprises and through unanticipated consequences of actions undertaken.

It is not far-fetched, on this view of "science" and "democracy," to see both as methods of re-education through which men seek to learn their way into an unknown future with the claims of valid knowledge and of moral growth of persons centrally in mind. It is, therefore, not alien to the enterprise of advancing the use of these methods in the practical affairs of men to see processes by which human beings receive help from and give help to each other as important to the enterprise. These processes have been lifted into consciousness and the values associated with their effectiveness or ineffectiveness identified in studies of pedagogy, counseling and psychotherapy. Unfortunately, the processes of giving and receiving help in these relationships are often seen as somewhat less than reciprocal and mutual. The receiver of help tends to be identified with only one side of the relationship because of the relative ignorance, immaturity, distress or alienation of the client when compared with the alleged or assumed knowledgeability, maturity and "needlessness" of the helper. In processes by which men and women try jointly to learn their way into an unknown future, they meet more as peers, as equals in ignorance, immaturity, distress and alienation. Exchanges in the helping relationship must, as a consequence, be more reciprocal and mutual.

This is not to discount the importance of childhood education, counseling or psychotherapy. It is rather to caution against taking the relationships in these uncritically as models for the relationships which ideally should come into being in processes of laboratory learning and changing. Nevertheless, the values identified in effective helping relationships can be used by users of laboratory method, if they are conceived reciprocally rather than in terms of a fixed and nonmutual relationship between helper and client. The values embodied in statements such as those of Carl Rogers concerning the conditions of an effective helping relationship—empathic understanding of the other, positive affective attitude toward the other, genuineness in expression—words coherent with inner feelings, and a match in intensity of affective expression in the exchange—have been incorporated in the norms, which should guide the use of laboratory method, that follow.

The moral orientation of proponents of laboratory method can be formulated more concretely in terms of norms that should be developed in processes of learning and changing. These represent an attempt to fuse and focus the value orientation of science, democracy and the helping relationship.

1. Processes of learning and changing should be experimental. Such processes are addressed to the clarification of a confused and conflicted present. They are aimed toward developing more adequate ways of thinking about, valuing and handling a future which by its very nature is partly unknown. Plans which emerge from transactions and deliberations in the present should be held provisionally as they are acted upon. Plans for continuing evaluation and revision, in the light of continuing experience in action, should be built into plans for action and re-education.

2. Processes of learning and changing should be collaborative. They should

involve living persons with a stake in the outcome in responsible participation, in reciprocal and responsible influence and interpersuasion in reaching the decisions which do affect and will affect their lives. Now muted voices need to be articulated and strengthened. Those with powerful and fashionable voices should learn to speak less and to listen more. Ultimately, each personal contribution is unique and common bases of action and evaluation are less adequate than they need be unless the widest possible range of personal contributions are woven into their fabric.

3. Processes of learning and changing should be oriented to the requirements of the confronting task and situation, not oriented to maintaining or augmenting the prestige and status systems which participants trail with them as they enter into processes of learning and changing. This means that contributions to a process of learning and changing are to be judged by their relevance to the confronting problematic situation, not by the prestige, position and credentials of the sources of the contributions. This is not meant to deny the importance or the necessity of authority in processes of learning and changing. It means rather that authority relations need continually to be built and rebuilt in relation to the changing situations which people confront. The right to exercise authority does not rest on past achievements but on the cogency and relevance of contributions to the presently confronting situation. This norm is most difficult to develop and maintain in exchanges in which some participants are "laymen" and others are "experts," in which some are young and others old, in which some are of "majority" and others are of "minority" status. But it is in such exchanges that the norm most needs to be developed and applied.

4. Processes of learning and changing should be educational (and re-educa-tional) for all participants. This may seem tautologous for processes of learning. But closer examination shows that it is not. Many learning situations are set up monologically—the students learn from the teacher, the teacher does not learn from the students, etc. This norm prescribes dialogic processes of learning in which all learn and in which, ideally, each learns what he most needs to learn. In any learning situation, each participant learns something different, whatever the core of common learning may be. In learning situations which employ laboratory method, this psychological fact is made into a virtue, not a blemish. Many changes in institutions and communities are "engineered" by those with greater power or prestige without attention to or responsibility for what participants learn in the process. This norm proscribes such "engineering."

Processes of learning and changing are re-educational when earlier enculturations of persons are brought up into consciousness and when persons develop a more adequate awareness of potentialities in themselves and in their environments which are inhibited from actualization by these previous enculturations. One of the important re-educative effects of desirable processes of learning and changing is an enlarged capacity in persons and groups participating to learn freshly and to revise old learnings more readily and wisely in future situations, in short, as they learn how to learn and to relearn for themselves.

5. Processes of learning and changing should make full use of available, relevant and validated information and experience. Laboratory methods of learning and changing emphasize the importance of using valid information as a basis of decisions and action policies. This includes the use of relevant objective, technical and factual knowledge. But it includes also relevant information about the subjective and personal states

of the persons and groups participating—feelings, attitudes, aspirations. The development of meaningful and rational responses in and to human situations requires a blending and integration of "objective" and "subjective" information, of public and personal knowledge.

6. Processes of learning and changing should be anti-individualistic but deeply respectful of personal and group uniqueness and identity. To understand this norm, two ideas and ideals of personal maturity need to be contrasted. The individualistic idea and ideal, still prominent in liberal cultures, envisage human maturity in terms of individual independence and self-sufficiency, in terms of freedom from responsibility for the welfare and growth of other persons. The communal idea and ideal conceives of maturity in terms of autonomous personal functioning in interdependence with other autonomous persons, in terms of a free assumption of responsibility to give and take with others in the service of mutual personal and group development. The latter idea and ideal seem more consistent with what we have come to know of the social development of persons. They seem also more conducive to the maintenance and extension of respect for persons in the webs of interdependence in which men now live their lives. They seem also more conducive to the task of building moral community within and among dangerously dehumanized collectivities which characterize life in contemporary societies.

7. Processes of learning and changing should be self-evaluative, self-correcting, and self-renewing. What is now known about the release of human potentialities for self-directed learning and changing is only a tiny fraction of what is still to be discovered and invented. Ideally, every program of training or of planned changing, involving as it does new people and new situations, presents an opportunity for gaining new knowledge and for inventing and testing new technologies. But such accumulation of refined insights, concepts and methods depends upon building self-critical evaluation into every program. And self-evaluation and self-criticism should extend beyond the cognitive and technological underpinnings of laboratory method. It should extend to the implicit and explicit value orientations which guide its use and application. The morality of laboratory method, as defined by the normative principles formulated here, is not a fixed morality. It represents in part an induction from experiences with laboratory method in various settings to date, though indeed it draws on moral wisdom derived from man's long cultural history as well. Self-evaluation should extend to the revision and reconstruction of these principles, as experience proves revision and reconstruction to be necessary. Only as continuing self-evaluation is directed to the cognitive, technological, axiological and moral dimensions of laboratory method can self-renewal of the method and of the persons, groups and larger human systems that accept it as a way of planning, learning and living into the future become a rational hope, if never a certainty.

One aspect of the morality of laboratory method deserves further comment. This is its reliance upon processes of consensual validation in forming and confirming decisions, policies and principles for the guidance and direction of human actions and transactions. Emphasis upon consensual validation for the guidance of planning and action not only characterizes life in teaching-learning, training and consultation situations but, as what is learned there is transferred by participants to other life situations, it will come to characterize validation methods in these situations as well.

Criticisms of this aspect of the morality of laboratory education come out of several perspectives. One of these stems from concern that the voices of prophet and of individual genius will be silenced in the councils of human affairs. It is pointed out that frequently the individual or the minority insight is proved to be right and the majority wrong, though the process of discovering this fact and of reevaluating the collective judgment of the earlier time may take decades, generations, even centuries. Does reliance upon consensual validation of decisions, policies and principles discourage divergent and original thinking? Does it elevate dead-level conformity to the level of a moral principle?

Other critics fear that dependence upon consensual validation undercuts the wisdom of traditions in the guidance and management of human affairs. Such traditions, it is claimed, embody the distilled wisdom of many generations of human life. To rely upon decisions made by the agreement of men and women in the present, with all of its temptations to elevate the urgent over the important, the immediate and prospective over the tested and the true, impulse over discipline, is to cut man off from his roots, to undercut authority, to encourage hubris rather than an appropriate humility among men.

Still another source of criticism is more openly "aristocratic" in its strictures upon reliance on consensual validation. The alternative appeal here is to reliance upon the decisions of some elite in the direction of human affairs rather than to the involvement of the ignorant, the immature, the alienated in processes of shaping the pattern of their own continuing life and culture. Some men, and perhaps women, it is alleged, are inherently better judges of the right and the good than are the masses of men. It is the better who should decide the direction and the way. If wider consent is required for action, such consent should be engineered in the masses of men by those best qualified to decide the valid direction of human affairs. In any event,

processes of engineering consent are not conceived as part of the process of validation. The former processes are, in a general sense, rhetorical *not* logical processes.

It is not enough of an answer to such criticisms to point out that they are at odds with some or all of the traditions from which proponents of laboratory methods of learning and changing have confessedly derived their moral orientations—science, democracy and the helping relationship. Yet such pointing out may help to answer the false claim that laboratory method is without traditional rootage. And it may help further to define the conflicts toward which a dialogue of reconciliation should be addressed. Nor is it enough of an answer to point out that the critics may stress the rightness of certain substantive values and goals, seen as somehow inherently or self-evidently "right," and underemphasize the methodological processes by which conflicts between these allegedly "right" goals and alternative "right" goals urged by others and equally based by them on claims of "genius," "tradition" and validation by "the best thinkers and judgers," are to be reconciled validly in today's divided world. For this would merely raise again the question of the merits and interrelations of "methodological" and "substantive" advocacies in humanly conflicted situations. Yet this latter pointing-out might induce critics of consensual validation to clarify their own alternative "methodological" assumptions so that the issues might be more fruitfully joined.

The most basic defense of consensual validation is the claim that it is inescapable in human affairs. Men and women do validate their private perceptions, beliefs and concepts, including their self-concepts, against the perceptions, beliefs and concepts of others in the very process of maintaining themselves as selves and persons. Selves are built in and through social processes. And they unavoidably are maintained and rebuilt in and through social processes. Kenneth Burke has expressed this idea trenchantly. "And in this staggering disproportion between man and no-man, there is no place for human boasts of grandeur, or for forgetting that men build their cultures by huddling together, nervously loquacious, at the edge of an abyss." Sensory deprivation and isolation "experiments," natural and contrived, have provided a factual underpinning to Burke's poetic statement concerning the human condition. When men are deprived of the resources of consensual validation, they literally become mad, the line between fantasy and "reality" is erased, the self, as reality-testing capacity of the organism, when unfed by communication with others, dissolves. In less extreme situations, we are typically unaware of the numerous occasions when we depend upon consensual validation to maintain ourselves in sane functioning.

On this view, to *argue against* consensual validation in human affairs is quite as futile as to *argue against* the gravitational pull between objects near the surface of the earth and the earth. In our fragmented society, men do not dispense with consensual validation. Often, they adopt some fragmentary group in society as the "validating community" against which they test the reasonableness, the sanity of their perceptions, opinions and beliefs. Under these conditions, public, social "reality" dissolves into many sub-social "realities" and communication and common deliberation become very difficult indeed. This is, in many areas of human life, our contemporary condition.

This suggests that consensual validation *can* indeed lead men to suppress dissenting voices in themselves and from their environments, even though these voices speak with the accents of genius and of prophecy. It *can* lead to the neglect of wisdoms inherent in the traditions of mankind. It *can* at times lead to neglect of the counsels of expertise and of

men and women of knowledge in the formation of dominant opinions, though this hardly justifies "the best men of expertise and of knowledge" in the "boast of grandeur" that their views concerning the future of mankind are universally valid and are in need of no validation against a wider community of men and women in justifying such a claim. Consensual validation *can* lead to narrow and mistaken conclusions.

But these facts, laboratory educators believe, hardly justify persons in dispensing with an indispensable human resource. It has seemed to them rather to justify efforts to examine the processes of consensual validation which people actually do use in making up their minds, to discover norms which make for adequacy of judgment in a person, a group or a community and those which militate against adequacy, to seek ways of overcoming barriers to widening and improving the validating community which men and women do use in forming their judgments about what to believe and to do, barriers which often inhere in group reenforced differences in orientation and outlook, in short, to help persons and groups improve processes of consensual validation rather than to deny their inescapable operation in their lives.

It is a gross misrepresentation of laboratory method to say that emphasis on consensual validation by its proponents means that agreement reached by a group or community is, by the social or psychological fact of agreement, justified as valid and correct. Their methodological commitment would lead them to examine the processes and methods by which any agreement was arrived at before venturing a judgment concerning the validity and correctness of the agreement actually reached. And, even if the methodological pedigree of the agreement proves to be as adequate as the group of people who made it could accomplish in their situation, the agreement must be held experimentally and revised in the light of consequent experience and of continuing inquiry and evaluation. The consensus to which proponents of laboratory method aspire is consensus in a methodology adequate to guide men wisely in dealing with the confusions and conflicts which they encounter in living out their lives, not some dead-level agreement in opinion, policy or principle reached by whatever means at some particular stage of historical development. Perhaps the "unlimited community of investigators," which Charles Peirce once proposed as the validating community of ultimately true beliefs, could grant absolute validity to human decisions. But the validation given to decisions by limited and finite communities of men living through history with commitments to the best formulable and usable norms of investigative conduct available to them provides the greatest degree of certainty to which time-bound men can reasonably aspire.

Index

Acceptant intervention, 48–53
Action, theories of, evaluating, 137–147
  congruence, 139–140
  effectiveness, 140
  internal consistency, 137–139
  testability, 140–143
  theory-building process and dilemmas, 144–146
  values for the world created by, 143
Adler, Alfred, 36
Alinsky, Saul, 177, 190*n*., 198*n*., 360, 361
Allport, F. H., 186
Andrews, K., 291
Argyris, C., 35*n*., 55, 57, 137–147, 190*n*., 191, 315, 331–352
Aries, Philippe, 438*n*.
Arnstein, Sherry R., 265
Art, science versus, in practice, 128–131
Ashby, W. R., 180*n*.
Assagioli, Robert, 75
Astrachan, Boris, 77*n*.
Axtelle, G., 33*n*.
Ayres, C. E., 131

Bacon, Francis, 151, 433
Balbus, I. D., 193*n*.
Baldwin, James, 393*n*., 398
Bannister, D., 265

Barber, T. X., 74*n*.
Barnard, Chester I., 38, 183
Barnett, H. G., 442
Barth, John, 460
Bartholomew, Susan, 205–219
Bauer, Raymond, 30
Beauvoir, S. de, 406, 407
Beckett, Samuel, 466
Beckhard, Richard, 55
Bell, Daniel, 461
Bellow, Saul, 460
Benne, Kenneth D., 4*n*., 13–22, 22–43, 46, 68–83, 127, 128–137, 151–164, 165–171, 186, 189, 190, 201*n*., 305*n*., 314, 315–327, 356*n*., 469, 470, 496–505
Bennett, Lerone, Jr., 388, 399*n*., 400*n*.
Bennis, Warren G., 13–22, 30*n*., 38, 39*n*., 55, 128–137, 177, 190, 191*n*., 219–227, 393*n*., 394*n*., 430, 470
Berg, Ivar, 208
Berger, Peter, 443
Bergson Henri, 421*n*.
Bernard, Jessie, 404
Berry, P. C., 285
Bertalanffy, L. von, 104, 178
Binet, Alfred, 26
Bioenergetics, 74
Bion, W. W., 76, 77*n*.

Bird, Carolyn, 404
Birnbaum, Max, 73, 79–80, 323
Blair, Ezell, Jr., 400n.
Blake, Robert R., 35n., 38, 47, 48–66, 68, 77, 78, 81
Blansfield, M. G., 61
Blauner, R., 193n., 201n.
Blecher, Earl, 268
Bloch, Marc, 439n.
Block, C. H., 285
Bloomberg, Warner, Jr., 245n.
Boas, Franz, 30
Bodin, Jean, 435
Body, the, rediscovery and reevaluation of, 73–74
Bolan, Richard, 413
Bookchin, M., 202
Boulding, Elise, 435n., 443n.
Boulding, Kenneth E., 179n., 183, 428, 431–444
Boulware, Marcus H., 395n.
Boundary, definition of, 92–93
Bradford, Ernest, 202, 392n., 397n.
Bradford, Leland P., 4n., 33, 34n., 73n., 202, 305n., 314, 315n., 356n., 496n.
Bradley, M., 193n.
Brager, G. A., 198n.
Brandt, John, 205–219
Braybrooke, D., 181
Brinton, Crane, 361
Brown, Norman O., 74, 418n.
Brownlow, Louis, 61
Brunswick, E., 180n.
Brymer, Richard A., 245
Buber, Martin, 190n., 383, 389n., 396, 414, 417n., 418, 422
Buckwalter, Paul, 268
Bunge, William, 268
Burke, Edmund M., 265
Burke, Kenneth, 504
Burris, B., 405, 406

Cage, John, 176, 360, 460
Caines, Ronald, 266
Campbell, J. P., 285
Camus, Albert, 389n., 418
Caplan, Gerald, 315
Carlson, Richard, 30
Carmichael, S., 190n., 201n.
Cartwright, Dorin, 186, 385, 386, 387n., 391n.
Cassirer, Ernst, 315–316
Castenada, Carlos, 75n.
Castro, Fidel, 173n., 396, 398

Chafetz, J. S., 404
Change, community, see Community change
  deliberate, strategies of, 44–45
  economic, see Economic change
  effecting, strategies for, general, 22–43
    empirical-rational, 23, 24–31, 39
    methods of, 2–3
    normative-re-educative, 23, 31–39
    power-coercive, 24, 39–43
    types of, 23–43
  empowering and legitimation of efforts, 228–259
  human individual as target of, 69–75
  opinion, see Opinion change
  organizational, see Organizational change
  personal, see Personal change
  planned, see Planned change
  resistance to, see Resistance to change
  social, see Social change
  technical, see Technical change
Change agent, 133–34, 273
  defender viewed by, 122–123
  models and, 99–101
  resistance to, 119–120
  school administrator as, 123–124
  value dilemmas of, 467–505
    consequences, assessment of, 492–494
    goals, choice of, 477–481
    means, choice of, 483–492
    social intervention, ethical issues in, 470–495
    target, definition of, 481–483
Cheever, Julia, 443n.
Chein, I., 180n.
Chesler, Mark A., 188–202
Chesler, P., 406
Chin, Robert, 13–22, 22–43, 46, 82, 89, 90–102, 103–112, 125, 128–137, 178n., 189, 190, 470
Chomsky, N., 486
Citizen participation, 245–246
Clarification groups, 73
Clark, B. R., 181
Clark, David, 29
Clark, James V., 36n.
Closed systems, 95–96
Cloward, R. A., 193n., 245
Cohen, A. M., 59
Coleman, J. S., 189
Commager, Henry, 15n.
Communal society, 417
Communities, planned changing in, current state of, 68–75, 77–81

Community change, planning of, structures in, 265–274
  action structures, 269–272
  knowledge structures, 265–269
Community change educator, style of, 352–358
  change agency, 358–359
  team concept, 356–357
Community drama, 253–255
Community interests, advocating, 252–253
Competence, mythology of, 439–440
Comte, Auguste, 25, 434
Concepts, feelings versus, in practice, 132–133
Conceptual tools, selection of, 133–135
Conflict, definition of, 93
  management variables, 114
  structures, community change planning, 269–270
Confrontation, strategies of change, 47, 56–58
Connectives, 96
Consciousness-raising, 231–244
Consequences, assessment of, in social intervention, 492–494
  direct, 493
  indirect, 493–494
Consulting-client relationships, explorations in, 331–352
  consultant, dilemma of, 333–340
  consultant group, values of, 332–333
  data available, nature of, 331–332
  discussion and conclusions, 346–352
  management interest, decrease in, 344–345
  new change program, 345–346
Cooper, C. L., 231n.
Cooper, G. O., 310n.
Corey, Kenneth E., 263–264, 265–274
Corey, Stephen M., 35
Coser, L., 192
Cottle, Thomas J., 80n.
Cotton, T. S., 285, 292n.
Cronkheit, Walter, 360
Crowfoot, James E., 178, 188–202
Culbert, Samuel A., 230, 231–244, 286
Culture, old and new, 370–381
  shared, future as basis for establishing, 444–458
Cyert, R. M., 181

Dahl, Robert A., 192, 388, 391n., 401n.
Dalton, G. W., 290
Darlington, C. D., 439n.
Darwin, Charles, 97, 178, 187, 454

Davidoff, Linda, 268n.
Davidoff, Paul, 268
Davis, Kingsley, 436
Davis, S. A., 191
Decentralized society, 416–417
Defense as part of process of innovation, 120–124
DeFoe, Daniel, 434
Delbecq, André L., 283–295
Deutsch, Morton, 315n.
Dewey, John, 2, 5, 6, 31, 32, 33, 34, 72, 167, 168, 430
Developmental models, 97–99
  direction, 97–98
  forces, 99
  identifiable state, 98
  potentiality, 99
  practitions, utility of, 99
  progression, form of, 98–99
Diagnosis/Development matrix, 47, 48–66, 68
  acceptant intervention, 48–53
  catalytic interventions, 47, 53–56
  confrontation, 47, 56–58
  prescriptive, 47, 58–61
  principles, theories, and models, 61–65
DiCara, L. V., 74n.
Dickson, William J., 34
Dickson-Roethlisberger counseling program, 66
Differentiation, 113
Differentiation-and-integration model, 112–117
  conceptual framework, summary of, 114–117
  differentiation, 113
  integration, 113–114
    conflict management variables, 114
Dilemmas, change agent, 467–505
  theory-building process and, 144–146
    of effectiveness, 145
    of inconsistency, 145
    of testability, 145–146
Dill, W. R., 186
Dively, George S., 211n.
Doctor-patient model, 329–330
Donleavy, J. P., 460
Douglass, William O., 310
Drucker, Peter F., 181, 432n.
Duality, perceptions of, 415
Dubos, René, 418
Dunn, Edgar, 415, 418n., 420n., 421n.
Dunnett, M. D., 285, 286
DuPont, Pierre, 219
Durkheim, E., 190

Easton, David, 382, 398n.
Eaton, Joseph W., 230, 245–250
Economic change, workforce, work-content and, 206–210
Economic Opportunity Act (1964), 245, 247n.
Edelman, Murray, 390n.
Education, 69–71, 314–358
    community change educator, style of, 353–358
    consulting-client relationships, explorations in, 331–352
    laboratory method of, moral orientation of, 496–505
    process consultation, 327–331
    re-education, processes of, 315–327
    research and dissemination of knowledge through, 25
    at Sanctum, 363–369
Educational field experience, as negotiation of different cognitive worlds, 164–171
Effectiveness, dilemmas of, 145
Eisley, Loren, 419
Emery, F. E., 104, 179, 180, 182, 185
Emmet, Dorothy, 385, 386n., 392n.
Empirical-rational strategies effecting change, 23, 24–31
    applied research and linkage systems for diffusion of research results, 27–30
    education, research and dissemination of knowledge through, 25
    personnel selection and replacement, 25–26
    reorganization, perceptual and conceptual, through clarification of language, 31
    system analysts as staff and consultants, 26–27
    utopian thinking, 30–31
Environment, contents of, 108–110
    models of, textures of and clustering in, utility of, 106–108
Epstein, Cynthia, 404
Equilibrium, definition of, 94
Erikson, Erik, 175
Escher, M. C., 415n.
Essien-Udom, E. E., 395n.
Esterson, A., 69n.
Etzioni, Amitai, 385, 386n, 387, 414n.
Evan, William, 183

Fairfield, R., 190n.
Fanon, F., 193n., 385n.
Fantini, Mario, 272, 273
Farris, Buford, 245
Feedback, definition of, 95

Feelings, concepts versus, in practice, 132–133
Fenton, J. M., 395n.
Ficklin, Jerry, 443
Filley, Alan, 283n.
Fillmore, Millard, 219
Firestone, Shulamith, 405, 422n.
Flack, Richard, 420n.
Flory, C. D., 59
Foegen, J. H., 55
Follett, Mary, 34
Fourier, Jean Baptiste, 434, 436
Franklin, Benjamin, 151
Franklin, Paula, 355n.
Franklin, Richard, 315, 352–358
Fransella, Fay, 265
Freel, James E., 443n.
Freire, Paulo, 81, 127, 171–174, 193n., 230, 437
French, John R. P., Jr., 384
Freud, Sigmund, 32, 34, 36, 117, 133
Fried, Morton, 398n.
Friedan, Betty, 404
Friedman, John, 265, 269, 272, 273, 297–305, 415
Friedrich, Carl, 382, 385, 386, 392n.
Fromm, Erich, 190n., 194, 217n., 414
Frost, Robert, 307–308, 309
Future, the, basis for establishing a shared culture, 444–458
    competence, mythology of, 439–440
    image-material, cultural reservoir of, 437–439
    learning communities, changing character of, 440–444
    learning to image, 431–444
    politics of imaging, 435–437
    self-process, protean style of, 458–466

Galbraith, John Kenneth, 14n.
Gamson, W. A., 82n., 190n., 192
Gandhi, Mahatma, 41, 396, 398, 443
Gans, Herbert J., 248n., 257
Gardner, J. W., 181, 271
Gauguin, Paul, 454
Gestalt therapy, 72
Gibb, J. R., 4n., 34n., 50, 73n., 305n., 314, 354, 356n., 496n.
Gibran, Kalhil, 306
Gilbert, Neil, 230, 245–250, 265
Goals, choice of, in social intervention, 477–481
Gold, Neil Newton, 268n.
Goldhamer, Herbert, 388n.
Goodman, Paul, 223

Goodman, Robert, 268
Gordon, G., 290
Gottschalk, L. A., 489
Gould, M. I., 53
Gouldner, Alvin W., 17, 81n.
Goulet, Denis, 473, 474, 485, 491
Grabbe, Paul, 314, 317, 325
Grabow, Stephen, 361, 363, 413–422
Grant, L. D., 285, 292n.
Grass, Günter, 460
Greenway, Robert, 443n.
Greer, Germaine, 404
Grimes, Andrew J., 283n.
Grimstad, K., 411
Grosser, Charles F., 248n.
Groups, planned changing in, current state of,
    68–75
    small group as medium and target of, 75–77
Guba, Egon, 29
Guetzkow, Harold, 5n.
Gustafson, J. M., 473
Gutkind, Erwin, 416, 417n.

Hagen, Everett, 91n., 473
Hainer, R., 143
Halkides, G., 397
Hall, Edward, 373
Hamilton, C., 190n., 201n.
Hampden-Turner, Charles, 419
Harrington, Michael, 417n.
Harsanyi, J. C., 403n.
Havelock, Ronald G., 28n., 29, 151–164, 191n.
Hayakawa, S. I., 31
Herrick, Neal Q., 177, 205–219
Heskin, Allan, 361, 363, 413–422
Higdon, H., 58
Hills, Jean, 26
Hoebel, E. A., 398
Hoffman, Abbie, 255
Holzman, P. S., 443n.
Hood, R. C., 181
Hoover, Herbert, 60, 61
Hoover Commission, 60
Hornstein, H., 189
Horvarth, Ronald J., 268n.
Howe, Florence, 403n.
Hudson, Barclay, 265, 272
Human development, facilitation of, 417–418
Humanizing structures, community change
    planning, 270–272
Humble, J. W., 54
Hunter, Floyd, 43
Hurwitz, Murray, 315n.
Huxley, Julian, 419n.

Hylton, L., 184, 185
Hyman, Herbert, 254

Image-material, cultural reservoir of, 437–439
Inconsistency, dilemmas of, 145
Inkeles, Alex, 475, 476
Innovation, process of, change agent views
    the defender, 122–123
    defender's role, 121–122
    outcome of, 123
    defense as part of, 120–124
    force field of the defender, 124
    school administrator, defender or change
        agent, 123–124
    social change, 120–121
Integration, 113–114
Integrity, maintenance of, 118–119
Intergroup relations level, planned change at,
    77–81
Inter-organizational analysis, 183–185
Intersystem model, 96–97
Interventions, acceptant, 48–53
    catalytic, 47, 53–56
    cathartic, 47, 48–53
    prescriptive, 47, 58–61
    sociology of, 219–227
Intervention structures, community change
    planning, 269–270

Jaastad, Kay, 285
Jacques, Elliot, 34, 181n.
Jaffe, Aniella, 419n.
Jasper, Karl, 18
Javits, Jacob, 211
Jayaram, G. K., 275–283
Jefferson, Thomas, 151
Johnson, Mrs. Lyndon B., 307
Jones, G. N., 27, 189
Jones, Maxwell, 70n.
Jones, W. Ron, 443n.
Jordan, W., 193n.
Jouvenel, Bertrand de, 382, 398n.
Judge, Anthony, 441
Jung, Carl G., 419n.

Kahn, Robert L., 196, 384, 439n.
Kahn, S., 190n., 198n.
Kamiya, I., 74n.
Kant, Immanuel, 434
Kaplan, A., 473
Kaplan, Marshall, 268, 382
Karenga, R., 201n.
Katz, D., 191

Katz, Elihu, 30
Kazantzakis, Nikos, 176
Keen, Sam, 75n.
Kelly, George A., 12
Kelman, Herbert C., 468, 469, 470–495
Kepner, C. H., 61
Kepner-Tregoe system, 61
Kerouac, Jack, 460
Keynes, John Maynard, 2
Keys, Langley, 258
King, Martin Luther, Jr., 41, 177, 359, 362, 387–390, 394–397, 403, 420, 455
Klein, Donald C., 89, 117–124, 292
Klein, Melanie, 76
Knowledge, application of, 22
    meaning of, 4
    research and dissemination of, through education, 25
    utilization of, 125–174
        action, theories of, evaluating, 137–147
        educational field experience as negotiation of different cognitive worlds, 164–171
        exploratory study of, 151–164
        oppressed, the, pedagogy of, 171–174
        science and practice, 128–137
        social research, 147–150
Knowledge structures, community change planning, advocate planning variations, 266–269
    citizen participation variations, 265–266
Korzybski, Alfred, 31
Kotler, Milton, 245
Kramer, Ralph, 249n., 250
Krassner, Paul, 255
Krichbaum, D., 193n.
Kropotkin, Peter, 417n.
Krimboltz, J. D., 59
Kuhn, Thomas, 416n., 421n.

Labor Department projections, U.S., 207–209
Laboratory methods of education and changing, moral orientation of, 496–505
Laing, R. D., 69n., 142, 310n., 394n., 417
Laissez faire doctrine, 15
Lakin, Martin, 83n.
Lasswell, H., 382, 473
Latent functions, community change planning, 270–272
Lawrence, Paul R., 35n., 89, 112–117, 191
Lazarus, S., 60
Leader, A. H., 285

Learning communities, changing character of, 440–444
Lenin, Vladimir, 171, 189n., 190n., 248
Levin, H. M., 206n., 216
Levine, S., 183, 184, 185
Levy, Marion, J., 393n.
Lewin, Gertrud Weiss, 4n.
Lewin, Kurt, 4, 32, 33, 35, 72, 314, 315–327
Lewis, R. W. B., 462
Liberation, power and, without control, 382–403
Liberation movements, 18
Lieberman, Morton S., 83n.
Life planning, 305–313
Lifton, Robert Jay, 430, 458–466
Likert, Rensis, 39, 54, 61, 115n., 190n.
Lilienthal, D. E., 64
Limiting objectives, community change planning, 270–272
Lindblom, C. E., 181, 414n.
Linkage systems for diffusion of research results, 27–30
Linke, W. R,, 60
Lippitt, Ronald O., 4n., 5n., 32n., 33, 38, 76n., 81n., 147–150, 186, 305n., 314, 316, 354, 470, 496n.
Lipsky, M., 287
Litwak, Eugene, 179n., 184, 185
Lomrantz, Jacob, 83n.
London, Peggy, 487, 488, 490
Loomis, M., 202
Lorsch, Jay W., 35n., 89, 112–117, 191
Lowen, Alexander, 74n., 309
Lundeen, Stan, 211

Maccoby, M., 216, 217n.
Machiavelli, Niccolò, 177
Macrosystems, planned changing in, 81–83
Maier, N. R. F., 286
Male power, women's movement and, 404–412
    change, approaches to, 407–412
    condition of women, contemporary, 404–407
Maniha, J., 181
Mann, Floyd, 357n.
Mann, Horace, 24
Mannheim, Karl, 31, 34, 168n.
Manuel, Frank E., 434n.
Mao Tse-tung, 126, 437
March, J. G., 181, 186, 191, 387n.
Marcuse, Herbert, 414, 417, 422n.
Martyn, Kenneth A., 247n.
Marx, Karl, 42–43, 189n., 385, 418, 419, 420, 422, 434

Marxism, 2, 43, 429, 449
Maslow, Abraham, 36, 417, 418, 419*n.*
Massarick, Fred, 36*n.*
May, Rollo, 484
Mayo, Elton, 34
McClelland, David, 482
McClusky, John E., 363, 382–403
McEwen, W. J., 184, 185
McGimsey, George, 247
McGregor, Douglas M., 36, 39, 61
McIntosh, D. S., 398*n.*
McNulty, J. E., 181
Mead, George Herbert, 72
Mead, Margaret, 19*n.*, 430, 436, 444–458
Means, choice of, in social intervention, 483–492
  coercion, 484–486
  environmental manipulation, 486–488
  facilitation, 491–492
  persuasion, 490–491
  psychic manipulation, 488–490
Means, Richard L., 21
Merleau-Ponty, 389*n.*
Merton, R., 201*n.*
Meyerson, Martin, 219, 220, 221, 225, 226
Miles, Matthew B., 29*n.*, 35*n.*
Miller, James, 186
Miller, N. E., 74*n.*
Miller, William Robert, 388*n.*, 390*n.*, 392*n.*, 400*n.*
Millett, K., 406
Mills, C. Wright, 43, 416
Mitchell, J., 407
Models, analytic, 91, 102
  application and utilization of, 47, 61–65
  change-agent and, 99–101
  consciousness-raising, for social and organizational change, 231–244
  developmental, *see* Developmental models
  differentiation-and-integration, *see* Differentiation-and-integration model
  doctor-patient, 329–330
  intersystem, 96–97
  limitations, 101–102
  organizational change, 185–187
  Program Planning (PPM), 283–295
  purchase, 328–329
  system, *see* System models
  utility of, of the environments of systems for practitioners, 103–112
    conceptions to practitioners, 110–112
    contents of the environment, 108–110
    system-environment relations, 103–106

    textures of and clustering in the environment, 106–108
Modern planning, 413–414
  critique of, 414–415
Mogulof, Melvin B., 267
Moorem Wilbert E., 436
More, Thomas, 385, 436
Moreno, J. L. 26, 82*n.*
Morgenthau, Hans, 388
Morphet, Edgar L., 432*n.*
Morrill, Justin, 27
Morse, E. V., 290
Mort, Paul R., 28
Mouton, Jane Srygley, 35*n.*, 47, 48–66, 68, 77, 78, 81
Moynihan, Daniel P., 287
Müller-Freienfels, 71*n.*
Mumford, Lewis, 377
Mumphrey, Anthony J., Jr., 269, 272
Myrdal, Gunnar, 477

National Training Laboratories, 5*n.*, 33, 34
Nearing, S. and H., 190*n.*
New Deal, 14, 17
New politics, power and, 359–422
  culture, old and new, 370–381
  education at Sanctum, 363–369
  liberating power, conditions conducive to, 393–403
    debilitating power and, 387–393
  liberation and, without control, 382–403
  planning, radical concept of, 413–422
  women's movement, male power and, 404–412
Nimkoff, M. F., 186
Nonviolence, strategies of, 41
Normative-re-educative strategies for effecting change, 23, 31–39
  persons in system, growth in, releasing and fostering, 36–39
  problem-solving capability, improving, 34–36

O'Connor, Bull, 362, 399
Ogburn, W. F., 186
Ohlin, L. E., 181, 186
Olmusk, K. E., 189
Open systems, 95–96
  planning, 275–283
Oppenheimer, Robert, 1*n.*, 2, 3–4
Oppressed, the, pedagogy of, 171–174
Organizational change, planned perspectives on, 175–227

environments, evolution of, 178–187
institutions, sociology of, 219–227
model for, consciousness-raising, 231–244
social change, perspectives on, 188–202
social experimentation, work world and, 205–219
Organizational environments, evolution of, 178–187
concepts of, 179–180
integrative framework, 185–187
inter-organizational analysis, 183–185
turbulence, evidence for, 181–183
Orwell, George, 142
Osborn, Alex, 442n.
O'Toole, James, 208, 214n.
Owen, Robert, 434, 436
Ozbekhan, Haran, 415n.

Pages, Max, 82
Parks, Rosa, 420
Parsons, T., 185, 191n., 392
Patterns, research utilization processes and, 147–150
Pattison, E. M., 489
Pearl, Arthur and Stephanie, 419
Peattie, Lisa R., 230, 251–259, 363
Pedagogy of the oppressed, 171–174
Peirce, Charles, 505
Perls, Fritz, 72n., 306, 326
Perrow, C., 181
Personal Growth Laboratory, 73, 74
Personnel selection and replacement, 25–26
Persons, planned changing in, current state of, 68–75
Peslikis, I., 193n.
Petzold, Hilarion, 83n.
Piaget, Jean, 168n.
Piven, Frances, 193n., 245
Planned change, current state of, in persons, groups, communities, and societies, 68–75
in America, 13–22
direction in, finding, 427–466
future, the, learning to image, 431–444
future as basis for establishing a shared culture, 444–458
self-process, protean style of, 458–466
historical perspective, 17–45
intergroup relations and community level, 77–88
macrosystems, 81–83
meaning of, 4

organizational, see Organizational change
practices of, 46–66
diagnosis/development matrix, 47, 48–66
small group as medium and target of, 75–77
social, see Social change
strategies for effecting, general, 22–43
Planning, community change, structures in, 265–274
action structures, 269–272
knowledge structures, 265–269
life, 305–313
modern, 413–414
critique of, 414–415
open systems, 275–283
policy, 266
program, 266
group process model for, 283–295
project, 266
radical concept of, foundations for, 413–422
communal society, 417
decentralized society, 416–417
duality, perceptions of, 415
ecological ethic, context of, 418–420
evolutionary experimentation, 420–421
human development, facilitation of, 417–418
modern, 413–415
new paradigm, 415–416
synthesis, 420
systems change, 416
structures and processes, 263–313
transactive, theory of, 297–305
Plato, 385, 435
Polak, Fred L., 431–435
Policy planning, 266
Political institutions, use of, to achieve change, 41–42
Politics, ecology of theater, 255–256
of imaging, 435–437
new, see New politics
Polk, Barbara Bovee, 361, 363, 404–412
Power, new politics and, 359–422
culture, old and new, 370–381
education at Sanctum, 363–369
liberating power, conditions conducive to, 393–403
debilitating power and, 387–393
liberation and, without control, 382–403
planning, radical concept, 413–422
women's movement, male power and, 404–412
Power-coercive strategies for effecting change, 23–24, 39–43

nonviolence, 41
political institutions, use of, 41–42
power elites, recomposition and manipulation of, 42–43
changing through, 42–43
Practice, science and, 128–137
art versus, 128–131
concepts versus feelings, 132–133
conceptual tools, selection of, 133–135
generalizations and cases, 131–132
pitfalls, 136–137
theory, aspects of, 135–136
Prawdin, Michael, 438n.
Price, Don K., 151n.
Principles, application and utilization of, 47, 61–65
Pringle, J. W. S., 182
Problem identification, group process model for, 283–295
Problem-solving capabilities of a system, improving, 34–36
Process, utilization as, 159–164
Process consultation, 327–331
assumptions underlying, 330
definition of, 330–331
difference from other consultation, 327–330
Program planning, 266
group process model for, 283–295
Program Planning Model (PPM), 283–295
Project planning, 266
Protest movements, 18–19
Purchase model, 328–329

Rabelais, François, 433
Radical planning, 421–422
Rasberry, Salli, 443n.
Raup, R. B., 33n.
Real communities, 256–257
Real threat, opposition to, 118
Reed, E., 407
Re-education, processes of, 315–327
Reich, Charles A., 19n., 177
Reich, Wilhelm, 74, 326
Reiss, Albert J., Jr., 247n.
Rennie, S., 411
Reorganization, perceptual and conceptual, through clarification of language, 31
Research, applied, 27–30
basic, through general education, 25
social, process of utilization of, 147–150
Resistance to change, change-agents, resistance to, 119–120
defender role, 117–120, 121–122

innovation, process of, defense as part of, 121–124
integrity, maintenance of, 118–119
real threat, opposition to, 118
Rhea, B., 193n.
Richards, I. A., 167n.
Rieff, P., 471
Riesman, David, 228
Roethlisberger, F. J., 34
Rogerian counseling, 72
Rogers, Carl R., 34, 36, 72n., 333, 354, 384, 394n., 418, 500
Rogers, E., 191n.
Rojas, Billy, 440n.
Rosengren, W. R., 181
Rosenstock, Florence W., 245n.
Rosenthal, R., 488
Rossi, Alice, 404
Rossman, Michael, 361, 363–369
Rostow, W. W., 479
Roszak, Theodore, 414, 422n., 463
Rothman, J., 189, 190
Rousseau, Jean Jacques, 385, 433
Rubin, Jerry, 255
Rubington, E., 181
Ryan, Charles O., 432n.

Saint-Simon, Claude Henri de, 434, 436
Sanford, Nevin, 384
Santayana, George, 6
Sarri, Rosemary, 179n.
Satir, Virginia, 77
Schein, E., 190n., 315, 327–331, 352, 393n.
Schein, E. H., 36n., 53, 54, 66
Schindler-Rainman, Eva, 76n., 81n.
Schlipp, Paul A., 316n.
Schon, Donald A., 137–147
School administrator, defender or change agent, 123–124
Schutz, W., 190n.
Schwartz, G. S., 74n.
Science, practice and, 128–137
art versus, 128–131
concepts versus feelings, 132–133
conceptual tools, selection of, 133–135
generalizations and cases, 131–132
pitfalls, 136–137
theory, aspects of, 135–136
Scott, W. E., 284
Seeman, Melvin, 315n., 383
Seley, John E., 269, 272, 471
Self, rediscovery and re-evaluation of, 71–73
Self-process, protean style of, 458–466

Self-sealing theory, 141
Sexton, Patricia C., 247n.
Shapiro, D., 74n., 193n.
Shepard, Herbert A., 39, 62, 305–313
Sheppard, H. L., 206n.
Sherif, Muzafer and Carolyn, 38
Shils, Edward, 387, 388n.
Shipler, David K., 251
Shoemaker, F., 191n.
Shostak, Arthur B., 249n.
Shull, Fremont A., 283n.
Silberman, Charles E., 249n.
Simon, H. A., 181, 186, 191, 414n.
Siu, Ralph Gildi, 310n.
Sjoberg, Gideon, 245
Skinner, B. F., 30, 65, 73n., 327, 435, 486, 487
Slater, Philip E., 177, 190n., 194, 363, 370–381,
    417, 430
Smith, Adam, 429
Smith, Everett Ware, 211n.
Smith, R. D., 33n., 59
Smith, W. C., 479
Smithburg, D. W., 284, 286
Social change, 2
    defense in, importance of, 120–121
    model for, consciousness-raising, 231–244
    planned, perspectives on, 188–202
        approaches to, 196–197
        countercultural, 194–195
        political, 192–194
        practical issues and, 195–202
        professional-technical, 190–192
Social intervention, ethical issues in, 470–495
    value preferences and value conflicts, 471–
    477
Social research, utilization of, process of,
    147–150
    roles and training of agent, 150
Societies, planned changing in, current state
    of, 68–75
Society, communal, 417
    decentralized, 416–417
Sofer, C., 191
Solanas, V., 405
Solomon, Barbara, 225
Spiegel, Hans, 359n.
Spinoza, Baruch, 7
Stark, Freya, 308n.
Steady date, definition of, 94–95
Steinem, Gloria, 404
Steiner, C., 195
Stinchcombe, A. L., 182
Stoyva, J., 74n.

Strain, definition of, 93
Stress, definition of, 93
Stretch, Bonnie Barrett, 443n.
Striner, H. E., 218n.
Sumner, William Graham, 15, 16
Supreme Court, U.S., 18n., 42, 375
Swift, Jonathan, 434
System models, 91–97
    intersystem, 96–97
    major terms, 92–95
    open and closed, 95–96
    utility of, 90–102
Systems, 87–124
    definition of, 92
    utilization as, 153–159
Systems analysis, 87
Systems analysts as staff and consultants, 26–
    27
Szasz, Thomas, 69n.

Tagore, Rabindranath, 455
Tannenbaum, Robert, 36n.
Tanner, Tony, 460
Tao, 302–305
Target, definition of, in social intervention,
    481–483
Tavistock Clinic, 34
Tavistock Model, 76
Taylor, D. W., 181, 183, 285, 286
Taylor, Frederick, 26
Teilhard de Chardin, Pierre, 359, 418n., 419n.,
    421
Tension, definition of, 93
Terreberry, S., 177, 178–187
Terry, R. W., 193n.
Testability, dilemmas of, 145–146
Thant, U, 455
Theories, application and utilization of, 47,
    61–65
Thomas, C., 201n.
Thomas, O. Pendleton, 211n.
Thompson, E. T., 60
Thompson, James D., 184, 185, 283n.
Thompson, Victor A., 284, 286
Thoreau, Henry David, 41
Thorndike, Edward L., 28
Tillich, Paul, 420
Toffler, Alvin, 435n.
Tolman, E. C., 180n.
Tomasi, Joseph, 211n.
Training group (T-group), 72, 76, 83, 326, 489
Transactional Analysis, 61, 72

Transactive planning, 297–305
Transpersonal, the rediscovery and reevaluation of, 74–75
Tregoe, B. B., 61
Trist, E. L., 34, 104, 179, 180, 182, 185, 211
Tucker, Robert C. 392
Tuden Arthur, 283n.
Tumin, Melvin, 436
Turbulence, evidence for, 181–183

Urban Planning Aid, 252–253, 258
Urwick, Lyndall, 38
Utopian thinking as strategy of changing, 30–31
Utterback, J. M., 291

Value, conflcts, in social intervention, 471–477
    dilemmas of change agent, 467–505
        consequences, assessment of, 492–494
        goals, choice of, 477–481
        means, choice of, 483–492
        moral orientation of laboratory methods of education and changing, 496–505
        social intervention, ethical issues in, 470–495
        target, definition of, 481–483
    preferences, in social intervention, 471–477
Variables, conflict management, 114
Van de Ven, Andrew H., 283–295
Van Til, Jon and Sally Bould, 266, 273
Veblen, Thorstein, 18, 131
Vietnam War, 14, 20–21
Vinter, Robert, 179n.
Vonnegut, Kurt, 460
Vroom, V. H., 285, 292n.

Wallace, George, 178
Walton, Richard E., 38, 83n.
Ward, Lester, F., 15, 16, 25
Warren, Roland L., 189, 271, 353n., 440
Warwick, Donald P., 468, 469, 470–495

Watson, G., 50, 190n., 191n.
Watson, J., 32n., 38, 470
Watts, Alan, 419
Weaver, Richard, 2
Weber, Max, 38, 183, 190n., 279, 391, 392n.
Weir, John and Joyce, 73
Wellman, D., 201n.
Weschler, I. R., 36n.
Westley, B., 32n., 38, 470
White, P. E., 183, 184, 185
White, Ralph, 316
Whitehead, Alfred North, 4, 420
Wieman, Henry N., 420n.
Willison, F. M. G., 61
Willner, Ruth Ann, 393n., 395n.
Wilson, Elizabeth, 403n.
Winter, D., 482
Wolff, Kurt, 394n.
Wolin, Sheldon, 385n.
Wolpert, Julian, 269, 272
Women's movement, male power and, 404–412
    change, approaches, to, 407–412
    condition of women, contemporary, 404–407
Wordsworth, William, 454
Work-content, change in, 207
Workforce, changes in, 206–207
Work world, changing, social experimentation and, 205–210
    institutional responses, 210–214
    pitfalls, potential benefits and, 214–219
    workforce, work-content, and economic change, 206–210
World War II, 17, 18

Yankelovich, Daniel, 207

Zander, Alvin, 387n., 391n.
Zetterberg, H., 190n.
Znaniecki, F., 167, 168n.